Serious Games

Serious Games provides a thorough exploration of the claim that playing games can facilitate learning that is deep, sustained and transferable to the real world. Contributors investigate the psychological mechanisms that take place not only during gaming, but also in game selection, persistent play, and gaming impact. Focusing on the desirable outcomes of digital game play, the volume editors distinguish between three possible effects—learning, development, and change. Contributions from internationally recognized scholars focus on five objectives:

- Define the area of serious games
- Elaborate on the underlying theories that explain suggested psychological mechanisms elicited through serious game play, addressing cognitive, affective and social processes
- Summarize the empirical evidence on the effectiveness of serious games
- Introduce innovative research methods as a response to methodological challenges imposed through interactive media
- Discuss the possibilities and limitations of selected applications for educational purposes.

Anchored primarily in social science research, the approaches included here emphasize the gaming process and the users' experiences. Additional perspectives, written from non-social science approaches by experts in academic game design and representatives of the gaming industry, conclude the volume.

This timely and singular work will appeal to scholars, researchers, and graduate students working in media entertainment and game studies in the areas of education, media, communication, and psychology. It serves a benchmark for serious games research, and will influence work in this area in the years ahead.

Serious Games

Mechanisms and Effects

Edited by
Ute Ritterfeld
Michael Cody
Peter Vorderer

NEW YORK AND LONDON

First published 2009
by Routledge
270 Madison Ave, New York, NY 10016

Simultaneously published in the UK
by Routledge
2 Park Square, Milton Park, Abingdon, Oxon OX14 4RN

Routledge is an imprint of the Taylor & Francis Group, an informa business

Typeset in Goudy and Gill Sans by EvS Communication Networx, Inc.
Printed and bound in the UK on acid-free paper by CPI Antony Rowe, Chippenham, Wiltshire

Library of Congress Cataloging in Publication Data
Serious games: mechanisms and effects / [edited by] Ute Ritterfeld, Michael Cody, and Peter
Vorderer.
p. cm.
1. Games—Psychological aspects. 2. Learning. 3. Games—Research. I. Ritterfeld, Ute. II. Cody,
Michael J. III. Vorderer, Peter.
GV1201.37.S47 2009
793.01—dc22
2008054273

ISBN 10: 0-415-99369-5 (hbk)
ISBN 10: 0-415-99370-9 (pbk)
ISBN 10: 0-203-89165-1 (ebk)

ISBN 13: 978-0-415-99369-2 (hbk)
ISBN 13: 978-0-415-99370-8 (pbk)
ISBN 13: 978-0-203-89165-0 (ebk)

To Geoffrey Cowan,
A great visionary and supporter of games research

Contents

Foreword: From *Virtual U* to Serious Games to Something Bigger

In 1999 I got a phone call that changed my life. On the other end of the call was a foundation program manager that I would learn right away doesn't take no for an answer. Jesse Ausubel of the Alfred P. Sloan Foundation chases big ideas. Aside from counting all the fish in the world with the Census of Marine Life project (http://www.coml.org), in 1999 Ausubel was working with former Stanford CFO William Massy and the game developer of *Capitalism I* and *II* Trevor Chan to develop a *Sim-City* styled simulation of universities which we would later title *Virtual U*.

Jesse told me that I would be on a plane the next day to visit the foundation and discuss how to finish the game, get it tested, and distributed to market. Despite my sense that getting a plane flight the next morning was sort of short notice, there I was on the plane flight from Portland, Maine to New York City that next morning wondering what I was about to get myself into. It was an eventful meeting and for the next 3 years *Virtual U* was a big part of my life. Given the part *VU* played in my life, it still is.

What *Virtual U* was to be was a method to explore a critical issue of management; namely, the effort to get people to manage complex systems more discretely as a sum of their most important parts and to infuse that system's culture throughout the organization thus breaking down the inevitable fiefdoms and blinders that inhibit how organizations function. The goal of course was to do this specifically for universities, which as organizations, are legendary for operating with a pervasive sense of parochial activity. I'm sure for many of the academic readers of this book I'm not providing you with breaking news. For the Sloan Foundation, to improve the management of the nation's universities was a leveraged means of improving all aspects of a university's output and it is an overall program that certainly has its roots in the foundation's namesake's career. Ausubel spoke about this in the context of *Virtual U* at an event held at MIT where we looked back on its early history:

> The story begins on a spring day in 1995 in Palo Alto. I was visiting Bill Massy, then a professor at Stanford. Bill was analyzing why graduate students took ever longer to obtain doctoral degrees. Managing the Sloan

Foundation's program on "the university as a system," I was concerned not only about specific problems such as the 9 years doctoral students averaged to acquire degrees but also about how the many problems connected to one another. The university was a jangly torso, in which the hip bone connected loosely to the thigh bone, and on down to the big toe. But no one seemed to have a working model of cause and effect. Indeed, perspectives on the university seemed to show it as all muscular thighs, all deft fingers, or a thick skull. I wanted a crude look at the whole.

There are many ways to improve university management and leadership. Books, conferences, films, and other methods were past, present, and future methods that were well known and utilized by the foundation. This time, however, the goal was to try something new, something that might move beyond the typical approaches, notions of audience, and baseline capability of other media efforts. Both Massy and Ausubel were on a collision course with an interesting bit of serendipity.

So, after hearing Bill's impressive analysis of the time required to reach a degree, I inquired, what would you really like to do? After a couple of tentative starts, Bill's eyes lit, exclamations began, and he ran to a file cabinet and pulled out a memo he had written some months earlier proposing to build an interactive video game of the U.S. University. I said, yes, yes, and we shook hands. The idea for a game-based approach wasn't so automatic though. There was an unique link of inspiration and history that further catalyzed faith in project's birth and approach.

Back in the mid-1980s I had edited a book on Cities and Their Vital Systems. Shortly after the book appeared, a call came from California in a very youthful voice, asking, "Hey, I am trying to build a game about building and managing a city. Would you mind if I draw on some of the ideas in your book?" A few weeks later a beta version of SimCity arrived in the mail for testing. The voice was that of Will Wright, the genius of simulation games, and the rest is history.

Looking back now it's interesting to see the intertwined paths of Wright and Ausubel, neither of whom attempt small projects. Both were interested in the unique systemic volume of urban life and now as Wright launches *Spore*, a game that is a simulation of digital life, Ausubel is finishing up a project of similar scale that is attempting to catalog all the unique (and often Spore-creature-like life) of the world's oceans. And if you ask me both Wright and Ausubel played big parts in establishing what many now call serious games. All of these series of anecdotal events and observations speak to the fact that the world of serious games and commercial entertainment games are inexorably linked.

The experience of *Virtual U* was at first unique: at the time we didn't call what we were doing serious games. It was just a game-based simulation. We did worry about the use of the word *game* then, an idea today I find ever more absurd. Our goal, simply, was to make it as good a game as possible, learn from our mistakes, and survive long enough to get a sequel out. Improving the software was my most important goal because frankly the first version of *Virtual U* wasn't that great.

Our biggest mistake was that the game had been designed to be a simulation of an "up and running" university whose growth and change state was measured by graphs and numbers and not by the idea that you built it from scratch. Regardless of the structure of the change state (i.e., what the player had achieved by playing), we also had a game that was poor at relating the picture of the journey the gamer had taken. What we heard most of all from its most important users was that the game had trouble working in a classroom environment (brick or distance) and that as a tool for teaching it needed some improvement. With some further funding from Sloan we were able to improve on some of these problems and others. Today the product is decent but still suffers, aside from age, from some of the structural approaches that were too big to overcome. However, what we did learn in going from launching the game and moving it from version 1.0 to 2.0 was a tremendous amount of nearly life lessons that still infuse my thinking concerning serious games and as a game designer today. I've often said that for all its success in providing a disruptive approach to exploring notions of university management and leadership, *Virtual U* will historically be remembered more for its contribution to the growth of serious games. The transition from *Virtual U* to serious games was catalyzed again by Jesse Ausubel.

In 2002, David Rejeski from the Woodrow Wilson Center for Scholars, influenced by watching his son play *Age of Empires* (*AoE*), was looking to explore the use of videogames for government policy planning. His Foresight in Governance Project at Wilson was charged with improving long-term government planning practices. Rejeski felt the way games such as *AoE* and *Sim-City* gave players a much more epic frame of reference and accessible interface that might prove useful for engaging policy makers, and the public at-large in bigger discussions about policies that sometimes take years to show their true effects (good or bad). Having heard of *Virtual U*, Rejeski reached out to Ausubel (whom he had known previously) and as a result I got another eventful phone call.

Rejeski and I agreed that what we needed to do first was explain the notion of why games could help the space of government simulations (at the time we were still thinking mostly about policy simulations) and that in doing so we'd be able to cheaply plant the seed that might lead to further funding and work. I worked on the idea for a couple of months and produced a paper, which I titled "Improving Public Policy through Game-Based Learning and Simulation." I felt it was suitably government sounding. Dave wanted it to have a bit more punch so, influenced by Clark Abt's book *Serious Games*, he added that term as a precursor to the title of the document. I only know this because I remember seeing the book in Dave's office one day. So that's the origin of the term *Serious Games* as used so fluently in the videogames industry today.

The paper was a modest hit. What we learned most of all from that, and from the *Virtual U* experience was that there were many more people pursuing the ideas we encapsulated in the serious games paper. What frustrated us, however, was that this network of pioneers had no real nexus. Without such a nexus there wasn't much of a way to organize and move forward on the specific ideas we had for government policy games.

With further help from Ausubel via the Richard A. Lounsbery Foundation we were able to begin hosting a series of topical meetings and travel to other meetings to expand on the idea of serious games. We also engaged in writing further articles and promoting the idea via press releases and general grassroots organizing. We called this effort the "Serious Games Initiative." The mere existence of this highly virtual effort served to add some nexus and through use of our e-mail discussion list and recruiting efforts a viable network of professionals began to emerge in unison and it was this group of connections that enabled more to happen quickly, including the birth of the Serious Games Summits and the creation of "The Games for Health" project.

As these new projects took hold I found myself traveling the country and other parts of the world expounding on an idea that had already taken root. Serious games wasn't birthed by *Virtual U* or *America's Army* or The Serious Games Initiative. To me it was clearly given its life by the amazing ascendancy of tools, techniques, talent, and tradecraft of the videogame development industry. There would be no serious games space as we define it today if the games industry's technical, cultural, and business growth hadn't been so meteoric in the last 10 to 15 years.

While we could dwell on certain aspects of games that drove the growth of serious games (e.g., the creation of real-time synchronous first-person 3D graphics engines) the key underlying current was that games were more rapidly taking advantage of what Moore's Law and Metcalfe's Law were doing on a fundamental technology level. As games mined the gap between the tops of these curves and traditional information technology companies, they increasingly created a disparity that prescient people began to try to exploit. That much of this prescience took place in academia certainly contributed to the focus on learning outcomes from games. However as Dave and I grew the Initiative and its network we soon realized that the use of games beyond entertainment was way beyond the scope of policy making, or learning.

Despite the efforts to widen people's eyes to the outlets for games and their related resources, the more I worked on the idea of serious games the more I realized that too much of the space resembled the story of the blind men and the elephant as recounted in the poem by John Godfrey Saxe. As the story goes six blind men examine different parts of an elephant and by virtue of their physical impairment cannot see the whole from its parts. By virtue of their mental impairment they then argue incessantly as to the elephant's true description:

> And so these men of Indostan
> Disputed loud and long,
> Each in his own opinion
> Exceeding stiff and strong,
> Though each was partly in the right,
> And all were in the wrong!

Too many people who work within, and study the notion of serious games are themselves casting too narrow a net. The worst case of all is the notion of games for learning, because despite it being the most prevalent use, the very proponents of this use have often succeeded in leaving many audiences for their work as equating serious games *only* as games for learning. As someone who has been deeply immersed in the serious games space, I can see the danger of allowing this shortsightedness to corrupt the very space of serious games, and in doing so we will destroy the ultimate potential of games beyond entertainment.

As leaders of a new emerging practice that we collectively call serious games (for lack of any other better label) we bear responsibility for ensuring that the descriptions we use and adhere to paint the entire picture of what serious games represents. Too often serious games is defined by the speaker or writer as "that which they do" and that is the very essence of narrowcasting, let alone quasi-snobbery. And as we argue the meaning and effectiveness and philosophy of games for learning we are swept into the tsunami of debate that permeates the general field of education. Again I am inspired by Saxe's words:

> So oft in theologic wars,
> The disputants, I ween,
> Rail on in utter ignorance
> Of what each other mean,
> And prate about an Elephant
> Not one of them has seen!

My journey in serious games is intensely personal. I've been playing games since pong and I can still remember so many large segments of my life devoted to games (I wrote my high-school economics paper on the games industry, describing ideas like affiliated developer agreements, distribution, and market segments that my teacher then called fascinating, which I think had more to do with the novel subject matter than the likely numerous spelling mistakes). What it has mostly been about, however, is a constant series of networked experiences and behind each of those experiences was the pervasive notion that games have and can be much more than what they have achieved at the present time. Serious games are a product of that sentiment (as are many other ideas like casual games, ARGs, Guitar Hero, machinima, and more) and for me that is the most special aspect to all of this.

I *love* games. I love the creativity, I love the software development challenges, I love the dynamics of the industry, I love that I live at both its dawn and perhaps several "golden age" cycles. As such I am heartened to know that games, serious games, can be applicable to so many aspects of life. It is amazing to turn the corner in my work and see some use for games that I had not even imagined before. Ideas like helping people overcome phobias, increasing productivity at work by the very virtue of doing their work inside a game, and changing our own biology as a result of exposed gameplay.

Assembled in the book are some great pieces of thought and work on serious games. However, if there is a warning that must prelude the fine work here, it is that this is but the tip of the iceberg and that it focuses predominantly on the educational power of games. I know many of the authors, and they are not all blind to the wider power and opportunities of games. However, you as a reader need to know that my own idea of serious games started out with my own blind senses and now, almost 10 years later, thanks to a wide and personal journey with games and many different walks of life I've managed to remove my own blindfolds and when I did I discovered a world that goes well beyond where it is now.

But you have to start somewhere and this wonderful collection of work is part of that. For me I will always remember it started as that phone call in the fall of 1999.

Ben Sawyer

Editors

Ute Ritterfeld, Professor of Media Psychology, received her education in the Health Sciences (Academy of Rehabilitation in Heidelberg) and in Psychology (University of Heidelberg), completed her PhD in Psychology (Technical University of Berlin), and habilitated at the University of Magdeburg, Germany. She was Assistant Professor at the University of Magdeburg, Adjunct Professor at the Universities of Berlin (Humboldt) and Hannover, and Associate Professor at the University of Southern California (USC) in Los Angeles, Annenberg School for Communication. At USC, Ritterfeld directed an interdisciplinary research team devoted to the studies of digital games and hosted the inaugural academic conference on serious games. In 2007, Ritterfeld joined the faculty of Psychology and Education at the VU University Amsterdam and co-founded the Center for Advanced Media Research Amsterdam (CAMeRA@VU) where she serves as director of interdisciplinary research. Ritterfeld co-edits the *Journal of Media Psychology* published by Hogrefe.

Michael Cody earned his PhD in Communication at Michigan State University in 1978, where he focused on research methods and face to face social influence processes. He has authored or edited books on persuasion, interpersonal communication, and entertainment education. He served as editor of *Communication Theory* (1999–2002) and is the current editor of the *Journal of Communication* (2009–2012).

Peter Vorderer (PhD, Technical University of Berlin) is Scientific Director of the Center for Advanced Media Research Amsterdam (CAMeRA) and head of the Department of Communication Science, VU University Amsterdam, The Netherlands. He specializes in media use and media effects research with a special focus on media entertainment and digital games. Together with Dolf Zillmann and Jennings Bryant, he has edited three well-recognized volumes on media entertainment and video games.

Contributors

Paul Robert Appleby, University of Southern California

Malcolm Bauer, Educational Testing Service, Princeton, NJ

Gary Bente, University of Cologne, Germany

Suzanne Biedenbach, Fordham University

Marije Nije Bijvank, VU University Amsterdam

Fran C. Blumberg, Fordham University

Johannes Breuer, University of Cologne, Germany

Jennings Bryant, University of Alabama

Brett Camper, Massachusetts Institute of Technology

Patrick Chipman, University of Memphis

Alex Chisholm, Massachusetts Institute of Technology

John L. Christensen, University of Southern California

Michael Cody, Michigan State University

Charisse Corsbie-Massay, University of Southern California

Jayson L. Dibble, Michigan State University

Marco Ennemoser, University of Gießen

Wes Fondren, University of Alabama

James Paul Gee, Arizona State University

Carlos G. Godoy, University of Southern California

Arthur Graesser, University of Memphis

Patricia Greenfield, University of California, Los Angeles and Children's Digital Media Center, Los Angeles

Neal Grigsby, Massachusetts Institute of Technology

Teo Chor Guan, Massachusetts Institute of Technology

Rodney Hoinkes, Parallel Labs, Inc.

Sabrina S. Ismailer, Fordham University

Jeroen Jansz, University of Amsterdam

Henry Jenkins, Massachusetts Institute of Technology

Younbo Jung, Nanyang Technological University

Yasmin B. Kafai, University of California, Los Angeles

Matias Kivikangas, Helsinki School of Economics

Christoph Klimmt, Johannes Gutenberg University of Mainz

Eric Klopfer, Massachusetts Institute of Technology

Elly A. Konijn, VU University Amsterdam

Frank Leeming, University of Memphis

Debra A. Lieberman, University of California, Santa Barbara

Margaret McLaughlin, University of Southern California

Lynn Carol Miller, University of Southern California

Scot Osterweil, Massachusetts Institute of Technology

Jorge Peña, University of Texas at Austin

Judy Perry, Massachusetts Institute of Technology

Joost Raessens, Utrecht University

Rabindra Ratan, University of Southern California

Niklas Ravaja, Helsinki School of Economics

Stephen J. Read, University of Southern California

Ute Ritterfeld, VU University Amsterdam

Albert Rizzo, University of Southern California

Michael A. Shapiro, Cornell University

Cuihua Shen, University of Southern California

John L. Sherry, Michigan State University

Valerie J. Shute, Florida State University, Tallahassee

Arvind Singhal, University of Texas, El Paso

Stacey Spiegel, Parallel Labs, Inc.

Kaveri Subrahmanyam, California State University, Los Angeles and Children's Digital Media Center, Los Angeles

Philip Tan, Massachusetts Institute of Technology

Matthew Ventura, Educational Testing Service, Princeton, NJ

Peter Vorderer, VU University Amsterdam

Mirjam Vosmeer, University of Amsterdam

Hua Wang, University of Southern California

James H. Watt, Rensselaer Polytechnic Institute

Matthew Weise, Massachusetts Institute of Technology

Carolee Winstein, University of Southern California

Shih-Ching Yeh, University of Southern California

Diego Zapata-Rivera, Educational Testing Service, Princeton, NJ

List of Figures and Tables

Figures

Tables

Part I

Serious Games

Explication of an Oxymoron

Chapter 1

Introduction

Ute Ritterfeld, Michael Cody, and Peter Vorderer

Over the past few years, *serious* games have become a hot topic at international conferences, conventions, and symposia. Interest in using games to educate, motivate, and change behavior has grown tremendously in a brief period of time, and by a truly international group of practitioners, civic leaders, health and human rights advocates, educators, gamers, and researchers. Ben Sawyer facilitated this movement when he launched the "Serious Games Initiative," which was followed quickly by the creation of important spin-off interest groups and Web sites like "Games for Health" and "Games for Change." A number of listservs and other discussion lists were initiated and have been successful in attracting an increasing number of game designers, educators, and academics alike. Indeed, as discussed in the chapters in this volume, an increasing number of disciplines are drawn to the topic of serious games, including health advocates, social advocates, immigration experts, political scientists, and others.

This vivid history is reflected in the term *serious games* that we have adopted for this volume. However, the term itself may easily be criticized for its literal meaning, which is an oxymoron: Games are inherently fun and not serious (Newman, 2004). Despite this apparent contradiction, many scholars and practitioners see serious games as involving fun, as well as being educational, engaging, impactful, meaningful, and purposeful.

When the video games industry began decades ago, few would have predicted its phenomenal success in profits and size. Who would have predicted that gaming would become bigger than the film industry? No one would have anticipated that digital games would one day be seen as a new educational tool that could fundamentally change learning, teaching, and training for upcoming generations. With new technologies at hand that allow for high resolution and 3D video and audio, social collaboration or competition, detachment from stationary equipment, and sensory-based input control, both genders and all age groups are now increasingly attracted to play (cf., Vorderer & Bryant, 2006). The evolution of digital games is clearly driven by entertainment purposes and interests, and their success is heavily associated with their entertainment value (Vorderer & Ritterfeld, in press).

Ideally speaking, serious games are building on this entertainment value, but they also add value through an educational component (Allen, 2004; Amroy, Naicker, Vincent, & Adams, 1999). In this respect, they represent a genre that was purposefully designed to be more than "just" fun (Dumbleton & Kirriemuir, 2006). At the same time, the educational value associated with serious gaming went beyond the academic purposes pursued by so called *edutainment applications*. *Edutainment*, at least in the beginning, was a rather unsuccessful attempt to involve play elements in more traditional curricular activities (Ritterfeld & Weber, 2006). Their focus was primarily on skill practice, and the entertainment value diminished substantially during exposure. The more recent serious games initiatives, however, refocused on deeper learning in the context of an enjoyable experience and on broader educational issues outside the school setting (Jenkins, 2006; Kline, 2004; Linderoth, Lindström, & Alexandersson, 2004).

In serious games we assume that the gaming element is prevalent; that is, the game is used as a toy (Goldstein, Buckingham, & Brougère, 2004). Using digital games as toys implies that the activity itself is intrinsically motivating because it provides fun (Vorderer, Steen, & Chan, 2006). Intrinsically motivating play implies deliberate selection of the toy, deliberate persistence of playing, and a high likelihood of repetitive usage (Oerter, 1999). Such forms of activity resemble what is known as enjoyment and entertainment (Vorderer, Klimmt, & Ritterfeld, 2004). The source of enjoyment, however, can be manifold and depends heavily on the user and the situation. While some consider challenges or competition as most enjoyable, others find enjoyment in role playing, creative work, or repetitive and low challenging activities.

Children's play is inseparably associated with learning. Children explore and acculturate the world through play, extend their skills and competencies, and experiment with possible selves. Only at a later point during elementary school do entertainment and learning start to drift apart. Older children may even associate play with being noneducational and learning with being anything but enjoyable. Media have long been considered to be a tool that would be able to reunite those two purposes: Educational radio or television shows, audio narratives, music, comic books, and more recently, digital, interactive media. There is considerable evidence from traditional media that such educational formats may work; that is, affect users by teaching them skills and content (see summaries in Singhal & Rogers, 1999; Singhal, Cody, Rogers, & Sabido, 2004), especially if the narrative transports the audience member into an emotionally involving and mentally stimulating, vivid world (Green, 2006; Green & Brock, 2002). But entertainment–education projects are often not as powerful as intended, and can be ineffective if sound social psychological theories are not appropriately applied. The successful educational outcome of embedding information in entertainment programming depends on a host of factors: capturing the attention of the users, making sure that the desired belief change or action to be adopted is discussed (repeatedly) or is visually shown (i.e., modeled), and reinforcing belief or behavioral changes by showing that there are rewards or advantages in adopting the changes. It is also important that the viewers are emotionally involved and affected by the entertainment story, identify with or have empathy for characters in the program, and are motivated to seek more information after viewing the entertainment program or discuss the program with friends. If some of these elements are missing, educational outcomes can be limited or nonexistent (see, for instance, a comparison of different storylines in Morgan, Movius, and Cody, in press).

Ritterfeld and Weber (2006) have differentiated three different models of entertainment education. They describe previous attempts as manifestations of a motivational and a reinforcement paradigm, respectively. The motivational paradigm suggests that entertainment features in a product elicit the specific selection of it by providing interesting, enjoyable add-ons. In a similar way, the reinforcement paradigm supports persistent usage by offering gratifications after successful completion of a task. Both models are most common in educational media formats. Although they may have some value, the full potential embedded in entertainment education has not been fully explored. In fact, entertainment and education still appear as two distinct, separate aspects of game play that follow each other and demand that the user shift his or her focus from one to the other. As such, the educational aspect of media use may be introduced or responded to by moments of enjoyment, but they themselves remain as bare from such experience as any other educational format that was not specifically designed for playful exploration. In order to blend educational purposes successfully with the entertainment experience, paralleled experiences are needed. The educational component needs to be enjoyable in its own right, and the entertainment component should be closely associated with education.

Since their emergence, serious games have been holding the promise to fulfill this requirement for three reasons: First, game play is intrinsically motivating. Second, the responsiveness of the game environment gives immediate feedback to the user. And third, the content has or can have the complexity that allows for ample learning opportunities. Possible educational impact is not limited to knowledge acquisition or skill practice; it also includes exploration, problem solving, or incidental learning.

However, ever since the implementation of serious games as a new promising genre, its promoters and critics have been struggling to find a consensus on the definition of the term itself. Unsatisfied with the generic but conflicting message of the label *serious games*, some turned to more specific alternatives, such as describing games for specific purposes (e.g., games for health, game-based learning, persuasive games) or proposed alternatives (e.g., meaningful games). But the inherent problem of defining a genre by characteristics of the media remains: What would be the features that turn a game into a serious game? Is it the purpose of the game, the intention of the content developer, or the goal of the user? Is an educational purpose a sufficient criterion to call a game serious? What if the effects of the game are not educational, and what if unintended effects are elicited? What about games that are designed from a pure entertainment perspective, but require substantial problem solving to be played? Are these games not serious because the publisher did not market them as such? Serious games can be customized digital games that were specifically and purposefully developed to educate (i.e., *Math* or *Reading Blaster*, *Tactical Iraqi*), or they can be over-the-counter games that primarily entertain its users while *also* providing educational opportunities (knowledge, skills) (i.e., *World of Warcraft*, *The Sims*).

Although advocates in the gaming industry often argue that game technology provides unique opportunities for deep, sustained learning (Michael & Chen, 2006), little systematic research is available to support this title. The central purpose of this book therefore is to examine critically the claim that playing games can provide learning that is deep, sustained, and transferable to the "real world." This volume is devoted to continuing this discussion in recognition of available scientific evidence. As this book is primarily social science driven, the reader will hereby be introduced to approaches that focus on the gaming process and the users' experiences more than on technological game elements.

To enter the discussion, however, we ask the reader to accept a fuzzy definition of serious games. As a starting point we define serious games as any form of interactive computer-based game software for one or multiple players to be used on any platform and that has been developed with the intention to be more than entertainment.

The second purpose of this volume is to provide a systematic overview of serious games research; that is, on theories that have been applied, on empirical evidence, and on methodological challenges. Although the development in this academic field is no doubt very impressive and there are a number of studies on the effectiveness of specific applications, we are still missing a comprehensive and systematic overview of the mechanisms that drive or don't drive the expected effectiveness. With this volume, we try to fill the gap in providing an academic overview on the mechanisms and effects of serious games from a primarily social science perspective. That means that we investigate the psychological mechanisms that take place during gaming, but also in game selection, persistent play, and gaming impact. Although we are far from introducing one theory that fits all applications, we have assembled solid scientific knowledge that guides our understanding of serious game play from various theoretical perspectives. We are specifically looking at the educational impact on the individual and on societies at large, while exploring the complex interplay of entertainment and learning in serious gaming. We use the term *educational* for any desired increase in skills, knowledge, competency, and mastery, and favored changes in attitudes, values, or behaviors.

Throughout the book we also use the generic term *digital games* to include all interactive video and computer games played on any platform by one or multiple players. We further decided to differentiate between a player and a gamer throughout the book: The term *player* refers to an individual (e.g., a research subject) who is playing a game, whereas the term *gamer* is used within the context of gaming as a cultural phenomenon.

This book is the result of a collaborative effort on the part of a research group that was formerly situated at the University of Southern California (USC), Annenberg School for Communication where Ute Ritterfeld and Peter Vorderer used to teach and do their research before they joined the VU University Amsterdam and where Michael Cody is still affiliated. In May 2007 a workshop, initiated by the USC games research group, on serious games for learning, development, and change involved many of the contributors of this book and served as a starting point for discussions that are reflected throughout this volume. Through much of 2007 and 2008 Shawna Kelly and Lauren Movius, two doctoral candidates at USC, worked as copyeditors and editorial assistants to help complete this volume. Their timely efforts helped make this volume a better one, and many chapters benefited from their skillful work in grammar, language use, and creative ideas. The editors are indebted to both for being so helpful over months of work on this book. Many thanks also to Dimitrina Chakinska who helped with proofreading.

The volume is divided into four parts. The chapters within each part are related and suggest linear reading. Besides this introductory chapter, part I (Serious Games: Explication of an Oxymoron) contains three additional chapters that build on each other in search of the nature of serious games (Ratan & Ritterfeld; Wang, Shen, & Ritterfeld; Shen, Wang, & Ritterfeld). Part II is devoted to Theories and Mechanisms, part III to Methodological Challenges, and part IV to Applications, Limitations, and Future Directions. For part II and III, we adopted the structure of pairing fundamental chapters written by renowned scholars from communication science and psychology who have been researching digital games (Gee; Graesser, Chipman, Leeming, & Biedenbach; Lieberman; Sherry & Dibble; Konijn & Nije Bijvank; Kafai; Klimmt; Shute, Ventura, Bauer, and Zapata-Rivera; Ennemoser; Shapiro and Peña) with a supplementing perspective in a corresponding social science discipline (Bryant & Fondren; Blumberg & Ismailer; Subrahmanyam & Greenfield; Ritterfeld; Jansz & Vosmeer; Wang & Singhal; Bente & Breuer; Watt; Ravaja & Kivikangas). Through this strategy we expect to connect the still young area of digital games research with the foundations of social science and to facilitate the exchange between two of its core disciplines, namely psychology and communication science.

We also distinguish between three desirable outcomes of digital game play: learning, development, and change. Learning is defined as the intentional acquisition of skills or knowledge through deliberate practice and training and has therefore a pedagogical focus. With development we emphasize the rather incidental psychological impact of game play on processes of human development such as identity or attitude formation or emotional regulation that may be facilitated or initiated through game play. Finally, change addresses social intervention; for example, political or health behavior. Although not completely distinct, focusing on these three dimensions should ensure that we cover a broad range of serious games' possible impacts.

The coming together of fundamental and applied communication as well as psychological concepts in the development of serious games is exemplified in the fourth and final part of this book (Jung, Yeh, McLaughlin, Rizzo, & Winstein; Miller, Christensen, Godoy, Appleby, Corsbie-Massay, & Read). This perspective will be supplemented by three concluding chapters that are written from a nonsocial science perspective: First, experts in academic game design (Jenkins, Camper, Chisholm, Grigsby, Klopfer, Osterweil, Perry, Tan, Weise, & Guan) and representatives of the gaming industry (Stacey Spiegel & Rodney Hoinkes) provide insights into most recent serious game developments. Although this book has an explicit focus on social science, we acknowledge the necessity for a broader interdisciplinary study of the phenomena. Our final chapter (Raessens) offers a humanistic perspective and was chosen as an outlook into a different paradigm in which meanings and contexts of games and gaming are investigated. We hereby try to contribute to overcome the methodological divide in games research as described by Williams (2005) and like to look ahead to a more integrated and interdisciplinary study of digital games.

References

Allen, M. (2004). Tangible interfaces in smart toys. In J. Goldstein, D. Buckingham, & G. Brougère (Eds.), *Toys, games, and media* (pp. 179–194). Mahwah, NJ: Erlbaum.

Amory, A., Naicker, K., Vincent, J., & Adams, C. (1999). The use of computer games as an educational tool: Identification of appropriate game types and game elements. *British Journal of Educational Technology, 30*(4), 311–321.

Dumbleton, T., & Kirriemuir, J. (2006). Digital games and education. In J. Rutter & J. Bruce (Eds.), *Understanding digital games* (pp. 223–240). London: Sage.

Goldstein, J., Buckingham, D., & Brougère, G. (2004). Introduction: Toys, games, and media. In J. Goldstein, D. Buckingham, & G. Brougère (Eds.), *Toys, games, and media* (pp. 1–10). Mahwah, NJ: Erlbaum.

Green, M. (2006). Narratives and cancer communication. *Journal of Communication, 56*, S163–S183.

Green, M. D., & Brock, T. C. (2002). In the mind's eye: Transportation-imagery model of narrative persuasion. In M. C. Green, J. J. Strange, & T. C. Brock (Eds.), *Narrative impact: Social and cognitive foundations* (pp. 315–341). Mahwah, NJ: Erlbaum

Jenkins, H. (2006). *Confronting the challenges of participatory culture: Media education for the 21th century.* MacArthur Foundation. Retrieved August 22, 2007, from http://digitallearning.macfound.org/atf/cf/%7B7E45C7E0-A3E0-4B89-AC9C-E807E1B0AE4E%7D/JENKINS_WHITE_PAPER.PDF.

Kline, S. (2004). Learners, spectators, or gamers? An investigation of the impact of digital media in the media-saturated household. In J. Goldstein, D. Buckingham, & G. Brougère (Eds.), *Toys, games, and media* (pp. 131–156). Mahwah, NJ: Erlbaum.

Linderoth, J., Lindström, B. & Alexandersson, M. (2004). Learning with computer games. In J. Goldstein, D. Buckingham, & G. Brougère (Eds.), *Toys, games, and media* (pp. 157–176). Mahwah, NJ: Erlbaum.

Math blaster [Digital game]. (n.d.). Knowledge Adventure School. http://www.knowledgeadventure.com/school/default.aspx

Michael, D., & Chen, S. (2006). *Serious games: Games that educate, train, and inform.* Tampa, FL: Thomson.

Morgan, S. E., Movius, L., & Cody, M. J. (in press). The power of narratives: The effect of entertainment television organ donation storylines on the attitudes, knowledge, and behaviors of donors and non-donors. *Journal of Communication.*

Newman, J. (2004). *Videogames.* London: Routledge.

Oerter, R. (1999). *Psychologie des Spiels: Ein handlungstheoretischer Ansatz* [Psychology of play from the perspective of action theory]. Weinheim, Germany: Beltz.

Ritterfeld, U., & Weber, R. (2006). Video games for entertainment and education. In P. Vorderer & J. Bryant (Eds.), *Playing video games: Motives, responses, and consequences* (pp. 399–413). Mahwah, NJ: Erlbaum.

Sims, The. [Digital game]. (2000). Redwood City, CA: Electronic Arts.

Singhal, A., Cody, M. J., Rogers, E. M., & Sabido, M. (Eds.). (2004). *Entertainment-education and social change: History, research and practice.* Mahwah, NJ: Erlbaum.

Singhal, A., & Rogers, E.M. (1999). *Entertainment-education: A communication strategy for social change.* Mahwah, NJ: Erlbaum.

Tactical Iraqi [Digital game]. (n.d.). Tactical Language Training. http://www.tactical-language.com/

Vorderer, P., & Bryant, J. (Eds.). (2006). *Playing video games: Motives, responses, and consequences.* Mahwah, NJ: Erlbaum.

Vorderer, P., Klimmt, C., & Ritterfeld, U. (2004). Enjoyment: At the heart of media entertainment. *Communication Theory, 4,* 388–408.

Vorderer, P., & Ritterfeld, U. (in press). Video games. In R. Nabi & M. B. Oliver (Eds.), *Handbook of media effects.* Thousand Oaks, CA: Sage.

Vorderer, P., Steen, F. F., & Chan, E. (2006). Motivation. In J. Bryant & P. Vorderer (Eds.), *Psychology of entertainment* (pp. 3–18). Mahwah, NJ: Erlbaum.

Williams, D. (2005). Bridging the methodological divide in game research. *Simulation & Gaming, 36,* 447–463.

World of Warcraft [Digital game]. (n.d.). Irvine, CA: Blizzard Entertainment. http://www.worldofwarcraft.com

Chapter 2

Classifying Serious Games

Rabindra Ratan and Ute Ritterfeld

The fundamental goal of this research is to elucidate the important characteristics of current serious games, thus providing a tool through which future
research can examine the impact of such games and ultimately contribute
to their development. Understanding the true impact of serious game play
requires first an understanding of what serious games are. The present research
lays the foundation for such an understanding by developing a classification
system of all serious games based on a dataset of over 600 serious games. This
classification system could potentially contribute to rigorous empirical investigations of serious games, such as those that are reviewed in part II of this book,
by presenting a framework within which such games could be analyzed systematically. By considering the dimensions and categories of serious games offered
here, such research would be better positioned to suggest promising directions
for the development of this valuable genre of digital games.

Serious games are an increasingly important medium with respect to education, training, and social change (Michael & Chen, 2006). Such games are
intended to facilitate deep and sustained learning (Gee, 2003, 2007) and to
reach wide audiences by building on the native language of the Games Generation (Prensky, 2006). The past few years have shown an increase in the prevalence of such games, marked by the emergence of various organizations, Web
sites, and conferences dedicated to advancing this medium. Educators, health
advocates, and CEOs of nonprofit organizations are joining industry officials
and game designers in advertising the assumed superiority of serious gaming
as an innovative means to educate the public. Indeed, interactive games may
prove more effective than other educational technologies and traditional pedagogy (cf. Prensky, 2006; Ritterfeld & Weber, 2006).

Educators are searching for innovative learning strategies that blend enjoyment with education. Games technology would, so the assumption goes, provide the entertainment frame in which serious content could be embedded,
resulting in the emergence of serious games as a distinct genre in the world
of interactive media. Although some researchers claim that any digital game
may provide (incidental) learning opportunities regardless of whether it is considered a serious game or a nonserious entertainment game (cf. Ritterfeld &

Weber, 2006), serious games is a genre that explicitly focuses on education. Thus, the genre has become associated with positively connoted features such as seriousness, education, or learning. Consequently, this recently developed genre may have the power to influence attitudes and selective exposure of digital gaming toward serious gaming by users, educators, and parents.

With the serious games genre, developers took a distinct stand against only-for-entertainment games, claiming that the content of serious games is highly desirable from an educator's perspective. The serious games genre implies that the outcome of playing these games is always advantageous for the player: first by facilitating learning experiences, and second by not having any negative or harmful impacts. Games that would elicit aggression or addiction would not qualify as serious games. On the contrary, serious games should always work as intended, contributing to a self-guided, enjoyable, and therefore deeply sustained learning experience.

Yet, not only is there a dearth of formal research about the true effectiveness of such games (Ritterfeld, Cody, & Vorderer, this volume, chapter 1), but even the definition of a serious game is vague and needs clarification. There is a common stereotype that serious games are synonymous with *edutainment* games, defined by the Entertainment Software Rating Board (ESRB) as those that "provide users with specific skills development or reinforcement learning within an entertainment setting" where "skill development is an integral part of product" (Entertainment Software Rating Board, 2007). While all edutainment games are certainly serious games, the body of serious games extends beyond edutainment, enveloping almost every digital game that has a purpose in addition to entertainment. Consistent with this notion, the Social Impact Games Web site defines serious games as "entertaining games with non-entertainment goals" (Social Impact Games, 2008). But a problem arises when attempting to identify such goals because the game producer's definition of its genre may not be consistent with the user's experience nor the psychological reality behind that experience. Hence, identifying an exact definition of serious games is neither a straightforward nor pragmatic endeavor. The simplest solution to this problem is to treat every game that has been called a serious game as a serious game.

In this chapter we temporarily accept the fact that some games are defined as serious by their publishers without reflecting on whether this claim does actually hold true in order to be able to describe and classify the current body of this new genre. Using only the qualification that a digital game has been deemed serious to some extent, we propose a classification system of serious games that categorizes each game along natural boundaries within the larger body of serious games. This classification system takes four dimensions into account: primary educational content, primary learning principle, target age group, and platform. The result is a basic map of the world of serious games intended to serve game scholars and developers to further their endeavors.

Developing a Classification System of Serious Games

In order to develop a classification system of serious games, it was necessary to assemble and analyze an extensive database of such games. Playing every single game was not possible, given the large number of serious games and limited amount of resources, so information about each game was collected from secondary resources. This information served as the basis for analysis through which natural groupings of certain characteristics were identified. The following sections describe the process of assembling this database and conducting this analysis.

Serious Games Database

The present classification system is based on a database of games that were self-proclaimed, by the game developers, or deemed by any other organization or Web site, as serious. The games in this database included English-language games, mostly developed in the United States with a minority from Asia or Europe, that were released between 1997 and 2007, though the number of games was skewed toward the latter half of the decade. They were collected via e-mail lists for serious game developers, Web sites dedicated to serious games, and simple Internet searches. The unit of analysis was a single game.

In the first wave of data collection, serious game developers were contacted through various professional organizations, specifically, the Serious Games Initiative (http://www.seriousgames.org), which includes the Games for Health (http://www.gamesforhealth.org) and Games for Change (http:// www.games-forchange.org) communities, as well as the Games Studies section of the International Communication Association (http://www.icahdq.org). E-mails were sent to these lists requesting that game developers enter information about their serious game into an online survey template. This survey included questions about the games' serious and narrative content, educational and entertainment methods, major purpose, and target demographics. The questions included both multiple choice and open-ended responses and were based on a preliminary analysis of a small sample of serious games identified through Internet searches.

A significant amount of descriptive information about serious games was gleaned from two Web sites dedicated to classifying digital games. The first was the official Web site for the ESRB (http://www.esrb.org). This Web site provides ratings and classifications of all types of digital games, including edutainment games. As discussed above, contrary to the common stereotype, not all serious games are edutainment games, but all edutainment games are serious games. Therefore, all of the 281 edutainment games from the ESRB list were included in the database.

The other aggregative Web site, dedicated entirely to games with a purpose beyond entertainment—their definition of serious games—was the Social

Impact Games Web site (http://www.socialimpactgames.com), sponsored by the Games to Train organization (http://www.games2train.com). Social Impact Games provides an extensive list of serious games, categorized according to the content types of the games. These content types are similar to the Primary Educational Content dimension of the present classification system. One hundred and seventy-five games were included in the database from this list.

The remainder of the information on serious games included in the database was collected through simple Internet searches. The Wikipedia entry on serious games (http://en.wikipedia.org/wiki/Serious_game) provided links that led to information on 50 additional serious games, and 83 further games were identified using Internet search engines. In some cases, the information collected on these games was similar to the information requested in the survey sent to the game developers, but the majority of these sources contained only basic descriptive information about the games.

In conclusion, 23 games were identified in the surveys filled out by game developers, 281 games and 175 games identified from the ESRB and the Social Impact Games Web sites, respectively, and 133 games identified through Internet searches. Hence, a total of 612 games are represented in the database and used to develop this classification system.

Iterative Analysis and Category Development

After the database was assembled, the classification system of serious games was developed by iteratively examining the information collected about the games from each of the sources. Two researchers consensually searched for natural groupings among the games based on characteristics of the game that related to the larger dimension in question. For example, researchers identified the different age groups that each game targeted and these groups eventually became the categories within the Target Age Group dimension. In order to refine these categories, the researchers classified all of the games according to the groupings and then redefined the groupings according to inconsistencies identified. This process was repeated numerous times until the groupings were as all-inclusive and as mutually exclusive as possible.

Dimensions of Serious Games

The classification system of serious games includes these four dimensions within which the games were categorized: primary educational content, primary learning principle, target age group, and platform. The following sections define each dimension, present the proportions of games found within the categories of each dimension, and provide some examples of games within the categories.

Primary Educational Content

To define the primary educational content dimension of the games, we catego-rized the driving force that makes the game serious and not simply entertain-ing into the following areas: academic education, social change, occupation, health, military, and marketing. Since many of the games contained more than one type of educational content, we identified which content the developer intended to be most important, gleaning clues about this intent from descrip-tions of the games and their potential effects. Figure 2.1 shows the proportions of games based on their primary educational content.

Games with primarily academic educational content are by far the most prevalent (63%) within the dataset. These games, not surprisingly, are inten-tionally designed to teach material traditionally taught within an academic environment. This material is often curriculum-based content, including alge-bra and biology, or extracurricular content, such as nanotechnology or religion. Examples of games in this category include the American Association for the Advancement of Science's *Kinetic City* (2005), "A program of standards-based online science games and other activities for kids in grades 3–5," Ramsbottom, Sidran, and Sharp's *Londoner* (2007), a game in which students experience life in 17th century London, and Nobel Web AB's *Electrocardiogram* (2008), in which players practice "as an ECG [electrocardiogram] technician in a health clinic…and perform ECGs on patients."

Games in which the primary educational content is related to social change make up 14% of games in the dataset. These games espouse particular social

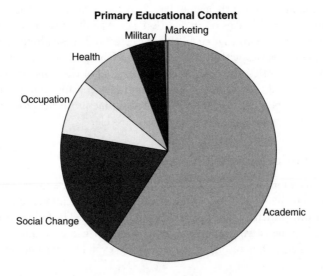

Figure 2.1 Proportions of games within each primary educational content category.

agendas, such as political issues, like supporting particular political candidates, and social issues, such as fighting world poverty or protecting the environment. Examples of games in this category include *Darfur is Dying* (2006), in which players assume the perspective of a displaced Darfurian, negotiating the forces that threaten survival in a refugee camp and learning about the crisis in Sudan, *Waterbusters* (2006), in which players learn how to conserve water around the home, and *Hate Comes Home* (2008), in which players go back in time to prevent a school dance from ending in a hate crime.

Games classified as having primarily occupational content are less prevalent, accounting for 9% of the games. These games give players knowledge and skills that can be applied specifically to the players' occupation, such as training to perform specific actions or imparting knowledge and skills that are broadly applicable to the players' occupations. Examples of games in this category include *Objection* (2008), a series of games to train lawyers in courtroom skills, *The Business Game* (2008), in which players develop and market a new business product, and *Stone City—Cold Stone Creamery, Inc* (2008)., a game designed to train Cold Stone ice cream employees to serve ice cream with specific proportioning to accomplish desired profitability.

Games with primarily health-related content make up 8% of the games. These games provide players with knowledge and habits that improve health, reduce risks, or enable coping with health problems in the player or others. The majority of the games in this category focus either on physical health, such as cancer or sexually transmitted diseases (STDs), mental health, such as dealing with depression, or on a combination of the two. An example of a game in this category is *Re-Mission* (2006), a game for cancer patients in which players manage realistic, life-threatening side effects associated with cancer with the intent of better understanding and managing their physical disease. Other examples include *Grow Your Chi* (2004), in which players grow their chi, thereby avoiding depression, by clicking on the appropriate clouds, and *Shagland* (2008), in which players collect condoms and avoid drinking alcohol in order to have safe sex.

Games in which the primary educational content is related to the military made up 5% of games in the dataset. These games provide players with knowledge and skills that can be applied to military activities, such as air strikes and infantry missions. The lack of prevalence of military-related games is an indication of the sampling bias within this research. Many more military-related simulations and pieces of software that can be considered serious games are likely to exist than those presented in this sample, but such games are most likely used exclusively within the military and so it would have been impossible to collect them within this sample or estimate their prevalence. Examples of games in this category include *America's Army* (2002), a first-person shooter game and recruitment device for the U.S. Army in which players go through basic training and develop their Army career, and *Anti-Terrorism*

Force Protection (2008), which trains officers to make decisions related to their command's antiterrorism posture.

Games with marketing related primary educational content were the least prevalent (<1%). These games reinforce brand awareness, promote products, or target players as potential customers. The lack of prevalence of such games is another indication of a sampling bias within this research. There are likely many more games that have a marketing intent, but such games have traditionally not been classified as serious and so these games were not identifiable through the methods used to collect the sample. Whether marketing can be considered educational is open to debate. This category is listed here as an indication of the potential for such games to be considered serious games, although additional research should be conducted in order to develop a more nuanced understanding of such games. Examples of games that were found in this category include *The Arcade Wire: Xtreme Xmas Shopping* (2008), in which players have a shopping list and must use whatever means necessary to purchase every item, and *Xtreme Errands* (2008), in which players must utilize the features of the new 2006 Jeep Commander in order to prepare for four big weekend events.

Primary Learning Principles

This dimension of the classification system is based on an understanding that the unique advantage of digital games is not so much in their delivery of curricular content but in providing opportunities for exploration, experimentation, and problem solving (Jenkins et al., this volume, chapter 26). Consistent with this notion, we identified the following four primary learning principles through which serious games attempt to impart skills, knowledge, or ideas to the players: practicing skills, knowledge gain through exploration, cognitive problem solving, or social problem solving. If a game utilized more than one learning principle, we determined the primary principle embedded in the game based on descriptions of the game play. Figure 2.2 shows the proportion of games in each primary learning principle category.

About half (48%) of the games within the dataset are classified as having the primary learning principle of practicing skills. These games induce players to practice and solidify basic or advanced skills. These games often focus repetitively on a narrow scope of information and activity. Games in this category include *Math Blaster* (2006), in which players use math skills to complete missions, *The Binary Game* (2008), in which players create binary numbers to learn how the binary numeral system works, and *River City* (2004), in which players use scientific inquiry and hypothesis testing to address 19th century health problems.

Games using the primary learning principle of cognitive problem solving were less prevalent than games that focus on practicing skills, representing about a quarter (24%) of the games in the dataset. In these games, the

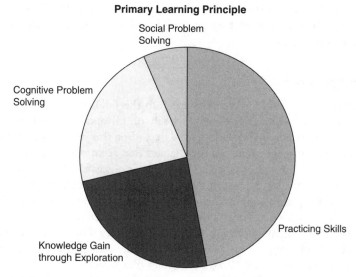

Primary Learning Principle

Social Problem
Solving

Cognitive Problem
Solving

Practicing Skills

Knowledge Gain
through Exploration

Figure 2.2 Proportions of games within each primary learning principle category.

player engages deeply, both cognitively and creatively, with material such as puzzles, brainteasers, or complex hypothetical situations. Games in this category include *Brain Booster* (2008), in which players engage in exercises such as Sudoku, word scrambles, and memory grids, *Urban Science* (2006), in which players learn about urban planning by developing a comprehensive, ecological plan for their community, and *Building Homes of Our Own* (2002), in which players manage the issues of building and selling a home.

The primary learning principle of knowledge gain through exploration was similarly represented (21%) within the dataset. In these games, players acquire information, such as historical or biological facts, but do not engage deeply with such information. Contrary to practicing-skills games, these games focus on a broad scope of information with a small amount of repetition. Games in this category include *Paestum Gate* (2008), in which players explore an archaeological site in southern Italy, and *Revolution* (2005), in which players experience the daily social, economic, and political life of colonial Williamsburg on the eve of the American Revolution.

Games with the primary learning principle of social problem solving were by far the least prominent (7%). In these games, players solve small- or large-scale social problems by interacting in teams, collaborating, or taking responsibility as members of society. It should be noted that games that have a positive social message do not necessarily focus on social interactions and thus may not fall into this category. Games in this category include *Entertech* (1998), in which players engage with coworkers and supervisors, learning about workplace ethics, teams, and company policies, *Quest for Independence* (2008), in which players engage in activities integral to living on their own, such as getting a job, using social services, getting food, and staying healthy, and *Hate Comes Home* (2008), in which players go back in time to prevent certain incidents from ending in a hate crime.

Target Age Group

All games in the dataset were classified into the following four age groups: (1) preschool and below; (2) elementary school; (3) middle school and high school; and (4) college, adult, and senior. Regarding this final group, it should be noted that although there are some games that seem more appropriate for college-age or senior players specifically, most serious games beyond the high school level do not target specific age ranges. Hence, it would not have been appropriate to split this group into smaller mutually exclusive groups. Figure 2.3 shows proportions of games within each target age group.

The most prevalent age groups were the elementary school and the middle and high school groups, with 39% of all the games targeting each age group, respectively. Less prevalent (16%) were games that targeted the college, adult, and senior age group, followed by the games in the preschool and below group (5%). Considering that the average entertainment digital game player is 33 years old (Entertainment Software Association, 2006), this indicates that serious games target younger players than other games, which makes sense given the prevalence of serious games with primarily academic educational content. An example game in the preschool and below category is *Baby Felix Creativity Center* (2007). An example game in the elementary school category is *Jump Start Advanced First Grade* (2008). An example game in the middle school and

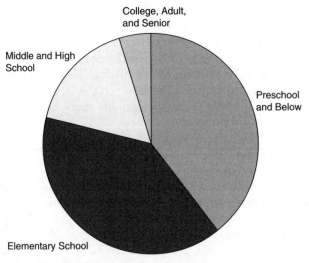

Target Age Group

Figure 2.3 Proportions of games within each target age group.

high school category is *Revolution* (2005). And an example game in the college, adult, and senior category is *The Enterprise Game* (2008).

Game Platform

While the effectiveness of a serious game is certainly dependent on the game's content, the game's platform may also play a role, so games in the dataset were classified according to whether they were made for play on computers or other platforms. The vast majority of the serious games in the dataset (90%) were developed for a computer platform. The remaining non-computer-based games (10%) included games made for DVD, Nintendo Game Boy, Nintendo 64, Nintendo DS, Palm Pilot, Playstation, and Plug-and-Play. Although playing experience and accessibility differ vastly between these non-computer-based platforms, the representation of each platform in the dataset was too small to categorize them separately.

According to Foehr (2006), computer-based digital games are among the most multitasked media among U.S. youth, while non-computer-based digital games are the least multitasked media. This loosely implies that players may pay more attention to non-computer-based digital games, the least represented faction within our dataset. Although current research does not explain this phenomenon, it may be easier to multitask with other computer programs while playing computer-based games simply because of the ease of accessibility on an Internet-linked computer or because the player does not need to turn to another screen. Another explanation may be that on average, non-computer-based games use more computing and video-processing resources than computer-based games, implying that these games have more engaging game play or graphics. Regardless, this discrepancy is important because it implies that the serious component of the game is likely to be more effective when players are not multitasking.

Aside from multitasking, platform differences may significantly impact the effectiveness of serious games based on various facets of the platforms. For instance, a computer's control interface, the keyboard and mouse, is quite different from typical noncomputer control interfaces, such as game pads and remotes. Perhaps different types of input devices facilitate learning in different ways. Or perhaps screen size or potential mobility of a platform affects the ways that serious games are played. Although the present categorization does not provide a comparison of non-computer-based platforms, it should still be apparent that these are worthy questions for serious games researchers to pursue.

Interactions between Educational Content and Learning Principles

By examining the interactions of the various categories of educational content and learning principles, we found that games with both the primary purpose

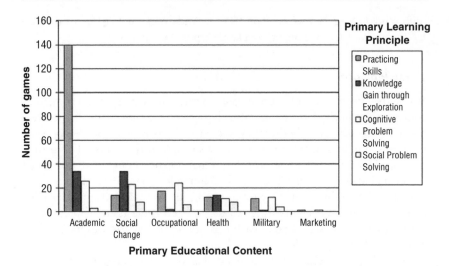

Figure 2.4 Distribution of games within the primary educational content and primary learning principle categories.

of academic education and the educational goal of skills practice were by far the most prevalent. However, in all other content areas, skills practice does not play this superior role and knowledge gain through exploration and cognitive problem solving are applied at least as extensively. Figure 2.4 shows the distribution of games within each combination of categories.

That the majority of serious games attempt to teach the same subject matter taught in schools, using the same methods of repetition and practice, is not surprising. In this sense, the majority of serious games classify as edutainment according to the ESRB's definition of the term. Unfortunately, most serious games do not go beyond this traditional role and are certainly not fulfilling the potential that serious games promise. Moreover, whether a game is the most suitable format for practicing skills is questionable. It can be argued that skill practice remains boring and uninteresting even if it is attached to interactive graphics and embedded in a narrative context. In this situation, the enjoyability features that games add only serve for initial motivation ("this is a different way of practicing") and more sophisticated, visualized gratification. In both cases, enjoyability and educational experiences remain detached, and the promise of an entertainment-education link is not fulfilled. As a consequence, such serious games would not be played deliberately over a longer period of time and would require similar external prompts or gratification schedules as any other skill practice. As Ritterfeld and Weber (2006) argued earlier, a successful blending of entertainment and education in game play requires parallel experiences and is best realized in game simulation that invites exploration and requires complex reasoning. We believe that applying these learning principles to many areas of academic education would significantly enrich the quality and effectiveness of serious games.

Final Remarks

The current research does not provide the basis for in-depth speculation about the future of serious games, but it does create a broad snapshot of the present state of serious games and a structure that could be utilized by future research in this area. Overall, the described trends indicate that serious games span a wide range of purposes and educational goals, with the academic education and practicing skills categories representing the vast majority of games, validating the stereotype that serious games consist mostly of edutainment games. Yet, considering that the sample contained over 600 games, the other categories are still important members of the serious games family. It seems obvious that the number of serious games has been increasing and will continue to do so, and this is supported by the finding that there are more games in the present database produced during the latter half of this past decade. A variety of industries and organizations are increasingly adopting serious games as a means of accomplishing their goals, so other learning principles and educational content areas, besides practicing skills within the realm of academic education, should ostensibly grow in representation. Future research might examine which categories of serious games are growing fastest and perhaps identify other trends in the development of the various serious games categories.

The classification system described in this chapter should serve as a guide to understanding and interpreting serious games as a medium. Future research on serious games could use this framework to situate the games of interest within the larger landscape of serious games. For example, by noting that a specific health-oriented game focuses on social problem solving and targets players who are over high school age, a researcher could argue that this game is relatively unique within the body of serious games and perhaps this has some bearing on its effectiveness. Thus, the classification system presented here provides a new tool for the analysis of serious games.

However, one limitation of this tool should be mentioned. As discussed earlier, creating the classification system was an iterative process of classifying the games according to the groupings and defining the groupings according to the games, in an attempt to develop groupings that were both as all inclusive and mutually exclusive as possible. While all inclusiveness was generally easy to achieve, mutual exclusivity was difficult to attain while maintaining a relatively small number of groupings. Exacerbating this dilemma, in some cases it was difficult to ascertain whether a game's primary purpose or educational goal was in fact primary or only secondary. For example, in *Anatomy of Care* (2008), the player acts as one of five hospital-team members, learning about the impact of their actions on patient care. This game is clearly related to health, but is it occupation related as well? The game developer's description does not specify whether the game is intended to be used by healthcare professionals or the general public, most likely implying that it is suitable for either type of player. Hence, health- and occupation-related categories are not mutually exclusive. Despite this caveat, the classification system developed in this chapter is flexible enough to absorb future development trends in serious games and is a strong foundation for future research in the field.

The potential applications of the present classification system are too diverse to anticipate completely at this time, but it seems likely that nearly all types of research on serious games could benefit from this framework. An important current question in the field is whether serious games fulfill their educational potential. Two chapters in this volume address this question in two subsequent steps: first, by examining the factors that make a game enjoyable (Wang, Shen, & Ritterfeld, this volume, chapter 3), and second, by asking whether these fun factors are sustained in games specifically developed for their serious content (Shen, Wang, & Ritterfeld, this volume, chapter 4). These chapters represent the first research to utilize the present classification system to explore a research question about serious games. Ideally, the findings from this and future research that employs this classification system will eventually be incorporated into serious game development, facilitating the creation of improved serious games that can accomplish their goals beyond entertainment as effectively as possible.

References

America's army—Operations [Digital game]. (2002). U.S. Army. Retrieved March 1, 2008, from http://www.americasarmy.com/

Anatomy of care [Digital game]. (2008). Potomac, MD: WILL Interactive.

Anti-terrorism force protection [Digital game]. (2008). Potomac, MD: WILL Interactive.

Arcade wire: Xtreme Xmas shopping [Digital game]. (2008). Persuasive Games. Retrieved March 1, 2008, from http://www.persuasivegames.com/games/game. aspx?game=arcadewirexmas

Baby Felix creativity center [Digital game]. (1997). Fox Interactive. Retrieved March 1, 2008, from http://www.answers.com/topic/baby-felix-creativity-center

Binary game [Digital game]. (2008). Cisco Systems. Retrieved March 1, 2008, from http://forums.cisco.com/CertCom/game/binary_game_page.htm?site=celc

Brain booster [Digital game]. Demand Entertainment. (2008). Retrieved March 1, 2008, from http://www.arcadetown.com/brainbooster/game.asp.

Building homes of our own [Digital game]. (2002). National Association of Home Builders. Retrieved March 1, 2008, from http://www.homesofourown.com

Business game [Digital game]. (2008). PIXELearning. Retrieved March 1, 2008, from http://www.pixelearning.com/services-the_business.htm

Electrocardiogram [Digital game]. (2008). Nobel Web AB. Retrieved March 1, 2008, from http://nobelprize.org/educational_games/medicine/ecg/

Enterprise game [Digital game]. (2008). PIXELearning. Retrieved March 1, 2008, from http://www.pixelearning.com/services-enterprise.htm

Entertainment Software Association. (2006). Top 10 industry facts. *Facts & Research.* Retrieved September 17, 2007, from http://www.theesa.com/facts/top_10_facts.php

Entertainment Software Rating Board. (2007). *Game ratings & descriptor guide.* Retrieved February 24, 2007, from http://www.esrb.org/ratings/ratings_guide.jsp

EnterTech Project. (1998). *Entertech* [Computer software]. Retrieved March 1, 2008, http://www.utexas.edu/depts/ic2/et/

Foehr, U. G. (2006). *Media multitasking among American youth: Prevalence, predictors and pairings.* Menlo Park, CA: Kaiser Family Foundation.

Gee, J. P. (2003). *What video games have to teach us about learning and literacy.* New York: Palgrave Macmillan.

Gee, J. P. (2007). *Good video games and good learning.* New York: Lang.

Grow your chi [Digital game]. (2004). Baldwin, M., & McGill University. Retrieved March 1, 2008, from http://selfesteemgames.mcgill.ca/games/chigame.htm

Hate comes home [Digital game]. (2008). Potomac, MD: WILL Interactive.

Jump start advanced first grade [Digital game]. (2008). Los Angeles, CA: Knowledge Adventure. Retrieved March 1, 2008, from http://shop.knowledgeadventure.com/Products/JumpStart-Advanced-1st-Grade__20518.aspx

Kinetic city [Digital game]. (2005). The American Association for the Advancement of Science. Retrieved March 1, 2008, from http://www.kineticcity.com/

Math blaster [Digital game]. (2006). Los Angeles, CA: Knowledge Adventure.

Michael, D., & Chen, S. (2006). *Serious games. Games that educate, train, and inform.* Boston, MA: Thomson.

Objection (Trial version) [Digital game]. (2008). TransMedia. Retrieved March 1, 2008, from http://www.objection.com.

Paestum gate [Digital game]. (2008). De Chiara, R., Erra, U., & Scarano, V. Retrieved March 1, 2008, from http://isis.dia.unisa.it/projects/paestumgate.

Prensky, M. (2006). *Digital game-based learning.* New York: McGraw-Hill.

Quest for independence [Digital game]. (2008). Kedzier, D. A., & Quinn, C. N. Retrieved March 1, 2008, from http://www.quinnovation.com/quest/options.html

Londoner [Digital game]. (2007). Urbana, IL. Ramsbottom, J., Sidran, D. E., & Sharp, R. E., III.

Re-mission [Digital game]. (2006). Redwood, CA: HopeLab.

Revolution [Digital game]. (2005). The Education Arcade. Retrieved March 1, 2008, from   http://www.educationarcade.org/revolution.

Ritterfeld, U., & Weber, R. (2006). Video games for entertainment and education. In P. Vorderer & J. Bryant (Eds.), *Playing video games: Motives, responses, and consequences* (pp. 399–413). Mahwah, NJ: Erlbaum.

River city [Digital game]. (2004). Harvard University. Retrieved March 1, 2008, from http://muve.gse.harvard.edu/rivercityproject/

Darfur is dying [Digital game]. (2006). Los Angeles, CA. Ruis, S., York, A., Stein, M., Keating, N., & Santiago, K.

Shagland [Digital game]. (2008). London: Rubberductions. Retrieved March 1, 2008, From http://www.lapoo.nl/shagland/shagland.htm

Social Impact Games. (2008). Homepage. Retrieved May 31, 2008, from http://www.socialimpactgames.com

Stone City—Cold Stone Creamery, Inc. [Digital game]. (2008). Persuasive Games. Retrieved March 1, 2008, from http://www.persuasivegames.com/games/game. aspx?game=coldstone

Urban science [Digital game]. (2006). The Epistemic Games Research Group. University of Wisconsin-Madison. Retrieved March 1, 2008, from http://epistemicgames. org/eg/?cat=14

Waterbusters [Digital game]. (2006). City of Seattle. Retrieved March 1, 2008, from http://www.savingwater.org/waterbusters.

Xtreme errands [Digital game]. (2008). Persuasive Games. Retrieved March 1, 2008, from http://www.persuasivegames.com/games/game.aspx?game=xtremeerrands

Chapter 3

Enjoyment of Digital Games
What Makes Them "Seriously" Fun?

Hua Wang, Cuihua Shen, and Ute Ritterfeld

Given the nature of their labeling, *games* are expected to be *fun!* Popular and commercially successful digital games are all fun entertainment games. But the fun appeal can be instantly diminished when a game is labeled a *serious* game—stereotyped by games designed for purposeful educational endeavors and prosocial causes. While Ratan and Ritterfeld (this volume, chapter 2) provided an overview of currently existing serious games, we focused on extracting fun factors in the context of *entertainment* games. What is fun may be contingent upon individual players and their play contexts; and what makes entertainment games enjoyable may not have the same magical effects in serious games. Yet, by identifying game elements that contribute to overall enjoyability, we can establish a useful frame of reference for understanding media enjoyment in both entertainment and serious games, and for exploring new strategies to improve the fun quality of serious games.

We begin this chapter by synthesizing the literature on enjoyment of media entertainment in general, and enjoyment of digital games in particular, providing a rationale for our unique expert-user approach and research methodology. We then describe in detail the procedure we adopted to develop a comprehensive list of game fun factors, using a combination of inductive and deductive reasoning. Finally, we discuss general trends, propose a potential "Big Five," and present the conceptualization of a three-level threshold model of digital game enjoyment.

Enjoyment: At the Heart of Digital Gaming

Communication scholars and media psychologists generally refer to *enjoyment* as the positive responses of individuals toward media technologies and content (e.g., Bryant, Roskos-Ewoldsen, & Cantor, 2003; Vorderer, Klimmt, & Ritterfeld, 2004). The same phenomenon has been studied under different terminology, such as *pleasure*, by researchers across the disciplines of communication, psychology, education, and neuroscience (e.g., Berridge, 2003; Bosshart & Macconi, 1998; Gee, 2005). Entertainment, via mass and interactive media, is a major source of enjoyment in contemporary societies (Bryant & Vorderer,

2006; Bryant & Zillmann, 2002; Zillmann & Vorderer, 2000). Enjoyment can come from unpleasant media entertainment experiences such as suspense, but most often from pleasant ones: (1) sensory pleasures, (2) ego-emotions, (3) cognitive competence, and (4) socioemotions (Bosshart & Macconi, 1998; Vorderer, 2001; c.f., Vorderer, Wulff, & Friedrichsen, 1996; Zillmann & Bryant, 1994). Vorderer, Klimmt, and Ritterfeld emphasized that enjoyment, which is at the heart of media entertainment, has multiple dimensions (i.e., physiological, affective, and cognitive). They further explicated a conceptual model that addresses the complex and dynamic nature of entertainment experiences, including specific prerequisites of enjoyment that must be fulfilled both by the media and the individual users (Vorderer, Klimmt, & Ritterfeld, 2004). Grounded in the above reviewed understandings of entertainment in general and enjoyment in media entertainment in particular, we focus on enjoyment in the context of digital games in this chapter.

Enjoyment Gaps between Game Developers and Players

Game developers intend to make games fun, and to this end for years they have been using heuristics as guiding tools for usability tests. These heuristics usually include game interface, game mechanics, game story, and game play (e.g., Clanton, 1998; Desurvire, Caplan, & Toth, 2004; Federoff, 2002; Fullerton, Swain, & Hoffman, 2004). However, what the game developers identify as key design factors for game enjoyment may not necessarily match with what the game players want. In fact, there can be substantial differences in fun factor preferences between the two groups (e.g., Choi, Kim, & Kim, 1999). Ultimately, what matters the most is how individual players feel about whether a game is fun or not. Therefore, it is not surprising to see that most of the scholarly discussions about game enjoyment come from the uses and gratifications perspective (e.g., Sherry, Lucas, Greenberg, & Lachlan, 2006). To summarize prior theoretical and empirical work, we organize the following review into three interrelated topical areas: *technological affordances*, *intrinsic motivations*, and *alternative reality*.

Different Approaches to Understanding Game Enjoyment

Vorderer (2001) suggested that Oerter's (1999) play theory offers a useful framework for understanding entertainment media experiences and proposed to (re) frame digital gaming as a form of play in coping with reality: "an intrinsically motivated action, accompanied by a change in perceived reality that is repeatedly used and highly attractive" (Vorderer, 2001, p. 256). Klimmt (2003) further proposed an integrated conceptual model of game enjoyment and argued that during game play the enjoyability of a game may be determined by different factors at three levels: At the first and basic level, the play process can be viewed as a series of quick and direct feedback loops between the player and the gaming system which result from unique technological affordances of digital games (e.g., interactivity) that enable players to have an experience of effectance. At the intermediate level, the play process is viewed as a sequence of interconnected episodes triggered by the player's intrinsic motivations (e.g., curiosity) that unfold with a sense of suspense-relief and increased self-esteem. At the last and most complex level, the play process is viewed as a whole, characterized by the player's active role in engaging with the narrative and their experience of perceived alternative reality in the gaming world (e.g., presence).

Gaming technologies include several features that are distinct from traditional media (for a comprehensive review on the technological affordances of digital games, see Klimmt, this volume, chapter 16; Wang & Singhal, this volume, chapter 17). One of the most obvious features is interactivity (Grodal, 2000; Vorderer, 2000). Based on their systematic review, Lee, Park, and Jin (2006) suggested adapting the concept of interactivity to capture the characteristics of digital games and define it as "a perceived degree that a person in a communication process with at least one more intelligent being can bring a reciprocal effect to other participants of the communication process by turn-taking, feedback, and choice behaviors" (p. 263). Compared with traditional leisure activities such as book reading and television watching, digital games engage more active and higher-level user participation by providing the player with opportunities (or sometimes require the player) to interact with elements in the gaming world and to experience the outcomes of their experimental decision making (Klimmt & Vorderer, 2007; Vorderer, 2000). Such experiences of effectance require only minimal input actions from the player but can result in immediate and multitude of responses from the gaming system, often providing the player a sense of control and empowerment (Klimmt, 2003; Klimmt & Hartmann, 2006). Recent experimental research has shown that game players enjoy watching the results of their own choices and actions in the gaming world (Klimmt, Hartmann, & Frey, 2007).

Intrinsic motivation is another approach of studying game enjoyment. Based on their pioneering work in the 1980s, Malone and Lepper developed a taxonomy of intrinsic motivations in the context of educational digital games for children with four theoretical categories: challenge, fantasy, curiosity, and control (Lepper & Malone, 1987; Malone, 1981a, 1981b; Malone & Lepper, 1987). Similarly, Cordova and Lepper (1996) summarized three basic underlying game factors as choice, fantasy, and challenge. Sherry et al. (2006) extracted six game uses and gratifications dimensions based on results from focus groups and surveys: competition, challenge, social interaction, diversion, fantasy, and arousal. With the increasing popularity of social computing, game researchers and practitioners have recently started to explore player motivations in the virtual worlds, such as massively multiplayer online gaming worlds. Bartle (1996, 2004) offered a typology of player types, placing four types of game players (i.e., killers, achievers, socializers, explorers) based on two intersecting behavioral dimensions (i.e., action vs. interaction, player vs. gaming world). Building on prior work, Yee (2005, 2007) adopted a factor analytic approach and classified three overarching motivations of play in online games: achievement, social, and immersion. Grounded in self-determination theory, Ryan, Rigby, and Przybylski (2006) looked into intrinsic motivations for digital game play, showing empirical evidence that players' perceived in-game autonomy, competence, and relatedness (i.e., sense of connection) are significant predictors of game enjoyment. Other theories such as mood management theory and affective disposition theory also hold potential for explaining game players' motives for selective media exposure and their association with game enjoyment (Bryant & Davies, 2006).

The last tenet of game enjoyment has to do with the digital gaming experience as a state of alternative reality. Scholars have approached this aspect from different, yet somewhat overlapping perspectives. For example, presence is a concept used to describe a psychological state in which virtual objects are experienced as actual objects, or perceptual illusion of non-mediation (e.g., Lee, 2004; Lombard & Ditton, 1997). Although how presence facilitates game play experience and contributes to game enjoyment is not yet clear, Tamborini and Skalski (2006) point out that the relationship between the two cannot be overlooked. Arguably, similar media phenomena have been studied under different terms with their own scholarly rationales and focuses: immersion (Hubbard, 1991), escapism (Oerter, 1999), absorption (Slater and Rouner, 2002), transportation (Green, Brock, & Kaufman, 2004), and realism (Shapiro, Peña-Herborn, & Hancock, 2006). However, the flow theory by Csikszentmihalyi (1997) is perhaps the most frequently adopted framework by game designers and researchers. Even a game-flow model was proposed with eight elements (i.e., concentration, challenge, skills, control, clear goals, feedback, immersion, and social interaction) as well as a set of criteria for evaluating player enjoyment in games (Sweetser & Wyeth, 2005). As well explained by Sherry (2004), although this theory was not developed with digital games in mind, enjoyment of media and game enjoyment in particular share many similar characteristics with the flow experience—"focused concentration, loss of self-consciousness, a sense that one is in control of the situation, distortion of temporal experience, and the experience of the activity as intrinsically rewarding" (p. 336). Sherry's version of media flow theory postulated that game enjoyment can be explained by the balance between individual differences in cognitive abilities and challenges presented by media messages.

Identifying Fun Factors from Game Reviews

Taken together, a significant number of scholars have provided theoretical reasoning and empirical evidence from a user's perspective that help understand the core of game enjoyment. However, this so-called uses and gratifications approach is often limited by the eloquence and insightfulness of the research participants. The implicit assumption that individuals are able to report their true motivations for media selection is questionable. The same applies to individuals reporting not only if, but why a game play experience was fun.

We adopted a unique strategy to overcome these limitations. In using elaborative justifications of enjoyment in the form of regularly published professional game reviews, we still designed our study from a user's perspective, but that of an expert user. Our assumptions are that professional game reviewers are experts who have a broad subject matter knowledge background as well as a diverse gaming experience. When writing reviews of a game, they often draw upon their prior knowledge and experience in making their judgment less idiosyncratic. Moreover, they make explicit arguments about their subjective play experiences in deliberative written evaluations. Therefore, the goal of this study was to identify fun factors of digital games articulated by professional game reviewers.

We conducted a content analysis of 60 game reviews retrieved from two highly credible sources. Results of our analyses rendered a total of 27 fun-factor-related content categories as well as their relative importance based on their weighted frequencies and valence in reviewer comments. The rest of this chapter summarizes and discusses general patterns among these identified fun factors and their implications for serious games.

Methods

Data Retrieval and Sampling

Players often go to popular Web sites to learn about newly released digital games. In fact, many professional game magazines also provide free game reviews on their Web sites. GamePro is one of the most popular professional game magazines published monthly in the United States, with its readership reaching almost 4 million in 2007 (Integrated Media Network, 2007). The game reviews in the magazine are also published on their Web site: GamePro.com. For both the magazine and the Web site, reviewed games are rated on a 5-point scale with fractional increments of 0.25. A newly released game is often given three specific fun factor ratings on graphics, sound, and control, and an additional overall fun factor rating. A game is placed in the Editor's Choice category if it receives an overall fun factor score of 4.50 or above. The site also provides an average critic score for each game based on expert ratings from other popular game magazines and Web sites. Given its prominent focus on fun factors, GamePro.com was chosen to be our primary data source.

IGN.com is another popular source of news and reviews on entertainment games, although it exists solely online. Formerly known as Imagine Games Network, the Web site was launched in 1996 and later became a unit of Fox Interactive Media owned by News Corporation. IGN.com provides comprehensive reviews of newly released games with five specific scores on presentation, graphics, sound, game play, and lasting appeal, and an overall IGN rating score, all on a 10-point scale. Similar to the average critic score on GamePro.com, this site also provides an average press rating for each game based on evaluations from other sources. To reduce the bias of a single source of game reviews and a limited number of in-house reviewers, IGN.com was selected as a complimentary data source in this study.

On both Web sites, game reviews are usually organized by game-playing platforms. The 10 most commonly listed game platforms are: PlayStation 2 (PS2), PlayStation 3 (PS3), Xbox, Xbox 360, Wii, GameCube, PlayStation Portable (PSP), DS, Game Boy Advance (GBA), and PC. For each of the 10 platforms the most recent 15 reviews by the end of January 2007 were retrieved from GamePro.com to create a primary data pool. Each review was assigned a unique identification number, such as 001.1, with the first three digits representing a particular game and the extension representing the source of database (i.e., .1 as from GamePro.com and .2 as from IGN.com). Then, three reviewed games on each platform were randomly sampled from the GamePro review data pool and retained when a review could also be retrieved from IGN.com for the same game. Thus, our final sample included 60 reviews for 30 games.

In terms of genre, 46.7% of our random sample was categorized by Game-Pro as action games, 20.0% were sports games, 13.3% were role playing games (RPGs), 6.7% were adventure games, 6.7% were simulations, and 6.7% were strategy games. In terms of ratings by the Entertainment Software Rating Board, 44.4% were rated as for "Teens," 22.2% for "Everyone," 22.2% for "Everyone 10+," and 11.1% for "Mature 17+." For all games reviewed we also obtained additional data on rating scores and sales ranking. From GamePro. com and IGN.com we compiled overall rating by their own experts, specific ratings focusing on different game play enjoyment dimensions by their own experts (appropriately delineated), and average ratings of other popular game Web sites. The games in our sample were rated by GamePro.com with overall fun factor ratings between 1.50 and 5.00, with a mean of 3.69. Amazon. com, a major American e-commerce company that often sells digital games, listed the sample's respective sales ranks as ranging from 140th to 5,366th with the smaller number indicating a higher sales rank. The average ranking of all games in the sample was 1,287th. For consistency, all sampled reviews were reformatted to contain only textual content with no graphics.

Coding Procedures

The coding schemes were created using both inductive and deductive approaches. Four experienced game players were asked to independently construct a list of commonsense fun factor categories. In addition, literature on game enjoyment was systematically reviewed to identify important fun factors suggested in previous studies and theoretical elaborations (detailed in previous literature review section). Initial coding schemes were pilot tested using a small sample of reviews and modified for final coding according to the following 30 identified content categories (see Table 3.1). The final coding scheme was applied to the text in each review.

Table 3.1 Content Categories, Definitions, and Examples

Content Category	Definition	Example
1. Overall Technological Capacity	General comments on the technological aspect of a game.	"*Liberation* makes great use of the PSP hardware and its capabilities – all of them – to establish its place as one of the best games on the system" [Review 068.2].
2. Usability	The functionality and stability of a game, such as loading time, frame rate, bugs, or navigability of menus.	"… we encountered bugs in flag activation…a couple of missions … stopped working mid-way for no reason" [Review 008.2].
3. Control	The ease, intuitiveness, and effectiveness of controls.	"On the field, the controls are sharp and swift" [Review 076.1].
4. Interactivity	The continuous action-and-reaction loops between the player(s) and the game world.	"Part of what makes it so rewarding is … how easily you interact with everything" [Review 068.2].
5. Artificial Intelligence	The design of and interaction with artificial intelligence in a game.	"Doing more to hamper the gameplay is the enemy A.I." [Review 097.2].
6. Overall Game Design	General comments on game design.	"While there was a lot to love about the original *Empire at War*, there were some design decisions that left many gamers, including us, feeling a little dissatisfied. Petroglyph seems to have taken all of those criticisms to heart and improved on nearly every single aspect of the game" [Review 084.2].
7. Novelty	The originality or innovativeness of a game, such as incorporating new ideas in a compelling manner versus rehashing old concepts.	"…when it comes to tricking, *Tony Hawk's Downhill Jam* is … a different experience from the traditional game" [Review 030.2].
8. Mechanics	The degree to which the basic game rules and core activities are well-established and enjoyable.	"Perhaps the most entertaining aspects of *Summon Night*'s gameplay is the battle system" [Review 041.1].
9. Complexity and Diversity	The quantity and quality of meaningful options presented to the player and how well those options build on each other to enable a deep and intriguing game-play experience.	"As the game progresses, more job classes are unlocked, creating more opportunities to determine what the best team combination is for each area" [Review 037.1].
10. Levels	The ability of game level designs to provide efficient structures to enhance the overall game play experience.	"If nothing else, a more sensible minimum level standard should have been adopted for each area of the game" [Review 062.2].

(continued)

Table 3.1 Continued

Content Category	Definition	Example
11. Challenge	The difficulty of a game and whether it is scaled to provide a balanced experience that is neither frustrating nor effortless for the player(s).	"The downside is that missions are either much easier or much more difficult depending on how many balls you have at the start" [Review 094.2].
12. Freedom	The degree to which the structure of a game allows players to pursue different courses of action at will.	"How you go about the game is entirely up to you, and the game allows for class switching at any time" [Review 037.2].
13. Gratification	When game elements provide players with a sense of reward upon completion of tasks.	"Included in the trick attack mode is the ability to grab double and triple point modifiers, which instantly add a ton of points to the trick total" [Review 030.2].
14. Overall Aesthetic Presentation	General comments on aesthetic presentation, such as visual look, sound effects, and style.	"The overall style is pretty solid" [Review 030.2].
15. Visual Presentation	The quality of the graphics in the game.	"The game has some of the finest graphics seen on the PS2" [Review 001.1].
16. Audio Presentation	The quality of music, sound effects, and voice acting.	"The worst offender is the song selection; it's a veritable cornucopia of musical variety" [Review 036.1].
17. Overall Entertainment Game Play Experience	General comments on the experience of entertainment during game play.	"...fun rhythm gameplay, in which you essentially tap markers that go along with the music" [Review 036.1].
18. Excitement	The pacing of a game and sensory pleasure and arousal experienced by the player.	"Giddy with excitement, I cranked up with the classic. Minutes later, I turned it off in anger" [Review 015.2].
19. Presence	The degree to which player(s) experience the virtual physical objects, virtual social actors, and virtual self generated by media technologies as if they were real.	"*Rogue Galaxy* is what every RPG should strive to be: an immersive experience that places you in a new world" [Review 001.1].
20. Social Interaction	The possibility, requirement, and quality of human interactions during game play, especially regarding multiplayer support / features.	"...this is one of the most addictive multiplayer titles ... With two or more people, it is transformed into one of those games that you just can't stop playing" [Review 076.2].

(continued)

Table 3.1 Continued

Content Category	Definition	Example
21. Length	Whether the game allows for a sufficient duration of play before it is beaten.	"…that stays fun for about an hour at most" [Review 017.2].
22. Replayability	Whether players want to play a game multiple times.	"There is not much point in running through it again" [Review 085.2].
23. Storyline	The existence and quality of storylines and plots in a game.	"*Bully* has a seriously poignant story with great dialogue" [Review 008.2].
24. Characters	The attractiveness, identifiability/relatablity, customizability, and depth of characters in a game.	"The biggest draw of this game is the goofy characters" [Review 017.2].
25. Humor	The use and effectiveness of humor in a game.	"The real joy of playing *Sam and Max* is in watching the hilarious interactions unfold and in spotting the throwaway jokes hidden in magazine racks and picture frames" [Review 085.2].
26. Realness	How a game resembles environments, situations, and social interactions in the physical world.	"*FFIII* has a more realistic feel" [Review 037.2].
27. Fantasy	Whether a game provides players with a fantastical and imaginative experience that is normally impossible in real life.	"I only wish that the writers had been willing to go just one step further and bring a little more absurdity into the whole thing. While the talking dog and rabbit thing are odd enough, everything else in the game seems just one shade too sane for you to totally lose yourself in the experience" [Review 085.2].
28. Other General Comments	Recommendations to the gamers and general comments about a game that don't explain what specifically makes the game fun to play.	"*Bully* is an interesting game" [Review 008.2].
29. Pure Descriptions	Pure descriptions of what is or what is not in a particular game.	"*Pocketbike Racer* has five tracks to choose from that range from short loops to longer jump and ramp filled course. Each course is filled with gates that fill up your power gauge when you cross through them …" [Review 017.2].
30. Irrelevant Content	Background information, general discussions about games or gaming that is not pertinent to the specific game under review.	"Burger King is offering three games for the low, low price of only four dollars with the purchase of a value meal" [Review 017.1].

To accommodate the evaluative nature of the reviews and the different reviewer writing styles, we defined the units of analysis, *arguments*, as verbal expressions which reflect a distinct point of view about a digital game. This allowed us the flexibility to identify words, phrases, sentences, and even short paragraphs that best reflected each of the content categories in this study. For instance, a complete sentence such as "*Bully* is easily one of the funniest PlayStation 2 titles we've ever seen and is one of the few pieces of software out there that can legitimately be called a 'comedy'" [review 008.2] would be coded as one argument or unit for our analysis. Sometimes, there can be multiple arguments within one single sentence. "Its cool boss fights and fighting engine overshadow sometimes repetitive design and occasional bugs" [review 008.2] would be coded as three distinct units as "Its cool boss fights and fighting engine," "sometimes repetitive design," and "occasional bugs" address three different aspects about game enjoyment in this study. Likewise, there are cases where an argument runs longer than a single sentence. "Like most Rockstar games, there's a ton to do in *Bully* whether you just started or have been playing for 40+ hours. Expect plenty of welcome distractions at just about every moment" [review 008.2] would be coded altogether as one unit of analysis.

Furthermore, all 30 content categories except for the last two were each divided into three subcategories in terms of the valence of an argument (i.e., whether it is a positive, negative, or neutral comment on the particular game under review). For instance, "humor in this game is top notch" [review 008.2] would not be coded just as an argument about humor, but a positive statement about humor; "the main gripe I have with *Liberation* is that it is too short" [review 068.1] would be coded as a negative statement about length; and "[T]here wasn't any noticeable lag in the matches we played" [review 017.2] would be coded as a neutral statement about usability. Thus, a coding sheet was created with a comprehensive list of content categories, their definitions, and corresponding variable names on one side; and a table to record the raw frequency counts of all content categories (including valence-specific subcategories), total number of units, as well as information about the game, the game review, and the coder on the other side.

All the 60 game reviews were independently coded by two primary coders, and a third person coded 20% of all reviews to check on intercoder reliability. Of the 30 content categories coded, the first 27 categories were pertinent to the specific fun factors in digital games that were of our research interest, whereas the last three (i.e., general comments about a game, pure descriptions, and irrelevant information) were necessary for our content-coding procedure, but did not provide any insights about game enjoyment and, therefore, were excluded from our data analysis and report.

For the purpose of checking intercoder reliability, the 27 fun-factor-related, evaluative content categories were consensually grouped within five distinct dimensions: (1) technological capacity, (2) game design, (3) aesthetic presentation, (4) entertainment game play experience, and (5) narrativity. Zero-order correlations and *Kappa* were separately calculated based on total frequency counts and modified three-level categorical coding (i.e., low, moderate, and high frequencies). High intercoder reliability was obtained for all five dimensions: technological capacity ($r = .99$, *kappa* = 1.00), game design ($r = .98$, *kappa* = 1.00), aesthetic presentation ($r = .97$, *kappa* = 1.00), entertainment game play experience ($r = .97$, *kappa* = .73), and narrativity ($r = .89$, *kappa* = .87).

Data Modification and Analysis

Sixty game reviews were analyzed in this study. The total number of words was 60,127. The total word counts of GamePro reviews were 13,610, ranged from 207 to 852 words, with an average of 454 words. And the total word counts of IGN reviews were 46,517, ranged from 637 to 2,579 words, with an average of 1,551 words. All reviews were marked with units of analysis, with each argument as a single unit. The review content was coded into a total of 2,292 units for further analysis, 575 units from GamePro and 1,717 units from IGN. Among all the coded units, about 20% fell into the three categories excluded from analysis: 9.9% were general comments such as "this is a great game," 7.2% were pure descriptions of the game, and 3.0% were irrelevant content to the particular game being reviewed. Therefore, fun-factor-related evaluative content in these game reviews only constituted 80% of all review texts. Given the substantial discrepancy in review length between GamePro and IGN, frequency counts of all fun factor categories were weighted by the number of units. Only weighted data were used in our analysis and hence the weighted frequency counts (in rounded whole numbers) are reported in this chapter.

Results

Overall Frequency

Table 3.2 shows the overall frequency of all content categories in descending order. The top five categories were: overall game design, visual presentation, control, audio presentation, and complexity and diversity. The bottom three were: fantasy, presence, and interactivity.

Positives, Negatives, and Relative Positions

Of all the review content related to fun factors, 55.4% were positive comments, 35.6% were negative comments, and 9.0% were neutral comments. As illustrated in Table 3.3, the most frequently mentioned categories in positive comments were: overall game design, visual presentation, audio presentation, complexity and diversity, and control. The least frequently mentioned categories in positive comments were: fantasy, interactivity, and presence.

The most frequently mentioned categories in negative comments were:

Table 3.2 Overall Frequency of Fun-Factor Content Categories

Fun-Factor Content Category	Frequency Counts Weighted by Units	% of All Fun-Factor-Related Content
Overall Game Design	800	17.7
Visual Presentation	591	13.1
Control	433	9.6
Audio Presentation	312	6.9
Complexity and Diversity	299	6.6
Overall Entertainment Game Play Experience	207	4.6
Usability	187	4.1
Mechanics	186	4.1
Novelty	180	4.0
Storyline	170	3.8
Characters	163	3.6
Social Interaction	162	3.6
Challenge	126	2.8
Artificial Intelligence	79	1.8
Length	77	1.7
Humor	71	1.6
Overall Technological Capacity	70	1.5
Levels	68	1.5
Overall Aesthetic Presentation	62	1.4
Excitement	59	1.3
Freedom	56	1.3
Replayability	42	0.9
Realness	37	0.8
Gratification	35	0.8
Interactivity	14	0.3
Presence	12	0.3
Fantasy	11	0.2

overall game design, control, visual presentation, usability, and complexity and diversity. The least frequently mentioned categories in negative comments were: presence, interactivity, gratification, and fantasy.

In general, five fun factor categories consistently appeared on top in the overall frequency ranking as well as the frequency rankings in positive, negative, and neutral comments: overall game design, visual presentation, audio presentation, complexity and diversity, and control.

Table 3.3 Frequency of Fun-Factor Content Categories by Valence

Positive Comments			Negative Comments			Neutral Comments		
Fun Factor	Weighted Freq	Percentage	Fun Factor	Weighted Freq	Percentage	Fun Factor	Weighted Freq	Percentage
Overall Game Design	412	16.5	Overall Game Design	286	17.8	Overall Game Design	102	25.3
Visual Presentation	361	14.4	Control	209	13.0	Visual Presentation	51	12.7
Audio Presentation	215	8.6	Visual Presentation	179	11.1	Control	38	9.5
Complexity and Diversity	195	7.8	Usability	117	7.3	Overall Entertainment Game Play Experience	32	7.9
Control	186	7.4	Complexity and Diversity	89	5.5	Audio Presentation	25	6.2
Mechanics	123	4.9	Audio Presentation	72	4.5	Storyline	23	5.7
Overall Entertainment Game Play Experience	117	4.7	Challenge	69	4.3	Challenge	21	5.2
Novelty	117	4.7	Overall Entertainment Game Play Experience	58	3.6	Length	17	4.2
Storyline	97	3.9	Novelty	57	3.6	Complexity and Diversity	15	3.7
Social Interaction	97	3.9	Characters	57	3.5	Usability	13	3.2
Characters	95	3.8	Social Interaction	54	3.4	Mechanics	12	2.9
Humor	60	2.4	Artificial Intelligence	52	3.2	Characters	11	2.7
Usability	57	2.3	Mechanics	52	3.2	Social Interaction	10	2.6
Overall Aesthetic Presentation	43	1.7	Storyline	49	3.1	Freedom	9	2.1

(continued)

Table 3.3 Continued

Positive Comments			Negative Comments			Neutral Comments		
Fun Factor	Weighted Freq	Percentage	Fun Factor	Weighted Freq	Percentage	Fun Factor	Weighted Freq	Percentage
Overall Technological Capacity	42	1.7	Levels	42	2.7	Overall Aesthetic Presentation	6	1.5
Excitement	37	1.5	Length	39	2.4	Novelty	6	1.4
Challenge	36	1.5	Freedom	28	1.7	Levels	3	0.7
Gratification	33	1.3	Overall Technological Capacity	26	1.6	Excitement	3	0.7
Realness	31	1.2	Excitement	19	1.2	Interactivity	3	0.7
Replayability	26	1.1	Replayability	16	1.0	Humor	2	0.5
Artificial Intelligence	25	1.0	Overall Aesthetic Presentation	13	0.8	Overall Technological Capacity	2	0.4
Levels	23	0.9	Humor	9	0.6	Artificial Intelligence	2	0.4
Length	21	0.8	Realness	6	0.4	Replayability	0	0.0
Freedom	20	0.8	Fantasy	3	0.2	Realness	0	0.0
Presence	12	0.5	Gratification	2	0.2	Fantasy	0	0.0
Interactivity	9	0.4	Interactivity	2	0.1	Gratification	0	0.0
Fantasy	8	0.3	Presence	0	0.0	Presence	0	0.0

A comparison of categorical rankings between positive and negative comments indicated that humor, mechanics, and gratification were more likely to be praised for their contribution to game enjoyment. However, game elements related to control, usability, challenge, and artificial intelligence came up more often when frustration and disappointment were expressed in the reviews.

Particularly "Fun" and "Not Fun" Games

Four games (eight reviews) in our sample were awarded the title of Editor's Choice with overall fun-factor scores of 4.50 or above on a 5-point scale. In these particularly "fun" games, 66.3% of all valenced comments were positive comments. The fun factors that appeared most frequently in those positive comments, as shown in Table 3.4, were: overall game design, control, characters, complexity and diversity, social interaction, and novelty. We also noticed that characters, social interaction, novelty, realness, and gratification rendered relatively more salient than they appeared in our general analysis.

Table 3.4 Frequency of Positively Valenced Comments on "Fun" Games

Fun Factor	Weighted Freq	Percentage
Overall Game Design	82	25.5
Control	33	10.1
Characters	20	6.1
Complexity and Diversity	20	6.1
Social Interaction	20	6.1
Novelty	19	5.9
Audio Presentation	15	4.5
Visual Presentation	14	4.4
Realness	13	4.1
Mechanics	11	3.3
Gratification	10	3.0
Usability	9	2.8
Storyline	9	2.7
Overall Technological Capacity	8	2.4
Overall Entertainment Game Play Experience	8	2.4
Levels	7	2.2
Humor	6	1.8
Artificial Intelligence	5	1.6
Freedom	4	1.2
Excitement	4	1.2
Challenge	3	0.9
Replayability	3	0.9
Overall Aesthetic Presentation	1	0.4
Length	1	0.4
Interactivity	0	0.0
Presence	0	0.0
Fantasy	0	0.0

Coincidentally, four games (eight reviews) in our sample were also given overall fun-factor scores of 2.50 or below. In these particularly "not fun" games, 36.7% of all valenced comments were negative comments. The categories that appeared most frequently in the negative comments, as shown in Table 3.5, were: overall game design, visual presentation, control, overall entertainment game play experience, audio presentation, and storyline. We also noticed that overall critical statements on entertainment game play experience, storyline, social interaction, and length rendered relatively more salient than they appeared in our general analysis.

Relevance of Fun-Factor Ratings for Games Sales

Prior research has suggested that media reviews can influence users' perceptions and their consumer behaviors as well (e.g., d'Astous & Colbert, 2002). Using our data set, we explored the connection between fun factors empha-

Table 3.5 Frequency of Negatively Valenced Comments on "Not Fun" Games

Fun Factor	Weighted Freq	Percentage
Overall Game Design	54	26.1
Visual Presentation	30	14.3
Control	17	8.2
Overall Entertainment Game Play Experience	17	8.0
Audio Presentation	15	7.1
Storyline	14	6.8
Complexity and Diversity	11	5.1
Social Interaction	10	4.8
Usability	10	4.6
Length	7	3.3
Novelty	5	2.7
Mechanics	5	2.2
Realness	4	1.9
Overall Aesthetic Presentation	3	1.5
Challenge	2	0.7
Freedom	2	0.7
Excitement	2	0.7
Artificial Intelligence	1	0.6
Gratification	1	0.6
Overall Technological Capacity	0	0.0
Levels	0	0.0
Characters	0	0.0
Humor	0	0.0
Replayability	0	0.0
Interactivity	0	0.0
Presence	0	0.0
Fantasy	0	0.0

sized in game reviews and consumer purchase behaviors. At first look, the prominent fun factor categories rendered from our content analysis generally corresponded to GamePro and IGN's rating dimensions. We understand that mere frequency counts of specific fun-factor categories cannot be used to predict rating scores in a linear fashion as each count may carry different weights (or degrees) in terms of valence that are not measured in the content coding procedure. For example, there is a qualitative difference in the same one count of positive comment between "humor in this game is top notch" [review 008.2] and "this game is one of the funniest titles on PS2 and one the few that can be legitimately called 'comedy'" [review 008.2]. So, in order to test the common assumption that these rating scores help promote game sales, we analyzed the dimensionality of the 10 fun-factor ratings (4 items from GamePro and 6 items from IGN) using maximum likelihood factor analysis. Based on the Scree Plot test, two factors were rotated using a Varimax rotation procedure, yielding two interpretable factors: IGN ratings (accounted for 37.4% of the item variance; $\alpha = .92$) and GamePro ratings (independently accounted for 31.4% of the item variance; $\alpha = .90$). We also included a unidimensional scale of average ratings posted on popular game Web sites other than GamePro.com and IGN.com, using principal components factor analysis (accounted for 97.7% of item variance; $\alpha = .96$). Factor scores were saved in both analyses. A multiple linear regression analysis was conducted to assess how well these three rating factors (GamPro, IGN, and averaged popular ratings) predicted sales reflected by Amazon.com game-sales ranking. The results of stepwise multiple regression indicated that the average popular ratings was the only significant predictor $[\beta = -.36, t(48) = -2.70, p = .01]$ and accounted for a significant portion of the variance in sales [adjusted $R^2 = .11, F(1,50) = 7.26, p = .01$]. Therefore, we can conclude that the various rating scores provided on popular game Web sites (taken together) do have a fair amount of influence on sales of entertainment titles.

Discussion

Game reviewers, unlike professional writers, are subject-matter experts. Their writing (i.e., the game reviews) may not be as structured or coherent as presidential speeches, but we trust them to provide precise arguments in their evaluations when it comes to what makes a game appealing, interesting, and, ultimately, *fun!* Although the pleasure of digital game play may be experienced and interpreted differently across individuals, platforms, genres, content, as well as the sociocultural contexts of play, we believe that the elaborative assessment presented in professional game reviews represents an effort to reduce idiosyncratic biases while still representing a user's perspective. In this sense, what is frequently discussed and how it is discussed in these game reviews provide important insights into our understanding of digital game enjoyment.

Trend Spotting: What's Attention Catching and What's Taken for Granted

Our content analysis indicated that certain fun-factor categories consistently appeared on the top in all of our frequency tables. They are *overall game design* (i.e., the different game elements, rules, procedures, objectives, and how they work together), *visual presentation* (i.e., the style and sophistication of graphics), *audio presentation* (i.e., the quality of auditory components and effects), *complexity and diversity* (i.e., the number, level, and interconnection of meaningful acts presented to the player in a game), and *control* (i.e., the ease of use and the comfortable feel of game control devices). These categories not only attracted the most attention of game reviewers, but that of game designers and developers as well. It is not news to anyone that large financial investments in high-end digital games would focus on innovative technological development and stylish, high-fidelity presentation. This attention and focus on technology and presentation are unavoidably transferred to the game rating systems as well. Both GamePro and IGN specifically include graphics, sounds, and control as their criteria for evaluating game enjoyment. As our regression analysis suggested, the rating scores offered by popular game Web sites do hold certain predictive power in the economic markets.

In contrast, three fun-factor categories consistently appeared the least frequently in the sampled reviews: *fantasy* (i.e., a fantastical and imaginative experience that is normally impossible in reality), *presence* (i.e., the player's feeling of immersion in the virtual world generated by media technologies), and *interactivity* (i.e., the continuous action-and-reaction loops between players and the game world). The low frequency of these categories does not necessarily mean that they barely contribute to game enjoyment. In our opinion, these factors are often taken for granted by experienced players, and, since the reviewers' perceived readers are game players as opposed to nonplayers, these factors might not be fully articulated in the context of game reviews. In fact, these factors are unique characteristics of digital games when compared with other media formats such as books and movies (Gee, 2005, 2007), and are main topics of study for many game researchers. They are also critical factors that offer players an emotionally engaging play experience, which is at the heart of game enjoyment (Klimmt, 2003, also this volume, chapter 16; Vorderer, 2000; Wang & Singhal, this volume, chapter 17).

Clustering Fun Factor Categories: The Big Five

In extracting the essence of our 27 fun-factor-related categories, we borrow the metaphorical label of the "Big Five" from research on personality psychology (e.g., John & Srivastava, 1999) and propose a potential Big Five of digital game enjoyment including (1) technological capacity, (2) game design, (3) aesthetic presentation, (4) entertainment game play experience, and (5) narrativity.

Like the Big Five of psychology, these are five very broad, abstract, and lexical dimensions that emerged from our content analysis. These five dimensions may be arguably positioned along a continuum with a more technological and designer-centered perspective on one end, and a more social psychological and player-centered perspective on the other end. Our proposal here is not meant to reduce all the possible aspects of game enjoyment to only five clusters, but rather to provide a potentially generic structure of taxonomy in understanding the subject, acknowledging the fact that each of these five dimensions should and does encompass a number of distinct and specific fun factors in digital games.

Leveling Up: Playability Threshold, Enjoyment Threshold, and Super Fun-Boosting Factors

Further comparisons of our content categorical rankings indicated that some factors (i.e., humor, mechanics, and gratification) tended to appear in positive comments more often while others (i.e., control, usability, challenge, and artificial intelligence) were more likely to appear in negative comments; and some factors (i.e., characters, social interaction, novelty, realness, and gratification) were perceived to have contributed more in the particularly "fun" games while others (i.e., overall entertainment game play experience, storyline, social interaction, and length) were thought to have diminished the entertainment value in the particularly "not fun" games. Relative ranking positions of these fun-factor categories implied that there are certain thresholds that a game has to pass in order to be playable or entertaining, and yet an additional set of factors are needed for a game to be super fun.

We arranged these patterns into a *playability threshold*, an *enjoyment threshold*, and a group of *super fun-boosting factors*. The *playability threshold* is based on common complaints related to technological capacity and basic game elements (such as usability, control, challenge, and visual presentation). These are things that are expected to be in place for a game to be playable, and serve as the prerequisites for game enjoyment. If they are not there, it is easy to generate a feeling of disappointment, frustration, and irritation. It is fairly understandable that not many people would be interested in playing a game that looks ugly, takes forever to load, has numerous glitches, and becomes easily repetitive. The *enjoyment threshold* constitutes common factors mentioned in both positive and negative ways and reflected in fun factors related to aesthetic presentation and game design (such as quality visual and audio presentation, complexity and diversity, mechanics, freedom, levels, balanced degree of challenge, and gratification). For example, the game should have decent graphic and sound effects; the player is given a variety of options to explore the game world at different levels, make decisions, and take actions; or their decisions and actions are reasonably connected to the consequences that follow, enabling the player to create a trajectory of personal experience through the game play. These things satisfy our innate human desires for discovery and problem solving and create genuine feelings of pleasure (Gee, 2005, 2007). Finally, the *super fun-boosting factors* make games extremely entertaining. These are the outstanding factors derived from the top games in our sample. These super fun-boosting factors are often related to extraordinary game design elements (such as complexity and diversity, novelty, mechanics, and gratification), superior quality of aesthetic presentation (such as highly sophisticated, stylish, and immersive visual and audio environments), but particularly the role of narrative in games (such as storylines, characters, and humor) and player's social interaction during and after the game-play experience. This has important implications for serious game developers. When making strategic decisions about allocating often limited financial resources, organizations and institutions interested in designing and developing serious games should consider investing in the narrative and social aspects of a game instead of solely focusing on improving the look and feel.

In summary, we identified 27 fun-factor-related categories in our content analysis, using a combination of inductive and deductive approaches. We then suggested a Big Five of digital game enjoyment that includes technological capacity, game design, aesthetic presentation, entertainment game play experience, and narrativity. We further proposed a three-level threshold perspective to understand the enjoyability of digital games. Overcoming the *playability threshold* provides a game higher probability of being picked up for a try by the players. Passing the *enjoyability threshold* offers possibilities of an appealing, fun play experience. Yet, it is when a game incorporates the *super fun-boosting factors* that it becomes exceptionally entertaining. The Big Five may overlap across these three levels. However, taken together, technological capacity roughly defines the playability threshold whereas game design and aesthetic presentation mostly account for the enjoyability threshold. Entertainment game play experience and narrativity best distinguish between fun and super fun games. There is no doubt that we found great variations in the distribution of game quality in the entertainment genre. Crucial for our further understanding of the serious game genre, however, is whether the enjoyment threshold can be realized or even passed with examples of super fun serious games.

Acknowledgments

The authors thank Daniel Ye for his invaluable input and contribution. We are also indebted to Dr. Michael Cody, Roy Alugbue, Brian Strumpf, and Khadeejah Raoof for their assistance with this project.

References

Bartle, R. (1996). Hearts, clubs, diamonds, spades: Players who suit MUDs. *Journal of MUD Research, 1*(1). Retrieved April 20, 2008, from http://www.mud.co.uk/richard/hcds.htm

Bartle, R. A. (2004). *Designing virtual worlds*. Berkeley, CA: New Riders.

Berridge, K. C. (2003). Pleasures of the brain. *Brain & Cognition, 52*, 106–128.

Bosshart, L., & Macconi, I. (1998). Defining "entertainment." *Communication Research Trends, 18*(3), 3–6.

Bryant, J., & Davies, J. (2006). Selective exposure to video games. In P. Vorderer & J. Bryant (Eds.), *Playing video games: Motives, responses, and consequences* (pp. 181–196). Mahwah, NJ: Erlbaum.

Bryant, J., Roskos-Ewoldsen, D. R., & Cantor, J. (Eds.). (2003). *Communication and emotion: Essays in honor of Dolf Zillmann*. Mahwah, NJ: Erlbaum.

Bryant, J., & Vorderer, P. (Eds.). (2006). *The psychology of entertainment*. Mahwah, NJ: Erlbaum.

Bryant, J., & Zillmann, D. (Eds.). (2002). *Media effects: Advances in theory and research*. Mahwah, NJ: Erlbaum.

Choi, D., Kim, H., & Kim, J. (1999). Toward the construction of fun computer games; differences in the views of developers and players. *Personal Technologies, 3*, 92–104.

Clanton, C. (1998). An integrated demonstration of computer game design. *Proceedings of CHI 98 Conference on Human Factors in Computing Systems*, Los Angeles: ACM.

Cordova, D. I., & Lepper, M. R. (1996). Intrinsic motivation and the process of learning: Beneficial effects of contextualization, personalization, and choice. *Journal of Educational Psychology, 88*, 715–730.

Csikszentmihalyi, M. (1997). *Finding flow: The psychology of engagement with everyday life*. New York: Basic Books.

d'Astous, A., & Colbert, F. (2002). Moviegoers' consultation of critical reviews: Psychological antecedents and consequences. *International Journal of Arts Management, 5*(1), 24–36.

Desurvire, H., Caplan, M., & Toth, J. A. (2004). Using heuristics to evaluate the playability of games. *CHI 2004*, 1509–1512. Vienna, Austria: ACM.

Federoff, M. A. (2002). *Heuristics and usability guidelines for the creation and evaluation of fun in video games*. Unpublished master's thesis, Indiana University.

Fullerton, T., Swain, C., & Hoffman, S. (2004). *Game design workshop: Designing, prototyping, and playtesting games*. New York: CMP Books.

Gee, J. P. (2005). *Why video games are good for your soul*. Australia: Common Ground.

Gee, J. P. (2007). *Good video games and good learning*. New York: Lang.

Green, M. C., Brock, T. C., & Kaufman, G. F. (2004). Understanding media enjoyment: The role of transportation into narrative worlds. *Communication Theory, 14*, 311–327.

Grodal, T. (2000). Video games and the pleasure of control. In D. Zillmann & P. Vorderer (Eds.), *Media entertainment: The psychology of its appeal* (pp. 197–214). Mahwah, NJ: Erlbaum.

Hubbard, P. (1991). Evaluating computer games for language learning. *Simulation and Gaming, 22*, 220–223.

Integrated Media Network. (2007). GamePro Magazine readership climbs to 3, 836, 000. Retrieved May 8, 2008, from http://www.idgentertainment.com/pr/pr.cfm?article_id=121.

John, O. P., & Srivastava, S. (1999). The big five trait taxonomy: History, measurement, and theoretical perspectives. In L. A. Pervin & O. P. John (Eds.), *Handbook of personality: Theory and research* (2nd ed., pp. 102–153). New York: Guildford Press.

Klimmt, C. (2003). Dimensions and determinants of the enjoyment of playing digital games: A three-level model. In M. Copier & J. Raessens (Eds.), *Level up: Digital games research conference* (pp. 246–257). Utrecht, The Netherlands: Faculty of Arts, Utrecht University.

Klimmt, C., & Hartmann, T. (2006). Effectance, self-efficacy, and the motivation to play video games. In P. Vorderer & J. Bryant (Eds.), *Playing video games: Motives, responses, and consequences* (pp. 133–145). Mahwah, NJ: Erlbaum.

Klimmt, C., Harmann, T., & Frey, A. (2007). Effectance and control as determinants of video game enjoyment. *CyberPsychology & Behavior, 10*(6), 845–848.

Klimmt, C., & Vorderer, P. (2007). Interactive media. In J. J. Arnett (Ed.), *Encyclopedia of children, adolescents, and the media* (pp. 417–419). London: Sage.

Lee, K. M. (2004). Presence, explicated. *Communication Theory, 14*(1), 27–50.

Lee, K. M., Park, N., & Jin, S. (2006). Narrative and interactivity in computer games. In P. Vorderer & J. Bryant (Eds.), *Playing video games: Motives, responses, and consequences* (pp. 259–274). Mahwah, NJ: Erlbaum.

Lepper, M. R., & Malone, T. W. (1987). Intrinsic motivation and instructional effectiveness in computer-based education. In R. E. Snow & M. J. Farr (Eds.), *Aptitude, learning and instruction: Vol. 3. Conative and affective process analysis* (pp. 255–286). Hillsdale, NJ: Erlbaum.

Lombard, M., & Ditton, T. (1997). At the heart of it all: The concept of presence. *Journal of Computer Mediated Communication, 3*(2). Retrieved May 6, 2008, from http://jcmc.indiana.edu/jcmc/vol3/issue2/lombard.html

Malone, T. W. (1981a). Toward a theory of intrinsically motivating instruction. *Cognitive Science, 5*(4), 333–369.

Malone, T. W. (1981b). What makes computer games fun? *BYTE, 5,* 258–277.

Malone, T. W., & Lepper, M. R. (1987). Ming learning fun: A taxonomy of intrinsic motivations for learning. In R. E. Snow & M. J. Farr (Eds.), *Aptitude, learning and instruction: Vol. 3. Conative and affective process analysis* (pp. 223–253). Hillsdale, NJ: Erlbaum.

Oerter, R. (1999). *Psychologie des Spiels. Ein handlungstheoretischer Ansatz [The psychology of play: An action-theoretical approach].* Weinheim, Germany: Beltz.

Ryan, R. M., Rigby, C. S., & Przybylski, A. (2006). The motivational pull of video games: A self-determination theory approach. *Motivation and Emotion, 30,* 347–363.

Shapiro, M. A., Peña-Herborn, J., & Hancock, J. T. (2006). Realism, imagination, and narrative video games. In P. Vorderer & J. Bryant (Eds.), *Playing video games: Motives, responses, and consequences* (pp. 275–290). Mahwah, NJ: Erlbaum.

Sherry, J. L. (2004). Flow and media enjoyment. *Communication Theory, 14,* 328–347.

Sherry, J. L., Lucas, K., Greenberg, B. S., & Lachlan, K. (2006). Video game uses and gratifications as predictors of use and game preference. In P. Vorderer & J. Bryant (Eds.), *Playing video games: Motives, responses, and consequences* (pp. 213–224). Mahwah, NJ: Erlbaum.

Slater, M. D., & Rouner, D. (2002). Entertainment-education and elaboration likelihood: Understanding the processing of narrative persuasion. *Communication Theory, 12,* 173–191.

Sweetster, P., & W. P. (2005). GameFlow: A model for evaluating player enjoyment in games. *ACM Computers in Entertainment, 3*(3), Article 3A, 1–24.

Tamborini, R., & Skalski, P. (2006). The role of presence in the experience of electronic games. In P. Vorderer & J. Bryant (Eds.), *Playing video games: Motives, responses, and consequences* (pp. 225–240). Mahwah, NJ: Erlbaum.

Vorderer, P. (2000). Interactive entertainment and beyond. In D. Zillmann & P. Vorderer (Eds.), *Media entertainment: The psychology of its appeal* (pp. 21–36). Mahwah, NJ: Erlbaum.

Vorderer, P. (2001). It's all entertainment—sure. But what exactly is entertainment? Communication research, media psychology, and the explanation of entertainment experiences. *Poetics, 29,* 247–261.

Vorderer, P., Klimmt, C., & Ritterfeld, U. (2004). Enjoyment: At the heart of media entertainment. *Communication Theory, 14,* 388–408.

Vorderer, P., Wulff, H. J., & Friedrichsen, M. (Eds.). (1996). *Suspense: conceptualizations, theoretical analyses, and empirical explorations.* Mahwah, NJ: Erlbaum.

Yee, N. (2005, March 15). *A model of player motivations.* Retrieved October 3, 2006, from http://www.nickyee.com/daedalus/archives/001298.php?page=1

Yee, N. (2007). Motivations of play in online games. *Journal of CyberPsychology and Behavior, 9,* 772–775.

Zillmann, D., & Bryant, J. (1994). Entertainment as media effect. In J. Bryant & D. Zillmann (Eds.), *Media effects: Advances in theory and research* (pp. 437–461). Mahwah, NJ: Erlbaum.

Zillmann, D., & Vorderer, P. (Eds.). (2000). *Media entertainment: The psychology of its appeal.* Mahwah, NJ: Erlbaum.

Chapter 4

Serious Games and Seriously Fun Games

Can They Be One and the Same?

Cuihua Shen, Hua Wang, and Ute Ritterfeld

As already elaborated in the previous chapters of this volume, serious games have been acclaimed for playing an increasingly important role in learning, psychological development, and social change (see Ratan & Ritterfeld, this volume, chapter 2; Ritterfeld, Cody, & Vorderer, this volume, chapter 1). Serious games represent the effort to facilitate education through digital entertainment media, as explicated in entertainment education models (Ritterfeld & Weber, 2006; Wang & Singhal, this volume, chapter 17). These models suggest a sweet spot to perfectly blend entertainment and education together in one game experience. Through this entertainment education blend, the advantage of fun game play calls attention to some important social and educational issues, spurring deeper thinking, discussion, and learning, as well as creating opportunities for vicarious experiences that would be otherwise impossible.

Although this approach has a tremendous theoretical appeal, it still remains unclear whether and to what extent the educational enrichment of media content into an entertainment format impacts the entertainment value. Many so-called edutainment game titles are developed with a tight budget and suffer from poor game design and presentation. The fun experiences elicited by these games are rather limited, and the hope that players would select those games and deliberately play them is often not fulfilled (e.g., Moore, Rosenberg & Coleman, 2005). Games that exclusively rely on repetitive structures and practices can hardly provide an immersive and engaging space that enables joyful gaming experiences.

However, there has been a notable increase of more sophisticated serious games (e.g., *Re-Mission*, 2006) in recent years (Ratan & Ritterfeld, this volume, chapter 2), and those games also face the challenge of being successful entertainment education. The seriousness of serious games may already diminish the pleasure even in some sophisticated games. Such an unintended effect may result from two different processes: (1) the *serious* label and (2) the seriousness of serious games, which is absent in entertainment games. First, simply labeling a game as serious or educational may already reduce its appeal to a player. Digital game play emerged from purely leisure oriented cultural practices, and if learning is prescribed through gaming it may inhibit the fun experience associated with deliberate leisurely game play. Second, the assumption that serious games can be modeled the same as entertainment games may not hold true. The educational enrichment may require changes in fundamental game features that ultimately compromise the entertainment experience.

Although researchers have looked at the effectiveness of serious games (e.g., Brown et al., 1997; Durkin, 2006; Lee & Peng, 2006; Lieberman, 2006a; Ritterfeld & Weber, 2006), the enjoyment of such games has received much less attention than their educational outcomes. Game play is often assumed to be enjoyable even with serious content. Some studies, however, reported low enjoyment values for serious games regardless of their successful educational impact (cf. Graesser, Chipman, Leeming, & Biedenbach, this volume, chapter 6; Wong et al., 2007). In this chapter, we examine case studies of seven serious games that aimed to explore enjoyment and the seeming differences between serious gaming and seriously fun gaming. Specifically, we explore whether the enjoyment value in serious games is inevitably encroached upon by their serious purpose and content and whether enjoyability of serious games is facilitated or inhibited by the same fun factors as in entertainment games.

In order to probe the enjoyability of serious games in more general terms, we examine games that cover a variety of subject matters. The great diversity of existing serious games makes it impossible to provide a representative sample in terms of subject matters, genres, underlying educational principles, targeted player populations, and game platforms. Therefore, we conducted in-depth examinations of selected examples from the 612 serious games identified by Ratan and Ritterfeld (this volume, chapter 2).

In order to acknowledge the complex character of game enjoyability, we applied Wang, Shen, and Ritterfeld's (this volume, chapter 3) fun factors which are grouped into five dimensions: technological capacity, game design, aesthetic presentation, game play entertainment experience, and narrativity. Although Wang, Shen, and Ritterfeld's enjoyability analysis referred to entertainment games exclusively and did not include any serious games, we need to establish the same benchmark for evaluation in order to answer the question of whether serious games can be as enjoyable as entertainment games. Our enjoyment assessment supplements the common averaged unidimensional enjoyment ratings (*not at all enjoyable* to *very enjoyable*) with multidimensional fun factors adapted from the Wang, Shen, and Ritterfeld study, thus ensuring comparability in the assessment of the entertainment value of both game genres.

Sample of Serious Games

Given the diverse nature of the serious games dataset generated by Ratan and Ritterfeld (this volume, chapter 2), we first decided to exclude games aimed only at children (61% of all games), including preschool and below, elementary school, middle school, and high school. This restriction eliminated the potential problem of assessing children's games from the perspective of adults.

In addition, non-PC games (5% of all games) and marketing games (less than 1% of all games) were excluded, as they only constituted a minimal portion of the serious games dataset (Ratan & Ritterfeld, this volume, chapter 2). From the remaining 215 games, we selected at least one game from each of the five primary content areas (academic education, occupation, health, social change, and military) identified by Ratan and Ritterfeld. We only included games that are freely accessible to the public, either through the World Wide Web (e.g., *Londoner*, 2007), or through freely distributed hard copies (e.g., *Re-Mission*, 2006). In addition, we included highly sophisticated, high-budget developments; for example, *America's Army—Operations* (2002) and *Re-Mission* (2006), as well as lower budget applications, such as *Darfur is Dying* (2006) and *Hate Comes Home* (2008). The following seven serious games were selected for case studies (see Table 4.1): *America's Army—Operations* (2002), *Objection* (2008), *Re-Mission* (2006), *Electrocardiogram* (2008), *Londoner* (2007), *Hate Comes Home* (2008), and *Darfur is Dying* (2006).

Serious Games Enjoyability Assessment

In order to identify the enjoyability of the selected serious games and contrast those findings with play experiences in entertainment games, we used both quantitative and qualitative approaches. For both strategies, we selected a player with 10 years of experience playing digital games in all genres and relevant content areas. He was not biased toward our selected serious games as he had not played or discussed them prior to this study.

Table 4.1 Sample Description

	Primary Content Area	Producer	Website
America's Army – Operations	Military	United States Army	http://www.americasarmy.com/
Objection	Occupation	TransMedia Productions Inc.	http://www.objection.com/
Re-Mission	Health	HopeLab	http://www.re-mission.net/
Electrocardiogram	Academic education	Nobel Web AB	http://nobelprize.org/educational_games/medicine/ecg/
Londoner	Academic education	Ramsbottom, J., Sidran, D. E., & Sharp, R. E., III	http://www.londonergame.com
Hate Comes Home	Social change	Will Interactive Inc.	http://www.willinteractive.com/hate-comes-home
Darfur is Dying	Social change	mtvU & USC	http://www.darfurisdying.com/

Our player was asked to play each of the seven serious games and report his enjoyment experiences afterwards. First, he had to rate the enjoyability of the serious game (quantitative strategy) and then to describe his experiences in a detailed written form (qualitative strategy). For quantitative assessment, our player's past experiences with entertainment games were used to establish a unidimensional scale to rate the enjoyability of digital game play. The scale was calibrated with entertainment games to ensure comparability of enjoyment ratings for serious games. To reasonably anchor our ratings on a 100-point scale, where 0 means not at all enjoyable, 50 means average, and 100 means very much enjoyable, we asked our player to think of two PC-based entertainment games for each of those three benchmarks on the enjoyability scale. Our player wrote down the name of the six games and provided a detailed reflection on why each game was fun or not fun for him. In so doing, the past experience was made salient to our player and the calibration of the scale was reinforced. In order to elicit a wide variety of enjoyment aspects, we provided our player with Wang, Shen, and Ritterfeld's (this volume, chapter 3) 27 specific fun factors along with the Big Five general conceptual dimensions extracted from a content analysis of 60 entertainment game reviews. Our player used this listing to supplement his own detailed explanations of the most enjoyable, average, and least enjoyable games where applicable. The resulting numerical scale, along with the detailed descriptions of examples at the lowest, middle, and highest points, were then used to anchor the enjoyability scale for the serious games rating (see Table 4.2). Thus, the enjoyability scale our player applied to serious games was reasonably comparable to the one for entertainment games.

To prime our player, the enjoyability scale and the fun factor categories were reviewed before playing each serious game. Our player tried each serious game in a random order with no defined time constraint so as to become familiar enough with the game content and rules to be able to assess its enjoyability. After game play, our player was asked to first rate the enjoyability of the serious game on the 100-point scale and then to write a detailed description of his experience that would particularly reflect on the specific factors contributing to or hindering its enjoyability. In the case of low enjoyment, he also provided suggestions for improvement. The assessment is included below with a brief description of each game's content, our player's enjoyability rating, and our player's evaluative remarks reflecting on the fun factor categories (in the order of technological capacity, game design, aesthetic presentation, game play entertainment experience, and narrativity) where applicable.

America's Army—Operations (70 out of 100)

America's Army—Operations seeks to provide civilians with understandings of various aspects of soldiering by re-creating the experience of an army recruit. Players start the game as new recruits and role play from the first-person

Table 4.2 Calibration of Enjoyability Scale

Enjoyability	Examples of Entertainment Games (Producer, Release Date)	Descriptions
100	–Bioshock (2k Boston, August 21, 2007) –Counterstrike: Source (Valve, October 7, 2004)	–The game design is original, with innovative features –The controls are very natural and simple –The game is non-linear and has many levels –Sophisticated AI –The game is challenging and winning is very gratifying –Very good graphic and sound effects –The game has a very intricate and deep storyline; there is no end to the game, it can be played indefinitely without losing its fun factor –The game maintains a high sense of immersion
50	–Postal 2 (Running With Scissors, April 14, 2003) –The Lord of the Rings: The Fellowship of the Ring (Surreal Software, October 22, 2002)	–The game has decent graphic and sound effects, with some glitches (e.g., the camera is stuck on walls from time to time) –Controls and game mechanics are of average quality –Game play experience is exciting but is not sustained over time –There is not much immersion throughout game play
0	–Beach Head 2000 (Digital Fusion, June 15, 2000) –Driv3r (Reflections Interactive, March 22, 2005)	–Simple, stiff and unnatural control –The game lacks complexity and replayability –It is not rewarding at all to advance to the next level –Sound and graphics are poor –The game is either too easy or too difficult, making it either boring or frustrating.

perspective, engaging in training exercises and classroom sessions. The game is freely accessible to the public, and players can team up with and play against other players around the world.

America's Army—Operations was rated the most enjoyable game among the seven reviewed in this study. Enjoyability is related to the game's superior production quality and especially to the immersive environment created by great graphics and sound effects. The game also has a high level of complexity and flexibility to maneuver the character as our player describes: "…while the controls were a little cumbersome compared to other first-person shooter games I've played, I was willing to put up with them because of the level of control they allowed me." Moreover, the game covers a wide spectrum of army opera-tions with incredibly realistic details: "I was even required to buckle my seat-belt before driving any vehicle in the game. The exercises covered all aspects of military operations including basic maneuvering/obstacle courses, firearm and equipment training, vehicle operation, first aid, surveillance and covert operations training, parachuting, marksmanship, etc." According to our player, the underlying design mechanisms of the game incrementally advance player skills, preparing them for more complicated combat sequences in subsequent missions. The tasks can be quite difficult and they make winning rewarding. All vital game statistics (kills, deaths, time played, weapons used, accuracy, etc.) are recorded and used to produce a worldwide ranking system for each player. As the player's rank moves up, he or she is able to unlock new items, which "made the game much more enjoyable because it provided an objective to strive for, as well as a sense of competition."

America's Army—Operations presents a sophisticated and realistic inter-active digital world with a wide breadth of new scenarios for the player to explore, both individually and competitively. Coupled with good technologi-cal and aesthetic capacities, this game is enjoyable and has long lasting appeal, meaning that players are likely to repeatedly engage with the game.

Objection (60 out of 100)

Objection is a set of games (*Criminal, Civil, Expert Witness*) designed to train lawyers in courtroom skills. In each game, the player must use trial skills to achieve the best possible jury verdict for his or her client. This game is designed for college students or adults and is certified by the Continuing Legal Educa-tion (CLE) to receive CLE credits throughout the United States.

Technologically, the game runs quite smooth and stable, with simple and intuitive controls. For this study, we utilized the free trial version of this game, which is identical to the full version in terms of technological capacity, game design, and game play experience. The trial version simulates the role of a defendant's attorney and allows the player to participate in the prosecutor's questioning of his first witness. The player must judge each of the prosecutor's 20 questions as either proper or as one of 12 objectionable categories. In the full version, obtaining a high score advances the player to a higher level. For someone with no background in law, this task is quite challenging and it took our player five times to reach a sufficient level of expertise to advance to the next level (not included in the trial version).

The game offers a variety of narratives and dialogues, increasing the appeal for game replay. A fairly fast pace also contributes to the game's enjoyability. In general, our player found the game "addictive," "rewarding," and "replayable," although, aesthetically, the game doesn't offer sophisticated sound or graphic effects. Our player described the graphics as "blocky and simplistic." However, our player thought the game had a nice style and humor. The theme song and opening video even made our player "laugh out loud." Therefore, even if the game lacks high quality sound or graphic effects, the simple but stylish artistic presentation contributed to the overall enjoyability of the game.

Re-Mission (50 out of 100)

Re-Mission is a PC-based health-promotion game in which players control a nanobot who destroys cancer cells, battles bacterial infections, and realistically manages the life-threatening side effects associated with cancer. The primary goal of this game is to help young cancer patients better understand and manage their disease. Researchers have also used it to increase cancer related awareness and promote healthy lifestyle among youth in general (Lieberman, 2006b).

Our player complimented the originality of the game concept, but lamented about the lackluster game play. He completed all three tutorial missions as well as the first five levels of the game, but found the game not fun enough to advance further. In each mission, he went through a patient's body to combat cancer cells. According to our player, the game play was " repetitive" and "difficult not in a skill mastery type of way, but rather in an awkward controls, hold down the fire button and hope for the best frustrating kind of way." Our player characterized his experience in each mission as "flying through stages of identical looking tunnels killing identical looking enemies while picking up identical looking power-ups." Conversely, an enjoyable element was the narrative elements of reading various patients' biographies and detailed description of their ailments. Our player found the sound and voice acting "engaging and fairly immersive," and the overall production of good quality. It was the monotonous and bland game play that inhibited his desire to play further.

Electrocardiogram (40 out of 100)

Electrocardiogram teaches players 16 years and older the basic elements and operations of electrocardiograms (ECGs). The player assumes the role of a medical doctor and practices performing ECGs on various patients. There are three main tasks to complete: choose and interview a patient, prepare and administer the cardiogram, and finally diagnose the patient.

Overall, our player found the game interesting but lacking complexity. In terms of technological capacity, the game is generally stable, and the controls are both effective and easy to use. According to our player, *Electrocardiogram* has a solid design, where the tasks "were clean and easy to understand, and did not interfere with the message of the game." Accomplishing a task such as correct diagnosis of a patient was rewarding because it required a fair amount of effort to make the right decision. Although our player spent much of his playtime reading detailed information rather than actually playing the game, he still found the game quite engaging: "I was intrigued enough to go back through more quickly with the other patients to see if I could diagnose them correctly as well." The main drawback of the game is its lack of complexity. There was very little actual game play and the game does not provide multiple levels. In addition, the game doesn't have sound, and its visual artwork is not particularly sophisticated, but of decent quality.

Londoner (35 out of 100)

Londoner is designed to supplement an undergraduate-level history class on 17th century England, and can be played by college students or adults. The player makes financial, career, and other life choices as a young Londoner in order to earn enough money for a living, raise a family, and increase social status. Different life choices are supposed to have different consequences, such as ending up in debtor's prison or leading a prosperous life. Historical information about London in the 17th century is presented throughout the game.

Technologically, the game offered very limited options to control the character. Our player noted: "It quickly became obvious that the financial choices I made had little bearing on the game. Unless I was totally irresponsible with the money I had it was almost guaranteed that I would finish the game wealthy and married. Because of this there was no real challenge to the game, which was a letdown." Because of the disconnect between the player's decisions and the outcome of the game, the game failed to engage our player, to provide a sense of challenge and reward, or to offer a pleasant game play experience. The educational content, presented as historical information in the game, was not imbedded in the game play or correlated with outcome. Therefore, the player quickly skipped the educational content. Aesthetically, the game didn't offer a rich representation of historical London since the only graphics employed are still images, and the game has no sound.

Hate Comes Home (20 out 100)

Hate Comes Home is a self-acclaimed serious game for social change, designed to educate middle/high school aged and above players on the dangers and consequences of discrimination. The technology behind this game is unique among the games rated in this study, because it is a series of short video clips that describe the scenarios and the different outcomes associated with the player's choice. It offers very few opportunities to actually play the game, such as making decisions as to whether or not the player should stick to his or her values or to let discrimination go unchallenged.

The game design of *Hate Comes Home* is primitive and there is no interaction between the player and the development of the story. Despite the stability of the system, this game is not enjoyable to play or to contemplate replaying. Our player explained that "The only task in the game was choosing whether or not to do 'the right thing' by choosing what action to take when a situation arose. While the ability to determine my own outcome in the game was a good idea, there were just not enough opportunities to do so. Out of the 35 minutes of total game time, I was only able to make 3 decisions about what to do. The rest of the time was filled with 12 videos ranging from 1 to 5 minutes in length as well as 14 pages of straight text.... While the videos were engaging to some extent (though fairly corny) I felt like I was just sitting there being lectured, not playing a game." Even when the player was given the opportunity to make a choice, there was little challenge involved since the right choice was crystal clear, which made the player felt "no sense of efficacy." Furthermore, the player's decision is completely disconnected from the outcome, as "discrimination still won" even if the player stood up for the right thing. Aesthetically, the videos are of decent quality, although our player described them as sometimes "cheesy and long."

Darfur is Dying (20 out of 100)

Darfur is Dying is played from the perspective of a displaced Darfurian, where the player must negotiate forces that threatened the survival of his or her family as well as the refugee camp at large. It seeks to raise societal awareness of the genocide taking place in Darfur, Sudan. The game has two major tasks: to collect water and to bring that water to the village to create food or building materials. The main objective is to allow the village to survive for 7 days.

The game suffers from technical glitches. For example, it produces a massive harsh sound every time a militia vehicle drives straight into the camera. Our player also had difficulty using controls in certain modes.

Although the concept of the game is intriguing, the game play is repetitive and awkward, as described by our player:

> The collecting of water was awkward and seemed superfluous, and I lost attention fairly quickly. In fact after collecting water a few times I just let my avatar get hit by the militia's truck so that I could advance to the village mode. As disappointing as the collecting water task was, the village mode was even worse. Moving my avatar around the map was frustrating at best, and although you could complete different objectives like bring water to the fields to create food, or bring water to a housing plot to allow for the construction of new houses, the tasks were exactly the same.

In addition, our player found little connection between the tasks and the intended outcomes: "There was no thinking involved, just walking from the water hole to the site and back again." Poor game play diluted the intended educational effect of the game: "The awkward mechanics and repetitive unrewarding nature of the tasks were so distracting that I forgot that they were even trying to make a point about the severe conditions in Darfur." Overall, this game is not considered as attractive for play, even though other parts of the game, such as visual presentation, are of good quality and style.

Discussion and Conclusion

We looked at the entertainment value of seven serious games by rating and reviewing them on a scale of enjoyability based upon the entertainment experience of entertainment games (see Figure 4.1). The enjoyability of two out of seven games was assessed above average (*America's Army—Operations,* and *Objection*), one was average (*Re-Mission*), two below average (*Electrocardiogram,* and *Londoner*), and two much below average (*Hate Comes Home,* and *Darfur is Dying*). This distribution suggests that our sample covered a wide range of serious games in terms of their entertainment value.

Our first goal was to explore whether serious games could hold the promise of containing as much pleasure as entertainment games. Our findings reveal that serious games can be reasonably enjoyable compared to their entertainment counterparts. Five out of seven games ranged between 30 and 70 assessment points and could therefore be placed roughly around average in the enjoyability calibration. For scholars as well as practitioners, this heartening finding suggests that the blend of entertainment and education in digital games is possible in reality. Serious games, although not primarily designed for entertainment purposes, can still fulfill our entertainment desires to some degree.

Our second goal was to explore whether the enjoyability of serious games would result from the same inhibiting and facilitating factors as in

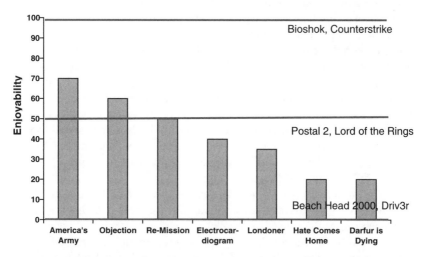

Figure 4.1 Enjoyability ratings of serious games (columns) with scale anchored by entertainment games (solid lines).

entertainment games. In evaluating the detailed reflections on game enjoyability of our sample, we did in fact find similar patterns discussed by Wang, Shen, and Ritterfeld (this volume, chapter 3). Our data suggest that in order for a serious game to be acceptable or playable, it has to meet certain thresholds in terms of technological capacity, aesthetic presentation, and game design elements. For example, it has to have a stable system with effective and intuitive control (when our player could not move the character around easily, it creates great frustration in *Darfur is Dying*, but when it worked smoothly, it offered tremendous pleasure in *America's Army—Operations*). A game must also have decent graphics and sound effects to attract the player (two games sampled here, *Electrocardiogram* and *Londoner* did not even have sound, which further inhibited their enjoyability). In addition, a game has to have some basic structure and formal game elements in place. It certainly diminishes the pleasure of play if the player is given limited options, as in *Hate Comes Home*, must take on repetitive actions, like in *Re-Mission* or *Darfur is Dying*, or when the actions do not result in logical consequences, like in *Londoner*, *Hate Comes Home*, and *Darfur is Dying*.

We have also recognized that a number of *super fun* factors contribute to a high level of enjoyment, even when the topic or content is serious (as opposed to pure entertainment). These super fun factors are namely: narrative-related elements such as character and dialogues (as in *Objection*), humor (also in *Objection*), and social interaction (as in *America's Army—Operations*). Of course, these games with super fun factors are often characterized by a more sophisticated and high-quality presentation and a game play structure with complexity and diversity.

For the serious games examined in this study, we found that most passed the threshold of technological capacity, aesthetic presentation, and game design. A few of the games were less enjoyable due to technological glitches. Most of the other games fell into a second category: they were playable, at rather average fun level, but not highly enjoyable. These games were generally stable technologically, but might have some problems with control or being less sophisticate aesthetically, which inhibited their enjoyability. In order to reach the third stage—to be a highly enjoyable game that is often deliberately selected and played over a longer period—a game must utilize both narrativity and social interaction to promote player emotional engagement and elevate the level of pleasure in game play (also see Wang, Shen, & Ritterfeld, this volume, chapter 3; Wang & Singhal, this volume, chapter 17).

As already noted above, some serious games proven to be effective in achieving educational goals may not be assessed as most enjoyable (cf. Graesser, Chipman, Leeming, & Biedenbach, this volume, chapter 6; Wong et al., 2007). The same pattern holds true for *Re-Mission*, where test results demonstrate that it has significant power to change adolescents' knowledge, attitudes, and even self-care behaviors related to cancer, but which only received average enjoyment ratings from our player. Our study, however, examined the enjoyability of serious games according to an enjoyability scale based on entertainment games. In other words, we found that although serious games are not yet as much fun as the top entertainment games, they can still be reasonably enjoyable. Other studies, specifically those comparing serious games with other forms of instruction, may report other findings about enjoyability levels because they adopt a different frame of reference.

The above conclusions, however, are merely a preliminary exploration of the link between serious games and enjoyability. As mentioned earlier, we only analyzed 7 serious games that are by no means representative of the more than 600 or more serious games currently on the market (Ratan & Ritterfeld, this volume, chapter 2), considering, for example, that the sample did not include games that charge a premium to play. Such games might have a larger investment figure and better production quality which could influence enjoyability. However, the enjoyability of games is not always a direct result of the budgetary investment in game development. *Re-Mission* was produced by a group of leading game developers with a budget similar to those for entertainment games (HopeLab, 2006), but it did not score very high in terms of enjoyability. The game boasts nice auditory and visual presentation, but monotonous game play. Thus, we cannot establish a clear connection between development budget and enjoyability. Budgetary investment seems crucial to enhance and raise enjoyability, but is not sufficient to ascertain high enjoyability.

On the other side, poor production effort is most likely inhibiting game enjoyability. Serious games such as *Hate Comes Home* and *Londoner* had a relatively low budget, as well as low enjoyability ratings, and were found to have inadequate technological capacity, less sophisticated presentation, and inferior game design. Current serious games development is usually supported by non- or small-profit agencies with limited resources available compared to high-end entertainment games development. Therefore, the crucial question for serious games is not whether this genre would be as enjoyable as successful entertainment games if the resources were invested, but what specific aspect(s) of serious games contributes most to the overall enjoyability and hence deserves the most attention and resources at the development phase.

This research suggests a relationship between several key aspects of serious games and enjoyability. First, technical elements such as smooth running and ease of use of the user interface are the backbone for an enjoyable game play experience. They ensure that the player is not distracted or frustrated because of technological glitches. Second, aesthetic presentation, visual and sound effects in particular, is not a sufficient condition for enjoyability. Several games examined in our study have good quality visuals but low enjoyability, such as *Re-Mission*. On the other hand, games like *Objection* manage to engage the player with very limited and even simplistic sound and visual effects. Since aesthetically appealing presentation may be very expensive to produce, it is worth reconsidering prioritizing sound and visual effects when game development resources are limited. Third, the game must have the basic game structure and formal elements of challenge and reward to be enjoyable. Some games with lower enjoyability scores suffer from a disconnection between the available actions and their respective consequences, which were not logical or meaningful to the player. Lastly, we found that humor in narrative and dialogues, diversity of tasks, and the ability to connect and play with other players over the Internet could contribute greatly to enjoyability. Serious games ventures should exploit these super fun factors to increase their enjoyability.

At this point we would like to draw the attention to the greater context of digital gaming in which serious games are a subset. As stated above, the mere labeling of some games as educational or serious may elicit negative reactance in a player. Utilizing games in an educational, occupational, military, or health setting could therefore be a double-edged sword. On the one hand, labeling these games as serious may elicit negative reactions if presented in a leisure context. On the other hand, serious games may simply represent an innovative way to teach and, thus, be highly appreciated by their players. If academic, education, health, or occupation related games do not compete with leisure activities, but with serious communication of less enjoyable format, they are most likely to fulfill their potential. In a gaming context, players may enjoy interacting with content that they are supposed to process anyway; however, whether they would deliberately choose this content over leisure activities is still unknown and could be explored by future research.

Given the patterns we've identified between entertainment and serious games, we believe that the supposed great potential and tremendous promise in serious gaming, as described in the beginning of this chapter, is well founded. In comparing examples of lower to high enjoyability, we identified similar causes for limited fun in both serious and entertainment games. The enjoyability aspects of digital games are very similar for both genres. Consequently, the dichotomous approach of establishing these genres as distinct must be challenged (cf. Jenkins et al., this volume, chapter 26; Gee, this volume, chapter 5), although whether the players of both genres follow the same motivational patterns remains unknown. Thus, in answering the question raised in the title of this chapter we conclude: Yes, serious games and seriously fun games can be one and the same.

Acknowledgments

The authors thank Michael Santa Cruz for his excellent research assistance.

References

America's army—Operations [Digital game]. (2002). U.S. Army. Retrieved Retrieved March 1, 2008, from http://www.americasarmy.com/

Brown, S. J., Lieberman, D. A., Gemeny, B. A., Fan, Y. C., Wilson, D. M., & Pasta, D.

J. (1997). Educational video game for juvenile diabetes: Results of a controlled trial. *Medical Informatics, 22*(1), 77–89.

Darfur is dying [Digital game]. (2006). Ruis, S., York, A., Stein, M., Keating, N., & Santiago, K. Retrieved March 1, 2008, from http://www.darfurisdying.com/

Durkin, K. (2006). Game playing and adolescents' development. In P. Vorderer & J. Bryant (Eds.), *Playing computer games: Motives, responses, and consequences* (pp. 415–428). Mahwah, NJ: Erlbaum.

Electrocardiogram [Digital game]. (2008). Nobel Web AB. Retrieved March 1, 2008, from http://nobelprize.org/educational_games/medicine/ecg/

Hate comes home [Digital game]. (2008). Potomac, MD: WILL Interactive.

Lee, K. M., & Peng, W. (2006). A brief biography of computer game studies. In P. Vorderer & J. Bryant (Eds.), *Playing computer games: Motives, responses, and consequences* (pp. 325–345). Mahwah, NJ: Erlbaum.

Lieberman, D. (2006a). What can we learn from playing interactive games? In P. Vorderer & J. Bryant (Eds.), *Playing computer games: Motives, responses, and consequences* (pp. 379–398). Mahwah, NJ: Erlbaum.

Lieberman, D. A. (2006b). *Re-Mission as an intervention for healthy lifestyles: Impacts of a cancer video game on healthy young adults.* Paper presented at the Annual meeting of the Games for Health conference, Baltimore.

Londoner [Digital game]. (2007). Ramsbottom, J., Sidran, D. E., & Sharp, R. E., III. Retrieved March 1, 2008, from http://www.londonergame.com/

Moore, D. R., Rosenberg, J. F., Coleman, J. S. (2005). Discrimination training of phonemic contrasts enhances phonological processing in mainstream school children. *Brain and Language, 94*, 72–85.

Objection (Trial version) [Digital game]. (2008). TransMedia. Retrieved March 1, 2008, from http://www.objection.com

Re-mission [Digital game]. (2006). Redwood, CA: HopeLab.

Ritterfeld, U., & Weber, R. (2006). Video games for entertainment and education. In P. Vorderer & J. Bryant (Eds.), *Playing video games—Motives, responses, and consequences* (pp. 399–413). Mahwah, NJ: Erlbaum.

Why re-mission? (2008). HopeLab. Retrieved March 1, 2008, from http://www.re-mission.net/site/about/why-remission.php

Wong, W. L., Shen, C., Nocera, L., Carriazo, E., Tang, F., Bugga, S. et al. (2007). Serious video game effectiveness. In *Proceedings of the International Conference on Advances in Computer Entertainment Technology* (pp. 49–55). New York: ACM.

Part II

Theories and Mechanisms

Serious Games for Learning

Chapter 5

Deep Learning Properties of Good Digital Games

How Far Can They Go?

James Paul Gee

In earlier work, I argued that good commercial digital games provide players with *good learning* (Gee, 2003, 2005, 2007). By good learning I mean learning that is guided by and organized by principles empirically confirmed by systematic research on effective and deep learning in the learning sciences (Bransford, Brown, & Cocking, 2000; Gee, 2004; Sawyer, 2006). This actually should not be surprising. Digital games are, at their heart, problem solving spaces that use continual learning and provide pathways to mastery through entertainment and pleasure. Not surprisingly, there has been a growing interest recently in so-called serious games that involve learning the sorts of domains, skills, or content that we associate with school, work, health, citizenship, knowledge construction, or community building, and not limited to pure popular form of entertainment (i.e., witchcraft, sorcery, fantasy war, etc.).

Games can be used for different types of learning. For example, we could, and do, use games for skill-and-drill, for a sort of Trivial Pursuit that takes knowledge to be memorizing and repeating "facts." Or we could seek to use games for the creation of deeper conceptual understandings and for problem-solving abilities that go beyond being able to pass paper-and-pencil tests. The creation of deep serious games for such deep learning remains today more a hope for the future than a realized possibility, though there are intriguing beginnings here and there.

There are lots of features of good entertainment games that make them good for learning. The most obvious learning is simply how to learn to play the game by learning rules, procedures, and causes and effects. A deep serious game would, of course, be a game we wanted people to learn how to play because we believed that learning to play it would involve content, skills, values, and conceptual understandings that we believe are important—a game, for example, devoted to urban planning, social activism, some type of science or business, or the exemplification of a particular perspective connected to ways of understanding and changing the world. There are, of course, examples of such games already available. How well they compare to entertainment games and in what ways is an open question.

What I want to do in this paper is discuss what I think are the deepest and most important properties of entertainment digital games that allow them to achieve powerful learning effects, in the sense both of learning to play the game (and the content and skills thereby involved) and of creating commitment and attachment to play and learning in the game. I would argue that if we are to make deep serious games that really use the power of gaming, then these features will have to be present and implemented well. In the end, I am not sure this can always be the case when we leave the domains (content) usually covered in entertainment games, though this is a matter for future research. That it can be done in some domains is certainly suggested by the fact that it has already been done to a certain extent in entertainment games like *Civilization* or *SimCity*, games that connect to domains (e.g., history, geography, urban planning) that we think of as serious. How far this paradigm can be extended is, again, an open question.

> *Property 1:* Gaming as psyching out how rules can be used for one's advantage to accomplish goals to which one is personally and emotionally attached.

Consider the phrase *gaming the system*, which means using the rules or policies of a system or institution against itself. Gaming the system, in this sense, is, oddly enough, close to the core meaning of *gaming* in the sense of playing digital games. At its foundation, gaming is about discovering how the rules of a game can be used to a player's advantage in order to accomplish the player's goals. When I use the term *rules* here I mean both rules that the game's designers have put in the game and rulelike properties players' discover and exploit (*emergent properties*). In this sense gaming is always about problem solving. But, crucially, this problem solving is integrated with self-interest. There is something personal at stake for the player in solving the problems. It is personal, not just in the sense of winning or losing, which is not required, but in the sense of accomplishing goals to which the player is personally and emotionally committed in the way in which people are often personally and emotionally committed to winning and losing.

It might be objected at this point that the goals in a digital game are set by the designers, not the players. Therefore, they are not really, or at least, not deeply, the player's goals. But this is not, in my experience, how players look at game goals. First, players accept game goals via the act of having chosen to play the game. Second, they adapt and transform the goals personally by seeking to accomplish them in their own way—style, skill level, their own standards of accomplishment. Thus, some players replay bosses they have beat, or repeat whole levels of games, to do it better. Good games allow for this and often offer multiple ways to solve a problem. Third, in many games, players can set goals of their own, which they must, of course, accomplish within the parameters afforded by the game's rules (e.g., getting through the museum level of *Thief: Deadly Shadows* (2004) without killing any guard or ever being seen).

Fourth, in some games (e.g., *The Sims*, 2000) players set almost all the goals themselves.

So gamers care about their goals in a game and problem solving is personal. We know from considerable research on the human brain that people learn more deeply when there is an emotional attachment to their learning and problem solving, when something is at stake for them personally (Damasio, 1994, 1999, 2003). Fear is often the effective emotion for learning in life, but it does not have to be—other emotions work as well. Saying there is an emotional attachment means that something is felt to be personally at stake for the player or learner in problem solving. Winning and losing is one way, though not the only way that this effect is created in games.

> *Property 2:* Gaming as microcontrol that gives rise to either embodied intimacy or a reach of power and vision.

Many but not all games have avatars which the player controls, like the master thief Garrett in the *Thief* games or Solid Snake in the *Metal Gear Solid* games. However, in digital games in general the player microcontrols one or more elements in the game. By microcontrol I mean that the player can affect the movements and actions of that element or elements at a fine-grained, detailed level.

Of course, microcontrol is readily apparent when we manipulate Lara Croft in the *Tomb Raider* games or the Prince of Persia in the *Prince of Persia* (1989) games. However, in *SWAT 4* the player manipulates one policeman and gives orders to three others; in *Full Spectrum Warrior* (2004) the player does not directly move any one character but gives orders to two, sometimes three, squads of four soldiers each. In *Rise of Nations* (2003) or *Age of Empires* (1997) the player builds and manipulates all sorts of elements: soldiers, workers, units, buildings, vehicles, and monuments. In *Tetris* (1985), the player manipulates the whole set of play pieces, being able to twist and turn each one as it falls.

Research on learning and the brain has discovered that such microcontrol has an interesting and important effect on humans (Clark, 1997). The space over which humans feel they have direct and immediate microcontrol is the space within which we humans feel we have embodied power. It is the space which we feel, in some sense, our body fills. This space has been, for most of human history, the space intimately close to the human body, just the area we can touch and feel. Blind people learn to extend this sense of the space they directly control out to the tip of their cane, thereby extending it. With the introduction of the Internet, strange effects can be achieved: if a person is using a web cam to manipulate a watering can in a fine grained way to water plants in another country, the person feels that his or her body has, in a sense, extended to that other country.

By giving players microcontrol over an element or elements in a virtual world, digital games create an effect where the player feels that his or her body has extended into and is intimately involved with the virtual world. This creates an effect that all gamers are aware of: a type of melding of one's self and one's character, especially with agile avatars like the Prince of Persia, the God of War, Lara Croft, Garrett, or Solid Snake, a melding of one's real body and one's surrogate body. What this means is that cognition (thinking and problem solving) in a game is embodied, and the research evidence shows that we humans learn best when we think and problem solve through experiences we are having as embodied beings in the world.

Games with single avatars, like Solid Snake or Lara Croft, create the most personally felt attachment, but games that allow the fine grained manipulation of multiple elements across a wide space, like *Full Spectrum Warrior* (2004), *Civilization*, or *Rise of Nations* (2003), allow for a more "god's eye" inspection of one's manipulation, at the cost of personal attachment perhaps, but with the gain of a wider reach. Such games widen vision, perhaps at the cost of intimacy. Neither sort of game is better nor worse, they just have different effects and are useable for different purposes.

> *Property 3:* Gaming as experiential learning with all the right conditions for learning from experience met.

Games put players in worlds where they experience things. This seems pretty simple, but it is, in fact, the foundation of how games recruit good learning. To see this, I need to talk briefly about contemporary research on human learning. Earlier learning theory argued that the mind works like a calculating device, something like a digital computer. On this view, humans think and learn by manipulating abstract symbols via logiclike rules.

Newer work, however, argues that people primarily think and learn through experiences they have had, not through abstract calculations and generalizations (Barsalou, 1999a, 1999b; Clark, 1993, 1997; Gee, 1992, 2004; Glenberg, 1997; Hawkins, 2005). People store these experiences in memory—and human long-term memory is now viewed as nearly limitless—and use them to run simulations in their minds to prepare for action and problem solving in new situations. These simulations help them form hypotheses about how to proceed in the new situation based on past experiences.

However, things are not quite that simple. There are conditions that experiences need to meet to be truly useful for learning (Kolodner, 2006, p. 227; see also diSessa, 2000; Gee, 2004; Kolodner, 1993, 1997). First, experiences are most useful for future problem solving if the experience is structured by specific goals. Humans store their experiences best in terms of goals and how these goals did or did not work out. We have already argued this is core to gaming, since gaming is about discovering how the rules of a game can be used to a player's advantage to accomplish the player's goals.

Second, for experiences to be useful for future problem solving, they have to be interpreted. Interpreting experience means thinking—in action and after action—about how our goals relate to our reasoning in the situation. In gaming this is just the requirement that good games make players think strategically—that they see through the "eye candy" to patterns and rules (what I will call *effectivity-affordance pairings* below) that will allow them to solve ever more challenging problems as they move through the game's levels.

Third, people learn best from their experiences when they get immediate feedback during those experiences so they can recognize and assess their errors and see where their expectations have failed. It is important, too, that they are encouraged to explain why their errors occurred and their expectations failed and what they could have done differently. Many games give good immediate feedback in terms of players being able to see and judge the results of their actions moment by moment and in terms of the sort of after-play assessments (in terms of graphs and charts) that real-time strategy games like *Rise of Nations* give players when they have finished a session of game play. Games, of course, do not require players to offer explanations for errors and expectation failures, but the social practices connected to multi-player gaming often do. Since people play multiplayer games, like *World of WarCraft*, together, and often hold each other to high standards of play, it is common for players to discuss and argue over strategy and other aspects of play on boards outside the game. Indeed, one will often see this sort of thing even on boards devoted to single player games, as players seek to help other players, for example.

Fourth, learners need ample opportunities to apply their previous experiences—as interpreted—to new similar situations, so they can "debug" and improve their interpretations of these experiences, gradually generalizing them beyond specific contexts. Of course, in good games, good level design pretty much ensures that this condition is met, as the player faces bosses and moves across the levels of the game, where later levels test previous skills, demand their mastery, and introduce new skills that must be integrated with old ones.

Fifth, learners need to learn from the interpreted experiences and explanations of other people, including both peers and more expert people. Social interaction, discussion, and sharing with peers, as well as mentoring from more advanced others, are important. Debriefing after an experience—that is, talking about why and how things worked in the accomplishment of goals—is important as well. Again, games themselves and by themselves don't meet this condition, but gamer communities often do. It is interesting to note that the Army, in using games for training, often requires collaboration in play and debriefing afterwards.

Humans learn from experience. These are the conditions experience must meet for effective and deep learning. Games, and the social practices and communities that accompany them, often meet these conditions pretty well.

Property 4: Gaming as finding and using effectivity-affordance matches between bodies or tools and worlds.

Games create a match between affordances and effectivities. Let me explain what I mean by this: An affordance is a feature of the world (real or virtual) that will allow for a certain action to be taken, but only if it is matched by ability (called *effectivity*) in an actor who has the wherewithal to carry out such an action (Gibson, 1979). For example, in the massively multiplayer game *World of WarCraft* stags can be killed and skinned (for making leather), but only by characters that have learned the skinning skill. So a stag is an affordance for skinning for such a player, but not for one who has no such skill (no such effectivity). Some creatures in the game are not an affordance for skinning for any players, since they cannot be skinned at all. Affordances are relationships between the world and actors (or, as we will see below, between tools and actors).

Let's first consider games that give the player an avatar that serves the player in the virtual world as a surrogate body. Take, for example, a game like one in *Thief: Deadly Shadows*. When you play this game, you get a surrogate body—namely Garrett, the master thief—that you as a player move around the virtual world and which you use to solve problems in that world. You also get a world, in this case a sort of medieval world of courtyards, towns, and castles. However, when you play as Garrett you realize that he has certain skills—he is good at some things (i.e., sneaking and hiding) and not so good at others (e.g., fighting out in the open). As a player, of course, since Garrett is your surrogate body in the virtual world, you inherit these skills.

Inheriting Garrett's skills means that if you want to solve problems in the game's world—that is, win the game—you have to look at the world in a specific way, not as eye candy, but as patches of light and dark and hidden nooks and crannies and edges and ledges that allow you to sneak and hide out of sight. Of course, the game's world is designed in such a way that the world can be readily seen and used in this way.

If you do see the virtual world of the game in this way—and use Garrett's body and skills well and appropriately—you get a perfect match between body (Garrett's built for sneaking and hiding) and world (seen effectively as places for sneaking and hiding). Of course, as player, you can, if you like, go against the grain of this match between body and world—you can, for instance, seek out well-lit open places and have Garrett directly attack foes. You can sort of succeed this way, in fact, but it is a continuous and frustrating struggle.

In games with a surrogate body that you microcontrol—or in games like *Full Spectrum Warrior* where you direct a squad of surrogate bodies as a group without being any one of them—there is always a match to be found between the surrogate body, or bodies, and the world. In *Full Spectrum Warrior* you must see the world as "cover" and move your squad carefully from cover to cover so they are never in danger—and their bodies and skills are perfectly suited for such movements and maneuvers (thanks to artificial intelligence). *Thief* shows you what the world looks like to a master thief, *Full Spectrum Warrior* shows you what it looks like to a combat soldier, and *SWAT 4* shows you what it looks like to a SWAT team member.

Garrett, the soldiers in *Full Spectrum Warrior*, and the policemen in *SWAT 4* have skills that players do not initially have. The player gets to participate in—to watch and use and think with—their skills thanks to having control over their bodies. This is a new thing in the world: an incompetent beginner gets to control a competent body. Of course, I, the player, can send the body into harm's way. I can misuse or squander its skills. However, as I learn to leverage the body-world match—to get Garrett sneaking and hiding in good synch with his world, to get the *Full Spectrum Warrior* soldiers moving from cover to cover in good synch with their world—I solve problems and learn to see the world (in this case a virtual world) in a new way. Anyone who has played *Thief: Deadly Shadows* or *Full Spectrum Warrior* or *SWAT 4* (2005) (or *Chibi-Robo*, 2005, for that matter) knows that once you have become adept at the game, you can, in fact, even look at the real world in the same way as you have learned to look at the virtual world.

Students in school cannot use their teacher's competent body (or mind) to see the world in a certain way (e.g., to do a certain type of biology) and solve problems from that perspective. However, Garrett, and the *Full Spectrum Warrior* soldiers, and the *SWAT 4* policeman can be viewed in a different way. They can be seen, not just as surrogate bodies, but also as tools—smart tools— tools that store knowledge and allow it to be leveraged and used. I, the player, use Garrett (with his built-in skills for sneaking and hiding) to solve problems in the virtual world of the game. And I do this by finding and using the match between the knowledge and skills built into Garrett and the affordances built into the world of the game.

When we view Garrett as a tool we see something interesting. Seeing Garrett as a tool (a sneaking, hiding tool) means we have to see his world in terms of affordances for solving the game's problems in certain ways (i.e., through sneaking and hiding) and not others. This means we see the game world not in terms of its eye candy, but now in a more abstract way. We see the graphically realistic and detailed world of the game as designed for sneaking and hiding. Its affordances for sneaking and hiding are foregrounded and other elements (pretty though they are) are backgrounded. Garrett's effectivities for hiding and sneaking are foregrounded and other aspects of Garrett—many of which are quite interesting—are backgrounded. The (virtual) world is now, in this sense, a more abstract place/space.

Games like *Civilization* and *Rise of Nations*, which let the player microcontrol a great many game elements, move away from an avatar to a set of tools (e.g., the soldiers, workers, fields, buildings, resources, vehicles, and so forth, of *Rise of Nations*). The player searches for a match between the effectivities of these tools (separately and as a set) and the affordances in the (virtual) world. The tools are smart tools; since they have knowledge and skills built into them that, in fact, constitute their effectivities (what they are good for, what affordances they can actually use). For example, workers know how to gather resources or build buildings. This can, of course, get to be quite complex and quite abstract. It is pretty clear in *Civilization* or *Rise of Nations* that you are carrying out plans, engaging in tactics and strategies, building economies and futures, not just moving avatars. However, this movement from avatar to tools is really a step on a continuum, since, as we have just seen, Garrett or Lara Croft can be viewed both as a surrogate body and as a smart tool.

Property 5: Gaming as modeling and using models to make learning from concrete experience more general and abstract.

I have just pointed out that games require players to look through eye candy to find effectivity-affordance matches. Players have to look at the game world in a certain way that fits with the body, bodies, or tools they have been given to micromanipulate. This renders a concrete experience—the experience of acting in and on a concrete real-looking world—somewhat more abstract, as one looks at the world as a system.

This combination of concrete experience and a more abstract view is crucial to learning. I have said above that humans learn and think through their embodied experiences, provided certain conditions are met. However, learning through experiences—experiential learning—has a problem: it can be too concrete, too tied to specific situations, not general enough.

I have already argued that this problem, as far as games are concerned, is partly solved by two things: first, the need to look for—and see the game world in terms of—effectivity-affordance pairings, and, second, the ways in which the conditions for learning from experience—conditions that require reflection, interpretation, and strategy, as well as comparing and contrasting multiple experiences (conditions which we discussed in above)—are met in good games. However, the problem of too much concreteness is solved in games in another way, as well, one that is quite powerful.

Players may be experiencing a game's virtual world, which might be quite graphically detailed, but very often they are using and thinking in terms of models. Models are crucial for good learning (diSessa, 2000, 2004; Lehrer & Schauble, 2000, 2005, 2006; Nersessian, 2002). They help bridge between concrete experiences and more abstract and systematic understandings. Models are crucial to games and gaming, as well.

Models are just depictions of a real thing (like planes, cars, or buildings) or a system (like atomic structure, weather patterns, traffic flow, eco-systems, social systems, and so forth) that are simpler than the real thing, stressing some properties of the thing and not others. They are used for imaginative thought, learning, and action when the real thing is too large, too complex, too expensive, or too dangerous to deal with directly.

Consider a model plane. A model plane closely resembles the thing it is modeling (a real plane). It could be used by a child for play or by a scientist studying aerodynamics. But models don't have to closely resemble what they are modeling. In fact, models can be arranged on a continuum of how closely they resemble the thing they are modeling. They can be more or less abstract or concrete. One model plane may have lots of details; another may be a simple balsa-wood wings and frame construction, no frills. Even more abstractly, the blueprint of the plane, on a piece of paper, is still a model, useful for some purposes (e.g., planning and building) and not others. It is a model that resembles the plane very little, but still corresponds to the real plane in a patterned way. It's an abstract picture.

We can go even further and consider a model of the plane that is presented as a chart with all the plane's different parts listed down a set of rows and a set of numbers ranged along the top in columns. The intersection of a part and number would stand for the amount of stress each part is under in flight. For each part we can trace along the row and see a number representing how much stress this part is under in flight. No resemblance, really, left here, but the chart still corresponds to the plane. We can still map from pieces of the chart to pieces of the plane. The chart still represents some properties of the plane, though this is a very abstract picture of the plane, indeed, and one useful for a narrow purpose.

However, this type of model—at the very abstract end of the continuum of resemblance—shows us another important feature of models and modeling. Such a model captures an invisible, relatively deep (that is, not so readily apparent) property of the plane, namely how parts interact with stress. Of course, we could imagine a much more user-friendly picture (model) of this property, perhaps a model plane all of whose parts are color coded (say in degrees of red) for how much stress they must bear in flight. This is more user friendly and it makes clear the mixture of what is readily apparent (the plane and its parts) and what is a deep (less apparent) property, namely stress on parts.

These are very basic matters. Models and modeling are basic to human play. They are basic to a great many other human enterprises, as well, for example, science (a diagram of a cell), architecture (model buildings), engineering (model bridges), art (the clay figure the sculptor makes before making the real statue), video and film (story boards), writing (outlines), cooking (recipes), travel (maps), and many more.

Models are basic to digital games, as well. Some digital games are simulations in which the player is inside the simulation thanks to the presence of an avatar. Of course, all simulations are models of what they are simulating. So *World of WarCraft* (2001) simulates (models) a world of mountains, lakes, roads, buildings, creatures, and so forth, which, while fantasy, is meant to resemble aspects of the real world. However, players for the most part pay very little attention to this modeling aspect of *World of WarCraft*, because it usually plays no important role in game play. Rather, players concentrate on the embodied experiences of play, problem solving, and socialization that *World of WarCraft* offers. By and large, the fact that it models environments does not matter all that much to the game play.

However, sometimes in *World of WarCraft* this is not true; sometimes the modeling aspect comes to the fore. For example, when I get stuck trying to walk up the inclines and crevices of a mountain in *World of WarCraft*, I begin to think about how the game's mountain is representing (modeling) gravity and resistance in the real world, sometimes with anger, because I realize that it did not model them well enough to ensure that I can get up an incline that in the real world I could, but in the game I can't. In other games, where one's character seems more than tall enough to jump over an obstacle, but can't, the player is well aware that the model is a model and isn't working well. So, in games like *World of WarCraft* the modeling aspect comes to the fore only when there are problems.

However, there are other games in which the modeling aspect of the simulation is crucial. Players in these games are having experiences, just as they are in *World of WarCraft* or *Half-Life* (1998), but the modeling aspect is also crucial at nearly all points, not just intermittently. In a game like *Civilization*, for instance, the depictions of landscapes, cities, and armies are not very realistic, not nearly as realistic as in *World of WarCraft*. For example, in *Civilization*, a small set of soldiers stands for a whole army and the landscape looks like a colorful map. However, given the nature of game play in *Civilization*, these are clearly meant to be models of real things, stressing only some of their properties. They are clearly meant to be used for quite specific purposes in the game, for example, modeling large scale military interactions across time and space and modeling the role of geographical features in the historical development of different civilizations.

However, even in games where, at the big picture level, modeling is not integral to game play in terms of their overall virtual worlds—games like *World of WarCraft* or *Half-Life*—very often models appear ubiquitously inside the game to aid the player's problem solving. For example, most games have maps that model the terrain (and maps are pretty abstract models) and allow players to navigate and plan. The bottom of *World of WarCraft*'s screen is an abstract model of the player's abilities and skills. Lots of games allow players to turn on and off a myriad of screens that display charts, lists, and graphs depicting various aspects of game play, equipment, abilities, skills, accomplishments, and other things. In a first-person shooter, the screen that shows all the guns a player has, their firing types, and their ammunition is a model of the game's weapon system, an abstract picture of it made for planning, strategizing, predicting, and problem-solving.

Models inside games go further, much further. Players and player communities often build modifications of games that are models used to solve certain sorts of problems. For example, *World of WarCraft* players can download a model that displays a chart (during actual fighting) that lists each player's class (e.g., Druid, Priest, Warrior, Mage, Paladin, etc.) and the amount of damage they are doing in a group raid inside a dungeon. This chart (*damage meter*) can be used to check publicly that each player is holding up his end of the group task. (So Warriors better be doing lots of damage and healing "holy" Priests better not be—they had better be concentrating on healing rather than attacking.) This is one of several models, almost all of them made by players, that help players solve a very real-world problem, namely the problem of individuals attempting to take a free ride in a group or attempting to hide their lack of skill. At the same time, such models generate a good deal of debate on fan forums about how good they are and how they should or should not used.

Models and modeling reach a new pitch in games like those in the *Tony Hawk* series. First, each game is a model of the practices and culture of skateboarders. Within that larger model, there are a myriad of models of boards, dress styles, tricks, and parks. However, players can readily design their own skaters, clothes, boards, tricks, points for tricks, and skate parks. That is, they can build their own models. When they build a model skate park, they interact with a set of more abstract models of environments (screens made up of grids and rotatable objects) that help them build the more specific and realistic looking model skate park they want—like a toy plane. Indeed, as skating in the real world changes, the models in the game and those made by players change, each time trying to capture things that are seen as important or essential, all the while balancing a variety of criteria about fidelity to different things and systems. This is modeling with a vengeance. Here modeling is integral to game play at all levels and in every way.

Models and modeling are important to learning because, although people learn from their interpreted experiences, as we have argued above, models and modeling allow specific aspects of experience to be interrogated and used for problem solving in ways that lead from concreteness to abstraction (diSessa, 2004; Lehrer & Schauble, 2006). Models and modeling are important to game design because in-game models are tools to facilitate, enrich, and deepen the problem solving the game designer is building.

Property 6: Games as player-enacted stories or trajectories.

There has been much controversy over the role of story in games. Of course, many, but by no means all, digital games have stories much in the way in which books and movies have stories—for example, the *Final Fantasy* games or the *Metal Gear Solid* games. This is what I will call the *designers' story*: The player has not made this story up, the games' designers have. I do not want to enter here into the controversies over the role of such stories in games, save to say that there is a second story in games that is, in my view, more important to game play than is the designers' story.

To see this second story, consider a game like *Castlevania: Symphony of the*

Night (1997). Any one who has played this great game and who does everything you can do in the game will, in the end, have done all the same things as any other player. A player who does less will have done some subset of this. This is just like a book. Everyone who reads the whole book will have read the same text. Any reader who reads less will have read some subset of this whole text.

However, each player of *Castlevania* will have done and found things in an entirely different order and in different ways from each other. Players will have ventured into the parts of the castle in a different order; they will have revisited them a different number of times. They will have faced the bosses in the game at different times and will have defeated them in different ways and with different degrees of difficulty. They will have found key items in the game in different orders. They will have made different choices of what strategies to use, when to save, and what equipment to wear and use. This is to say that each player has enacted a different *trajectory* through the game.

There is no sense (or not much of one, or not one in the same sense) of different trajectories in a game like *Tetris*. What allows each of us to feel and recognize a different trajectory in a game like *Castlevania* is that such games are composed of events that we, as players, created and set into motion. We can recognize that a distinctive event (e.g., Me as Alucard killed his/my first Sword Lord) happened before or after another distinctive event (e.g., Me as Alucard who found the gold ring). Such events give the player a way to mark time, and against this marking each player comes to see that he or she has enacted a unique trajectory through the game space.

This trajectory has an important consequence. Your Alucard is different from my Alucard; yours has had a different trajectory from mine. This means that the virtual character in the game world, Alucard in this case, is different for each player in a significant and meaningful way. The hero is, thus, not Alucard from the designer's story, nor is it you the real-world player (you are, after all, playing Alucard). It is "Alucard-you," a melding of the virtual character, Alucard, and you, the real-world player who has steered Alucard on a unique trajectory through the game.

The hero in my own personal trajectory through the game was "Alucard-Jim," a blend between a virtual (Alucard) and real person (me). This is why players can so readily switch between saying, "Alucard killed the Sword Lord" and "I killed the Sword Lord." The real actor here is a composite or blend: Alucard-you (me).

This trajectory is the second story. Let's call it, to distinguish it from the designer's story, the *trajectory story*. This is the important story in *Castlevania*. Players can play the game over again to gain another trajectory—good games lend themselves to such replay, to the building of new trajectories. This trajectory is personal and individual in a game like *Castlevania*. It can be both personal and social in a multiplayer game.

So when I play *Castlevania*, I generate a unique story—the trajectory story. This story is the enacted tale of Alucard-Jim and I can lard it up with all the fantasies, values, and morals I want to—no permissions needed, no critics allowed.

In the Alucard-Jim story, Alucard-Jim was only able to beat the large knight with the owl on his shoulder at the front of the castle (the Owl Knight) after Alucard-Jim became more powerful (Alucard by gaining experience and Jim by getting more practice and skill). For some other player, let's say "Jane," Alucard-Jane had a much easier time killing the Owl Knight early on with less hassle and effort than did Alucard-Jim. Alucard-Jim had, in fact, tried unsuccessfully several times earlier to kill the Owl Knight. After Alucard and Jim had gained enough experience, Alucard-Jim proudly marched to the front of the castle and, with great glee, mastered him easily.

This event (Alucard-Jim finally kills the Owl Knight at the front of the castle) became one of my own unique high points in the story I was performing in playing the game. Though the designers' own the designer's story, I own the Alucard-Jim story, the trajectory story, which has its own unique high and low points. Jane has a different trajectory story. Each of us human beings has a unique trajectory through life. Indeed, the trajectory (second story) I am talking about in *Castlevania* is much more similar to our own life trajectories than it is to the linear and intricately predesigned stories in books and movies.

The trajectory story is apparent and immediate in games with an individual avatar like Alucard, whether this is played in the first or third person. But the effect, with different nuances, is present in other sorts of games, as well. In *Full Spectrum Warrior*, the player still says things like "we lost," identifying with the team (the squads he or she controls). In *Civilization*, players identify with their civilization. In both cases—*Full Spectrum Warrior* or *Civilization*—players have unique trajectories through the games. So, too, for yet other types of games, as long as there are player enacted events that can be lined up in time.

The trajectory a player takes through a game—the virtual-real story—can, in certain circumstances, give space a special sort of deep meaning in a game. If I can revisit spaces (places) in a game, and different things happen there at different times (e.g., I have different experiences with the Owl Lord each time I go to the front of the castle in *Castlevania* or I have different quest and social experiences in the Bone Wastes in *World of WarCraft* over time), then there are layers of meaning (layers of my trajectory story) laid down, one on top of the other, at that place.

Space becomes a patchwork of such meaning-layered places, connected in a myriad of ways through the meaningful (storied, in the trajectory sense) connections across layers (this event that happened *here* is connected, in some fashion, with that event that happened *there*). Anyone who has played *World of WarCraft* a great deal has had this feeling of layered and connected space as they fly over regions of the game, looking down at a now fully storied space— storied in the sense of my trajectory story. Connections within and across layers can be meaningful in many different ways to players, most certainly including emotionally meaningful.

Conclusion

I restate the deep learning properties of good digital games here in terms of questions. Deep games—entertainment or serious—not only have these properties, but implement them powerfully. There are, of course, perfectly entertaining games that meet none of these conditions—for example, the delightful *Sam and Max* games do not. Games do not have to be long and complicated to meet the conditions—*Diner Dash* meets them and is neither. *Sam and Max* probably helps people with mental alertness and general problem solving skills, but *Diner Dash* does more—in addition, it makes the player embody and empathize with a set of connected problems (a problem space) connected to a certain identity or way of being in the world. So do *Thief: Deadly Shadows*, *Full Spectrum Warrior*, *SWAT 4*, *Civilization 4* (2008), and *Rome: Total War* (2004). A game like *The Sims* invites players to create these properties for themselves, offering them resources that allow them to do so in powerful and entertaining ways.

For me, it is an interesting question to ask if we can make games beyond games like *America's Army*, *Full Spectrum Warrior*, and *SWAT 4* (and their more official training versions), games that focus on armed conflict or controlling armed conflict. At their best, the properties below allow players to have powerful experiences that compete with experience in the real world precisely because experiences in the real world, at their best—when we humans feel control, agency, deep learning, and mastery—meet just these properties. But that is a story for another day.

Property 1: Does game play allow and encourage the player to "psych out" and take advantage of an underlying rule system to accomplish personally held goals to which the player is emotionally attached?

Property 2: Does the game allow the player microcontrol that creates either a sense of embodied intimacy or a feeling of reach in power and vision?

Property 3: Does the game offer the player experiences that meet the conditions for good learning (discussed above)?

Property 4: Does the game allow, encourage, and help players find and use effectivity–affordance matches between smart bodies or tools and worlds?

Property 5: Does the game use modeling or models to make learning from experience more general and abstract?

Property 6: Does the game allow and encourage the player to enact his or own unique trajectory through the game, thereby creating his or her own story?

References

Age of empires [Digital game]. (n.d.). Dallas, TX: Ensemble Studios. Retrieved March 20, 2009, from http://www.microsoft.com/GAMES/EMPIRES/

Barsalou, L. W. (1999a). Language comprehension: Archival memory or preparation for situated action. *Discourse Processes, 28,* 61–80.

Barsalou, L. W. (1999b). Perceptual symbol systems. *Behavioral and Brain Sciences, 22,* 577–660.

Bransford, J., Brown, A. L., & Cocking, R. R. (2000). *How people learn: Brain, mind, experience, and school* (Rev. ed.). Washington, DC: National Academy Press.

Castlevania: Symphony of the night [Digital game]. (n.d.). Tokyo, Japan: Konami. Retrieved March 20, 2009, from http://castlevania.classicgaming.gamespy.com/ Games/sotn.html

Chibi-Robo, (2005). Retrieved March 20, 2009, from http://www.chibi-robo.com

Civilization IV [Digital game]. (2008). Hunt Valley, MD: Firaxis Games. Retrieved March 20, 2009, from http://www.civilization.com/

Clark, A. (1993). *Associative engines: Connectionism, concepts, and representational change.* Cambridge, England: Cambridge University Press.

Clark, A. (1997). *Being there: Putting brain, body, and world together again.* Cambridge, MA: MIT Press.

Damasio, A. (1994). *Descartes' error: Emotion, reason, and the human brain.* New York: Penguin.

Damasio, A. (1999). *The feeling of what happens: Body and emotion in the making of consciousness.* Orlando, FL: Harvest Books.

Damasio, A. (2003). *Looking for Spinoza: Joy, sorrow, and the feeling brain.* Orlando, FL: Harcourt.

Diner dash [Digital game]. (2008). New York: Gamelab.

diSessa, A. A. (2000). *Changing minds: Computers, learning, and literacy.* Cambridge, MA: MIT Press.

diSessa, A. A. (2004). Metarepresentation: Native competence and targets for instruction. *Cognition and Instruction, 22,* 293–331.

Full spectrum warrior [Digital game]. (n.d.). Los Angeles: Pandemic Studios. Retrieved March 20, 2009, from http://www.fullspectrumwarrior.com/

Gee, J. P. (1992). *The social mind: Language, ideology, and social practice.* New York: Bergin & Garvey.

Gee, J. P. (2003). *What video games have to teach us about learning and literacy.* New York: Palgrave/Macmillan.

Gee, J. P. (2004). *Situated language and learning: A critique of traditional schooling.* London: Routledge.

Gee, J. P. (2005). *Why video games are good for your soul: Pleasure and learning.* Melbourne, Australia: Common Ground.

Gee, J. P. (2007). *Good video games and good learning: Collected essays on video games, learning, and literacy.* New York: Lang.

Gibson, J. J. (1979). *The ecological approach to visual perception.* Boston: Houghton Mifflin.

Glenberg, A. M. (1997). What is memory for. *Behavioral and Brain Sciences, 20,* 1–55.

Half-life [Digital game]. (n.d.). Bellevue, WA: Valve Software.

Hawkins, J. (2005). *On intelligence.* New York: Henry Holt.

Kolodner, J. L. (1993). *Case based reasoning.* San Mateo, CA: Morgan Kaufmann.

Kolodner, J. L. (1997). Educational implications of analogy: A view from case-based reasoning. *American Psychologist, 52,* 57–66.

Kolodner, J. L. (2006). Case-based reasoning. In R. K. Sawyer (Ed.), *The Cambridge handbook of the learning sciences* (pp. 225–242). Cambridge, England: Cambridge University Press.

Lehrer, R., & Schauble. (2000). Modeling in mathematics and science. In R. Glaser (Ed.), *Advances in instructional psychology: Educational design and cognitive science* (Vol. 5, pp. 101–159). Mahwah, NJ: Erlbaum.

Lehrer, R., & Schauble, L. (2005). Developing modeling and argument in the elementary grades. In T. Romberg, T. P. Carpenter, & F. Dremock (Eds.), *Understanding mathematics and science matters* (pp. 29–53). Mahwah, NJ: Erlbaum.

Lehrer, R., & Schauble, L. (2006). Cultivating model-based reasoning in science education. In R. K. Sawyer (Ed.), *The Cambridge handbook of the learning sciences* (pp. 371–387). Cambridge, England: Cambridge University Press.

Metal gear solid [Digital game]. (n.d.). Tokyo: Kojima Productions. Retrieved March 20, 2009, from http://www.konami.jp/kojima_pro/english/index.html

Nersessian, N. J. (2002). The cognitive basis of model-based reasoning in science. In P. Carruthers, S. Stich, & M. Siegal (Eds.), *The cognitive basis of science* (pp. 133–155). Cambridge, England: Cambridge University Press.

Prince of Persia [Digital game]. (n.d.). Montreuil sur Bois, France: Ubisoft. Retrieved March 20, 2009, from http://prince-of-persia.uk.ubi.com/intro/

Rise of nations [Digital game]. (n.d.). Baltimore, MD: Big Huge Games. Retrieved March 20, 2009, from http://www.microsoft.com/games/RiseofNations/

Rome: Total war [Digital game]. (n.d.) Horsham, England: Creative Assembly. Retrieved March 20, 2009, from http://www.totalwar.com

Sawyer, R. K. (Ed.). (2006). *The Cambridge handbook of the learning sciences*. Cambridge, England: Cambridge University Press.

Sam and Max [Digital game]. (n.d.). San Raphael, CA: Telltale Games.

SimCity [Digital game]. (n.d.). Emeryville, CA: Maxis Software.

Sims,The [Digital game]. (2000). Retrieved March 20, 2009, from http://thesims.ea.com/

SWAT 4 [Digital game]. (n.d.). Boston, MA: Irrational Games. Retrieved March 20, 2009, from http://www.activision.com

Tetris [Digital game]. (1985). Pajitnov, A. Honolulu, HI: Tetris.

Thief: Deadly shadows [Digital game]. (n.d.). Austin, TX: Ion Storm. Retrieved March 20, 2009, from http://www.eidos.co.uk/gss/thief_ds/

Tomb raider [Digital game]. (n.d.). Derby, England: Core Design. Retrieved March 20, 2009, from http://www.tombraider.com/server.php?change=LandingPage

Tony Hawk [Digital game]. (n.d.). Woodland Hills, CA: Neversoft.

World of warcraft [Digital game]. (2001). Irvine, CA: Blizzard Entertainment.

Chapter 6

Deep Learning and Emotion in Serious Games

Arthur Graesser, Patrick Chipman,
Frank Leeming, and Suzanne Biedenbach

Serious games are designed with the explicit goal of helping students learn about important subject matter, problem solving strategies, and cognitive or social skills. Instead of learning about biology by reading a textbook, listening to a lecture, or interacting with a conventional computer-based training system, the learner plays a game that successfully integrates the game with curriculum. If we could manage to design serious games, the impact would be revolutionary because the learning of difficult content would end up being an enjoyable, engaging experience for the learner. Intellectual hard work would be transformed into play.

Unfortunately, at this point in the learning sciences, very few serious games have been developed that would impress experts in education. This has led some researchers and game developers to speculate that game design may be inherently incompatible with pedagogy (see Prensky, 2000). The optimistic view is that there needs to be careful analysis of how the features of games are systematically aligned with the features of pedagogy and curriculum (Gee, 2004; Gredler, 1996; O'Neil, Wainess, & Baker, 2005; Rieber, 1996; Shaffer, 2007; Van Eck, 2007). For example, Van Eck (2007) analyzed how Gagne's principles of instructional design (Gagne, Wager, Golas, & Keller, 2005) are mapped onto particular features of games. O'Neil et al. (2005) presented a similar mapping of game features to Kirkpatrick's (1994) four levels of evaluating training (student reaction, learning, behavioral transfer, and systemic results) and to Baker and Mayer's (1999) model of learning that has five major families of cognitive demands (content understanding, problem solving, self-regulation, communication, and collaborative teamwork).

The design, development, and testing of serious games are at an early stage of evolution so there is not a large empirical literature on how well they facilitate learner's reactions and learning. Ideally, the learner's reaction to serious games would increase enjoyment, interest in the topic, and what Csikszentmihaly (1990) has called the *flow* experience. Flow is experienced when the learner has such intense concentration that time and fatigue disappear. Such engagement in the game would be expected to facilitate learning by virtue of time on task, motivation, and self-regulated activities, as long as the focus is on the instructional curriculum rather than exogenous game components. Available reviews and meta-analyses have not provided overwhelming support that serious games enhance learning of content, strategies, or skills (Fletcher & Tobias, 2007; O'Neil et al., 2005; Randel, Morris, Wetzle, & Whitehead, 1992). O'Neil et al. (2005) reported that there are less than 20 published journal articles that have the scientific rigor for a meaningful quantitative assessment of learning gains compared to control conditions. Nevertheless, these reviews uniformly recommend that adequate assessments require a behavioral, cognitive, and social task analysis between the game features and the desired learning objectives. There are documented success cases that show the promise of serious games, such as Gopher, Weil, and Bareket's (1994) transfer of the *Space Fortress* game to piloting real aircraft, Green and Bavelier's (2003) transfer of action digital games to visual selective attention, and Moreno and Mayer's (2005) use of experimenter-constructed games to train explanations of scientific mechanisms.

Theoretical analyses of games, game taxonomies, and game features have frequently been proposed by game designers (Gredler, 1996; Salen & Zimmerman, 2004) and researchers (Gee, 2004; Malone & Lepper, 1987; O'Neil et al., 2005; Rieber, 1996; Shaffer, 2007; van Eck, 2007; Vorderer, Bryant, Pieper, & Weber, 2006). A consensus has not yet emerged on the necessary, sufficient, and primary features of games, but there is reasonable agreement on the basic categories of games that can classify the wide diversity of games in the market (Green & McNeese, 2007; Smith, 2006). Some example genres of games in these taxonomies are first-person shooter (e.g., *Halo 3*, 2007), action/adventure (*Myst*), strategy (chess), puzzle (*Tetris*, 2008), trivia (*Jeopardy*; Friedman, 2008), simulation (*SimCity*), role playing (*Dungeons & Dragons*), and massively multiplayer online (*EverQuest*) genres.

The game genres can be aligned with specific behavioral, cognitive, or social skills that are acquired and automatized as a function of increasing playing time, practice, tests, and challenges. These skills span perception-attention-motor skills, working memory management, memory for content, reasoning, planning, problem solving, and social interaction. The field needs a theoretical framework that maps the game genres and game features onto theoretical components of cognition, emotion, motivation, and social interaction (Moreno & Mayer, 2005; O'Neil et al., 2005). Deeper levels of learning would involve many different elements, including an analysis of causal mechanisms, logical explanations, creation and defense of arguments, management of limited resources, tradeoffs of processes in a complex system, and a way to resolve conflicts. These activities require reasoning and are taxing on cognitive resources (Bloom, 1956; Chi, Siler, Jeong, Yamauchi, & Hausmann, 2001; VanLehn et al., 2007). More shallow levels include perceptual learning, motor skills, definitions of words, properties of objects, and memorization of facts. Aside from the depth of skills afforded by a game, there is the persistent question of their utility and relevance to the real world.

The scientific status of the game features proposed by game designers is greatly in need of computational and empirical inquiry. All games have rules, actions of the player, uncertainty in outcomes as the game progresses, and feedback on the outcomes that occur. The uncertainty creates suspense, one of the prominent entertaining features that sustain one's attention (Cheong & Young, 2006; Vorderer, Wulff, & Friedrichsen, 1996; Zillman, 1996). Many games have points, rewards, competition, winners versus losers, and different levels of privilege that are tied to prior successes, but these features are not universal to games. Aside from the computational essence of games, there is the question of what makes them successful psychologically (Loftus & Loftus, 1983; O'Neil et al., 2005; Vorderer & Bryant, 2006). At this point in the science, there are few firm answers to such questions about the essence of games and their psychological impact, but the available literature offers a number of suggestions, as illustrated below.

1. *Interest, Challenge, and Fantasy.* When Malone and Lepper (1987) analyzed the features of successful digital games on the market, the features they identified were the arousal of interest, challenge, and fantasy. Ideally these features would be endogenous to educational content and skills in a serious game, rather than to the frivolous aspects of the game that are exogenous to content.

2. *Play.* Games have the potential of integrating work and play (Rieber, 1996; Van Eck, 2007) by incorporating different forms of play that appeal to progress, fate, power, identity, imagination, and self. However, the integration is tricky because many players become turned off if the environment looks similar to formal education. Players do not want to read or listen to a lecture on technical content; instead this content needs to be seamlessly integrated with play.

3. *Challenge and the Goldilocks Principle.* Games have an optimal level of challenge that is at a level of not being too hard or too easy, but just right (i.e., the Goldilocks principle). A good game is at the zone of proximal development (Vygotsky, 1978) or at the brink of other zones of ability, cognition, and emotion (Conati, 2002; Rieber, 1996). A game that is slightly more challenging than the learner's skill and knowledge may sustain interest by providing accomplishment while maintaining effort. Success breeds self-efficacy, which is highly correlated with interest in games and learning environments in general (Lepper & Woolverton, 2002).

4. *Feedback.* Feedback on performance in the form of immediate corrections, explanations, cumulative points, mastery of specific content, and skillometers can facilitate engagement, effort, and self-efficacy in many instructional technologies (Anderson, Corbett, Koedinger, & Pelletier, 1995; Foltz, Gilliam, & Kendall, 2000; Jackson & Graesser, 2007; Shute, 2006). However, game designers emphasize that the feedback should not appear too much like taking a test in a formal educational environment.

5. *Instructional Support.* Instructional support can facilitate learning from games (Moreno & Mayer, 2005; Rieber, 1996; Shaffer, 2007; Swaak & de Jong, 2001), including guidance, explanations on feedback, and prompted reflection. Shaffer (2007) has encouraged a tutor or mentor for complex games to assist the player in getting started, articulating strategies, and modeling important interactions with the game.

6. *Narrative.* Many games are embedded in a story narrative with characters/ players, a setting, a conflict/competition, action episodes of players, and outcomes. Narrative has a special status in the cognitive system (Bruner, 1986; Graesser, Singer, & Trabasso, 1994; Read & Miller, 1996; Schank & Abelson, 1995), being comprehended quickly and remembered well compared with other genres (Graesser & Ottati, 1996). Unlike text or film, narrative in games has a distinctive status because the story plans are coconstructed interactively between the player and game system (with or without other players) and because a player can experience hundreds of game threads rather than a single episodic sequence (Gee, 2004; Van Eck, 2007; Vorderer, 2000; Young, 2006).

7. *Hypothetical Worlds and Eventualities.* Games allow the learner to explore many hypothetical worlds and eventualities rather than being constrained to a single situation model. O'Neil et al. (2005) have contrasted simulation and games with respect to the integrity of the simulated trajectories and outcomes, with the former having some integrity in the causal mechanisms but games potentially following arbitrary rules or algorithms. However, serious games would be expected to have an accurate simulation that instantiates the targeted causal mechanism.

8. *Entertainment and Enjoyment.* Vorderer, Klimmt, and Ritterfeld (2004) pointed out that enjoyment is the core of the entertainment process, including the experience of games. The entertainment value of a game can be predicted by (a) sensory pleasure, which comes with photorealism and immersion; (b) the emotions of suspense, thrill, and relief, which are influenced by one's caring for characters and a strong narrative; and (c) the motivational factors of achievement, control, and self-efficacy, which should be influenced by the degree of interactivity.

9. *Types of Interest.* Interest signifies that underlying needs or desires of learners are energized (Alexander, Murphy, Woods, Duhon, & Parker, 1997). Motivation researchers contrast *individual interest* that springs from the desire to develop competence and personal investment versus *situational interest* that reflects a transitory, short-lived interest within an immediate situation or context (Alexander et al., 1997; Hidi & Harackiewicz, 2000).

From our perspective, the primary challenge in designing serious games is to find ways to facilitate deep learning rather than shallow learning. There are several games that help learners acquire shallow knowledge and skills, (i.e., perceptual learning, motor skills, definitions of words, properties of objects, and memorization of facts). It remains an open question how efficient the games are from the standpoint of the amount learned per unit time compared to alternative learning environments. In contrast, there a very few games that promote the acquisition of deep knowledge, strategies, and skills, such as: understanding causal mechanisms; generating explanations and well-formed arguments; critical reasoning; precise monitoring of tradeoffs between variables; managing limited resources; resolving conflicts in complex systems; satisfying multiple constraints; and applying old solutions to new problems in the real world. Yet deep learning is essential in modern societies where there is a serious shortage of expertise in science, technology, engineering, and mathematics (STEM).

Intelligent Tutoring Systems (ITSs) are the best example of computer environments that promote deep learning, so it would be worthwhile to explore the advantages of incorporating the above features of games into existing ITSs. Serious games presumably engage students more than traditional tutoring environments. However, we do not know which components of games are most critical for capitalizing on the seductive aspects of games for deep learning. It is an open question how to develop *serious deep games*, as we will explore throughout this chapter.

Is Deep Learning Compatible with Serious Games?

Serious games presumably need to be buttressed by psychological theories of behavior, cognition, emotion, and social psychology. Links between games and psychology have been identified in a number of books, papers, and research efforts (Loftus & Loftus, 1983; O'Neil et al., 2005; Vorderer & Bryant, 2006), but the empirical evidence is modest at best. Given the growing popularity of games in the United States and throughout the world, one might have expected a generation of psychologists to be forming new societies and journals as they investigate the psychology of games. But that has not happened. Somehow psychology has ended up being detached from the $10 billion game industry in the United States, where half of the citizens play games (Entertainment Software Association, 2004). Mainstream game industries are not currently hiring psychologists in droves, but perhaps that opportunity will be realized in the future.

Why is psychology functionally out of the loop of the entertainment game market? The argument we want to advance in this chapter is that there are complex reasons for the detachment, but we hope these will not be insurmountable in the future. The crux of our argument is that the constraints of complex learning, emotions, and game architecture are often very different from each other and that it will take some systematic, detailed science and engineering to satisfy the constraints of all three systems. Indeed, there are sometimes tradeoffs or incompatibilities between the three systems that present challenges and nontrivial obstacles. Solutions will require some tedious wiring between the components of very different systems.

We have one example that very much gets at the heart of the issue. A doctoral student, Tanner Jackson, recently completed his dissertation on the role of feedback in a learning environment that we developed in the interdisciplinary Institute for Intelligent Systems at the University of Memphis (Jackson & Graesser, 2007). The learning environment was *AutoTutor*, an intelligent tutoring system that helps people learn by holding a conversation in natural language. Students work on difficult questions on the topic of computer technology or physics by having a turn-by-turn dialogue with *AutoTutor* (Graesser, Chipman, Haynes, & Olney, 2005; Graesser, Lu, Jackson, et al., 2004; VanLehn et al., 2007). The details of the system are irrelevant from the present standpoint, other than to say that the system was designed to promote deep explanatory reasoning about mechanisms in technology and science, as opposed to shallow knowledge (e.g., definitions of terms, properties of entities, recognition of explicit ideas). College students learned with different versions of *AutoTutor* and were given pretests, posttests, and rating scales of how much they liked the learning experience. The pretests and posttests were multiple-choice questions and open-ended essay questions that tapped deep levels of comprehension. One of the interesting results of the dissertation was the negative relationship between learning and the students' self-report ratings on how much they liked the learning environments. As more deep learning occurred, the less the students liked the learning environment. The results were compatible with the adage "No pain, no gain." There was clearly a tradeoff between complex learning and positive emotional valences: the deeper the learning, the more negative the emotional response.

It is conceivable that a serious game architecture could mitigate the negative correlation between liking and deep learning. We could add on another layer to *AutoTutor* in which there is an increase in points, choice options, fantasy worlds, or empowering tools when the player exhibits deeper learning. Will there still be a tradeoff between deep learning and affect with these components of reinforcement? There is no empirical research that has investigated the complex interactions among complex learning, emotions, and game architecture.

Another practical example of the difficulties of these interactions is in our recent work on learning communities for serious games. In the fall of 2006, the four authors of this chapter organized a college freshmen focused learning community on the design of serious games. Each of the 26 students in the learning community took a common set of four courses on game design, psychology, problem solving with computers, and English composition. The students were divided into groups, and each group spent the semester designing a serious game on psychology content by integrating what they learned in the four courses. There were six groups and their games were designed, revised, and refined over the course of the semester as the students integrated these various bodies of knowledge. The students read books on game theory and design (Gee, 2004; Salen & Zimmerman, 2004) while they designed the games in the design teams. One of the courses helped them learn how to program the computer with software for novices to design games and multimedia environments (Sherrell, Francisco, Tran, & Bowen, in press). However, the games they designed ended up being board games because there was not enough time in a single semester for students to implement the games on computer.

The learning community was very successful in many respects. The attendance of the students was extremely high in the courses and the morale of the students was unusually positive by all objective indicators. They also acquired the typical amount of traditional content in each of the academic courses in psychology, computer science, and composition. However, the games did not integrate a sophisticated level of knowledge about psychology. The games had analogies to traditional games like *Trivial Pursuit*, *Monopoly* (e.g., a game called *Psychopoly*), and *Pictionary*. The psychology content referred to trivial facts and shallow knowledge, such as Freud being the father of clinical psychology, the composition of neurons, and the distinction between short-term memory and long-term memory. One group attempted to integrate knowledge about the behaviors exhibited in psychological disorders through a game like charades, but this game only required exhibiting shallow knowledge in the diagnosis of such disorders. Deep knowledge about psychological mechanisms was conspicuously absent.

It is perhaps not surprising that the students' games were pitched at shallow levels because the students had only introductory knowledge of psychology, textbooks and other reading materials in introductory psychology tend to be shallow, and the students had to design the game before they were finished with the course. In fact, the learning community we taught in 2007 was modified so the students learned more about psychology and more about game designs to promote deeper learning before the groups started designing their games. Nevertheless, it just might be the case that the constraints of games make it extremely difficult to integrate deep content, strategies, and skills. The complex mechanisms of psychology may have very few alignments or may even be incompatible with the essential hooks of engaging interesting games. This may explain why there are very few entertainment games that would be considered serious games for promoting deep learning of science, technology, engineering, and mathematics. One of the challenging research questions for the future is how to design serious deep games.

Relationships between Deep Learning and Emotions

Connections between emotions and learning are receiving more attention in the fields of psychology (Dweck, 2002; Lepper & Henderlong, 2000), education (Meyer & Turner, 2006), neuroscience (Damasio, 2003), and computer science (Kort, Reilly, & Picard, 2001). A satisfactory understanding of such emotion-learning connections is necessary to design engaging learning environments that motivate students to learn. Consequently, factors that promote emotions and motivation have been surfacing in advanced learning environments such as intelligent tutoring systems (De Vicente & Pain, 2002; Graesser, McDaniel, et al., 2006; Litman & Forbes-Riley, 2004) and serious games (Conati, 2002; Gee, 2004).

What mechanisms might theoretically relate emotions with learning? Psychologists have developed theories that link cognition and emotions very generally (Barrett, 2006; Mandler, 1984; Ortony, Clore, & Collins, 1988; Russell, 2003; Stein & Hernandez, in press), but most of these do not concentrate on the process of learning per se. Ekman's (2003) classic work on the detection of emotions from facial expressions examined primarily the six basic emotions of sadness, happiness, anger, fear, disgust, surprise. However, these emotions have minimal relevance to complex learning (Graesser, McDaniel, et al., 2006; Kort et al., 2001). Pervasive affective states during complex learning in a 1-hour tutorial session include confusion, boredom, flow/engagement, curiosity/interest, delight/eureka, and frustration from being stuck (Burleson & Picard, 2004; Craig, Graesser, Sullins, & Gholson, 2004; Csikszentmihalyi, 1990; Graesser et al., 2006; Kort et al., 2001).

There are a number of theoretical frameworks that predict systematic relationships between emotions and learning of complex material. Most of these have direct relevance to the design of serious games. Meyer and Turner (2006) identified three major theories that they called academic risk taking, flow theory, and goal theory. The *academic risk theory* contrasts the adventuresome learners versus cautious learners. Adventuresome learners are typically, but not always, those with high ability. They want to be challenged with difficult tasks, take risks of failure, and manage negative emotions when they occur. Cautious learners prefer easier tasks, take fewer risks, and minimize learning situations in which they fail and experience negative emotions. These differences in learners could be accommodated in serious games if the system could somehow infer the learner's emotional profile and proclivities for taking academic risks, and then present challenges within an optimal zone of risk.

According to *flow theory*, the learner is in a state of flow (Csikszentmihaly, 1990), when the learner is so deeply engaged in learning the material that time and fatigue disappear. A model proposed by Metcalfe and Kornell (2005) predicts that the flow experience is optimized when the learning rate is high and the learner eventually achieves a high level of mastery. Thus, engagement is lower when the learner starts out performing well, when minimal learning occurs, or when his or her achievements never reach an acceptable level. Serious games would benefit from a mechanism that optimizes the pleasurable flow experience by dynamically adjusting parameters of learning rate, game challenges, feedback on achievements, and so on.

Goal theory emphasizes the role of goals in predicting emotions. Outcomes of behaviors that achieve goals are reinforcing and result in positive emotions whereas outcomes that jeopardize goal accomplishment result in negative emotions (Dweck, 2002; Stein & Hernandez, in press). Obstacles to goals are particularly diagnostic of both learning and emotions. The affective state of confusion correlates positively with learning gains presumably because it is accompanied by deep thinking (Craig et al., 2004; Guhe, Gray, Schoelles, & Ji, 2004). Confusion is diagnostic of *cognitive disequilibrium*, a state that occurs when learners face obstacles to goals, contradictions, incongruities, anomalies, uncertainty, and salient contrasts (Festinger, 1957; Graesser, Lu, Olde, Cooper-Pye, & Whitten, 2005; Graesser & Olde, 2003; Piaget, 1952). Cognitive equilibrium is restored after thought, reflection, problem solving, and other effortful deliberations. Serious games could be designed to place the players in cognitive disequilibrium and have them conquer the impasses, thereby boosting self-efficacy. This would occur in multiple cycles throughout the game. Parameters such as cycle phase duration and degree of challenge would need to be tailored to the emotional and cognitive profile of the learner.

As mentioned earlier, human tutoring and intelligent tutoring systems (ITSs) are regarded as the best learning environments to promote deep learning of content, strategies, and skills (Aleven & Koedinger, 2002; Chi et al., 2001; Cohen, Kulik, & Kulik, 1982; Dodds & Fletcher, 2004; Van Lehn et al., 2007). Researchers have considered the possibility that a tutoring environment that is sensitive to a learner's emotions would enhance learning from tutors even further (D'Mello, Picard, & Graesser, 2007; Graesser, Jackson, & McDaniel, 2007; Lepper & Woolverton, 2002; Litman & Forbes-Riley, 2004). If the learner is frustrated, for example, the tutor would generate hints to advance the learner in constructing knowledge or would make supportive empathetic comments to enhance motivation. If the learner is bored, the tutor would need to present more engaging or challenging problems for the learner to work on. If the learner is engaged in the flow state, then the tutor would presumably lay low and let the learner maintain control over the learning experience. If the learner is confused, then the tutor might attempt to keep the learner in the confused state for a period of time to encourage thinking, but would eventually need to step in to prevent the learner from getting dispirited. Since a state of confusion is positively correlated with learning events (Craig et al., 2004), it will be important to have the tutor's actions manage the learner's confusion productively. Some learners tend to give up when they are confused because they attribute their confusion to having the trait of low ability (Dweck, 2002; Meyer & Turner, 2006); these learners need to be encouraged and also informed that working on the problem will be fruitful and that confusion is a sign of thoughtful progress. Other learners get motivated when they are confused because it is a signal that they are being challenged and they have confidence in their ability to conquer the challenge. These relations between emotions and complex learning are of course quite relevant to the design of serious games that promote deep learning.

We are currently in the process of developing a version of *AutoTutor* that is sensitive to both the cognitive and affective states of the learner (D'Mello et al., 2007; Graesser, Jackson, & McDaniel, 2007). Assessments of *AutoTutor* on learning gains have shown effect sizes of approximately 0.8 standard deviation units in the areas of computer literacy (Graesser et al., 2004) and Newtonian physics (VanLehn et al., 2007). *AutoTutor* presents challenging questions to the learner that require about a paragraph of information to answer correctly. The typical response from the learner on any one conversational turn is very short, usually only one word to two sentences in length. Therefore, *AutoTutor* uses a series of pumps ("What else?" "uh huh") to request additional information, and prompts for the learner to express specific words. *AutoTutor* also uses hints, assertions, and feedback to elicit responses from the learner that lead to a complete answer to the question.

An automated emotion classifier is needed to make *AutoTutor*, other learning environments, and serious games responsive to learner emotions. We have previously reported some empirical studies that collect the dialogue history, facial action units, position of their body, and other sensory channels while they learn with *AutoTutor* (D'Mello et al., 2007). There are systematic relations between these sensing channels and particular emotions. For example, learner emotions are predicted by (1) the occurrence of *AutoTutor*'s feedback; (2) relations to the type of feedback (positive, neutral, negative); (3) the directness of *AutoTutor*'s dialogue moves (hints are less direct than assertions); and (4) the quality of learner's contributions. Regarding the nonverbal channels, emotions are correlated with particular facial expressions (Ekman, 2003; Kaliouby & Robinson, 2005), posture, and face–posture combinations (D'Mello et al., 2007). When speech is recorded, affective states may be induced from a combination of lexical, acoustical, and prosodic features (Litman & Forbus-Riley, 2004). The features from the various modalities can be detected in real time automatically on computers, so we are currently integrating these technologies with *AutoTutor*.

These emotion-sensing technologies could be used to track the relations between learning and emotions in serious games. The above sensing channels are nonintrusive and indirect in the sense that the learners are not hooked up to sensors and equipment that the learner believes is recording their physiological arousal or brain states. Intrusive technologies directly measure the arousal of the autonomic systems, as in the case of GSR and heart rate, or brain mechanisms, as in fMRI (Mathiak & Weber, 2006), evoked potentials, or transcranial stimulation. One direction for future research is to track both intrusive and nonintrusive sensing channels while learners interact with games. Which of these channels are most diagnostic of different emotions during the experience of playing a serious game? How are the measures from these different channels inter-correlated within and across emotions?

Prospects of Developing Serious Deep Games

Psychology has already had a theoretical impact on game design by virtue of operant and classical conditioning. We see operant conditioning at work whenever we go into a casino and observe hundreds of people pulling handles and pushing buttons under a variable interval or a variable ratio schedule of reinforcement. We see classical conditioning at work when we see marketers of games casting their products in sex and violence. These are obvious examples of applying psychology principles to the design of games per se, but not necessarily serious educational games that attempt to facilitate deep learning. Operant and classical conditioning do not go the distance in optimizing and explaining serious games that promote deep learning.

This section explores the prospects of building serious deep games. The games we have in mind are serious in the sense that the users end up learning content that is aligned with curricula in school systems. The games are deep in the sense that the content and skills tap deep reasoning, critical thinking, complex systems, causal chains and networks, and other difficult material that is part of science, technology, engineering, and mathematics (STEM). As discussed earlier, there are few examples of serious deep games and precious little empirical research on their effectiveness in promoting learning.

Costs of Modern Learning Environments

There has been a revolution in technology-based training since the advent of the computer. Fifty years ago there were none of the following genres of learning environment: (1) computer-based training; (2) multimedia; (3) interactive simulation; (4) hypertext and hypermedia; (5) intelligent tutoring systems; (6) inquiry-based information retrieval; (7) animated pedagogical agents; (8) virtual environments with agents; (9) serious games; and (10) computer supported collaborative learning. Most of these (3–10) were not available 20 years ago, and most are not mainstream technologies in schools today. However, the Web has either exemplars or mature technologies for all 10 of these technologies, so they are potentially available to all Web users. These learning environments implement pedagogical mechanisms, such as mastery learning with presentation-test-feedback-branching, building on prerequisites, practice with problems and examples, multimedia learning, modeling-scaffolding fading, reciprocal training, problem-based learning, inquiry learning, and collaborative knowledge construction (Graesser, Chipman, & King, 2007). Nearly all of these mechanisms emphasize that the learner actively constructs knowledge and builds skills, as opposed to merely being exposed to information delivered by the learning environment.

The learning environments vary significantly in development costs, with games being at the high end of the continuum. We recently estimated the ball-park costs of some of the alternative learning environments (Graesser, Chipman, & King, 2007). Approximate costs for an hour training session with conventional computer-based training would be $10,000, for a 10-hour course with conventional computer-based training and rudimentary multimedia would be $100,000, for an information-rich hypertext-hypermedia system would be $1,000,000, for a sophisticated intelligent tutoring system without authoring tools would be $10,000,000, and for a serious game on the Web with thousands of users would be $100,000,000. These cost estimates are of course gross approximations, but it is important to acknowledge that a successful entertainment game requires $5 to $10 million to develop.

The costs of the sophisticated ITSs and immersive virtual environments are dramatically reduced by using authoring tools or by modifying existing game engines. However, it is widely acknowledged that it is nearly impossible to use the authoring tools and game engines without knowledge of computer science (Murray, Ainsworth, & Blessing, 2003; Van Eck, 2007). It is impractical to expect an instructor or curriculum developer to use these tools and engines without a substantial amount of training in computer technologies. It would be more practical to have a research team that covers expertise in pedagogy, psychology, computer science, art, economics, and marketing. Such a research team would presumably be an expensive proposition. The academic communities have pursued this team approach (Johnson & Beal, 2005; Young, 2006; Zyda, 2006) on projects funded by the government for several million of dollars, but the entertainment game industry does not incorporate expertise in pedagogy and psychology.

Immersive Worlds with Animated Conversational Agents

Animated conversational agents have become increasingly popular in advanced learning environments (Atkinson, 2002; Baylor & Kim, 2005; Graesser et al., 2005; McNamara, Levinstein, & Boonthum, 2004; Reeves & Nass, 1996). The agents take on roles of mentors, tutors, peers, players in multiparty games, and avatars in the virtual worlds. They can be designed to have different cognitive abilities, expertise, personalities, physical features, and styles. The agents in some of these systems are carefully scripted and choreographed, whereas agents in other systems are dynamic and adapt to the user. The users communicate with the agents through speech, keyboard, gesture, touch panel screen, joystick, or conventional input channels. In turn, the agents express themselves with speech, facial expression, gesture, posture, and other embodied actions. When an agent reaches the sophistication of having speech recognition and natural language generation, it holds a face-to-face, mixed-initiative dialogue with the student, just as people do in everyday conversations (Cole et al., 2003; Gratch et al., 2002; Johnson & Beal, 2005). Quite clearly, these worlds create a presence that is akin to everyday experiences in our social and physical worlds.

The animated agents will continue to be prevalent in most game environments. The field is on the brink of designing intelligent cyber agents that are indistinguishable from avatars controlled by humans. As we discussed earlier, learning will be facilitated by a tutor or mentor who guides and scaffolds interactions with a game (Shaffer, 2007). Such tutors and mentors will be extremely important additions to serious deep games because students are prone to settle for shallow learning without such external scaffolding to encourage deep learning.

Psychological Principles and Mechanisms

This chapter has already identified some of the psychological principles and mechanisms that drive successful games. The primary challenge is to identify which of these principles and mechanisms should be aligned with particular subject matter content, skills, and categories of learners. For example, the principles/mechanisms described earlier included curiosity, interest, control, fantasy, feedback, adaptivity, narrative experience, enjoyment, cognitive challenge, and the Goldilocks principle (i.e., the game should not be too hard and not too easy, but just right). Under what conditions should each of these principles and mechanisms be recruited by game designers who have the goal of building a serious deep game? It probably would not be prudent, for example, to have fantasy guide the design of a game to help Navy personnel operate a ship.

It may be difficult to have narrative experience aligned with deep learning of science. How would the game designer weave in a captivating story that keeps the player engaged? It is difficult enough to write a captivating story, so the difficulty is compounded by incorporating deep knowledge about the subject matter. We can learn about history, shallow knowledge, and trivia though story games, but how can we learn about complex scientific mechanisms? Perhaps we could learn about blood circulation through an interesting story about the journey of a drop of blood that gets transformed in its travel. But as soon as the constraints of the circulatory system appear, the story runs the risk of meandering and becoming boring. As soon as we get on a roll with an interesting story, the integrity of the circulatory system runs the risk of degenerating. Detailed mappings between the world of science and the world of narrative are needed but there is no guarantee that there will end up being any mapping that satisfies the mutual constraints.

SimCity is one example of an entertainment game with educational value. In SimCity, the player takes on the role of a mayor and city manager who is tasked with building a thriving metropolis from an empty plot of land. The player has a wide variety of controls available to accomplish this goal, ranging from specifying the zoning of parts of the city to implementing ordinances to change the behavior of its inhabitants. The game provides little immediate guidance on what actions the player should take; instead, it offers feedback over time as the simulation progresses, as well as more immediate feedback from both virtual "advisors" who can be consulted about the needs of the city and also a "news ticker" that scrolls across the scene to warn of problems that require direct, prompt action (such as natural disasters or missing infrastructure).

SimCity does not provide a drill and practice environment or any form of direct didactic content delivery. However, it does educate in a constructivist framework that incorporates most of the principles and mechanisms of serious games. Players learn by doing and trial and error as they approach both the larger problem of building a large city from nothing as well as the smaller sub-problems presented by the effects of the choices they make and the vicissitudes of city growth. The simulation provides feedback by modeling the results of the player's decisions. A choice to bring in a casino, for example, would bring in vastly increased tax revenue from tourism, but simultaneously would have the side effects of increased crime and reduced property values. An understanding of the unwanted side effects requires the discovery of a causal network of variables, propagation of constraints, tradeoffs, and resource limitations. By manipulating the system and observing the results, players can implicitly (through reasoning) or explicitly (through experimentation) learn the rules of the city simulation that are aligned with the complex social system. Given that the simulation is designed to be reasonably accurate, players of *SimCity* should be able to transfer this knowledge to related management scenarios.

What we need are more example games like *SimCity* that are both absorbing and afford deep learning of complex systems. In this chapter we have argued that this will not be easy to accomplish because the constraints of domain knowledge, emotions, and games are more frequently incompatible than they are aligned. However, rather than giving up trying, researchers need to conduct the systematic mappings between the systems and to perform the detailed behavioral, cognitive, and social task analyses. The world of games has not only captured the lives of the younger generations but has also penetrated adults of all ages. It is an empirical question whether it will be possible to smuggle deep knowledge, strategies, and skills into the entertainment games that are so engaging and entertaining. It is also an empirical question whether serious deep games will yield higher learning gains than alternative advanced learning environments.

Acknowledgments

The research on *AutoTutor* was supported by the National Science Foundation (SBR 9720314, REC 0106965, REC 0126265, ITR 0325428, REESE 0633918), the Institute of Education Sciences (R305H050169, R305B070349), and the Department of Defense Multidisciplinary University Research Initiative (MURI) administered by ONR under grant N00014-00-1-0600. Any opinions, findings, and conclusions or recommendations expressed in this material are those of the authors and do not necessarily reflect the views of NSF, IES, or DoD. The Tutoring Research Group (TRG) is an interdisciplinary research team comprised of researchers from psychology, computer science, physics, and education (visit http://www.autotutor.org). Correspondence concerning this article should be addressed to Art Graesser, Department of Psychology,

202 Psychology Building, University of Memphis, Memphis, TN 38152-3230, a-graesser@memphis.edu.

References

Aleven, V., & Koedinger, K. R. (2002). An effective metacognitive strategy: Learning by doing and explaining with a computer-based cognitive Tutor. *Cognitive Science, 26,* 147–179.

Alexander, P. A., Murphy, P. K., Woods, B. S., Duhon, K. E., & Parker, D. (1997). College instruction and commitment changes in students' knowledge, interest, and strategy use: A study of domain learning. *Contemporary Educational Psychology, 22,* 125–146.

Anderson, J. R., Corbett, A. T., Koedinger, K. R., & Pelletier, R. (1995). Cognitive tutors: Lessons learned. *The Journal of the Learning Sciences, 4,* 167–207.

Atkinson, R. K. (2002). Optimizing learning from examples using animated pedagogical agents. *Journal of Educational Psychology, 94,* 416–427.

Baker, E. L., & Mayer, R. E. (1999). Computer-based assessment of problem solving. *Computers in Human Behavior, 15,* 269–282.

Barrett, L. F. (2006). Emotions as natural kinds? *Perspectives on Psychological Science, 1,* 28–58.

Baylor, A. L., & Kim, Y. (2005). Simulating instructional roles through pedagogical agents. *International Journal of Artificial Intelligence in Education, 15,* 95–115.

Bloom, B. S. (1956). *Taxonomy of educational objectives: The classification of educational goals: Handbook 1: Cognitive domain.* New York: McKay.

Bruner, J. (1986). *Actual minds, possible worlds.* Cambridge, MA: Harvard University Press.

Burleson, W., & Picard, R. W. (2004, September). Affective agents: Sustaining motivation to learn through failure and a state of stuck. In *Proceedings of the 7th International Conference on Intelligent Tutoring Systems: Workshop on social and emotional intelligence in learning environments.* Maceio-Alagoas, Brazil: ITS.

Cheong, Y., & Young, M. R. (2006, July). A computational model of narrative generation for suspense. Paper presented at the AAAI 2006 Workshop on Computational Aesthetics, Boston, MA.

Chi, M. T. H., Siler, S. A., Jeong, H., Yamauchi, T., & Hausmann, R. G. (2001). Learning from human tutoring. *Cognitive Science, 25,* 471–533.

Cohen, P. A., Kulik, J. A., & Kulik, C. C. (1982). Educational outcomes of tutoring: A meta-analysis of findings. *American Educational Research Journal, 19,* 237–248.

Cole, R., van Vuuren, S., Pellom, B., Hacioglu, K., Ma, J., Movellan, J., et al. (2003). Perceptive animated interfaces: First steps toward a new paradigm for human computer interaction. *Proceedings of the IEEE, 91,* 1391–1405.

Conati, C. (2002). Probabilistic assessment of user's emotions in educational games. *Journal of Applied Artificial Intelligence, 16,* 555–575.

Craig, S. D., Graesser, A. C., Sullins, J., & Gholson, B. (2004). Affect and learning: An exploratory look into the role of affect in learning. *Journal of Educational Media, 29,* 241–250.

Csikszentmihalyi, M. (1990). *Flow: The psychology of optimal experience.* New York: Harper Row.

Damasio, A. R. (2003). *Looking for Spinoza: Joy, sorrow, and the feeling brain.* Orlando, FL: Harcourt.

De Vicente, A., & Pain, H. (2002). Informing the detection of students' motivational state: An empirical study. In S. A. Cerri, G. Gouarderes, & F. Paraguacu (Eds.), *Proceedings of the sixth international conference on intelligent tutoring systems* (pp. 933–943). Berlin, Germany: Springer.

D'Mello, S. K., Picard, R., & Graesser, A. C. (2007). Toward an affect-sensitive Auto-Tutor. *IEEE Intelligent Systems, 22,* 53–61.

Dodds, P., & Fletcher, J. D. (2004). Opportunities for new "smart" learning environments enabled by next-generation web capabilities. *Journal of Educational Multimedia and Hypermedia, 13*(4), 391–404.

Dweck, C. S. (2002). Messages that motivate: How praise molds students' beliefs, motivation, and performance (in surprising ways). In J. Aronson (Ed.), *Improving academic achievement: Impact of psychological factors on education* (pp. 61–87). Orlando, FL: Academic Press.

Ekman, P. (2003). *Emotions revealed.* New York: Times Books.

Entertainment Software Association. (2004). (n.d.). Industry facts. Retrieved August 7, 2008, from http://www.theesa.com/facts/index.asp

EverQuest [Digital game]. (n.d.). San Diego, CA: Sony Online Entertainment.

Festinger, L. (1957). *A theory of cognitive dissonance.* Evanston, IL: Row, Peterson.

Fletcher, J. D., & Tobias, S. (2007). *What research has to say (thus far) about designing computer games for learning.* Unpublished manuscript, Institute for Defense Analysis, Alexandria, VA.

Foltz, P. W., Gilliam, S., & Kendall, S. (2000). Supporting content-based feedback in on-line writing evaluation with LSA. *Interactive Learning Environments, 8,* 111–127.

Friedman, H. (Executive producer). (2008). *Jeopardy* [Television series]. Culver City, CA: Sony Pictures Television.

Gagne, R. M., Wager, W. W., Golas, K. C., & Keller, J. M. (2005). *Principles of instructional design* (5th ed.). Belmont, CA: Wadsworth/Thompson Learning.

Gee, J. P. (2004). *What video games have to teach us about language and literacy.* New York: Palgrave/Macmillan.

Gopher, D., Weil, M. & Bareket, T. (1994). Transfer of skill from a computer game trainer to flight. *Human Factors, 36,* 387–405.

Graesser, A. C., Chipman, P., Haynes, B. C., & Olney, A. (2005). AutoTutor: An intelligent tutoring system with mixed-initiative dialogue. *IEEE Transactions in Education, 48,* 612–618.

Graesser, A. C., Chipman, P., & King, B. G. (2007). Computer mediated technologies. In J. M. Spector, M. D. Merrill, J. J. G. van Merrienboer, & M.P. Driscoll (Eds.), *Handbook of research on educational communications and technology* (3rd ed., pp. 211–224). Mahwah, NJ: Erlbaum.

Graesser, A. C., Jackson, G. T., & McDaniel, B. (2007). AutoTutor holds conversations with learners that are responsive to their cognitive and emotional states. *Educational Technology, 47,* 19–22.

Graesser, A. C., Lu, S., Jackson, G. T., Mitchell, H., Ventura, M., Olney, A., & Louwerse, M. M. (2004). AutoTutor: A tutor with dialogue in natural language. *Behavioral Research Methods, Instruments, and Computers, 36,* 180–193.

Graesser, A. C., Lu, S., Olde, B. A., Cooper-Pye, E., & Whitten, S. (2005). Question asking and eye tracking during cognitive disequilibrium: Comprehending illustrated texts on devices when the devices break down. *Memory and Cognition, 33,* 1235–1247.

Graesser, A. C., McDaniel, B., Chipman, P., Witherspoon, A., D'Mello, S., & Gholson, B. (2006). Detection of emotions during learning with AutoTutor. In R. Son (Ed.), *Proceedings of the 28th annual meetings of the Cognitive Science Society* (pp. 285–290). Mahwah, NJ: Erlbaum.

Graesser, A. C., & Olde, B. A. (2003). How does one know whether a person understands a device? The quality of the questions the person asks when the device breaks down. *Journal of Educational Psychology, 95*(3), 524–536.

Graesser, A. C., & Ottati, V. (1996). Why stories? Some evidence, questions, and challenges. In R. S. Wyer (Ed.), *Knowledge and memory: The real story* (pp. 121–132). Hillsdale, NJ: Erlbaum.

Graesser, A. C., Singer, M., & Trabasso, T. (1994). Constructing inferences during narrative text comprehension. *Psychological Review, 101,* 371–95.

Gratch, J., Rickel, J., Andre, E., Cassell, J., Petajan, E., & Badler, N. (2002). Creating interactive virtual humans: Some assembly required. *IEEE Intelligent Systems, 17,* 54–63.

Gredler, M. E. (1996). Educational games and simulations: A technology in search of a research paradigm. In D. H. Jonassen (Ed.), *Handbook of research for educational communications and technology* (pp. 521–540). New York: Simon & Schuster.

Green, C. S., & Bavelier, D. (2003). Action video game modifies visual selective attention. *Nature, 423,* 534–537.

Green, M., & McNeese, M. N. (2007). Using entertainment software to enhance online learning. *International Journal on E-Learning, 6,* 5–16.

Guhe, M., Gray, W. D., Schoelles, M. J., & Ji, Q. (2004). Towards an affective cognitive architecture. In K. D. Forbus, D. Gentner, & T. Regier (Eds.), *Proceedings of the 26th annual meeting of the Cognitive Science Society* (pp. 1565). Hillsdale, NJ: Erlbaum.

Halo 3 [Digital game]. (n.d.). Seattle, WA: Microsoft Game Studios.

Hidi, S., & Harackiewicz, J. M. (2000). Motivating the academically unmotivated: A critical issue for the 21st century. *Review of Educational Research, 70,* 151–179.

Jackson, G. T., & Graesser, A. C. (2007). Content matters: An investigation of feedback categories within an ITS. In R. Luckin, K. Koedinger, & J. Greer (Eds.), *Artificial Intelligence in Education: Building technology rich learning contexts that work* (pp. 127–134). Amsterdam: IOS Press.

Johnson, W. L., & Beal, C. (2005). Iterative evaluation of a large-scale intelligent game for language learning. In C. Looi, G. McCalla, B. Bredeweg, & J. Breuker (Eds.), *Artificial intelligence in education: Supporting learning through intelligent and socially informed technology* (pp. 290–297). Amsterdam: IOS Press.

Kaliouby, R., & Robinson, P. (2005). Generalization of a vision-based computational model of mind-reading. In J. Tao, T. Tan, & R.W. Picard (Eds.), *ICII, LNCS* (pp. 582–589). Berlin, Germany: Springer.

Kirkpatrick, D. L. (1994). *Evaluation training programs: The four levels.* San Francisco: Berrett-Koehler.

Kort, B., Reilly, R., & Picard, R. (2001). An affective model of interplay between emotions and learning: Reengineering educational pedagogy—Building a learning companion. In T. Okamoto, R. Hartley, Kinshuk, & J. P. Klus (Eds.), *Proceedings IEEE international conference on advanced learning technology: Issues, achievements and challenges* (pp.43–48). Madison, WI: IEEE Computer Society.

Lepper, M. R., & Henderlong, J. (2000). Turning "play" into "work" and "work" into "play": 25 years of research on intrinsic versus extrinsic motivation. In C. Sansone & J. M. Harackiewicz (Eds.), *Intrinsic and extrinsic motivation: The search for optimal motivation and performance* (pp. 257–307). San Diego, CA: Academic Press.

Lepper, M. R., & Woolverton, M. (2002). The wisdom of practice: Lessons learned from the study of highly effective tutors. In J. Aronson (Ed.), *Improving academic achievement: Contributions of social psychology* (pp. 133–156). Orlando, FL: Academic Press.

Litman, D. J., & Forbes-Riley, K. (2004). Predicting student emotions in computer-human tutoring dialogues. In *Proceedings of the 42nd annual meeting of the association for computational linguistics* (pp. 352–359). East Stroudsburg, PA: Association for Computational Linguistics.

Loftus, G. R., & Loftus, E. F. (1983). *Mind at play: The psychology of video games*. New York: Basic Books.

Malone, T. W., & Lepper, M. R. (1987). Making learning fun: A taxonomy of intrinsic motivations for learning. In R. E. Snow & M. J. Farr (Eds.), *Aptitude, learning and instruction: Vol. 3. Conative and affective process analyses* (pp. 223–253). Hillsdale, NJ: Erlbaum.

Mandler, G. (1984). *Mind and body: Psychology of emotion and stress*. New York: Norton.

Mathiak, K., & Weber, R. (2006). Toward brain correlates of natural behavior: fMRI during violent video games. *Human Brain Mapping, 27,* 948–956.

McNamara, D.S., Levinstein, I. B., & Boonthum, C. (2004). iSTART: Interactive strategy trainer for active reading and thinking. *Behavioral Research Methods, Instruments, and Computers, 36,* 222–233.

Metcalfe, J., & Kornell, N. (2005). A region or proximal of learning model of study time allocation. *Journal of Memory and Language, 52,* 463–477.

Meyer, D. K., & Turner, J. C. (2006). Reconceptualizing emotion and motivation to learn in classroom contexts. *Educational Psychology Review, 18,* 377–390.

Moreno, R., & Mayer, R. E. (2005). Role of guidance, reflection, and interactivity in an agent-based multimedia game. *Journal of Educational Psychology, 97*(1), 117–128.

Murray, T., Blessing, S., & Ainsworth, S. (Eds.). (2003). *Authoring tools for advanced technology learning environments: Towards cost-effective adaptive, interactive and intelligent educational software*. Dordrecht, The Netherlands: Kluwer.

Myst [Digital game]. (n.d.). Chicago: Midway Games.

O'Neil, H. F., Wainess, R., & Baker, E. L. (2005). Classification of learning outcomes: Evidence from the computer games literature. *The Curriculum Journal, 16,* 455–474.

Ortony, A., Clore, G. L., & Collins, A. (1988). *The cognitive structure of emotions*. New York: Cambridge University Press.

Piaget, J. (1952). *The origins of intelligence*. Madison, CT: International Universities Press.

Prensky, M. (2000). *Digital game-based learning*. New York: McGraw-Hill.

Randel, J. M., Morris B. A., Wetzle, C. D., & Whitehead, B. V. (1992). The effectiveness of games for educational purposes: A review of recent research. *Simulation and Gaming, 23,* 261–276.

Read, S. J., & Miller, L.C. (1996). Stories are fundamental to meaning and memory: For social creatures, could it be otherwise? In R. S. Wyer, Jr. (Ed.), *Knowledge and memory: The real story, advances in social cognition* (Vol. 8, pp. 139–152). Hillsdale, NJ: Erlbaum.

Reeves, B., & Nass, C. (1996). *The media equation: How people treat computers, televisions, and new media like real people and places.* Cambridge, England: Cambridge University Press.

Rieber, L. P. (1996). Animation as feedback in a computer-based simulation: Representation matters. *Educational Technology Research & Development, 44*(1), 5–22.

Russell, J. A. (2003). Core affect and the psychological construction of emotion. *Psychological Review, 110,* 145–172.

Salen, K., & Zimmerman, E. (2004). *Rules of play: Game design fundamentals.* Cambridge, MA: MIT Press.

Schank, R. C., & Abelson, R. P. (1995). *Knowledge and memory: The real story.* In R. S. Wyer (Ed.), *Advances in social cognition* (pp. 1–85). Mahwah, NJ: Erlbaum.

Shaffer, D. W. (2007). *How computer games help children learn.* New York: Palgrave.

Sherrell, L., Francisco, L., Tran. Q, & Bowen, S. (in press). Computer games for mathematics and science: A Tri-P-LETS initiative. *Journal of Computing Sciences in Colleges.*

Shute, V. J. (2006). *Focus on formative feedback* (ETS Research Report). Princeton, NJ: ETS.

SimCity [Digital game]. (n.d.). Emeryville, CA: Maxis Software.

Smith, B. P. (2006). The (computer) games people play. In P. Vorderer & J. Bryant (Eds.), *Playing video games: Motives, responses, and consequences* (pp. 43–56). Mahwah, NJ: Erlbaum.

Stein, N. L., & Hernandez, M.W. (in press). Assessing understanding and appraisals during emotional expereince: The development and use of the Narcoder. In J. A. Coan & J. J. Allen (Eds.), *Handbook of emotion elicitation and assessment.* New York: Oxford University Press.

Swaak, J., & de Jong, T. (2001). Discovery simulations and the assessment of intuitive knowledge. *Journal of Computer Assisted Learning, 17,* 284–294.

Tetris [Digital game]. (1985). Pajitnov, A., & Gerasimov, V. Moscow: Academy of Science of the USSR.

Van Eck, R. (2007). Building artificially intelligent learning games. In D. Gibson, C. Aldrich, & M. Prensky (Eds.), *Games and simulations in online learning research & development frameworks* (pp. 271–307). Hershey, PA: Idea Group.

VanLehn, K., Graesser, A. C., Jackson, G. T., Jordan, P., Olney, A., & Rose, C. P. (2007). When are tutorial dialogues more effective than reading? *Cognitive Science, 31,* 3–62.

Vorderer, P. (2000). Interactive entertainment and beyond. In D. Zillman & P. Forderer (Eds.), *Media entertainment: The psychology of its appeal* (pp. 21–36). Mahwah, NJ: Erlbaum.

Vorderer, P., & Bryant, J. (2006). (Eds.). *Playing video games: Motives, responses, and consequences.* Mahwah, NJ: Erlbaum.

Vorderer, P., Bryant, J., Pieper, K. M., & Weber, R. (2006). The (computer) games people play. In P. Vorderer & J. Bryant (Eds.), *Playing video games: Motives, responses, and consequences* (pp. 1–7). Mahwah, NJ: Erlbaum.

Vorderer, P., Klimmt., C., & Ritterfeld, U. (2004). Enjoyment: At the heart of media entertainment. *Communication Theory, 14,* 388–408.

Vorderer, P., Wulff, H. J., & Friedrichsen, M. (Eds.). (1996). *Suspense: Conceptualizations, theoretical analyses, and empirical explorations.* Mahwah, NJ: Erlbaum.

Vygotsky, L. S. (1978). *Mind in society.* Cambridge, MA: Harvard University Press.

Young, R. M. (2006). Story and discourse: A bipartite model of narrative generation in virtual worlds. *Interaction Studies, 8,* 177–208.

Zillman, D. (1996). The psychology of suspense in dramatic exposition. In P. Vorderer, H. J. Wulff, & M. Friedrichsen, M. (Eds.). (1996). *Suspense: Conceptualizations, theoretical analyses, and empirical explorations* (pp. 199–231). Mahwah, NJ: Erlbaum.

Zyda, M. (2006, June). Educating the next generation of game developers. *IEEE Computer,* 30–34.

Chapter 7

Psychological and Communicological Theories of Learning and Emotion Underlying Serious Games

Jennings Bryant and Wes Fondren

With the prominent, if not preeminent, role of digital gaming in contemporary entertainment firmly established (e.g., Vorderer, Bryant, Pieper, & Weber, 2006), game developers and social scientists have begun to examine the potential of video and digital games to transcend entertainment and teach lessons as well as to model and motivate positive social change. As Gudmundsen (2006) claimed, "there's a movement afoot that's quietly trying to do something more substantial.... Known as the Serious Games Movement, this genre is about taking the resources of the (video) games industry and applying them outside of entertainment" (p. 1). A small sample of recent news headlines reveals that media gatekeepers have found such efforts newsworthy:

> Saving the World, One Video Game at a Time (Thompson, 2006)
>
> Three Winners Announced in Competition to Discover Innovative Video and Computer Games that Improve Health and Health Care ("Three Winners," 2007)
>
> Virtual-Reality Video Game to Help Burn Patients Play Their Way to Pain Relief ("Virtual-reality," 2008)
>
> Video Games Stimulate Learning (BBC, 2002)
>
> LA Kids Learning Via Video Games ("LA Kids," 2008)

The serious games movement's birth is often traced to the U.S. Army's release of the digital game *America's Army* as a free online download in 2002, and its rapid expansion typically is linked to a series of focused conferences held jointly by scholars and industry practitioners between 2003 and 2007 (Gudmundsen, 2006). The movement has espoused numerous methodologies and principles, among them:

> Action learning, learning by doing.... Instead of remembering facts or processes, students perform real tasks, employing both the knowledge and

the method as they do it. It is the difference between reading the manual and building the machine. It is experience over information. ("Software: Serious Games," 2007, p. 1)

An article in *The New York Times* (Thompson, 2006) offered some important reasons for the rapid expansion of serious games:

> The proposition may strike some as dubious, but the "serious games" movement has some serious brain power behind it. It is a partnership between advocates and nonprofit groups that are searching for new ways to reach young people, and tech-savvy academics keen to explore video games' educational potential. (p. 1)

Not everyone has been so positive about the efforts or potential of serious games. Peters (2007) noted, "Ever since video games were invented, parents and teachers have been trying to make them boring.... Making games educational is like dumping Velveeta on broccoli" (p. 1). Peters continued:

> All of these ideas are premised on the notion that video games can and should be more than mindless fun. But all of this noodling about games' untapped potential raises some philosophical questions: When does a game stop being a game and turn into an assignment? Can a game still be called a game if it isn't any fun? (p. 1)

Value judgments aside, scholarship in media psychology offers some valuable lessons about how to utilize communicological and psychological principles to undergird and inform the design of serious games. Moreover, recent research in entertainment theory, consumer behavior, and user engagement and education (e.g., Bryant & Anderson, 1983; Bryant & Vorderer, 2006; Vorderer & Bryant, 2006) can be invaluable in better enabling game designers to inform and motivate targeted consumers.

The Need for Theory in Serious Games

A precursor question that should be answered, however, is would theory from media psychology even be considered, much less utilized, by those in the media industries that design, promote, and distribute digital games? Actually, several clarion calls have been issued of late from some very unusual fronts clamoring for more durable and valid research and theory to guide the development of digital games and interactive software of all sorts. Moreover, several of these calls have come from the professions that design and develop communication networks, software, and message systems, which is a dramatic departure from traditional media industry practices. Here are three examples:

1. Two years ago our University of Alabama Institute for Communication and Information Research received a call from a midsized company that designs, produces, markets, and distributes casino games. Obviously the purposes of casino games are very different from those that were the focus of most serious games developers and scholars, but the process of game development is at least somewhat similar. In our initial meetings in Las Vegas, their officers emphatically emphasized that they needed to move forward to a different level of sophistication in game development, and to do that they were convinced they needed guidance from basic research in entertainment theory and media psychology.

2. Recently a remarkable international consortium of sponsors gathered for a meeting of advisors of the Interactive Television Research Institute (ITRI), directed by Duane Varan and located at Murdock University in Australia. These sponsors included many of the world's largest brands and advertisers (e.g., Coca-Cola, General Motors, Kellogg, Microsoft, Proctor & Gamble, Nike) and media companies (e.g., ABC, NBC, Sky TV, Comcast, ESPN, Turner, Nickelodeon). When these influential executives were asked what they most needed to know about interactive television, including gaming components, they charged ITRI with helping them understand the most basic questions about how to make their media and advertising more effective and successful, but from a theoretical perspective. In other words, they needed to know about factors leading to effective interactivity at the propositional level, and they wanted to know about principles for how to make better use of interactive technologies for learning, advertising, gaming, and the like (Varan, 2007).

3. A few years ago an officer of the U.S. Telephone Association (USTA) asked one of us (JB) to make sense of all of the many "technology trials" USTA members had funded to demonstrate how to use broadband to improve education and facilitate social change, including the use of digital games for educational purposes. After we presented the report—which was in large part a critique of their conventional scattergun approach of one-shot applications of an innovation followed by a single posttest—we brainstormed ways to improve future funding and research initiatives. The USTA officer concluded that their largely atheoretical approach had been less productive than it would have been if the trials had employed rigorous research designs and theoretical hypotheses, and they committed to attempting to motivate their members to launch a series of theory-guided research initiatives that would employ rigorous research designs.

In other words, it would seem that emerging perspectives from the most progressive industry practitioners who create and manage advanced communication and information systems and networks, including digital games, recognize the need for theory and programmatic research on serious games. That represents a major philosophical change on the part of media institutions. How do we begin to take advantage of this shift in the intellectual tectonic plates of the media industries?

The More Things Change, the More They Stay the Same

First we might want to take advantage of some of the intellectual history in cognate areas and update related theoretical musings. For example, more than a decade ago, Bryant and Love (1996) published a chapter titled "Entertainment as the Driver of New Information Technology," in which they advanced an argument that it was essential to move from inductive reasoning (i.e., industry trials) to deductive reasoning (i.e., theory trials) in order to productively design educational programs, games, and other content that would both push and pull the adoption of broadband. Moreover, these authors articulated several processes and mechanisms that would have to be more fully researched and much better understood for this to happen efficiently. The processes and mechanisms they proffered are remarkably similar to those that need to be better understood in order to advance research in serious games.

Selectivity

The first process considered by Bryant and Love (1996) was selectivity, also known as *selective exposure* and *media choice*. For serious games, the problem is similar to that which educational television shows like *Sesame Street* faced more than 30 years ago and continue to face today—"capturing and holding an audience in the face of competition from commercial entertainment programming" (Bryant, Zillmann, & Brown, 1983, p. 222). However, today the number and range of competing choices are vastly larger than they were in the infancy of educational television.

Fortunately, the state of selective-exposure research has advanced considerably of late. For example, in two reviews Bryant and Davies (2006a, 2006b) noted that research evidence indicated that selective exposure to games and other media fare is in part a function of (1) level of excitatory homeostasis of the digital game player; (2) the involvement potential or intervention potential of the game's message system; (3) message-behavioral affinity between attributes of the game and those of the player; and (4) hedonic valence of the message system of the game. Although empirical evidence to test these components within the context of serious games is generally lacking, using these criteria, empirical generalizations from selective exposure research on other media message systems would suggest theoretical principles that should guide game development so as to facilitate selective exposure to serious games.

Diet

The concept of diet refers to the specific media fare selected by a consumer from the constellation of choices available to him or her. In this information-age era, digital gamers have a plethora of choices available to them, including games of different genres (e.g., strategy, role play, adventure), styles (e.g., first-person, third-person), etc. One unanswered empirical question is whether having an abundance of games available creates more patterned behavior (i.e., playing more of the same sorts of games) or if gamers take advantage of the diversity of game types available and become more diverse in their game diet. In other words,

> Given that we have access to a smorgasbord of…fare, what diet plan will we follow? Will we binge on our favorite sweets? Will usage be biased toward light, easily digestible fare? Will entertainment bulimia or anorexia result? Will we quickly become satiated with one type of treat and then graze on more varied, healthy fare? (Bryant & Love, 1996, p. 111)

Bryant and Love asked these questions about broadband fare more generally, and obviously no equivalent abundance in serious game fare is currently available to make their questions germane, but in the future, such issues of diet may well be critical to digital game developers.

Interactivity

Long considered to be the key to the emerging supremacy of digital gaming in the entertainment arena, interactivity it would appear is equally if not more potent in the world of serious games. Technically, interactivity is the capacity of media users to respond to messages, act on them, and alter them in some way. Or, as Vorderer et al. (2006) suggested, "Interactivity…assumes that content evolves as the user participates with the medium" (p. 2).

As Grodal (2000) emphasized, the entertainment experience will be fundamentally different in digital games than in more traditional media fare, because when a player takes an active role in altering or constructing content, the role of curiosity, surprise, and suspense fundamentally change. In digital games, "the experience of given situations will change over time, due to learning processes that will change arousal and will change the cognitive labeling of the arousal" (Grodal, 2000, p. 207). These elements are as fundamental to learning and motivation as they are to entertainment, so we would anticipate that the degree of and nature of interactivity in serious games would be a fundamental marker of their success.

Agency

The concept of agency refers to the degree of control the user has over the technology or system, in this case, over the serious game being utilized. Bryant and Love (1996) noted, "the term can be used as a psychological personality factor (e.g., locus of control) or it can be referred to as the potential of the medium for user empowerment" (p. 111). In the context of gaming, agency can refer to the degree to which the user can customize an avatar, the control that one has over the selection of tools or weapons, the degree of personalization available, the potency of the user in alerting the motivational structure or outcome criteria, and numerous other elements of play. We assume that the closer a player comes to being omnipotent in this instance, the more desirable and productive the gaming experience, but such assumptions sorely want empirical verification in the serious-gaming environment.

Personalization

A combination of agency and interactivity are closely related to personalization, or how closely the game is aligned to the preferred persona of the player. In traditional mass media, messages were addressed "to whom it may concern," whereas in gaming the potential for making the messages addressable to the specific consumer is almost unlimited. Such personalization has long been considered to be an element of parasocial interaction (e.g., Klimmt, Hartmann, & Schramm, 2006), but the place of parasocial interaction in the learning or motivational context is not nearly so well developed as it is in entertainment. Many players of serious games may well want a degree of anonymity, especially when dealing with highly threatening issues such as personal health and safety, but it is anticipated that at least some degree of personalization would be beneficial in serious games, at least for many people in some contexts.

Dimensionality

The nature of messages in the digital world permits designers to manipulate dimensionality (e.g., 2D, 3D, hologram) in addition to numerous other message features. High definition display screens and advanced audio (e.g., 7.1 surround sound) facilitate such potential. Obviously designers of entertainment games have taken advantage of such potential, which appears to have been a major factor in recent marketing successes. It is equally obvious that there is no reason for designers of serious games not to fully exploit the multimedia and multidimensional potential of their games. Empirical investigations of the nuances of such effects are sorely needed.

In an earlier, more-expansive version of their 1996 chapter, Bryant and Love (1993) had suggested two additional dimensions of new technologies that could enhance the entertainment experience: (1) level of complexity and (2) potential for competition. Both features would also appear to have potential for the adoption and employment of serious games.

Complexity

Considering ideal level of complexity games and other interactive communication technologies, Bryant and Love (1993) suggested beginning with the Wundt curve (e.g., Blumenthal, 2001), which provides an iconic analog for the notion that moderate levels of complexity create intermediate levels of cortical arousal, which is both optimally pleasing to most interpreters and maximally efficient for learning in most instances. The authors also noted that designers should expect considerable individual differences on this factor, because personality factors relevant to the complexity variable often are only moderately highly correlated (e.g., not everyone high in intelligence as measured on traditional IQ tests score high on cognitive complexity, nor is need for cognition particularly highly correlated with either IQ or cognitive complexity). They advised the use of extensive formative research to assess optimal level of complexity of any game, taking into account developmental considerations. That advice would appear to be equally valid for designers of serious games.

Competition

Bryant and Love (1993) noted that with the rapid growth and improved quality of digital games, including digital games like *DOOM* (which was released in 2003), the potential for player competition was apt to be a major factor in the success of new game software. Although the language of this paper reflected the primitive status of computer networking at the time (i.e., lots of talk about modems, LANs, and intelligent networks), the authors' claim for the importance of competition has proven to be at least somewhat prescient. Results of a survey by the Annenberg School for Communication (ASC) Games Group at the University of Southern California revealed that competition was the number one rated factor why players said they chose and liked particular games (Vorderer et al., 2006). Given the well-established place of competition in learning and other motivational environment, competition surely will play a vital role in the success of serious games. In many such situations, competition with one's own self to improve on prior performance may be as important as interpersonal or group competition.

Entertainment Features

Finally, Bryant and Love (1996) delineated several entertainment features—such as drama, conflict, storytelling, and empathy (e.g., Zillmann & Vorderer, 2000)—that would be essential for developers to understand and utilize in information-system development and message design before the potential of broadband IT could be fully realized. Entertainment features, including humor, drama, and special effects, have been shown to effectively drive attention as well as information acquisition in educational television, so long as the entertainment features do not mask or "swamp" the educational messages (Bryant, Zillmann, & Brown, 1983). It would seem that entertainment features would likewise serve to advance the curriculum goals of many serious games.

One thing that should be noted when discussing the place of entertainment features in serious games is that when entertainment is used in the service of education, it is imperative that it serves the cause of engagement rather than mirth per se. Although entertainment features may motivate attention in educational media fare, mirth reactions like laughter may prove to distract from educational points, if such elements are not used judiciously. Peters (2007) noted, "The basic issue here is that it's easier to make a fun game educational than it is to inject fun into an educational game" (p. 2). Mixing learning with fun is a difficult task that often requires formative evaluation, even with designers and writers who are sensitive to edutainment issues.

What Do We Need to Know from Psychology?

Social, clinical, psychophysiological, and personality psychology—among other subdisciplines of psychology—offer quite a few theories of learning and emotion that would seem to apply directly to the scientific examination of serious games.

Learning Theory

After discussing the potential application of traditional learning theories to serious games, Graesser, Chipman, Leeming, & Biedenbach (this volume, chapter 6) concluded, "Operant and classical conditioning have little to say about serious games that promote deep learning ." Many so-called traditional learning theories go way beyond the "Skinner Box" in applying systematic extensions of operant- and classical-conditioning models in ways that do have relevance to contemporary gaming behaviors. For example, psychologist Arthur W. Staats (e.g., 1963, 1964, 1996) wrote several books and articles that extended traditional learning theories to a variety of complex learning behaviors that involved interactivity and various forms of transactional behaviors. So Graesser et al.'s claim technically may be correct in the sense that traditional learning theory has not been successfully applied to serious games in the past, but that certainly does not mean that systematic extensions of learning theory into the serious-games arena could not be fruitful. In fact, when cognitive-based learning theories are considered, it might be useful to apply the principle of Occam's razor, asking if all of their cognitive components and constructs are necessary to gain a veridical view of the learning process. Sometimes the cognitive mechanisms proffered are not necessary to explain mediated learning.

Game Theory

A couple of intellectual generations ago in psychology, adaptations of game theory (Morgenstern & von Neumann, 1944/2007) were in vogue. Although game theory has not infiltrated cognitive psychology to the extent it did social psychology, fully explaining learning via games without some consideration of game theory often seems incomplete, if for no other reason than for face validity. Moreover, in employing game theory many proponents examine each of five elements systematically: (1) players, or decision makers; (2) strategies available to each player; (3) rules governing players' behavior; (4) outcomes that result from particular choices made by each player at any given point in the game; and (5) payoffs accrued by each players as a result of each decision and outcome (Smith, 2003). Such a systematic review process would provide a valuable heuristic for designers of serious games.

Learning Styles

When the senior of us (JB) published his first coedited scholarly book 25 years ago, entitled *Children's Understanding of Television: Research on Attention and Comprehension* (Bryant & Anderson, 1983), he was fortunate to obtain a chapter on different learning styles for different media by fledgling psychologist Howard Gardner. Gardner published his own book that same year, entitled *Frames of Mind: The Theory of Multiple Intelligences* (Gardner, 1983), which changed the way most educational psychologists think about learning. The wisdom acquired from research on learning styles has immense value to designers of serious games.

What is Special about Serious Games?

What is special psychologically about educational and prosocial gaming? Such questions need to be given much greater attention. Psychologically, what separates this genre of software from casino gaming, other entertainment-gaming genres, online play of other forms, and the like? Does serious digital gaming hold any special potential for understanding human motivation, gratification, information acquisition, and knowledge generalization that other forms of technology-assisted learning do not? To us, these are fundamental questions that psychological theories of gaming and learning must address if the scientific study of serious games is to be all that it can be.

Similarly, the relationship between emotions and learning in serious gaming need to be considered most systematically. Undoubtedly strong emotions, such as sadness, happiness, anger, fear, disgust, surprise, confusion, boredom, flow/engagement, curiosity/interest, delight/eureka, and frustration, need to be taken into account in creating serious games, because such emotions as may be produced via game play are likely to introduce cognitive as well as affective distraction into the learning environment. As previously mentioned in our discussion of the Wundt curve in complexity, optimal performance typically takes place under conditions of moderate arousal. Other affective states, such as amusement and embarrassment, would appear to be equally relevant to the psychological study of scientific games, and both emotions have been studied extensively as they relate to learning in the digital environment (e.g., Ekman, 2003). In other words, because serious games ultimately are about learning and motivation, the effects of emotional states that are precursors to playing such games, as well as the emotions produced via game playing, need to be systematically considered when assessing the impact of serious games.

What Would We Add from Disciplines Outside Psychology?

We are media psychologists and communicologists, and we operate largely from the purviews of these knowledge communities, as well as with different intellectual histories, epistemological underpinnings, and the like. Let us offer some different theoretical perspectives of the role of learning and emotion in serious games from our Weltanschauung and disciplinary biases.

Entertainment-Education

The specialized work on entertainment-education (e.g., Singhal, Cody, Rogers, & Sabido, 2004; Singhal & Rogers, 1999) is directly related to learning and emotion and has considerable application to games for learning, development, and change.

> Entertainment-education (E-E) is the process of purposely designing and implementing a media message to both entertain and educate, in order to increase audience members' knowledge about an educational issue, create favorable attitudes, shift social norms, and change overt behavior. (Singhal et al., 2004, p. 5)

E-E is still at a rather rudimentary level of development and has not generated much dedicated theory. In fact, typically it has ignored the principles of entertainment theory (An, 2008), which could enhance its effectiveness dramatically. Yet it would seem to have veridical applications to the development of many types of serious games, and the knowledge base its literature yields needs to be accommodated in study and designing serious games.

Theory of Affective Dynamics

Speaking of entertainment theory, one comprehensive schema developed from state-of-the-art theory and research in entertainment theory is Zillmann's

(2003) theory of affective dynamics: emotions and moods. This theory appears to be particularly well suited for incorporation into serious-games assessments, because it systematically integrates dimensions such as enjoyment, moral judgment, perceptions of justice, and the like in ways that make it clear how they should be a critical part of our ultimate theories of the role of learning and emotion as well as entertainment. Looked at very simplistically, at the very least it is highly likely that the more enjoyable our games are—even our so-called serious games—the more successful they will be, if not in educating and informing, at least in motivating usage. In other words, let us not forget the lessons of *Sesame Street* (Fisch & Truglio, 2001; Lesser, 1974).

Social Perspectives

Our previous recognition of the place of competition in the motivational mix leads to recognition of the importance of peers, learning groups, collaborators and collaboratories, and task teams. This suggests the importance of assuming a social perspective on serious games from the outset. Obviously there are many ways that one can approach this, ranging from taking an organizational/instructional perspective to undertaking a full-scale network analysis. Whatever the approach taken, it is likely that incorporation of social factors, social networking, and the like into our motivational models will be essential if our theories are to be veridical (e.g., Monge & Contractor, 2003).

Aesthetic Dimensions

Another element that research in media psychology suggests will prove to be critical to the success of our learning and social-action games is their aesthetic value. Aesthetic dimensions often are important intrinsic factors in motivation and have long been shown to affect mediated learning (e.g., Bryant & Anderson, 1983). Aesthetic theory (e.g., Cupchik, 2001; Cupchik & Kemp, 2000) has made considerable progress of late, and many of its contributions have been from the humanities, rather than from the social or cognitive sciences. The place of aesthetic judgment in learning and emotion undoubtedly will prove to be more difficult to access than some other factors, but it is likely to be an important component to our understanding of learning and social development from games.

Hierarchical Theories

Finally, as theory in serious games becomes more sophisticated, we would anticipate that hierarchical theories that simultaneously integrate emotion, cognition, and at least one other element (e.g., experiential, direction) would prove invaluable. Theories such as Zillmann's three-factor theory of emotion (Bryant & Miron, 2003) offer a sophisticated blend of psychological and communicalogical factors. Such theories ultimately will be required to even begin to understand the place of emotion, cognition, motivation, and the like in determining the effectiveness and effects of serious games.

References

America's army—Operations [Digital game]. (2002). U.S. Army. http://www.americasarmy.com/

An, S. (2008, May). *Where is the entertainment? A thematic macro-analysis of entertainment-education campaign research.* Paper presented at the International Communication Association convention, Montreal, Canada.

BBC. (2002, March 18). Video games "stimulate learning." Retrieved April 2, 2008, from http://news.bbc.co.uk/1/hi/education/1879019.stm

Blumenthal, A. L. (2001). A Wundt primer: The operating characteristics of consciousness. In R. W. Reiber & D. K. Robinson (Eds.), *Wilhelm Wundt in history: The making of a scientific psychology* (pp. 123–184). Amsterdam: Kluwer Academic.

Bryant, J., & Anderson, D. R. (Eds.). (1983). *Children's understanding of television: Research on attention and comprehension.* Orlando, FL: Academic Press.

Bryant, J., & Davies, J. (2006a). Selective exposure processes. In J. Bryant & P. Vorderer (Eds.), *Psychology of entertainment* (pp. 19–33). Mahwah, NJ: Erlbaum.

Bryant, J., & Davies, J. (2006b). Selective exposure to video games. In P. Vorderer & J. Bryant (Eds.), *Playing video games: Motives, responses, and consequences* (pp. 181–194). Mahwah, NJ: Erlbaum.

Bryant, J., & Love, C. (1993, April). *Factors to consider and test when creating viable multimedia for enjoyment and learning in the broadband environment.* Paper presented at the annual conference of the Broadcast Education Association, Las Vegas, NV.

Bryant, J., & Love, C. (1996). Entertainment as the driver of new information technology. In R. R. Dholakia, N. Mundorf, & N. Dholakia (Eds.), *New infotainment technologies in the home: Demand-side perspectives* (pp. 91–114). Mahwah, NJ: Erlbaum.

Bryant, J., & Miron, D. (2003). Excitation-transfer theory and three-factor theory of emotion. In J. Bryant, D. Roskos-Ewoldsen, & J. Cantor (Eds.), *Communication and emotion: Essays in honor of Dolf Zillmann* (pp. 31–59). Mahwah, NJ: Erlbaum.

Bryant, J., & Vorderer, P. (Eds.). (2006). *Psychology of entertainment.* Mahwah, NJ: Erlbaum.

Bryant, J., Zillmann, D., & Brown, D. (1983). Entertainment features in children's educational television: Effects on attention and information acquisition. In J. Bryant & D. R. Anderson (Eds.), *Children's understanding of television: Research on attention and comprehension* (pp. 221–240). New York: Academic Press.

Cupchik, G. C. (2001). Aesthetics and emotion in entertainment media. *Media Psychology, 3,* 69–89.

Cupchik, G. C., & Kemp, S. (2000). The aesthetics of media fare. In D. Zillmann & P. Vorderer (Eds.), *Media entertainment: The psychology of its appeal* (pp. 249–264). Mahwah, NJ: Erlbaum.

Doom. [Computer Game Software]. (1993). Mesquite, TX: id Software.

Ekman, P. (2003). *Emotions revealed.* New York: Times Books.

Fisch, S. M., & Truglio, R. T. (Eds.). (2001). *G is for growing: Thirty years of research on children and Sesame Street.* Mahwah, NJ: Erlbaum.

Gardner, H. (1983). *Frames of mind: The theory of multiple intelligences.* New York: Basic Books.

Grodal, T. (2000). Video games and the pleasures of control. In D. Zillmann & P. Vorderer (Eds.), *Media entertainment: The psychology of its appeal* (pp. 197–213). Mahwah, NJ: Erlbaum.

Gudmundsen, J. (2006, May 18). Movement gets serious about making games with purpose. *Press Connects.* Retrieved April 3, 2008, from http://pressconnects.gns.gannettonline.com/apps/pbcs.dll/article?AID=/20060518/Tech05.htm

Klimmt, C., Hartmann, T., & Schramm, H. (2006). Parasocial interactions and relationships. In J. Bryant & P. Vorderer (Eds.), *Psychology of entertainment* (pp. 291–313). Mahwah, NJ: Erlbaum.

LA kids learning via video games. (2008, April 2). Retrieved April 2, 2008, from http://kotu.com/gaming/education/la-kids-learning-via-video=games-305632.php

Lesser, G. S. (1974). *Children and television: Lessons from Sesame Street.* New York: Vintage Books.

Monge, P. R., & Contractor, N. S. (2003). *Theories of communication networks.* Oxford, England: Oxford University Press.

Morgenstern, O., & von Neumann, J. (2007). *The theory of games and economic behavior.* Princeton, NJ: Princeton University Press. (Original work published 1944)

Peters, J. (2007, June 27). Gaming: World of borecraft. *Slate.* Retrieved April 3, 2008, from http://www.slate.com/id/2169019/

Serious games in virtual worlds. (2007, December 12). *Science Daily.* Retrieved April 2, 2008, from http://sciencedaily.com/releases/2007/12/0712212254.htm

Singhal, A., Cody, M. J., Rogers, E. M., & Sabido, M. (Eds.). (2004). *Entertainment-education and social change: History, research, and practice.* Mahwah, NJ: Erlbaum.

Singhal, A., & Rogers, E. M. (1999). *Entertainment-education: A communication strategy for social change.* Mahwah, NJ: Erlbaum.

Smith, M. S. (2003). *Game theory.* Retrieved April 2, 2008, from http://www.beyond-intractability.org/essay/prisoners_dilemma/

Staats, A. W. (1963). *Complex human behavior.* New York: Holt, Rinehart & Winston.

Staats, A. W. (Ed.). (1964). *Human learning.* New York: Holt, Rinehart & Winston.

Staats, A. W. (1996). *Behavior and personality: Psychological behaviorism.* New York: Springer.

Thompson, C. (2006, July 23). Saving the world, one video game at a time. *New York Times.* Retrieved April 2, 2008, from http://www.nytimes.com/2006/07/23thom.html

Three winners announced in competition to discover innovative video and computer games that improve health and health care. (2007, November 19). Retrieved April 2, 2008, from http://www.rwjf.org/pr/products.jsp?id=23753

Varan, D. (2007, April). *Television's changing landscape.* Presentation at the College of Communication & Information Sciences, University of Alabama, Tuscaloosa, AL.

Virtual-reality video game to help burn patients play their way to pain relief. (2008, March 22). *Science Daily.* Retrieved April 2, 2008 from http://www.sciencedaily.com/releases/2008/03/080319152744.htm

Vorderer, P., & Bryant, J. (Eds.). (2006). *Playing video games: Motives, responses, and consequences.* Mahwah, NJ: Erlbaum.

Vorderer, P., Bryant, J., Pieper, K. M., & Weber, R. (2006). Playing video games as entertainment. In P. Vorderer & J. Bryant (Eds.), *Playing video games: Motives, responses, and consequences* (pp. 1–7). Mahwah, NJ: Erlbaum.

Zillmann, D. (2003). Theory of affective dynamics: Emotions and moods. In J. Bryant, D. Roskos-Ewoldsen, & J. Cantor (Eds.), *Communication and emotion: Essays in honor of Dolf Zillmann* (pp. 533–567). Mahwah, NJ: Erlbaum.

Zillmann, D., & Vorderer, P. (Eds.). (2000). *Media entertainment: The psychology of its appeal.* Mahwah, NJ: Erlbaum.

Chapter 8

Designing Serious Games for Learning and Health in Informal and Formal Settings

Debra A. Lieberman

Digital interactive games for entertainment have been commercially available for 37 years, and, almost from the start, serious games made for learning, skill development, attitude and behavior change, and other purposes beyond entertainment have also been part of the landscape (Malone & Lepper, 1987; Rieber, Smith, & Noah, 1998). Even before the advent of digital interactive games as consumer products, games and simulations supported by mainframe computers were used in education (Coleman, 1971; Suppes, 1967; Suppes, Jerman, & Groen, 1966). The use of games for serious purposes has been controversial amid concerns about the violent and stereotyped content of certain popular entertainment games and the enticement of yet one more screen that could lead people to be more sedentary. However, the resistance has subsided in the past few years, and digital games and game technologies have been gaining wider general acceptance as viable platforms for learning, skill development, behavior change, and other serious aims.

This change in acceptance may be due to several converging factors. First, game technologies are becoming more advanced and powerful and yet also more easy and intuitive to use. A prime example of intuitive ease-of-use is the *Nintendo Wii* console's motion-sensitive remote control interface, with its immediate and strong appeal across age groups, from toddlers to seniors, and across demographic categories. As a result, an increasing number and variety of people are playing entertainment games and experiencing first-hand how engaging and impactful they can be. Second, a fair number of well designed serious games, many of them aimed at learning or health outcomes, are now available that successfully use interactive game-based entertainment as the learning environment, and so the potential of serious games is becoming a reality for all to see and experience (Gee, 2003; Prensky, 2006; Squire & Jenkins, 2003). Off-the-shelf commercial entertainment games are also being repurposed to attain learning and health goals with impressive results (Lieberman, 2006a). The popular dance pad game *Dance Dance Revolution* (1999) is an example of repurposing, as schools and health clinics are using the game to improve students' and patients' physical fitness and weight management (Murphy et al., 2006; Unnithan, Houser, & Fernhall, 2005). Third, a growing body of research has provided substantial evidence of the effectiveness of serious games mainly in the areas of learning and health (Baranowski, Baranowski, et al., 2003; Baranowski, Buday, Thompson, & Baranowski, 2008; Blumberg & Ismailer, this volume, chapter 9; Lieberman, 1997, 2006b; Raessen & Goldstein, 2005), and this has influenced opinion leaders and decision makers to engage in more advocacy and implementation. Fourth, research on serious games is producing validated design principles that are improving each consecutive generation of serious games (see this volume; Vorderer & Bryant, 2006).

Because of these trends, momentum in the serious games field is growing and so is the amount of available support. A wide-ranging array of stakeholders has become interested in serious games, including educators, health care providers, game producers, technology companies, investors, funding agencies, and policy makers. Professional and academic associations are holding well-attended conferences with names such as CDC's Strategic Look at eGames; Game Education Summit; Games for Health; Gaming to Learn; Meaningful Play; Serious Games Summit; and Virtual Learning in Health Communication. Online discussion groups such as Games for Change, Games for Health, Games Network, and Serious Games are lively forums for debate, discussion, and information sharing. Online reviews and blogs are also contributing to the marketplace of ideas, including Grand Text Auto, Kotaku, The Ludologist, Terra Nova, and Water Cooler Games. Recent books discuss serious game design and the cultural or educational significance of games (e.g., Bergeron, 2006; Bogost, 2007; Gee, 2003, 2007; Prensky, 2006), and some books present empirical research on the processes and effects of game play and use this evidence to recommend advances in the research, design, and implementation of serious games (this volume; Raessen & Goldstein, 2005; Vorderer & Bryant, 2006). New journals and more established ones are publishing peer-reviewed research in the field. University-based undergraduate and graduate programs are emerging to teach the art and science of game development. Federal agencies such as the National Science Foundation, the U.S Department of Education, the National Institutes of Health, and the Centers for Disease Control and Prevention are supporting research and development projects that incorporate serious games, and foundations such as the MacArthur Foundation and the Robert Wood Johnson Foundation are sponsoring research grants and national programs to help advance theory, evidence, evaluation, design, and innovation in the areas of digital interactive media for learning and health. These valuable forms of support have helped spur the field's momentum and have helped attract interest and participation. More research support, funding, investment, and innovation are needed because many key questions are still unaddressed, new questions are always arising as technology and innovation continue to advance, and the potential of this form of learning and behavior change is not nearly fully realized, even though this young field is off to a strong start.

Why are digital interactive games such effective learning environments? The most compelling games are immersive, experiential, responsive, and adaptive, activating at certain times players' emotional, social, and even kinesthetic processes of learning, in addition to the cognitive. They are popular, fun, cool, and played enthusiastically during leisure time, they offer dramatic stories and characters or compelling game-play challenges, and they are played by a broad spectrum of people who might otherwise be hard to reach or unreceptive to certain topics or activities.

Aimed at goals beyond pure entertainment, serious games have been designed to enhance and support a variety of outcomes, and here are a few:

- Knowledge gain, insight, and deeper understanding
- Skill development and transfer
- Health behavior change
- Medical diagnosis, treatment, and therapy
- Physical activity and fitness
- Decision-support
- Social skills
- Work collaboration
- Civic engagement
- Political campaigning
- Recruitment to causes and organizations
- Persuasion and attitude change

With today's advances in game technologies, formats, and genres, it is especially important to pay attention to the context for game play, in order to design and implement a serious game appropriately for the targeted population and the setting in which the game will be played. A major distinction to consider is the contrast between informal and formal learning environments. These two contexts for serious game play should point designers and practitioners toward distinct choices in game formats and goals. Informal learning—the definition of learning here goes beyond knowledge gain because it includes the changes in attitudes, beliefs, skills, and behavior that may also be intended in the game, such as with health games—takes place during leisure time and the player is likely to have chosen to play the game, sometimes with no learning goals in mind but simply for entertainment, while formal learning involves assignment, assessment, and a specific curriculum chosen for the player by the educational institution.

This chapter focuses on informal and formal learning with serious games intended for learning and health, two areas that touch people's lives every day and have huge institutional infrastructures behind them—schools and the health care system—with carefully developed and well vetted curricula geared to important, and often vital, learning and behavioral goals. First, the chapter discusses a few concepts and theories in the learning sciences and the health communication sciences that provide principles that could be integrated into the design of serious games for learning and health. It then contrasts the use of games for informal learning during leisure time versus formal learning in school classrooms and health education settings, and concludes with two lists of issues involved in the design and implementation of serious games for learning and health; one set aimed at informal leisure-time learning and the other at formal classroom-based learning.

Some Game Design Concepts

Learning tends to be more enjoyable and the learner more motivated when there is a compelling reason to learn (Bruner, 1960, 1961; Locke & Latham, 1990). Good teachers know how to make a subject worth knowing, so that students are eager to learn in order to attain an outcome that matters to them. These teachers establish clear goals, their students know why they are learning, and there are plenty of opportunities to apply what they have learned (Bransford, Brown, & Cocking, 1999). Furthermore, these teachers adapt to their students' skills, interests, and learning styles to make learning more personally meaningful and achievable (Hannafin & Land, 1997).

Constructivist learning is a well tested and validated approach that situates learning in an experiential and applied environment, where learners take an active role and personally construct their own knowledge in authentic situations that allow them to build on what they already know (Honebein, Duffy, & Fishman, 1993). By building on students' prior knowledge and learning styles, and giving them choice and autonomy, learning becomes more relevant and interesting.

During leisure time, digital interactive games can deliver constructivist learning opportunities that people will eagerly play for the fun of it. Games involve challenge to reach a goal, and serious games can pose compelling and motivating challenges during leisure time that require the player to learn new content, engage in higher-order thinking and problem solving, make decisions, interact with others collaboratively and in leadership roles, and try out new experiences that would be difficult or impossible in the physical world. Within a well designed game, learners have a safe and private environment in which they can try out and rehearse new skills, receive helpful feedback, progress at their own pace, and learn how and why things work beyond simply memorizing a series of facts. In addition to the sometimes desirable private aspects of learning with games, learners interested in social interaction can talk with others about a game, show it to others, or play it with others either face-to face or, in some cases, online.

Examples of constructivist games that have been played for leisure-time learning are *Oregon Trail*, *SimCity*, *Re-Mission* (2006), and *Pulse!*, to name just a few. *SimCity* challenges the player to build cities that succeed or fail based on the player's city planning decisions and allocation of resources. *Re-Mission*, a cancer education video game, challenges players to save the lives of various cancer patients by shooting their cancer cells with chemotherapy and administering other treatments. A randomized controlled study found that playing *Re-Mission* improved adolescent and young adult cancer patients' cancer-related knowledge, self-efficacy (belief in one's ability to carry out a specific behavior; in this case it was self-efficacy for engaging in certain cancer treatment-related behaviors), and adherence to their prescribed cancer treatment plan (Kato, Cole, Bradlyn, & Pollock, 2008). Other studies of *Re-Mission's* health effects have been conducted with healthy young adults who do not have cancer, and have found that (1) playing the game strengthens beliefs and attitudes about cancer that are predictors of better cancer prevention and self-care, and (2) inclusion of dramatic story elements and a focus on the cancer patient characters' needs, personalities, and aspirations enhance players' learning about cancer, empathy and caring about the characters, and beliefs and attitudes about cancer that are predictors of better cancer prevention and self-care, such as self-efficacy and perceptions about one's own susceptibility to getting cancer. On the other hand, exclusion of dramatic story elements and exclusion of the cancer patient characters' needs, personalities, and aspirations focuses the player on game mechanics, which in this case involve the shooting of cancer cells with chemotherapy, and this pure game-play focus enhances players' positive attitudes and self-efficacy related to the use of chemotherapy, which in essence is a "health mechanic" taught in the game (Lieberman, 2008). *Re-Mission*, like *Oregon Trail*, *SimCity*, *Pulse!*, and many other constructivist games, puts players into a challenging environment where, in order to succeed within the simulated virtual game world, they must learn and then apply new knowledge and skills.

With the constructivist approach—in which learners are often eager to learn so they can succeed in reaching a goal—the desire to find facts, solve problems, develop skills, and understand how and why systems work is internally driven. The game is not delivering "stealth learning," hidden behind some frothy entertainment that sugar coats the learning to make it invisible or at least more palatable. Instead, learning is front and center as a process to enjoy and an achievement to be proud of. Learning is more likely to be experienced as fun when there is a good reason to learn, the material is tailored to the individual learner's abilities, the system provides helpful feedback and support, and the learner has some personal control over the process.

Immersiveness and perceived reality are also characteristics of digital interactive games that help make them effective environments for learning and behavior change. Games, like many other media formats, elicit feelings of presence, of really being there (Lee, 2004; Lombard & Ditton, 1997), an authentic experience that can bring up the same kinds of arousal, physiological response, and empathy that real experiences do (Picard, 1997; Reeves & Nass, 1996). This is not necessarily due to the realism of the graphics or animation or sound track, because very simple and low-resolution games can create strong feelings of immersion and presence (see Reeves & Nass, 1996). On an emotional level, players may strongly identify with a character that is like them in some ways or that they aspire to be like (Cohen, 2001), and when a game requires that they assist a character who needs help they may develop caring and nurturing feelings toward that character and may identify so strongly with that character's plight that they begin imagining that they too might some day have similar problems to confront in their own lives, and this could motivate them to learn more and take action on their own behalf (Lieberman, 2008). Game players are directly engaged in the world of the game and receive feedback for their own actions. They gain first-hand experience of mastering problems in the virtual world of a game, and this experience of mastery and seeing it lead to effective decisions can be a powerful way to learn, compared to carrying out problem-solving exercises on paper and receiving external acknowledgment in the form of a grade (Prawat & Flowden, 1994).

Simulations in games provide a rich environment for understanding systems and the causes and effects of change within those systems. They lend themselves to learning in a variety of subject areas ranging from math to science to social studies to health. A simulation is a representation of a physical or social system that lets the user adjust its conditions and components and then observe the changes that unfold (Aldrich, 2003; Heinich, Molenda, Russell, & Smaldino, 1996; Rieber, 1996). They are algorithm-based artificial worlds that have some properties of the real world. For example, there are simulations that enable users to learn how businesses and economic systems work, how organizations can be led effectively, how cells grow and change, how to keep a family happy and prosperous, and how to use medications and avoid environmental triggers to keep a virtual character's asthma under control. Simulations can simplify a view of a system by eliminating some of the variables; they can speed up or slow down time so that processes and outcomes are easier to observe; they allow the user to manipulate variables that are not immediately alterable in the real world (such as raising and lowering the earth's temperature to observe the impact of global warming); and they are safe because any dangerous outcomes are depicted but not physically experienced. Simulations are often used as the basis for serious games because they provide a world in which the player can make decisions and see or even virtually experience the consequences.

Research has investigated the learning that can occur with simulation-based games, such as multidisciplinary learning across the curriculum, where students see how academic subjects are interrelated when they try to solve real-world problems using information and methods from various fields (Betz, 1995); insight into cause and effect within complex systems, where learners make decisions and immediately see the consequences (Corbeil, 1999); development of skills in logic and decision making (Aldrich, 2003; Goldstein, 2003); and moral and ethical development as learners see how their decisions can affect others (Aldrich, 2003; Millians, 1999; Reigeluth & Squire, 1998).

In addition to using constructivism, immersion, and simulations to enhance learning, educational games can be designed with other pedagogical features that have been shown to foster learning, such as role modeling (Bandura, 1977a, b); self-directed learning in environments where the individual learns how to learn (Lieberman & Linn, 1991); placing learning and problem solving in a familiar context so that learners can more readily draw on their prior experiences in that setting (Cordova & Lepper, 1996); scaffolding, feedback, and other forms of learner help and support (Arroyo, Beal, Walle, Murray, & Woolf, 2004); adaptive instruction that adjusts to the learner's performance and abilities to keep the material challenging but not too easy or difficult (Schwartz, Lin, Brophy, & Bransford, 1999); intelligent tutoring and coaching (Mayer & Moreno, 2002); the use of multiple media modalities to enhance learner understanding and transfer of skills (Moreno & Mayer, 2002); the development and rehearsal of planning skills and other basic academic skills (Mayer, Schustack, & Blanton, 1999); and the use of fantasy and narrative to enhance engagement and to provide a framework for remembering and applying what was learned (Parker & Lepper, 1992).

Another pedagogical approach that serious games can be designed to support is learning-by-teaching (Biswas, Leelawong, Schwartz, & Vye, 2005). Games can provide teachable agents that motivate the player to learn the material so they can teach it to a virtual agent character. Games can also build peer teaching into the activity. For example, cooperative games can create situations in which two or more players must teach and help each other in order to win the game (Brown, Lieberman, et al., 1997).

Interactive media, including digital interactive games, can provide dynamic assessment in which the game or the teacher measures the learner's performance, helps the learner reflect on her or his performance and strategies, provides help and suggestions for improvement, allows opportunities to practice, and then assesses again (Vye et al., 1998; Yeomans, 2008). With this approach, assessment and learning are seen as linked and not separate, interrelated in a continuous and interactive process that leads to deeper learning and understanding through testing, intervening, and retesting. Dynamic assessment could be used in both informal and formal learning settings. In formal settings the data generated by dynamic assessment could be collected by an educational management system that the teacher could use to track each student's progress and identify areas that need more work.

Health games can incorporate all the learning theories and strategies mentioned above and also apply health communication and health behavior change theories and strategies into the game design. Examples include tailoring, or customizing, of health messages to more closely match the characteristics, interests, culture, and health status of the individual, which can lead to improvements in attention to health messages, engagement, perceived quality and relevance, learning, retention, and health behaviors (Kreuter, Farrell, Olevitch, & Brennan, 2001); use of gain frames to depict the benefits of engaging in a health behavior and loss frames to depict the risks of not doing so, and selecting either a gain frame or a loss frame strategy based on the individual's dispositions and motivations (Mann, Sherman, & Updegraff, 2004); designing media differently, according to the elaboration likelihood model, for people who are highly involved and interested in a health issue (e.g., give them plenty of the information they seek) versus those who are not highly involved (e.g., use humor, vividness, sex appeal, and other techniques to attract attention to a simple but powerful health message), and in these ways increase cognitive processing of health messages, a strategy known to lead to more significant learning and attitude change (Petty & Cacciopo, 1986); using role modeling and rehearsal of skills, among other approaches, to increase the individual's sense of self-efficacy, or self-confidence, to carry out desirable prevention and self-care behaviors (Bandura, 1997); using the extended parallel process model with its emphasis on changing health behavior by increasing people's perceptions of the severity of a health problem and of their own susceptibility to experiencing it, as well as perceptions of efficacy related to one's own abilities (self-efficacy) and related to the benefits of the recommended health behavior (response efficacy) (Witte, Meyer, & Martell, 2001); and fostering communication and social support through game play because social connections are associated with better prevention behaviors, coping skills, and health outcomes (Lieberman, 1997, 2001, 2006b).

This quick tour of a few relevant learning and health behavior change theories and concepts is meant to provide a glimpse at just some of the many learning processes and media design principles and strategies that have been, or could be, applied to the design of games for learning and health. (For further reading about applicable theories, concepts, models, and research, see books about digital interactive game research and design, such as this volume; Vorderer & Bryant, 2006; Raessen & Goldstein, 2005.)

Informal versus Formal Settings for Serious Games

Serious games for informal learning must compete with all the other leisure-time options available to the individual. They must be engaging, either because they are fun, challenging, cool, social, interesting, or entertaining, or because they offer other gratifications, including serious purposes such as a desire to improve cognitive fitness with a brain game or to get some physical activity with a dance pad game or other exergame such as *Dance Dance Revolution* (1999) or *Wii Fit*. While leisure-time games for informal learning and health behavior change should be assessed and evaluated to assure that they lead to significant benefits and avoid serious drawbacks, still they are supplementary activities that do not take the place of other more traditional ways of delivering instruction or health interventions. If they turn out to have little or no educational or health impact for any particular individual, it would be regrettable that they were not more impactful, but there would be no need for deep concern. Even the lamest of learning or health games could, at the very least, expose the player to important learning concepts or valuable reminders about healthy lifestyle, self-care, prevention, adherence, or chronic condition self-management. Since leisure-time games are supplements, a relatively ineffective serious game would not be a major problem.

However, the bar is raised tremendously higher when a serious game is implemented in a formal learning environment, such as a school classroom or a worksite training session or a health care provider's health education classes. The teacher or facilitator is responsible for attaining significant outcomes and students deserve to have state-of-the-art forms of instruction, be it game-based learning or any other learning method. Every student is different yet must be taught appropriately. A game may be an excellent mode of learning for certain students, such as those who already play digital interactive games, enjoy them, and are skillful at playing them, while a game may not be very effective for students who don't already play games or who do not like the assigned game's format or genre.

One size rarely fits all when it comes to games for learning and health, and classroom teachers and health educators will need to develop variations in the way they assign games, so that all learners can be served. For example, teachers could offer a game as one of several learning activities the student may choose, or they could use games as homework supplements to the material that was presented and explored during class meeting times, thereby using the game to support the curriculum but not serve as its focus. Another approach would be to assign pairs or groups of students to play learning games cooperatively as a team, so that advanced and novice players could succeed when their skills are shared and all could find something interesting and fulfilling within the assignment. Students could also be assigned to modify existing games or create new games of their own, and this would allow them to pursue their interests and create the kinds of games they would like to play, learning a great deal in the process of making a game that they think would motivate others to learn. And lastly, there are some games that have such broad appeal that everyone likes to play them, at least to some extent. They don't have to like the game as much as they have to like one that they would choose themselves in an informal leisure-time setting. Students may willingly play games at school that would not be their first choice at home, because the school-based game is part of an assigned curriculum and the orientation is toward learning the content.

Not only is it desirable that a game, or the way a game is assigned, align with student interests and abilities, it must align with the curriculum. This is difficult to achieve when all 50 states have their own K-12 curriculum standards, and when health care providers differ in their standards of clinical care and their recommendations to patients for self-care. Curriculum leaders in each state's department of education and in a health plan or clinic's health education department can play an important role in selecting appropriate learning and health games to match their curriculum goals and standards, and they can develop accompanying curriculum materials that expand on the content of a game in ways that present more of the specific curriculum that they need to cover. They can also take a proactive role in obtaining games that align with their curricula, either by funding or creating the games themselves or by advising game developers who want to make games that suit customer needs.

And, some of their own students and teachers can create games that address the curriculum precisely.

Following are some of the issues involved in designing and implementing serious games for learning and health, for informal leisure-time learning and for formal classroom-based learning.

Serious games for informal learning:

- Compete with many other leisure-time activities, so they must be highly entertaining or personally useful to the target user group.
- Have more latitude than games for formal learning, in terms of the issues addressed, story lines presented, opportunities to test and play around with failure states, social interactions with other players, and other parameters that make games fun, edgy, and exciting to play.
- Do not need to motivate a great deal of learning or skill development related to the topic; a serious game that takes 40 hours to play yet does nothing more than expose the player to a concept could serve a valuable role during leisure time, but formal classes in schools and health care settings could not afford to devote this amount of time to a game like that.
- Do not need to be evaluated before they reach consumers. While evaluation of their impact is always a tremendous benefit to the consumer and could make a strong selling point, games for informal learning do not require careful review or evidence of effectiveness in order to enter the marketplace.
- Do not need to align with specific curriculum standards; however they will have wider credibility and acceptance if they show that they were developed with advice from content area experts, instructional designers, behavioral health specialists, and game designers.
- Could be targeted to a small population with specific and unique characteristics, without the requirement that they serve a group of diverse learners.

Serious games for formal learning:

- Do not have to be highly appealing to learners, who are a captive audience.
- Must have at least moderate appeal to all learners, who are often a diverse group with a wide range of game playing interest and skill, academic skill, and content interest and knowledge.
- Could be used as the focus of the curriculum or could serve as a supplement as homework, or could be an option the student could choose among other learning materials and activities.
- Should adapt to the learner's interests and abilities, and continuously adapt as the learner demonstrates improvements or setbacks while playing the game.

- Should provide scaffolding and guidance to serve learners who need help and feedback.
- Should be aligned with curriculum standards and goals.
- Usually must have outcomes that are measurable, as K-12 education is becoming more focused on assessing student performance and preparing students for standardized tests.
- Could embed assessment within the game, and generate results that are transmitted to the teacher's course management system or to a clinic's patient management system.
- Could support dynamic assessment that integrates assessment and learning into a continuous process.

To serve learners well, serious games for informal and formal learning must be well designed for learning and behavior change. Fundamentally, they have a lot in common. They should meet the highest standards of quality. They should be well researched during formative stages of development and then evaluated in the field after completion to ensure effectiveness. They should make use of the unique strengths of games as environments for learning and behavior change, such as the experiential and applied learning they can provide and the performance feedback and adaptiveness they can deliver. They should avoid content that condones gratuitous violence or demeans others, and they should avoid bias or errors in the cause-and-effect scenarios they portray. For example, it would not be accurate to portray a character drinking five alcoholic drinks and then being able to excel at sports with no performance impairment. There are many other game development procedures and game features that go into making excellent and effective serious games, and they are pertinent to games made for both informal and formal settings. The two lists above point to some of the special concerns for each setting and are presented here as guidelines for designers and practitioners to consider.

References

Aldrich, C. (2003). *Simulations and the future of learning: An innovative (and perhaps revolutionary) approach to e-learning*. New York: Jossey-Bass/ Pfeiffer.

Arroyo, I., Beal, C., Walle, R., Murray, T., & Woolf, B. P. (2004). Web-based intelligent multimedia tutoring for high stakes achievement tests. In *Intelligent tutoring systems: Proceedings from the 7th International Conference, ITS* (pp. 468–477). Heidelberg: Springer Berlin.

Bandura, A. (1997a). *Self-efficacy: The exercise of control*. New York: Freeman.

Bandura, A. (1997b). Toward a unifying theory of behavioral change. *Psychological Review, 84*(2), 191–215.

Baranowski, T., Baranowski, J., Cullen, K. W., Marsh, T., Islam, N., Zakeri, I., et al. (2003). *Squire's Quest!* Dietary outcome evaluation of a multimedia game. *American Journal of Preventive Medicine, 24*(1), 52–61.

Baranowski, T., Buday, R., Thompson, D. I., & Baranowski, J. (2008). Playing for real:

Video games and stories for health-related behavior change. *American Journal of Preventive Medicine, 34*(1), 74–82.

Bergeron, B. (2006). *Developing serious games.* Hingham, MA: Charles River Media.

Betz, A. J. (1995). Computer games: Increased learning in an interactive multidisciplinary environment. *Journal of Educational Technology Systems, 24*(2), 195–205.

Biswas, G., Leelawong, K., Schwartz, D., & Vye, N. (2005). Learning by teaching: A new agent paradigm for educational software. *Applied Artificial Intelligence, 19*(3–4), 363–392.

Bogost, I. (2007). *Persuasive games: The expressive power of videogames.* Cambridge, MA: MIT Press.

Bransford, J. D., Brown, A. L., & Cocking, R. R. (Eds.). (1999). *How people learn: Brain, mind, experience, and school.* Washington, DC: National Academy Press.

Brown, S. J., Lieberman, D. A., Gemeny, B. A., Fan, Y. C., Wilson, D. M., & Pasta, D. J. (1997). Educational video game for juvenile diabetes: Results of a controlled trial. *Medical Informatics 22*(1), 77–89.

Bruner, J. S. (1960). *The process of education.* Cambridge, MA: Harvard University Press.

Bruner, J. S. (1961). The act of discovery. *Harvard Educational Review, 31,* 21–32.

Cohen, J. (2001). Defining identification: A theoretical look at the identification of audiences with media characters. *Mass Communication and Society, 4*(3), 245–264.

Coleman, J. (1971). Learning through games. In E. Avedon & B. Sutton-Smith (Eds.), *The study of games* (pp. 322–329). New York: Wiley.

Corbeil, P. (1999). Learning from the children: Practical and theoretical reflections on playing and learning. *Simulation & Gaming, 30*(2), 163–180.

Cordova, D. I., & Lepper, M. R. (1996). Intrinsic motivation and the process of learning: Beneficial effects of contextualization, personalization, and choice. *Journal of Educational Psychology, 88*(4), 715–730.

Dance dance revolution [Digital game]. (1999). Tokyo, Japan: Konami.

Gee, J. P. (2003). *What video games have to teach us about learning and literacy.* New York: Palgrave Macmillan.

Gee, J. P. (2007). *Good video games + good learning: Collected essays on video games, learning and literacy.* New York: Lang.

Goldstein, J. (2003). People @ play: Electronic games. In H. van Oostendorp (Ed.), *Cognition in a digital world* (pp. 25–45). Mahwah, NJ: Erlbaum.

Hannafin, M. J., & Land, S. M. (1997). Student centered learning and interactive multimedia: Status, issues, and implications. *Contemporary Education, 68*(2), 94–99

Heinich, R., Molenda, M., Russell, J. D., & Smaldino, S. E. (1996). *Instructional media and technologies for learning* (5th ed.). Englewood Cliffs, NJ: Prentice-Hall.

Honebein, P., Duffy, T., & Fishman, B. (1993). Constructivism and the design of learning environments: Context and authentic activities for learning. In T. M. Duffy, J. Lowyck, & D. H. Jonassen (Eds.), *Designing environments for constructive learning* (pp. 87–108). New York: Springer Verlag.

Kato, P. M., Cole, S. W., Bradlyn, A. S., & Pollock, B. H. (2008). A video game improves behavioral outcomes in adolescents and young adults with cancer: A randomized trial. *Pediatrics, 122*(2), e305–e317.

Kreuter, M., Farrell, D., Olevitch, L., & Brennan, L. (2001). *Tailoring health messages: Customizing communication with computer technology.* Mahwah, NJ: Erlbaum.

Lee, K. M. (2004). Presence, explicated. *Communication Theory, 14,* 27–50.

Lieberman, D. A. (1997). Interactive video games for health promotion: Effects on knowledge, self-efficacy, social support, and health. In R. L. Street, W. R. Gold, & T. Manning (Eds.), *Health promotion and interactive technology: Theoretical applications and future directions* (pp. 103–120). Mahwah, NJ: Erlbaum.

Lieberman, D. A. (2001). Management of chronic pediatric diseases with interactive health games: Theory and research findings. *Journal of Ambulatory Care Management, 24*(1), 26–38.

Lieberman, D. A. (2006a). Dance games and other exergames: What the research says. Unpublished report, University of California, Santa Barbara. Retrieved June 21, 2008, from http://www.comm.ucsb.edu/faculty/lieberman/exergames.htm

Lieberman, D. A. (2006b). What can we learn from playing interactive games? In P. Vorderer & J. Bryant (Eds.), *Playing video games: Motives, responses, and consequences* (pp. 379–397). Mahwah, NJ: Erlbaum.

Lieberman, D. A. (2007). What is a "game?" Retrieved June 21, 2008, from http://www.changemakers.net/en-us/node/1308

Lieberman, D. A. (2008). *Health games that work: Examples of well designed health games and related research findings.* Presentation to the CDC's National Conference on Health Communication, Media and Marketing, Atlanta, GA.

Lieberman, D. A., & Linn, M. C. (1991). Learning to learn revisited: Computers and the development of self-directed learning skills. *Journal of Research on Computing in Education, 23*(3), 373–395.

Locke, E., & Latham, G. (1990). *A theory of goal setting and task performance.* Englewood Cliffs, NJ: Prentice-Hall.

Lombard, M., & Ditton, T. (1997). At the heart of it all: The concept of presence. *Journal of Computer-Mediated Communication, 3*(2).

Malone, T. W., & Lepper, M. R. (1987). Making learning fun: A taxonomy of intrinsic motivations for learning. In R. E. Snow & M. J. Farr (Eds.), *Aptitude, learning and instruction: Vol. 3. Cognitive and affective process analysis* (pp. 223–253). Hillsdale, NJ: Erlbaum.

Mann, T., Sherman, D., & Updegraff, J. (2004). Dispositional motivations and message framing: A test of the congruency hypothesis in college students. *Health Psychology, 23*(3), 330–334.

Mayer, R. E., & Moreno, R. (2002). Aids to computer-based multimedia learning. *Learning and Instruction, 12*(1), 107–119.

Mayer, R. E., Schustack, M. W., & Blanton, W. E. (1999). What do children learn from using computers in an informal, collaborative setting? *Educational Technology, 39,* 27–31.

Millians, D. (1999). Simulations and young people: Developmental issues and game development. *Simulation & Gaming, 30*(2), 199–226.

Moreno, R., & Mayer, R. E. (2002). Learning science in virtual reality multimedia environments: Role of methods and media. *Journal of Educational Psychology, 94,* 598–610.

Murphy, E. C., Donley, D., Carson, L., Ullrich, I., Vosolo, J., Mueller, C., Richison, K., & Yeater, R. (2006). An innovative home-based aerobic exercise intervention improves endothelial function in overweight West Virginia children. *Medicine & Science in Sports & Exercise, 38*(5), S571.

Parker, L. E., & Lepper, M. R. (1992). Effects of fantasy contexts on children's learning and motivation: Making learning more fun. *Journal of Personality and Social Psychology, 62,* 625–633.

Petty, R., & Cacioppo, J. (1986). *Communication and persuasion: Central and peripheral routes to attitude change.* New York: Springer Verlag.

Picard, R. W. (1997). *Affective computing.* Cambridge, MA: MIT Press.

Prawat, R. S., & Flowden, R. E. (1994). Philosophical perspectives on constructivist views of learning. *Educational Psychologist, 29*(1), 37–48.

Prensky, M. (2006). *Don't bother me Mom—I'm learning!* New York: Paragon House.

Raessen J., & Goldstein, J. (2005). *Handbook of computer game studies.* Cambridge, MA: MIT Press.

Reeves, B., & Nass, C. (1996). *The media equation: How people treat computers, television, and new media like real people and places.* New York: Cambridge University Press.

Reigeluth, C. M., & Squire, K. D. (1998). Emerging work on the new paradigm of instructional theories. *Educational Technology, 38*(4), 41–47.

Re-Mission [Digital game]. (2006). Redwood, CA: HopeLab.

Rieber, L. P. (1996). Seriously considering play: Designing interactive learning environments based on the blending of microworlds, simulations, and games. *Educational Technology Research & Development, 44*(2), 43–58.

Rieber, L. P., Smith, L., & Noah, D. (1998). The value of serious play. *Educational Technology, 38*(6), 29–37.

Riverdeep Interactive Learning. (2007). The Oregon Trail, enhanced educator version, 5th ed. Retrieved December 14, 2008, from http://web.riverdeep.net

Schwartz, D. L., Lin, X., Brophy, S., & Bransford, J. D. (1999). Towards the development of flexibly adaptive instructional design. In C. Reigeluth (Ed.), *Instructional design theories and models: New paradigms of instructional theory* (pp. 183–214). Mahwah, NJ: Erlbaum.

SimCity [Digital game]. Emeryville, CA: Maxis Software.

Squire, K., & Jenkins, H. (2003). Harnessing the power of games in education. *Insight, 3,* 7–31.

Suppes, P. (1967). On using computers to individualize instruction. In D. D. Bushnell & D. W. Allen (Eds.), *The computer in American education* (pp. 11–24). New York: Wiley.

Suppes, P., Jerman, M., & Groen, G. (1966). Arithmetic drills and review on a computer-based teletype. *The Arithmetic Teacher, 13,* 303–309.

Unnithan, V. B., Houser, W., & Fernhall, B. (2005). Evaluation of the energy cost of playing a dance simulation video game in overweight and non-overweight children and adolescents. *International Journal of Sports Medicine, 26,* 1–11.

Vorderer, P., & Bryant, J. (Eds.). (2006). *Playing video games: Motives, responses, and consequences.* Mahwah, NJ: Erlbaum.

Vye, N. J., Schwartz, D. L., Bransford, J. D., Barron, B. J., Zech, L., & Cognition and Technology Group at Vanderbilt. (1998). SMART environments that support monitoring, reflection, and revision. In D. Hacker, J. Dunlosky, & A. Graesser (Eds.), *Metacognition in educational theory and practice* (pp. 305–346). Hillsdale, NJ: Erlbaum.

Wii Fit (n.d.). Retrieved March 23, 2009, from http://www.nintendo.com/wiifi

Witte, K., Meyer, G., & Martell, D. (2001). *Effective health risk messages.* Thousand Oaks, CA: Sage.

Yeomans, J. (2008). Dynamic assessment practice: Some suggestions for ensuring follow up. *Educational Psychology in Practice, 24*(2), 105–114.

Chapter 9

What Do Children Learn from Playing Digital Games?

Fran C. Blumberg and Sabrina S. Ismailer

According to the Nielsen Media Research State of the Console report (2007), 33% of individuals aged 2 and older had used an in-home digital game console in the United States in the last 4 months of 2006. One crucial aspect of this appeal, particularly among child and preadolescent players, is the developmental appropriateness of the games they play independent of the required ratings that may be ascribed to them, for example, by the Entertainment Software Rating Board.

As in the watching of educational and leisure-based television programming, the developmental level of a digital game may very well have ramifications for what players will glean from the game experience (Valkenburg & Cantor, 2000). For example, preschool-age television viewers are more likely than elementary school-age viewers to learn educational content associated with perceptually attractive qualities such as fast pacing and animation (Calvert, 1999; Calvert, Huston, Watkins, & Wright, 1982). Unlike the watching of television, however, the playing of digital games is interactive and offers an opportunity to master the intricacies of a complex, multicued, rule-governed environment that players of all ages presumably find intrinsically motivating. According to seminal research by Malone (1981), contributors to children's willingness to continue playing despite frequent opportunities for failure and impasse reflects the level of challenge, fantasy, and curiosity inherent in a given game. Presumably, the games that are played most frequently are those presenting child and adolescent players with optimal levels of one or more of these variables, as exemplified in adventure games. In fact, industry data about top-selling games in the United States indicates that adventure games have the broadest appeal among child and adult players (see Entertainment Software Association, 2007).

The attractiveness of digital games also may be based on the level of developmental tasks presented to the children who play them (von Salisch, Oppl, & Kristen, 2006). Developmental tasks, as defined by Havighurst (1953), are age-graded milestones such as learning to read during the late preschool or elementary school years or mastering a bicycle without training wheels during middle childhood. Thus, children's attraction to a specific game may be motivated by the cognitive or physical skills promoted through the playing of that game. These competencies have been cited as the refinement of spatial skills (De Lisi & Wolford, 2002; Greenfield, Brannon, & Lohr, 1994; Subrahmanyam & Greenfield, 1996), problem solving and inductive reasoning (Greenfield, 1984; Greenfield, Camaioni, & Ercolani, 1994; Rosas et al., 2003), and visual attention (Castel, Pratt, & Drummond, 2005; Green & Bevalier, 2003, 2006a, 2006b). Recent evidence also shows that the playing of action digital games may reduce gender differences in mental rotation and spatial attention (Feng, Spence, & Pratt, 2007).

Similarly, different game genres have been linked to the enhancement of specific skills such as those cited above and acquisition of content knowledge. The latter may be promoted through the playing of serious games to facilitate children's understanding of chronic diseases such as cancer (see *Ben's Game* at http://www.makewish.org) or asthma (Lieberman, 2001). Simulations such as *SimCity* may be used to advance knowledge about civics, puzzle games such as *Tetris* (1985) may promote spatial cognition, and adventure games such as *Sonic the Hedgehog* may facilitate problem solving ability (Blumberg, Rosenthal, & Randall, 2008; Rosas et al., 2003).

As clearly demonstrated in the chapters throughout this text, the rapidly growing body of research that demonstrates the linkage between the playing of digital games and the enhancement of cognitive and perceptual skills has contributed to researchers' and educators' keen interest in the educational value and ramifications of digital game play for academic activities (Gee, 2003; Squire, 2006). Notably, the incorporation of digital games specifically designed for use in classroom settings remains an arduous and contrived effort that is not necessarily appreciated by the intended learners (Tüzün, 2007; Van Eck, 2006).

One question that we have examined in our research is what it is that players do learn while playing digital games as influenced by their game experience and more importantly, their developmental level. We explore this question below by examining differential learning and motivation to play in the context of more formal academic and informal leisure-based games, and how these factors contribute to effective game design. Our research has focused on what children learn while playing informal digital games and the extent to which the goals and strategies they enact in the leisure setting may be used when they learn in school.

We initiate our discussion by considering game design elements that contribute to the developmental appropriateness of the digital games. We then turn to an examination of what it is that players learn from the playing of digital games and the implications of this understanding for educational practice in school settings.

Factors That Contribute to the Developmental Appropriateness of Digital Games

Explication of digital game appeal is evident in research within diverse disciplines such as communications (e.g., Sherry, Lucas, Greenberg, & Lachlan, 2006); education (e.g., Gee, 2003; Squire, 2006); media (e.g., Herz, 1997); and psychology (e.g., Greenfield, 1984; Greenfield & Cocking, 1994). Specification of factors that contribute to a digital game's accessibility and comprehensibility among its child and adolescent players is less apparent, especially in the context of formal digital games. We discuss below variables that we see as influencing preadult players' ability to effectively negotiate and learn from a digital game; namely that of formal features and interactivity.

Formal Features

One factor linked to children's preference and learning from television programming is that of formal features (Bickham, Wright, & Huston, 2001; Calvert, 1999; Calvert et al., 1982; Fisch, 2004; Wright & Huston, 1983). Wright and Huston (1983) and Calvert (1999) have defined formal features as the auditory and visual production and editing techniques used in television, including action and pace, sound effects, narration, pans, and zooms. According to Calvert (1999), formal features draw the child's attention to the information needed to comprehend relevant content and provide the child with a developmentally appropriate mode of representation, either visual or verbal, with which to encode program content.

Formal features are typically used to mark content that is child-relevant and ultimately appealing. These markers include female voices, child dialogue, nonhuman voices, animation, and music (Wright & Huston, 1983). Adult-relevant content (that is presumably incomprehensible for preschool and early elementary school-age children) may be marked by male voices, adult dialogue, and narration (Bickham et al., 2001; Huston & Wright, 1998; Valkenburg & Cantor, 2000). According to Valkenburg and Janssen (1999), children's choice of television programs to watch may reflect the comprehensibility of those programs, which in turn, may be flagged by formal features appropriate to the developmental level of the child. For example, preschool viewers may be more likely than older, elementary school-age viewers to learn content in the context of educational television programs associated with perceptually attractive qualities such as animation and fast-paced action (Calvert, 1999; Calvert et al., 1982). Elementary school viewers, by comparison, may be more likely to learn content associated with features that are less perceptually salient such as character dialogue or narration portrayed without moderate or rapid action (Calvert, 1999). Older children also may appreciate more fast-paced, adventurous programs than younger children who appear to enjoy slow-paced programs that stress repetition of content (Fisch, 2004; Valkenberg & Cantor, 2000).

Viewers of all ages may prefer programs that feature cuts and movements (Schmitt, Anderson, & Collins, 1999).

Formal features, or the "grammar of television content" (Calvert, 1999, p. 455), may have a counterpart in digital games referred to as "language of digital games" (Prensky, 2001, pp. 5–29). This language may be reflected in production techniques or game devices that are used to promote comprehension of the story line. For example, in the popular genre of action digital games, two common devices include back-story and cut scenes (Dickey, 2006). The former is used to set the context of the story which may be included as a short video sequence used to open the game or as a brief synopsis of the game presented on the packaging. Cut scenes are used to advance the story line and comprise brief bits of narrative that are often presented following the player's achievement of the goal needed to reach a new level of game play. This game device may take the form of brief narration by a story protagonist, or a page drawn from that character's diary that presages obstacles that players may confront as they play.

Prensky (2001) characterizes electronic game language as including shared understanding among players that game design elements other than those very small in size should be clicked on and similarly, that characters can be moved if clicked on; repetitions of actions are frequently warranted to attain a goal or circumvent an impasse; codes or "cheats" are typically embedded in the game to expedite game progress, and that the game may contain surprise elements, or "Easter Eggs." This language also may include game design features, as noted by DiPietro, Ferdig, Boyer, and Black (2007), as the availability of feedback and the player's ability to control the game pace (a point that we revisit in our discussion below of interactivity).

Unlike the television literature, little empirical information is available about the linkage between specific features of game design and different-aged players' ability to learn game content. Beyond middle childhood, in fact, age may be incidental to game performance as compared with actual game experience (Rosenthal & Blumberg, 2005). For younger players, however, one might hypothesize that developmentally appropriate games, as in the case of far less interactive venues such as television programs, are those with perceptually attractive graphics, appealing music, cartoonlike characters, and simple rules to follow, given that young players may be most inclined to use trial and error as a strategy for learning a digital game (Blumberg & Sokol, 2004). The first author is reminded of a second-grader's comment when asked what he liked most about digital games. The majority of his second grade peers showed great difficulty providing a cogent response. His point, however, was highly succinct, if grammatically compromised, "Because I like the way it looks like and the songs."

Interactivity

A key contributor to the strong appeal of electronic games stems from their interactivity. The efficacy of this game feature for encouraging, sustaining, and managing game play has been well documented (Vorderer, 2000). Sellers (2006) characterizes interactivity within the context of digital games as that which "presents state information to the user; enables the user to take actions indirectly related to that state; changes state based on the user's action, and displays that new state" (p. 13). According to Lieberman (2006), games that are interactive involve feedback and help messages that become tailored to the individual game player, much the same way that a tutor provides feedback to a tutee.

Clearly, interactivity allows players the flexibility to control and customize the pace, interface, complexity of the game experience, and to receive immediate feedback (DiPietro et al., 2007; Prensky, 2001). This game feature serves to maintain players' attention, which in turn has ramifications for their enjoyment and immersion in the game and their ability to learn from it (Grodal, 2000; Sellers, 2006). Similarly, players can form the schemas needed to master a game in the context of a play experience appropriate for their current cognitive and physical skill level. This form of scaffolding conforms to Vygotsky's contention that learning is maximized when framed within the learner's zone of proximal development (DiPietro et al., 2007).

What Do Players Learn in the Context of Digital Games?

An extensive body of research attests to the efficacy of digital games for promoting child and adolescent players' learning. Within this literature, emphasis is placed on the cognitive and social skills players use to negotiate game challenges and obstacles such as metacognition (VanDeventer & White, 2002), selective attention (Blumberg, 1998), problem solving, and perspective taking (DiPietro et al., 2007; Kafai, 1995). These skills are inferred, as is the case with most social science research, from behaviors demonstrated by participants after playing the game or having performed some act during it. Questions still remain as to what it is that child and adolescents learn as they play digital games and their perceptions and evaluation of that activity. We have assumed this focus in our research among child, adolescent, and adult players representing both frequent and infrequent digital game players.

Learning in the Context of Informal Digital Games

One research tactic we have used to better elucidate players' interpretations of their mental behavior while playing is to have them think aloud. Specifically, players are trained to think aloud while solving a training problem and are then asked to continue to think aloud while playing a novel adventure digital game. This approach has yielded a rich corpus of information about players' attention to game content, and their identification and selection of game strategies and goals in situ.

For example, Blumberg, Rosenthal, and Randall (2008) recently found differential patterns of strategies used to negotiate and anticipate impasses encountered during digital game play among an adult sample of frequent and infrequent digital game players. Players were asked to think aloud while playing *Sonic the Hedgehog 2 for Game Gear* for 20 consecutive minutes. The particular game was selected for its potential novelty among participants, given its initial introduction into the digital game market in the early 1990s and for its use in our prior investigations of digital game play (Blumberg, 1998, 2000). Participants' comments then were categorized into five major categories, as adapted from our prior research and reviewed below.

Cognitive Processes

This category included reference to cognitive processes that occurred during game play. These comments were subcategorized into *impasse recognition*, which includes acknowledgment that further actions are unsuccessful or that progress is halted and *insight*, which reflects the sudden recognition of a new strategy or how to negotiate an impasse. We focused on impasse recognition given that digital games sustain player interest and attention by presenting increasingly challenging problems or obstacles to overcome. We had surmised that an impasse and its resolution would serve as a catalyst for the acquisition of new knowledge and problem-solving strategies, which would be reflected in comments suggestive of new insights.

Goal Oriented

This category included references to specific goals for game play. These comments were subcategorized as *process goals*, or goals pertaining to completion of a specific subgoal such as avoiding an obstacle or determining how to use a feature integral to the game console, such as a control button, or *outcome goals*, which included comments pertaining to completing or reaching certain levels of the game. The basis for inclusion of these goals was research within the area of self-regulated learning, which concerns the processes learners use to negotiate their cognitive abilities, motivation, and performance while striving toward task mastery (Schunk, 2005). As part of self-regulated learning, students may use either process or outcome goals (Schunk & Zimmerman, 2007) and may use them in a developmental fashion, such that process goals are used during the initial phases of task mastery, after which, outcomes goals are used to maximize the task performance (Zimmerman & Kitsantas, 1997).

Game Oriented

This category included comments that referenced specific game aspects, techniques, and prior experience with digital games. These comments were further classified as *game strategies*, that pertained to specific moves utilized within game play with reference to the consequences of an action or inaction; *game mechanics*, that pertained to using game functions integral to the game console to enact a move, change parameters of the game presented, or to pause or turn the game console on and off; *game cues*, that referenced specific game features, such as the landscape, or game characters; *game rules*, that pertained to how specific icons could be used or how many lives one had; and *background knowledge*, that reflected prior experience with comparables games played in the past.

Affective

This category included comments referencing *game evaluations* that referred to how much the player enjoyed the game and *performance evaluations*, which were personal appraisals of game performance.

Context Oriented

This category included comments that referenced the experimental context, which were further delineated into *experimental context*, or comments that concerned participation in the study and had limited to no relationship to actual game play, and *off task* comments.

We found that frequent players made significantly greater reference to insight and game strategies than infrequent players. No significant differences in reference to impasse were found, counter to our expectations that frequent players would be keenly aware of impediments to their game progress given their presumably more enriched game schemas. In fact, frequent and infrequent players were less inclined to make references to impasses than other types of comments reflective of general problem-solving.

To examine changes in participants' problem-solving approach over the course of game play and to control for the number of games that participants initiated over the course of the 20 minutes, we examined the proportion of participants' comments across 10 blocks of codeable comments, roughly equivalent in size. Thus, for a participant with 400 total comments, 10 blocks of 40 comments were created. Across all participants, the proportion of impasse, insight, and game strategy comments significantly increased over time. In contrast, the proportion of game mechanics, background knowledge, and experimental context comments decreased over time. Frequent players, in particular, made significantly fewer game rules and experimental context comments than frequent players, potentially attesting to their greater engagement in the game. Better game performance was associated with greater reference to insight about how to negotiate game play.

We viewed our findings as demonstrating players' greater emphasis on problem solving (as reflected by their increased mention of impasse, insight, and game strategy comments) and engagement (as reflected by their decreased consideration of background knowledge and game context) as they played the game. Notably, the players' evaluation of the game was fairly low. We hypothesized that the subjective appeal of the game was secondary to mastering it, as evidenced by the patterns of comments over time.

Digital Game Play and Classroom Learning

We are now in the midst of replicating this study among a preadolescent and adolescent population in the New York City area. This investigation is designed to directly address the issue of what problem-solving behaviors preadolescents and early adolescents use while playing digital games (via think alouds) and their beliefs about the transferability of these behaviors from leisure to academic activities (via focus groups). Our target group includes frequent and infrequent fifth through seventh grade digital game players.

These students, as the adult participants, are instructed to play a digital game for 20 consecutive minutes and to think aloud while playing *Sonic the Hedgehog 2 for Game Gear*, as in prior studies (Blumberg, 1998, 2000). The archaic nature of the game has not been necessarily salient for our middle childhood and adolescent participants who have been more inclined to evaluate the game positively than the adults.

We also are conducting focus groups organized by age group and frequency of digital game play to further clarify the strategies and approaches used by children for problem solving in digital games and academic tasks encountered in school. Our goal here is to better understand why differential approaches may be used in the presumably high risk academic contexts and low risk digital game contexts, and how these approaches may differ developmentally.

Concluding Comments

Evidence attesting to the positive ramifications of digital games for the skills they can foster and content knowledge they can impart continues to accrue. The design of developmentally appropriate informal, or what Van Eck (2006) refers to as "commercial off-the-shelf" games, that promote learning seems a nonissue. Informal games already have an eager consumer market and a low stakes agenda to entertain or serve as a diversion for their players (see research by Sherry et al., 2006 for greater consideration of how players needs are served through the playing of digital games). Players can revisit their "failures" with little consequence and limited stipulations on the steepness of their learning curve. However, challenges do loom large for the effective incorporation of serious or formal learning games that are often linked to specific, high stakes curricula-based objectives in the lives of the students they are designed to teach. These stakes alone may hinder the efficacy of formal games to instruct, particularly if the stakes are developmentally or culturally inappropriate. This issue certainly warrants greater investigation.

Clearly, not all informal games are exciting any more than not all formal or serious games are tedious. However, as noted throughout this volume, the goals for learning in the context of each of the two games differ markedly. A related question, that we are currently addressing, is the relationship between learning in the context of informal leisure-based digital games and learning in the context of more formal academic-based tasks.

References

Ben's Game. [Digital game]. Make a Wish Foundation. Retrieved from http://www.makewish.org

Bickham, D. S., Wright, J. C., & Huston, A. C. (2001). Attention, comprehension, and the educational influences of television. In D. G. Singer & J. L. Singer (Eds.), *Handbook of children and the media* (pp. 101–119). Thousand Oaks, CA: Sage.

Blumberg, F. C. (1998). Developmental differences at play: Children's selective attention and performance in video games. *Journal of Applied Developmental Psychology, 19*, 615–624.

Blumberg, F. C. (2000). The effects of children's goals for learning on video game performance. *Journal of Applied Developmental Psychology, 21*, 641–653.

Blumberg, F. C. (2002). The effects of children's goals for learning on video game performance. *Journal of Applied Developmental Psychology, 21*, 641–653.

Blumberg, F. C., Rosenthal, S. F., & Randall, J. D. (2008). Impasse-driven learning in the context of video games. *Computers in Human Behavior, 24*, 1530–1541.

Blumberg, F. C., & Sokol, L. M. (2004). Boys' and girls' cognitive strategy use when learning to play video games. *Journal of General Psychology, 131*, 151–158.

Calvert, S. L. (1999). The form of thought. In I. E. Sigel (Ed.), *Development of mental representation* (pp. 453–470). Mahwah, NJ: Erlbaum.

Calvert, S. L., Huston, A. C., Watkins, B. A., & Wright, J. C. (1982). The relation between selective attention to television forms and children's comprehension of content. *Child Development, 53*, 601–610.

Castel, A. D., Pratt, J., & Drummond, E. (2005). The effects of action video game experience on the time course of inhibition of return and the efficiency of visual search. *Acta Psychologia, 119*, 217–230.

De Lisi, R., & Wolford, J. L. (2002). Improving children's mental rotation accuracy with computer game playing. *Journal of Genetic Psychology, 163*, 272–282.

Dickey, M. D. (2006). Game design narrative for learning: Appropriate adventure game design narrative devices and techniques for the design of interactive learning environments. *ETR&D, 54*, 245–263.

DiPietro, M., Ferdig, R. E., Boyer, J., & Black, E. W. (2007). Towards a framework for understanding educational gaming. *Journal of Educational Multimedia and Hypermedia, 16*, 225–248.

Entertainment Software Association. (2007). Game player data. Retrieved September 19, 2007, from http://www.theesa.com/facts/gamer_data.php

Feng, J., Spence, I., & Pratt, J. (2007). Playing an action video game reduces gender differences in spatial cognition. *Psychological Science, 18*, 850–855.

Fisch, S. M. (2004). Characteristics of effective materials for informal education: A cross-media comparison of television, magazines, and interactive media. In M. Rabinowitz, F. C. Blumberg, & H. T. Everson (Eds.), *The design of instruction and evaluation: Affordances of using media and technology* (pp. 3–18). Mahwah, NJ: Erlbaum.

Gee, J. P. (2003). *What video games have to teach us about learning and literacy*. New York: Palgrave Macmillan.

Green, C. S., & Bevalier, D. (2003). Action video game modifies visual selective attention. *Nature, 423*(6939), 534–538.

Green, C. S. & Bevalier, D. (2006a). Enumeration versus multiple object tracking: the case of action video game players. *Cognition, 101,* 217–245.

Green, C. S., & Bevalier, D. (2006b). Effect of action video games on the spatial distribution of visuospatial attention. *Journal of Experimental Psychology: Human Perception and Performance, 32,* 1465–1478.

Greenfield, P. M. (1984). *Mind and media: The effects of television, video games, and computers.* Cambridge, MA: Harvard University Press.

Greenfield, P. M., Brannon, G., & Lohr, D. (1994). Two-dimensional representation of movement through three-dimensional space: The role of video game expertise. *Journal of Applied Developmental Psychology, 15,* 87–103.

Greenfield, P. M., Camaioni, L., & Ercolani, P. (1994). Cognitive socialization by computer games in two culture: Inductive discovery or mastery of an iconic code? *Journal of Applied Developmental Psychology, 15,* 59–85.

Greenfield, P. M., & Cocking, R. R. (1994). Effects of interactive entertainment technologies on development. *Journal of Applied Developmental Psychology, 15,* 1–2.

Grodal, T. (2000). Video games and the pleasure of control. In D. Zillman & P. Vorderer (Eds.), *Media entertainment: The psychology of its appeal* (pp. 197–213). Mahwah, NJ: Erlbaum.

Havighurst, R. J. (1953). *Developmental tasks and education*. New York: Longman.

Herz, J. C. (1997). *Joystick nation: How videogames ate our quarters, won our hearts, and rewired our minds.* New York: Little, Brown.

Huston, A. C., & Wright, J. C. (1998). Mass media and children's development. In W. Damon (Ed.-in-Chief), I. E. Sigel, & K. A. Renninger (Vol. Eds.), *Handbook of child psychology: Vol. 4. Child psychology in practice* (5th ed., pp. 99–1058). New York: Wiley.

Kafai, Y. (1995). *Minds in play: Computer game design as a context for children's learning.* Mahwah, NJ: Erlbaum.

Lieberman, D. (2001). Management of chronic pediatric diseases with interactive health games. *Journal of Ambulatory Care Management, 24,* 26–38.

Lieberman, D., (2006). What can we learn from playing interactive games? In P. Vorderer & J. Bryant (Eds.), *Playing video games. Motives, responses, and consequences* (pp. 379–397). Mahwah, NJ: Erlbaum.

Malone, T. W. (1981). Toward a theory of intrinsically motivating instruction. *Cognitive Science, 4,* 333–369.

Nielsen Media Research. (2007). *The state of the console.* Retrieved September 16, 2007, from http://www.nielsenmedia.com/nc/nmr_static/docs/Nielsen_Report_State_Console_03507.pdf.

Prensky, M. (2001). *Digital game-based learning.* New York: McGraw-Hill.

Rosas, R., Nussbaum, M., Cumsille, P., Marianov, V., Correa, M., Flores, P., et al. (2003).

Beyond Nintendo: Design and assessment of educational games for first and second grade students. *Computers & Education, 40,* 71–94.

Rosenthal, S. F., & Blumberg, F. C. (2005, August). *Developmental differences in goals for video game play.* Poster presented at the annual meeting of the American Psychological Association, Washington, DC.

Schmitt, K. L., Anderson, D. R., & Collins, P. A. (1999). Form and content: Looking at visual features of television. *Developmental Psychology, 35,* 1156–1167.

Schunk, D. H. (2005). Self-regulated learning: The educational legacy of Paul R. Pintrich. *Educational Psychology, 40,* 85–94.

Schunk, D. H., & Zimmerman, B. J. (2007). Influencing children's self-efficacy and self-regulation of reading and writing through modeling. *Reading & Writing Quarterly, 23,* 7–25.

Sellers, M. (2006). Designing the experience of interactive play. In P. Vorderer & J. Bryant (Eds.), *Playing computer games: Motives, responses, and consequences* (pp. 9–22). Mahwah, NJ: Erlbaum.

Sherry, J. L., Lucas, K., Greenberg, B. S., & Lachlan, K. (2006). Video game uses and gratifications as predictors of use and game preference. In P. Vorderer & J. Bryant (Eds.), *Playing computer games: Motives, responses, and consequences* (pp. 213–224). Mahwah, NJ: Erlbaum.

SimCity [Digital game]. Emeryville, CA: Maxis Software.

Sonic the Hedgehog [Digital game]. Ota, Tokyo, Japan: Sega.

Squire, K. (2006). From content to context: Videogames as designed experience. *Educational Researcher, 35,* 19–29.

Subrahmanyam, K., & Greenfield, P. M. (1996). Effect of video game practice on spatial skills in girls and boys. In P. M. Greenfield & R. R. Cocking (Eds.), *Interacting with video* (pp. 95–114). Norwood, NJ: Ablex.

Tetris [Digital game]. (1985). Pajitnov, A., & Gerasimov, V. Moscow: Academy of Science of the USSR.

Tüzün, H. (2007). Blending video games with learning: Issues and challenges with classroom implementations in the Turkish context. *British Journal of Educational Technology, 38,* 465–477.

Valkenburg, P. M., & Cantor, J. (2000). Children's likes and dislikes in entertainment programs. In D. Zillman & P. Vorderer (Eds.), *Media entertainment: The psychology of its appeal* (pp. 135–152). Mahwah, NJ: Erlbaum.

Valkenburg, P. M., & Janssen, S. (1999). What do children value in entertainment programs? A cross-cultural investigation. *Journal of Communication, 49,* 3–21.

VanDeventer, S. S., & White, J. A. (2002). Expert behavior in children's video game play. *Simulation and Gaming, 33*(1), 28–48.

Van Eck, R. V. (2006 March/April). Digital game-based learning. *Educause Review, 41*(2), 17–30.

von Salisch, M., Oppl, C., & Kristen, A. (2006). What attracts children? In P. Vorderer & J. Bryant (Eds.), *Playing video games. Motives, responses, and consequences* (pp. 147–179). Mahwah, NJ: Erlbaum.

Vorderer, P. (2000). Interactive entertainment and beyond. In D. Zillman & P. Vorderer (Eds.), *Media entertainment: The psychology of its appeal* (pp. 21–34). Mahwah, NJ: Erlbaum.

Wright, J. C., & Huston, A. C. (1983). A matter of form: Potential of television for young viewers. *American Psychologist, 38*, 835–843.

Zimmerman, B. J., & Kitsantas, A. (1997). Developmental phases in self-regulation: Shifting from process goals to outcome goals. *Journal of Educational Psychology, 89*, 29–36.

Section II

Serious Games for Development

Chapter 10

The Impact of Serious Games on Childhood Development

John L. Sherry and Jayson L. Dibble

In March of 2007 the U.S. Department of Education (DOE) announced the results of a yearlong natural experiment: educational software does not work (Paley, 2007). The study had been commissioned by the DOE as required by the No Child Left Behind Act to determine the effectiveness of computer software in the classroom context. A group of researchers from Mathematics Policy Research, Inc. and SRI International tested 16 educational software products designed to enhance reading and mathematics in first (7 years old), fourth (10 years old), and sixth (12 years old) grade students. The researchers randomly assigned 132 schools from 33 districts to treatment (software use) or control (no software use) conditions. The experiment took place over the course of an entire school year. The results showed no significant difference in learning between software and nonsoftware students.

The news came at a time when the serious game movement was riding a tide of positive publicity with the Federation of American Scientists calling for federal support, the MacArthur Foundation pledging $50 million to support serious games work, and chief strategist Ichiro Otobe of Square Enix announcing the software giant's entry into the educational software market at the 2007 Game Developers Conference. Further, games remain very popular among school age children. According to a 1999 Kaiser Family Foundation study, nearly 70% of 2- to 18-year-olds have a digital game console or computer at home, and even more have access to computers through school. The same study found that children aged 1 to 13 years played an average of 32 minutes of digital games per day with some playing much more. Even toddlers are getting into playing; Rideout, Vandewater, and Wartella (2003) found that 9% of children from birth to 6 years old play digital games daily.

Given the strong interest in digital games and serious games, one would think that there is ample empirical evidence to contradict the DOE study. However, this is not the case. A search of the term *serious games* in electronic databases including PsychINFO, PsychARTICLES, Comm Abstracts, Sage Journals On-line, and Education Abstracts results in very few empirical articles and a large number of theory/speculation articles on serious games (other search terms don't improve the results much). When empirical results are provided, they are often so idiosyncratic to a particular game that they cannot be generalized beyond that game.

A Brief Description of Serious Games

Whereas there is little generalizable empirical research on serious games, there appears to be no shortage of articles offering definitions of serious games.

What is a Serious Game?

Here are some examples of comments on serious games:

> The Serious Games Initiative is focused on uses for games in exploring management and leadership challenges facing the public sector. (*Serious Games Initiative*, n.d.)

> Serious games (SGs) or persuasive games are computer and video games used as persuasion technology or educational technology. They can be similar to educational games, but are often intended for an audience outside of primary or secondary education. Serious games can be of any genre and many of them can be considered a kind of edutainment. (*Wikipedia*, n.d. http://en.wikipedia.org/wiki/Serious_game)

> Serious Games are games with a purpose beyond entertainment, including but not limited to games for learning, games for health, and games for policy and social change. (Michigan State University, MSU Serious Games MA Program, n.d.)

> Serious games usually have a message promoting education, science, health care or even the military. They're meant to educate people by simulating real-world events and are often created with the best of intentions. (Terdiman, 2006)

These definitions illustrate important characteristics of serious games. First, all the definitions emphasize that serious games are designed with a purpose beyond entertainment, often for prosocial change. Next, there is a broad array of goals for serious games. Game purposes may emphasize education, social change, or training. Finally, there is an understanding that the fun of games must be leveraged to achieve the goals of the game, even though entertainment is not the purpose of the game.

Potential Advantages of Serious Games

Most articles and books on serious games extol their potential for affecting positive change or for education (e.g., Gee, 2003; Lieberman, 2006; Ritterfeld

& Weber, 2006; Sherry & Pacheco, 2006). There are several reasons to believe this. In addition to commanding tremendous amounts of player attention and time, games can be tailored to individual ability levels, can facilitate individual learning through repetition or discovery, and can simulate just about any phenomenon that the designer might want players to understand. In fact, digital games can be used to do many things that are not otherwise possible (e.g., simulate a billion years of geophysical development). The game playing experience consists of strong engagement in a set of complex cognitive puzzles. In uses and gratifications studies, the most popular reason for playing games among players of elementary school age through young adults is the challenge of beating the game and advancing to the next level (Sherry, Lucas, Greenberg, & Lachlan, 2006). In order to conquer each level, the player must learn the basic rules of the game universe and apply those rules to puzzles presented. As such, games provide an opportunity for inductive and deductive reasoning in real time. A well designed game engages players in a flow experience by gradually increasing cognitive challenges as the skill level of the player increases (Sherry, 2004). The flow state offers an intrinsic intellectual reward, referred to by flow theorist Mahayi Czikszentmahayi (1988) as an autotelic experience. Players are engaged in a mental task for hours—probing options, learning rules, and making sense of the underlying logic of the environment. Due to the dynamics of flow that emerge in a well designed game, the experience tends to hold the attention of the player for as long as it takes to master the material (Sherry, 2004). The game is a great example of the process of equifinality because there is typically one answer, but an almost limitless number of ways of getting that answer. As such, digital games can be tailored to a wide variety of designer purposes, player backgrounds, and learning styles.

Finally, like cartoons and books, games are not limited by what is plausible in the real world. Games can simulate any existing world, worlds that do not exist, or worlds that are unperceivable to the naked eye. *The Fantastic Voyage* (Asimov, 1966) through the body is not only possible, but the interactive nature of the medium allows the player to navigate, investigate, and make sense of the diegesis of the body in a variety of ways. Complex dynamic phenomena that are difficult to explain in the linear confines of lecture or printed word come alive as the player explores the game world. Students can encounter worlds through both time and space that they normally would not be able to interactively access.

Empirical Results

Literature Search

A broad search was undertaken using communication, education, and psychology databases to locate empirical articles on serious games. The search terms used included *serious games,* "*video game, computer game, game,* and *learn, game,* and *education*, and various combinations of these search terms. The results of the search can be classified into four groups: empirical articles on general game effects (nonviolence related); theory articles on games and learning; tests of specific software products; and nondigital games for learning. Because there is very little empirical literature on serious games, only the first category, empirical articles on general game effects, was used in this chapter. Theory articles will be covered in a separate chapter, tests of specific software offer no insight into generalizable principles of games and learning, and there are currently no empirical data showing that success of nondigital based games will transfer to serious game applications.

The search resulted in 121 research reports on a wide variety of topics. Among those articles, the most popular categories included: physiological reactance studies (*n* = 20), learning processes (*n* = 15), attentional processes (*n* = 12), gender differences in game choice and effects (*n* = 9), and game usage patterns (*n* = 7). There were a wide variety of other research topics including addiction, social facilitation, overall game performance, motivations for game play, neurophysiology, games and physical activity, and several others. The majority of the studies were done with adult subjects (48%), while the remainder used adolescent (14%) and middle childhood (22%) subjects—the remaining 16% are reviews of literature. This review will focus on the main categories of research that are germane to serious games: usage studies, gender differences, physiological reactance, attentional processes, and learning. The first two sections set the context of game play, the next two are preliminary steps tied to learning outcomes, and the final section examines results indicating actual learning from digital games.

Game Use Across the Lifespan—Empirical Results

The digital game industry trade group, the Electronic Software Association (n.d.), conducts an annual survey of game use. According to recent surveys, the current average age of digital game players is 33 years old, with children comprising about 31% of the $10 billion per year digital gaming market. In a recent analysis of 90 media use studies since 1949, Marshall, Gorely, and Biddle (2006) estimate that children spend an hour and 20 minutes per day playing digital games.

However, digital game play varies primarily by age and gender. Bickham et al. (2003) examined data across European-American, African-American, and Hispanic-American samples from the Panel Study of Income Dynamics and found that amount of game play was predicted across the three ethnic groups primarily by age and gender. In the most recent study of media use among the very young (ages 0–6), digital game play was the least common activity in children's lives by far (Rideout et al., 2003). Whereas over three quarters of young children play outside (83%), read (79%), or listen to music (79%) on a typical day, only 9% of young children play digital games on a typical day despite three quarters of them having a computer (73%) or around half of them having a game system (49%) in their home. This compares to 73% of very young children who watch television or DVD/videocassettes on a typical day. Further, only 3% of children under the age of 2 years have ever played a digital game. Daily use increases to 16% among children 4 to 6 years of age despite the fact that fully half of children between the ages of 4 to 6 years have experienced playing games. This may suggest the games simply are not holding the attention of very young children or that parents are monitoring access to computers. Further, when the study was conducted in 2003, most parents were not optimistic about the educational effects of digital games, with 40% feeling that gaming will mostly hurt their child's learning and only 22% thinking it will help. It would be interesting to see if these numbers have changed since the recent high profile studies showing that surgeons who play digital games are much better and faster surgeons than their colleagues who don't play (Rosser et al., 2007).

As children get older, their media use increases until it peaks in the preteen years. A November 1999 Kaiser Family Foundation national sample survey (Roberts et al., 1999) of the media use of 2- to 18-year-old children found that although children typically spend 5.5 hours a day using media, only 20 minutes of that time is dedicated to digital game play. Nearly 70% of 2- to 18-year-olds have a digital game console or a computer in their homes, so access is available for most children. Despite having access, children spent little time playing digital games in 1999: children 2 to 4 years played only 4 minutes per day on average, children 5 to 7 years played 13 minutes per day (across the entire sample of 2 to 7 years, digital game play amounts to only 8 minutes per day), children 8 to 13 years played 32 minutes per day, and adolescents 14 to 18 years played 20 minutes per day. These data compare to average television viewing per day of 2 hours and 45 minutes (accounting for 42% of daily media use) and average reading per day of 45 minutes. The minutes/day averages are probably suppressed by nonplayers. Roberts et al. (1999) found that 16% of 2- to 7-year-olds play digital games daily (as defined by having played the day before the survey administration) with an average of 50 minutes a day. This compares to 45% of 8- to 13-year-olds who were daily players (at 1 hour and 9 minutes per day) and 30% of 14- to 18-year-olds who are daily players (at 1 hour and 5 minutes per day). Not all children play, but those who do spend a good amount of time with digital games.

Recent academic studies have also shown that the amount of game play increases with age. For example, one study (Sherry, Lucas, Greenberg, & Lachlan, 2006) found that 5th graders (age 11 years) report playing about 1.81 hours per day, 8th graders (14 years old) report 2.46 hours per day, 11th graders (16 years old) report 1.62 hours per day, and young adults aged 18 to 22 report report playing for 1.73 hours per day. This more recent study shows longer playing time in all age groups, but it is not clear whether the magnitude of the difference is substantial. The Roberts et al. (1999) study questioned parents about child game use while the Sherry et al. (2006) survey reported on child responses. It is common to see sizable media use differences dependent on who fills out the survey, parent or child. Greenberg et al. (2005) showed that accounts of media use also vary according to how usage is measured. They showed that survey estimates of media use were consistently higher than diary estimates, though the two methods are significantly correlated. The important point is that the trend in data is consistent across the two studies.

Whereas patterns of game genre preference primarily differ by sex, game play uses and gratifications vary by developmental stage. Sherry et al. (2006) showed that, although competition and challenge are the highest rated reasons for playing digital games across all age groups and genders, the variance in the amount of time spent playing digital games by older teens (16-year-olds) and young adults (20-year-olds) is explained by social interaction and diversion motivations. Among 14-year-olds, variance in the amount of game play per week is best explained by diversion, challenge, and social interaction, while amount of game play is explained for 10-year-olds by competition, challenge and the fantastical desire to be strong. It appears that games begin as an intellectual challenge and as an expression of fantasy in the younger years, but becomes more of a social event as children progress through adolescence and into young adulthood. In a study of a unique game playing subculture, Wood, Griffiths, Chappell, and Davies (2004) found that realism was considered to be one of the most important factors among online game players. In Wood's study, realism was captured as realistic sound, graphics, and settings.

Gender Differences in Game Choice and Effects

The biggest differences in usage patterns have always been found between boys and girls, with boys averaging an hour and a half more game play per day than girls across all developmental stages in the Sherry et al. (2006) study. Similarly, the Roberts et al. (1999) study found that boys from 8 to 13 years average 47 minutes of game play per day as compared to girls' 16 minutes. The gender difference stays the same among 14 to 18 year olds with boys (34 minutes), playing significantly longer per day than girls (7 minutes). Also dramatic are the clear differences in genre preferences between boys and girls. Across four studies (Lucas & Sherry, 2004; Roberts et al. 1999; Sherry, Lucas, Rechtsteiner, Brooks, & Wilson, 2001; von Salisch, Oppl, & Kristen, 2006), boys prefer action, fighting, shooting, adventure, and sports games, while girls prefer classic platform games, puzzle games, and educational games. Lucas and Sherry (2004) have offered two possible explanations for these patterns. First, the games reflect gender differences in well-established orientations to play. For example, boy games tend to involve direct competition, as in sports and fighting games, while girl games tend toward turn-taking, as found in puzzle games. Second, gender differences in game play may reflect well established patterns of sex differences in cognitive skills needed to play the game. In support of this idea, Sherry, Rosaen, Bowman, and Huh (2006) have shown in a series of experiments that cognitive skill is a more powerful predictor of game play enjoyment and success than sex.

Differences in game performance between males and females have also been observed in other experiments. Brown (1997) found that males outperformed females in the game *Pong* even after controlling for game experience, trait sex role identification, and sports competition anxiety. After finding that differences in cognitive skill predict game ability, both Okagaki and Frensch (1994) and Subrahmanyam and Greenfield (1994) found that game practice does not close the gap in cognitive skill. Instead, Okagaki and Frensch found that practicing a digital game improved the cognitive ability of young adult males, but not young adult females, effectively widening the gap. However, Subrahmanyam and Greenfield found that both boys and girls (M = 11 years) improved significantly on spatial ability, maintaining the gender gap. This suggests an interaction of learning and age such that younger females may be more open to learning spatial skills at a younger age than they are at an older age. Gender differences are observed and internalized by children aged 10 and 11, as shown in a study by Funk and Buchman (1996). According to their survey, children endorsed statements containing game gender stereotypes and showed clarity on which types of games are "boy games" or "girl games."

Physiological Effects of Digital Game Play

Measures of physiological responses to various social psychological phenomena are becoming more frequent among social scientific researchers. This may be due in part to certain advantages gained over traditional social scientific methods. To illustrate, cortisol is a hormone commonly secreted in the adrenal cortex in response to a stressful encounter, and an individual's cortisol level can be determined through the analysis of easy to obtain saliva samples. Moreover, it is difficult to imagine a respondent consciously and actively manipulating his or her cortisol level in response to a stressful encounter. For stress researchers, examining cortisol levels might lend an advantage when typical self-report questionnaire designs are not optimal (e.g., when the accuracy of reports or the avoidance of social desirable reports are in question).

Physiological indicators are of particular value to researchers who are interested in exploring links between their phenomena of interest and health or behavioral outcomes. This is often the case with those who study the effects of digital game playing, where physiological measures are frequently taken as indicators of arousal. This section offers a cursory summary of what is currently known about how digital games impact individuals on a physiological level. The section is organized according to the more common physiological measures being employed, and special attention is given to human developmental differences where data exist. Two caveats preface the discussion that follows. First, readers will note the glaring dearth of research that looks at physiological effects of digital games on younger children. This is unfortunate, and one hopes that at some point this knowledge gap might begin to be filled. Like much social scientific research, the studies reviewed here rely overwhelmingly on undergraduate samples. Nonetheless, those studies dealing with younger populations that could be located are reported.

The second caveat is that these studies depart from typical game research in an important way: the primary goal is to note physiological responses to phenomena other than qualities associated with the digital games. In these studies the games are commonly used to induce some psychological variable (e.g., stress) or to serve as a task for all participants to complete when other variables have been induced (e.g., self-efficacy). In other words, the game is treated as one of the conditions to which the study's participants are exposed. Very few of the studies that involved a digital game did so with the purpose of determining the ways digital games themselves impact participants' psychophysiology. Thus, it is often difficult to determine the extent of the physiological impact of digital games. In this section, studies of both types are reviewed for whatever rudimentary evidence can be gleaned from them.

Cardiovascular Measures: Heart Rate

Indicators of cardiovascular activity appear to be the most common physiological measures taken in response to digital game playing. The most common and easiest to obtain is heart rate. The youngest samples for which heart rate was measured as a response to digital game playing were 9-year-olds. Denot-Ledunois, Vardon, Perruchet, and Gallego (1998) measured several physiological variables in 10 young people (M = 9.2 years). They reported no change in heart rate as participants played a digital game that became progressively more difficult. In contrast, Musante and Raunikar (1994) had 341 children aged 9 to 14 play a challenging digital game as one of three separate stress inductions (the others being postural change and forehead cold), and noted that heart rates increased an average of 9.3 beats per minute from resting baseline. Another study (Murphy, Alpert, Walker, & Willey, 1991) used a digital game as a constant stimulus to induce cardiovascular reactivity in 477 3rd graders (9-year-olds) with the specific goal of tracking racial differences. Heart rate was measured before and during the playing of the digital game, and this procedure was repeated for all participants one year later. Murphy et al. observed that Black participants demonstrated greater heart rate reactivity than did White participants. With regard to adolescents, Murphy, Alpert, and Walker (1994) conducted a study (N = 451, 14-year-olds) to test whether order effects would obtain when resting heart rate measures were taken either before or well after the playing of a digital game. Although it was not the primary finding sought by their study, they did observe an increase in heart rate while the adolescent was playing the game compared to his or her resting measure.

Studies featuring adult participants are much more common. However, most of these use the digital game as an induction of some stressor (e.g., Anguiano-Serrano & Reynoso, 2000), or as the vehicle for accomplishing some sort of task. When digital games are used as stress-inducers, the primary goal is to research the effects of some other moderating variable (e.g., gender: Lawler, Wilcox, & Anderson, 1995; female hormone levels: Sita & Miller, 1996; self-efficacy: Gerin, Litt, Deich, & Pickering, 1996; social support: Gerin, Milner, Chawla, & Pickering, 1995; and Type A behavior: Sveback, Knardahl, Nordby, & Aakvaag, 1992), and any increases in heart rate were compared between experimental groups. Overall, these studies indicate that heart rates increased during or immediately following the playing of the digital game.

Wolfson and Case (2000) conducted a study that examined the effects of background color (red or blue) and sound level (loud or quiet) of a digital game on heart rate. Participants who saw a blue screen had heart rates that gradually increased over the course of their playing. Red screen participants had heart rates that peaked midway through playing and decreased back toward baseline as play continued. The authors concluded only that arousal was implicated in this effect.

Other Cardiovascular Measures

A few other measures of cardiovascular activity have been employed. Examples include blood pressure (BP) and total peripheral resistance (TPR), which assesses blood flow. A number of the studies mentioned above that assessed heart rate also assessed these other indicators, and the results are generally convergent with the expected indicators of being aroused. Again, however, each of these studies utilized the digital game as a constant stress-inducer, which means little can be said regarding any effects of the games themselves.

A longitudinal study was conducted by Newman, McGarvey, and Steele (1999) in order to assess the relationship between blood pressure reactivity to a digital game and resting blood pressure 3 to 4 years later. Eighty-three Samoan adolescents (aged 11–14 years) played a digital game during which blood pressure reactivity was measured. These same adolescents returned 3 to 4 years later and their resting blood pressure was taken. Digital game play was again a constant, and the authors found that adolescents who showed the most reactivity to the digital game did have higher resting blood pressure levels during follow-up.

Respiratory Measures

Breath duration and breathing rate are relatively easy to measure, and would seem to be the most common respiratory measures employed. With regard to digital games, however, only one study measured respiratory responses specifically. Denot-Ledunois et al. (1998) observed that breath duration increased as children played a game that became progressively more difficult. Denot-Ledunois et al. interpreted their findings to mean that focusing one's attention inhibits breathing.

Hormonal Response Indicators

The body's hormonal response to stressful situations is another domain rich in physiological indicators. Recently, social scientists have concerned themselves with the stress hormone cortisol, which is secreted by the adrenal glands and is detectable in saliva. Denot-Ledunois et al. (1998) took cortisol level measurements in their 9-year-old participants and observed no substantial change as the game became more difficult.

Recall, however, that only 10 participants comprised the sample for Denot-Ledunois et al. (1998), perhaps leaving statistical power in question. In contrast, Hebert, Beland, Dionne-Fournelle, Crete, and Lupien (2005) did note changes in cortisol levels of adult participants ($N = 52$, $M = 24.3$ years), particularly in response to techno music built into the digital game they played. Players in the "music" condition displayed significantly higher salivary cortisol levels than players in the "silence" condition. Hebert et al. concluded that the music featured in digital games is a key predictor of the stress associated with playing digital games. Sveback et al. (1992) utilized a digital game as a constant stressor, but did observe increases in participants' postplay cortisol levels.

Neural Responses and Brain Imaging

Until recently, information having to do with brain activation came from older methods such as electroencephalography (EEG) (e.g., Smith, McEvoy, & Gevins, 1999). The development of noninvasive brain-scanning technology (e.g., functional magnetic resonance imaging [fMRI]) has permitted researchers a peek into the inner-workings of the brain as individuals play digital games. Although access to this technology is limited and generally involves tremendous cooperation and collaboration among several fields, studies are beginning to emerge which reveal interesting insights. However, the insights thus far have come from adult samples. Weber, Ritterfeld, and Mathiak (2006) noted that the virtual violence encountered while playing a violent digital game was enough to suggest that portions of the brain were operating as if the player was in a live-action violent encounter. Izzetoglu, Bunce, Onaral, Pourrazaei, and Chance (2004) manipulated task difficulty and task load in a digital game, and used functional near infrared monitoring to note changes in brain oxygenation. Their results indicated that the rate of change in prefrontal cortical blood oxygenation was significantly sensitive to changes in task load, and that brain oxygenation was positively correlated with eventual performance.

Attentional Processes

Attention has long been positively associated with learning outcomes. In the case of serious games, many theorists believe that attention to and engagement with digital games will lead to positive learning outcomes. In this section, we review the literature on games and attention to determine the efficacy of games for learning. There are three general questions addressed of studies in this area: (1) Do game players have better attention? (2) Do games improve attention? (3) Does attention predict better game performance?

In an early study, Arthur et al. (1995) showed that trait attention ability predicted higher performance both in an initial test and after training. In fact, the advantage of subjects with high trait attention grew over the course of the 10-session, 2-week training period. However, they also found that the 10 training sessions accounted for more variance in attention ability than trait attention. Another series of studies has shown that regular digital game players have better attention than their nonplaying counterparts. In a series of four experiments reported in *Nature*, Green and Bavelier (2003) compared players to nonplayers on an attention distraction task and an enumeration task. The distraction task tests the amount of visual information processing attention that individuals have by pushing their limits of attention. In two experiments, players demonstrated residual attention after nonplayers had exhausted their attentional load. In the enumeration task, subjects are asked to count the number of squares flashed on the screen while they are involved in a primary attention task. Again, players had greater attention resources than non-players. It is unclear from the study whether frequent players acquire attentional resources from play, or if those who possess high attentional resources are more likely to become players. In a fifth study, Green and Bavelier began to address this question by showing that nonplayers could improve their attention resources through game play.

Following this stream of research, Castel, Pratt, and Drummond (2005) tested the ability of players and nonplayers to detect targets, speed of response time to easy and difficult visual search tasks, and whether the type of processing strategies differ between the two groups. As in the prior studies, players were faster to detect targets in both easy and difficult visual search tasks. Further, there was evidence that players and nonplayers use similar search strategies, but that players processed information faster. Recently, Green and Bavelier (2006) expanded on their prior research by attempting to identify where player advantage lies. They compared center and peripheral attention in players and nonplayers in two separate experiments and found that players were faster and more accurate in all forms of attention. In a third experiment, they tested whether nonplayers could improve visual attention ability by playing an action-adventure (*Quake Tournament*, 2004) digital game for 30 hours. Subjects in the control group trained on a game that emphasized eye–hand coordination but did not require the participant to process multiple objects at once at a fast pace (*Tetris*, 1985) for the same 30 hours. Subjects who played the action-adventure digital game showed significantly greater increases in visual attention abilities over those in the control group. In a study comparing children with ADHD with nonsymptomatic children, Davison (2004) found that non-ADHD children who frequently play digital games showed a higher level of vigilance than infrequent players and ADHD children. In fact, the ADHD children scored lower in performance than all non-ADHD children.

Learning Processes

In the digital game literature, there have been three major categories of studies addressing learning. First, and most abundant, are studies of learning of specific information from specific games. These highly idiosyncratic studies have focused on such diverse topics as the importance of wearing a hockey helmet (Goodman, Bradley, Paras, Williamson, & Bizzochi, 2006) to better social behavior for children with ADHD (Goldsworthy, Barab, & Goldsworthy, 2000) to handheld social studies games in Singapore (Lim & Wang, 2005). Unfortunately, the specific nature of the learning tasks and the noncontrolled or qualitative nature of the majority of the studies provided very little information that can be generalized. The most we can say about these studies is that players learn some short term facts from game play versus not playing the game.

More useful are the two other types of studies which address actual learning processes and transfer of learned skills to other situations. Several scholars have looked into the strategies involved in learning skills from games. In one of the earliest studies in this category, Subrahmanyam and Greenfield (1994) showed that children could enhance spatial skill deficits by playing a digital game that provided practice in spatial skills. Similarly, Greenfield, Brannon, and Lohr (1994) found that 3D action arcade game expertise was correlated with spatial representation ability and that game expertise, over the long term, improved spatial representation ability. Sims and Mayer (2002) also found that skilled *Tetris* players were better at spatial rotation than nonskilled *Tetris* players, despite using the same mental procedures. Like Greenfield et al. (1994), they did not find a short term effect of practicing *Tetris* on mental rotation ability, but did show that players were adapting new strategies to the game.

In a study with 2nd and 5th grade students (8- and 11 years old respectively), Blumberg (1998) asked children about features of a game that they had played for 10 minutes. She found that frequent players performed better in the unfamiliar game than infrequent players. However, differences in postplay responses indicated that developmental differences accounted for more of the difference in response than player/nonplayer status. Older children focused on the goals of the game while younger players primarily focused on evaluative assessments of the game, suggesting motivational differences by development stage. Older children were much more in tune with the intrinsic motivational tasks (goals) of the game than younger children.

Day, Arthur, and Gettman (2001) later found that the type of knowledge structures used to play games mediated the relationship between general cognitive ability and game performance. Specifically, subjects using the predetermined '"expert" knowledge structure for the game performed significantly better than those who did not. Green and Flowers (2003) observed that kindergarteners in their study were able to learn game play strategy by offering an explanation of game play that revealed their strategies. In fact, the children in the study persisted with their own strategies and goals despite possible distractions of other players' strategies. Similarly, Blumberg and Sokul (2004) found that players approach games differently in terms of goals and strategies. They classified these strategies as internal and external and found that frequent and older players were more likely to use internal strategies than their younger and less experienced counterparts. Finally, Green and Flowers (2003) found that an implicit, nonrule based strategy led to better digital game performance than rule discovery and rule application learning models. Engagement may be leading to higher level processing of the games.

These findings are of significance to serious games researchers as several studies have shown that game players prefer games that require cognitive skills consistent with their own cognitive strengths. For example, Quaiser-Pohl, Geiser, and Lehmann (2005) recently found that children with strong mental rotation ability prefer games that feature that skill. In a series of experiments, Sherry et al. (2006) showed that players liked and performed better in games matching their cognitive skill strengths across a range of skills including 3D mental rotation, targeting, object location memory, and verbal fluency. Sherry and Pacheco (2006) have argued, using media flow theory, that lack of specific cognitive skill will diminish enjoyment of serious games, and thus will inhibit longer engagement and learning.

The final major category of game learning research addresses is whether skills and strategies can be transferred between digital game play and other contexts. This has particular importance for the ultimate effectiveness of serious games. In one series of experiments, Paredes-Olay, Abad, Gamez, and Rosas (2002) tested whether strategies taught to game players prior to play would transfer to actual game play situations. Their college-aged subjects learned the optimal strategy presented and were able to transfer the strategy to game play despite a number of experimentally manipulated distractions. These findings suggest that players of serious games can benefit from a mix of traditional education (strategy) and game play.

Other researchers have addressed the transfer question from the opposite direction—that of transferring knowledge gained in the game to the real world. Okita (2004) tested whether children transfer knowledge about characters found in games from the virtual world to the real world. Subjects were introduced to a toy dog character in one of three modalities (e.g., digital game, stuffed animal, book) and later shown a similar character in a different modality. She found that younger children were most likely to transfer information across modalities, while the technology and the interactivity had little effect on transfer. It would appear to be a cognitive stage that children grow out of, probably the preoperational stage in which fantasy is dominant. However, she did not test for other types of transfer, and such studies will be important to understanding the effects of serious games.

Attitudinal and Health Effects of Digital Games

Indicators of the effects of game play on attitudes can be found in the large literature on the link between digital game play and negative consequences for both adults and young people. For example, Sheese and Graziano (2005) examined the relationship between violent digital game play and eventual cooperative behavior in a Prisoner's Dilemma game with undergraduates. Game play condition made no difference in three out of four indicators of cooperation, but was significant on one measure. Compared to the nonviolent condition, male undergraduates who played a violent digital game for 10 minutes in a study by Brady and Matthews (2006) experienced greater negative affect, more permissive attitudes toward using controlled substances including alcohol, and more uncooperative behavior in a Prisoner's Dilemma game. In a survey, Griffiths, Davies, and Chappell (2003) found that adolescents (M = 17 years) were more likely to report that violence was their favorite aspect of the game *Everquest* than adults were (M = 30 years).

A few studies focusing on personal health outcomes also examined negative consequences of digital game play. The proposed link between digital game play and adolescent obesity has been the topic of several studies. Some studies find effects between digital game play and weight status (e.g., Vandewater, Shim, & Caplovitz, 2003), while other studies find no relationship between digital game play and weight (e.g., Burke et al., 2006). These studies appear to operate under assumption that digital game play inherently represents sedentary behavior. A study by Brodersen, Steptoe, Boniface, and Wardle (2007) goes so far as to operationalize sedentary behavior as hours spent watching television and playing digital games.

Other studies, however, consider the possibility that digital games can be used toward positive ends. The positive consequences relating to digital game technology uncovered thus far can be grouped according to two types: the first type of outcome involves actual physiological health and direct health outcomes as they relate to digital game technology. The second type tests the viability of using digital games for educational purposes.

An example of the first type includes the collection of digital games that are anticipated to provide positive physiological benefits. For example, Lanningham-Foster et al. (2007) hold the view that certain digital games can promote physical activity. They distinguish between games that involve what they term sedentary screen time (played while seated, e.g., *Disney's Extreme Skate*

Adventure, 2003) and active screen time (e.g., *Dance Dance Revolution*, 1999). The 8- to 12-year-old participants who played *Dance Dance Revolution* (DDR) expended more than twice the amount of energy than those who played the traditional digital game while seated, suggesting that games like *DDR* can be employed to combat obesity and stimulate physical activity. Another study took a different approach, using digital games as reward motivation for engaging in physical activity (Saelens & Epstein, 1998). Obese children aged 8 to 12, for whom playing digital games or watching television was contingent upon first riding an exercise bicycle, increased their physical activity level and watched less television compared to a control group for whom digital games and television viewing was freely available. These studies stand in stark contrast to the studies mentioned earlier where digital games were thought of as being merely sedentary activities.

Another vein of research explores ways to educate young people about a variety of health issues. For example, Goodman et al. (2006) developed and successfully tested a game designed to teach adolescent hockey players about concussion symptoms. As predicted, playing the game led to increased knowledge of concussion symptoms. Additionally, players' enjoyment ratings and reports that they would like to play the game again appear to provide evidence that the entertainment dimension of the game was intact and successful.

The work of Lieberman and her colleagues represents well over a decade of pursuit to develop digital games designed to promote health behavioral change. One game entitled *Packy & Marlon* (1995) promotes various positive outcomes involving juvenile diabetes management and education (Brown et al., 1997). This game, created for the Super Nintendo Entertainment System (SNES) platform, has players managing a character that has diabetes. For the character, players must monitor blood glucose, insulin use, and food intake as the character tries to save a diabetes summer camp from marauding rats and mice. Another game called *Bronkie the Brachiosaurus* (1994) again developed for the SNES platform, teaches children how to manage their asthma (Lieberman, 2001). The documented benefits of either game include increased knowledge of the health condition, increased communication with parents regarding the health condition, and increased self-efficacy for self-management of these conditions.

Improving the quality of life of young people with cancer was the aim of a digital game intervention and study by Christen, LaPointe, Kato, Marin-Bowling, and Cole (2006). Consultation with various oncologists, biologists, parents, and juvenile cancer patients led to the development of a third-person shooter type game that featured a "nanobot," who was piloted through the body of a cancer patient. The nanobot's mission was to identify and destroy cancer cells, prevent infections, and deal with various side effects. Again, games such as these have been shown to provide a benefit that warrants their being considered as far more than simply another sedentary activity.

Conclusions

Given the increasing number of researchers and designers interested in the dynamics associated with digital game play, it is safe to say that digital games and education are here to stay. We know that young children currently do not play digital games to any significant degree; not surprising given their fine motor and cognitive capacity. Across a person's lifespan, one's game play increases during the preteen years and continues into adulthood. What is not known is the extent to which patterns of game use across the lifespan are tied to development. Is it possible that game play is most popular among those who have reached formal operations? Certainly many of the challenges of high level games require abstract thinking. Data collected with college student samples tend to show higher amounts of game play than data collected on a representative sample. This may point to evidence of the importance of formal operations, or may simply be a methodological artifact. Because most research is done with college undergrads, who have probably reached formal operations, it is impossible to determine the interaction of cognitive stage and game play with existing data.

There are clearly significant differences with respect to sex and gender when it comes to digital game playing and the choices made by females and males. In a world where more and more scholars agree that important and practical psychological gender differences are rare, the fact that consistent evidence for sex differences in the digital game domain exist certainly deserves more attention. More importantly for serious game researchers and designers, some educational games may alienate female players, simply due to design assumptions of popular entertainment games. Until recently, gender differences in game genre preference have been largely ignored, or games have been designed for girls with the assumption that boys will enjoy any type of game (but see chapter 14 this volume). A better approach may be to use research to isolate and minimize the observed gender differences. For example, our group at Michigan State's MIND Lab is isolating cognitive skill differences that enhance or detract from game play enjoyment. These cognitive skills have been shown to be significantly different between males and females in many studies. For example, games that require 3D rotation (a typically male cognitive skill) are more typically played by males. We are using a number of different strategies to eliminate the effect of 3D rotation ability on game success and enjoyment. Games taking advantage of the techniques we discover will be fun for both female and male students.

Overall, physiological indicators appear to be a fruitful source of information regarding the body's arousal and other responses to digital game playing. One broad conclusion might be drawn in this regard: Digital games have the potential to operate as stressors that indeed induce arousal, across a variety of arousal measures. This makes sense when one considers that physiology is always implicated (to some degree) whenever a cognitive response is recorded.

The inclusion of physiological indicators should not result in biological reductionism, but rather should be viewed as an additional means by which researchers can triangulate sources of information about the effects of digital games. Arousal has been associated with learning in a number of studies, though the mechanism is not yet clear. Further, researchers will need to determine cases in which arousal, perhaps in the form of stress, may be harmful to learning. The task becomes balancing arousal that enhances memory and enjoyment without inducing stress or frustration. Finally, future research will be needed to determine which formal features of games have the intended effect on arousal and which features might lead to stress. Formal features implicated may involve the pace of the game, music, number of tasks/sensory modalities required, content attributes, and graphic features.

There is little doubt that digital game playing requires high degrees of attention. Attention is critical to the learning process, but the literature tells us nothing about how to engage high levels of attention or what that attention may mean for learning and enjoyment. Importantly, studies have shown that visual attention ability can be increased by game play. Perhaps increased attention can be embraced as a serious game goal that has implications for the types of skills required of the new multimedia work force that children will be entering. Will employers and employees benefit from increased attentional ability? Will games improve players' abilities to multitask or process multiple streams of information? What will be the cognitive costs and benefits? Finally, there is continuing research on the use of games to address attentional problems such as ADHD. Perhaps games have a therapeutic use in this domain.

The preliminary evidence suggests that strategic thinking ability and transfer can be enhanced by playing a digital game that requires those skills. At this point, the literature is simply too light and the studies are too disparate to make any meaningful conclusions. However, the acquisition and transfer of strategy represents high level learning. This should be a strong focus of future research.

Finally, all these research topics need to be examined from a developmental perspective. How does the interaction of formal game features interact with our focal dependent variables (e.g., arousal, attention, strategic learning, etc.) by age? It is likely that some game features will simply not make sense to very young children, while other features will contribute to learning for the same age group. It is also likely that formal learning strategies will need to vary by life stage. Toddlers may be excited to play a game portrayed as educational, but educational content may need to be more subtle in games designed for teens. It may be that the types of things that games can teach teenagers may be quite different from the types of things that will work for younger children.

Future Directions for Research

We hope that this chapter has at least awakened a realization that digital games constitute a part of the human experience that certainly holds the potential to significantly affect the lives of those who play. Moreover, computer technology and the digital game industry it drives have already been marshaled toward creating "the impossible" (e.g., bringing a web-slinging Spider-Man to life through a sweeping cityscape). Because there is no visible limit to what can be realized through the use of computer technology, it follows that these same resources can be harnessed for learning and prosocial causes beyond mere entertainment.

Several areas emerge from this review for future focused research attention. These areas include:

- Games and developmental stages.
- Biological and social processes driving gender differences in game play.
- Manipulation of game features in physiological studies to determine the drivers of hormone release, arousal, etc.
- A developmental and gender approach to biological reactance differences.
- Further focused research on the types of skills (e.g., 3D rotation, visual attention), strategies, thinking processes, and information learned and transferred from game play.

This is a broad and relatively large agenda for empirical work on serious games. However, a more generalizable approach will advance the field faster than a large series of idiosyncratic evaluation studies. Unfortunately, funding mechanisms available favor design and testing over basic research. This needs to change in order to gain a set of successful design principles. There are more than enough good ideas available to test; the challenge for serious games research is to engage in strong empirical testing of social, cognitive, and neural processes involved in both game engagement/enjoyment and game learning.

References

Anguiano Serrano, S. A., & Reynoso, L. (2000). Evaluacion de respuestas psicofisiologicas en estudiantes sometidos a estres mediante un videojuego [Assessment of physiological responses in students under stress caused by a video game]. *Revista Mexicana de Analisis de la Conducta, 26*(3), 355–366.

Arthur, W., Strong, M. H., Jordan, J. A., Williamson, J. E., Shebilske, W. L., & Regian, J. W. (1995). Visual attention: Individual differences in training and predicting complex task performance. *Acta Psychologica, 88*(1), 3–23.

Asimov, I. (1966). *The fantastic voyage.* New York: Bantam.

Bickham, D. S., Vandewater, E. A., Huston, A. C., Lee, J. H., Caplovitz, A. G., & Wright, J. C. (2003). Predictors of children's electronic media use: An examination of three ethnic groups. *Media Psychology, 5*(2), 107–137.

Blumberg, F. C. (1998). Developmental differences at play: Children's selective attention and performance in video games. *Journal of Applied Developmental Psychology, 19*(4), 615–624.

Blumberg, F. C., & Sokol, L. M. (2004). Boys' and girls' use of cognitive strategy when learning to play video games. *Journal of General Psychology, 131*(2), 151–158.

Brady, S. S., & Matthews, K. A. (2006). Effects of media violence on health-related outcomes among young men. *Archives of Pediatrics and Adolescent Medicine, 160,* 341–347.

Brodersen, N. H., Steptoe, A., Boniface, D. R., & Wardle, J. (2007). Trends in physical activity and sedentary behaviour in adolescence: Ethnic and socioeconomic differences. *British Journal of Sports Medicine, 41,* 140–144.

Bronkie the Brachiosaurus [Digital game]. (1994). Wavequest. Redwood City, CA: Health Hero Network.

Brown, R. (1997). Gender and video game performance. *Sex Roles, 36*(11–12), 793–812.

Brown, S. J., Leiberman, D. A., Gemena, B. A., Fan, Y. C., Wilson, D. M., & Pasta, D. J. (1997). Educational video game for juvenile diabetes: Results of a controlled trial. *Medical Informatics, 22,* 77–89.

Burke, V., Beilin, L. J., Durkin, K., Stritzke, W. G. K., Houghton, S., & Cameron, C. A. (2006). Television, computer use, physical activity, diet and fatness in Australian adolescents. *International Journal of Pediatric Obesity, 1,* 248–255.

Castel, A. D., Pratt, J., & Drummond, E. (2005). The effects of action video game experience on the time course of inhibition of return and the efficiency of visual search. *Acta Psychologica, 119*(2), 217–230.

Christen, P., LaPointe, E., Kato, P. M., Marin-Bowling, V. M., & Cole, S. (2006). Model for developing and evaluating video games or other technology-based solutions to improve the health and quality of life of young people with cancer or other chronic illnesses. *Cyberpsychology & Behavior, 9,* 665.

Csikszentmihalyi, M. (1988). The flow experience and its significance for human psychology. In M. Csikszentmihalyi & I. S. Csikszentmihalyi (Eds.), *Optimal experience: Psychological studies of flow in consciousness* (pp. 15–35). New York: Cambridge University Press.

Dance dance revolution [Digital game]. (1999). Tokyo, Japan: Konami.

Davison, L. L. (2004). Media viewing and the neurological development of ADHD: Voluntary and involuntary processing. (Doctoral dissertation, Claremont Graduate University, 2004) *Dissertation Abstracts International: Section B: The Sciences and Engineering, 65*(3 B).

Day, E. A., Arthur, W., & Gettman, D. (2001). Knowledge structures and the acquisition of a complex skill. *Journal of Applied Psychology, 86*(5), 1022–1033.

Denot-Ledunois, S., Vardon, G., Perruchet, P., & Gallego, J. (1998). The effect of attentional load on the breathing pattern in children. *International Journal of Psychophysiology, 29*(1), 13–21.

Disney's Extreme Skate Adventure [Digital game]. (2003). Santa Monica, CA: Activision.

Electronic Software Association. (n.d.). http://www.theesa.org

Entertainment Software Association. (2008). *Essential facts about the computer and video game industry.* Retrieved March 17, 2009, from http://www.theesa.com/press-room.html

Funk, J. B., & Buchman, D. D. (1996). Children's perceptions of gender differences in social approval for playing electronic games. *Sex Roles, 35*(3–4), 219–232.

Gee, J. P. (2003). *What video games have to teach us about learning and literacy.* New York: Palgrave Macmillan.

Gerin, W., Litt, M. D., Deich, J., & Pickering, T. G. (1996). Self efficacy as a component of active coping: Effects on cardiovascular reactivity. *Journal of Psychosomatic Research, 40*(5), 485–493.

Gerin, W., Milner, D. v., Chawla, S., & Pickering, T. G. (1995). Social support as a moderator of cardiovascular reactivity in women: A test of the direct effects and buffering hypotheses. *Psychosomatic Medicine, 57*(1), 16–22.

Goldsworthy, R., Barab, S. A., Goldsworthy, E. L. (2000). The STAR Project: enhancing adolescents' social understanding through video-based, multimedia scenarios. *Journal of Special Education Technology, 15*(2), 13–26.

Goodman, D., Bradley, N. L., Paras, B., Williamson, I. J., & Bizzochi, J. (2006). Video gaming promotes concussion knowledge acquisition in youth hockey players. *Journal of Adolescence, 29*(3), 351–360.

Green, C., & Bavelier, D. (2003). Action video game modifies visual selective attention. *Nature, 423*(6939), 534–537.

Green, C., & Bavelier, D. (2006). Enumeration versus multiple object tracking: The case of action video game players. *Cognition, 101*(1), 217–245.

Green, T. D., & Flowers, J. H. (2003). Comparison of implicit and explicit learning processes in a probabilistic task. *Perceptual and Motor Skills, 97*(1), 299–314.

Greenberg, B. S., Eastin, M., Skalski, P., Cooper, L., Levy, M., & Lachlan, K. (2005). Comparing survey and diary measures of internet and traditional media use. *Communication Reports, 18*(1), 1–8.

Greenfield, P. M., Brannon, G., & Lohr, D. (1994). Two dimensional representation of movement through three dimensional space: The role of video game expertise. *Journal of Applied Developmental Psychology, 15*(1), 87–103.

Griffiths, M. D., Davies, M. N. O., & Chappell, D. (2003). Online computer gaming: A comparison of adolescent and adult gamers. *Journal of Adolescence, 27*, 87–96.

Hebert, S., Beland, R., Dionne Fournelle, O., Crete, M., & Lupien, S. J. (2005). Physiological stress response to video game playing: The contribution of built in music. *Life Sciences, 76*(20), 2371–2380.

Id Software, Inc. (2004). Quake Tournament [Digital game]. Tustin, CA: Loki Software, Inc.

Izzetoglu, K., Bunce, S., Onaral, B., Pourrezaei, K., & Chance, B. (2004). Functional optical brain imaging using near infrared during cognitive tasks. *International Journal of Human Computer Interaction, 17*(2), 211–227.

Lanningham-Foster, L., Jensen, T. B., Foster, R. C., Redmond, A. B., Walker, B. A., Heinz, D., et al. (2007). Energy expenditure of sedentary screen time compared with active screen time for children. *Pediatrics, 118*, 1831–1835.

Lawler, K. A., Wilcox, Z. C., & Anderson, S. F. (1995). Gender differences in patterns of dynamic cardiovascular regulation. *Psychosomatic Medicine, 57*(4), 357–365.

Lieberman, D. A. (2001). Management of chronic pediatric diseases with interactive health games: Theory and research findings. *Journal of Ambulatory Care Management, 24*, 26–38.

Lieberman, D. A. (2006). What can we learn from playing interactive games? In P. Vorderer & J. Bryant (Eds.), *Playing computer games: Motives, responses, and consequences* (pp. 379–398). Mahwah, NJ: Erlbaum.

Lim, K. Y. T., & Wang, J. Y. Z. (2005). Collaborative handheld gaming in education. *Educational Media International, 42*(4), 351–359.

Lucas, K., & Sherry, J. L. (2004). Sex differences in video game play: A communication based explanation. *Communication Research, 31*(5), 499–523.

Marshall, S. J., Gorely, T., & Biddle, S. J. (2006). A descriptive epidemiology of screen based media use in youth: A review and critique. *Journal of Adolescence, 29*(3), 333–349.

Michigan State University, MSU Serious Games MA Program. (n.d.). Retrieved August 6, 2008, from http://seriousgames.msu.edu/

Murphy, J. K., Alpert, B. S., & Walker, S. S. (1994). When to measure resting values in studies of children's cardiovascular reactivity. *Journal of Behavioral Medicine, 17*(5), 501–510.

Murphy, J. K., Alpert, B. S., Walker, S. S., & Willey, E. S. (1991). Children's cardiovascular reactivity: Stability of racial differences and relation to subsequent blood pressure over a one year period. *Psychophysiology, 28*(4), 447–457.

Musante, L., & Raunikar, R. (1994). Consistency of children's hemodynamic responses to laboratory stressors. *International Journal of Psychophysiology, 17*(1), 65–71.

Newman, J. D., McGarvey, S. T., & Steele, M. S. (1999). Longitudinal association of cardiovascular reactivity and blood pressure in Samoan adolescents. *Psychosomatic Medicine, 61*(2), 243–249.

Okagaki, L., & Frensch, P. A. (1994). Effects of video game playing on measures of spatial performance: Gender effects in late adolescence. *Journal of Applied Developmental Psychology, 15*(1), 33–58.

Okita, S. Y. (2004). Effects of age on associating virtual and embodied toys. *CyberPsychology and Behavior, 7*(4), 464–471.

Packy & Marlon [Digital game]. (1997). Miller, A. Palo Alto, CA: Click Health.

Paley, A. R. (2007). Software fails as student aid, report finds. Indystar. Retrieved April 7, 2007, from http://www.indystar.com/apps/pbcs.dll/article?AID=2007704050552

Paredes-Olay, C., Abad, M. J. F., Gamez, M., & Rosas, J. M. (2002). Transfer of control between causal predictive judgments and instrumental responding. *Animal Learning and Behavior, 30*(3), 239–248.

Quaiser-Pohl, C., Geiser, C., & Lehmann, W. (2006). The relationship between computer-game preference, gender, and mental-rotation ability. *Personality and Individual Differences, 40*(3), 609–619.

Quake III: Arena [Digital game]. (2000). Id Software. Tustin, CA: Loki Software.

Rideout, V. J., Vandewater, E. A., & Wartella, E. A. (2003). *Zero to six: Electronic media in the lives of infants, toddlers, and preschoolers.* Menlo Park, CA: The Henry J. Kaiser Family Foundation.

Ritterfeld, U., & Weber, R. (2006). Video games for entertainment and education. In P. Vorderer & J. Bryant (Eds.), *Playing computer games: Motives, responses, and consequences* (pp. 399–413). Mahwah, NJ: Erlbaum.

Roberts, D.F., Foehr, U.G., Rideout, V.J., & Brodie, M. (1999). *Kids and media at the new millennium: A comprehensive national analysis of children's media use.* Menlo Park, CA: Kaiser Family Foundation.

Rosser, J. C., Lynch, P. J., Cuddihy, L., Gentile, D. A., Klonsky, J., & Merrell, R. (2007). The impact of video games on training surgeons in the 21st century. *Archives of Surgery, 142,* 181–186.

Saelens, B. E., & Epstein, L. H. (1998). Behavioral engineering of activity choice in obese children. *International Journal of Obesity, 22,* 275–277.

Serious Games Initiative. Retrieved August 6, 2008 from http://www.seriousgames.org/index2.html

Sheese, B. E., & Graziano, W. G. (2005). Deciding to defect: The effects of video game violence on cooperative behavior. *Psychological Science, 16*, 354–357.

Sherry, J. L. (2004). Media enjoyment and flow. *Communication Theory, 14*(4), 328–347.

Sherry, J. L., Lucas, K., Greenberg, B., & Lachlan, K. (2006). Video game uses and gratifications as predictors of use and game preference. In P. Vorderer & J. Bryant (Eds.), *Playing computer games: Motives, responses, and consequences* (pp. 213–224). Mahwah, NJ: Erlbaum.

Sherry, J. L., Lucas, K., Rechtsteiner, S., Brooks, C., & Wilson, B. (2001, May). *Video game uses and gratifications as predictors of use and game preference.* Paper presented at the International Communication Association Annual Convention, Washington, DC.

Sherry, J. L., & Pacheco, A. (2006). Matching computer game genres to educational outcomes. *Electronic Journal of Communication, 16*(1 & 2). Retrieved from http://www.cios.org/www/ejc/v16n1.htm

Sherry, J. L., Rosaen, S., Bowman, N. D., & Huh, S. (2006, June). *Cognitive skill predicts video game ability.* Paper presented at the International Communication Association Annual Convention, Dresden, Germany.

Sims, V. K., & Mayer, R. E. (2002). Domain specificity of spatial expertise: The case of video game players. *Applied Cognitive Psychology, 16*(1), 97–115.

Sita, A., & Miller, S. B. (1996). Estradiol, progesterone and cardiovascular response to stress. *Psychoneuroendocrinology, 21*(3), 339–346.

Smith, M. E., McEvoy, L. K., & Gevins, A. (1999). Neurophysiological indices of strategy development and skill acquisition. *Cognitive Brain Research, 7*(3), 389–404.

Subrahmanyam, K., & Greenfield, P. M. (1994). Effect of video game practice on spatial skills in girls and boys. *Journal of Applied Developmental Psychology, 15*(1), 13–32.

Svebak, S., Knardahl, S., Nordby, H., & Aakvaag, A. (1992). Components of Type A behavior pattern as predictors of neuroendocrine and cardiovascular reactivity in challenging tasks. *Personality and Individual Differences, 13*(6), 733–744.

Terdiman, D. (2006). What's wrong with serious games? C/net news. Retrieved March 22, 2006, from http://news.com.com/Whats+wrong+with+serious+games/2100-1043_3-6052346.html

Tetris [Digital game]. (1985). Pajitnov, A. Honolulu, HI: Tetris.

Vandewater, E. A., Shim, M., & Caplovitz, A. G. (2003). Linking obesity and activity level with children's television and video game use. *Journal of Adolescence, 27*, 71–85.

von Salisch, M., Oppl, C., & Kristen, A. (2006). What attracts children? In P. Vorderer & J. Bryant (Eds.), *Playing computer games: Motives, responses, and consequences.* (pp. 147–164). Mahwah, NJ: Erlbaum.

Weber, R., Ritterfeld, U., & Mathiak, K. (2006). Does playing violent video games induce aggression? Empirical evidence of a functional Magnetic Resonance Imaging study. *Media Psychology, 8*(1), 39–60.

Wolfson, S., & Case, G. (2000). The effects of sound and colour on responses to a computer game. *Interacting with Computers, 13*(2), 183–192.

Wood, R. T. A., Griffiths, M.D., Chappell, D., & Davies, N. M. O. (2004). The structural characteristics of video games: A psycho-structural analysis. *CyberPsychology and Behavior, 7*(1), 1–10.

Chapter 11

Designing Serious Games for Children and Adolescents

What Developmental Psychology Can Teach Us

Kaveri Subrahmanyam and Patricia Greenfield

Digital games are part and parcel of young people's lives today. Using data from several recent studies conducted by the Kaiser Family Foundation, Roberts and Foehr (2008) report that 50% of households with children younger than 6 years and 83% of households with children 8 to 18 years of age have a game console. Not surprisingly, children spend considerable amounts of time playing these games—in 2004, 8- to 10-year-olds played for 65 minutes per day and 15- to 18-year-olds played for 33 minutes per day. Within this context, Sherry and Dibble's chapter (this volume, chapter 10) presents a timely review of the research on the relation between digital games and development. Unfortunately, we are severely limited in the conclusions that we can draw from these studies. A limited number of studies on a topic, a small number of subjects in those studies, with only a few of them focusing on children—these are only some of the problems with this body of work. Regardless, what we learn from the chapter is that digital game playing does have an effect on a variety of dimensions including physiological measures, attentional processes, and learning. It is the expectation of such effects that has fueled the serious games movement.

Our goal in this chapter is to go beyond current research to inform the development of serious games for children and adolescents. Our starting point is Sherry and Dibble's correct assertion that research on these topics needs to adopt a developmental perspective. This lack of a developmental perspective is perhaps one of the biggest limitations of work they reviewed in their chapter. Most of the studies are on young adults, typically introductory psychology students. Very few studies have included children and adolescents and very few to none systematically compared participants of different ages. Yet we know from developmental theory and research that timing is all-important in development. For instance, timing has been found to be important in diverse aspects of development including the effects of teratogens (e.g., drugs and alcohol) in prenatal development (Hogge, 1990), the effects of poverty during childhood (Duncan & Brooks-Gunn, 2000), and the learning of a second language (Johnson & Newport, 1989). To our knowledge, the few digital game studies that have used such an approach have yielded unequivocal results. For instance, the Blumberg (1998) study cited in Sherry and Dibble's chapter suggests that children of different ages focus on different aspects of a game; when asked about the features of game they had played, 11-year-olds were able to describe the goals of the game, whereas 8-year-olds focused on evaluative assessments of the game. However, another study which examined the effect of digital game playing on mental rotation skill found no differences in the effects between fifth, seventh, and ninth grade students (McClurg & Chaille, 1987).

Thus, we have no way of knowing whether the effects of game playing that have been reported to date are specific to the age group of the participants in the study, whether the effects may generalize to players of other ages, and how developmental trends might mediate these effects. Yet they must be taken into account when designing serious games, if they are supposed to be seriously effective for a broad cross-section of the child population. In the absence of such developmental research, we turn to recent theoretical and empirical work to present a theoretical framework for understanding the effects of digital games, as well as to present some other important considerations for designers of serious games.

A Developmental Framework for Understanding the Effects of Digital Games

We start with our developmental framework of media understanding and use that we have described in detail elsewhere (Maynard, Subrahmanyam, & Greenfield, 2005; Subrahmanyam & Greenfield, 2008). This theory draws from the Russian psychologist, Lev Vygotsky's (1962, 1978) proposal that the tools (e.g., abacus, language, and mathematics) provided by a culture enable individuals to develop their higher mental functions. Extending this idea we suggested that using the particular tools provided by a culture elicits and develops particular sets of cognitive skills (Maynard et al., 2005). On this view, digital games are tools provided by our culture and one would expect them to influence our thinking and learning. In this chapter, we argue that understanding how these influences come about is key for designers of serious games.

To understand how media such as radio, television, and digital games influence learning, we have suggested that a distinction must be made between the formal features of a medium, such as the audiovisual production features that characterize it, and the content it presents, such as the topic of a software program. In the following we will first focus on how formal features might affect learning and will then discuss the role of content.

The Role of Formal Features: What is Internalized?

The formal features of a medium are independent of content and consist of symbol systems that a user must decode to understand the content of the message. Different media use different symbol systems. A solid body of work has identified the formal features of television, including action, pace, visual techniques, such as camera zooms, cuts, and visual special effects, and auditory features such as music, dialogue, and sound effects (Wright & Huston, 1983). Television also uses other symbol systems such as text, pictures, and diagrams, both stationary and in motion (Kozma, 1991). In Subrahmanyam and Greenfield (2008), we pointed out that digital games are even more complex than television when it comes to presenting two-dimensional representations of three-dimensional space. Most digital games use action and pace, are dynamic, have multiple, often simultaneous, things happening at different locations and utilize a variety of attentional, spatial, and iconic representations.

But how do the formal features of a medium bring about a change in our thinking and learning? Saloman (1979) has proposed that the symbol systems utilized by a medium become internalized by the user, leading to changes in his or her representations. Greenfield (1993) has called this process *cognitive socialization*—it is the process of internalization by which cultural tools such as digital games come to influence users' processing skills. There are several studies that have demonstrated that digital game playing can influence specific cognitive skills such as attention as well iconic and spatial representational skills (see Subrahmanyam & Greenfield, 2008). Sherry and Dibble refer to some of these studies in their chapter as well. Most of the studies reviewed by Sherry and Dibble under *attention* and *learning* actually deal with the effect of the formal features of games.

Unfortunately, existing studies have not systematically analyzed the formal features of games as has been done with television (see Subrahmanyam & Greenfield, 2008, for a review of some of this research). Similarly, most studies of game effects have not separated the effects of formal features from those of game content. One way to address this issue is by holding one feature constant and systematically varying the other to assess how symbols and content might interact to bring about the effects of digital games on cognitive skills. Such an approach was used by Salomon and Cohen (1977) to assess the effects of television grammar; they showed children the identical television content, but varied formal features such as zoom in and zoom outs, fragmented spaces, logical gaps, and close-ups. They found that the children were more knowledgeable about the relation between parts and whole when they viewed the version with close-ups, but showed better comprehension of logical structure and continuity when they viewed the version with logical gaps. Such an approach would be a first step toward understanding the symbolic grammar of digital games.

A related issue is that because of individual differences in processing style (e.g., Childers, Houston, & Heckler, 1985), there may be individual differences in users' ability to process and internalize different symbol systems. Sherry and Dibble (this volume, chapter 10) report that game players prefer games that require "cognitive skills consistent with their own cognitive strength." Thus, it is not only important for game designers to recognize that formal features of games have effects on users, but also that there are differences across users in how they are able to process these features and internalize them.

Developmental Factors Affect the Processing of Formal Features

Bruner (1966) has distinguished three different kinds of representation appearing in a developmental order: enactive representation through action, iconic representation through images that resemble their referent, and symbolic representation through symbols that bear no resemblance to their referent, are arbitrary, and are therefore established by social agreement or convention. That enactive representation develops first implies that even very young children will be able to use a mouse, a prerequisite for any type of digital game, serious or not. Using a mouse involves creating an action representation on the part of the user, so it makes developmental sense, in terms of Bruner's representational theory, that children who are quite young should be able to master the basics of this technology. The 2003 (Rideout, Vandewater, & Wartella) Kaiser Report, Zero to Six, found that 64% of children between 4 and 6 years of age know how to use a computer mouse to point and click (Rideout, Vandewater, & Wartella, 2003). In doing so, they are integrating their own enactive representations using the mouse with the icons and iconic representations they find on the screen.

We have recently developed a theoretical proposal that the more real-world perceptual and cognitive cues a media representation makes available, the less mental transformation it will require and the earlier it will become accessible and usable to a child (Subrahmanyam & Greenfield, 2008). This is really an extension of Piaget's emphasis on mental transformation as a hallmark of cognitive development (Gruber & Voneche, 1977). As game design has moved to increasingly realistic (dynamic, three-dimensional, full color) graphics and sound, and games increasingly look like film or television, they require much less mental transformation to be comprehended and become accessible to increasingly younger audiences. Indeed, the Kaiser Report (2003) indicates that the age for using digital games is declining rapidly. Parents report that 14% of their 6-month to 3-year-olds and 50% of their 4- to 6-year-old children have played a digital game. A casual exploration of games available for this age group on the Internet shows that games such as those on the Nickelodeon Junior Web site are utilizing multimodal cues and realistic graphics, including a voice to tell the child every move to make with the joystick. Clearly such formal features make serious learning games accessible to ever-younger children.

However, there can be costs as well as benefits to this early accessibility of digital games. Sigel uses the term *distancing* to refer to "a class of cognitive demands that serve to activate a separation of self cognitively from the here and now" (Sigel, 1993, p. 142). Digital games are one manifestation of the fact that children are increasingly growing up in a virtual world. This means that they are spending less and less time in face-to-face interaction, in physical activity, and interacting with solid objects. To use Sigel's terminology, digital games, whether serious or not, are a medium that serves to separate the child both cognitively and socially from the here and now. The reduction of a relationship to the real is a cost of the expansion of virtuality to serious games for child and adolescent development.

Last but not at all least, serious games will be able to build upon the skills in processing particular kinds of formal features that entertainment games develop. One such skill is the use of iconic imagery. Experimental study has demonstrated that experience with a digital game can shift representation from the symbolic toward the iconic (Greenfield, Camaioni, et al., 1994). For university students in Los Angeles and Rome, iconic representation was also correlated with better understanding of Robinett and Grimm's, *Rocky's Boot* (1982), a learning game designed to teach about the logic of electronic circuitry. Generalizing from this finding, we see that serious games to teach science and engineering can, because of the prevalence of entertainment games, utilize iconic representation as a teaching tool with confidence that basic skill in processing this formal feature has already been developed through experience with digital games for entertainment.

Serious games can utilize the development of other visual skills that nonserious action games develop—skills such as interpreting a two-dimensional display in terms of three dimensions (Greenfield, Brannon, & Lohr, 1994) or monitoring multiple locations on a computer screen (Green & Bavelier, 2003; Greenfield, DeWinstanley, Kilpatrick, & Kaye, 1994). The widespread experience with the entertainment games of today means that children and adolescents will be better able to process visual features such as iconic imagery, three-dimensional representation, and action at multiple locations when these formal features are used for serious learning processes. Unknown at this point is how formal features of a game might interact with game content, the topic we turn to next.

The Role of Game Content: What is Learned?

We define game content as the topic area or message conveyed by the formal features; for example, a game's thematic focus (e.g., geography, algebra). Research on game content has mostly consisted of studying games that teach specific academic skills (such as reading or mathematics) or subject content (e.g., science, math, personal health). Although it appears that games may promote health behavioral changes (Christen, LaPointe, Kato, Marin-Bowling, & Cole, 2006; Lieberman, 2001), research has yielded very little evidence that their use in the classroom yields consistent benefits. Kafai (2006) wrote that "a survey of the past 20 years of educational publications reveals a rather sparse bounty, in particular if one is interested in hard-core academic benefits rather than motivational or social aspects of playing games for learning" (p. 37).

Furthermore, Sherry and Dibble (this volume, chapter 10) point out that the idiosyncratic nature of the studies make it very difficult to draw any conclusions and generalizations.

More promising in our opinion is an effort that provided students with an opportunity to design games for learning. Relevant here is Kafai and colleagues' research in which students were provided with the opportunity to construct their own games; for instance in one study students were given the opportunity to create their own games (with their own worlds, characters, storylines, etc.) to teach fractions to a group of younger students in their school (Kafai, Franke, Ching, & Shih, 1998). By analyzing the games designed, the authors hypothesized that designing games helped the students develop more sophisticated and complex representations of fractions. Making games for learning seemed to allow learners to develop new understandings of content knowledge.

This work points out the importance of analyzing in detail learners' representations of a content area. In particular, when designing serious games for children, game designers must start with learners' representations of the content matter. They must proceed systematically by examining how these representations differ among children of different ages, at different levels of cognitive development, and at different levels of expertise in the content area. Only then can we design games that will be effective in bringing about change in those representations. In the next sections, we identify some themes that should be kept in mind when designing games for children.

Gender and Games

Gender differences have consistently emerged from research on children and games, and the chapters by Sherry and Dibble (this volume, chapter 10) as well as Kafai (this volume, chapter 14) address this issue. Relevant to us are two findings: that more boys play digital games and do so for more time than girls; second there seem to be differences in game preferences between boys and girls. Getting girls to play games is not an inconsiderable challenge—when we conducted our digital game study in the late 1980s (Subrahmanyam & Greenfield, 1994), we found it very difficult to recruit girls to participate in the study and to keep them engaged in the game training we provided. The gender disparity in game playing has remained and is even found in online games (Griffiths, Davies, & Chappell, 2003).

As Kafai notes, the challenge for designers of serious games is to create games that are appealing and accessible to all players, whether boys or girls. A similar goal motivated the Girls' Games movement and Kafai (this volume, chapter 14) has discussed this along with several games (e.g., *Barbie Fashion Designer*, *Rockett's New World*) that were produced as part of this effort. Here we discuss our work on the *Barbie Fashion Designer* game (Subrahmanyam & Greenfield, 1998). To understand girl appeal in digital games, we analyzed the game as well as gender differences in other aspects of children's lives, such as their play and their media (television) preferences. Our analysis suggested that girls like nonaggressive play activities that allow them to create fantasies set in familiar settings with familiar characters, compared to boys who seemed to prefer more aggressive and fantasy based activities. These preferences were also mirrored in the virtual world—boys dove into action games with their aggressive and fantasy-based content, whereas girls overwhelmingly rejected violent action games and instead took to an electronic game that allowed them to construct real life themes in the virtual world. In other words, we found that girls' and boys' preferences in electronic play mirrored their preferences in real-life play and media (e.g., print and television).

This is a powerful theoretical finding, and one that shows that in seeking to design games that have broad appeal, game developers must be informed by existing research on individual differences in children's play and everyday activities. But more broadly, this finding also suggests that for young people, physical and virtual worlds may be connected; this is an observation that has recently emerged from our own and other people's work on young people and the Internet (Subrahmanyam, Garcia, Harsono, Li, & Lipana, 2009; Subrahmanyam, Smahel, & Greenfield, 2006). Although this work deals with the Internet, we think it is relevant for game designers because it speaks more generally to young peoples' virtual worlds.

Psychological Connectedness of Physical and Virtual Worlds

The psychological connectedness of physical and virtual worlds is becoming apparent via the gender differences that are emerging in online behavior (Griffiths et al., 2003; Subrahmanyam et al., 2007). Although the gender gap that is typically found in digital game playing is not found with regard to Internet access and use (Subrahmanyam, Greenfield, Kraut, & Gross, 2001), some gender differences from the physical world continue to be mirrored in the online virtual world. Thus, among adolescents, males seem to prefer gaming (Griffiths et al., 2003) and females prefer blogging (Subrahmanyam et al., 2009); interestingly, the majority of blog entries written by adolescents contain themes related to peers and everyday life. Another finding refers to social networking sites, and girls report using social networking sites more to reinforce pre-existing friendships, whereas boys report using them to flirt and make new friends (Lenhart & Madden, 2005). These trends seem to parallel the gender differences noted earlier in other areas of young peoples' lives (Subrahmanyam & Greenfield, 1998; Subrahmanyam et al., 2009).

Evidence for the connectedness of the two worlds also comes from studies indicating that young people use instant messaging to communicate with offline friends (Gross, Juvonen, & Gable, 2002) and chat rooms to enact real-life issues such as sexuality, identity, and partner selection (Smahel &

Subrahmanyam, 2007; Subrahmanyam et al., 2006). Closer to computer games, are computer-generated virtual worlds such as *Second Life*, and behavior in these newer contexts appear to mimic off-line behavior, so much so that they may be providing social psychologists with a new way for studying human behavior and complex social interactions (Miller, 2007).

Thus it appears that when given the opportunity to coconstruct their virtual worlds, young people do so in ways that are psychologically connected to their physical life. For designers of serious games this may mean that games and game worlds have to be psychologically connected to users' physical lives to be maximally appealing and effective to bring about learning in young people. There have also been reports in the media that *Second Life* is being used for learning in higher education (Wong, 2006). How successful these efforts will be we do not know as yet. But together they suggest that when designing games for young children, it is important to be informed by what is happening in other spheres of their lives.

Potential Role of Developmental Issues and the Development of Game Understanding

Issues such as sexuality, identity, and partner selection are highly salient at a particular stage of life—adolescence and young adulthood. These stage-specific issues in social development may explain why playing digital games is less popular in adolescence than in middle childhood (Roberts & Foehr, in press), whereas communication functions of the Internet are so dominant in adolescence (Subrahmanyam & Greenfield, 2008).

One clue as to why digital games are increasingly popular through middle childhood lies in Piaget's research on the development of children's understanding of games (Piaget, 1932). Interviewing children about the game of marbles, Piaget found three stages in the understanding of the rules of the game. Up to age 4 to 5, children in Geneva did not really understand rule-bound games at all; they simply engaged in personal exploration and individual ritual acts when given a set of marbles to play with. At this point true games with rules would be futile in the digital game arena. Only software that provided an opportunity for individual exploration without obvious constraints or goals would be functional for this age group.

Around age 5 or 6, children began to see the rules of a game as sacred and unchangeable, given by authorities such as parents or God. In actual play, however, children at this stage tended to play their own individual games rather than trying to compete with each other. This might be the stage at which digital games could first be successful, given that the rules are in fact programmed into the game (therefore given by authority and unchangeable). But because competition is still not understood, games for this stage should not be for more than one player. Indeed, a quick survey of online games for young children indicates that they generally are single-player games. For example, in the online version of *Candyland*, a board game for young children, interaction with the computer is substituted for the social interaction of the offline game. Applying Piaget's findings, we would guess that this change would make this game (or other games) able to be played by younger children than the multiplayer board game versions.

By around age 10, a third stage was reached in Piaget's research on the game of marbles. At this point children no longer saw game rules as sacred, laid down by external authority. Instead, they saw them as established by mutual consent; rules could therefore be changed by agreement among the players. For the first time, children had the concept that they themselves can construct and coconstruct the rules of a game. The implications of this progression would be that multiplayer games with changeable rules might be the best way to provide learning experiences through digital gaming at this last stage. In addition, the idea that that they themselves can make the rules of a game would allow children, at this point in development, to program and construct their own games for the first time. In the light of this general developmental stage in game understanding, it is undoubtedly no coincidence that children between the ages of 9 and 11 were Kafai's choice as designer/programmers of serious games (1996; this volume, chapter 14); this choice of ages must be one reason that the children were so successful as designers of games to teach fractions.

Formal and Informal Contexts of Learning

One final point—in recent years, developmental psychologists have begun to recognize that learning is not restricted to the formal context of the classroom, but can also occur in the informal contexts of everyday life, such as museums, at home, in the kitchen, when interacting with peers, and in after-school settings (Rogoff, 1990; Scribner & Cole, 1973). In contrast to the direct instruction from an expert that is characteristic of the learning in a typical classroom, learning in informal settings is characterized by the learner's active participation as well as collaboration between people with different levels of knowledge and expertise (Rogoff, 1990). Anecdotal observation of digital game playing in the home suggests that these characteristics are present when children play games, particularly in the company of their peers.

Unfortunately, research on the effects of digital games has not systematically examined game effects using the theoretical distinction between formal and informal learning. We do not as yet understand the informal learning mechanisms that take place during game playing or how the setting itself can influence whether learning takes place or not. Another thorny issue is that of transfer, a topic that Sherry and Dibble address in their chapter in this volume. Do children transfer the skills/knowledge gained when playing games to the formal setting of the classroom, and do skills learned in the classroom transfer to game contexts? What game features are more likely to ensure such transfer? Evidence that the online worlds coconstructed by young people are psychologically connected to their physical lives leads us to speculate that transfer might be more likely to occur when game worlds are similarly connected to players' offline lives. In the absence of systematic research to support or refute our contention, the very least that game designers can do is to keep these issues in mind when designing games for children.

Conclusions

In conclusion, although research to date suggests that playing digital games may have effects on our learning and thinking, many questions remain as to the factors that mediate these effects. In the absence of such research, we have used developmental theory and research to provide some considerations and themes that should be kept in mind when developing serious games for children and adolescents. Our analysis suggests that when designing games, designers should pay attention to the formal features of games as separate from content, look to young people's offline lives, and take into account the context in which the game will be used.

References

Barbie Fashion Designer [Digital game]. (1995). El Segundo, CA: Mattel.

Bruner, J. S. (1966). On cognitive growth. In J. S. Bruner, R. R. Olver, & P. M. Greenfield (Eds.), *Studies in cognitive growth* (pp. 1–67). New York: Wiley.

Childers, T. L., Houston, M. J., & Heckler, S. E. (1985). Measurement of individual differences in visual versus verbal information processing. *The Journal of Consumer Research, 12*, 125–134.

Christen, P., LaPointe, E., Kato, P. M., Marin-Bowling, V. M., & Cole, S. (2006). Model for developing and evaluating video games or other technology-based solutions to improve the health and quality of life of young people with cancer or other chronic illnesses. *Cyberpsychology & Behavior, 9*, 665.

Duncan, G. J., & Brooks-Gunn, J. (2000). Family poverty, welfare reform, and child development. *Child Development, 71*, 188–196.

Green, C. S., & Bavelier, D. (2003). Action video game modifies visual selective attention. *Nature, 423*, 534–537.

Greenfield, P. M. (1993). Representational competence in shared symbol systems: Electronic media from radio to video games. In R. R. Cocking & K. A. Renninger (Eds.), *The development and meaning of psychological distance* (pp. 161–183). Hillsdale, NJ: Erlbaum.

Greenfield, P. M., Brannon, C., & Lohr, D. (1994). Two-dimensional representation of movement through three-dimensional space: The role of video game expertise. *Journal of Applied Developmental Psychology, 15*, 87–103.

Greenfield, P. M., Camaioni, L., Ercolani, P., Weiss, L., Lauber, B., & Perucchini, P. (1994). Cognitive socialization by computer games in two cultures: Inductive discovery or mastery of an iconic code? *Journal of Applied Developmental Psychology, 15*, 59–85.

Greenfield, P. M., deWinstanley, P., Kilpatrick, H., & Kaye, D. (1994). Action video games and informal education: Effects on strategies for dividing visual attention. *Journal of Applied Developmental Psychology, 15,* 105–123.

Griffiths, M. D., Davies, M. N. O., & Chappell, D. (2003). Online computer gaming: A comparison of adolescent and adult gamers. *Journal of Adolescence, 27,* 87–96.

Gross, E. F., Juvonen, J., & Gable, S. E. (2002). Online communication and well-being in early adolescence: The social function of instant messages. *Journal of Social Issues, 58,* 75–90.

Gruber, H. E., & Voneche, J. J. (1977). *The essential Piaget: An interpretive reference and guide.* New York: Basic Books.

Hogge, W. A. (1990). Teratology. In I. R. Merkatz & J. E. Thompson (Eds.), *New perspectives on prenatal care* (pp. 117–122). New York: Elsevier.

Johnson, J., & Newport, E. (1989). Critical period effects in second language learning: The influence of maturational state on the acquisition of English as a second language. *Cognitive Psychology, 21,* 60–99.

Kafai, Y. B. (1996). Gender differences in children's construction of video games. In P. M. Greenfield & R. R. Cocking (Eds.), *Interacting with video* (pp. 39–66). Norwood, NJ: Ablex.

Kafai, Y. B. (2006). Playing and making games for learning: Instructions and constructionist perspectives for game studies. *Games and Culture, 1,* 36–40.

Kafai, Y. B., Franke, M., Ching, C., & Shih, J. (1998). Game design as an interactive learning environment fostering students' and teachers' mathematical inquiry. *International Journal of Computers for Mathematical Learning, 3,* 149–184.

Kozma, R. F. (1991). Learning with media. *Review of Educational Research, 61,* 179–211.

Lenhart, A., & Madden, M. (2005). *Teen content creators and consumers.* Washington, DC: Pew Internet and American Life Project. Retrieved August 9, 2007, from http://www.pewinternet.org/pdfs/PIP_Teens_Content_Creation.pdf.

Lieberman, D. A. (2001). Management of chronic pediatric diseases with interactive health games: Theory and research findings. *Journal of Ambulatory Care Management, 24,* 26–38.

Maynard, A. E., Subrahmanyam, K., & Greenfield, P. M. (2005). Technology and the development of intelligence: From the loom to the computer. In R. J. Sternberg & D. Preiss (Eds.), *Intelligence and technology: The impact of tools on the nature and development of human abilities* (pp. 29–53). Mahwah, NJ: Erlbaum.

McClurg, P. A., & Chaille, C. (1987). Computer games: Environments for developing spatial cognition? *Journal of Educational Computing Research, 3,* 95–111.

Miller, G. (2007). The promise of parallel universes. *Science, 317,* 134–343.

Piaget, J. (1932). *The moral judgment of the child.* London: Routledge & Kegan Paul.

Rideout, V. J., Vandewater, E. A., & Wartella, E. A. (2003). *Zero to six: Electronic media in the lives of infants, toddlers and preschoolers* (Kaiser Family Foundation Report). Menlo Park, CA: Kaiser Family Foundation.

Rockett's New World [Digital game]. Mountain View, CA: Purple Moon Product.

Roberts, D. F., & Foehr, U. G. (2008). Trends in media use. *The Future of Children, 18,* 11–37.

Rocky's Boot [Digital game]. (1982). Robinett, W., & Grimm, L. San Francisco: Learning Company.

Rogoff, B. (1990). *Apprenticeship in thinking: Cognitive development in social context.* New York: Oxford University Press.

Salomon, G. (1979). *Interaction of media, cognition, and learning*. San Francisco: Jossey-Bass.

Salomon, G., & Cohen, A. A. (1977). Television formats, mastery of mental skills and the acquisition of knowledge. *Journal of Educational Psychology, 69*, 612–619.

Scribner, S., & Cole, M. (1973). Cognitive consequences of formal and informal education: New accommodations are needed between school-based learning and learning experiences of everyday life. *Science, 182*, 553–559.

Second Life [Digital game]. San Francisco, CA: Linden Lab.

Sigel, I. E. (1993). The centrality of a distancing model for the development of representational competence. In R. R. Cocking & K. A. Renninger (Eds.), *The development and meaning of psychological distance* (pp. 141–158). Hillsdale, NJ: Erlbaum.

Šmahel, D., & Subrahmanyam, K. (2007). Any girls want to chat press 911: Partner selection in monitored and unmonitored teen chat rooms. *Cyberpsychology & Behavior, 10*, 346–353.

Subrahmanyam, K, Garcia, E. C., Harsono, L. S., Li, J. S., & Lipana, L. (2009). In their words: Connecting online weblogs to developmental processes. *British Journal of Developmental Psychology, 27*, 219–245.

Subrahmanyam, K., & Greenfield, P. M. (1994). Effect of video game practice on spatial skills in girls and boys. *Journal of Applied Developmental Psychology 15*, 13–32.

Subrahmanyam, K., & Greenfield, P. M. (1998). Computer games for girls: What makes them play? In H. Jenkins & J. Cassell (Eds.), *From Barbie to Mortal Kombat: Gender and computer games* (pp. 46–71). Cambridge, MA: MIT Press.

Subrahmanyam, K., & Greenfield, P. (2008). Media symbol systems and cognitive processes. In S. Calvert & B. Wilson (Eds.), *The Blackwell handbook of children, media, and development* (pp. 166–187). Oxford, England: Blackwell.

Subrahmanyam, K., Greenfield, P. M., Kraut, R., & Gross, E. (2001). The impact of computer use on children's development. *Journal of Applied Developmental Psychology, 22*, 7–30.

Subrahmanyam, K., Šmahel, D., & Greenfield, P. M. (2006). Connecting developmental processes to the Internet: Identity presentation and sexual exploration in online teen chatrooms. *Developmental Psychology, 42*, 1–12.

Vygotsky, L. S. (1962). *Thought and language*. Cambridge, MA: MIT Press.

Vygotsky, L. S. (1978). *Mind in society: The development of higher psychological processes*. Cambridge, MA: Harvard University Press.

Wong, G. (2006). Educators explore "Second Life" online. *CNN*. Retrieved March 5, 2008, from http://www.cnn.com/2006/TECH/11/13/second.life.university/index.html

Wright, J. C., & Huston, A. C. (1983). A matter of form: Potentials of television for young viewers. *American Psychologist, 38*, 835–843.

Chapter 12

Doors to Another Me

Identity Construction Through Digital Game Play

Elly A. Konijn and Marije Nije Bijvank

Tell me and I will forget,
Show me and I may remember,
Involve me and I will understand. (Confucius, 450 B.C.)

Digital games are all about identity (Gee, 2007). Imagine a 15-year-old boy, who wants to impress his classmates, wants to chase that lovely girl next door, wants to be popular among his friends, and wants to acquire a well-paid job in the future. Where does he look for inspiration? Where can he find examples of how to build and maintain the right "identity" as a popular, attractive, and competent person? Very likely, nowadays, he will acquire a great deal of information through playing digital games, because today's adolescent worldwide plays games intensively (both in frequency and in duration). Therefore, although it is reasonable to expect that game play may influence developmental processes in adolescents, it is thus far an understudied area in game research. To address this, the present paper will discuss how the underlying mechanisms of contemporary digital game play make it so entertaining for adolescents to play them intensively, and therefore, why and how digital games can be used as a tool for learning and adolescent identity development. We will bring together theories from media entertainment (especially those relating to digital game play and television) and developmental psychology (especially regarding adolescence). The purpose of this chapter is to explicate underlying processes of the use of serious digital game characters as role models for the development of an adolescent's identity. We include serious games as well as entertainment games that may have "incidental" impact on learning and development. We assume that similar underlying mechanisms hold for both types of games; processes that enhance learning and development in an entertainment environment will do so in a serious game environment (cf. Ritterfeld & Weber, 2006). Finally, because male adolescents are heavy users of entertainment media (Roberts, Foehr, Rideout, & Brodie, 1999), and more specifically of digital games (Gentile, Lynch, Linder, & Walsh, 2004), the following will primarily hold for adolescent males. While Turkle (1995) believes that digital game play may cause a fragmented self, we believe that game play may help to develop a flexible, yet stable, identity. Because the adolescent developmental stage is a critical period in life, in which identity construction is a most important developmental process, identity construction through playing games could be studied and exploited in a more serious way.

Serious and Entertainment Games as Tools for Learning and Development

Playing digital games is highly popular worldwide, especially among adolescents (Durkin, 2006; Raney, Smith, & Baker, 2006; Vorderer, Bryant, Pieper, & Weber, 2006), although the average age of the digital game player has increased (the 2006 ESA report listed an average age of 33). Studies in the United States show that among 8- to 13-year-old boys the average digital game playing was 7.6 hours a week already in 1999 and the numbers are increasing rapidly (Anderson & Bushman, 2001). A study in 2003 showed that 87% of U.S. children play digital games (Walsh, Gentile, Gieske, Walsh, & Chasco, 2003). Another study (N = 600, M age = 14) showed that adolescent boys in the United States played 13 hours per week (Gentile et al., 2004).

It is clear that adolescents love to occupy their free time with playing digital games, and that games can hold their attention and concentration for a long time. In their leisure time, young people deal with many of their developmental tasks such as developing a sense of self, handling peer relations, and managing emotions (Durkin, 2006; Vorderer, Klimmt, & Kurcke, 2006). Traditionally, adolescents' engagement in media use and social pastime functioned to facilitate the establishment of social identity and group membership (Arnett, 2003; Christenson, 2003). Today, adolescents' engagement in media use most often pertains to playing entertainment games. Therefore, it is important to explore why games are so appealing, to identify what mechanisms in games may foster developmental tasks related to identity construction, and to understand how serious games can become effective tools for adolescent identity construction.

Michael and Chen define serious games as "games that do not have entertainment, enjoyment, or fun as their primary purpose" (2006, p. 21). Nevertheless, we believe that the entertainment value of serious games should not be underestimated. In addition, commercial digital games designed merely for entertainment may have a high educational potential. Most of the available serious digital games were expressly developed to teach specific skills or content, and any entertainment value is only a means to arrive at a learning experience. An example is *America's Army* (2002) developed by the U.S. Army. It is one of the first online digital games to make recruitment an explicit goal and it is among the most popular games that have an overt political aim. Critics have charged that the game serves as a propaganda device (2002). However, many players play this game merely for entertainment purposes and possibly don't even want to join the Army in real life. Yet, playing games that were primarily developed for entertainment can still impact knowledge, skills, and other learning outcomes. An example is the *Civilization* series of games, where the players learn how to think strategically, and to build a complex civilization as a statesman. Thus, it is hard to define the border between the (so-called) serious games and the entertainment games, and even more to measure the degrees to which they are fun to play and to which they are a tool for learning and development, implicitly or explicitly, to the player. Distinguishing between entertainment and educational digital games actually simplifies the understanding of what is educational (Ritterfeld & Weber, 2006). Therefore, similar mechanisms may underlie both types of games—processes that enhance learning and development in an entertainment environment will do so in a serious game environment.

Nadolski, van der Hijden, Tattersall, and Slootmaker (2006) describe a series of motives for educational use of digital games and simulations that can be of value here. Among their most important motivations are: (1) games stimulate fantasy, challenge, and stir curiosity; (2) games offer safe and cheap environments to experiment with daily-life affairs or one's dreams; (3) games provide practical and relevant contexts for learning, while creating a good fit between learning and future professions; (4) games activate learning through competition-based education in addition to active knowledge construction; and (5) games may adjust to youth culture (e.g., through the use of digital narratives). While these motivations were explicitly formulated for serious games for educational purposes, we also believe that there are other motivations that impact learning and development through playing games. Specifically, a key factor to explain adolescents' interest in playing digital games can be found in their developmental stage, in which their primary task is to develop and construct their identity. Adolescents pay close attention to and get involved in almost anything that can contribute to the construction of identities—who they are today, who they may become, and how they may add or modify their sense of self (Erikson, 1982; Meeus, Iedeman, Maassen, & Engels, 2005; Vleioras & Bosma, 2005). The interactive nature of digital games offers a unique opportunity to experiment with different identities. Furthermore, digital games simulate emotions in a form that is closer to typical real life experiences than film (Grodal, 2000).

Compared to traditional media, games provide more intense and more flexible possibilities for identity exploration. Until the introduction of digital games, adolescents were constrained to observing examples from more passive media, such as television, literature, movies, and music. With no virtual contexts in traditional media, adolescents were left to try out the various identities in real life, with real-life consequences, such as the risk of losing face, and without access to the proper material, physical, and emotional resources of their media heroes. Obviously, the virtual worlds provided by digital games present a far more attractive option for identity exploration. In virtual worlds, youngsters can freely experiment with taking on different identities and identity-related issues (Subramanyam, Greenfield, & Tynes, 2004).

Adolescents and Identity Construction

According to the well-known psychologist Erik Erikson (1968, 1982), the primary developmental task of the teen years is to form a sense of identity. In addition to increased hormonal secretions and the need to adjust to increased sexual feelings and physical growth, adolescents have to adjust to new cognitive and socio-emotional challenges at school, and to changes in their emotional and social relations with their parents and peers (Keniston, 1971; Steinberg & Morris, 2001). These readjustments can lead to conflicts and insecurities about the adolescent's sense of self or identity with the emotions being experienced.

Essentially, adolescents need to make up their minds on important issues in their lives, such as what profession to follow, in what religion to believe, or what political ideas to adopt. Identity construction is the successful resolution of the so-called identity crisis, presented in Erikson's (1982) psychosocial theory (Vleioras & Bosma, 2005). The degree to which relational and societal identity commitments develop during adolescence is important for adolescents' emotional adjustment (Meeus et al., 2005). At the end of adolescence (> 18 years of age), identity becomes less diffuse and more clearly articulated (Adams & Fitch, 1982; Erikson, 1968; Waterman, 1993). Furthermore, clarity of self-definition is associated with a low level of depression and a high level of self-esteem (Campbell, 1990; Campbell, Trapnell, Heine, Lavallee, Katz, & Lehman, 1996). Therefore, the stability of the identity construction before reaching the end of adolescence is crucial for one's life-long well-being.

The question of "who am I" is not one that teens think about at a conscious level. Instead, over the course of the adolescent years, teens begin to integrate the opinions of influential others into their own likes and dislikes. Developmental psychologists emphasize that many of the developmental and learning processes in youth are incidental and implicit (Bjorklund, 2000). Digital game play offers possibilities to experience the execution of developmental tasks without being aware of the developmental goal (Ritterfeld & Weber, 2006). The ultimate goal is to have a clear sense of their selves, having a secure identity, and know where they fit in their world (Huebner, 2000). A distinction can be made between relational and societal identity. These domains refer to two key developmental tasks in adolescence: (1) building a satisfactory relationship with peers and (2) securing an attractive occupational career and through it a good position in society (Dunkel, 2000). Marcia (1966) and Meeus et al. (2005) regard identity as the outcome of two processes: first, exploring developmental alternatives in a certain domain and, second, selecting one of these alternatives (i.e., entering into a commitment). Commitment indicates the structure and the strength of identity, while exploration refers to the process whereby identity is formed. Both the processes of exploration and commitment can benefit from playing digital games, because digital games (1) offer a wide variety of identities to explore and (2) require (temporary) commitment to the roles offered through the interactive nature of digital games.

Exploration is the way in which adolescents seek and use information (Berzonsky, 1989; Berzonsky & Neimeyer, 1994; Stephen, Fraser, & Marcia, 1993) and is therefore important for the way in which commitments are formed and maintained (Meeus et al., 2005). Adolescents experiment with different roles (Erikson, 1968; Keniston, 1971), by storing (and trying out) small components of others' personalities. Therefore, it is important for adolescents to transfer these initially compartmentalized identities into an integrated self (Josselson, 1994; Marcia, 1993; Valkenburg, Schouten, & Peter, 2005).

Turkle (1995) argues that digital game play threatens this process of developing an integrated self from compartmentalized identities: "When each player can create many characters and participate in many games, the self is not only decentered but multiplied without limit" (p. 185). She illustrates her point of fragmentation of the self with the case of a MUD-player who stated that "I'm not one thing, I'm many things" and "even though I play more than one self on MUDs, I feel more like 'myself' when I'm MUDding" (p. 185). The use of multiple personas as a means for self-exploration is making us reconsider our view of the development of the self (Turkle, 1995). Contrary to Turkle, we believe that digital games may help develop a flexible, yet stable identity, because the player is able to explore which roles may suit him or her. Therefore, the more roles an individual explores, the clearer the sense of self can become by finding out what does and does not fit with him or her. Otherwise, roles to which he or she feels attracted may remain unexplored and cause an underlying, restless sense of unfulfillment, especially in these days of continuous exposure to all kinds of possible "other me's."

In line with the identity processes of Marcia (1966) and Meeus et al. (2005), we believe that commitment to one of many alternatives will be much stronger when it occurs after thorough exploration. Instead of fragmenting, this will strengthen one's sense of identity by strengthening the level of commitment. Thus, the constructive process of creating one's own identity may begin by fully exploring possible selves, which digital games offer in a wide variety. According to Durkin (2006), we know relatively little about how salient digital game characteristics and environments are to young people exploring identity issues. Thus far, the potential that games may offer for identity development has hardly been examined and is a fruitful area for future research on digital games.

Role Modeling in Digital Games

Especially for identity exploration, adolescents are looking for role models both in the real world and, increasingly, in the mediated world, encountering many models which attract them and from which they distance themselves. The exploration phase of identity construction involves actively "trying on" different selves (Harter, 1999; Kerpelman & Pittman, 2001). Media figures play an important part in this process, because they offer a variety of distinctive and attractive possible selves that adolescents can experiment with and today's adolescents engage themselves for many hours in media offerings (Giles & Maltby, 2004; Oyserman, Bybee, Terry, & Hart-Johnson, 2004; Wood, Griffiths, Chappell, & Davies, 2004). Possible selves are defined as the representations of "individual" ideas about what they might become, what they would like to become, and what they are afraid of becoming (Markus & Nurius, 1986). Possible selves emerge out of social experiences and form a link from the past to the present to the future development of a self identity—what people strive to become in the future is important to their present self-concept (Dunkel, 2000).

Social learning theory emphasizes the importance of observing and modeling the behaviors, attitudes, and emotional reactions of others (Bandura, 1977, 2001). Small children play roles to search for who they are and how to behave, and to explore the boundaries of good and evil, an essential part of developing their own identity (Carlson & Taylor, 2005). Role modeling and imitation are some of the primary ways children try out the characteristics of media characters (McDonald & Kim, 2001). The evolutionary function of play is behavioral adaptation (Ohler & Nieding, 2006) and serves to prepare adolescents for adulthood and provides a safe setting to practice skills necessary for later life (Parker, 1984; Raney, Smith, & Baker, 2006). The appeal of role play continues throughout one's lifetime.

In 1955, Kelly introduced his fixed-role therapy, that is, the theory of personal constructs, that focused at establishing an enduring behavior change in individuals through roles and scripts with which his clients had to exercise intensively (cited in Bonarius, 1967). Individually tailored scripts were constructed to explore novel ways of acting and understanding and to promote new ways of coping with challenging behavior. This promised to be a developmentally appropriate approach for adolescents; however, Kelly's theory and practice are poorly documented (Green, 1997). Perhaps digital games, especially role-playing games, provide the right stage for Kelly's fixed-role therapy and may give game researchers a way to take a fresh look at this theory.

Digital games map onto the four themes of play identified by Pellegrini (1995). Typically, games (1) acknowledge progression—finishing levels, advancing in complexity; (2) represent power—having characteristics not possessed in the real world, using them to manipulate one's environment; (3) contain fantasy—simulation games alike; and, finally (4) involve the self—specifically an avatar or alter ego. Thus, the four themes of play connect to the learning through playing potential that games generally offer. Virtual worlds offer adolescents safe environments for exploring and experiencing developmental issues (Subrahmanyam et al., 2004) and games offer a chance to interact with media characters in many different social and affective contexts without immediate real-life consequences. Therefore, games can be seen as a private laboratory in which an adolescent can experiment safely with the uncertain status of his identity (Goldstein, 1998; Jansz, 2005; Kestenbaum & Weinstein, 1985; Lieberman, 2006).

Problematic Role Models in Digital Games

Role models offered in most digital games are rather stereotypical, emphasizing the "macho male" and "sexy female" characters (Dietz, 1998; Lee & Peng, 2006). Male role models in digital games, like traditional mass media, are generally tough and brave heroes, with (super) male-gender characteristics, such as being courageous, fast, dexterous, remorseless, competitive, destructive, and strong (Vorderer, Klimmt, & Kurcke, 2006). Therefore, attractive role models possess extremes of gender characteristics that adolescents believe they should possess themselves or characteristics that represent the highest level of a real man (or a real woman). In developing their identity, adolescent boys who take ideals of what "real men" are like from the media may use these ideals to guide their own behavior (Epstein, Kehily, Mac an Ghaill, & Redman, 2001; Greenberg, Siemicki, Dorfman, Heeter, Soderman, & Linsangan, 1986; Phoenix & Frosh, 2001). In selecting role models, adolescents will seek for the most attractive and distinctive heroes they can find. They may find deviant role models curious, exciting, or fascinating and like to experiment with them. For males, such heroes are often tough, aggressive men with guts and glory. Identifying with these "real heroes" may also help boys feel more independent and mature (Arnett, 2003; Keniston, 1971; Moffitt, 1993; Zillmann, 1998).

The achievement of autonomy also is one of the fundamental tasks of a healthy adolescence and digital games offer worlds where one has symbolic agentic autonomy (Durkin, 2006). Especially avatar-based games (e.g., massively multiplayer online role playing games; MMORPGs) offer ample opportunities to adopt, enhance, hide, and disguise identities (Chan & Vorderer, 2006). For example, gender switching is a popular activity in role playing games, which relates to the important developmental task of developing one's sense of gender. Although there is some literature about this phenomenon (e.g., Roberts & Parks, 1999), to our knowledge, no systematic studies are available yet that investigate adolescent online gender switching as a means to explore their identity.

It would be worthwhile for serious games research to explore the above implications for serious games that can contribute to adolescents' development. Further research should address what happens if games are designed in such a way that the players encounter a wide variety of highly attractive and distinct models for possible selves, not only the stereotypical models that most current games offer. Furthermore, do game characters that come with features that can be adjusted to varied personal standards for boys or girls create more nuances in available role models? For example, would a boy choose to explore being a soldier while taking on a homosexual identity? Likewise, would a girl take on the perspective of a political ambassador or a scientific engineer, while having children? How can interviewing adolescents to find out what they consider cool, distinct, and desirable features in role models and characters help designers develop more attractive prosocial role models?

Underlying Mechanisms of Digital Games' Impact on Identity Construction

The central position of role models in digital games is for the role models to serve as tools for exploring adolescent identity. We derived four underlying mechanisms that support this process. In this section, we will explicate the underlying mechanisms of the impact of playing digital games on identity development, which make playing digital games appealing to adolescents for experimenting and exploring different situations, actions, characters, and emotions. That is, (1) the opportunity to wishfully identify with role models; (2) the games' potential to master hard-to-get goals and challenges; (3) the level of immersion and presence while playing; and (4) the level of perceived realism of the virtual world and its inhabitants.

Wishful Identification (Mechanism 1)

Role play offers the possibility to experience what something would be like and can be like, and provides players with the simulation of being their ideal self. Adolescents will select models that are both similar to themselves (e.g., models that look and act like themselves), and also select models that possess qualities they do not have, but wish they did—"real heroes" they look up to (Bandura, 1986; Hoffner & Cantor, 1991; Huesmann & Eron, 1986; Oyserman et al., 2004). There is an important distinction between similarity identification and wishful identification (Von Feilitzen & Linné, 1975), concepts often studied in film and television research. In similarity identification, the observer identifies with the character because they share salient characteristics. Most identification conceptions in media effects research focus on similarity as an important underlying mechanism for attractiveness of role models. Meanwhile, the concepts of involvement, identification, and empathy are not clearly distinct from liking and are often measured as general liking of a character (Cohen, 2001; Konijn & Hoorn, 2005; Wirth, 2006; Zillmann, 1994). However, from the perspective of observing role models and exploring possible selves through media figures (i.e., from a social learning and developmental perspective), wishful identification is a more appropriate concept here. In adolescents' development, the power and charisma of heroes to be found in the media probably are more important than similarity.

In wishful identification, the observer desires to emulate the character, either in general terms (as a role model for future action or identity development) or in specific terms (extending responses beyond the viewing situation or imitating a particular behavior; Hoffner & Buchanan, 2005; Hoffner &

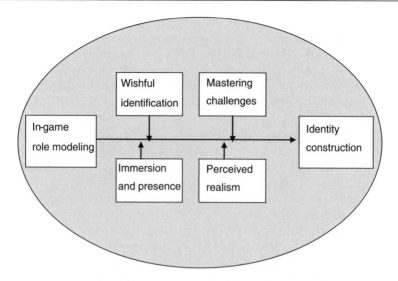

Figure 12.1 Model of the underlying mechanisms of the process of identity construction through role play in digital games. *Note.* The model should be perceived as within the broader context of learning and development in adolescent lives.

Cantor, 1991; Von Feilitzen & Linné, 1975). Because an adolescent's identity is in development, an aspired identity rather than a finished personality constellation is more logically related to the exploration of possible selves (Vorderer, Klimmt, & Kurcke, 2006). Adolescents may not seek only role models who are similar to them, as most adolescents face so many uncertainties and insecurities in life that they do not yet have a secure feeling about their own identity. Rather, they may seek role models that are dissimilar to them, yet dissimilar in certain positive ways—role models who, in their view, possess attractive features that the adolescent would like to possess for his or her own future sense of self. Wishful identification provides a glimpse of "what if," and these glimpses are powerful predictors of future behavior, especially in adolescents (Cohen, 2001). Thus, wishful identification is closer than similarity identification to the concept of vicarious learning (Bandura, 1986). In many games, the player assumes an adult role and lives and acts in a virtual adult world, obtaining confidence in being able to master such adult situations in the future in reality (Raney, Smith, & Baker, 2006).

Identifying with digital game characters may also provide (male) adolescents a way to deal with the insecurities and emotional doubts that often accompany adolescence (Piko, Keresztes, & Pluhar, 2006). Therefore, adolescent boys may be more likely to chose a digital game hero as a role model and imitate the character's behavior. For example, a recent study showed that boys who wishfully identified with the violent character expressed more aggression after playing a violent digital game than boys who did not wishfully identify with the aggressive hero (Konijn, Nije Bijvank, & Bushman, 2007). Socially unacceptable activities seem particularly appealing to low-achieving adolescents, who find it difficult to enhance self-esteem and social reputation via the conventional system (Emler & Reicher, 1995). In a similar vein, a recent study (Nije Bijvank, Konijn, & Bushman, 2007) showed that lower-educated boys were more attracted to the violence in games and reported a stronger need to wishfully identify with the games' heroes than the higher-educated boys.

However, wishful identification with characters may not only lead to negative impact, it may guide positive outcomes. If digital game players could use the prosocial messages that role models portray to guide their everyday decisions, then important benefits can be gained from these mediated models. Youth who become emotionally involved with media characters as their role models become engaged in their experiences "as if the model" and potentially transfer to their own lives what they learn from the imaginary stories (Bandura, 1986). Adolescents become motivated through affective experiences with characters, through the wish to be more like ideal selves (McDonald & Kim, 2001). Wishful identification with game heroes might therefore be considered a mechanism through which players construct their identity.

Explicating wishful identification with role models as an underlying mechanism of a role model's impact on adolescents playing digital games raises the question of how the concept of wishful identification relates to the different role-perspectives in digital games. In most contemporary digital games, players either (1) inherit a character, or (2) they get to build a character from the ground up. Some games offer a character so intriguing, strongly formed, and appealing, that players want to inhabit the character and can readily project their own fantasies, desires, and pleasures onto the character. Other games offer a relatively empty character whose traits the player must determine; for example, in *World of Warcraft* or *Second Life*. With either type of game character, players become committed to the new virtual world in which they will live, learn, and act through their commitment to their new virtual identity (Gee, 2005). In addition, there is a difference in visual portrayals of characters between different types of games. For instance, a player sees his character on the screen differently in a first-person shooter than in a third-person perspective, like in *World of Warcraft*. Because in the first-person perspective, the player actually does not see his embodied character, and because the player's view equals the character's view, one could argue that "wishing to look like this character" is not possible. However, the player can wish to act like this character or to be in the character's situation. Thus, wishful identification with the actions or situations of the game character can arouse strong feelings of "as-if it were me," even from a first-person perspective. Future studies should explore in more detail how the concepts of similarity identification and wishful identification may apply to one's ideal self and ideal others, as reflected or created in different role perspectives in interactive digital games such as in first-person shooters and in MMORPGs such as *World of Warcraft*.

Mastering Challenges (Mechanism 2)

Media heroes (role models) with whom adolescents like to identify generally encounter dangerous situations, are at risk, face insurmountable challenges, and pursue almost unattainable goals: in general, heroes face the risk of failure, yet (almost) always conquer and dare to do things most people would never dare to do in real life (Konijn, 2000). That may make them particularly attractive to adolescents, who are facing uncertainties and insecurities in their own unstable lives, and who long for such heroic glory (cf. Raney, Smith, & Baker, 2006). Therefore, such independent heroes may look attractive to adolescents, who strive for independence and maturity and can experience this feeling of being in control through the game (Moffitt, 1993; Moffitt, Caspi, Dickson, Silva, & Stanton, 1996). Games constantly offer clear and attainable goals.

When playing a digital game, players as game-heroes are confronted with difficult and challenging goals. When there is an optimal balance between risk of failure (difficulty) and the chance to attain the goals (skills), the challenges evoke the experience of flow. Csikszentmihalyi's (1990) description of activities that are most likely to create the flow state can also be explicated for digital game play, since digital games (1) frequently have concrete goals and manageable rules; (2) provide action that can be manually or automatically adjusted to our capabilities; (3) provide clear feedback in terms of running scores; and (4) have abundant visual and aural information that screens out distraction and facilitates concentration. This is related to Bandura's (1977) concept of self-efficacy, that is, the more individuals believe they are able to deal with given tasks or situations successfully, the stronger their motivations to engage in those situations and the more effort they will invest. Challenging games, therefore, confront their players with opposing forces or obstacles that can still be overcome, otherwise playing a game would not be enjoyable (Klimmt & Hartmann, 2006). In other words, to be enjoyable, games offer a carefully designed balance between challenge and mastery. So, exploring risks through heroes may increase self-efficacy.

Thus, digital games possess ideal characteristics to create and maintain flow experiences, because the flow experience of digital games is brought on when the skills of the player match the difficulty of the game (Malone & Lepper, 1987; Reid, 1997). This points at the importance of many difficulty levels and presents the player with ever-increasing goals. For example, attaining the in-game goal can be made difficult by an artificial conflict and limiting in-game rules (Salen & Zimmerman, 2003). After all, pushing yourself to new limits grabs your attention and allows new information to connect with your already existing knowledge. Furthermore, to overcome something that had seemed just too difficult at the start provides you with feelings of contentment and self-assurance. Vorderer and Hartmann (2006) argue that challenge is an important aspect for media users to maintain their basic organism's need to "stay in control." The player can stay in control by the improvement of skills through engagement and mastering challenges in the digital game environment. Fascination with digital games has also been attributed to the ability of players to control the game in terms of outcomes, progress, and mastering the game or competing with other players (Grodal, 2000; Sherry, 2004). An integral element of digital games is their goal-driven character—an element that is also acknowledged as important for learning and development processes in general. Learning goes best when win states are created—rewarding states which can be arrived at through achieving in-game goals, such as through points made, achieving the next level, or whatever goal the player has set for himself (Gee, 2007; Lieberman, 2006). In order to reach these goals, the players must recognize problems and solve them from within the game world (Gee, 2007). Achieving these goals implies that the player achieves control of the challenges provided by the game, and the player reaches a win state. Once all of the challenges within a game have been mastered, the game is conquered and the player triumphs.

Furthermore, the interactive interface of digital games enables the player to control actions by an ability to control the point of view; that is, to control the point from which, and the direction by which, the game world is represented (Grodal, 2000). Contemporary views on learning and development processes position learners as active participants, and attribute to them an important level of control over their own learning and development activities. Thus, both the contemporary learner and the digital game player are in charge of realizing their desired outcomes (Westera, 2007). Feeling in control and mastery of challenges are key issues in adolescents' development of a stable identity and should therefore be part and parcel of serious games. Specifically, when players perceive their mastery and success in terms of their own decisions and skills, adolescents will feel pride and an increase in self-esteem (Lieberman, 2006).

Immersion and Presence (Mechanism 3)

Immersion is a term widely used in the digital game industry to promote, review, and describe the gaming experience (Cheng & Cairns, 2005). Entertainment game designers put considerable effort into making digital games increasingly immersive. The implicit assumption is that getting immersed in the game world leads to greater enjoyment and more positive attitudes toward the game (Schneider, Lang, Shin, & Bradley, 2004). Digital games also allow the player to become deeply involved in the game as an experiential space. In a digital game the attributes of the game create the illusion that the player is actually within the space. The degree to which the player feels integrated with the game space is a measure of her or his sense of immersion (Taylor, 2002). Immersion ultimately may lead to a state of presence—the feeling of being "there" while physically in another space (Biocca, Kim, & Levy, 1995; Lombard & Ditton, 1997; Witmer & Singer, 1998).

The difference between immersion and presence is not always easy to discern in how they are used by various scholars. Immersion is defined by Coomans and Timmermans (1997) as an experience, a feeling of being deeply engaged in a make-believe world as if it is real. However, other definitions also exist that focus more on the technical side of the interaction, such as an emotional response presented by a virtual world (Menetta & Blade, 1998) or the ability to enter a game through its controls (Radford, 2000). In defining presence, Slater (1999; see also Slater, Usoh, & Steed, 1994; Slater & Wilbur, 1997) distinguishes presence from the concept of immersion. He describes immersion as an objective description of the technology: "the extent to which the computer displays are capable of delivering an...illusion of reality to the senses of a human participant" (Slater & Wilbur, 1997, p. 604–616). Slater sees immersion as objectively quantifiable, whereas presence (or, more precisely, the sense of presence) is a subjective experience and only quantifiable by the user experiencing it. Lombard and Ditton (1997) suggest that presence is the perceptual illusion of nonmediation. Technological factors (e.g., screen size, image quality, and sound) all contribute to this sense of presence. According to Laurel (1993) and Schneider, Lang, Shin, and Bradley (2004) the correct use of a story line should further help to ease players into a game and make them feel more like they are actually part of the environment.

In sum, researchers seem to agree that presence is the sense of being there when it relates to the digital game experience (Tamborini & Skalski, 2006), but there are at least three discernable dimensions of presence: (1) spatial presence—a sense of being physically located in a virtual environment (Ijsselsteijn, de Ridder, Freeman, Bouwhuis, & Avons, 1998); (2) social presence—the experience of virtual social actors as though they are actual social actors (Lee, 2004); and (3) self-presence—to experience the virtual self as if it were their actual self (Lee, 2004). In view of the above discussion of adolescents' identity construction, the latter element of self-presence, seems most relevant. Social presence might also contribute to being able to identify role models from game characters.

Biocca's (1997) definition of self-presence identifies three bodies that are present in a virtual world: the actual body, the virtual body, and the body schema; that is, the user's mental model of the self. He argued that when we see a graphic representation of ourselves within a virtual environment, the representation evokes mental models of our body as well as our identity. Parallels can be drawn with stage or screen acting, where similar identified bodies are defined: (1) the actual actor as a craftsman (the professional) (cf. actual body); (2) the performed character (cf. virtual body); and (3) the "inner model" (cf. body schema) (Konijn, 1995, 2000). In former days, before digital games existed, playing theater roles provided a popular outlet and exploration stage for identity development. Therefore, it would be an interesting endeavor for theory building and research to compare taking on a character in stage acting with taking on a role in playing games.

Digital games provide the player with an experience of being totally immersed in a virtual reality (Grodal, 2000) and an immersive environment may be very helpful in adolescents' identity development because it helps youths to concentrate and focus on the task at hand for long periods of time. Designers often focus on maximizing realism in images in virtual reality environments, including digital games, in order to enhance immersion and presence (Hoorn, Konijn, & Van der Veer, 2003). Recent technical developments in digital game production have made digital games increasingly lifelike and realistic (Carnagey & Anderson, 2004). For example, sensory input and feedback introduces real sound, real feel, and real touch into game play and future technological advances may continue this trend, which may ultimately affect our mental models, our social interactions, and even our self-perceptions (Tamborini & Skalski, 2006).

The immersive nature of digital games, therefore, provides an excellent learning environment because learning through experience is more effective than passive learning (Gee, 2007). The intrinsic captivating power may increase the educational potential of games. Games demand active involvement, and they also provide a wide arrange of occasions to respond to constantly changing conditions. Because of the player's embodied experience of the immediate effects of their in-game actions, playing digital games is a form of personalized learning by doing "pur sang" (Westera, 2007). Thus, immersion and the feeling of presence only add to digital games' potential as a learning and developmental tool.

Perceived Realism (Mechanism 4)

Players rate realistic digital games more favorably than unrealistic ones (Griffiths & Hunt, 1995; Wood, Griffiths, Chappell, & Davies, 2004). Expanding findings in television viewers to digital games, it seems that games may influence players' real-world knowledge structures the more they perceive realism in them (cf. Busselle & Greenberg, 2000; Potter & Tomasello, 2003; Shapiro & Chock, 2003). Perceived realism is defined as the subjective viewer interpretation of the extent to which media content contains a reflection of daily life reality (including events, characters, behavior, stories, etc.), irrespective of the program makers' intentions (Konijn, Walma van der Molen, & Van Nes, in press). In other words, it reflects how representative of real-life affairs a particular (segment of a) digital game is considered by its players. Several unpublished exploratory interviews with adolescent boys indicated that, on the one hand, they considered it extremely important that a game is realistic (e.g., "I don't play a game if it's fake, it has to be real") while on the other hand, they claim to know that it is fiction (e.g., "Of course, I know the difference between real life and life in the game"; expressed during debriefing in the study of Konijn, Nije Bijvank, & Bushman, 2007). Although various studies already pointed to the complexity of perceived realism as a construct (e.g., Busselle & Greenberg, 2000; Shapiro, Peña-Herborn, & Hancock, 2006), the concept seems to be even more complex in game environments. A more flexible, multidimensional or multileveled notion of perceived realism seems indicated (Bailenson, Yee, Merget, & Schroeder, 2006; Rothmund, Schreier, & Groeben, 2001). For example, the perception of realism in audiovisual contents may pertain to any of the following: to the program at a global level, to the program at a more specific level, to its literal contents, to the story line (narrative realism), to the images conveyed (graphic realism), to the depicted people (character realism), to the depicted places, and situations (situational realism) or even to the behaviors (behavioral realism), as well as to the psychological realism. Furthermore, in game environments, perceived realism also coincides with the properties of the medium, hardware features such as the interface, formal features such as the game mechanics, and instrumental editing techniques such as point of view. From various perspectives, perceived realism appears to be an elusive variable whose contribution to the effects of digital game play should be further studied.

Contemporary adolescents grew up with media (including digital games) and might therefore have a different conception of perceived realism of media than today's older persons (as most researchers are). The idea that younger respondents perceive media content differently than older people is consistent with Potter's (1992) conclusion that the magic window conception of television is stronger for younger individuals than for more mature ones. Likewise, younger people may be more prone to source-confusion (Mares, 1996) than grown-ups (cf. Rössler & Brosius, 2001). Also, younger people may pay less attention to, ignore, or attend in a different way to the program features that reveal the fiction-status than older viewers do. For example, in assessing the reality-fiction status of a program, younger viewers may weigh specific program cues, for example, emotion-evoking cues, more heavily than program labeling. Furthermore, in judging the perceived realism of a program, younger individuals may let themselves be guided more strongly by their emotional responses while viewing than do older individuals (Konijn, Walma van der Molen, Van Nes, in press; Walma van der Molen & Konijn, 2007). Future games research may systematically study what adolescents mean when they judge certain (features of) media as more or less realistic.

Because of the hybrid status of most current audiovisual media productions, including digital games, people will need to make ever more sophisticated reality judgments to understand what information can be derived from it. Given adolescents' increased dependency on media information, it is increasingly important to understand how they interpret the level of realism in media content (cf. Konijn, 2008; Lea & Spears, 1995; Rothmund, Schreier, & Groeben, 2001; Shapiro & Lang, 1991; Shapiro, Peña-Herborn, & Hancock, 2006). The few studies that have been conducted among adolescents reveal that today's adolescents find it rather difficult to judge the perceived realism of media content; for example, pornography on the Internet (Peter & Valkenburg, 2006).

Nevertheless, if a game was judged realistic by the male adolescent players, the players identified more with game characters (Konijn et al., 2007). Therefore, we have reason to believe that perceived realism plays an important role and adds to potential effects for learning and development in adolescents playing digital games.

In sum, a higher level of perceived realism in a digital game, such as its graphical representation of environments, experiences, and actions, makes it more attractive to adolescents. To take the presented possible selves seriously as their future ideals, adolescents must somehow attribute realism to the game characters—either in outer appearances, situations, acts, professional outlook, peer relationships, or whatever relevant aspect, they should somehow be realistic. Even fictional portrayals may contain a good deal of realism when it comes to the information provided (cf. Hoorn et al., 2003; Konijn & Hoorn, 2005). Therefore, the level of perceived realism serves as one of the underlying mechanisms of the impact of digital game play on identity development through role modeling.

Conclusion

In 1938, John Dewey stated that "…there is an intimate and necessary relation between the processes of actual experience and education" (pp. 19–20). In this chapter, we argued that digital games may come close to the actual experience through role play and capture players through identity construction issues (cf. Gee, 2007). Digital games have a lot of potential to support the developmental task of adolescent identity construction. Adolescents get easily absorbed in anything that can contribute to the construction of their own identity, because this is such a central task in their lives. We explicated four underlying mechanisms of the appeal and impact of playing digital games: wishful identification, immersion and presence, mastery of challenges, and perceived realism.

The underlying mechanisms that we defined to support the process of identity construction as a function of role modeling are graphically represented in Figure 12.1. The model shows how adolescents may use digital games in the process of identity construction through role play as part of the broader process of learning and development in adolescent's lives. Wishfully identifying with digital game characters, increased immersion and feelings of presence in the game environment, mastery of challenges offered by the game's difficulty levels, and a certain degree of perceived realism of digital game play all contribute to the game's potential as a tool for learning and development. Wishful identification, immersion and presence, mastery of challenges, and perceived realism are considered moderators in the broader process of learning and development. Future research should test the viability of this model. The process of identity construction through role modeling in digital games may play a key role in achieving broader educational and developmental goals of serious games in adolescents.

While we believe that the underlying processes may likewise hold for girls, the emphasis in the present chapter was on adolescent males because they are mostly studied, thus far. Generally, as is also known from television and film research, most attractive media models are male and males generally occupy most interesting parts. Furthermore, many media models are fairly stereotypical and conform to simplified societal roles. Therefore, digital games may provide nice opportunities for research to study various role models; for example, by systematically varying specifics of the game characters from the angle of adolescents' identity construction.

Based on the existing literature on adolescents' identity development and entertainment games, we argued that serious games could focus on providing a variety of attractive, distinct, and flexible role models with which adolescents can freely experiment and that can be easily adjusted to their own tastes. Role variety and exploration in gaming may promote more stable development of identity later on. The exploration of possible selves is greatly enhanced if the game offers role models with whom adolescents wish to identify. Obviously, the need for role models in serious games may vary with the goals and the emphasis of the game. Researchers may study whether the need for role models is less or different in serious games that focus primarily on exercising specific skills such as grammar, organic chemistry, or statistics. Offering a variety of modifiable role models however allows the player to create a personalized learning environment, which is very powerful.

Empirical tests are needed to establish to what extent playing various roles supports a stable identity construction or rather leaves the adolescent with a split self, a fragmented conception of one's identity (cf. Turkle, 1995). Related, playing heroic roles in virtual lives may enhance self-esteem, which may extend to daily life. Furthermore, it should be studied to what extent short-term effects of in-game role modeling may affect long-term developmental identity formation. To know what kind of characters may serve developmental purposes in serious games, researchers and designers may look around at adolescents' profile sites, serve lists, but also conduct research with adolescents to learn what is most appealing to them and to get to know their heroes. However, in doing so, one should be aware that such sites may be dominated by a selective subculture; it might be helpful to also design alternatives to the dominant views given essentially appealing details. Furthermore, such information should be carefully balanced with the educational and developmental goals specified. Such complicated processes should be dealt with in a more detailed and empirical manner in future research.

In all, we have provided arguments to support our notion that digital games offer ample opportunities for learning and development, especially to support the developmental task of adolescent identity construction. We have outlined four underlying mechanisms that may support this process. On the way, we encountered many bare fields for future game researchers to explore. While many theoretical building blocks have already been outlined, now it is time to systematically and empirically pursue studies to support theoretical notions.

Acknowledgments

This study was funded by a grant from the Faculty of Social Sciences at the VU University Amsterdam. Correspondence should be addressed to Dr. Elly A. Konijn or Drs. Marije Nije Bijvank, Department of Communication Sciences, VU University Amsterdam, Metropolitan Building, De Boelelaan 1081, 1081 HV Amsterdam – NL. Electronic mail may be sent to ea.konijn@fsw.vu.nl

References

America's army—Operations. (2002). [Digital game]. U.S. Army. Retrieved March 23, 2008, from http://www.americasarmy.com/

Adams, G., & Fitch, S. (1982). Ego stage and identity status development, a cross-sequential analysis. *Journal of Personality and Social Psychology, 43,* 574–583.

Anderson, C. A., & Bushman, B. J. (2001). Effects of violent video games on aggressive behavior, aggressive cognition, aggressive affect, physiological arousal, and prosocial behavior: A meta-analytic review of the scientific literature. *Psychological Science, 12,* 353–359.

Arnett, J. J. (2003). Conceptions of the transition to adulthood among emerging adults in American ethnic groups. In J. J. Arnett & N. L. Galambos (Eds.), *New directions for child and adolescent development: Exploring cultural conceptions of the transition to adulthood.* San Francisco: Jossey-Bass.

Bailenson, J. N., Yee, N., Merget, D., & Schroeder, R. (2006). The effect of behavioral realism and form realism of real-time avatar faces on verbal disclosure, nonverbal disclosure, emotion recognition, and copresence in dyadic interaction. *Presence: Teleoperators and Virtual Environments, 15*(4), 359–372.

Bandura, A. (1977). Self-efficacy: Toward a unifying theory of behavioral change. *Psychological Review, 84,* 191–215.

Bandura, A. (1986). The social learning perspective: Mechanisms of aggression. In H. Toch, (Ed.), *Psychology of crime and criminal justice* (pp. 198–236). Prospect Heights, IL: Waveland Press.

Bandura, A. (2001). Social cognitive theory of mass communications. *Media Psychology, 3,* 265–299.

Berzonsky, M. (1989). Identity style: Conceptualization and measurement. *Journal of Adolescent Research, 4,* 267–281.

Berzonsky, M., & Neimeyer, G. (1994). Ego identity status and identity processing orientation the moderating role of commitment. *Journal of Research in Personality, 28,* 425–435.

Biocca, F. (1997). The cyborg's dilemma: Progressive embodiment in virtual environments. *Journal of Computer-Mediated Communication, 3*(2). Retrieved from http://www.ascusc.org/jcmc/vol3/issue2/biocca2.html

Biocca, F., Kim, T., & Levy, M. (1995). The vision of virtual reality. In F. Biocca & M. Levy (Eds.), *Communication in the age of virtual reality* (pp. 3–14). Hillsdale, NJ: Erlbaum.

Bjorklund, D. F. (2000). *Children's thinking: Developmental function and individual differences* (3rd ed.). Belmont, CA: Wadsworth.

Bonarius, J. C. (1967). The fixed role therapy of George A. Kelly. *Nederlands Tijdschrift voor de Psychologie [Dutch Journal for Psychology], 22*(8), 482–520.

Busselle, R. W., & Greenberg, B. S. (2000). The nature of television realism judgments: A re-evaluation of their conceptualization and measurement. *Mass Communication and Society, 3,* 249–268.

Brosius, H. (1993). The effects of emotional pictures in television news. *Communication Research, 20,* 105–124.

Campbell, J. (1990). Self-esteem and the clarity of the self-concept. *Journal of Personality and Social Psychology, 59,* 538–549.

Campbell, J., Trapnell, S., Heine, L., Lavallee, R., Katz, I., & Lehman, D. (1996). Self-concept clarity measurement, personality correlates, and cultural boundaries. *Journal of Personality and Social Psychology, 70,* 141–156.

Carnagey, N. L., & Anderson, C. A. (2004). Violent video game exposure and aggression: A literature review. *Minerva Psichiatrica, 45,* 1–18.

Chan, E., & Vorderer, P. (2006). Massively multiplayer online games. In P. Vorderer & J. Bryant (Eds.), *Playing computer games: Motives, responses, and consequences* (pp. 77–88). Mahwah, NJ: Erlbaum.

Carlson, S. M., & Taylor, M. (2005). Imaginary companions and impersonated characters: Sex differences in children's fantasy play. *Merrill-Palmer Quarterly, 51,* 93–118.

Cheng, K., & Cairns, P. (2005). Behaviour, realism and immersion in games. Paper presented at ACM Conference on Human Factors in Computing Systems. *CHI 2005,* 1272–1275.

Christenson, P. G. (2003). Equipment for living: How popular music fits in the lives of youth. In D. Ravitch & J. P. Viteritti (Eds.), *Kid stuff: Marketing sex and violence to America's children* (pp. 196–124). Baltimore: Johns Hopkins University Press.

Civilization. [Digital game]. (2001). New York: Infogames.

Cohen, J. (2001). Defining identification: A theoretical look at the identification of audiences with media characters. *Mass Communication and Society, 4*(3), 245–264.

Coomans, M. K. D., & Timmermanns, H. J. P. (1997). Towards a taxonomy of virtual reality user interfaces. *Proceedings of the International Conference on Information Visualisation (IV97), London, UK* (pp. 27–29).

Csikszentmihalyi, M. (1990). *Flow.* New York: Harper & Row.

Dietz, T. L. (1998). An examination of violence and gender role portrayals in video games: Implications for gender socialization and aggressive behavior. *Sex Roles, 38,* 425–442.

Dunkel, C. S. (2000). Possible selves as a mechanism for identity exploration. *Journal of Adolescence, 23,* 519–529.

Durkin, K. (2006). Game playing and adolescents' development. In P. Vorderer & J.

Bryant (Eds.), *Playing computer games: Motives, responses, and consequences* (pp. 165–179). Mahwah, NJ: Erlbaum.

Emler, N., & Reicher, S. (1995). Adolescence and delinquency: The collective management of reputation. Oxbehaviour: A multiyear, multischool study. *American Educational Research Journal, 30*(1), 179–215.

Erikson, E. H. (1968). *Identity, youth and crisis.* New York: Norton.

Erikson, E. H. (1982). *The life cycle completed.* New York: Norton.

Epstein, D., Kehily, M., Mac an Ghaill, M., & Redman, P. (2001). Boys and girls come out to play: Making masculinities and femininities in school playgrounds. *Men and Masculinities, 4,* 158–172.

Gee, J. P. (2005). Learning by design: good video games as learning machines. *E learning, 2,* 5–16.

Gee, J. P. (2007). *Good video games and good learning: Collected essays on video games, learning and literacy.* New York: Lang.

Gentile, D. A., Lynch, P. J., Linder, J. R., & Walsh, D. A. (2004). The effects of violent video game habits on adolescent aggressive attitudes and behaviors. *Journal of Adolescence, 27,* 5–22.

Giles, D. C., & Maltby, J. (2004). The role of media figures in adolescent development: relations between autonomy, attachment, and interest in celebrities. *Personality and Individual Differences, 36,* 813–822.

Goldstein, J. (1998). Children and advertising: The research. *Commercial Communications, 7,* 4–7.

Green, D. (1997). An experiment in fixed-role therapy. *Clinical Child Psychology and Psychiatry, 2*(4), 553–564.

Greenberg, B., Siemicki, M., Dorfman, S., Heeter, C., Soderman, A., & Linsangan, R. (1986). *Sex content in R-rated films viewed by adolescents.* (Project CAST Report No. 3). East Lansing: Michigan State University.

Griffiths M. D., & Hunt, N. (1995). Computer game playing in adolescence, prevalence and demographic indicators. *Journal of Community and Applied Social Psychology, 5,* 189–193.

Grodal, T. (2000). Video games and the pleasures of control. In D. Zillmann & P. Vorderer (Eds.), *Media entertainment* (pp. 197–212). Mahwah, NJ: Erlbaum.

Harter, S. (1999). *The construction of the self: A developmental perspective.* New York: Guilford Press.

Hoffner, C., & Buchanan, M. (2005). Young adult's wishful identification with television characters: The role of perceived similarity and character attributes. *Media Psychology, 7,* 325–351.

Hoffner, C., & Cantor, J. (1991). Perceiving and responding to mass media characters. In Bryant, J. & Zillmann, D. (Eds.), *Responding to the screen: Reception and reaction processes* (pp. 63–101). Hillsdale, N.J.: Erlbaum.

Hoorn, J. F., Konijn, E. A., & Van der Veer, G. (2003). Virtual reality: Do not augment realism, augment relevance. *Upgrade: Human-Computer Interaction, 4*(1), 18–26. http://www.upgrade-cepis.org/issues/2003/1/upgrade-vIV-1.html

Huebner, A. (2000). Adolescent growth and development. http://www.ext.vt.edu/pubs/family/350-850/350-850.html

Huesmann, L. R., & Eron, L. D. (1986). *Television and the aggressive child: A cross-national comparison.* Hillsdale, NJ: Erlbaum.

IJsselsteijn, W. A., de Ridder, H., Hamberg, R., Bouwhuis, D., & Freeman, J. (1998). Perceived depth and the feeling of presence in 3DTV. *Displays, 18,* 207–214.

Jansz, J. (2005). The emotional appeal of violent video games for adolescent males. *Communication Theory, 15*(3), 219–241.

Josselson, R. (1994). Identity and relatedness in the life cycle. In H. A. Bosma, T. L. G. Graafsma, H. D. Grotevant, & D. J. de Levita (Eds.), *Identity and development: An interdisciplinary approach* (pp. 81–102). Thousand Oaks, CA: Sage.

Keniston, K. (1971). *Youth and dissent: The rise of a new opposition.* New York: Harcourt Brace Jovanovich.

Kerpelman, J. L., & Pittman, J. F. (2001). The instability of possible selves: Identity processes within late adolescents' close peer relationships. *Journal of Adolescence, 24,* 491–512.

Kestenbaum, G. I., & Weinstein, L. (1985). Personality, psychopathology, and developmental issues in male adolescent video game use. *Journal of the American Academy of Child Psychiatry, 24,* 325–337.

Klimmt C., & Hartmann, T. (2006) Effectance, self-efficacy, and the motivation to play video games. In P. Vorderer & J. Bryant (Eds.), *Playing video games: motives, responses, and consequences* (pp. 133–145). Mahwah, NJ: Erlbaum.

Konijn, E. A. (1995). Actors and emotions; a psychological analysis. *Theatre Research International, 20*(2), 132–140.

Konijn, E. A. (2000). *Acting emotions. Shaping emotions on stage.* Amsterdam, The Netherlands: Amsterdam University Press.

Konijn, E. A. (2008). Affects and media exposure. In W. Donsbach (Ed.), *The international encyclopedia of communication* (Vol. 7, pp. 123–129). Oxford, England: Blackwell.

Konijn, E. A., & Hoorn, J. F. (2005). Some like it bad. Testing a model on perceiving and experiencing fictional characters. *Media Psychology, 7*(2), 107–144.

Konijn, E. A., Nije Bijvank, M., & Bushman, B. J. (2007). I wish I were a warrior: The role of wishful identification in the effects of violent video games on aggression in adolescent boys. *Developmental Psychology, 43,* 1038–1044.

Konijn, E. A., Walma van der Molen, J. H., & Van Nes, S. (in press). Emotions bias perceived realism of audiovisual media. Why we may take fiction for real. *Discourse Processes.*

Laurel, B. (1993). *Computers as theatre.* Reading, MA: Addison-Wesley.

Lea, M., & Spears, R. (1995). Love at first byte? Building personal relationships over computer networks. In J. T. Wood & S. Duck (Eds.), *Understudied relationships: Off the beaten track* (pp. 197–233). Newbury Park, CA: Sage.

Lee, K. M. (2004). Why presence occurs: Evolutionary psychology, media equation, and presence. *Presence: Teleoperators and Virtual Environments, 13,* 494–505.

Lee, K. M., & Peng, W. (2006). What do we know about social and psychological effects of computer games? A comprehensive review of the current literature. In P. Vorderer & J. Bryant (Eds.), *Playing video games: Motives, responses, and consequences* (pp. 101–115). Mahwah, NJ: Erlbaum.

Lieberman, D. A. (2006). What can we learn from playing interactive games? In P. Vorderer & J. Bryant (Eds.), *Playing video games: Motives, responses, and consequences* (pp. 379–399). Mahwah, NJ: Erlbaum.

Lombard, M., & Ditton, T. B. (1997). At the heart of it all: The concept of presence. *Journal of Computer-Mediated Communication, 13*(3).

Malone, T. W., & Lepper, M. R. (1987). Making learning fun: A taxonomy of intrinsic motivations for learning. In R. E. Snow & M. J. Farr (Eds.), *Aptitude, learning and instruction: Vol. 3. Connative and affective process analyses* (pp. 223–253). Hillsdale, NJ: Erlbaum.

Marcia, J. E. (1966). Development and validation of ego identity status. *Journal of Personality and Social Psychology, 3,* 551–558.

Marcia, J. E. (1993). The ego identity status approach to ego identity In J. Marcia, A. Waterman, D. Matteson, S. Archer, & J. Orlofsky (Eds.), *Ego identity* (pp. 3–21). New York: Springer Verlag.

Mares, M. L. (1996). The role of source confusions in television's cultivation of social reality judgments. *Human Communication Research, 23*(2), 278–297.

Markus, H., & Nurius, P. (1986). Possible selves. *American Psychologist, 41,* 954–969.

McDonald, D. G., & Kim, H. (2001). When I die, I feel small: Electronic game characters and the social self. *Journal of Broadcasting & Electronic Media. 45*(2), 241–258.

Meeus, W., Iedema, J., Maassen, G., & Engels, R. (2005). Separation-individuation revisited: on the interplay of parent–adolescent relations, identity and emotional adjustment in adolescence. *Journal of Adolescence, 28*(1), 89–106.

Menetta, C., & Blade, R. A. (1998). Glossary of virtual reality terminology. *International Journal of Virtual Reality.* http://ijvr.uccs.edu/manetta.htm

Michael, D., & Chen, S. (2006) *Serious games: Games that educate, train, and inform.* Boston, MA: Thomson Course Technology.

Moffitt, T. E. (1993). Adolescence-limited and life-course persistent antisocial behavior: A developmental taxonomy. *Psychological Review, 100,* 674–701.

Moffitt, T. E., Caspi, A., Dickson, N., Silva, P., & Stanton, W. (1996). Childhood-onset versus adolescent-onset antisocial conduct problems in males: Natural history from ages 3 to 18 years. *Development and Psychopathology, 8,* 399–424.

Nadolski, R., Van der Hijden, P., Tattersall, C., & Slootmaker, A. (2006) *Multiuser online serious games: Beleid, ontwerp en gebruik.* Utrecht: Stichting Digitale Universiteit.

Nije Bijvank, M., Konijn, E. A., & Bushman, B.J. (2007, May). *Bridging the video game gap: Relating games, players, and their motivations.* Paper Presented at the International Communication Association (ICA), San Francisco, CA.

Ohler, P., & Nieding, G. (2006). Why play? An evolutionary perspective. In P. Vorderer & J. Bryant (Eds.), *Playing video games: Motives, responses, and consequences* (pp. 101–115). Mahwah, NJ: Erlbaum.

Oyserman, D., Bybee, D., Terry, K., & Hart-Johnson, T. (2004). Possible selves as roadmaps. *Journal of Research in Personality, 38*(2), 130–149.

Parker, S. T. (1984). Playing for keeps. An evolutionary perspective on human games. In P. K. Smith (Ed.), *Play in animals and humans* (pp. 271–293). Oxford, England: Blackwell.

Pellegrini, A. D. (Ed.). (1995). *The future of play theory: A multidisciplinary inquiry into the contributions of Brian Sutton-Smith.* Albany, NY: State University of New York Press.

Peter, J., & Valkenburg, P. M. (2006). Adolescents' exposure to sexually explicit material on the Internet. *Communication Research, 33,* 178–204.

Phoenix, A., & Frosh, S. (2001). Positioned by "Hegemonic" masculinities: A study of London boys' narratives of identity. *Australian Psychologist, 36,* 27–35.

Piko, B. F., Keresztes, N., & Pluhar, Z. F. (2006). Aggressive behavior and psychosocial health among children. *Personality and Individual Differences, 40*, 885–895.

Potter, W. J. (1992). How do adolescents' perceptions of television reality change over time? *Journalism Quarterly, 69*, 392–405.

Potter, W. J., & Tomasello, T. K. (2003). Building upon the experimental design in media violence research: The importance of including receiver interpretations. *Journal of Communication, 53*, 315–329.

Radford, A. (2000). Games and learning about form in architecture. *Automation in Construction, 9*, 379–385.

Raney, A. A., Smith, J., & Baker, K. (2006). Adolescents and the appeal of video games. In P. Vorderer & J. Bryant (Eds.), *Playing computer games: Motives, responses, and consequences* (pp. 165–179), Mahwah, NJ: Erlbaum.

Reid, E. R. (1997). *Teaching literal and inferential comprehension.* Salt Lake City, UT: Cove.

Ritterfeld, U., & Weber, R. (2006). Video games for entertainment and education. In P. Vorderer & J. Bryant (Eds.), *Playing computer games: Motives, responses, and consequences* (pp. 399–415). Mahwah, NJ: Erlbaum.

Roberts, D. F., Föhr, U. G., Rideout, V. J., & Brodie, M. (1999). *Kids and media at the new millennium: A comprehensive national analysis of children's media use* (A Kaiser Family Foundation Report). Menlo Park, CA: Kaiser Family Foundation.

Roberts, L. D., & Parks, M. R. (1999). The social geography of gender-switching in virtual environments on the Internet. *Information, Communication & Society, 2*(4), 521–540.

Rössler, P., & Brosius, H.-B. (2001). Do talk shows cultivate adolescents' views of the world? A prolonged-exposure experiment. *Journal of Communication, 51*, 143–163.

Rothmund, J., Schreier, M., & Groeben, N. (2001). Fernsehen und erlebte Wiklichkeit II: Ein integratives Modell zu Realitäts-Fiktions-Unterscheidungen bei der (kompetenten) Mediennutzung [Television and perceived reality II: An integrative model on reality-fictionality-distinction in (literate) media usage]. *Zeitschrift für Medienpsychologie, 13*(2), 85–95.

Salen, K., & Zimmerman, E. (2003). *Rules of play: Game design fundamentals.* Cambridge, MA: MIT Press.

Schneider, E. F., Lang, A., Shin, M., & Bradley, S. D. (2004). Death with a story: How story impacts emotional, motivational, and physiological responses to first-person shooter video games. *Human Communication Research, 30*, 361–375.

Shapiro, M. A., & Chock, T. M. (2003). Psychological processes in perceiving reality. *Media Psychology, 5*, 163–198.

Shapiro, M. A., & Lang, A. (1991). Making television reality. *Communication Research, 18*, 685–706.

Shapiro, M. A., Peña-Herborn, J., & Hancock, J. T. (2006). Realism, imagination, and narrative video games. In P. Vorderer & J. Bryant (Eds.), *Playing computer games: Motives, responses, and consequences* (pp. 275–291). Mahwah, NJ: Erlbaum.

Slater, M. (1999). Measuring presence: A response to the Witmer and Singer presence questionnaire. *Presence: Teleoperators and Virtual Environments, 8*(5), 560–565.

Slater, M., Usoh, M., & Steed, A. (1994). Depth of presence in virtual environments. *Presence, Teleoperators and Virtual Environments, 3*(2), 130–140.

Slater, M., & Wilbur, S. (1997). A framework for immersive virtual environments

(FIVE): Speculations on the role of presence in virtual environments. *Presence: Teleoperators and Virtual Environments* 6, 603–616.

Steinberg, L., & Morris, A. S. (2001). Adolescent development. *Annual Review of Psychology, 52*, 83–110.

Stephen, J., Fraser, E., & Marcia, J. E. (1993). Moratorium-achievement (Mama) cycles in lifespan identity development value orientations and reasoning system correlates, *Journal of Adolescence, 15*, 283–300.

Subramanyam, K., Greenfield, P. M., & Tynes, B. (2004). Constructing sexuality and identity in an online teen chat room. *Applied Developmental Psychology, 25*, 651–666.

Tamborini, R., & Skalski, P. (2006). The role of presence in the experience of electronic games. In P. Vorderer & J. Bryant (Eds.), *Playing video games: Motives, responses, and consequences* (pp. 225–241). Mahwah, NJ: Erlbaum.

Taylor, L. N. (2002). *Video games: Perspective, point-of-view, and immersion.* Unpublished master's thesis, University of Florida, Gainesville.

Turkle, S. (1995). *Life on the screen.* New York: Simon & Schuster.

Valkenburg, P. M., Schouten, A. P., & Peter, J. (2005). Adolescents' identity experiments on the internet. *New Media & Society, 7*(3), 383–402.

Vleioras, G., & Bosma, H. A. (2005). Are identity styles important for psychological well-being? *Journal of Adolescence, 28*, 397–409.

Von Feilitzen, C., & Linné, O. (1975). Identifying with television characters. *Journal of Communication, 25*, 51–55.

Vorderer, P., Bryant, J., Pieper, K. M., & Weber, R. (2006). Playing video games as entertainment. In P. Vorderer & J. Bryant (Eds.), *Playing computer games: Motives, responses, and consequences* (pp. 1–9). Mahwah, NJ: Erlbaum.

Vorderer, P., & Hartman, T. (2006, May). *On the nature of media entertainment: An integrative account.* Paper presented at the annual meeting of the International Communication Association, Dresden International Congress Centre, Dresden, Germany.

Vorderer, P., Klimmt, C., & Kurcke, T. (2006, May). *Why is virtual fighting fun? Motivational predictors of exposure to violent video games.* Paper presented at the annual meeting of the International Communication Association, Dresden International Congress Centre, Dresden, Germany.

Walma van der Molen, J. H., & Konijn, E. A. (2007). Dutch children's emotional reactions to news about the second Gulf war: Influence of media exposure, identification, and empathy. In D. Lemish & M. Götz (Eds.), *Children, media, and war: The case of the Iraq war* (pp. 75–97). Cresskill, NJ: Hampton Press.

Walsh, D. A., Gentile, D. A., Gieske, J., Walsh, M., & Chasco, E. (2003). *The eighth annual MediaWise video game report card.* Minneapolis, MN: National Institute on Media and the Family.

Waterman, A. S. (1993). Developmental perspectives on identity formation from adolescence to adulthood. In J. Marcia, A. Waterman, D. Matteson, S. Archer, & J. Orlofsky (Eds.), *Ego identity* (pp. 42–68), New York: Springer.

Westera, W. (2007, January, 26). Games en simulaties in het onderwijs: Hype of voorbode? [Games and simulations in education: Hype or predecessor?] In P. Fisser (Ed.), *Compendium Media Nu Symposium.* Universiteit Twente, Enschede, The Netherlands.

Wirth, W. (2006). Involvement. In P. Vorderer & J. Bryant (Eds.), *The psychology of media entertainment*. Mahwah, NJ: Erlbaum.

Witmer, B. G., & Singer, M. G. (1998). Measuring presence in virtual environments: A presence questionnaire. *Presence: Teleoperators & Virtual Environments, 7*(3), 225–240.

Wood, R. T. A., Griffiths, M. D., Chappell, D., & Davies, M. N. O. (2004). The structural characteristics of video games: A psycho-structural analysis. *CyberPsychology & Behavior, 7*, 1–10.

World of WarCraft [Digital game]. Irvine, CA: Blizzard Entertainment.

Zillmann, D. (1994). Mechanisms of emotional involvement with drama. *Poetics, 23*(1), 33–51.

Zillmann, D. (1998). The psychology of the appeal of portrayals of violence. In J. H. Goldstein (Ed.), *Why we watch: The attractions of violent entertainment* (pp. 179–211). New York: Oxford University Press.

Chapter 13

Identity Formation and Emotion Regulation in Digital Gaming

Ute Ritterfeld

This chapter builds on the chapter by Konijn and Nije Bijvank (this volume, chapter 12), who make a provocative statement in considering all digital games as potentially serious. According to this perspective, game play that is personally meaningful or relevant to the player (e.g., for his or her identity) may be considered serious. However, this seriousness does not necessarily imply being of desirable value, which is another prerequisite for serious games. If we accept the potential qualification as serious, we need to show how these serious effects present a positive outcome for the player. In this chapter I will extend the argument made by Konijn and Nije Bijvang in suggesting that successful completion of emotion regulation episodes qualifies for desirable impact in some game play. I hereby parallel the idea of games as suitable environments to apply and practice rather than to cognitively problem solve (Gee, this volume, chapter 5; Graesser, Chipman, Leeming & Biedenbach, this volume, chapter 6; Lieberman, this volume, chapter 8).

Problem solving is usually considered an educational activity and games that elicit, facilitate, or practice problem solving strategies should qualify as serious games. An emotion regulation episode, I will argue, may be considered as educational, too, if it helps to develop and fine tune coping strategies in high intensity emotional states, as at times elicited in digital game play. In order to support this line of argumentation, I will turn to the potential of emotion regulation embedded in digital gaming and its relevance for identity formation. Specifically, I am discussing the psychological reality of virtual experiences with respect to recent studies in neuropsychology and suggest to model online gaming experiences along a continuous oscillation between virtual and nonmediated experiences during game play that are guiding episodes of emotion elicitation and regulation. On the background of these explications I will finally return to the question what defines a serious game.

Personal Relevance of Digital Gaming

Many digital games require a substantial amount of effort from the player in order to be enjoyed (Juul, 2003). The complexity and high velocity of game play elicited in recent generation games even require considerable practice in order to master successful or competent game playing. Interestingly, this prerequisite has not inhibited digital games from becoming the fastest growing segment of the entertainment industry from 2004 to 2007 (Entertainment Software Association [ESA], 2004, 2007). Digital games are the prototype of the so-called lean-forward media (Newman, 2004), because they require active engagement by the user, and as such are fundamentally different from television or other lean-back media. Consequently, digital games create a high sense of *presence* or *immersion*, typically defined as a mental state of taking the virtual for real (Biocca, 2002; Klimmt & Vorderer, 2003; Lee, 2004).

Clearly, perceiving game environments as a casual pastime activity cannot fully explain their tremendous appeal. Fighting boredom or filling time when waiting could be more easily accomplished by using traditional lean-back media. Digital game play, however, requires engagement, endurance, and a commitment to confront and overcome significant challenges and potentially frustrating experiences. The gratification of gaming comes when it is more than just distraction, when the activity itself is intrinsically valuable for the player.

One of the motivators for digital gaming may be its relevance for identity formation. As today's games allow the player to represent him/herself as an avatar in the game, be it from a first or a third person perspective, she or he can utilize the game environments as "safe private laboratories" (Jansz, 2005, p. 221) to explore possible selves. Adopting this proposition, I look at game play from a functional perspective, asking what the game experience can actually do for the player that is meaningful for his or her identity formation.

As Konijn and Nije Bijvank (this volume, chapter 12) argue, one of the most important developmental tasks in adolescence is identity formation. The media play at least three supporting roles in creating, adapting, and maintaining identities among youth.

First, adolescents define who they are in reference to the media they use. Social identification, social integration, and peer formation are substantially influenced by shared media preferences and even shared media usage (e.g., joint digital game play, especially of entertainment media; Durkin, 2006). With media usage, both media format (e.g., preferred digital game platform or music player) and content (e.g., genres) provide ample opportunities for peer communication. One may even consider media usage as social norms in which deviation is at least not encouraged, possibly even punished, and may contribute to alienation from peers and, subsequently, even to social exclusion. Some empirical evidence supports this assumption in revealing a positive association between digital game play and social connectedness (Durkin & Barber, 2002).

Second, social cognitive theory of human behavior (Bandura, 1986) suggests that media characters can serve as models for media users. Although initially proposed to explain aggressive behavior, the theory is also used to explain positive behavior changes and to design effective campaigns (e.g., Bandura, 2001). However, the framework is shaped by traditional media usage, where the model and the user represent distinct entities. Interactive media with the inherent potential of representing the player him- or herself are challenging this understanding of media models: The player both engages with the virtual environment and observes him- or herself engaging with the environment. Thus, imitation is supplemented and, to some extent even replaced by (self-)exploration. This leads us to our third aspect of media usage and identity development: the exploration of possible selves in the virtual environment, which will be examined more closely in the following paragraphs.

Gaming as *Probehandeln*:[1] Playing with Possible Selves

Digital games provide players with opportunities of mastery and control that are not usually available in the physical world. These experiences may elicit feelings of potency that contribute to self-enhancement and, in the long run, to the development of positive self-esteem. Some authors (e.g., Klimmt & Hartmann, 2006) warn that virtual experiences of control and mastery that are not reflected in the nonmediated world may also lead to illusionary self-perceptions. Such self-perceptions may result in stressful disillusion when confronted with reality or even result in incremental withdrawal from reality. However, retraction into the virtual world does not necessarily result in withdrawal from peers. With the increasing accessibility of virtual communities embedded in massively multiplayer online role-playing games and other online communities, social participation is no longer limited to the physical world. Virtual social interactions are no less meaningful for identity formation than social encounters in the physical world. In fact, virtual environments provide a stage for self-exploration (*Probehandeln*) that is unmatched in the physical world.

According to recent studies, adolescent digital gamers in the United States spend an average of 22 hours per week interacting with other people via their avatars (Griffiths, Davies & Chappel, 2003; Yee, 2006a, 2006b). Game players represent themselves as one or more avatars in these virtual environments. It seems highly plausible that the construction of an avatar identity is not random, but is closely associated with the self of the player, as Gee (this volume, chapter 5) argues. The connection between the physical and the virtual self can affect representational sex and appearance, but also personality and behavior. Taking this argument a step further, one may consider the virtual representation as an extension of self. Not surprisingly, players frequently comment on their avatar's virtual encounters with reference to themselves (e.g., "He got *me!*").

The crucial question is whether the virtual world is mainly mimicking the physical world or whether it can help overcome the physical boundaries and offer significant experiences that go beyond those made in the physical world, as Konijn and Nije Bijvank argue (this volume, chapter 12). Several studies indicate that virtual encounters do, in fact, parallel social behavior in real life (e.g., Schilbach et al., 2006; Yee, Bailenson, Urbanek, Chang, & Merget, 2007). In the same vein, normal social phenomena travel with players into the virtual world(s). For example, cultural events, social group formation, civic engagement (Williams, 2006), economic trade (Castronova, 2006), or even legal debate (Balkin & Noveck, 2005) are often restaged in virtual worlds. Possibly, human fantasy is limited to the familiar and only reproduces itself. On the other hand, utopian ideas of liberation from physical boundaries may emerge in the virtual, giving room for socially and personally meaningful new identities (cf., Konijn & Nije Bijvank, this volume, chapter 12; Ritterfeld & Hünnerkopf, in press). In this sense, virtual identities are constructed as possible selves. Encounters in those identity roles may inform the person about his or her potencies for feelings, cognitions, behaviors, and social interaction.

Konijn and Nije Bijvank (this volume, chapter 12) apply the concept of wishful identification to explain why adolescents are drawn to powerful and often stereotypically portrayed heroes or heroines. However, events documented by Levine (2007) suggest that some virtual identities go beyond such stereotypical representations: He reports the example of a delicate and shy Filipino mother who believed that others, in the real world, treated her with little respect and rarely took her seriously. After giving herself a virtual identity of a bold masculine individual in the *City of Heroes*, she began to enjoy a sense of strength and authority in her virtual encounters. A young man with cerebral palsy whose physical limitations bound him to the constraint of a wheelchair revealed a profound sense of liberation and freedom when his avatar in *Second Life* rises from the wheelchair to dance (cf., Wheeling in *Second Life*). Similarly, a gentleman who suffered from an advanced stage of Duchenne muscular dystrophy, emerged as a super hero in *Star Wars Galaxies*, which earned him respect among the playing community, and a chance to be treated no differently than anybody else in this multiplayer online game (Levine, 2007). These reports are significant because they suggest that a virtual experience can elicit strong feelings about self. In each of these examples, the feeling of positive esteem evolves through the self-conscious contrast between the limitations in physical life and the liberation in the virtual. That supports Gee's (this volume, chapter 5) argument that both the physical and the virtual self are present in the mediated experience.

Other authors have elaborated on the concept of immersion in media as a temporary suspension of disbelief (e.g., Tamborini, Eastin, Skalski, Lachlan, Fediuk & Brady, 2004). The resulting psychological state of *presence* is defined as an experience that appears to be nonmediated (Lombard & Ditton, 1997) or the sense of actually being in the virtual world. The player's immersion results from a sense of spatial presence defined by environmental cues or social presence defined by the social reality represented in the virtual one. This line of research implies that the player enters the virtual world as the same person he or she is in the physical world; however, self-presence has not yet been explored as a significant concept.

Over the last decade, research in psychology has demonstrated that identity or the self needs to be conceptualized as dynamic and context-dependent rather than as a stable and consistent entity (cf. Hannover & Kühnen, in press). Although some aspects of self may be stable, others vary significantly depending on context salience and intentions. Taking this argument a step further, self-presence in virtual experiences may vary significantly depending on the stability of a player's concept of physical self, the virtual and the gaming context, and the player's intentions during the game play.

Assuming a distinctive virtual identity extends our understanding of the nonmediated self in two ways. First, the virtual self possesses features or attributes that may be significantly distinct from the self-concept applicable in the physical world—for example, being able to walk and dance in the virtual while physically being wheelchair bound. The distinctiveness of these attributes and their significance for the virtual encounters make them salient in the virtual self-awareness and contribute to a self-construction that is independent of the physical self (Kühnen, Hannover, & Schubert, 2001). Second, the virtual context provides an environment in which specific aspects of self can be requested. As such, contexts may function as primes, eliciting those virtual selves that match the game logic. As a consequence, virtual extensions of selves can be manifold; gamers may represent themselves in a virtual environment with various possible selves. Such rich opportunities for experiences of self-exploration can be beneficial if they are psychologically real to the players.

The Psychological Reality of the Virtual

Evidence from studies that employ physiological or neuropsychological measures supports the psychological reality of virtual experiences. Physiological measures demonstrate consistently strong responses in some game play and include blood pressure, heart rate, electrodermal activity, or oxygen consumption (Anderson, Carnagey, Flanagan, Benjamin, Eubanks, & Valentine, 2004; Baldaro, Tuozzi, Codispoti, Montebarocci, Barbagli, Trombini, et al., 2004; Ballard & Wiest, 1996; Calvert & Tan, 1994; Gwinup, Haw & Elias, 1983; Murphy, Alpert, & Walker, 1991; Murphy, Stoney, Alpert, & Walker, 1995; Schneider, Lang, Shin, & Bradley, 2004; Segal & Dietz, 1991). A neuroimaging study reported convincing evidence for not only game-elicited, but also game-content-elicited neural activity (Weber, Ritterfeld, & Mathiak, 2006). Results demonstrate that the virtual experiences of suspenseful content account for the observed neurophysiological changes during game play.

The study points to another aspect worth mentioning: If distinct episodes of content are considered, on average, only a rather small percentage of game play involves strong emotions (Weber, Behr, Tamborini, Ritterfeld, & Mathiak, 2008). While playing digital games, players spend part of the time in emotional states that presumably do not involve presence. The emotions elicited during game play vary significantly in strengths and duration, although this largely depends on game mechanics as well as the players' choices. The gaming experience can therefore be described as highly dynamic in emotional intensity. That means that players deliberately navigate through the virtual environment of a digital game encountering moments of increased arousal which are counterbalanced by lengthy episodes of anticipation and relieve. If we assume that less intense experiences correspond with less immersion, gaming can be described as a constant pull and push between the virtual and the physical worlds. Thus, players also alternate between experiencing their virtual and physical selves. As such, digital games are of potentially high personal relevance. If a connection can be made between the virtual and physical selves, the virtual encounters may indeed play a critical role for identity development.

A Deliberate Choice: Eliciting Intense Emotions

Gaming fulfills the criteria of deliberate activity. Players select a game genre and a particular game before they decide on how to play the game (e.g., script and setting) and how to navigate through the virtual environment. We need to ask whether player choices about games are made despite or because of the potential to elicit strong emotions.

Since the 1950s, researchers have acknowledged that choices about media is rarely limited to mere exposure, but media usage and effects are the result of sophisticated processes of selection of media formats and various contents. Notions about self-selection of entertainment media is supported by the selective exposure paradigm developed in communication research (see the overviews in Bryant & Davies, 2006; Hartmann, 2009). In a nutshell, individuals select specific media that fulfill cognitive, affective, social or behavioral needs for entertainment or information. Fulfilled expectations and satisfying one's needs are rewarding, resulting in the persistence of media usage and future selection. Applying this to gaming, if a person continues to play digital games he or she is assumed to benefit from this activity; that is, some needs or expectations are fulfilled (Vorderer & Ritterfeld, in press).

Exploring this phenomenon more closely, Jansz (2005) looked at the strong emotional appeal that especially violent games hold for young males. This appeal may contribute to the fact that the best selling games contain high levels of violence (ESA, 2004). Jansz (2005) explains this appeal by seeing the potential especially of those games to help individuals to cope with the increasing insecurities of male adolescent life. Specifically, some games offer the safe, private laboratory to explore control, competition, and challenge involving basic emotions relevant for masculine identity such as joy and compassion, anger and fear. In contrary to traditional lean-back media, the emotions elicited in interactive media are derived from the status of being an active participant. This is especially pronounced in shooter or combat games. Here, the player is the one who pursues a mission, defends his or her team, shoots an opponent, or loses his or her virtual life. The player can decide whether to engage in virtual combat or to hide in a safe spot while waiting for virtual agents to act. Thus, digital games offer the possibilities of committing versus witnessing assaults and thereby giving the player control over the amount of personal involvement. Reexperiencing emotionally loaded situations may be applied for coping strategies. Users may choose to either mimic their past experiences or to explore alternative routes. For example, a person who witnessed a fatal explosion in real life may choose to immerse him- or herself in the photo-realistic graphics of exploding avatars to cope with horror and grief. Another individual may opt to act bravely and compensate for feelings of shame or guilt derived from a fear reaction in a past experience.

One might argue that virtual and physical experiences are incomparable. For example, virtual violence allows the expression of anger in the brutal beating of a virtual agent, which is tolerated in the virtual environment and may be experienced as gratifying (Kestenbaum & Weinstein, 1985). A digital game can be switched off, and, although virtual experiences may be highly immersive, the user is not physically endangered, suffers no pain, and won't be killed by virtual violence. The safe environment of virtual spaces allows for as-if experiences that may elicit deep emotions such as fear, aggression, anger, or relief, without the consequences that "real" experiences would have. However, the structural similarities that exist in both environments may be relevant for coping. For example, like real combat, war games simulate combat within a narrative, establishing a mission in which a military team member in a command hierarchy fights an enemy using strategy and weapons; like real combat, a digital game can be set within a variety of environments; like "real" experiences, virtual experiences may include any form of combat such as attacks, random explosions, or shootings.

Thus, it comes as no surprise that data reveal that playing digital games, specifically involvement in virtual violence, is often engaged in by military personnel and game play may even be more pronounced after deployment (Henderlite, 2005). Air Force veterans who were personally involved in combat spent on average almost twice as many hours per day playing digital games after returning home compared to soldiers who had not been involved in violent interactions. According to Henderlite, the subjects indicated a strong preference for violent games, including first-person shooters, war, and battle games. Thus, most subjects selected games in which virtual violence is integral to the narrative and game play experience. These games offered a high level of resemblance to their expected or factual experiences during past deployment in Iraq and Afghanistan. Interestingly, most subjects also rated the content of the games they played as rather violent. This suggests that although they were expecting or had been exposed to factual violence in a war environment, even veterans who were involved in combat don't downplay the content of the games as harmless. Therefore, it seems rather unlikely that virtual violence, especially if presented in a war setting similar to Iraq or Afghanistan, is simply a form of entertainment for the veterans. Instead, their tendency to spend more time playing violent digital games may reflect a need to relive situations similar to factual combat again and again. In this manner, the usage of digital games may serve as a coping strategy or a tool for self-induced therapy. This reasoning is confirmed by the effective usage of virtual environments for therapy in anxiety and posttraumatic stress disorders (Rizzo, Rothbaum, & Graap, in press; Rizzo, Schultheis, Kerns, & Mateer, 2004; Rothbaum, Hodges, Ready, Graap, & Alarcon, 2001). Since these studies indicate that virtual encounters can be well suited to simulate crucial real-life experiences, I would even argue that it is possible to facilitate emotion regulation processes through digital gaming, which can be transferred to the physical world.

Creating Episodes of Emotion Regulation

I argued that digital games have the potential to elicit intense and self-relevant emotions which can be experienced during game play. Moreover, playing is a deliberate activity; that is, a player selects a specific game and chooses to make time to play the game. Although the reasons for game play are no doubt manifold, elicitation of intense emotions and the subsequent coping strategies applied should be considered one of the driving motives for gaming.

The field of psychology elaborates on several forms of coping strategies. For example, Gross (2002) introduced the term *emotion regulation* to describe consequences of positive or negative emotional states in order to maintain or to regain a positive balance. Emotions are hereby defined as circumscribable responses to a specific situation (in contrast to mood), involving central and peripheral physiology, behavior, and subjective experience. Successful emotion regulation results in either increase of positive or in decrease of negative emotions (Gross & Thompson, 2007). This offers an explanation for players' use of the combat games discussed above. In applying this concept, we expect emotion regulation, such as reduction of fear, anger, or shame and facilitation of pride or joy, as a consequence of enhanced self-esteem during game play. Although it remains an open question how long the in vitro experiences last and whether they translate into the physical world at all, we may consider virtual worlds as being suitable platforms to exercise emotion regulation processes.

However, emotion regulation processes in the virtual environment differ significantly from those described in the physical world (Gross, 2002; Gross & Thompson, 2007; John & Gross, 2007). First, the player has chosen to participate in the specific virtual situation, and second, the situation may be cancelled at any time. Strictly speaking, a player elicits emotions in the virtual that have no substantiate correlate in the nonmediated world. To illustrate this argument let's consider the following example:

A player is immersed in fighting an opponent who endangers her virtual life. She is hiding behind a wall waiting for the killer to detect her, preparing to attack and defend herself. Her heart is beating, she feels fear, and all of her attention is focused in the virtual. Just when the opponent becomes visible, a blackout interrupts the game; the screen turns blank. No doubt, the player immediately realizes her return into the physical world. Fear declines, and physiological arousal fades quickly.

The crucial question, however, is whether the player is delighted or frustrated about the blackout. At first glance, the sudden return into the physical world could represent the most effective emotion regulation possible. But game players are reportedly not at all amused by such experiences. Obviously, virtually elicited emotions need to be regulated in the mediated world in order to provide a satisfying gaming experience. In other words, playing the game exercises the whole cycle of emotion elicitation and coping behavior.

As mentioned before, episodes of intense emotions do not account for all playing time. On the contrary, they only account for a small percentage of time spent playing (Weber et al., 2008). Often, after completing a cycle of emotion elicitation and coping behavior, the player returns to a state in which he or she is at least somehow aware of the virtuality of the situation. Players therefore describe their experiences as "fun," refer to them as "winning a game" and thereby chose a vocabulary that stands in contrast to the intensity of "existential" emotional experiences. Awareness of virtuality also explains that some players repeatedly choose a situation that elicits fear: the choice is made before being immersed. I therefore propose a conceptualization of game play in which the state of gaming is oscillating between various states of presence and involving more or less pronounced awareness of the virtual character of game play. Figure 13.1 illustrates the gaming dynamics between the poles of presence (sense of nonmediation) and virtuality awareness. Presence is hereby understood as a gradually variable state rather than a distinct state of immersion.

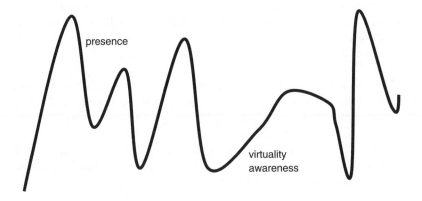

Figure 13.1 In-N-Out Presence

However, current research does not yet address whether and to what extent a player is aware of the virtuality of his or her experiences during game play, nor do we know whether the player can intentionally regulate this awareness.

Obviously, some players purposefully elicit intense emotions in a state of presence that represses virtuality awareness. Surprisingly, such emotion elicitation is not limited to positive emotions, but will also apply to negative emotions, such as fear. One may argue that negative emotions are sought after to overcome them. For example, a player exposes him- or herself to strong fear responses in order to cope with the emotion. In other words, a player elicits not only emotions, but also emotion regulation processes. Thus, emotion eliciting game play can be described in cycles of emotion elicitation and emotion regulation processes that, if the episode can be completed within the virtual frame—are enjoyed. It is therefore not the elicitation of emotion itself that accounts for a gratifying experience—but a successfully completed episode of emotion regulation.

Again: What are Serious Games?

There are two drawbacks involved in using combat games to elaborate on the thesis that games can be used to regulate emotional states: First, virtual violence contributes to aggression at least in noncombat personnel (see the overview in Weber, Ritterfeld, & Kostygina, 2006). Even if war games may be considered self-selected coping tools for combat-experienced veterans, the harmful effects of such games on some youth cannot be disregarded. Second, combat games are not usually included in the generic term serious games. In fact, with the attribute serious, we implicitly exclude game content that is not explicitly serving the well-being of its users and is not at all potentially harmful.

In general, I support a conceptualization of serious games as games that serve the physical and or mental well-being of their user. However, in contrast to the perspective taken by many game developers (cf., Ratan & Ritterfeld, this volume, chapter 2), I suggest an approach in which the kind of individual effect of usage is the ultimate criterion for seriousness, not the producer's intention, nor the game or its content. Strictly speaking, only post-usage evidence can help decide whether a game has positive, none, or negative effects on a particular person, whether they were intended by the game developer or evolved unexpectedly.

Ritterfeld and Weber (2006) previously argued that learning can take place in any digital game, and the question is whether the outcome is desirable or not. This normative quality is necessary to distinguish between serious and nonserious games. With that in mind, a violent game that enables a person to improve his or her anger management has a desirable outcome for one person, although it may be harmful in inducing aggression in another individual. Thus, content or genre analysis cannot predict the impact a game has, nor can it affect studies that rely on average statistical data to provide meaningful results. We need a combination of both content and user information for progress in our understanding of the complex interaction between the two (Nieding & Ritterfeld, 2008).

Finally, taking a developmental perspective in the study of games (whether labeled serious or not) shifts the perspective of media usage toward a functional framework: The self-selected exposure that such media undoubtedly represent can be considered an answer to a person's acquaintance with his or her developmental tasks (cf., Durkin, 2006; Havighurst, 1971). I hereby consider processes of emotion regulation and identity formation as developmental tasks and suggest that players actively seek out games that are appropriate in order to master them. Accordingly, a player may lose interest in a specific game if the game no longer provides support in resolving current developmental tasks. An opening gap between the challenges imposed by a specific game and the personal relevance of these challenges for the user may present itself simply as a loss of fun. The player does not necessarily have to be aware of the complex processes of identity formation and emotion regulation that lie beyond his or her entertainment experience. In fact, entertainment may only be the surface phenomena, indicating the fit between substantial needs and competencies of a gamer on one side, and game-imposed—not only cognitive, but also emotional—challenges on the other side. In this respect, serious gaming is the result of a good fit between game and gamer, and thus, a truly enjoyable experience.

Notes

1. I am using the untranslatable German term *Probehandeln* (Ueckert, 1989) to describe imaginative cognitions intentionally chosen to explore strategies for problem solving and self-exploration.

References

Anderson, C. A., Carnagey, N. L., Flanagan, M., Benjamin, A. J., Jr., Eubanks, J., & Valentine, J. C. (2004). Violent video games: Specific effects of violent content on aggressive thoughts and behavior. *Advances in Experimental Social Psychology, 36,* 199–249.

Baldaro, B., Tuozzi, G., Codispoti, M., Montebarocci, O., Barbagli, F., Trombini, E., et al. (2004). Aggressive and nonviolent videogames: Short-term psychological and cardiovascular effects on habitual players. *Stress and Health, 20*(4), 203–208.

Balkin, J., & Noveck, B. (Eds.). (2005). *The state of play: Law and virtual worlds.* New York: New York University Press.

Ballard, M. E., & Wiest, J. R. (1996). Mortal Combat: The effects of violent video game play on males' hostility and cardiovascular responding. *Journal of Applied Social Psychology, 26,* 717–730.

Bandura, A. (1986). *Social foundations of thought and action: a social cognitive theory.* Englewood Cliffs, NJ: Prentice-Hall.

Bandura, A. (2001). Social cognitive theory: An agentic perspective. *Annual Review of Psychology, 52,* 1–26.

Biocca, F. (2002). The evolution of interactive media: Toward "being there" in nonlinear narrative worlds. In M. C. Green, J. J. Strange, & T. C. Brock (Eds.), *Narrative impact: Social and cognitive foundations* (pp. 97–130). Mahwah, NJ: Erlbaum Associates.

Bryant, J., & Davies, J. (2006). Selective exposure processes. In J. Bryant & P. Vorderer (Eds.), *Psychology of entertainment* (pp. 19–34). Mahwah, NJ: Erlbaum.

Calvert, S. L., & Tan, S. (1994). Impact of virtual reality on young adults' physiological arousal and aggressive thoughts: Interaction versus observation. *Journal of Applied Developmental Psychology, 15,* 125–139.

Castronova, E. (2006). *Synthetic worlds: The business and culture of online games.* Chicago: University of Chicago Press.

City of Heroes (n.d.). [Digital game]. Retrieved March 8, 2009, from http://www.cityofheroes.com

Durkin, K. (2006). Game playing and adolescents' development. In P. Vorderer & J. Bryant (Eds.), *Playing video games: Motives, responses, and consequences* (pp. 415–428). Mahwah, NJ: Erlbaum.

Durkin, K., & Barber, B. (2002). Not so doomed: Video game play and positive adolescent development. *Applied Journal of Developmental Psychology, 23,* 73–392.

Entertainment Software Association (ESA). (2004). *Essential facts about the computer and video game industry.* Retrieved September 2, 2004, from http://www.theesa.com/pressroom.html

Entertainment Software Association (ESA). (2007). U.S. video game industry's growth outpaces national economy. Retrieved December 13, 2007, from http://www.theesa.com/archives/2007/11/us_video_game_i.php.

Griffiths, M., Davies, O., & Chappel, D., (2003). Breaking the stereotype: The case of online gaming. *CyberPsychology and Behavior, 6,* 81–91.

Gross, J. J. (2002). Emotion regulation: Affective, cognitive, and social consequences. *Psychophysiology, 39,* 281–291.

Gross, J. J., & Thompson, R. A. (2007). Emotion regulation: Conceptual foundations. In J. J. Gross (Ed.), *Handbook of emotion regulation* (pp. 3–24). New York: Guilford Press.

Gwinup, G., Haw, T., & Elias, A. (1983). Cardiovascular changes in video-game players. Cause for concern? *Postgraduate Medicine, 74*(6), 245–248.

Hannover, B., & Kühnen, U. (in press). Culture, context, and cognition. The semantic-procedural-interface model of the self. *European Review of Social Psychology.*

Hartmann, T. (2009). (Ed.). *Media choice: A theoretical and empirical overview.* New York: Routledge.

Havighurst, R. J. (1971). *Developmental tasks and education.* (3rd ed.). New York: Longman.

Henderlite, A. (2005). *Real involvement in violence: It's relationship to video game usage and aggression.* Unpublished master's thesis, University of Southern California, Los Angeles.

Jansz, J. (2005). The emotional appeal of violent video games for adolescent males. *Communication Theory, 15,* 219–241.

John, O. P., & Gross, J. J. (2007). Individual differences in emotion regulation strategies: Links to global trait, dynamic, and social cognitive constructs. In J. J. Gross (Ed.), *Handbook of emotion regulation* (pp. 351–372). New York: Guilford Press.

Juul, J. (2003). The game, the player, the world: Looking for a heart of gameness. In M. Copier & J. Raessens (Eds.), *Level up: Digital games research conference* (pp. 30–46). Utrecht, The Netherlands: University of Utrecht and DIGRA.

Kestenbaum, G. L., & Weinstein, L. (1985). Personality, psychopathology, and developmental issues in male adolescent video game use. *Journal of the American Academy of Child Psychiatry, 24*, 329–337.

Klimmt, C., & Hartmann, T. (2006). Effectance, self-efficacy, and the motivation to play video games. In P. Vorderer & J. Bryant (Eds.), *Playing video games: Motives, responses, and consequences* (pp. 133–146). Mahwah, NJ: Erlbaum.

Klimmt, C., & Vorderer, P. (2003). Media psychology "is not yet there": Introducing theories on media entertainment to the presence debate. *Presence, Teleoperators and Virtual Environments, 12*, 346–359.

Kühnen, U., Hannover, B., & Schubert, B. (2001). Procedural consequences of semantic priming: The role of self-knowledge for context-bounded versus context-independent modes of thinking. *Journal of Personality and Social Psychology, 80*, 397–409.

Lee, K. M. (2004). Presence, explicated. *Communication Theory, 14*, 27–50.

Levine, K. (2007). Alter egos in a virtual world. *National Public Radio*. Retrieved Dec. 20, 2007, from http://www.npr.org/templates/story/story.php?storyId=14087749&sc=emaf

Lombard, M., & Ditton, T. (1997). At the heart of it all: The concept of presence. *Journal of Computer-Mediated Communication, 3*.

Murphy, J. K., Alpert, B. S., & Walker, S. S. (1991). Whether to measure change from baseline or absolute level in studies of children's cardiovascular reactivity: A two-year follow up. *Journal of Behavioral Medicine, 14*, 409–419.

Murphy, J. K., Stoney, C. M., Alpert, B. S., & Walker, S. S. (1995). Gender and ethnicity in children's cardiovascular reactivity: 7 years of study. *Health Psychology, 14*, 48–55.

Newman, J. (2004). *Videogames*. London: Routledge.

Nieding, G., & Ritterfeld, U. (2008). Mediennutzung, Medienwirkung und Medienkompetenz bei Kindern und Jugendlichen [Media use, effects, and literacy in children and adolescents]. In F. Petermann & W. Schneider (Eds.), *Enzyklopädie der Psychologie* [Encyclopedia of Psychology]: *Vol. 2. Angewandte Entwicklungspsychologie* [Applied Developmental Psychology] (pp. 331–388). Göttingen, Germany: Hogrefe.

Ritterfeld, U., & Hünnerkopf, M. (in press). Medien und medienvermittelte Umwelten [Media and mediated environments]. In V. Linneweber & E. D. Lantermann (Eds.), *Enzyklopädie der Psychologie* [Encyclopedia of psychology]: *Vol. 2. Umweltpsychologie* [Psychological Environment]. Göttingen, Germany: Hogrefe.

Ritterfeld, U., & Weber, R. (2006). Video games for entertainment and education. In P. Vorderer & J. Bryant (Eds.), *Playing video games: Motives, responses, and consequences* (pp. 399–413). Mahwah, NJ: Erlbaum.

Rizzo, A. A., Rothbaum, B. O., & Graap, K. (in press). Virtual reality applications for the treatment of combat-related PTSD. In C. R. Figley & W. P. Nash (Eds.), *Combat and operational stress management: Theory, research, and practice*.

Rizzo, A. A., Schultheis, M. T., Kerns, K., & Mateer, C. (2004). Analysis of assets for virtual reality applications in neuropsychology. *Neuropsychological Rehabilitation, 14*(1), 207–239.

Rothbaum, B. O., Hodges, L. F., Ready, D., Graap, K., & Alarcon, R. D. (2001). Virtual reality exposure therapy for Vietnam veterans with posttraumatic stress disorder. *Journal of Clinical Psychiatry, 62*, 617–622.

Schilbach, L., Wohlschlaeger, A., Krämer, N. C., Newen, A., Zilles, K., Shah, J. N., et al. (2006). Being with virtual others: Neural correlates of social interaction. *Neuropsychologia, 44*, 718–730.

Schneider, E. F., Lang, A., Shin, M., & Bradley, S. D. (2004). Death with a story: How story impacts emotional, motivational, and physiological responses to first-person shooter video games. *Human Communication Research, 30*, 361–375.

Second Life [Digital game]. (n.d.). Retrieved March 8, 2009, from www.secondlife.com

Segal, K. R., & Dietz, W. H. (1991). Physiologic responses to playing a video game. *American Journal of Diseases of Children, 145*, 1034–1036.

Tamborini, R., Eastin, M. S., Skalski, P., Lachlan, K., Fediuk, T. A., & Brady, R. (2004). Violent virtual video games and hostile thoughts. *Journal of Broadcasting & Electronic Media, 48*, 335–357.

Ueckert, H. (1989). Denken als Probehandeln. Zur Untersuchung komplexen Problemlösens an Simulationsmodellen [Cognition as Probehandeln. On the study of complex problem solving within simulations]. In W. Schönpflug (Ed.), *Bericht über den 36. Kongress der Deutschen Gesellschaft für Psychologie in Berlin 1988* [Report on the 36th Congress of the German Psychological Society, 1988], pp. 384–391. Göttingen, Germany: Hogrefe.

Vorderer, P., & Ritterfeld, U. (in press). Video games. In R. Nabi & M. B. Oliver (Eds.), *Handbook of media effects*. Thousand Oaks, CA: Sage.

Weber, R., Behr, K.-M., Tamborini, R., Ritterfeld, U., & Mathiak, K. (2008). *Event-related, high-resolution content analysis of first-person-shooter games*. Unpublished manuscript, Department of Communication, University of California, Santa Barbara.

Weber, R., Ritterfeld, U., & Kostygina, A. (2006). Aggression and hostility as effects of playing violent games. In P. Vorderer & J. Bryant (Eds.), *Playing video games: Motives, responses, and consequences* (pp. 374–361). Mahwah, NJ: Erlbaum.

Weber, R., Ritterfeld, U., & Mathiak, K. (2006). Does playing violent video games induce aggression? Empirical evidence of a functional magnetic resonance imaging study. *Media Psychology, 8*, 39–60.

Williams, D. (2006). Groups and goblins: The social and civic impact of online gaming. *Journal of Broadcasting and Electronic Media, 50*, 651–670.

Yee, N. (2006a). The demographics, motivations and derived experiences of users of massively-multiuser online graphical environments. *Presence: Teleoperators and Virtual Environments, 15*, 309–329.

Yee, N. (2006b). The labor of fun: How video games blur the boundaries of work and play. *Games and Culture, 1*, 68–71.

Yee, N., Bailenson, J. N., Urbanek, M., Chang, F., & Merget, D. (2007). The unbearable likeness of being digital: The persistence of nonverbal social norms in online virtual environments. *CyberPsychology and Behavior, 15*, 309–329.

Serious Games for Social Change

Section III

Serious Games for
Social Change

Chapter 14

Serious Games for Girls?

Considering Gender in Learning with Digital Games

Yasmin B. Kafai

Since the late 1990s, we have witnessed some remarkable changes in the field of digital games. The most obvious one concerns the move of digital games into mainstream entertainment. People of all ages and backgrounds, and not just young boys and men, can be seen playing digital games. New gaming formats and platforms have expanded participation into mobile, massive online, and alternative reality gaming anytime, anywhere, and with anyone. Equally important is the recognition of digital games for their educational benefits amplified by the creation of the serious games[1] movement. But arguably one of the most significant changes has been the increased presence of girls and women as gamers. Industry reports (Entertainment Software Association [ESA], 2006) list over 40% of women as gamers with casual gamers consisting of over 70% of women players.

Thus the worry about gender issues, which has been documented so prominently in the research literature (Cassell & Jenkins, 1998a; Yelland & Rubin, 2002), might seem misplaced and could explain why it has been put to rest in some discussions. Jim Gee (2003), who has helped popularize digital games as examples of promising learning environments, said that he had "nothing whatsoever to say about this issue" (p. 10) given the large number of existing publications. Gee admitted that digital games, like other popular cultural forms, overstress sexualized women in their content and usually portray them as minor characters, but foresaw that "as more girls and women play these games, this will change" (p. 11). As I will argue, this is an overly simplistic view because gender in digital games has always been about more than just having larger numbers of female players and fewer virtual bosoms in games.[2]

Two different arguments have been prominent in discussions on why gender should matter in digital games. The technology pipeline argument has been discussed most extensively because boys' early access to digital games presumably provided them with a home advantage (Hayes, 2008). Consequently, increasing girls and women's participation in gaming has been seen as one way to address the lack of women's involvement with technology. It was also assumed, as visible in Gee's (2003) argument, that with the increased presence of female gamers, we should have witnessed visible shifts in game content, mechanics, and the industry at large. Yet, the trends seem to indicate otherwise: since the late 1990s, the participation of women and minorities in IT fields has decreased. Games as such have changed little, and women have made few inroads into the game design industry (Consalvo, 2008).

A second argument as to why gender should matter in digital games concerned their content, most notably the violence and stereotypical representations (Hartmann & Klimmt, 2006). Provenzo (1991) conducted one of the first content analyses of characters in digital games and found that most of them portrayed women as victims or prizes and provided no choice for female gamers. In a similar vein, the violence prominent in many games was seen as another deterrent for girls.[3] Researchers like Gailey (1992) have debated to what extent these messages are received as transmitted when analyzing how young players interpret the play process and what children get out of the games. One of her findings was that children did not accept the universals provided in digital games; they made up their own descriptions. In contrast, Kinder (1991) argued that the values embedded in movies, toys, television, and digital games provide powerful stereotypes for children's thinking. More recent research documents that strong female protagonists such as Lara Croft are now prominent in many games (Jansz & Martis, 2006), but stereotyping continues to exist.

These two arguments, among many others, have made gender in games an issue that we cannot ignore. Now that digital games are part of everyday media, we also need to consider their role in positive youth development (Bers, 2006). In light of all these changes, the question of whether we need serious games for girls[4] doesn't seem so farfetched. But, as I will argue in this chapter, there is more than one answer to this question, because how we think about gender in digital games is far more complex than a representational bias. Industry and academia have developed different proposals of what kind of digital game might appeal to girls and why. As a first step, we need to untangle these different proposals before we can address the issue of how gender should be considered in serious games. Also, when referring to serious games, it is important to distinguish between two different approaches that have been prominent in the research literature: playing and making games for learning. Most discussions in academia and industry have been about playing games for learning, but now players' participation in the design of levels and characters are desired components of game play. Thus, gender in serious games will be discussed in both contexts even though we recognize that ultimately the boundaries between playing and making serious games are less distinct than claimed for rhetorical purposes.

Gender in the Design of Digital Games

In the early 1990s, digital games were mostly seen as toys for boys. During those years, there was little interest in the game industry in creating and marketing games for girls because all the research had shown that girls just weren't interested in computers, and, by extension, in digital games. Yet, others wondered whether this untapped market segment could be mined by designing games for girls. These discussions crystallized in the Girl Game movement—an unlikely alliance between academics and industry (for an extensive discussion, see Cassell & Jenkins, 1998b). Within the Girl Game movement, games were created for girls only, based on the premise of gender differences emphasizing traditional notions of femininity. This approach to gender in game design will be called *games for girls*. In contrast, approaches under the premise of gender as a social construct have favored games that challenge stereotypes and will be called *games for change*. The following sections will provide more detail on the different approaches using selected games as examples that illustrate similarities and differences in game character design, mechanics, and context.

Games for Girls: Building on Gender Differences

A large body of research has established significant gender differences in various aspects such as performance and experience related to digital game play (for an overview, see Greenfield & Cocking, 1996). Other research focused on differences in game playing interests and used these as an explanation for why girls were not playing digital games (Hartmann & Klimmt, 2006; Klawe, Inkpen, Phillips, Upitis, & Rubin, 2002). Industry designers and academics thus argued that games needed to emphasize different content, mechanics, and characters in order to appeal to girls. The Barbie series exemplifies the characteristics of a typical girl game aimed at 6- to 11-year-olds. *Barbie Fashion Designer* released by Mattel in 1996 was the most popular package produced in this series. It let players design clothes for the Barbie doll and model them on a catwalk before printing them out on special clotheslike paper and gluing or "sewing" them together to dress an actual Barbie doll. The software provides dozens of clothes patterns that fit the actual Barbie doll body and a large array of different colors and print patterns. Other software packages in this series let the player via Barbie explore the ocean environment (e.g., *Barbie Ocean*) or create dresses for collaborative doll play (e.g., *Barbie Print 'n' Play*). These game activities emphasized traditional notions of femininity, such as being beautiful and fashionable. Subrahamayan and Greenfield (1998) explained the success of *Barbie Fashion Designer* with its focus on girls' traditional play patterns with dolls. When Mattel released *Barbie Fashion Designer*, the title outsold all other console games in the traditional boys market. This commercial success indicated for the first time that girls could be interested in computers, given the right software.

Other efforts, most notably the *Friendship* series developed by Purple Moon under the direction of Brenda Laurel, promoted different interests of girls, those of social interaction and helping. The *Friendship* series focused on girls ages 8 to 12 years old. For instance, *Rockett's New World* released by Purple Moon in 1997 presented a player with the situation of moving to a new school and navigating her way through the social maze of making friends. In the game, Rockett would face different social situations with classmates and could rehearse answers and experience their outcomes. Rockett and her six friends were dressed in casual fashion. A diary provided additional information about Rockett's feelings and interests (Laurel, 1998). Other packages in this series would allow Rockett and her friends to explore secret pathways in a forest and design friendship bracelets. The game activities focused on gaining access and social status among peers. This group of girl games has often been called purple software because of its purple packaging while the Barbie software, and others alike, were called pink software because of their pink packaging.

The successes and failures behind these two developments have been extensively discussed elsewhere (Jenkins, 2003; Jenkins & Cassell, 2008; Laurel, 2003). But what's important here is that this focus on gender differences in game play and interests produced clear prescriptions on how to design games for girls: offer female player protagonists, afford realistic feature choices, use cooperation not competition, and provide positive but not violent feedback. Studies by Kafai (1996a), which asked children to design their own digital games, found that girls incorporated many of these features in their games when compared to the games designed by boys, which often only featured male protagonists and violent feedback. More recent research by Denner and Campe (2008) confirmed these features in their analyses of teen's game designs.

Games for Change: Supporting Gender Play

The pink and purple games that appealed to large numbers of girls (based on their commercial successes) and used girls rather than boys as a starting point for their designs, created considerable concern among feminist researchers (Cassell & Jenkins, 1998b; De Castell & Bryson, 1998): the promotion of traditional values about what it meant to be a girl, the limited choices of identification with femininity, and the creation of separate, girls-only spaces leading to a possible ghettoization of girls (Seiter, 1993). But one of the most problematic aspects was for many the essentialization of girls and boys—the assumption that all same sex children share the same likes and dislikes. This view ignores the substantial differences that exist within a group of girls or boys. A recent meta-analysis found that most of the observed differences between men and women in psychological studies are rather small, with the exception of motor performances and views on aggression (Hyde, 2005). Many researchers now focus on contextual factors and their impact on situating gender. For instance, a follow-up study of Kafai (1998) revealed that most of the observed gender differences disappeared in children's digital game designs once the context for the instructional games was changed from teaching mathematics to teaching science.

While games for girls movement was based on the premise that all girls are alike, games for change was predicated on the notion that gender is a socially constructed identity (De Castell & Bryson, 1998). Theorists like Butler (1990) have introduced the notion of *gender play*, meaning that both girls and boys, and men and women, experiment with gendered expressions within different contexts. She conceptualizes gender from a human feminist perspective as "an attribute of a person, who is characterized essentially as a pregendered substance, or 'core,' called the person..." (p. 14). Much of the research has focused on where and how society places constraints on gender performances and thus impacts a gendered identity formation. The basic premise of these games is to challenge existing gender stereotypes and provide room for exploration.

This take on gender obviously leads to games with different game mechanics, contexts, and characters. One example is *SiSSYFiGHT 2000* developed by Zimmerman and colleagues (2003) to illustrate how one can challenge norms about social interactions. *SiSSYFiGHT 2000* focuses on girl groups who are all out to ruin each other's popularity and self-esteem. The object of the game is to attack and "dis" enemies both physically and verbally until they are mortified beyond belief. The game involves six online players and each round establishes who comes out as a winner or loser; the final results are published on an online board reset on a weekly basis. The game activities focus on abusive practices used by girls to establish popularity in their groups, and thus explicitly challenge stereotypes that all girls are nice and supportive.

A different approach provides room for exploration by creating tools to design games. Flanagan (2006) incorporated game mechanics such as cooperation, sharing, and fair representation in the multiplayer game *Rapunsel* which is programmed by the players themselves. *Rapunsel*, aimed at 11- to 14-year-olds, presents a multiplayer game world populated by two sets of creatures called Peeps and Gobblers who like to dance. Peeps design and program all of their dance moves while Gobblers learn them from copying the Peeps. Players control Peeps characters by programming increasingly complex dance moves that can be stolen by Gobblers. Players have the choice of two modes: battle or exploratory. In exploratory mode, players can decorate their houses in their home base and make music. In the battle mode, players confront Gobblers and put voodoolike spells on them to protect their moves. Players collect credits for their home designs, new music loops, dance moves, and character designs. *Rapunsel* includes both cooperation and competition, thus allowing players to choose whichever mode they prefer.

Each of these approaches incorporates expression of and play with gender in different ways. The games for girls' approaches stress different notions of femininity: Mattel's Barbie series focuses on beauty and fashion while Purple Moon's Friendship series focuses on popularity and friendship. The games for change approaches challenge these traditional notions: Zimmerman's *SiSSYFiGHT 2000* explicitly asks players to engage in psychological and physical attacks whereas Flanagan's *Rapunsel* allows players to choose their mode of interaction of being either collaborative or competitive. Each approach has built-in challenging or confirming notions of what is considered to be appropriate for a girl.

More recently, research has expanded beyond the game itself to focus on physical locations in which games are played (Beavis & Charles, 2005; Bryce & Rutter, 2002; Carr, 2005; Schott & Horrell, 2000). In these studies researchers examine the ways in which girls' access to and participation in game play is supported when various family members compete for access to consoles or how locations structure game play.[5] It is clear that multiple factors—design, mechanics, and contexts—impact gender differences and performances.

Gender in the Design of Serious Games

As we move from entertainment into serious games, we need to consider gender in two different approaches: the playing games and the making games for learning. The interest in playing games for learning is not new in education. Games have always been around schools, except that for the most part they have been used for motivational rather than academic purposes. Many teachers use board and digital games in classrooms as a reward for students completing their assignments. In the past, when researchers focused on playing games for learning, they considered the impact of either motivational principles (Bright, Harvey, & Wheeler, 1985; Malone, 1981) or spatial reasoning skills (Loftus & Loftus, 1983). It is only in the last few years, since the publication of Gee's (2003) examination of cultural and social aspects of learning in gaming environments, that the academic appeal of games has gathered more momentum.

Much less prominent has been the approach of making serious games for learning introduced in the 1990's by Kafai (1995) as a promising alternative. We have evidence from numerous studies that the design of games can be a context for the forms of learning and participation that Gee (2003) described both in and outside of school (Peppler & Kafai, 2007). A study of designing serious games within school illustrates how young designers engage in complex and extended planning and develop design blueprints for their games (Kafai, 1996b), provide assistance and consultancy to each other (Evard, 1998), and also learn valuable programming strategies, skills, and academic content (Kafai, 1995). In making serious games, we found evidence of different types of peer pedagogy, informal teaching strategies that young game designers develop (Ching & Kafai, in press) and conversation strategies to facilitate design and science dialogue among peers (Kafai & Ching, 2001). Most importantly, we paid close attention to aspects that could either foster or hinder equitable participation in such collaborative design contexts (Ching, Kafai, & Marshall, 2000). The research and discussion on gender and serious games will thus focus on the two approaches, playing serious games and making serious games, in more detail.

Playing Serious Games

There are few studies that have examined gender in playing serious games with an exclusive focus on gender differences. Malone's (1981) seminal work, "What Makes Things Fun to Learn," investigated various motivational features of a dart game that would increase the learning and engagement of mathematical content. He found only one instance with significant differences between boys and girls in what they liked about games: "The boys seemed to like the fantasy of popping balloons and the girls seemed to dislike this fantasy. The addition of musical rewards, on the other hand, appeared to increase for girls, but to decrease for boys, the intrinsic interest of the activity" (p. 226; Malone & Lepper, 1987). The dart game investigated by Malone presented simple graphics on black screens with no customization options for the players. In contrast, Rubin, Murray, O'Neil, and Ashley (1997) examined students' interactions with Broderbund's *Logical Journey of the Zoombinis*, which focuses on discrete mathematics and logical reasoning. They found both groups were equally engaged in the game, but girls tended to spend more time customizing the design of the Zoombini features (color and shape of eyes, mouth, hair, nose, and shoes) while the boys spent more time on solving logical puzzles. These results suggest that boys and girls find many (but not all) of the same game features appealing, but that differential engagement could be consequential for learning outcomes when girls don't get to the core content of the game.

More recent developments have focused on the new genre of multiplayer online games, which promote explicit educational goals such as science inquiry skills in *River City* (Nelson, Ketelhut, Clarke, Bowman, & Dede, 2005), ecological thinking in *Quest Atlantis* (Barab, 2006), historical thinking (Squire, 2006), or science engagement in *Whyville* (Kafai, Feldon, Fields, Giang, & Quintero, 2007). Nelson (2007) documented that girls ask for less instructional guidance in *River City* but otherwise little attention, if any, has been given to gender issues. For the most part, existing studies have examined entertainment games such as *World of Warcraft* and documented how adult players engage in extended investigations of growing complexity, collaborate with others to solve problems, search for information, and engage in discussions (Steinkuehler, 2006). Note that these games are obviously not the type of first person shooter or violent games often discussed in the media for promoting problematic cultural values or being of less interest to girls. The multiplayer online games considered here fall more into the category of simulation games that already have a long-standing history of successful classroom use and learning, with or without computers.

But youth are not the only ones making decisions about playing and learning with serious games. We found that gender concerns often fall to the wayside when teachers examine serious games (Kafai, Franke, & Battey, 2002). Few teacher reviewers considered whether the design of game contexts, activities, and characters could be biased toward one group. For instance, many serious games feature sports contexts such as football or baseball, which are not widely practiced by girls. The reviews also revealed that most teachers focus on motivational and not content related criteria when discussing serious games. When Huff, Fleming, and Cooper (1987) asked designers to develop gender-specific educational software, they found game designs for boys and learning tools for girls. When asked to design generic software, designers replicated the same patterns. While this is not a comprehensive body of research, the few studies seem to suggest that gender differences can come into play in the design and review of serious games.

Most of the available research on this topic focuses on learning with computers in schools, and not games per se, revealing significant gender differences in access, use, attitudes, and achievement (Kirkpatrick & Cuban, 1998; Volman & van Eck, 2001). Here, studies have documented, over and over again, that girls' access and participation with computers is not the same as those of boys. Schofield (1995) painted a dramatic picture of the cultural and social forces that shape girls' inclusion or exclusion in computer classrooms and school clubs. Jenson, De Castell, and Bryson (2003) provided an example of a feminist intervention project that created opportunities for girls to develop and experience new identities as technology experts within their school by allowing them to voice their concerns about inequitable access. Ito (2007) and others have argued that we cannot neglect the social and cultural factors when considering learning with serious games which situate when, how, and who is learning what.

Making Serious Games

For the most part, discussions about serious games and gender have focused on playing such games. The alternative, making serious games, proposes a very different paradigm that puts the players in charge of designing the game(s) themselves (Kafai, 2006). Gender has been a much more prominent concern in programs that promote and study the making of serious games. It was seen as a particularly promising way to get girls interested in computers and competent in technology by asking them to design applications, rather than to focus on the learning of decontextualized algorithms (American Association of University Women [AAUW], 2000). In her early work, Kafai (1996a) found significant differences in girls and boys' game designs but no differences in their abilities to make the games. In the project, students aged 9 to 11 years were asked to design fraction games to teach other students at their school about fractions. Most of the boys' designs featured violent feedback, were situated in fantasy settings, and assumed a male player, while most of the girls designed games with no violent feedback, selected realistic settings, and made provisions for players of different gender. An alternative interpretation of these findings would propose that the boys positioned themselves in their games as savvy game players by choosing established conventions that reaffirm their gender while the girls did the same with their choices (Pelletier, 2008). A later study (Kafai, 1998), in which students were asked to design and implement astronomy games, found no differences in game designs—suggesting that context plays an important role in how students position themselves in relation to particular subject matters and game designs.

In these serious games made by players (Kafai, Franke, Ching, & Shih, 1998), we also observed other cultural stereotypes, in particular pedagogical conceptions in which teaching is about asking questions and learning about giving answers. For example, a large number of commercial serious games, such as the *MathBlaster* series by Davidson, fall into this category. This is perhaps because of the children's extensive experience with many drill-and-practice games but also what others have termed the *Hollywood curriculum*, which promotes stereotypical views on learning and teaching. It resonates with Ito's (2007) observations of differential game use in school and after-school settings where peers can subvert or support the educational agendas incorporated in serious games.

One key aspect in making serious games is that players can customize and personalize avatars, levels, and activities or even design their own game (Seif El Nasir & Smith, 2006). Today, most entertainment games are released with such modding features or game engines, which in the early 1990s were only available to hackers. There is now a whole range of different game design tools under development, ranging from modding to programming tools. But even tools that allow for the design of games can be designed to incorporate features that promote more equitable access, as Kelleher (2008) has shown with *Alice*. Here the inclusion of the popular *Sims* characters engaged girls in storytelling and connected them to aspects of game design. Akin to this is the *Rapunsel* program by Flanagan (2006) discussed earlier in this paper. Similar successes have been seen with media-rich environments such as *Scratch* that allow for a range of game designs by boys and girls (Kafai, Peppler, & Chiu, 2007). While there is some debate about the differences in using either modding or programming tools for making serious games, in the end both efforts involve interfaces and some form of scripting language designed to allow players to manipulate different aspects of the game.

Final Thoughts

There are obviously many ways to answer the question whether or not we need serious games for girls. What we can gather from this review is that our efforts should be more directed toward providing opportunities for players to define the meaning and personalize assets in the games. For those who subscribe to the games for girls approach, the goal would be to offer games with more choices, and different game mechanics. For those who favor games for change, the answer would be to offer game modding and making features. Our ultimate goal should be to make serious games more accessible and enrich gaming experiences for all. For that, we not only need different games but also different design approaches.

Because different designs can result when considering gender in digital games, several proposals have been put forward to address gender and learning issues in the design process and participation. Cassell and Jenkins (1998a) proposed what they called underdetermined design for software and games that would encourage boys and girls (and by implication, men and women) to express aspects of self-identity that transcend stereotyped gender categories. In this approach, activities involving girls and boys are not neutral or isolated acts but involve the person becoming and acting in the world as part of the construction of a complex identity. Flanagan and Nissenbaum (2008) called for a design approach that reveals the values designers bring to their games' designs, as revealed in Huff, Fleming, and Cooper's (1987) research findings. They argue that designers and producers need to pay attention to safeguarding critical values in all phases of the game design process: delineation of a project, specification of game mechanics, implementation, and revisions. In the same vein, we need to apply criteria for educational activities and content. One way to address a wide range of activities and themes based on different interests is to create wide walls, not just low thresholds for learners to enter the game (Resnick & Silverman, 2005).

We also need to be careful with the boundaries that we draw, oftentimes for rhetorical purposes, between game playing and game making. For one, most games today come with modding features to keep players in the game and extend playability as the next version is being developed. Thus, former distinctions between players and makers, or media consumers and producers (Jenkins, 2006), have become less clear. In fact, we now have games or player-generated environments such as *Second Life* by Linden Lab and *Whyville* by Numedeon that seem to suggest that players, girls and boys alike, are drawn to these participatory features. Rather than defining up front the end goal of the game, a new genre of alternative reality games (MacGonigal, 2007) uses player participation as a design directive to create the next steps in the game. What is defined as a game is a moving target. It seems then that many entertainment games embody features that are of interest to those considering gender in the design of serious games. Many of the changes in teaching and learning situations that came out of the gender equity movement improved the situation for all students, and not just for girls and women. In any case, serious games are not stand-alone applications, but should be seen as a part of a larger learning community. Having learners become game designers and creators is a small yet achievable step as the examples have shown—but one with big implications for those interested in closing the divide or participation gap in the digital culture (Jenkins, Clinton, Purushotma, Robison, & Weigel, 2006). Perhaps this will lead us to lay the foundation to achieve more equitable participation in the computer culture at large.

Acknowledgments

The writing of this paper was supported by a grant of the National Science Foundation (NSF-0411814). The views expressed are those of the author and do not necessarily represent the views of NSF or the University of California. Many thanks are due to Deborah Fields and Kylie A. Peppler for their comments on earlier drafts of this paper.

Notes

1. The term *serious games* has been recently coined to describe what previously have been called *educational games*, *edutainment* or even *epistemic games* (Shaffer, 2006), referring to the combination of educational software with games.
2. Gee (2007) is aware of the criticism he has received for this statement about gender and games.
3. A number of different studies have tried to establish a link between digital game playing and violence, but Goldstein (2005) argued that the methodological shortcomings of this research, such as short time frames and nonvoluntary play, made it difficult to support this connection.
4. The title of my chapter is a variation on the now iconic Saturday Night Live (SNL) TV skit "Chess for Girls" that prefaced the first work on gender and digital games *From Barbie to Mortal Kombat* (Cassell & Jenkins, 1998). In the SNL skit, the chessboard was transformed into a dollhouse with clothes for the king and queen to get girls interested playing chess.
5. I should also note that there is now a significantly richer body of research on gender differences and performances in game play, but it refers to adult women and not the age group discussed in this article. Most notable here is T. L. Taylor's work (2006).

References

Alice. [Digital game]. (2000). Redwood City, CA: Electronic Arts.

American Association of University Women (AAUW). (2000). *Tech-savvy: Educating girls in the new computer age*. Washington, DC: Educational Foundation of the American Association of University Women.

Barab, S. A. (2006, Winter). From Plato's Republic to Quest Atlantis: The role of the philosopher-king. *Technology, Humanities, Education, and Narrative, 2*, 22–53.

Barbie Fashion Designer. [Digital game]. (1996). El Segundo, CA: Mattel.

Barbie Ocean. [Digital game]. (1997). El Segundo, CA: Mattel.

Barbie Print 'n' Play. [Digital game]. (1997). El Segundo, CA: Mattel.

Beavis, C., & Charles, C. (2005). Challenging the notions of gendered game play: Teenagers playing the Sims. *Discourse: Studies in the Cultural Politics of Education, 26*(3), 355–367.

Bers, M. (2006). The role of new technologies to foster positive youth development. *Applied Developmental Science, 10*(4), 200–219.

Bright, G. W., Harvey, J. G. & Wheeler, M. M. (1985). Learning and mathematics games. *Journal for Research in Mathematics Education* (Monograph, Vol. 1). Reston, VA: National Council of Teachers in Mathematics.

Bryce, J., & Rutter, J. (2002). Killing like a girl: Gendered gaming and girl gamers' visibility. In F. Mayra (Ed.), *Proceedings of Computer Games and Digital Cultures Conference* (pp. 243–255). Tampere, Finland: Tampere University Press.

Butler, J. (1990). *Gender trouble*. New York: Routledge.

Carr, D. (2005). Contexts, pleasures and preferences: Girls playing computer games. *Proceedings of DiGRA 2005 Conference*. Retrieved May 21 2007, from http://www.digra.org/dl/db/06278.08421.pdf

Cassell, J., & Jenkins, H. (Eds.). (1998a). *From Barbie to Mortal Kombat: Gender and computer games*. Cambridge, MA: MIT Press.

Cassell, J., & Jenkins, H. (1998b). Chess for girls? Feminism and computer games. In J. Cassell & H. Jenkins (Eds.), *From Barbie to Mortal Kombat: Gender and computer games* (pp. 2–45). Cambridge, MA: MIT Press.

Ching, C. C., & Kafai, Y. B. (in press). Peer pedagogy: Student collaboration and reflection in learning through design. *Teachers College Record*.

Ching, C. C., Kafai, Y. B., & Marshall, S. (2000). Spaces for change: Gender and technology access in collaborative software design projects. *Journal for Science Education and Technology* 9(1), 45–56.

Consalvo, M. (2008). Crunched by passion: Women game developers and work place challenges. In Y. B. Kafai, C. Heeter, J. Denner, & J. Sun (Eds.), *Beyond Barbie and Mortal Kombat: New perspectives on gender and computer games* (pp. 177–191). Cambridge, MA: MIT Press.

De Castell, S., & Bryson, M. (1998). Retooling play: Dystopia, dysphoria, and difference. In J. Cassell & H. Jenkins (Eds.), *From Barbie to Mortal Kombat: Gender and computer games* (pp. 2–45). Cambridge, MA: MIT Press.

Denner, J., & Campe, S. (2008). What games by girls can tell us. In Y. Kafai, C. Heeter, J. Denner, & J. Sun (Eds.), *Beyond Barbie and Mortal Kombat: New perspectives on gender and gaming* (pp. 129–144). Cambridge, MA: MIT Press.

Entertainment Software Association [ESA]. (2006). *2006 essential facts about the computer and video game industry*. Washington, DC: Author. Retrieved May 28, 2007, from http://www.theesa.com/archives/2006/05/2006_essential.php

Evard, M. (1998). *Twenty heads are better than one: Communities of children as virtual experts*. Unpublished doctoral dissertation, MIT Media Lab, Cambridge, MA.

Flanagan, M. (2006). Making games for social change. *AI & Society, 20*, 493–505.

Flanagan, M., & Nissenbaum, H. (2008). Value added design. In Y. B. Kafai, C. Heeter, J. Denner, & J. Sun (Eds.), *Beyond Barbie and Mortal Kombat: New perspectives on gender and computer games* (pp. 265–279). Cambridge, MA: MIT Press.

Friendship series. [Digital Game]. (n.d.). Mountain View, CA: Purple Moon Product.

Gailey, C. (1992). Mediated messages: Gender, class, and cosmos in home video games. *Journal of Popular Culture, 15*(2), 5–25.

Gee, J. (2003). *What videogames have to teach us about learning and literacy*. New York: Palgrave.

Gee, J. (2007). Introduction. In C. L. Selfe & G. E. Hawisher (Eds.), *Gaming lives in the twenty-first century* (pp. ix–xiii). New York: Palgrave Macmillan.

Goldstein, J. (2005). Violent video games. In J. Raessens & J. Goldstein (Eds.), *Handbook of computer game studies* (pp. 341–358). Cambridge, MA: MIT Press.

Greenfield, P. M., & R. R. Cocking (1996). (Eds.). Effects of interactive entertainment technology on development. In P. Greenfield & R. Cocking (Eds.), *Interacting with video* (pp. 1–5). Norwood, NJ: Ablex.

Hartmann, T., & Klimmt, C. (2006). Gender and computer games: Exploring females' dislikes. *Journal of Computer-Mediated Communication, 11*, 910–931.

Hayes, B. (2008). Girls, gaming, and trajectories of technological expertise. In Y. B. Kafai, C. Heeter, J. Denner, & J. Sun (Eds.), *Beyond Barbie and Mortal Kombat: New perspectives on gender and computer games* (pp. 217–230). Cambridge, MA: MIT Press.

Huff, C. W., Fleming, J. H., & Cooper, J. (1987). The social bias of gender differences in human computer interaction. In C. D. Martin (Ed.), *In search of gender-free paradigms for computer-science education* (pp. 19–32). Eugene, OR: ISTE Research Monographs.

Hyde, J. S. (2005). The gender similarities hypothesis. *American Psychologist, 60*(6), 581–592.

Ito, M. (2007). Education v. entertainment: A cultural history of children's software. In K. Salen (Ed.), *Ecology of games* (pp. 89–116). Chicago: MacArthur Foundation.

Jansz, J., & Martis, R. G. (2006). The Lara phenomenon: Powerful female characters in video games. *Sex Roles, 56*, 141–148.

Jenkins, H. (2003). From Barbie to Mortal Kombat: Further reflections. In: A. Everett & J. T. Caldwell (Eds.), *New media: Theories and practices* (pp. 243–254). New York: Routledge.

Jenkins, H. (2006). *Convergence culture: Where old and new media collide.* New York: New York University Press.

Jenkins, H., & Cassell, J. (2008). From Quake Grrls to Desperate Housewives: A Decade of gender and computer games. In Y. Kafai, C. Heeter, J. Denner, & J. Sun (Eds.), *Beyond Barbie and Mortal Kombat: New perspectives on gender and gaming* (pp. 5–20). Cambridge, MA: MIT Press.

Jenkins, H., Clinton, K., Purushotma, R., Robison, A., & Weigel, M. (2006). *Confronting the challenges of participation culture: Media education for the 21st century* (White Paper). Chicago: MacArthur Foundation.

Jenson, J., De Castell, S., & Bryson, M. (2003). "Girl talk": Gender equity, and identity discourses in a school-based computer culture. *Women's Studies International Forum, 26*(6), 561–573.

Kafai, Y. (1995). *Minds in play. Computer game design as a context for children's learning.* Hillsdale, NJ: Erlbaum.

Kafai, Y. B. (1996a). Gender differences in children's constructions of video games. In P. M. Greenfield & R. R. Cocking (Eds.), *Interacting with video* (pp. 39–66). Norwood, NJ: Ablex.

Kafai, Y. B. (1996b). Learning through making games: Children's development of design strategies in the creation of a computational artifact. In Y. Kafai & M. Resnick (Eds.), *Constructionism in practice* (pp. 71–96). Mahwah, NJ: Erlbaum.

Kafai, Y. B. (1998). Video game designs by children: Consistency and variability of gender differences. In J. Cassell & H. Jenkins (Eds.), *From Barbie to Mortal Kombat: Gender and computer games* (pp. 90–114). Cambridge, MA: MIT Press.

Kafai, Y. B. (2006). Playing and making games for learning: Instructionist and constructionist perspectives for game studies. *Games and Culture, 1*(1), 34–40.

Kafai, Y. B., & Ching, C. C. (2001). Affordances of collaborative software design planning for elementary students' science talk. *The Journal of the Learning Sciences, 10*(3), 323–363.

Kafai, Y., Feldon, D., Fields, D. A., Giang, M., & Quintero, M. (2007). Life in the time of Whypox: A virtual epidemic as a community event. In C. Steinfield, B. Pentland, M. Ackerman, & N. Contractor (Eds.), *Communities and technologies 2007* (pp. 171–190). New York: Springer.

Kafai, Y. B., Franke, M. L., & Battey, D. S. (2002). Educational software reviews under investigation. *Education, Communication & Information, 2*(2/3), 163–180.

Kafai, Y. B., Franke, M., Ching, C., & Shih, J. (1998). Games as interactive learning environments fostering teachers' and students' mathematical thinking. *International Journal of Computers for Mathematical Learning, 3*(2), 149–193.

Kafai, Y., Peppler, K., & Chiu, G. (2007). High tech programmers in low income communities: Seeding reform in a community technology center. In C. Steinfield, B. Pentland, M. Ackerman, & N. Contractor (Eds.), *Communities and technologies 2007* (pp. 545–564). New York: Springer.

Kelleher, C. (2008). Learning computer programming as storytelling. In Y. B. Kafai, C. Heeter, J. Denner, & J. Sun (Eds.), *Beyond Barbie and Mortal Kombat: New perspectives on gender and computer games* (pp. 247–264). Cambridge, MA: MIT Press.

Kinder, M. (1991). *Playing with power.* Berkeley: University of California Press.

Kirkpatrick, H., & Cuban, L. (1998). Should we be worried? What the research says about gender differences in access, use, attitudes and achievement with computers. *Educational Technology, 45,* 56–61.

Klawe, M., Inkpen, K., Phillips, E., Upitis, R., & Rubin, A. (2002). E-GEMS: A project on computer games, mathematics and gender. In N. Yelland, A. Rubin, & E. McWilliam (Eds.), *Ghosts in the machine: Women's voices in research with technology* (pp. 209–227). New York: Lang.

Laurel, B. (1998). Interview. In J. Cassell & H. Jenkins (Eds.), *From Barbie to Mortal Kombat: Gender and computer games* (pp. 118–135). Cambridge, MA: MIT Press.

Laurel, B. (2003). *Utopian entrepreneur.* Cambridge, MA: MIT Press.

Loftus, G. R., & Loftus, E. F. (1983). *Minds at play.* New York: Basic Books.

Logical Journey of the Zoombinis. [Digital Game]. (n.d.). Boston Riverdeep Interactive Learning.

MacGonigal, J. (2007). The success of I love bees: Study in massively collaborative puzzle gaming. In K. Salen (Ed.), *Ecologies of games* (pp. 199–227). Cambridge, MA: MIT Press.

Malone, T. W. (1981). What makes computer games fun? *BYTE, 258–277.*

Malone, T. W., & Lepper, M. R. (1987). Making learning fun: A taxonomy of intrinsic motivations for learning. In R. E. Snow & M. J. Farr (Eds.), *Aptitude, learning and instruction: Vol. 3. Conative and affective process analyses* (pp. 223–253). Hillsdale, NJ: Erlbaum.

MathBlaster. [Digital Game]. (n.d.). Los Angeles, CA: Knowledge Holdings, Inc.

Nelson, B. (2007). Exploring the use of individualized, reflective guidance in an educational multi-user virtual environment. *The Journal of Science Education and Technology, 16*(1), 83–97.

Nelson, B., Ketelhut, D. J., Clarke, J., Bowman, C., & Dede, C. (2005). Design-based research strategies for developing a scientific inquiry curriculum in a multi-user virtual environment. *Educational Technology, 45*(1), 21–27.

Pelletier, C. (2008). Gaming in context: How young people construct their gendered identities in playing and making games. In Y. B. Kafai, C. Heeter, J. Denner, & J. Sun (Eds.), *Beyond Barbie and Mortal Kombat: New perspectives on gender and computer games* (pp. 145–160). Cambridge, MA: MIT Press.

Peppler, K., & Kafai, Y. B. (2007). From SuperGoo to Scratch: Exploring creative media production. *Journal of Learning, Media & Technology, 32*(2), 149–166.

Provenzo, E. F. (1991). *Vide kids: Making sense of Nintendo*. Cambridge, MA: Harvard University Press.

Quest Atlantis. [Digital game]. (n.d.). (2001). Bloomington Indiana University Learning Sciences. http://atlantis.crlt.indiana.edu

Rapunsel [Digital game]. (2003). http://rapunsel.org.

Resnick, M., & Silverman, B. (2005). Some reflections on designing construction kits for kids. In *Proceeding of the 2005 Conference on Interaction Design and Children* (pp. 117–122). New York: ACM Press.

River City. [Digital game]. (2004). Cambridge, MA: Harvard University. Retrieved from http://muve.gse.harvard.edu/rivercityproject

Rockett's New World [Digital game]. (n.d.). Mountain View, CA: Purple Moon Product.

Rubin, A., Murray, M., O'Neil, K., & Ashley, J. (1997, March). *What kind of educational computer games would girls like?* Paper presented at the annual meeting of the American of Educational Research Association, Chicago.

Schofield, J. W. (1995). *Computers and classroom culture*. New York: Cambridge University Press.

Schott, G., & Horrell, K. R. (2000). Girls' gamers and their relationship with the gaming culture. *Convergence, 6*(4), 36–53.

Scratch. [Digital game]. (n.d.). Cambridge, MA: MIT Media Lab.

Second Life. [Digital game]. (2003). San Francisco, CA: Linden Lab.

Seif El Nasir, M., & Smith, B. (2006). Learning through game modding. *Computers in Entertainment, 4*(1), 5–9.

Seiter, E. (1993). *Sold separately: Children and parents in consumer culture*. New York: Rutgers University Press.

Shaffer, D. W. (2006). How computer games can help us learn. New York: Palgrave Macmillan.

Sims, The. [Digital game]. (2000). Redwood City, CA: Electronic Arts.

SiSSYFiGHT 2000. [Digital game]. (2000). Zimmerman, E. Retrieved from http://www.sissyfight.com

Squire, K. D. (2006). From content to context: Video games as designed experiences. *Educational Researcher, 35*(8), 19–29.

Steinkuehler, C. (2006). The mangle of play. *Games and Culture, 1*(3), 199–213.

Subrahmanyam, K., & Greenfield, P. M. (1998). Computer games for girls: What makes them play? In H. Jenkins & J. Cassell (Eds.), *From Barbie to Mortal Kombat: Gender and computer games* (pp. 46–71). Cambridge, MA: MIT Press.

Taylor, T. L. (2006). *Play between worlds*. Cambridge, MA: MIT Press.

Volman, M., & van Eack, E. (2001). Gender equity and information technology in education: The second decade. *Review of Educational Research, 71*(4), 613–634.

Whyville. [Digital game]. (1999). Pasadena, CA: Numedeon.

World of WarCraft. [Digital game]. (n.d.). CA: Blizzard Entertainment.

Yelland, R., & Rubin, A. (Eds.). (2002). *Ghosts in the machine: Women study women and technology*. New York: Lang.

Zimmerman, E. (2003). *Play as research: The iterative design process*. Retrieved May 28, 2007, from http://www.ericzimmerman.com/texts/iterative_design.htm

Chapter 15

Girls as Serious Gamers
Pitfalls and Possibilities

Jeroen Jansz and Mirjam Vosmeer

The common observation that women and girls not only play fewer digital games than men and boys, but also generally spend less time playing games, could be attributed to a simple matter of taste. If females prefer other kinds of entertainment, so be it. Men tend to prefer fishing, too, and are noticeably more enthusiastic about football and model railways than most women. Although it might be interesting to investigate the social and cultural causes of these gender stereotypes, there is no real necessity to fully understand, let alone try to change, the demographics of football fandom, for example. In contrast, gender participation in digital games parallels professional participation, namely that women are as underrepresented among players of digital games as they are in information technology (IT) careers (American Association of University Women [AAUW], 2000; National Center for Women and Information Technology [NCWIT], 2007). This chapter discusses how this parallel might be understood and utilized for change by looking at how gender and equity issues are impacted by digital game content and contextual factors.

Why Should We Care About Girls Playing Games?

In chapter 14 of this volume, Yasmin Kafai suggests the *technology pipeline* as a significant reason for why the study of gender and games is important. A better understanding of why girls tend to either like or dislike digital games might result in digital entertainment designed to appeal from an early age, thereby contributing to girls developing a positive attitude toward IT. In other words, girls playing digital games could be instrumental in achieving a more equitable participation in the computer culture at large.

Design issues must be taken into account as soon as we start to think about the role that games play in the issue of gender equity. Kafai (this volume, chapter 14) proposes that there should be two approaches to game design: (1) *games for girls* and (2) *games for change*. Each approach continues along the path taken by Justine Cassell and Henry Jenkins in their seminal work *From Barbie to Mortal Kombat* (1998):

We examine the different ways in which we might strive for equity: equity through separate but equal computer games, equity through equal access to the same computer games, equity through games that encourage new visions of equity itself. (p. 5)

Kafai's games for girls approach elaborates on realizing "equity through separate but equal computer games" (Cassell & Jenkins, 1998, p. 5), and criticizes the biased content of most digital games, emphasizing the need for content that will appeal to girls. We agree with Kafai not only about gender bias in the content of games, but also the importance of content with respect to equity. However, in this chapter, we argue that it is first necessary to focus on the specific meanings that female players attribute to the content of games, rather than on the actual content itself.

Kafai's games for change approach continues Cassell and Jenkins's (1998) goal of using games to encourage new perspectives on gender equity. As this goal relates to games that challenge gender stereotypes, both within a digital game itself and in the wider world, it also embraces the context of play. Yet the role of context is perhaps not as fully developed in Kafai's argument as it should be. In our view, context involves much more than either the setting of a game, or the environment in which it is played (Kafai, this volume, chapter 14). It must also take into account wider cultural factors, such as society's different perceptions of the appropriateness of girls versus boys playing particular digital games or digital games in general.

The Content of Digital Games: Does it Matter Much?

Emphasizing game content as a way of realizing gender equity has strong intuitive appeal and is supported by social cognitive theory (Bandura, 2001). If players were able to play a game that did not include stereotypical characters, this might lead to a proper appreciation of the content and a consequential effect on their own behavior. Smith (2006) argues that the biased representation of females in games is partly responsible for women's disinterest in them. Research about game content reveals that almost all games portray gender in a stereotypical way (Beasly & Standly, 2002; Dietz, 1998; Jansz & Martis, 2007). Indeed, although representation of powerful women in recent games should be applauded, the overall portrayal of them has not improved significantly because the emphasis on their physical attributes and female sexuality remains (Jansz & Martis, 2007).

Another important element that alienates women and girls from digital games is the notion that they often contain violent confrontations and scenes. In fact, research conducted among female Dutch secondary school students between the ages of 12 and 18 found that when asked about the games that they disliked most, the girls identified games which contained blood, killing, violence, or aggression. Interestingly, none of them mentioned those in which highly sexualized female characters were featured (Vosmeer, Jansz, & Van Zoonen, 2007b). In a study that specifically focused on female gaming dislikes, Hartmann and Klimmt (2006) also identified a similarly negative female attitude toward violent game content.

The concept *technology of gender* (De Lauretis, 1987) suggests that reception of media contributes to everyday gender roles, or, in other words, is an enabler of masculinity and femininity. Digital games can function as a technology of gender when players express their engagement or identification with the characters they are playing as they discuss their looks and actions with other players (Vosmeer, Jansz, & Van Zoonen, 2006). But dominant game content only promotes contemporary masculinity, providing a one-sided technology of gender (Walkerdine, 2006). To understand the potential of digital games to also be a technology of gender for girls, we will explore what kind of game content has been successful with a female audience, and what game content has been actively appropriated by female players.

The Women Are Playing: Game Content That Works

The success of Mattel's *Barbie Fashion Designer* (1995), which became the pinnacle of the so-called pink games (e.g., games for girls), showed that many girls were eager to play if provided with attractive game content. However, these games have been criticized for their traditional, if not stereotypical, portrayal of female gender roles (Cassell & Jenkins, 1998). The continued presence and development of these pink games cast doubt on how relevant this criticism is. The pink games on shelves in game stores and toyshops emphasize bright colors and game content that relates to traditional female roles, like nursing and caring. Yet the amount of shelf space that is dedicated to pink games is considerably less than that reserved for the "green-brown games" that are targeted at a young male audience. The green and brown colors aptly reflect a content that is often about fighting wars in camouflage attire, or playing sports matches on green fields. Indeed, the abundance of green-brown games still reflects the male dominance of the contemporary game culture (Ivory, 2006; Walkerdine, 2006).

Alternatives to pink games, namely games for change, are scarce. *SISSY-FiGHT 2000* (2000) is an example of a game with nontraditional content that appeals to girls (Kafai, this volume, chapter 14). *PowerBabes* (2002) is another example (Krotoski, 2004). Both games reflect empowerment and the concept of girl power that was successfully introduced and commodified by *The Spice Girls* franchise. However, the content of *SISSYFiGHT 2000* merely trades the stereotype of the nice, supportive girl for a girl who is a nasty "teen-bitch" obsessed with popularity. Similarly, the *PowerBabes* characters are very much occupied with clothing and partying, despite their obvious control of the situation. This raises the crucial question of whether the intention behind games for change is really being met by games that may give girls an opportunity to experiment with the image of what it means to be female, but nevertheless still confirm existing stereotypes of adolescent female behavior.

Regardless, this discussion still rests on the assumption that game content has a direct effect on a gamer's identity and neglects to consider the active role that a player takes in attributing meaning to a game. Insight gained by research into uses and gratification (Ruggiero, 2000) and audience studies (Jansz, 2005; Jenkins, Clinton, Purushotma, Robison, & Weigel, 2006; Livingstone, 2004) highlights the active role of the user in the attribution of meaning to media content, which is even more apparent in the case of interactive digital games. Players process the information that they are confronted with, and their interventions may result in changes in the ways that they experience the actual content on their screens. In other words, if we want to understand the effects of particular character representations, we must also take players' experiences into account.

The Affordances of Game Content: It's Not About the Virtual Money

The analytical link between game content and player experience is realized by the concept of *affordance*, which was originally developed by perception psychologist J. J. Gibson (1979) in his attempt to systematically link perception and action to the world in which the perceiver/actor is functioning. Affordance refers to the opportunities for action offered up to an organism by a given environment (Gibson, 1979). Affordances are part of nature, but also occur in man-made, artificial environments. As an example, humans approaching a staircase perceive it as being climbable without explicit instruction or even thought. Conceptualizing particular game features as affordances allows them to appeal to gamers (Linderoth, Lindström, & Alexandersson, 2004; Yates & Littleton, 1999). Obviously, the perceiver/actor side of any affordance involves capacity and skill. Most titles require players to have attained certain levels of cognitive development (e.g., literacy). Specific titles require specific abilities— for example, background knowledge of soccer's rules when playing a title in the FIFA series.

The active appropriation of these affordances results in a different evaluation of a game's content among players, and some of them may not be at all bothered by the dominant stereotypical portrayal of male and female characters. Game researchers have stretched the argument about active appropriation by pointing to differences between novice and experienced players. Newman (2004) observed that experienced players are less interested in how a character is portrayed, than in its competence. For them, a character becomes a cursor with a particular functionality. Carr (2005) made a similar point when she argued "seasoned gamers routinely distinguish between the 'look' of a game and its game-play" (p. 478). Less-experienced players, by contrast, tend to overestimate the importance of representational factors. In a study that focused on female gaming dislikes, Hartmann and Klimmt (2006) found that these players disliked the emphasis on competition, but they were not overly concerned by the hypersexualized and biased imagery.

The active appropriation of game content makes an ironic or even opposite interpretation of the content feasible. An ironic player stance is possible in both "pink" and "green-brown games" as well as in alternative games for change. For example, some female players interviewed by Royse and her colleagues took pleasure in challenging gender norms (Royse, Lee, Undrahbuyan, Hopson, & Consalvo, 2007). While they admitted to the hypersexualization of female images in games, they deliberately choose to pick (or create) avatars that were feminine, sexy, and strong (Royse et al., 2007). Generally, there is only one prerequisite: the game must promise an enjoyable experience, since research suggests that enjoyment is the principal reason for individuals spending time on media content (Vorderer, Klimmt, & Ritterfeld, 2006). Obviously, an educational game that instructs girls in gender play has less appeal than one that turns gender play into an entertaining experience. Female players could enjoy themselves by ridiculing what is on display, and elaborating on the absurd possibilities that a game presents, instead of being impressed or offended by the hypersexualized nature of their game character. Their gender performances in daily life are constrained by social norms, but the virtual reality of a game enables them to experience and even ridicule gender performance in a way that is not possible outside of the game's environment (Jansz, 2005). If new games for change are to be developed, the process should begin with an investigation into the conditions in which digital games function as technologies of gender for female players. In addition, it is essential to have detailed knowledge of how adolescent female gamers appropriate the affordances of a variety of digital games, including the ones with allegedly offensive content.

Context is Crucial

Kafai (this volume, chapter 14) acknowledges that context is one of the factors that has an impact on gender differences and performances, although she does not make it absolutely clear what the context of play embraces. It may, for example, refer to the physical location in which a game is played, to the social context of enjoying a game with other players, or to cultural notions about the appropriateness of gaming for boys and girls. Earlier research enables us to distinguish between the influence of the immediate context of play and the wider social context of game culture. A study by Yates and Littleton (1999) identified the importance of the immediate social context for the actual appropriation of the game's affordances. Boys and girls were asked to execute a computer-based task. The researchers varied the context of the instructions without making any changes to the software itself. In the experiment, the task was presented as either a game or as a skills test. In the skills condition there was no gender difference in performance, but when the same task was introduced as a game, there were considerable differences between the boys' and girls' performances, with the boys achieving much higher scores than the girls.

Carr (2005) took a different approach by showing how the immediate physical location of play influenced girls' game preferences. In her study, girls participated in an all-girl gaming club at school, and this setting shaped their preferences by boosting their enthusiasm for specific titles. But the preferences were shaped equally by the girls' earlier experiences, leading Carr to conclude that preferences are gendered, but not static. The girls' choices depended on where they were and the games to which they had previous access.

A recent study about girls and boys designing digital games provided further insight into cultural context and preexisting ideas about the appropriateness of gaming and IT for girls and boys. Vosmeer, Jansz, and Van Zoonen (2007b) looked at the Dutch national *Make a Game* competition, in which secondary school students designed digital games. The games were developed in teams of about five students coached by a teacher. One of the explicit aims of *Make a Game* (2007) was to enhance the levels of interest in IT of both female and male students, although the goal of recruiting female students was not given particular emphasis in either the presentation or the set-up of the contest. The results confirmed several stereotypes about women, games, and IT.

First, there were seven times as many male as there were female competitors. Consequently, most teams consisted exclusively of male students. Second, the coaches observed that task differentiation in mixed-sex teams followed dominant gender stereotypes, in that the male members of a team programmed the games, whereas female members engaged in the narrative aspects and design features. The overrepresentation of male students in the *Make a Game* contest could be easily explained, since participation in it was organized by IT teachers in almost all of the schools. Dutch secondary school students have some freedom in choosing subjects for their curriculum, and since relatively small numbers of girls had chosen to take IT classes, the number of girls who participated in the contest was therefore equally limited. As far as the issue of gendered task differentiation is concerned, because gender differences in attitudes towards digital games and IT was not specifically addressed, Vosmeer et al. (2007b) assume that existing patterns of gender preferences were merely reproduced. As a result, the *Make a Game* contest could not succeed in inspiring girls' interest in the "hard" technology aspects of IT (i.e., programming). The results also highlighted the importance of addressing existing gender differences when serious gaming projects are introduced within the classroom so that both male and female students can fully benefit from the opportunities that these projects have to offer.

Bryce and Rutter (2003) analyzed a wider social context when they considered the issue of the gendered nature of contemporary game culture. They argued that the social and spatial positioning of gaming strongly influences the way in which the gendered nature of game culture is experienced. Public game culture is manifested in gaming events, game reviews, Websites and advertisements that are dominated by stereotypical masculine values (see also Ivory, 2006), hence the lack of enthusiasm by female adolescents for public events such as local-area network (LAN) parties and gaming competitions, even though some of them may play the kind of online games that are popular at LAN parties in the privacy of their homes (Bryce & Rutter, 2003; Jansz & Martens, 2005).

In conclusion, several studies have shown that the immediate social context of play and the wider cultural context of games and play are both important influences on the gendered nature of game choices and preferences. There is, however, a further contextual factor that must be taken into account if we want to explain the gendered nature of gaming, and that is the issue of adolescent development.

Age seems to be an important factor when it comes to games and gender. Although there is no significant gender difference in the playing of digital games among young children, when girls reach their early teens their interest in gaming drops dramatically, while boys continue to play. For many girls this change is final, although some do (re-)embrace gaming in early adulthood (Durkin, 2006; Jones, 2003; Pratchett, 2005; Roberts, Foehr, & Rideout, 2005; Royse et al., 2007). These changes coincide with the approximate onset of adolescence in most girls, meaning that consideration of the effect of adolescent development on game choice and preference is crucial. Research about adolescence in the Western world has tended to characterize this period as a series of changes, conflicts, and challenges. Adolescents must adjust to physical growth and increased sexual feelings, to new cognitive and socioemotional challenges at school, and to changes in their emotional and social relationships with their parents and peers (Harter, 1998; Steinberg & Morris, 2001). These readjustments may lead to conflict and insecurity about who they are (identity), and what they feel (emotion), as well as doubts about where they fit in socially (Bosma & Kunnen, 2001).

Leisure activities are particularly important in adolescent development because they offer more opportunities for playfully probing identities than school and work. This is particularly relevant to playing digital games. Recent studies have found that there is an important gender difference in motives for play. In a survey by Lucas and Sherry (2004), social interaction was the second most important motive (after challenge) for male participants, whereas female participants rated social interaction as the least important of the six motives. Jansz, Avis, and Vosmeer's (2008) research into *The Sims* (2000) corroborated this result, with male players scoring high on social interaction than their female counterparts. Interviews with female players of *The Sims* also revealed that they enjoyed playing the game to experience individual pleasure and relaxation (Vosmeer, Jansz, & Van Zoonen, 2007a). In the same vein, female players interviewed by Royse et al. (2007) reported that games provided a needed distraction from their daily worries. These different studies showed that playing allowed female gamers to refrain from social interaction, and to separate themselves from domestic and family duties, in the same way that reading romance novels and women's magazines resulted in temporary, comfortable isolation (Hermes, 2005; Radway, 1984). Boys and young men, by contrast, are attracted to gaming because playing enables them to interact with friends. In this sense it has a lot in common with, for example, playing football. Playing digital games offers ample opportunities for male bonding where social and emotional ties are based on sharing an activity, rather than on disclosing oneself in intimate conversation (Durkin, 2006; Jansz, 2000).

This research suggests that the ordinary social context of (most) adolescent girls is not conducive to gaming. Social interaction is an important leisure activity for them, but digital games are not generally appreciated for their interaction. In fact, the results from *The Sims* study suggest that the opposite is true, namely that women and girls like to play games because it creates a comfortable isolation (Vosmeer, Jansz, & Van Zoonen, 2007b). Whether this observation can be generalized across genres is a pressing empirical question. *Everquest* (1999) for example, attracts a substantial group of female players (about 19%; Griffiths, Davies, & Chappell, 2004). The gameplay of this massively multiplayer online role-playing game (MMORPG) is very much about online interaction with other players, but women can still appreciate it because it allows them to isolate themselves from their immediate social context. Yee (2006) also studied gender differences in motivational factors between players of MMORPGs, and found that while male players scored significantly higher on achievement components, female players scored higher on relationship components. However, he also found that male players socialized just as much as female players, but were apparently looking for very different things in those relationships.

The results of these studies indicate that the choices and preferences of girls and women are determined by a complex interplay between game content, genre, and personal motives. Deci and Ryan's self-determination theory (SDT; Deci & Ryan, 2000) has been proposed as an explanation for the motive behind certain preferences in forms of entertainment media (Vorderer, Steen, & Chan, 2006). Female game preferences, for example, may be explained by the extent to which a game (or genre) satisfies the three fundamental requirements of SDT: autonomy, competence, and relevance. In their study among male and female players, Ryan and his colleagues did not find any gender differences in any of the three requirements (Ryan, Rigby, & Przybylski, 2006). In other words, the specific group of women that plays digital games does not differ from male players in what motivates them during the game. But this study did not address the gender differences in initial preferences for games and genres. Therefore, we suggest employing SDT in future research to study how girls satisfy their needs for autonomy, competence, and relevance through different media content, in different social contexts. Detailed insight into what motivates girls to prefer certain digital games to other forms of media is necessary if we want to determine what is needed to develop serious games for girls.

Designing Serious Games for Girls

Kafai considers the ability to mod a game as key to making serious games for girls (this volume, chapter 14). The possibility of customizing and personalizing avatars may be attractive to girls, and to a certain extent, we share Kafai's optimism about the appeal of modding. This kind of digital tinkering fits into existing play patterns, because, for example, it has a lot in common with what girls do when they play with their dolls' houses. Game modding is a productive activity, and girls who engage with modding and share the results with others on the Internet may have enhanced digital skills, thus reducing the participation gap in digital culture between boys and the female gender (Jenkins et al., 2006).

However, we are skeptical about the extent of the appeal of modding. Its appeal may be limited only to younger age groups, because adolescent girls (12 and older) have different patterns of play in their daily lives and may be less attracted to modding games. The play and leisure activities of adolescent girls are generally concerned with the construction of a female identity by negotiating and performing it in the public arena. A (serious) game for change could contribute to an alternative negotiation or performance by affording girls the opportunity to perform different kinds of gendered practices inside and outside the digital game arena. The likely success of this type of serious gaming depends on the entertainment value attributed to this kind of digital gender play. A promising prospect is that adolescent girls are enthusiastic users of digital communication technology, despite being less interested in digital games and information technology. They are actively engaged in emailing, instant messaging, and presenting their profiles on the Internet, and recent research found that using these communicative technologies was positively related to real-life social relationships (Valkenburg & Peter, 2007; Valkenburg, Schouten, & Peter, 2005). Apparently, the mobile phone- and Internet-based social networks are attractive technologies that afford users the opportunity to relate virtual communication to ordinary interactions. The conditions under which girls' enthusiasm for digital communication translates into other digital domains, including digital games, is a fertile area for further research.

Conclusion

The chapters in this volume highlight the opportunities that serious games offer. When linked with issues of gender, serious games, and equity, the focus generally is on game content, especially on what pitfalls in game design prevent girls from playing digital games, or how serious games invite or persuade their players to engage in gender play that contributes to equity. We argue that a focus just on content is too restrictive because it doesn't consider the ways in which active players appropriate the affordances of the game or the broader social and cultural context in which the game is played.

Because of hegemonic male values in gaming culture, it is difficult to change existing gaming patterns; however, it may be useful to change the context of gaming locally. The examples discussed above show that specific local contexts may radically change girls' interpretation of and preferences for games, and that they can be persuaded to forego their negative perceptions about gaming entertainment and game culture. Access to a gaming environment within an educational setting may be determined by factors that date back to earlier in the children's time in the school, in particular their original choices of certain subject matters. Accordingly, when introducing serious games in schools, teachers should take into account existing gendered patterns of leisure, just as a creative teacher who uses fishing or building a model railway as an exercise for learning about biology or mathematics must consider that fishing and model railways are more attuned to male patterns of leisure activities than to female, and that female students may feel inhibited from embracing such exercises enthusiastically. With respect to serious games, it is therefore important to be aware of existing gender attitudes toward gaming and the contextual determinants of game choice and appreciation in order to create situations in which girls are likely to benefit from and enjoy the possibilities that serious games have to offer.

References

American Association of University Women (AAUW). (2000). *Tech-savvy. Educating girls in the new computer age.* Washington, DC: American Association of University Women Educational Foundation.

Bandura, A. (2001). Social cognitive theory of mass communication. *Media Psychology, 3*(3), 265–299.

Barbie Fashion Designer. [Digital game]. (1995). El Segundo, CA: Mattel.

Beasly, B., & Standly, C. T. (2002). Shirts vs. skins: Clothing as an indicator of gender role stereotyping in video games. *Mass Communication & Society, 5,* 279–293.

Bosma, H. A., & Kunnen, E. S. (2001). Determinants and mechanisms in ego identity development: A review and synthesis. *Developmental Review, 21*(1), 39–66.

Bryce, J., & Rutter, J. (2003). Gender dynamics and the social and spatial organization of computer gaming. *Leisure Studies, 22,* 1–15.

Carr, D. (2005). Contexts, gaming pleasures, and gendered preferences. *Simulation and Gaming, 36*(4), 464–482.

Cassell, J., & Jenkins, H. (Eds.). (1998). *From Barbie to Mortal Kombat: Gender and computer games.* Cambridge, MA: MIT Press.

Deci, E. L., & Ryan, R. M. (2000). The "what" and "why" of goal pursuits: Human needs and the self-determination of behavior. *Psychological Inquiry, 11*(4), 227–268.

De Lauretis, T. (1987). *Technologies of gender: Essays on theory, film, and fiction.* Bloomington: Indiana University Press.

Dietz, T. L. (1998). An examination of violence and gender role portrayals in video games: Implications for gender socialization and aggressive behavior. *Sex Roles: A Journal of Research, 38*(5–6), 425–442.

Durkin, K. (2006). Game playing and adolescents' development. In P. Vorderer & J. Bryant (Eds.), *Playing video games* (pp. 415–428). Mahwah, NJ: Erlbaum.

Everquest. [Digital game]. (1999). San Diego, CA: Sony Online Entertainment.

Gibson, J. J. (1979). *The ecological approach to visual perception.* Boston, MA: Houghton Mifflin.

Griffiths, M. D., Davies, M. N. O., & Chappell, D. (2004). Demographic factors and playing variables in online computer gaming. *CyberPsychology & Behavior, 7*(4), 479–487.

Harter, S. (1998). The development of self-representations. In N. Eisenberg (Ed.), *Handbook of child psychology: Vol. 3. Social, emotional and personality development* (5th ed., Vol. 3, pp. 553–618). New York: Wiley.

Hartmann, T., & Klimmt, C. (2006). Gender and computer games: Exploring females' dislikes. *Journal of Computer-Mediated Communication, 11*(4), 910.

Hermes, J. (2005). *Reading women's magazines.* Cambridge, England: Polity Press.

Ivory, J. D. (2006). Still a man's game: Gender representation in online reviews of video games. *Mass-Communication-and-Society, 9*(1), 103–114.

Jansz, J. (2000). Masculine identity and restrictive emotionality. In A. H. Fischer (Ed.), *Gender and emotion. Social psychological perspectives* (pp. 166–186). Cambridge, England: Cambridge University Press.

Jansz, J. (2005). The emotional appeal of violent video games for adolescent males. *Communication Theory, 15,* 219–241.

Jansz, J., Avis, C., & Vosmeer, M. (2008). *Playing the Sims2: An exploratory survey among female and male gamers.* Manuscript submitted for publication.

Jansz, J., & Martens, L. (2005). Gaming at a LAN-event: The social context of playing video games. *New Media & Society, 7,* 333–355.

Jansz, J., & Martis, R. G. (2007). The Lara phenomenon: Powerful female characters in video games. *Sex Roles, 56,* 9–34.

Jenkins, H., Clinton, K., Purushotma, R., Robison, A. J., & Weigel, M. (2006). *Confronting the challenges of participatory culture: Media education for the 21st century.* Chicago: MacArthur Foundation.

Jones, S. (2003). *Let the games begin: Gaming technology and entertainment among college students.* Washington, DC: Pew Internet & American Life Project.

Krotoski, A. (2004). *Chicks and joysticks: An exploration of women and gaming.* London: Entertainment & Leisure Software Publishers Association.

Linderoth, J., Lindström, B., & Alexandersson, M. (2004). Learning with computer games. In J. Goldstein, D. Buckingham, & G. Brougère (Eds.), *Toys, games, and media* (pp. 157–176). Mahwah, NJ: Erlbaum.

Livingstone, S. (2004). The challenge of changing audiences: Or, what is the audience researcher to do in the age of the Internet? *European Journal of Communication, 19*(1), 75–86.

Lucas, K., & Sherry, J. L. (2004). Sex differences in video game play: A communication-based explanation. *Communication Research, 31*(5), 499–523.

Make a Game. (2007). Retrieved December 19, 2007, from http://www.make-a-game. nl/

National Center for Women and Information Technology (NCWIT). (2007). *Women and information technology: By the numbers.* Retrieved December 19, 2007, from http://www.ncwit.org/pdf/Stat_sheet_2007.pdf

Newman, J. (2004). *Video games.* London: Routledge.

Pratchett, R. (2005). *Gamers in the UK: Digital play, digital lifestyles.* BBC New Media & Technology.

PowerBabes. [Digital game]. (2002). Copenhagen, Denmark: Egmont Serieforlaget.

Radway, J. A. (1984). *Reading the romance: Women, patriarchy, and popular literature.* Chapel Hill: University of North Carolina Press.

Roberts, D. F., Foehr, U. G., & Rideout, V. J. (2005). *Generation M: Media in the lives of 8-18 year-olds.* Menlo Park, CA: Kaiser Family Foundation.

Royse, P., Lee, J., Undrahbuyan, B., Hopson, M., & Consalvo, M. (2007). Women and games: technologies of the gendered self. *New Media & Society, 9*(4), 555–576.

Ruggiero, T. E. (2000). Uses and gratifications theory in the 21st century. *Mass Communication & Society, 3*(1), 3–37.

Ryan, R., Rigby, C., & Przybylski, A. (2006). The motivational pull of video games: A self-determination theory approach. *Motivation & Emotion, 30*(4), 344–360.

Sims, The. [Digital game]. (2000). Redwood Shores, CA: Electronic Arts.

SiSSYFiGHT 2000. [Digital game]. (2000). Zimmerman, E. http://www.sissyfight.com

Smith, S. L. (2006). Perps, pimps, and provocative clothing: Examining negative content patterns in video games. In P. Vorderer & J. Bryant (Eds.), *Playing video games—Motives, responses, and consequences* (pp. 57–75). London: Erlbaum.

Steinberg, L., & Morris, A. S. (2001). Adolescent development. *Annual Review of Psychology, 52*(1), 83–110.

Valkenburg, P. M., & Peter, J. (2007). Preadolescents' and adolescents' online communication and their closeness to friends. *Developmental Psychology, 43*(2), 267.

Valkenburg, P. M., Schouten, A. P., & Peter, J. (2005). Adolescents' identity experiments on the Internet. *New Media & Society, 7*(3), 383.

Vorderer, P., Klimmt, C., & Ritterfeld, U. (2006). Enjoyment: At the heart of media entertainment. *Communication Theory, 144,* 388–408.

Vorderer, P., Steen, F. F., & Chan, E. (2006). Motivation. In J. Bryant & P. Vorderer (Eds.), *Psychology of entertainment* (pp. 3–17). Mahwah, NJ: Erlbaum.

Vosmeer, M., Jansz, J., & Van Zoonen, L. (2006, June). *Video games as technologies of gender: Analyzing Final Fantasy forums.* Paper presented at the annual meeting of the International Communication Association, Dresden, Germany.

Vosmeer, M., Jansz, J., & Van Zoonen, L. (2007a, May). *I'd like to have a house like that. A study of adult female players of The Sims.* Paper presented at the annual meeting of the International Communication Association, San Francisco, CA.

Vosmeer, M., Jansz, J., & Van Zoonen, L. (2007b, April). *Make a game. An analysis of girls making games.* Paper presented at Women in Games Conference, Newport, UK.

Walkerdine, V. (2006). Playing the game. Young girls performing femininity in video game play. *Feminist Media Studies, 6*(4), 519–537.

Yates, S. J., & Littleton, K. (1999). Understanding computer game cultures: A situated approach. *Information, Communication & Society, 2*(4), 566–583.

Yee, N. (2006). Motivations for play in online games. *CyberPsychology & Behavior, 9*(6), 772–775.

Chapter 16

Serious Games and Social Change
Why They (Should) Work

Christoph Klimmt

Of the content areas discussed in this volume, social change presents a special challenge for theorists and for game designers. Social change, in contrast to learning and development, typically refers to much broader, multicomponent phenomena closely connected to peoples' daily lives, often in conjunction with others in the family and community. Health-related behaviors, for instance, are targets of entertainment education media striving for social change (Singhal, Cody, Rogers, & Sabido, 2004), and cannot be limited simply to providing new knowledge about a certain disease. Rather, several communication goals have to be achieved if social change is likely to occur, including changes in beliefs and attitudes, learning how to perform selected behaviors, (e.g., how to become an organ donor or how to use a condom), and instilling motivation to change among members in the targeted audience. Ideally, a successful serious game may be able to produce significant changes in all of these outcomes, or at least modest changes that are sustained over time.

In this chapter, I argue that serious games have an important place in communication campaigns for social change. I will do so by constructing a conceptual model of serious game outcomes that combines a variety of well-established psychological mechanisms. After discussing these mechanisms, I will outline empirical research perspectives and, more importantly, reflect on the nature of playful action that provides conceptual reasons underlying possible outcomes.

Conceptualizing Social Change

The theoretical difficulty associated with the notion of social change is its connection to multiple levels of social analyses (e.g., Sherry, 2002). Ultimately, social change can (and needs to) be construed at the level of society (Papa et al., 2000). If a certain social change is to occur in a relevant, notable, and measurable way, then a substantial portion of a society's members needs to adjust their behavior. For instance, a society's position towards domestic violence will only be regarded as having changed if a significant number of men have adjusted their behavior in certain ways sustained over time. In this sense, social change is societal change, and it is the ultimate goal of any communication campaign. If successful, a critical mass of behavioral alteration is achieved, producing future chain-reactions and ultimately leading to self-stabilizing processes (Papa et al., 2000). For instance, shifts in public opinion about certain behaviors (say, using tobacco) may lead to altered legislation that stabilizes the desired change: It guides public behavior, institutionalizes the endorsement of the desired behaviors, and thus expands the change process beyond the (small) social movement that had initialized the shift in public opinion originally.

In addition to the societal level, social change can be construed at the level of organizations and groups, both formal or informal, large or small. Social life is organized in very different ways, including tribal structures, core families, schools, and companies. At this level of analysis, decision-making bodies relevant for a campaign are simple to identify, which opens access points for communication that address a change of behavior within the social structure. For example, heads of tribes, chief executive officers, or school directors are important partners (or targets) of campaigns for social change at the mesolevel. On the other hand, mesolevel structures typically display strong internal coherence and long-grown social bonds among members, which can result in significant capacities to resist or counteract change messages concerning traditional behaviors now seen as threatened. A community of immigrants that adheres to a traditional social behavior, such as arranged marriages of young girls, for instance, would resist communication activities that threaten traditions if the campaign strategy is not carefully designed and executed. Nevertheless, since mesolevel social structures are important reference points for individuals and their behavior (Tajfel & Turner, 1986), communication for social change cannot ignore this dimension, but rather, has to face the challenges associated with it.

Finally, social change must be explicated at the level of individual cognition and behavior. Society-level and group-level effects of communication campaigns depend on the ability to reach and influence a sufficiently large number of individuals, including opinion leaders, innovators, or influencers (Keller & Berry, 2003; Rogers, 2003; Singhal et al., 2004). Because social change involves complex processes of knowledge acquisition, attitude change, follow-up interpersonal communication, and collective action (Papa et al., 2000; Singhal et al., 2004), a potentially large number of cognitive/attitudinal, motivational/affective, and behavioral media effects needs to be assumed as part of the communication process for social change, which can complicate serious games research.

These conceptualizations of social change have guided previous projects on entertainment education campaigns that utilize conventional mass media, such as radio or television (Singhal & Rogers, 1999, 2002; Singhal et al., 2004). Entertainment education has been developed as a strategy to render change-related messages so appealing that target audiences reluctant to select serious, instructional media would find exposure to the messages gratifying (Singhal

& Rogers, 1999). The model of serious games effects outlined later in this chapter looks at serious games as an interactive delivery medium for entertainment education (see also Wang & Singhal, this volume, chapter 17). This perspective allows the direct application of established theory to the uses and consequences of playing serious games. By reviewing the specific properties of digital games, especially interactivity (Klimmt & Vorderer, 2007; Vorderer, 2000), existing assumptions on entertainment education effects in the domain of social change can be adopted or modified.

Important Properties of Serious Games

A model of the possible effects of serious games on social change needs to be based on the unique properties of digital games that could be relevant for such effects. Five characteristics of digital games will be considered: multimodality, interactivity, narrative, option for social (multiplayer) use, and the specific frame of gaming experiences (cf. Ritterfeld & Weber, 2006).

Multimodality

The history of digital games is dominated by continuous improvement of game technology, which has primarily focused on better graphics and better sound. With the availability of more powerful computing hardware, the richness of audiovisual representation in digital games has increased dramatically over the years. Contemporary shooter games share the basic principles of the early *Pac Man* games, but have proceeded from the formerly abstract and symbolic to a very natural, concrete, and lifelike representation of the game world (Tamborini & Skalski, 2006). More recently, haptic modality has been included in the technological improvements of digital games. Force feedback input devices stimulate players' hands and transmit, for instance, simulated vibrations of moving vehicles to the driver (player). More complex motion-oriented devices, such as the controller of Nintendo's *Wii*, allow natural movements to create input to the game. For example, a tennis game on the *Wii* is played by moving the controller similar to the way one would move a tennis racket in a real tennis match. The latest technological advances include speech recognition, which enables new modes of input and, among other advantages, "natural" conversations with digital characters in the game world (Johnson et al., 2004). In sum, contemporary digital games are high-fidelity simulation environments that (can) involve various senses and create very convincing, immersive experiences (Steuer, 1992; Wirth et al., 2007).

While commercial games companies strive for fidelity or lifelike multimodal representation to increase the games' entertainment value (Tamborini & Skalski, 2006), the technological capabilities of modern digital game systems (engines) also allow for creative, multiperspective representation of complex, abstract spaces (Wolf, 1995), issues, and processes, which are potentially useful in terms of didactics (Amory, Naicker, Vincent, & Adams, 1999; Ritterfeld & Weber, 2006). Thus, the multimodality property of modern digital game technology is relevant to both motivational and cognitive issues in the modeling of serious games' impact on social change. Furthermore, it is a quality that distinguishes digital games from the conventional mass media that have been used in prior entertainment education projects (Singhal et al., 2004).

Interactivity

Interactivity has a long history in the communication literature, especially in the literature on computer-mediated communication and Internet use (e.g., Kiousis, 2002) and virtual reality media (e.g., Steuer, 1992). The implications of interactivity for new media entertainment, especially digital games, have also been discussed (e.g., Grodal, 2000; Klimmt, Hartmann, & Frey, 2007; Vorderer, 2000). In the context of digital games, interactivity is defined as a game property that allows users to influence the quality and course of events occurring in the game world (see Klimmt & Vorderer, 2007). Depending on the game genre, interface technology, and player skill, interactive game use can manifest in very different ways, including simulated motion within three-dimensional virtual spaces, manipulation of complex ecologic or economic systems, communication with virtual characters, and adjustment of visual perspectives onto the game world's processes and events.

A very important commonality of all the conceivable manifestations of digital game interactivity is the increased self-reference they create for players. Interactive use creates a game experience in which players perceive themselves as the center of events, as the driver of change and progress. Game events are closely connected to player action through interactivity. Whatever happens in the game world becomes relevant to the player's self due to interactivity: The player has caused the event through her or his input (Klimmt & Hartmann, 2006)—perhaps based on plans and intentions, perhaps without intention or in spite of contradicting intentions. The player is immediately affected by the event, as it is relevant to her or his own situation within the game world, namely the individual's performance and further options to proceed and act. In contrast, when watching a noninteractive movie, events on the screen are neither caused by viewers nor are viewers directly affected by them. Rather, the movie characters are agents of and affected by the events. Movie characters may be highly relevant to viewers (e.g., Klimmt, Hartmann, & Schramm, 2006), which also renders movie events caused by or relevant to the characters important for viewers. But interactive digital game use clearly creates a more direct, self-related connection between player and game world events. This self-connection holds important implications for game experience (Vorderer, 2000) and cognitive processing of game content, such as mental model construction.

Narrative

Early digital games did not include much of a notable narrative. If anything, they incorporated simple narrative structures such as good triumphs over evil. Modern games contain much more complex narrative structures, and specific techniques to integrate player interactivity with a coherent narrative framework have emerged (Klimmt, 2003; Kücklich, 2003; Lee, Park, & Jin, 2006). In contemporary story-driven games, players explore a rich world with hundreds of smaller stories connected to one main plot—a structure similar to that of a modern novel. Careful balance of (1) open elements that players can explore interactively and (2) predefined closed elements that secure the coherence and logical structure of the story, allows one to integrate voluminous and very appealing narrative frameworks in contemporary games. Just like multimodality and interactivity, the capacity of digital games to tell reasonable, comprehensive, and interesting stories is, in terms of serious games effects theory, relevant both to issues of playing motivation and to processing of game content.

Social (Multiplayer) Use

With the technological improvements of computer networks (LAN) and broadband Internet connections, more and more digital games include options to bring several or even a very large number of players together. Small-scale multiplayer sessions are run on local networks ("LAN-party," cf. Jansz & Martens, 2005) or by an Internet server to which individual players hook up (e.g., Griffiths, Davies, & Chappel, 2003). Large-scale social game play is organized within virtual game worlds that exist permanently online (massively multiplayer online role-playing games (MMOs) (cf. Chan & Vorderer, 2006; Yee, 2006). Playing together alters the experiential quality of digital games substantially and opens new possibilities for entertainment (Klimmt & Hartmann, 2008). In terms of serious games, multiplayer gaming is a feature that should be considered in terms of both cognitive and motivational dimensions of game impact. Specifically, online interaction among players and possibilities to create or cocreate parts of a game world together hold implications for the appeal and the impact power of serious game applications.

Specific Frame of Play Situations

The final characteristic of digital games introduced here as potentially relevant for serious games is the situation of playing a game that is attached to digital game use. At first glance, the observation that digital game players perceive the playing situation as playing a game is of course trivial. However, the psychology of play assigns very important consequences to the condition that a situation is framed as playing (Ohler & Nieding, 2006). Play as a mode of human action serves as a bridge between reality and fantasy (Sutton-Smith, 1997). Playful action is focused on the execution of activity and the immediate results of the activity. Consequences of the results that would connect a given activity to other subsequent activities are, in contrast, irrelevant for playful action (Oerter, 1999). For instance, the action category *work* is characterized by the fact that its outcomes (e.g., a product manufactured), are always related to further consequences (e.g., the product can be sold), and the individual receives payment for the result, which are already anticipated during the execution of action (i.e., when manufacturing the product), and thus affect the action (e.g., in terms of motivation to work accurately and fast). Playful action, however, is intentionally limited to a situational frame that blocks out further consequences of action results. Play stands for itself; it is executed in its own right, and players want their play to differ from nonplayful, consequential kinds of action. The special frame that is given to playful action comes along with a variety of interesting implications. One of them is reduction of complexity, because players do not have to keep consequences of action results in mind. Another is a strict enforcement of a limited set of rules, which can only function within a specific situation frame. A third important property is the accessibility of imagined contexts and activities. By blocking out connections to other events and actions (consequences), fantasy can occupy players' minds and facilitate role-play in contexts that would not be feasible, appropriate, or desirable in nonplayful action.

For instance, children can imagine they are fighter pilots or princesses, and they can act within these role descriptions if they create the situational frame of playing. Because they are playing, their behaviors as pilots or princesses do not affect their life after play is over— nobody will, for instance, question their mental health because they talk about launching missiles or marrying a prince. Therefore, the situation frame of playing a game allows an individual to enter realms of fantasy and imagination—a characteristic that applies to any mode of playing, including playing digital games. Consequently, playing digital games is, from the perspective of players, a specific mode of action that allows and legitimizes "as-if" experiences, and the trying out of actions and simulated confrontations with unknown, impossible, even immoral or socially disagreeable events and behaviors. This experimental, obligation-free nature of game play has important implications for serious game effects on social change.

Serious Games and Social Change: A Model of Potential Effect Mechanisms

Based on the description of key properties of contemporary digital games that are or could be included in serious games as well, this section outlines a model of how serious games could facilitate social change on an individual level. The model considers only those effects that may come out of individual players' game use or the social-psychological consequences of individual exposure to a serious game. Meso- and macrolevel perspectives on social change are not integrated into this particular model. The reason for this conceptual focus is that playing digital games is an activity that creates highly individualized, potentially unique experiences, in each user. Collective game play is possible and popular, but it is very hard to derive implications of MMO use on mesolevel social change. Rather, it is argued that individual exposure to and involvement with serious games (including games with online and massively multiplayer functionality) will result in specific individual processes that affect individual players in ways beneficial for the occurrence of behavioral change, which in turn represents the base for large-scale social change, as discussed above.

The structure of the model is a matrix of three stages of game exposure (stage of activity/medium selection, stage of exposure itself, stage of post-play thinking and communication behavior) and three effect categories relevant to serious games (motivation to elaborate on content of desired social/behavioral change, knowledge acquisition/comprehension, and attitude change/persuasion). Table 16.1 visualizes this matrix and presents the proposed mechanisms through which serious games are argued to be potential facilitators of social change. Fifteen mechanisms are introduced that can but do not necessarily have to be active in serious games' effects on social change. Conceptually, the mechanisms are founded on previous work in entertainment education, entertainment research, cognitive and social psychology. In the following description, mechanisms are organized through their effect categories: those related to (1) exposure and elaboration motivation; (2) comprehension and knowledge acquisition; and (3) persuasion and attitude change.

Mechanisms Related to Exposure and Elaboration Motivation

Players' readiness to select media messages that include change-related content and their motivation to process and elaborate on that content are processes relevant to serious games' effects. Motivation has been identified as a key facilitator of successful information processing both in learning (e.g., Renninger, Hidi, & Krapp, 1993) and in persuasion (e.g., Petty & Wegener, 1999). It is proposed that serious games gain capabilities to induce social/behavioral change due to their ability to trigger relevant motivational processes, especially the motivation to select change-related messages, to process their content during exposure, and to elaborate on them beyond the exposure situation.

Entertainment Capacity of Serious Games Increases Likelihood of Selection of Change-Related Message (Mechanism 1)

In traditional entertainment education, the combination of entertainment and educational content serves communicators' goal to facilitate any contact of target audiences with the change-related message. While this strategy works very well in countries with media systems that are not fully developed, there

Table 16.1 A Matrix Visualization of the Potential Effect Mechanisms Underlying Playing Serious Games on Social Change

Stage Effect Category	Preexposure / Selection of Medium	Exposure / Processing of Content	Postexposure
Motivation to elaborate content of desired social change	(1) Entertainment capacity of serious games increases likelihood of selection of change-related message (2) As-if quality of game play weakens refusal to expose to change-related content	(4) Enjoyment generates attention and interest for game world and content (5) Social game play renders elaboration of change-related content as socially acceptable ("I am not the only one doing it")	(11) Enjoyment promotes involvement with game and thus facilitates motivation for repeated, prolonged game play (redundancy) (12) Enjoyment promotes involvement with game and thus facilitates motivation to think about game content (e.g. planning strategies for next session) (13) Enjoyment promotes involvement with game and thus facilitates motivation to talk about the game (content) with other individuals
Knowledge acquisition / comprehension		(6) Multimodality increases likelihood of knowledge acquisition about the content of desired behavioral/social change (7) Interactivity increases likelihood of connection of content to player self (8) Narrative creates sense-making framework that facilitates comprehension (9) Multi-user play facilitates in-game communication that may resolve comprehension problems and support further elaboration of change-related content	(14) Multimodality and interactivity increase likelihood of knowledge application to real-world settings, which substantiates learning processes ("This situation is just like in that game")
Attitude change/persuasion	(3) Activation of inoculation-based anti-persuasion-stance less likely through entertainment-quality of serious game (no attempt to persuade expected)	(10) Narrative persuasion theory: Suppression of Counterarguing, increased salience of values connected to desired change	(15) Narrative persuasion theory: misattribution of attitude to serious/real-life source and argumentation

is much competing communication available to audiences in media-saturated countries (Sherry, 2002). Serious games that facilitate enjoyment (similar to popular entertainment games) can nevertheless claim the same motivational advantage that entertainment education programming claims in comparison to serious instructional media materials. Moreover, using serious games as a vehicle for change-related messages adapts a communication strategy for social change to specific target audiences' media preferences. Especially male adolescents, but also older males, can be reached via sophisticated digital games very well today, perhaps even better than via television. Female audiences can be addressed through digital games as well, if certain conditions are met (Cassell & Jenkins, 1998; Klimmt & Hartmann, 2006; Nutt & Railton, 2003). In this sense, the integration of serious games into a communication campaign can include the likelihood of target audiences selecting change-related messages (i.e., they are more likely to play the game than to work through a change-related multimedia course), especially among game-affine target audiences such as adolescent males (e.g., Jansz, 2005).

Play Situation Reduces Resistance to Being Confronted With Change-Related Message (Mechanism 2)

Media choice is an extremely complex process with numerous variables (LaRose & Eastin, 2004), but it can also be construed in terms of avoidance motivation (Fahr & Böcking, 2005). In many cases, messages on social change create cognitive conflict in target audiences: Behaviors to be changed are common and well-accepted, maybe even rooted in tradition and cultural norms. Messages that suggest a change of such well-known and widely practiced behavior can thus appear as a threat to receivers' self-image, as uncomfortable, and even embarrassing (e.g., Papa et al., 2000). Serious games can, because they are framed as play (Sutton-Smith, 1997), potentially override the refusal of target audiences to receive such uncomfortable messages: By creating a sense of fantasy and imagination, they may let confrontation with the change-related message appear less binding, serious, and consequential.

Green (2006) argues that narratives can facilitate mental simulation of unknown, difficult, or frightening events. The same could be argued for digital games: If a serious message concerning the problems associated with a well-accepted behavior causes cognitive conflict in target audiences, the as-if quality of a game may increase chances that people would agree to receive that message, because they perceive the message as fictional and thus less striking in terms of real-life contexts and self-image.

Enjoyment Generates Attention and Interest During Exposure (Mechanism 4)

Motivational variables are also important to the construal of serious game effects during exposure. For instance, motivated students will invest more energy and thinking in solving the assigned tasks, which leads to better learn-ing outcomes (e.g., Lepper & Malone, 1987). Cognitive models of knowledge acquisition rely (sometimes implicitly) on learners' attention. Attention is modeled as perceptual gateway to information processing (e.g., Lang, 2000); successful knowledge gain can only occur if attention is directed towards a learning content. Entertaining media content is argued to attract users' controlled attention (Schneider & Shiffrin, 1977), that is, enjoyable media motivate users to actively allocate their attentional resources to process their content. Users benefit from this attention allocation, because they can exploit the full entertainment capacity of the medium (for instance, they do not miss a joke or miss comprehending the complete story of a crime show). Controlled attention allocation thus serves audiences' desire to obtain as much (enjoyable) information as possible from the media product. For serious games, the ability of the entertainment elements to attract attentional resources to their process-ing is potentially helpful for knowledge transfer efficiency, because chances that the change-related messages within the game will be processed and elabo-rated are higher if users are devoting attention to the game (cf. Ritterfeld, Klimmt, Vorderer, & Steinhilper, 2005).

Sense of Community in Multiplayer Gaming Legitimizes Interest in Controversial Change-Related Message (Mechanism 5)

Various frameworks from social psychology, including social identity theory (Tajfel & Turner, 1986) and self-determination theory (Deci & Ryan, 2000) argue for people's strong tendency toward social cohesion: Individuals prefer to engage in behaviors that are common within their social reference group and tend to avoid behaviors that the reference group finds disagreeable. That means that perceptions of being the only member of one's social reference group (e.g., tribe, clan, community, or neighborhood) who thinks about or simply receives a change-related message will undermine people's willingness to process that message. Multiplayer serious gaming may overcome this barrier: If target users recognize that the (large) community of other players are also involved in the serious game, the perception of deviance from social norms through exposure to the change-related message in the game could be countered, which would result in greater motivation to deal with the game and its message(s). This is especially true if the gaming community actively communicates about the game's content and provides motivational and emotional support to individual players (e.g., Bracken & Lombard, 2004).

Enjoyment Promotes Involvement and Motivation for Repeated Exposure (Mechanism 11)

One of the most important properties of media entertainment is its capability to motivate audiences to return to them. Many people are willing to consume the very same piece of entertainment several times, because it was (is) so enjoyable (Tannenbaum, 1985). One enjoyable episode of a television series creates an appetite for subsequent episodes. One level of an entertaining digital game motivates players to play the game again tomorrow to see what will happen in the next level. Involvement with an entertaining media product thus creates motivation for continued and repeated exposure (Wirth, 2006), which is an important element in cognitive processing, especially in learning and knowledge acquisition from media messages (e.g., Ritterfeld & Weber, 2006; Vorderer, Böcking, Klimmt, & Ritterfeld, 2006). Enjoyment-based involvement with a serious game should thus increase motivation for repeated game play, which would cause redundant processing of the game's change-related information—with positive implications for comprehension and retention.

Enjoyment Promotes Involvement and Motivation to Elaborate on Game Content between Exposure Situations (Mechanism 12)

In times of nonexposure, involved digital game players frequently reflect on what they did during the past sessions of game play and plan ahead what to do (and how to do it) in future gaming situations. Unresolved challenges and puzzles as well as ongoing events (e.g., large-scale events in multiplayer worlds) are especially likely to trigger cognitions about the game while one is not playing it. Parasocial relationship theory argues that television viewers who are strongly involved with a media persona will think about the persona frequently in everyday life (e.g., Klimmt et al., 2006), with important consequences for the parasocial relationship itself and the viewer's further selective exposure behavior. Similar cognitive processes are likely to occur in players heavily involved in a serious game (or with game characters). Such elaboration processes can also promote the impact of the change-related message of a serious game (to the extent the message is effectively intertwined with the motivating/appealing elements of the game; e.g., opponents who symbolize a behavior to be changed).

Enjoyment Promotes Involvement and Motivation to Talk about Game Content (Mechanism 13)

Studies on noninteractive entertainment education suggest that stimulating interaction among members of the target audience and promoting communication about the issues of the campaign are critical to success (Papa et al., 2000; Sood, 2002). Highly entertaining serious games could therefore contribute to social change by motivating players to talk about their game experiences with other players (and with nonplayers), for instance, to manage their social reputation as a game expert within their peer group or to seek advice how to proceed in the game successfully. Communication that addresses game issues can be facilitated online, offline, and, in the case of multiplayer gaming, even within the game environment (Klimmt & Hartmann, 2008). Consequently, the communication-inspiring capacity of high-involvement games could also support serious games' effectiveness in terms of social change.

Mechanisms Related to Comprehension and Knowledge Acquisition

So far, properties ascribed to serious games show that they can affect players' motivational system in ways beneficial for the facilitation of social change. The second major class of effect processes is comprehension of the change-related message and the acquisition of knowledge. For instance, a change of social behavior in the domain of health must necessarily be grounded on improved knowledge of the target audience on the (negative undesirable) consequences of the behavior currently practiced, and about the advantages of the behavioral alternative introduced by a communication campaign (e.g., Sood, 2002). This section describes the mechanisms of serious games' effects that support players' message comprehension and knowledge acquisition.

Multimodality Increases Likelihood of Knowledge Acquisition (Mechanism 6)

The immersive capacity of modern digital game technology is mostly exploited for entertainment purposes (Tamborini & Skalski, 2006). However, a lot of research has also shown the importance of multimodal content presentation for the effectiveness for computer-based instruction. Moreno and Mayer (2002), for instance, explain the effectiveness of multimodal content presentation as a better fit of the instructional communication form to learners' working memory structure. Other researchers argue that multimodal presentation of content can enhance learners' understanding of complex and abstract phenomena (Jones, Minogue, Tretter, Negishi, & Taylor, 2006). While there is a substantial risk of cognitive overload, distraction, and other effects dysfunctional to comprehension and knowledge acquisition, multimodality is proposed as a potentially powerful factor in serious games' effects on social change, since the behavior to be changed, its causes and consequences, as well as its broader social and historical context can be presented to players in a very illustrative way (see also Ritterfeld, Weber, Fernandes & Vorderer, 2004).

Interactivity Increases Likelihood of Connection of Game Content to the Player's Self (Mechanism 7)

In contrast to television-based instructional material, computer-based instruction is mostly interactive. It is hoped that interactivity will affect a variety of processes in media-based learning in positive ways. For instance, Kritch, Bostow, and Dedrick (1995) report that adding a simple element of interactivity to a video-disc instruction on AIDS (e.g., a fill-in-a-response task on screen after each chapter of the video course) improved knowledge acquisition. Conceptually, interactivity of learning environments is a potential resolution to learners' cognitive overload (Kirschner, 2002) and to individual differences in learning capacity and speed, because through interactive navigation through the instructional material, learners (may be able to) adjust the complexity and speed of the tasks and information presented to them to their personal capacities and preferences (Ritterfeld & Weber, 2006; see also Blumberg & Ismailer, this volume, chapter 9; Gee, this volume, chapter 5; Lieberman, this volume, chapter 8; Shute, Ventura, Bauer, & Zapata-Rivera, this volume, chapter 18).

In the context of digital games, interactivity may be an important facilitator for game effects on social change because it increases the connection between players' self and the content of the game. Because players can act within the virtual game world and see the results of their input, their role is completely different from the role of a television viewer, for instance (Klimmt & Hartmann, 2006). Television viewers observe other people, their actions, and the events happening to them. Game players do the action by themselves and witness what is happening to themselves (Vorderer, 2000). Whatever happens in the game thus automatically holds a close, personal, and individual connection to the player—either because it is a result of player action or it is an event that is or could be relevant to the player; for example, in terms of success, failure, discovery, or other enjoyment-related issues.

The increased self-relevance of digital game play would also apply to the change-related message built into a serious game. Interactive confrontation with a social behavior to be changed, for instance, shapes the learning experience differently from the conventional "Behavior X holds negative consequences Y for character Z and should thus be replaced by behavior A" (the kind of learning experience a narrative entertainment education broadcast would create). Rather, the interactive learning experience would be "If I perform behavior X, this holds negative consequences Z for me (or my player character at least), but if I perform behavior A, I (or my player character) am doing better." Such increase of self-connection may be important to motivational issues, for example, increased personal relevance of the change-related message, but also to issues of comprehension and knowledge transfer, because myself-focused learning experiences are potentially useful to facilitate procedural learning through simulation ("I am performing a behavior" instead of "Character X performing a behavior" or "Performing a behavior in general"). As social change typically refers to behavioral change, such procedural and self-directed ways of looking at the content of media-based instruction (including serious games) may thus be especially effective in this domain of serious game application.

Narrative Creates Sense-Making Framework that Facilitates Comprehension (Mechanism 8)

Conventional entertainment education approaches rely on narratives into which change-related messages are integrated (Singhal et al., 2004). Narratives are also widely used in traditional education (e.g., McEwan & Egan, 1995). Contemporary digital games can contain substantial narrative (see above), so interactive stories within serious games could be used for instructional purposes as well. One specific function that narratives serve is sense-making; that is, the integration of individual real-world views and knowledge into the comprehension of mediated information. By making personal sense out of a story, audience members increase their comprehension and memory performance and can identify the personal relevance of the message more easily (e.g., Brendlinger, Dervin, & Foreman-Wernet, 1999). Serious games tell stories interactively (see above), which creates a unique capability to allow sensemaking processing: Because interactivity evokes stronger self-connections in players, a narrative that unfolds through player interaction should be most comprehensive to individual players.

Multiuser Play Facilitates In-Game Communication that Supports Comprehension (Mechanism 9)

The importance of communication among members of the target audience for the impact of entertainment education has already been mentioned (see explication of mechanism 13). Serious games that offer online play can create spaces for such connected communication within the game context and thus very close to the actual change-related message. Talking about the message does not require a change of communication channels from receiving and processing the message, as it is the case with television or radio consumption, which does not enable interpersonal communication among (larger groups of) audience members. Such interplayer communication can serve emotional motivational purposes (Pena & Hancock, 2006) and also support comprehension and knowledge acquisition, because talking to other players may help to resolve individual problems with understanding parts of the message or simply lead to repeated confrontation with the change related message. Interaction with a larger player community and support received from other players when playing online (Klimmt & Hartmann, 2008) is a potential facilitator of cognitive effects for serious games (given that the games provide the option to play online). Of course, such interplayer communication may also lead to resistance to the change related message (Singhal & Rogers, 2002). However, as communication campaigners can participate in online player interaction, their moderation and input may be able to override such barriers potentially associated with communication among players (see the previous section on social change).

Interactivity and Multimodality Increase Likelihood of Knowledge Application (Mechanism 14)

The process of acquiring knowledge is not limited to when the learner is exposed to the target information. The postexposure stage is also relevant to knowledge processes, because a sufficient degree of cognitive integration of the target information can be assumed only if the individual can apply (acquired) knowledge in subsequent situations or tasks. In the context of social change, sufficient knowledge acquisition means that an individual has memorized and understood the change-related message to an extent that would allow her or him—given personal motivation and situational conditions supporting that person—to execute the desired social behavior some time after the exposure stage, potentially in a situation of choice between the traditional problematic behavior and the newly introduced behavioral alternative (e.g., Bandura's 2001 social-cognitive framework). Such action-focused knowledge integration may be promoted by serious games' interactivity and multimodality. These properties allow one to simulate target audiences' personal, geographic, cultural, and social environment in a very realistic and authentic way (Tamborini & Skalski, 2006). Interactive game use provides procedural perspectives on the social behavior to be changed (see explication of mechanism 7). The combination of interactivity and multimodality can result in a life-simulation of social behavior (e.g., Nutt & Railton, 2003) that provides relevant knowledge in a structure and quality that is especially well suited for integration in action-oriented memory contexts and easily applicable to real life situations of decision making and action planning.

Effect Mechanisms Related to Persuasion and Attitude Change

To the extent that social change is bound to individual behavioral change such as health behavior or domestic violence, changing attitudes is a priority for many communication campaigns (e.g., Slater & Rouner, 2002). The relevance for persuasion within communication for social change is justified by various theories of human behavior that assign a key role in the genesis of behavior to attitudes and values. For instance, the theory of reasoned action (Ajzen, 1991) heavily relies on attitudinal processes as determinant of behavior. Another example is moral disengagement theory (Bandura, 2002) that proposes moral reasoning as important precursor to social behavior, especially in situations of conflict. Changing people's attitudes is thus an important access point for communication campaigns to change people's actual behavior. Therefore, issues of persuasion are most important to conventional entertainment education for social change and also for serious games designed for this purpose.

Except for the cognitive effects of violent digital games, there is not much empirical evidence for persuasive digital game effects. One cross-sectional survey found weak correlations between digital game play and aggressive political opinions (Eyal, Metzger, Lingsweiler, Mahood, & Yao, 2006); a pilot survey in Germany (Klimmt, 2006) revealed more substantial associations between use of war, police, and fighting games and right-wing conservative political attitudes. A set of theoretical mechanisms that could underlie such persuasive game effects is outlined in this section.

Situation Definition as Play Prevents Persuasion-Resistance Stance (Mechanism 3)

One of the most interesting properties of entertainment based communication strategies for social change is that they differ formally and notably from explicit persuasive communication such as advertising or textbooks. Most persuasive effects of media based communication for social change are assumed to be undermined by a preexisting antipersuasion stance. With this resistance oriented stance, audience members will not be open to the change related message at all, but will rather cognitively counteract the message; for example, by questioning the source credibility or blaming the communicators for wrong ideologies. Entertainment education as well as serious games for social change open unique pathways for attitude change by appearing to be entertainment products (e.g., a story) (Green & Brock, 2000; Slater & Rouner, 2002). The situation frame of play that digital games establish (see above) differs sharply from the serious instructional style of multimedia products and other media used in educational settings. Therefore, the persuasive impact of serious games may already occur before the actual exposure situation: Because people do not expect a formal persuasion attempt (that would, for example, cause cognitive conflict by questioning accepted social norms), they are less likely to adopt an antipersuasion stance before playing.

An antipersuasion stance could follow from *inoculation*; that is, the preparation of the person for a persuasion attempt (Pfau et al., 1997). Inoculation has been demonstrated to reduce effects of counterattitudinal messages (e.g., An & Pfau, 2004) and is thus a problem for communication for social change. This may be especially salient at the mesolevel of analysis (see above) where there may be communities or institutional agents resisting social change and performing effective inoculation of group members. A digital game offered as an entertainment medium may avoid such inoculation effects, because a counterpersuasion stance is much more likely to be activated when the individual person is confronted with explicit persuasive material than when she or he is exposed to a digital game. Without such a resistance-oriented stance taken before exposure to the change related message begins, persuasive effects of the message are more likely to occur.

Game Narrative Contributes to Persuasion (Mechanism 10)

Research on entertainment education has demonstrated some processes through which attitude change can be facilitated during entertainment consumption. Slater and Rouner (2002) and Slater, Rouner, and Long (2006) argue for reduced counterarguing to the attitudinal message for the same reasons that have been mentioned above in the context of the antipersuasion stance (see mechanism 3). They also argue that entertainment media will reduce the attitudinal importance of trait ideology; that is, the attitudes audience members hold before exposure to the change related message. Rather, entertainment media can render specific values more important to audience members than these values were before exposure. This happens via the temporal change of the value structure (e.g., assigning more importance to the value of gender equality), which may allow specific attitudes to be shaped accordingly (e.g., more positive attitude toward sending girls to school; cf. Slater et al., 2006).

Similarly, transportation theory (Green, 2006; Green & Brock, 2000) argues for narrative's persuasive power, as fictional media content is processed less critically (e.g., in terms of questioning credibility and truthfulness of the information), while it is still perceived as being a relevant source of information for real-world beliefs and attitudes. Such persuasive effects could also be assumed for serious games, which display both fictional and virtual worlds (see the above discussion on the situation definition as play). While modifications to the existing accounts for narrative persuasion may be required to address the peculiarities of interactive narrative in digital games, exposure to a serious game is proposed to result in attitude change similar to conventional entertainment education and fictional narrative which has been partly demonstrated empirically (see Brock, Strange, & Green, 2002; Shrum, 2004).

Attitude Change May Result From Misattribution of Attitude to Real-Life Source (Mechanism 15)

Finally, advantages in persuasion may be found in serious games for social change after actual exposure. Mares (1996) has argued that people tend to confuse sources of information (especially fact and fiction sources), which opens a pathway for fictional information to affect real-world beliefs and thoughts. Such attitudinal effects are proposed for serious games as well, especially because their life like appearance (interactivity and multimodality, see above) renders game experiences increasingly similar to real-world experience, e.g., in terms of spatial environments, and, in multiplayer settings, also in terms of social interaction (see Yee, 2006). For instance, confrontation with a change related message in a highly interactive and multimodal digital game might display a social behavior in a context that is extremely similar to a context that a player is confronted with weeks later in real life. Attitudes that have been emphasized by the game may thus be accessed in the real situation without the complete reconstruction of the acquisition of that attitude as coming out of a virtual fictional game world. Such source confusions could thus complete the narrative persuasion process in the postexposure stage of confrontation with a serious game (see also Green, 2006).

Summary

The model outlined in this chapter relies on specific properties of digital games that can be adopted for serious games addressing social change. These properties have been connected to player motivations, cognitions, and behaviors that are related to the game experience or to the change-related content within the game in order to derive 15 mechanisms which all can contribute to a serious game's impact on social/behavioral change. The mechanisms from which serious game impact on social change can or could benefit refer to: (1) preexposure (selective exposure and cognitive stance); (2) exposure and information processing; and (3) post exposure (elaboration and communication) and address issues of (a) player motivation; (b) comprehension/knowledge acquisition; and (c) attitude change/persuasion. Much of this 3 x 3 cell argumentation matrix is identical or similar to what is discussed about conventional noninteractive entertainment education (Singhal et al., 2004). Substantial additions and conceptual variations have been proposed, however, to deal with the peculiarities of the digital game medium (Vorderer & Bryant, 2006). The main assumption of the model is, however, that many properties of contemporary digital games that are currently exploited for entertainment purposes only (e.g., stunning graphics and sound, rich narrative, discovery experiences, social interaction among players) can be very helpful for serious games for social change as well— if the integration of the change related message into the enjoyable elements of the game does not undermine the entertaining capacity of the game.

Conclusion

Up to this point, the model of serious games' effects for social change outlined in this chapter has been extremely enthusiastic about the possibilities of serious games. Indeed, the model outlines many justifiable arguments for potential effects of serious games on individual variables relevant to social/behavioral change. But this should not be mistaken for the assumption that one, some, or all of these mechanisms are operating in any given serious game and that, consequently, serious games are a guaranteed success for communication campaigns. Rather, the working model is proposed to stimulate more detailed theory building (for which 15 directions have been described), more empirical research, and experimental serious game development. Much more detailed knowledge is required to identify those mechanisms that are most promising in terms of effect potential and that are practically manageable at the same time. For instance, a multiuser game is extremely expensive, both in programming and daily running. The benefits for game impact coming along with online game play would have to be calculated against these costs. Another important economic-technical issue is the equipment of the target population. In media saturated countries (Sherry, 2002), high end gaming technology (on which many of the proposed effect mechanisms rely) is certainly a good choice for communication campaigners; the opposite holds true for audiences in countries with high poverty. Finally, and most importantly, whether any of the proposed mechanisms can be exploited by a serious game for social change is a question of design and implementation. Suboptimal design not only can fail to exploit a given effect mechanism to evoke social change, it can also have contraproductive consequences; for example, an interactive narrative that leaves space for undesired message interpretations such as the Archie Bunker effect (Singhal & Rogers, 2002).

One issue for which the model does not offer a suitable, generalizable strategy is how to build a change related message into a serious game. In conventional entertainment education, characters, and plots are the general tools used for this purpose (Singhal et al., 2004), and to a certain extent, these general strategies can also be integrated into serious game design (see the model's mechanisms 3, 8, 10, 11, 12, 13, and 15).

However, a critical question to serious games is how to synthesize the change related message(s) with the interactivity of the medium. Predefined narrative structures and interactivity are not always compatible (Lee et al., 2006; Murray, 1997). While there are certain techniques to blend narrative and game play available to game designers, it is still most challenging and important to think about how change related messages can be installed in digital games in ways that resonate with interactivity, multimodality, and online game play. Theoretical arguments that games with such built-in messages should work have been compiled in this paper; however, without practical implementation and game design, all theory is useless for the facilitation of social change. Therefore, research on serious games for social change needs collaboration between scholars from communication and computer science in order to develop real prototype (pilot, testing) games to explore the theorized capabilities of serious games to facilitate social change. Because in theory, digital games are very powerful facilitators of social change—this paper attempts to motivate scholars to take on the research challenges necessary to add serious games to the repertoire of modern entertainment education.

References

Ajzen, I. (1991). The theory of planned behavior. *Organizational Behavior and Human Decision Processes, 50*, 179–211.

Amory, A., Naicker, K., Vincent, J., & Adams, C. (1999). The use of computer games as an educational tool: Identification of appropriate game types and game elements. *British Journal of Educational Technology, 30*(4), 311–321.

An, C., & Pfau, M. (2004). The efficacy of inoculation in televised political debates. *Journal of Communication 54* (3), 421–436.

Bandura, A. (2001). Social cognitive theory of mass communication. *Media Psychology, 3*(3), 265–299.

Bandura, A. (2002). Selective moral disengagement in the exercise of moral agency. *Journal of Moral Education, 31*(2), 101–119.

Bracken, C., & Lombard, M. (2004). Social presence and children: Praise, intrinsic motivation, and learning with computers. *Journal of Communication, 54*(1), 22–37.

Brendlinger, N. H., Dervin, B., & Foreman-Wernet, L. (1999). When respondents are theorists: An exemplar study in the HIV/AIDS context of the use of sense-making as an approach to public communication campaign audience. *The Electronic Journal of Communication, 9*(2, 3, & 4). Retrieved from http://www.cios.org/www/ejcmain. htm

Brock, T. C., Strange, J. J., & Green, M. C. (Eds.). (2002). *Narrative impact: Social and cognitive foundations.* Mahwah, NJ: Erlbaum.

Cassell, J., & Jenkins, H. (Eds.). (1998). *From Barbie to Mortal Kombat: Gender and computer games.* Cambridge, MA: MIT Press.

Chan, E., & Vorderer, P. (2006). Massively multiplayer online games. In P. Vorderer & J. Bryant (Eds.), *Playing video games: Motives, responses, and consequences* (pp. 77–90). Mahwah, NJ: Erlbaum.

Deci, R. M., & Ryan, E. L. (2000). Self-determination theory and the facilitation of intrinsic motivation, social development, and well-being. *American Psychologist, 55*(1), 68–78.

Eyal, K., Metzger, M. J., Lingsweiler, R. W., Mahood, C., & Yao, M. Z. (2006). Aggressive political opinions and exposure to violent media. *Mass Communication & Society, 9*(4), 399–428.

Fahr, A., & Böcking, T. (2005). Nichts wie weg? Ursachen der Programmflucht [Just out of here! Reasons for avoiding TV programs]. *Medien- und Kommunikationswissenschaft, 53*(1), 5–25.

Green, M. C. (2006). Narratives and cancer communication. *Journal of Communication, 56*, 163–183.

Green, M. C., & Brock, T. C. (2000). The role of transportation in the persuasiveness of public narratives. *Journal of Personality and Social Psychology, 79*(5), 701–721.

Griffiths, M. D., Davies, M. N. O., & Chappel, D. (2003). Breaking the stereotype: The case of online gaming. *CyberPsychology & Behavior, 6*(1), 81–91.

Grodal, T. (2000). Video games and the pleasures of control. In D. Zillmann & P. Vorderer (Eds.), *Media entertainment: The psychology of its appeal* (pp. 197–212). Mahwah, NJ: Erlbaum.

Jansz, J. (2005). The emotional appeal of violent video games for adolescent males. *Communication Theory, 15*(3), 219–241.

Jansz, J., & Martens, L. (2005). Gaming at a LAN event: The social context of playing video games. *New Media & Society, 7*(3), 333–355.

Johnson, L., Choi, S., Marsella, S., Mote, N., Narayanan, S., Vilhjlmsson, H., et al. (2004). *Tactical language training system: Supporting the rapid acquisition of foreign language and cultural skills.* Presentation at the InSTIL/ICALL 2004 Symposium on Computer-Assisted Language Learning, June 17–19, Venice (Italy).

Jones, M. G., Minogue, M., Tretter, T. R., Negishi, A., & Taylor, R. (2006). Haptic augmentation of science instruction: Does touch matter? *Science Education, 90*(1), 111–123.

Keller, E., & Berry, J. (2003). *The influentials.* New York: Free Press.

Kiousis, S. (2002). Interactivity: A concept explication. *New Media & Society, 4*(3), 355–383.

Kirschner, P. A. (2002). Cognitive load theory: Implications of cognitive load theory on the design of learning. *Learning and Instruction, 12*, 1–10.

Klimmt, C. (2003). Dimensions and determinants of the enjoyment of playing digital games: A three-level model. In M. Copier & J. Raessens (Eds.), *Level up: Digital games research conference* (pp. 246–257). Utrecht, The Netherlands: Utrecht University.

Klimmt, C. (2006, October). *Computerspielkonsum und politischer Konservatismus unter*

Jugendlichen [Video game play and political conservatism among adolescents]. Presentation at the Workshop Konstruktion von Politik und Gesellschaft in Computerspielen, Munich, Germany.

Klimmt, C., & Hartmann, T. (2006). Effectance, self-efficacy, and the motivation to play video games. In P. Vorderer & J. Bryant (Eds.), *Playing video games: Motives, responses, and consequences* (pp. 132–145). Mahwah, NJ: Erlbaum.

Klimmt, C., & Hartmann, T. (2008). Mediated interpersonal communication in multiplayer video games: Implications for entertainment and relationship management. In E. Konijn, M. Tanis, S. Utz, & S. Barnes (Eds.), *Mediated interpersonal communication* (pp. 309–330). New York: Routledge.

Klimmt, C., Hartmann, T., & Frey, A. (2007). Effectance and control as determinants of video game enjoyment. *CyberPsychology & Behavior, 10*(6), 845–847.

Klimmt, C., Hartmann, T., & Schramm, H. (2006). Parasocial interactions and relationships. In J. Bryant & P. Vorderer (Eds.), *Psychology of entertainment* (pp. 291–313). Mahwah, NJ: Erlbaum.

Klimmt, C., & Vorderer, P. (2007). Interactive media. In J. J. Arnett (Ed.), *Encyclopedia of children, adolescents, and the media* (pp. 417–419). London: Sage.

Kritch, K. M., Bostow, D. E., & Dedrick, R. F. (1995). Level of interactivity of video-disc instruction on college students' to a video-disc instruction. *Journal of Applied Behavior Analysis, 28*(1), 85–86.

Kücklich, J. (2003). The playability of texts versus the readability of games: Towards holistic theory of fictionality. In M. Copier & J. Raessens (Eds.), *Level up: Digital games research conference* (pp. 100–107). Utrecht, The Netherlands: Utrecht University.

Lang, A. (2000). The information processing of mediated messages: A framework for communication research. *Journal of Communication, 50*, 46–70.

LaRose, R., & Eastin, M. S. (2004). A social cognitive theory of internet uses and gratifications: Toward a new model of media attendance. *Journal of Broadcasting and Electronic Media, 48*(3), 358–377.

Lee, K. M., Park, N., & Jin, S.-A. (2006). Narrative and interactivity in computer games. In P. Vorderer & J. Bryant (Eds.), *Playing video games: Motives, responses, consequences* (pp. 259–274). Mahwah, NJ: Erlbaum.

Lepper, M. R., & Malone, T. W. (1987). Intrinsic motivation and instructional effectiveness in computer-based education. In R. E. Snow & M. J. Farr (Eds.), *Aptitude, learning, and instruction: Vol. 3. Conative and affective process analyses* (pp. 255–286). Hillsdale, NJ: Erlbaum.

Mares, M. L. (1996). The role of source confusions in television's cultivation of social reality judgements. *Human Communication Research, 23*, 278–297.

McEwan, H., & Egan, K. (Eds.). (1995). *Narrative in teaching, learning, and research.* New York: Teachers College Press.

Moreno, R., & Mayer, R. E. (2002). Verbal redundancy in multimedia learning: When reading helps listening. *Journal of Educational Psychology, 94*(1), 156–163.

Murray, J. (1997). *Hamlet on the holodeck: The future of narrative in cyberspace.* Boston: MIT Press.

Nutt, D., & Railton, D. (2003). The Sims: Real life as genre. *Information, Communication and Society, 6*(4), 577–592.

Oerter, R. (1999). *Psychologie des Spiels. Ein handlungstheoretischer Ansatz* [Psychology of play: An action-oriented approach]. Weinheim, Germany: Beltz.

Ohler, P., & Nieding, G. (2006). Why play? An evolutionary perspective. In P. Vorderer & J. Bryant (Eds.), *Playing video games: Motives, responses, consequences* (pp. 101–114). Mahwah, NJ: Erlbaum.

Papa, M. J., Singhal, A., Law, S., Pant, S., Sood, S., Rogers, E. M., et al. (2000). Entertainment-education and social change: An analysis of parasocial interaction, social learning, collective efficacy, and paradoxical communication. *Journal of Communication, 50,* 31–55.

Pena, J., & Hancock, J. T. (2006). An analysis of socioemotional and task communication in online multiplayer video games. *Communication Research, 33*(1), 92–109.

Pfau, M., Kyle, J. Tusing, J., Koerner, A. F., Lee, W., Godbold, L. C., et al. (1997). Enriching the inoculation construct: The role of critical components in the process of resistance. *Human Communication Research, 24*(2), 187–215.

Petty, R. E., & Wegener, D. T. (1999). The elaboration likelihood model: Current status and controversies. In S. Chaiken & Y. Trope (Eds.), *Dual-process theories in social psychology* (pp. 41–72). New York: Guilford Press.

Renninger, K. A., Hidi, S., & Krapp, A. (Eds.). (1993). *The role of interest in learning and development.* Hillsdale, NJ: Erlbaum.

Ritterfeld, U., Klimmt, C., Vorderer, P., & Steinhilper, L. K. (2005). The effects of a narrative audio tape on preschoolers' entertainment experience and attention. *Media Psychology, 7*(1), 47–72.

Ritterfeld, U., & Weber, R. (2006). Video games for entertainment and education. In P. Vorderer & J. Bryant (Eds.), *Playing video games: Motives, responses, consequences* (pp. 399–414). Mahwah, NJ: Erlbaum.

Ritterfeld, U., Weber, R., Fernandes, S., & Vorderer, P. (2004). Think science! Entertainment education in interactive theaters. *Computers in Entertainment: Educating Children through Entertainment, 2*(1). Retrieved from http://www.acm.org/pubs/cie.html

Rogers, E. M. (2003). *Diffusion of innovations* (5th ed.). New York: Free Press.

Schneider, W., & R. M. Shiffrin. (1977). Controlled and automatic human information processing: 1. Detection, search, and attention. *Psychological Review, 84,* 1–66.

Sherry, J. L. (2002). Media saturation and entertainment-education. *Communication Theory, 12*(2), 206–224.

Shrum, L. J. (Ed.). (2004). *Blurring the lines: The psychology of entertainment media.* Mahwah, NJ: Erlbaum.

Singhal, A., Cody, M., Rogers, E., & Sabido, M. (Eds.). (2004). *Entertainment education and social change: History, research and practice.* Mahwah, NJ: Erlbaum.

Singhal, A., & Rogers, E. M. (1999). *Entertainment education: A communication strategy for social change.* Mahwah, NJ: Erlbaum.

Singhal, A., & Rogers, E. M. (2002). A theoretical agenda for entertainment-education. *Communication Theory, 12*(2), 117–135.

Slater, M. D., & Rouner, D. (2002). Entertainment-education and elaboration likelihood: Understanding the processing of narrative persuasion. *Communication Theory, 12*(2), 173–191.

Slater, M. D., Rouner, D., & Long, M. (2006). Television dramas and support for controversial public policies: Effects and mechanisms. *Journal of Communication, 56*(2), 235–254.

Sood, S. (2002). Audience involvement and entertainment-education. *Communication Theory, 12*(2), 153–172.

Steuer, J. (1992). Defining virtual reality: Dimensions determining telepresence. *Journal of Communication, 42*(4), 73–93.

Sutton-Smith, B. (1997). *The ambiguity of play*. Cambridge, MA: Harvard University Press.

Tajfel, H., & Turner, J. C. (1986). The social identity theory of intergroup behavior. In S. Worchel & W. Austin (Eds.), *The social psychology of intergroup behavior* (pp. 7–24). Chicago: Nelson-Hall.

Tamborini, R., & Skalski, P. (2006). The role of presence in the experience of electronic games. In P. Vorderer & J. Bryant (Eds.), *Playing video games: Motives, responses, and consequences* (pp. 225–240). Mahwah, NJ: Erlbaum.

Tannenbaum, P. (1985). "Play it again, Sam": Repeated exposure to television programs. In D. Zillmann & J. Bryant (Eds.), *Selective exposure to communication* (pp. 225–241). Hillsdale, NJ: Erlbaum.

Vorderer, P. (2000). Interactive entertainment and beyond. In D. Zillmann & P. Vorderer (Eds.), *Media entertainment: The psychology of its appeal* (pp. 21–36). Mahwah, NJ: Erlbaum.

Vorderer, P., Böcking, S., Klimmt, C., & Ritterfeld, U. (2006). What makes preschoolers listen to narrative audio tapes? *Zeitschrift für Medienpsychologie, 18*(1), 9–18.

Vorderer, P., & Bryant, J. (Eds.). (2006). *Playing video games. Motives, responses, consequences*. Mahwah, NJ: Erlbaum.

Wirth, W. (2006). Involvement. In J. Bryant & P. Vorderer (Eds.), *Psychology of entertainment* (pp. 199–213). Mahwah, NJ: Erlbaum.

Wirth, W., Hartmann, T., Böcking, S., Vorderer, P., Klimmt, C., Schramm, H., et al. (2007). A process model of the formation of spatial presence experiences. *Media Psychology, 9*(3), 493–525.

Wolf, M. J. P. (1995). Inventing space. Toward a taxonomy of on- and off-screen space in video games. *Film Quarterly, 51*(1), 11–23.

Yee, N. (2006). The psychology of massively multiplayer online role playing games: Motivations, emotional investment, relationships, and problematic use. In R. Schroeder & A. Axelson (Eds.), *Avatars at work and play: Collaboration and interaction in shared virtual environments* (pp. 187–207). London: Springer.

Chapter 17

Entertainment-Education Through Digital Games

Hua Wang and Arvind Singhal

Imagine yourself living in the United States as an asylum seeker from Haiti; an Indian green-card holder; a Polish-American citizen with legal paperwork issues and a record of a misdemeanor; a Japanese foreign student; or an undocumented migrant worker from Mexico. What happens to you if you drink and drive and are caught? Or if you engage in petty shoplifting and the shop owner calls the local police? How can these bad choices come back to haunt you? Or how about if you make better choices: For instance, not knowing a word of English, you purposefully enroll in English-language classes?

These are not hypothetical scenarios, but rather based on real cases. In early 2008, Breakthrough, an international human rights organization based in New York and New Delhi, launched *ICED! I Can End Deportation* (2007), a free, 3D downloadable game that teaches players about the unjust nature of U.S. immigration laws. Primarily aimed at high school and college students, the game seeks to increase awareness about how immigration laws violate human rights by denying due process, and what resources may exist if one finds oneself in such an unfortunate situation (Breakthrough, 2008).

Why use digital games to explore social issues such as immigration? "Games are really good at exploring complex issues, and what issue is more complex than immigration?" noted Suzanne Seggerman, President of Games for Change, an organization that supports social uses for digital games (quoted in Gorman, 2007). Immigration is only one of the important social topics being addressed via digital games. Health educators have used games to promote self-efficacy among children and help build self-management skills for those with diabetes or other chronic diseases; corporations like Starbucks have collaborated with NGOs to create games to bring attention to global warming; and university students have designed games to raise empathy for migrant laborers and express their opinions about U.S.-Mexico border crossing (e.g., Brown et al., 1997; Gorman, 2007; Lieberman, 2001). U.N.'s aid-relief game *Food Force* had 4 million downloads in 15 months; more than 800,000 people played *Darfur Is Dying* between April and August, 2006; and over 110,000 copies of *Re-Mission* have been distributed in 78 countries since its release—"techno do-gooders are proliferating, and gamers are saving the world" (*Do-Gooder Games*, 2006; *Impact*, 2008).

The present chapter analyzes the rise of digital games as a vehicle for entertainment-education (hereafter E-E). A (re)definition of E-E is provided to account for the present-day digital phenomena, and a conceptual distinction is made between serious games and E-E games available in a digital format. Then building on Klimmt's explication of the common characteristics of digital games, including their potential for social change based on psychosocial models (this volume, chapter 16), we emphasize the connection between these properties of digital games and crucial concepts and components identified from existing E-E theories and practices. Further, through illustrations, we discuss the possibilities of incorporating E-E paradigms in serious games to address complex and sensitive social issues, reach population groups beyond conventional gaming market, and stress the importance of coproduction and the use of infrastructure in games for change. We conclude this chapter by sharing prior E-E experience of creating alternative realities through collective efficacy and action and by problematizing the dominant psychosocial centered scholarship in conceptualizing the effects of serious games.

Redefining Entertainment-Education in the Digital Era[1]

The idea of using entertainment media for educational or persuasive purposes is not new, but to consciously combine entertainment and education in mass and mediated communication is a relatively recent phenomenon (Singhal & Rogers, 1999). Seamlessly coupling the two to achieve positive sociocultural and behavioral change is a great challenge (e.g., Nariman, 1993; Papa, Singhal, & Papa, 2006; Papa et al., 2000; Slater, 2002a), although not insurmountable. E-E has emerged as a field of scholarship and practice focusing on "the process of purposely designing and implementing a media message to both entertain and educate, in order to increase audience knowledge about an educational issue, create favorable attitudes, and change overt behavior" (Singhal, Cody, Rogers, & Sabido, 2004, p. 5; Singhal & Rogers, 1999, p. 9). Over the past three decades, several hundred E-E interventions have been designed and implemented, addressing important public health and social issues in countries of Asia, Africa, and Latin America, primarily through the use of television and radio soap operas and now increasingly in Europe and North America employing more diversified communication channels and genres (Singhal & Rogers, 2004).

Taking into account the recent developments in the field, especially the popularity of digital entertainment media and the emerging participatory culture,[2] we propose a reformulation of the previous definition: Entertainment-education is a theory-based communication strategy for purposefully embedding educational and social issues in the creation, production, processing, and dissemination process of an entertainment program, in order to achieve desired individual, community, institutional, and societal changes among the intended media user populations.

By saying *theory based* we emphasize the crucial role of theory in each part of the E-E strategy—from design to evaluation. This phrase also refers to the multiplicity and interdisciplinary nature of human communication theories that E-E has incorporated as it has evolved. Additionally, the use of the word *embedding* is purposeful as the idea behind E-E is not just about message manipulation or about simply inserting an educational message in an entertainment program, but rather incorporating the issue, in all its nuance and subtlety, through the entire process. Thus, the social issue, the problems contained therein, and the solutions for social change are an integral part of the E-E process. Here *process* signifies all the steps that go into an effective E-E intervention, including the development of creative ideas for programming, the actual production of media programs, as well as the dissemination, information processing, and dialogue that follows. In this definition, we also explicitly specify that the intended outcome can be "individual, community, institutional, and societal changes." A review of effective E-E interventions indicate that although the bulk of the research has focused on assessing effects at the individual level, E-E programs often contribute to social change at the meso- and macrolevel by influencing social dynamics among cultural groups, communities, organizations, and social systems at large. These changes take place across multiple levels and often in a nonlinear manner, as E-E may induce unintended consequences and encounter resistance due to selective message decoding and competitive political and economic forces. Further, we use the term *intended media user populations* to include consumers of increasingly diverse media formats such as digital games and virtual environments that E-E programs seek to engage.

In the context of the above definition of E-E, we make the distinction between what constitute serious games and what represent E-E interventions in the form of digital games. A number of organizations such as Robert Wood Johnson Foundation, Games for Change, and Games for Health have been instrumental in attracting interest in health promotion and social change among the professional gaming community. However, games that happen to address a health-related issue or happen to factor in some socio-cultural circumstances, as they are commonly defined as within the realm of serious games, are not necessarily designed, developed, and distributed with the consciousness of E-E principles. In fact, a great majority of these games are not what we can strictly call as E-E digital games. Nonetheless, many initiatives undertaken in this area hold tremendous potential and promise. Through this chapter, we hope to explore the unique contributions that serious games can make to the field of E-E, as well as the additional value that digital games can bring to traditional mass media E-E programs.

Connecting Social Affordances of Digital Games with Entertainment-Education

The rise of Internet and interactive digital entertainment media technologies afford social possibilities that were not realized previously (Baym, 2002; also see Parks & Roberts, 1998; Sproull & Faraj, 1997). *Social affordance*[3] of technologies has been defined as possibilities generated by properties of information and communication technologies that enable social interactions among individuals or groups, as well as between human and computer intelligence (Bradner, 2001; Bradner, Kellogg, & Erickson, 1999; Hutchby, 2001; Mynatt, O'Day, Adler, & Ito, 1998; Ruhleder, 2002; Wellman & Hogan, 2004; Wellman et al., 2003).

Klimmt (this volume, chapter 16) highlighted five properties of digital games that enable or afford certain social activities through game play: multimodality, interactivity, narrative, option for social (multiplayer) use, and the game frame of experience. They are explicated in a matrix of well-grounded psychological mechanisms of game play stages for change at the individual level and validated in previous research (e.g., Grodal, 2000; Lee, Park, & Jin, 2006; Ritterfeld & Weber, 2006; Vorderer, 2000). Here, we elaborate on each of these properties highlighting its relevance to key elements of E-E models. We think of *experiential game play*[4] as the most unique feature of digital games, supported by increasingly sophisticated technological capacity that is closely associated with multimodality and interactivity. We also want to call attention to the important role of *persuasive, interactive narrative*[5] and *social interaction*[6] in enhancing the structure and infrastructure of E-E in its digital forms of communication.

Experiential Game Play

Play is one of the "basic dramatic elements" identified by expert game designers that help create player's emotional engagement (Fullerton, Swain, & Hoffman, 2004, p. 81). This game frame of experience or play perspective is crucial to achieve any outcome, whether enjoyment and relaxation, or knowledge gains and skill building, or other attitudinal and behavioral change (Bryant & Vorderer, 2006; Gee, 2005, 2007; Singhal, Cody, et al., 2004; Singhal & Rogers, 1999; Vorderer & Bryant, 2006; Zillmann & Vorderer, 2000). Digital games share many common outcome possibilities with other entertainment media such as arousal and diversion. But perhaps what differentiates digital games from most other entertainment vehicles is its attribute of experiential play.

Many games now allow players to embody a human being (or an animal, or another subject) and be playful in the game world. Such playfulness fosters curiosity and experimentation, allowing gamers to explore multiple identities and experiential possibilities. "A playful approach can be applied to even the most serious or difficult subjects because playfulness is a state of mind rather than an action" (Fullerton et al., 2004, p. 88). For instance, in the game *Squeezed*, the player takes on the role of a tree-hopping, bandana-wearing frog who leaves home to seek work abroad as a fruit picker, experiencing the trials and tribulations of living in a foreign country, under highly oppressive conditions, and preoccupied with the thought of sending monies back home to the family (Gorman, 2007). In *Darfur Is Dying*, a player may embody the role of a refugee girl who needs to fetch water in an environment fraught with threats and danger. If the refugee girl is caught, you (as player) are caught. If she suffers, you (as player) suffer (Gorman, 2007).

Such immersive game play experience is qualitatively different from the kind of vicarious experience an audience member may derive from traditional mass media entertainment genres. Through serendipitous discoveries and random encounters, players—often at the center of the actions—are more likely to understand or accept different points of view and learn lessons from unexpected consequential scenarios. Such a world that combines realistic representation and imaginative fantasies provide enormous opportunities for creativity, participation, and collaboration where alternative perspectives, collective actions, and new social norms may emerge. Games for social change need to strike a balance between individualized dynamic play experience and the game structure to optimize the ultimate outcome.

Multimodality

Multimodality is an attribute of most new information and communication technologies. Digital games, as entertainment products, often assemble cutting-edge technologies that are developed to increase the enjoyment of play experiences. Compared to traditional entertainment media, multimodality is enriched in digital games in terms of content presentation and channels of communication. Sophisticated audiovisual (re)presentation, increasingly integral haptic devices, and speech recognition capacity allow the possibility of sensory and realistic simulations (Johnson et al., 2004; McLaughlin, 2006; McLaughlin et al., 2006; Ritterfeld & Weber, 2006) and enable a sense of realness and presence (Lee, 2004; Shapiro, Peña-Herborn, & Hancock, 2006; Steuer, 1992; Tamborini & Skalski, 2006; Wirth et al., 2007). This enhanced multimodality capacity of digital games, in addition to gaming associated activities on the Internet, offers immense opportunities for establishing infrastructure and facilitating discussions about the social content during and after game play.

Interactivity

Despite the conventional static view, traditional mass media genres of entertainment can also be interactive. For instance, radio and television programs have been taking phone calls for years and now also casting votes via the Internet and mobile technologies. Interactivity in digital games, however, is "a perceived degree that people in a communication process with at least one more intelligent being can bring a reciprocal effect to other participants of the communication process by turn-taking, feedback, and choice behavior" (Lee et al., 2006, p. 263). This multilateral, real-time interactivity in digital games provides a different way of exposure, information processing, and social interaction between the player and the virtual environment, artificial intelligence-based software agents, avatars controlled by human actors, and other known and unknown game players (Lee et al. 2006; Sellers, 2006; Vorderer, 2000).

A player's freedom to make choices changes the pathways of individual game play experiences and subsequent outcomes (Lee et al., 2006; Ritterfeld & Weber, 2006). Instant reactions allow for quick feedback loops to provoke deeper thinking and learning with player engagement in the plot development through dialogues, constant decision making, as well as sense making of previous decisions which can be limited in television and radio programs due to air time constraints (Gee, 2005, 2007; also see this volume, chapter 5). With player's personal well-being at stake (as Klimmt refers to as "increased self-reference," also see Klimmt & Vorderer, 2007), the situated awareness/learning becomes more powerful in stimulating and sustaining changes through increased player engagement and participation.

Persuasive, Interactive Narrative

Much of the early work on mass-mediated E-E was influenced by Mexican writer-producer-director Miguel Sabido, who formulated a methodology for the production of social soap operas grounded in multiple theoretical frameworks: social learning/cognitive theory (Bandura, 1977, 1986, 1997); dramatic theory (Bentley, 1967); archetypes (Jung, 1958, 1970); triune brain theory (MacLean, 1973); and the theory of the tones (Sabido, 2004). Key elements in the Sabido methodology include: a values grid derived from the moral framework of a specific educational issue; social modeling through the protagonist, antagonist, and satellite characters (esp., similarity modeling which evokes deep emotions as audiences watch their favorite characters suffer, doubt, and ultimately triumph over the obstacles and "win"; and also transitional modeling, as often shown in the satellite/minor characters who take actions after they see positive changes in the main character); using cliffhangers to engage the audience, epilogues to spur discussions, and infrastructure and resources to provide accurate information and further assistance to change (Cody & Sabido, in press; Nariman, 1993; Sabido, 2002, 2004, in press). Based on his methodology, Sabido created and produced a series of social content telenovelas in Mexico in the 1970s and early 1980s (Singhal & Rogers, 1999). The success of these E-E programs snowballed in the years that followed into a global wave by using narratives (especially melodramas) to address social problems across the world (Singhal & Rogers, 2004; see examples in Case Box 1, and also Singhal, Cody, Rogers, & Sabido, 2004).

Case Box I Examples of Successful E-E Programs

From November 1975 to December 1976, 30 minutes a day, 5 times a week, millions of Mexicans tuned in to watch a phenomenally popular telenovela *Ven Conmigo* (Come with Me), depicting the journeys of a dozen adults who overcame obstacles to enroll in literacy classes and obtain a primary school diploma. With positive role models set by main characters, epilogues delivered by a celebrity, and display of free material distribution locations all carefully incorporated in the episodic serial, adult literacy class enrollment in Mexico increased ninefold during the broadcast and doubled the following year (Singhal & Rogers, 1999).

Taru, a radio soap opera broadcast weekly for a year from 2002 to 2003, in four states of India, told the story of a young woman with feminist sensibilities who worked at the village health center. The program addressed entrenched social problems in a highly engaging storyline, showing the young woman protagonist in conflict with community members. Coupling mass media with community mobilization and service delivery, the program achieved a listenership of an estimated 20 to 25 million people, spurring multiple listening clubs and enthusiastic discussions on gender equality, small family size, reproductive health, caste and communal harmony, and community development (Singhal, Sharma, Papa, & Witte, 2004).

Such E-E dramas hold persuasive powers to induce social change. As the audience members become immersed in the story and develop parasocial relationships with their favorite characters, they tend to be distracted from seriously questioning the educational messages, and at least temporarily accept the values and attitudes advocated by the characters. The power of narrative persuasion thus lies, in part, in the inhibited counterarguing and suspension of disbelief (Green & Brock, 2000; Green, Garst, & Brock, 2004; Prentice & Gerrig, 1999; Slater, 2002b; Slater & Rouner, 2002). The use of narratives may be "one of the only strategies available for influencing the beliefs of those who are predisposed to disagree with the position espoused in the persuasive content" (Slater, 2002a, p. 175).

A majority of the dramatic elements in game design have to do with narrative (Fullerton et al., 2004): Premise helps situate digital games in a setting or metaphor beyond the abstract concepts of the game system, often with introductions of a specific time and place, the main character(s) and objective, as well as the starting action to propel the story forward. A premise that unifies the formal and dramatic elements can make a game more enjoyable and enrich game play experience. Character and story may not be found in all games, but when included in a game as they increasingly are, they often create "a sense of connection for the players" (p. 81). The dramatic arc (or conflict) is at the heart of any good drama and any good game system, going through the classic pattern of exposition, rising action, climax, falling action, and resolution (p. 101), which are inherently built in the Sabido methodology for producing E-E soap operas. These dramatic elements allow for possibilities of role modeling, identification, empathy, and efficacy that facilitate the achieving of E-E goals.

Lee et al. (2006) proposed that "interactivity and narrative can coexist and should be integrated in interactive media environments" (p. 266). Interactive narrative has many built-in psychological motivation mechanisms that help empower game players by allowing them to make choices that change the structure of the story and take actions that affect the eventual outcomes (Laurel, 1993; Lee et al., 2006; Murray, 1997; Plowman, 1996; Schneider, Lang, Shin, & Bradley, 2004; Wolf, 2001). In the present time, narratives constitute, for the most part, the background subtext in most digital games (Fullerton et al. 2004), and hence the advantages offered by complex, interactive digital media narratives (over the more linear traditional narratives) are not being fully exploited. As per Schell (2004), it is a myth that interactive storytelling in digital games is fundamentally different from traditional storytelling. In fact, it is this coupling of narrative and interactivity embedded in games that offers the greatest promise for E-E in the digital era. Fortunately, game design techniques, such as branching storyline and emergent storytelling, are rapidly developing (Fullerton et al., 2004).

Social Interaction

The evolution and diffusion of the Internet (and associated digital entertainment games) have important social implications (e.g., Wellman & Hogan, 2004; Wellman et al., 2003), especially with the extreme popularity of massively multiplayer online role-playing games such as *World of Warcraft*. Games increasingly include multiplayer modalities; this option not only grants gaming access to more than one person, but also opens doors to opportunities for group or collective change.

So the number of players matter. The interactions between an individual player, the game system, and other players may be presented in many different patterns: single player versus game; multiple individual players versus game; player versus player; unilateral competition; multilateral competition; cooperative play; and team competition (Fullerton et al., 2004, p. 46). Social interaction in and around digital games can often take place on a much larger scale if you compare millions of players to one or just a few. The nature of game play requires communication in a more direct, spontaneous, informal, and potentially intimate fashion, which provides possibilities of social influence through these interwoven networks of computers and human players. This kind of social interaction may enhance the enjoyment of game play experience

(Sellers, 2006), encourage collective learning (e.g., Kafai, 2006; Lieberman, 2006), creating both opportunities and barriers for community building and cultural coconstruction (e.g., Greenfield 1997; Steen, Greenfield, Davies, & Tynes, 2006).

The provision of a service delivery infrastructure, such as the availability of family planning clinics and adult literacy classrooms, has proved to be essential to the success of E-E initiatives centering around traditional media genres (Singhal, Cody, Rogers, & Sabido, 2004; Singhal & Rogers, 1999). Some scholars have studied the role of the Internet in information searching behaviors, and suggested that the two-step flow (Katz, 1957; Lazarsfeld, Berelson, & Gaudet, 1944) has become a multistep, multiloop flow as people switch between online resources and human capital (Kayahara & Wellman, 2007). E-E digital games certainly need to consider taking advantage of the infrastructure on- and off-line to provide accurate and reliable information as well as a safe space for dialogues.[7]

In short, the social affordances of digital games in relation to E-E are: (1) experiential game play; (2) multimodality; (3) interactivity; (4) persuasive, interactive narrative; and (5) social interaction. These five properties are interrelated and work together to provide an enjoyable and fruitful play experience (also see Wang, Shen, & Ritterfeld, this volume, chapter 3) and make digital games a promising platform for E-E interventions.

Opening Possibilities for Entertainment-Education through Digital Games

We believe that serious games open up possibilities to strategically incorporate E-E principles in game design to: (1) address complex and sensitive social issues such as political conflicts, public policy, and sex education; (2) serve population groups that are beyond common gaming market reach, such as children and young people with medical conditions and senior citizens; and (3) provide a space for active participation in content generation and taking actions in the real world. In this section, we describe some promising examples in each of the three areas mentioned above. These examples are not necessarily what we have defined as E-E digital games in this chapter, but their stories shed light on a bright future where important social issues can be purposefully embedded in the game design, creation, and play experience to achieve desired attitudinal or behavioral change among the intended user populations.

Serious Games: Seriously Complex and Sensitive Content

Digital games "not only deliver messages, but also simulate experiences" and can be used as "rhetorical tools" (Persuasive Games, 2008). Bogost (2007) argues that digital games can reinforce existing social structures and positions, but also disrupt the existing social structures and persuade people to change their positions, leading to potentially significant and long-term social change. Under Bogost's leadership, Persuasive Games has been an active player in creating new genres of digital games for change such as antiadvergames (e.g., *Disaffected*), editorial news games (e.g., *Points of Entry*), and political games (e.g., *Airport Insecurity*).

Another rising trend in games for change is the creation of what are termed public policy games, designed to educate the public on some aspect of a policy and help them better understand and fulfill their role as citizens in a democracy (Social Impact Games, 2008). For example, the French government launched an online game *Cyber-Budget* to try and find a solution to the country's financial challenges. The game allows people to balance the books. The challenge is to ensure the €300 billion budget is spent wisely. The players have the ability to cut taxes but such should be done in a way that government-run services do not fall into deficit. Every decision is thus whetted by fiscal and social considerations, and one can even avail oneself of the opportunity to present the budget to a virtual parliament, invite questions, feedback, and challenges (Social Impact Games, 2008). Another example is *Peacemaker*, winner of the Reinventing Public Diplomacy through Games Competition in 2006. The game challenges the player who takes on the role of either the Israeli Prime Minister or Palestinian President to come up with a resolution to the conflict as they react to various events in the game from military attacks to diplomatic negotiations, as well as interactions with other political leaders and social groups (Hong, 2006).

Digital games are also seen as a potential and powerful tool for highly sensitive content, such as sex education. The unique properties of digital games make it relatively easy to customize and tailor messages toward individual needs and provide a more effective learning tool through experiential and fun game play, especially with immediate, direct, and corrective reinforcement. A group of scholars at the University of Connecticut is developing a game based on well-established learning strategies to promote safer sex among urban young adults (Farrar, Snyder, Barta, & Lin, 2007). Digital games have also been used for sexual health promotion in other countries. A highly popular online game in the Netherlands, *Super Shagland*, promotes responsible sexual behavior and specifically stresses the importance of using condoms and abstinence from drinking while engaging in sex (Social Impact Games, 2008). Also, an interactive computer-based multimedia game was an effective intervention to educate marginalized Peruvian youth about sexual and reproductive health (Chib, 2008).

From Typical Gamers to "Atypical" Gamers

Players of digital games are arguably dominated by young males, with some education and stable income, living in urban or suburban areas (Newman, 2004; Voderer & Bryant, 2006). However, as more and more people with diverse background from all corners of the world come to play, digital games can be a powerful and effective tool to reach and better serve the population groups not considered as typical gamers.

One of the earlier issues discussed about digital games are addiction and violence. Parents and teachers are often concerned about the physical and psychological well-being of children and young adults who tend to spend excessive hours playing games, and the prevalence of violent content in games would lead to aggressive behaviors (e.g., Egli & Meyers, 1984; Fisher, 1994; Gee, 2007; Griffiths & Davies, 2005; Sherry, 2006; Weber, Ritterfeld, & Kostygina, 2006). However, since late 1990s, games have been particularly designed and developed to help children and adolescents with certain medical conditions to learn about their diseases, practice self-management skills, and improve overall quality of life. Some examples of games for health include *Packy & Marlon* and *Bronkie: The Bronchiasaurus* both designed by ClickHealth. Children who played those games regularly showed significantly higher self-efficacy and self-care ability, increased communication with parents about the disease, and a dramatic decline of emergency and urgent care hospital visits by 40 to 77% (Brown et al., 1997; Lieberman, 2001; also see Lieberman, this volume, chapter 8). *Re-Mission* is another excellent example of a game and community built for young people, in this case to help them cope with cancer. Research from large-scale, randomized, controlled trials has shown evidence that digital games can be very effective to help educate individuals about cancer-related matters, provide young patients with a sense of empowerment, and motivate them to adhere to medication.

The gaming community is largely made up of, but certainly not restricted to, youth and teenagers. Senior citizens, at least in the United States, are increasingly turning to digital games to maintain mental acuity and also to use games for personal recreation and networking (e.g., IJsselsteijn, Nap, de Kort, & Poels, 2007; Riddick, Drogin, & Spector, 1987; Schueren, 1986; Vanden Abeele, & Van Rompaey, 2006). Spurred by the popularity of the Nintendo Wii game system among older players, Erickson Retirement Communities, based in Baltimore, which manages 18 campuses with 19,000 total residents, is installing the consoles at each location. Also, Norwegian Cruise Line, whose client base includes a fair percentage of senior citizens, is also in the process of installing Wii systems on all its ships (Schiesel, 2007). A recent study on game design with and for seniors suggested that digital games can be a useful tool for the elderly to connect with their children, grandchildren, and friends, fulfill their continued desire of personal growth, and keep a sense of self-value and connection to the society (Vanden Abeele & van Rompaey, 2006).

Coproduction and Collective Action!

Digital media have lowered the threshold of user participation. A study conducted by Pew Internet and American Life Project in 2005 suggested that over half of the American teens online consider themselves "media creators"[8] and a third of them share their creations with others (Lenhardt & Madden, 2005). The 2008 Digital Future Project reported that since 2003 an increasing number of people have shared original content on the Internet—through a blog, display of photos, or by maintaining a personal Web site (Center for the Digital Future, 2008). This emerging participatory culture not only encourages individual creative expressions, but provides a safe space for sharing, a sense of community, and strong incentives for active participation (Jenkins, 2007).

Prior experience of designing traditional E-E programs suggests that it is crucial to include intended user groups in the content generation process (Usdin, Singhal, Shongwe, Goldstein, & Shabalala, 2004). The same idea can be applied to digital games and is highly recommended. It is often in this process of coproduction that the designers can truly listen to the people that their program aims to serve, incorporate original concepts in the stories that they are about to tell, and in a language that can be easily understood. We are glad to see some digital game projects have taken the lead in making an effort to reach their intended user groups and produce high quality products through their collaborations. For example, in creating *ICED*, Breakthrough partnered with various community-based organizations, and also included more than 100 high school students and their teachers in New York City. Similarly, the production team of *Re-Mission* also made sure that teens and young adults with cancer were involved in the entire design and development process so the game can speak to their concerns that stem from their day-to-day struggles but still be entertaining at the same time.

ICED and *Re-Mission* also did a fine job of establishing infrastructure. Creating compelling and dramatic content is important, but only when service delivery resources are provided that real change can take place. On the Web site of *ICED*, topics labeled as "What are the issues?" and "Get the word out!" are side by side with instructions for downloading and playing the game. Fact sheets of current U.S. immigration laws on detention and deportation are provided. And players are encouraged to include *ICED* character trading cards and game logos to their personal Web sites, blogs, social networking Web pages, and e-mail signatures. *Re-Mission* has also made a deliberate effort to build a community for young cancer patients. People can participate in their forums, read blogs, and benefit from many other resources. In both cases, the change does not stop at the finish of game play, but rather starts from there.

To sum up, many of the principles and key learning gleaned from traditional E-E initiatives can be incorporated in the design, development, and distribution of digital games. Digital games can be used to address complex social phenomena and sensitive topics, to reach and better serve population groups that are normally not considered as of interest to game developers, and to encourage collaborative learning and collective actions. In the next section, we discuss the role of digital games in broaching and presenting new alternative social realities.

Digital Games and Alternative Realities

To what extent might digital games help in opening up a slate of new interventional possibilities beyond the computer screen which may not have been broached before? How might digital games help social change practitioners to (virtually) suspend certain rules of existing social reality so that they can come up with new and more effective interventional strategies? Might the playing of a game that deals with a real social problem empower players to identify alternative intervention strategies that are otherwise difficult to fathom or propose?

Here the experience of E-E soap operas may be a useful starting point. One of the most promising aspects of E-E narratives lies in their potential to disseminate "new" behavioral models of collective action (Singhal, Cody, et al., 2004). E-E programs can question existing patterns of social behavior and model new ways of dealing with past social practices. For instance, in the 1999 *Soul City* E-E television series in South Africa, a new collective behavior was modeled to portray how neighbors might intervene in a spousal abuse situation (Singhal & Rogers, 2002). The prevailing cultural norm in South Africa was for neighbors, even if they wished to help a victim, not to intervene in a spousal abuse situation. Wife (or partner) abuse is seen as a private matter, carried out in a private space, with curtains drawn and behind closed doors. In the *Soul City* series, neighbors collectively decide to break the ongoing cycle of spousal abuse. When the next wife-beating episode occurred, they gathered around the abuser's residence and collectively banged pots and pans, censuring the abuser's actions (Usdin et al., 2004).

This prime-time television soap opera episode, which earned one of the highest audience ratings in South Africa in 1999, demonstrated the importance of creatively modeling *collective efficacy* in order to energize neighbors, who, for social and cultural reasons, felt previously inefficacious. By watching the neighbors collectively act against an abuser on screen, viewers learned new ways to break the cycle of spousal abuse. Several weeks after this episode was broadcast, pot banging to stop partner abuse was reported in several communities in South Africa. Clearly, in these communities, the newly modeled behavior was discussed, debated, and decisions were made. Interestingly, patrons of a local pub in Thembisa Township in South Africa also reinvented the new collective behavior they learned from *Soul City*. They collectively banged bottles in the bar when a man physically abused his girlfriend (Singhal & Rogers, 2002).

What implication does *Soul City's* experience with the modeling of new alternative realities (for domestic violence) hold for serious games? For one, digital games offer tremendous generative potential for broaching alternative interventional possibilities. Here the focus is not just on what a digital gaming experience yields for an individual user (or a community of users), which is in itself important, but on how these individual/collective outcomes can broaden the slate of interventional possibilities for social change. Here the argument is that creatively crafted digital games can provide useful inputs in generating new plotlines for other E-E narratives (e.g. soap operas). This coupling of digital gaming outputs as formative inputs for designing large-scale E-E initiatives can be a potentially very exciting area of theorizing and practice, something that has not been addressed before. However, in so doing, we problematize the dominant psychosocial theoretical frameworks that have been dominant in conceptualizing the effects of serious games, and call for alternative conceptualizations.

Problematics and Wicked Questions

We end this chapter by problematizing past and current scholarship on serious games, raising two key "wicked questions" for E-E and serious games researchers/practitioners to address in the future. Wicked questions, unlike "trick" questions, have no right answers but can expose straitjacketed assumptions about an issue, context, or situation, opening up options and possibilities not considered before.

Wicked Question 1. How might one capture the complexity of social change in a serious game without trivializing it? Some years ago, at an African E-E summit in Kenya, a participant asked: "Professor Singhal, you can't be serious about studying soap operas?" When this assertion was politely questioned, the counterassertion went something like: "Can you really address serious social topics in a genre that is mindless and escapist?" The response: "Yes, mindless and escapist but acknowledge that a soap opera is a highly complex narrative involving various characters who find themselves in different situations and face multiple consequences, and it is this open-ended narrativity of possibilities that makes it one of the most popular genres of mass media programming, cutting across geographic, national, and cultural boundaries. So, why does this genre need to be trashy, mindless, and escapist? Why can't it be mindful and thought-provoking?"

Similarly, can a serious game—in its design and implementation—capture the complexity of the social change process in an engaging manner without grossly simplifying or trivializing it? That is the challenge. A corollary question that naturally follows is: Are there limits to what social issues serious games can and should explore?

Wicked Question 2. Why are serious game scholars, driven by psychological leanings, so wedded to theorize complex social change problems in individualistic, cognitive-processing frameworks? Behavior change models, driven by psychosocial frameworks (for instance, Klimmt, this volume, chapter 16) focus on individuals as the locus of change. The change mechanisms revolve around plugging knowledge, attitude, and practice (KAP) gaps, targeting the existing "deficiencies" at the individual level. However, such models subscribe implicitly to questionable assumptions: For example, individuals are capable of controlling their context, are on an "even playing field," make decisions on their own free will, and through a rational cognitive processing framework. While these assumptions may hold more water in cultures that value independence (e.g., in individualistic cultures such as the United States), they are less useful in understanding human behavior in collectivistic cultures—where an individual's behavior is highly regulated and influenced by her or his other salient relationships. Also, in cultures where there are highly entrenched social hierarchies, or in dyadic relationships characterized by power differentials, psychosocial models of individual-level changes can be highly limiting in their explanatory power.

Can designers of serious games pay careful attention to values and beliefs embedded in specific cultural contexts, and be mindful of the social, political, and economic differentials that may mediate individual "play" decisions? An understanding of how individual decisions are grounded in sociocultural contexts can open new possibilities for enacting individual, group, or community-level collective actions. For instance, in a serious game which involves various scenarios to help a commercial sex worker reduce her risk of HIV infection, alternatives may range from her individual skills in negotiating condom usage with a client to all commercial sex workers taking a collective decision that "no condom, no sex."

In summary, the present chapter analyzed the role of digital games in the growing practice of entertainment-education. We argued that serious games should not be automatically labeled as E-E digital games just because they include some social content. Connections were drawn between the social interactional possibilities afforded by the technology of digital games vis-à-vis the more traditional mass-mediated E-E programs, expounding on the five key attributes of experiential game play, multimodality, interactivity, persuasive, interactive narrative, and social interaction. We concluded by noting that digital games offer tremendous generative potential for broaching alternative interventional possibilities for social change, and that scholarship on digital games would benefit from questioning the dominant psychosocial theoretical leanings that privilege linearity, causality, reductionism, and individual-centeredness.

Notes

1. We would like to acknowledge the contribution of Joyee S. Chatterjee and Michael J. Cody to the thinking and writing of this section.
2. Here, we borrow the term and definition of *participatory culture* from Jenkins (2007), *Confronting the challenges of participatory culture: Media education for the 21st century*: "A participatory culture is a culture with relatively low barriers to artistic expression and civic engagement, strong support for creating and sharing one's creations, and some type of informal mentorship whereby what is known by the most experienced is passed along to novices. A participatory culture is also one in which members believe their contributions matter, and feel some degree of social connection with one another" (p. 3).

3. While it originated in environmental psychology (Gibson, 1977, 1979), the term *affordance* was largely appropriated by Norman (1988, 1990) as a conceptual tool for discussing the design of interactive systems.
4. We have purposefully chosen to use the term *experiential game play* instead of Klimmt's *game frame of experience* to emphasize both the "play" perspective and the "experiential" way of play related to E-E.
5. We intentionally add "persuasive" and "interactive" to the label of "narrative" in this case to emphasize these characteristics of narrative in relation to its implications of E-E.
6. Likewise, here we prefer the term *social interaction* over *option for social/multiplayer use* to promote the use of this element in serious game design.
7. Here it is important to be mindful about the different types of play in terms of level of engagement—namely *spectator play, participant play*, and *transformational play* (Fullerton et al., 2004), because the social interaction behaviors and outcomes may vary given different personalities and expectations.
8. A media creator is defined as "someone who created a blog or webpage, posted original artwork, photography, stories or videos online or remixed online content into their own new creations" (Jenkins, 2007, p. 6).

References

Airport Insecurity. [Digital game]. (2005). Atlanta, GA: Persuasive Games.

Bandura, A. (1977). *Social learning theory*. Englewood Cliffs, NJ: Prentice-Hall.

Bandura, A. (1986). *Social foundation of thought and action: A social cognitive theory*. Englewood Cliffs, NJ: Prentice-Hall.

Bandura, A. (1997). *Self-efficacy: The exercise of control*. New York: Freeman.

Do-gooder games. (2006, August 6). Batchelder, H. Retrieved February 24, 2008 from http://www.time.com/time/magazine/article/0,9171,1223388,00.html

Baym, N. K. (2002). Interpersonal life online. In L. A. Lievrouw & S. Livingstone (Eds.), *Handbook of new media* (pp. 62–76). Thousand Oaks, CA: Sage.

Bentley, E. (1967). *The life of drama*. New York: Atheneum.

Bogost, I. (2007). *Persuasive games: The expressive power of videogames*. Cambridge, MA: MIT Press.

Bradner, E. (2001). Social affordances of computer-mediated communication technology: Understanding adoption. In *Conference on Human Factors in Computing Systems*. Extended Abstracts on Human Factors in Computing Systems (pp. 67–68). New York: ACM.

Bradner, E., Kellogg, W., & Erickson, T. (1999). The adoption and use of "Babble": A field study of chat in the workplace. *Proceedings of the 6th European Conference on Computer Supported Cooperative Work (ECSCW'99)* (pp. 139–157). Lyngby, Denmark. Retrieved October 23, 2007, from http://www.research.ibm.com/SocialComputing/Papers/AdoptionOfBabble.htm

Breakthrough. (2008). *Just launched! ICED video game*. Retrieved February 24, 2008 from http://www.breakthrough.tv/product_detail.asp?proid=92&id=7

Bronkie: The Bronchiasaurus. [Digital game]. (1995). Mountain View, CA: Click Health, Inc.

Brown, S. J., Lieberman, D. A., Gemeny, B. A., Fan, Y. C., Wilson, D. M., & Pasta, D. J. (1997). Educational video game for juvenile diabetes: Results of a controlled trial. *Medical Informatics, 22*(1), 77–89.

Bryant, J., & Vorderer, P. (Eds.). (2006). *Psychology of entertainment*. Mahwah, NJ: Erlbaum.

Center for the Digital Future. (2008). *The 2008 digital future report—Surveying the digital future: Year seven*. Los Angeles: USC Annenberg School for Communication. Retrieved January 21, 2008, from http://www.digitalcenter.org

Chib, A. (2008, May). *Network influences in health initiatives: Multimedia games for youth in Peru*. Paper presented at the annual meeting of International Communication Association, Montreal, Canada.

Cody, M. J., & Sabido, M. (in press). Entertainment-education. In W. Donsbach (Ed.), *The International encyclopedia of communication*. Oxford, England: Blackwell.

Cyber-Budget. [Digital game]. (2006). French government. France.

Darfur is Dying. [Digital game]. (2006). Ruis, S., York, A., Stein, M., Keating, N., & Santiago, K.

Disaffected! [Digital game]. (2006). Atlanta, GA: Persuasive Games LLC.

Egli, E. A., & Meyers, L. S. (1984). The role of video game playing in adolescent life: Is there reason to be concerned? *Bulletin of the Psychonomic Society, 22*(4), 309–312.

Farrar, K., Snyder, L., Barta, W., & Lin, C. A. (2007, May). *Creating positive sexual media effects using a video game*. Paper presented at the annual meeting of International Communication Association, San Francisco, CA.

Fisher, S. (1994). Identifying video game addiction in children and adolescents. *Addictive Behaviors, 19*(5), 545–553.

Food Force. [Digital game]. (2005). United Nations World Food Programme.

Fullerton, T., Swain, C., & Hoffman, S. (2004). *Game design workshop: Designing, prototyping, and playtesting games*. New York: CMP Books.

Gee, J. P. (2005). *Why video games are good for your soul: Pleasure and learning*. Melbourne, Australia: Common Ground.

Gee, J. P. (2007). *Good video games and good learning: Collected essays on video games, learning, and literacy*. New York: Lang.

Gibson, J. J. (1977). The theory of affordances. In R. E. Shaw & J. Bransford (Eds.), *Perceiving, acting, and knowing: Toward an ecological psychology* (pp. 67–82). Hillsdale, NJ: Erlbaum.

Gibson, J. J. (1979). *The ecological approach to visual perception*. Boston: Houghton Mifflin.

Gorman, A. (2007, July 9). *Immigration debate finds itself in play*. Retrieved May 23, 2007, from http://www.breakthrough.tv/event_details.asp?eventid=181&id=4

Green, M. C., & Brock, T. C. (2000). The role of transportation in the persuasiveness of public narratives. *Journal of Personality and Social Psychology, 79*, 401–421.

Green, M. C., Garst, J., & Brock, T. C. (2004). The power of fiction: Determinants and boundaries. In L. J. Shrum (Ed.), *The psychology of entertainment media: Blurring the lines between entertainment and persuasion* (pp. 161–176). Mahwah, NJ: Erlbaum.

Greenfield, P. M. (1997). Culture as process: Empirical methods for cultural psychology. In J. W. Berry, Y. Poortinga, & J. Pandey (Eds.), *Handbook of cross-cultural psychology: Vol. 1. Theory and method* (pp. 301–346). Boston: Allyn & Bacon.

Griffiths, M. D., & Davies, M. N. O. (2005). Does video game addiction exist? In J. Raessens & J. Goldstein (Eds.), *Handbook of computer game studies* (pp. 359–369). Boston: MIT Press.

Grodal, T. (2000). Video games and the pleasure of control. In D. Zillmann & P.

Vorderer (Eds.), *Media entertainment: The psychology of its appeal* (pp. 197–214). Mahwah, NJ: Erlbaum.

Hong, Q. (2006). *Peacemaker wins USC public diplomacy prize.* Retrieved February 25, 2008 from http://seriousgamessource.com/item.php?story=9230

Hutchby, I. (2001). *Conversation and technology: From the telephone to the Internet.* Malden, MA: Polity.

ICED: I Can End Deportation! [Digital game]. (2007). New York: Breakthrough.

IJsselsteijn, W. A., Nap, H. H., de Kort, Y. A. W., & Poels, K. (2007). Digital game design for elderly users. *Proceedings of Future Play 2007,* 17–22.

Impact. [Digital game]. (2008). Retrieved February 24, 2008, from http://www.hopelab. org/impact/

Jenkins, H. with Clinton, K., Purushotma, R., Robinson, A. J., & Weigel, M. (2007). *Confronting the challenges of participatory culture: Media education for the 21st century.* (White paper). Chicago: MacArthur Foundation.

Johnson, L., Choi, S., Marsella, S., Mote, N., Narayanan, S., Vilhjlmsson, H. et al. (2004). Tactical language training system: Supporting the rapid acquisition of foreign language and cultural skills. *Proceedings of InStil, Venice.*

Jung, C. G. (1958). *Psychology and religion* (R. F. C. Hall, Trans.). New York: Pantheon Books.

Jung, C. G. (1970). *Archetypes and the collective unconscious.* Buenos Aires: Editorial Paidos.

Kafai, Y. B. (2006). Playing and making games for learning: Instructionist and constructionist perspectives for game studies. *Games and Culture, 1*(1), 36–40.

Katz, E. (1957). The two-step flow of communication: An up-to-date report on an hypothesis. *Public Opinion Quarterly, 21*(1), 61–78.

Kayahara, J., & Wellman, B. (2007). Searching for culture- high and low. *Journal of Computer-Mediated Communication, 12*(3), article 4. Retrieved November 20, 2007, from http://jcmc.indiana.edu/vol12/issue3/kayahara.html

Klimmt, C., & Vorderer, P. (2007). Interactive media. In J. J. Arnett (Ed.), *Encyclopedia of children, adolescents, and the media* (pp. 417–419). London: Sage.

Laurel, B. (1993). *Computers as theater.* Reading, MA: Addison-Wesley.

Lazarsfeld, P. F., Berelson, B., & Gaudet, H. (1944). *The people's choice: How the voter makes up his mind in a presidential campaign.* New York: Columbia University Press.

Lee, K. M. (2004). Presence, explicated. *Communication Theory, 14,* 27–50.

Lee, K. M., Park, N., & Jin, S. (2006). Narrative and interactivity in computer games. In P. Vorderer & J. Bryant (Eds.), *Playing video games: Motives, responses, and consequences* (pp. 259–274). Mahwah, NJ: Erlbaum.

Lenhardt, A., & Madden, M. (2005). *Teen content creators and consumers.* A report by Pew Internet and American Life Project. Retrieved Feburary 24, 2008, from http:// www.pewinternet.org/PPF/r/166/report_display.asp

Lieberman, D. A. (2001). Management of chronic pediatric diseases with interactive health games: Theory and research findings. *Journal of Ambulatory Care Management, 24*(1), 26–38.

Lieberman, D. A. (2006). What can we learn from playing interactive games? In P. Vorderer & J. Bryant (Eds.), *Playing video games: Motives, responses, and consequences* (pp. 379–397). Mahwah, NJ: Erlbaum.

MacLean, P. D. (1973). A triune concept of the brain and behavior, including psychology of memory, sleep, and dreaming. In V. A. Kral et al. (Eds.), *Proceedings of the Ontario Mental Health Foundation Meeting at Queen's University.* Toronto: University of Toronto Press.

McLaughlin, M. L. (2006). Simulating the sense of touch in virtual environments: Applications in the health sciences. In P. Messaris & L. Humphreys (Eds.), *Digital media: Transformations in human communication* (pp. 265–274). New York: Lang.

McLaughlin, M. L., Zimmermann, R., Liu, L., Jung, Y., Peng, W., Jin, S., et al. (2006, March). *Integrated voice and haptic support for tele-rehabilitation.* Proceedings of the 4th Annual IEEE International Conference on Pervasive Computing and Communications Workshops (pp. 13–17).

Murray, J. H. (1997). *Hamlet on the Holodeck: The future of narrative in cyberspace.* New York: Free Press.

Mynatt, E. D., O'Day, V. L., Adler, A., & Ito, M. (1998). Network communities: Something old, something new, something borrowed… *Computer Supported Cooperative Work: The Journal of Collaborative Computing, 7,* 123–156.

Nariman, H. N. (1993). *Soap operas for social change: Toward a methodology for entertainment-education television.* Westport, CT: Praeger Press.

Newman, J. (2004). *Videogames.* New York: Routledge.

Norman, D. (1988). *The psychology of everyday things.* New York: Basic Books.

Norman, D. (1990). *The design of everyday things.* New York: Doubleday.

Packy & Marlon. [Digital game]. (1994). Mountain View, CA: Click Health, Inc.

Papa, M. J., Singhal, A., & Papa, W. H. (2006). *Organizing for social change: A dialectic journey of theory and praxis.* New Delhi: Sage.

Papa, M., Singhal, A., Law, S., Pant, S., Sood, S., Rogers, E. M. et al. (2000). Entertainment-education and social change: An analysis of parasocial interaction, social learning, collective efficacy, and paradoxical communication. *Journal of Communication, 50,* 31–55.

Parks, R. R., & Roberts, L. D. (1998). "Making MOOsic": The development of personal relationships on line and a comparison to their off-line counterparts. *Journal of Social and Personal Relationships, 15,* 517–537.

Peacemaker. [Digital game]. (2006). Pittsburgh, PA: Impact Games.

Persuasive Games. (2008). *We design, build, and distribute electronic games for persuasion, instruction, and activism.* Retrieved February 24, 2008 from http://persuasivegames.com/

Plowman, L. (1996). Narrative, linearity and interactivity: Making sense of interactive multimedia. *British Journal of Educational Technology, 27,* 92–105.

Points of Entry. [Digital game]. (2007). Atlanta, GA: Persuasive Games LLC.

Prentice, D. A., & Gerrig, R. J. (1999). Exploring the boundary between fiction and reality. In S. Chaiken & Y. Trope (Eds.), *Dual-process theories in social psychology* (pp. 529–546). New York: Guilford.

Re-Mission. [Digital game]. (2006). Redwood, CA: HopeLab.

Riddick, C. C., Drogin, E. B., & Spector, S. G. (1987). The impact of videogame play on the emotional states of senor center participants. *Practice Concepts, 27*(4), 425–427.

Ritterfeld, U., & Weber, R. (2006). Video games for entertainment and education. In P. Vorderer & J. Bryant (Eds.), *Playing video games: Motives, responses, and consequences* (pp. 399–413). Mahwah, NJ: Erlbaum.

Ruhleder, K. (2002). Understanding on-ling community: The affordances of virtual space. *Information Research*, 7(3). Retrieved October 23, 2007 from http://InformationR.net/ir/7-3/paper132.html

Sabido, M. (2002). *The tone, theoretical occurrences, and potential adventures, and entertainment with social benefit* [in Spanish]. Mexico City: National Autonomous University of Mexico Press.

Sabido, M. (2004). The origins of entertainment-education. In A. Singhal, M. J. Cody, E. M. Rogers, & M. Sabido (Eds.), *Entertainment-education and social change: History, research, and practice* (pp. 61–74). Mahwah, NJ: Erlbaum.

Sabido, M. (in press). *The structure of the telenovela* [in Spanish]. Mexico City: National Autonomous University of Mexico Press.

Schell, J. (2004). The two great myths of interactive storytelling. In T. Fullerton, C. Swain, & S. Hoffman, *Game design workshop: Designing, prototyping, and playtesting games* (pp. 98–99). New York: CMP Books.

Schiesel, S. (2007, March 30). Video games conquer retirees. *New York Times*. Retrieved May 23, 2007 from http://www.gamesforchange.org/main/entry/a_rise_in_games_for_social_change/

Schneider, E. F., Lang, A., Shin, M., & Bradley, S. D. (2004). Death with a story: How story impacts emotional, motivational, and physiological responses to first-person shooter video game. *Human Communication Research*, 30(3), 361–375.

Schueren, B. (1986). Video games: An exploration of their potential as recreational activity programs in nursing homes. *Activities, Adaptation, and Aging*, 8(1), 49–58.

Sellers, M. (2006). Designing the experience of interactive play. In P. Vorderer & J. Bryant (Eds.), *Playing video games: Motives, responses, and consequences* (pp. 9–24). Mahwah, NJ: Erlbaum.

Shapiro, M. A., Peña-Herborn, J., & Hancock, J. T. (2006). Realism, imagination, and narrative video games. In P. Vorderer & J. Bryant (Eds.), *Playing video games: Motives, responses, and consequences* (pp. 275–290). Mahwah, NJ: Erlbaum.

Sherry, J. L. (2006). Would the great and mighty Oz play Doom? A look behind the curtain of violent video game research. In P. Messaris & L. Humphreys (Eds.), *Digital media: Transformations in human communication* (pp. 225–236). New York: Lang.

Singhal, A., Cody, M. J., Rogers, E. M., & Sabido, M. (Eds.). (2004). *Entertainment-education and social change: History, research, and practice*. Mahwah, NJ: Erlbaum.

Singhal, A., & Rogers, E. M. (1999). *Entertainment-education: A communication strategy for social change*. Mahwah, NJ: Erlbaum.

Singhal, A., & Rogers, E. M. (2004). The status of entertainment-education worldwide. In A. Singhal, M. J. Cody, E. M. Rogers, & M. Sabido (Eds.), *Entertainment-education and social change: History, research, and practice* (pp. 3–20). Mahwah, NJ: Erlbaum.

Singhal, A., Sharma, D., Papa, M. J., & Witte, K. (2004). Air cover and ground mobilization: Integrating Entertainment- Education broadcasts with community listening and service delivery in India. In A. Singhal, M. J. Cody, E. M. Rogers, & M. Sabido, M. (Eds.), *Entertainment-education and social change: History, research, and practice* (pp. 351–375). Mahwah, NJ: Erlbaum.

Slater, M. D. (2002a). Entertainment education and the persuasive impact of narrative. In M. C. Green, J. J. Strange, & T. C. Brock (Eds.), *Narrative impact: Social and cognitive foundations* (pp. 157–181). Mahwah, NJ: Erlbaum.

Slater, M. D. (2002b). Involvement as goal-directed, strategic processing: The extended ELM. In J. P. Dillard & M. Pfau (Eds.), *The persuasion handbook: Developments in theory and practice* (pp. 175–194). Thousand Oaks, CA: Sage.

Slater, M. D., & Rouner, D. (2002). Entertainment-education and elaboration likelihood: Understanding the processing of narrative persuasion. *Communication Theory, 12,* 173–191.

Social Impact Games. (2008). *Entertaining games with non-entertaining goals.* Retrieved February 24, 2008 from http://www.socialimpactgames.com

Sproull, L., & Faraj, S. (1997). Atheism, sex, and databases: The net as a social technology. In S. Kiesler (Ed.), *Culture of the Internet* (pp. 35–52). Mahwah, NJ: Erlbaum.

Squeezed. [Digital game]. (2006). Denver, CO: University of Denver.

Steen, F. F., Greenfield, P. M., Davies, M. S., & Tynes, B. (2006). What went wrong with *The Sims Online*: Cultural learning and barriers to identification in a massively multiplayer online role-playing game. In P. Vorderer & J. Bryant (Eds.), Playing video games: Motives, responses, and consequences (pp. 307–323). Mahwah, NJ: Erlbaum.

Steuer, J. (1992). Defining virtual reality: Dimensions determining telepresence. *Journal of Communication, 42*(4), 73–93.

Super Shag Land. [Digital game]. (2008). Retrieved February 25, 2008, from http://socialimpactgames.com/modules.php?op=modload&name=News&file=article&sid=151

Tamborini, R., & Skalski, P. (2006). The role of presence in the experience of electronic games. In P. Vorderer & J. Bryant (Eds.), *Playing video games: Motives, responses, and consequences* (pp. 225–240). Mahwah, NJ: Erlbaum.

Usdin, S., Singhal, A., Shongwe, T., Goldstein, S., & Shabalala, A. (2004). No short cuts in entertainment-education: Designing Soul City step-by-step. In A. Singhal, M. Cody, E. M. Rogers, & M. Sabido (Eds.), *Entertainment-education and social change: History, research, and practice* (pp. 153–176). Mahwah, NJ: Erlbaum.

Vanden Abeele, V., & Van Rompaey, V. (2006). Introducing human-centered research to game design: Designing game concepts for and with senior citizens. *CHI'06,* 1469–1474.

Vorderer, P. (2000). Interactive entertainment and beyond. In D. Zillmann & P. Vorderer (Eds.), *Media entertainment: The psychology of its appeal* (pp. 21–36). Mahwah, NJ: Erlbaum.

Vorderer, P., & Bryant, J. (Eds.). (2006). *Playing video games: Motives, responses, and consequences.* Mahwah, NJ: Erlbaum.

Weber, R., Ritterfeld, U., & Kostygina, A. (2006). Aggression and violence as effects of playing violent video games? In P. Vorderer & J. Bryant (Eds.), *Playing video games: Motives, responses, and consequences* (pp. 347–362). Mahwah, NJ: Erlbaum.

Wellman, B., & Hogan, B. (2004). The immanent Internet. In J. McKay (Ed.), *Netting citizens: Exploring citizenship in a digital age* (pp. 54–80). Edinburgh, Scotland: St. Andrew's Press.

Wellman, B., Quan-Haase, A., Boase, J., Chen, W., Hampton, K., de Diaz, I. I., et al. (2003). The social affordances of the Internet for networked individualism. *Journal of Computer-Mediated Communication, 8*(3). Retrieved November 22, 2007, from http://jcmc.indiana.edu/vol8/issue3/wellman.html

Wirth, W., Hartmann, T., Böcking, S., Vorderer, P., Klimmt, C., Schramm, et al. (2007). A process model of the formation of Spatial Presence experiences. *Media Psychology, 9*(3), 493–525.

Wolf, M. J. (2001). *The medium of the video game*. Austin, TX: University of Texas Press.

World of WarCraft. [Digital game]. CA: Blizzard Entertainment.

Zillmann, D., & Vorderer, P. (Eds.). (2000). *Media entertainment: The psychology of its appeal*. Mahwah, NJ: Erlbaum.

Methodological Challenges

Melding the Power of Serious Games and Embedded Assessment to Monitor and Foster Learning

Flow and Grow

Valerie J. Shute, Matthew Ventura, Malcolm Bauer, and Diego Zapata-Rivera

> We already have too much medicine that is (cognitively) good for the patient—who will not take it—and medicine that patients find delicious—but that contributes little to their cognitive abilities. (Simon, 1995, p. 508)

There is an enormous chasm between what kids do for fun and what they are required to do in school. School covers material we deem "important," but kids, generally speaking, are unimpressed. These same kids, however, are highly motivated by what they do for fun (e.g., interactive, entertainment games). Imagine these two worlds united. Student engagement is strongly associated with academic achievement (e.g., Finn & Rock, 1997; Fredricks, Blumenfeld, & Paris, 2004; Fredricks & Eccles, 2006). Thus, combining school material with games has tremendous potential to increase learning, especially for lower performing, disengaged students.

This chapter will describe a viable solution to methodological obstacles[1] that surround such an important unification. Our strategy involves a two-stage approach. The first stage is the focus of this chapter and defines a systematic way to use engaging games as the venue to extract academically relevant information from students during game play. This method could be applied to validate the claim that there are, in fact, important knowledge and skills being learned during the course of playing. If the first stage is successful, we will find that educationally valuable learning is going on during game play and that we can measure it accurately. This will inform the second stage of the approach, which entails adaptation of existing, or the design of new, engaging games that monitor and support students' learning of academically relevant skills. In short, we are proposing a two-stage strategy and then illustrating in this chapter how the first stage might be accomplished and evaluated.

After defining serious games and embedded (or stealth) formative assessment, we will show how the two (i.e., games and stealth assessment) may be joined by employing (1) evidence-centered design (ECD; Mislevy, Steinberg, & Almond, 2003), and (2) Bayesian networks (e.g., Pearl, 1988) to monitor and support learning in the context of gaming environments. The ECD approach allows us to embed assessments directly into the gaming environment, which should permit the unobtrusive collection and analysis of meaningful, emergent data to be used to enhance the efficiency and effectiveness of the gaming and learning experience. We will illustrate the approach of merging stealth assessment into digital environments in two contexts: (1) an ECD-based simulation that was developed for training Cisco network administrators (Bauer, Williamson, Mislevy, & Behrens, 2003), and (2) a fairly well-known immersive game used to elicit evidence about current and emergent cognitive and noncognitive attributes (*The Elder Scrolls IV: Oblivion*, 2006). We conclude with a call for future research needed in the area.

In general, the goal of this chapter is to present an innovative methodological approach for extracting important data relating to valued educational constructs, while concurrently sustaining (not disrupting) the students' engagement. Ultimately (i.e., within stage 2 of the research—beyond the scope of this chapter), we envision using the data obtained from the stealth assessment to inform changes to the gaming environment to support student learning and also to inform the creation of new games. Our current aim, however, is to examine existing immersive games to assess the degree of actual and important learning that goes on therein. The main assumptions underlying this chapter are that: (1) learning by doing (required in game play) may improve learning processes and outcomes; (2) different types of learning may be verified and measured during game play; (3) strengths and weaknesses of the student may be capitalized on and bolstered, respectively; and (4) formative feedback can be used to further support student learning. Additionally, we want students to come to consider knowledge and skills as additionally important currencies in the game world—on a par with health and weapons. In short, the more we learn about the game play experience—the valuable competencies being acquired and honed—the more we can exploit such games to really support learning.

Serious Games

Serious games are virtual environments explicitly intended to educate or train. As Squire (2006) points out, groups as diverse as the U.S. military and the National Association of Home Builders invest in games that represent and instruct their particular content and views. Such serious games are designed to impart their content as players are immersed in game playing activities. The U.S. Army's game, *America's Army 3* (2009), is a good example of a serious game. In fact, it was the first digital game to make recruitment an explicit goal. It teaches, via game play, what it is like to be a soldier in the U.S. Army.

Another way to understand serious games is in contrast to more typical digital games that have no explicit goals about being educational or informational—such as *Dance Dance Revolution* (1999) and *Diner Dash* (2008). The raison d'être of such casual games is to entertain. In contrast, and according to Carey (2006), serious games (as well as educational simulations, like physics or chemistry simulations) represent a unique product category with functional requirements that are different from casual games. Two key features of serious games are educational and immersive. Casual games are typically not viewed as educational, but they can be immersive.

Players may experience immersion within a virtual world because of features such as interactive stories that provide context and clear goal structures for problem solving in the game environment. Researchers have noted that features that are common to all intrinsically motivating environments include elements of challenge, control, and fantasy to pique curiosity and engage attention (Lepper & Malone, 1987; Malone, 1981; Rieber, 1996). These characteristics all work together to induce what is commonly called *flow*, defined as the state of optimal experience, where a person is so engaged in the activity that self-consciousness disappears, sense of time is lost, and the person engages in complex, goal-directed activity not for external rewards, but simply for the exhilaration of doing (Csikszentmihalyi, 1990).

Our aim is to identify what players do and learn within immersive games, specifically immersive games that are not explicitly educational. While these games are not by definition serious games, the purpose of this chapter is to describe how learning and assessment can be accomplished in immersive games that have the *potential* for being educational. We focus on immersive games because they have the greatest potential for inducing and sustaining flow (i.e., finding the perfect spot between too hard and too easy; see Csikszentmihalyi, 1990). Along the same lines, Pausch, Gold, Skelly, and Thiel (1994) describe the essence of digital game design as: (1) presenting a goal; (2) providing clear-cut feedback to the user as to their progress toward the goal; and (3) constantly adjusting the game's challenges to a level slightly beyond the current abilities of the player. Similarly, Rieber (1996) contends that challenge must be matched to the player's current skill or ability level; that is, boredom or frustration may ensue to the degree that there is a mismatch.

Embedding assessments within such immersive games would permit us to monitor a player's current level on valued competencies, and then use that information as the basis for adjusting game features, such as the difficulty of challenges. This is intended to maximize both our "flow" and "grow" (i.e., learning) goals. Integrating the flow state of immersive games with learning theories has tremendous potential to enhance students' learning—both in the short- and long-term (e.g., Gee, 2003; Lieberman, 2006; Squire & Jenkins, 2003). The idea is to exploit animation and immersive characteristics of game environments to create the flow needed to keep the students engaged in solving progressively more complex learning tasks. In other words, we want to use the flow to facilitate the growth in terms of students' acquisition of valued proficiencies.

As more and more researchers are pointing out (e.g., Cannon-Bowers, 2006; de Freitas & Liver, 2006; Squire, 2006), there is currently a shortage of experimental studies that examine learning through game play, despite the fact that games represent a very rich venue for conducting learning research. For practical purposes, and in line with the ideas presented in this chapter (i.e., to leverage immersive games to support learning), we first need to ascertain exactly what it is that players are taking away from games such as *Grand Theft Auto IV* (2008) and *Civilization IV* (2008). Gee (2003), Lieberman (2006), and others in the field firmly believe that a lot of important learning and development is going on within these games. But are these educationally valuable skills and strategies? As mentioned, many immersive games are intrinsically motivating, likely because they employ such features as challenge, control, and fantasy, as well as opportunities for social interaction, competition, and collaborative play (Malone, 1981). Additionally, we realize that immersive games can potentially have adverse effects, such as players acquiring undesirable attitudes or learning maladaptive social behaviors. This occurs due to the freedom enabled by immersive games.

We now turn our attention to the general topic of embedded formative assessments (FAs), that have the potential to improve student learning directly (e.g., via feedback on personal progress) or indirectly (e.g., through modifications of the learning or gaming environment). In this context, the term *embedded* refers to assessments that are unobtrusively inserted into the curriculum (or game). Their formative purpose is to obtain useful and accurate information about student progress, on which the teacher, instructional environment, or the student can act.

Embedded Formative Assessment

> If we think of our children as plants…summative assessment of the plants is the process of simply measuring them. The measurements might be interesting to compare and analyze, but, in themselves, they do not affect the growth of the plants. On the other hand, formative assessment is the garden equivalent of feeding and watering the plants—directly affecting their growth. (Clarke 2001, p. 2)

When teachers or computer-based instructional systems know how students are progressing and where they are having problems, they can use that information to make real-time instructional adjustments such as reteaching, trying alternative instructional approaches, altering the difficulty level of tasks or assignments, or offering more opportunities for practice. This is, broadly speaking, formative assessment (Black & Wiliam, 1998a), and it has been shown to improve student achievement (Black & Wiliam, 1998b; Shute, Hansen, & Almond, 2008).

In addition to providing teachers with evidence about how their students are learning so that they can revise instruction appropriately, formative assessments (FAs) may directly involve students in the learning process, such as by providing feedback that will help students gain insight about how to improve. Feedback in FA should generally guide students toward obtaining their goal(s). The most helpful feedback provides specific comments to students about errors and suggestions for improvement. It also encourages students to focus their attention thoughtfully on the task rather than on simply getting the right answer (Bangert-Drowns, Kulik, Kulik, & Morgan, 1991; Shute, 2008). This type of feedback may be particularly helpful to lower-achieving students because it emphasizes that students can improve as a result of effort rather than be doomed to low achievement due to some presumed lack of innate ability (e.g., Hoska, 1993).

A more indirect way of helping students learn via FA includes instructional adjustments that are based on assessment results (Stiggins, 2002). Different types of FA data can be used by the teacher or instructional environment to support learning, such as diagnostic information relating to levels of student understanding, and readiness information indicating who is ready or not to begin a new lesson or unit. Formative assessments can also provide teachers or computer-based learning environments with instructional support based on individual student (or classroom) data. Examples of instructional support include: (1) recommendations about how to use FA information to alter instruction (e.g., speed up, slow down, give concrete examples), and (2) prescriptions for what to do next, links to Web-based lessons and other resources, and so on.

Conjoining Games and Embedded Assessments

New directions in educational and psychological measurement allow more accurate estimation of student competencies, and new technologies permit us to administer formative assessments during the learning process, extract ongoing, multifaceted information from a learner, and react in immediate and helpful ways, as needed. When embedded assessments are so seamlessly woven into the fabric of the learning environment that they are virtually invisible, we call this *stealth assessment*. Such stealth assessment can be accomplished via automated scoring and machine-based reasoning techniques to infer things that would be too hard for humans (e.g., estimating values of evidence-based competencies across a network of skills).

One big question is not about collecting this rich digital data stream, but rather, how to make sense of what can potentially become a deluge of information. Another major question concerns the best way to communicate student-performance information in a way that can be used to easily inform instruction or enhance learning. Our solution to the issue of making sense of data and thereby fostering student learning within gaming environments is to extend and apply evidence-centered design (ECD; e.g., Mislevy, Steinberg, & Almond, 2003). This provides (1) a way of reasoning about assessment design, and (2) a way of reasoning about student performance whether in gaming or other learning environments.

The Methodology

There are several problems that must be overcome to incorporate assessment in serious games. Bauer et al. (2003) address many of these same issues with respect to incorporating assessment within interactive simulations in general. Here we outline several of the issues and provide an example of how they may be addressed using ECD. There are many factors that may influence learning in games and simulations. Are immersive games more engaging than more typical venues such as lectures, textbooks, and even serious games? If so, does simply providing a more engaging environment (and hence increasing time on task) produce increased learning outcomes? Can one provide richer learning experiences and new venues for learning that could not be explored otherwise? Consider, for instance, the prospect of learning by playing out "what-if" scenarios in history, such as through the games *Civilization III* (Meier, 2004) or *Revolution* (Education Arcade, 2008; for more scenarios, see Squire & Jenkins, 2003).

Two good reviews of studies that have been conducted with games' effects on learning outcomes include the dissertation of Blunt (2006) and a recent chapter by Lieberman (2006). However, compared to other types of instructional environments, there are currently too few experimental studies examining the range of effects of immersive environments and simulations on learning. For instance, Cannon-Bowers (2006) recently challenged the efficacy of game-based learning, "We are charging head-long into game-based learning without knowing if it works or not. We need studies." Furthermore, of the evaluation studies that have been conducted, the results of games and simulations effects on learning are mixed. For example, Kulik (2002) reports that a meta-analysis of six studies of classroom use of simulations found only modest learning effects, and two of the six studies could not find any increase in learning at all. In addition, research on the use of simulations to enhance students' understanding of physics has also yielded mixed results (e.g., Ranney, 1988).

In playing games, students naturally produce rich sequences of actions while performing complex tasks, drawing upon the very skills we want to assess (e.g., critical thinking, problem solving). Evidence needed to assess the skills is thus provided by the students' interactions with the game itself—the processes of play, which may be contrasted with the product(s) of an activity, as is the norm within educational settings. Making use of this stream of evidence to assess skills and abilities presents problems for traditional measurement models used in assessment. First, in traditional tests the answer to each question is seen as an independent data point. In contrast, the individual actions within a sequence of interactions in a simulation or game are often highly dependent on one another. For instance, what one does in a flight simulator at one point in time affects subsequent actions later on. Second, in traditional tests, questions are often designed to get at one particular piece of knowledge. Answering the question correctly is evidence that one knows a certain fact; that is, one question—one fact. By analyzing students' responses to all of the questions, each providing evidence about students' understanding of a specific fact or concept, teachers or instructional environments can get a picture of what students are likely to know and not know overall. Because we typically want to assess a whole constellation of skills and abilities from evidence coming from students' interactions within a game or simulation, methods for analyzing the sequence of behaviors to infer these abilities are not as obvious. Evidence centered design is a method that can address these problems and enable the development of robust and valid simulation- or game-based learning systems.

Evidence-Centered Design

A game that includes stealth assessment must elicit behavior that bears evidence about key skills and knowledge, and it must additionally provide principled interpretations of that evidence in terms that suit the purpose of the assessment. Figure 18.1 sketches the basic structures of an evidence-centered approach to assessment design (Mislevy et al., 2003). Working out these variables, and models, and their interrelationships is a way to answer a series of questions posed by Sam Messick (1994) that get at the very heart of assessment design:

What complex of knowledge, skills, or other attributes should be assessed? A given assessment is meant to support inferences for some purpose, such as a licensing decision, provision of diagnostic feedback, guidance for further instruction, or some combination. Variables in the competency model (CM) describe the knowledge, skills, and abilities on which the inferences are to be based. The term *student model* is often used to denote a student-instantiated version of the competency model; that is, values in the student model express the assessor's current belief about a student's level on variables within the CM.

What behaviors or performances should reveal those constructs? An evidence model expresses how the student's interactions with, and responses to a given problem constitute evidence about student-model variables. Observables describe features of specific task performances.

What tasks or situations should elicit those behaviors? Task-model variables describe features of situations that will be used to elicit performance. A task model provides a framework for characterizing and constructing situations with which a student will interact to provide evidence about targeted aspects of knowledge.

In games with stealth assessment, the student model will accumulate and represent belief about the targeted aspects of skill, expressed as probability distributions for student-model variables (Almond & Mislevy, 1999). Evidence models will identify what the student says or does that can provide evidence about those skills (Steinberg & Gitomer, 1996) and express in a psychometric

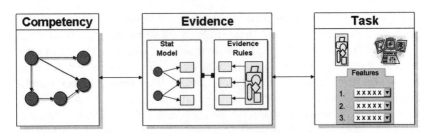

Figure 18.1 The central models of an evidence-centered assessment design.

model how the evidence depends on the competency-model variables (Mislevy, 1994). Task models will express situations that can evoke required evidence.

An Example of Embedding Assessment in a Simulation

Bauer et al. (2003) describe a simulation and assessment system developed for the Cisco Networking Academy Program (CNAP). Based on the needs of CNAP, an online simulation-based training system with stealth assessment was designed and developed. The system uses realistic scenarios to set the stage for authentic design, configuration, and troubleshooting tasks that are provided via Flash simulations and remote access to actual computer networks. The system is used by students to practice networking skills, and students receive detailed feedback on their performance on each problem. The system also accumulates evidence, via stealth assessment and gleaned from students' performances across tasks, to estimate their overall skills and abilities. The simulation environment was structured to support learning, based on accepted psychological principles that include active construction of knowledge, use of multiple representations, performance on realistic complex tasks, and support for abstraction and reflection.

Here we describe the competency, evidence, and task models within the interactive simulation and assessment design to provide a concrete example of how the ECD methodology works. The CM in Figure 18.2 represents the constellation of knowledge, skills, and abilities that are important for success as a student of Cisco's networking academy. The CM was generally developed to support the claims that instructors would like to make about the skills their students have. It was specifically developed on the basis of a cognitive task analysis, a preexisting job-task analysis of computer networking professionals, and judgments of subject matter experts. The CM was structured to reflect the dependencies among competencies in the domain.

As shown in Figure 18.2, the CM is composed of a number of variables that represent aspects of knowledge, skill, and ability. The domain disciplinary knowledge variable represents the declarative knowledge of network components and operation. There are a number of elements of declarative knowledge

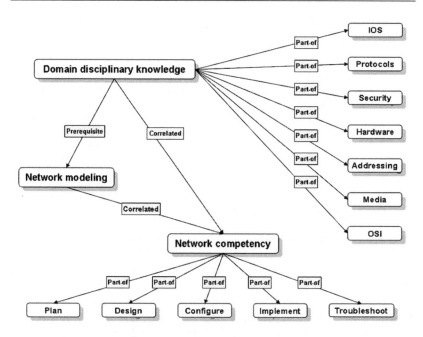

Figure 18.2 The competency model (conceptualization).

that are part of domain disciplinary knowledge, such as addressing schemes, hardware components of a network, media, protocols, etc. The network competency variable represents the overall networking ability including the subskills of planning, designing, configuring, implementing, and troubleshooting a network. As each of these network activities requires some declarative knowledge in order to conduct the procedures required to perform these tasks, there is a modeled relationship between the declarative knowledge represented in domain disciplinary knowledge and the procedural knowledge and skills required for network competency. The network modeling variable is the ability of the student to explain and predict the behavior of a network. Experts identified this skill as a key to the highest levels of skill in network competency; hence the two variables have a link between them. The ability to produce a model of a network requires domain disciplinary knowledge, which is therefore represented as a prerequisite of network modeling ability.

The evidence model describes what specific behaviors or observables are indicative of different levels of skill in the CM. On the basis of the results from a cognitive task analysis, the statistical portion of the evidence model is constructed by positing CM variables to be "parents" of observables, which are meant to bear evidence about their (inherently unobservable) values. Table 18.1 presents an outline of several evidence model observables used to update the CM variables for design, implement, and troubleshoot. The italicized

Table 18.1 Example of Observables in the Evidence Model

Design	Implement	Troubleshoot
Correctness of Outcome	*Correctness of Outcome*	*Correctness of Outcome*
Functionality of design	*Correctness of Procedure*	Error of Identification
Core requirements	Efficiency of procedure	Error Over-Identification
Peripheral requirements	Help usage	*Correctness of Procedure*
	IOS syntax	Efficiency of procedure
	Volume of actions	Help usage
	Procedural sequence	IOS syntax
		Volume of actions
		Procedureal sequence
		Sequence of actions
		Sequence of targets

composite variables are included in probabilistic models (i.e., Bayes net objects; see Koller & Pfeffer, 1997) as observable variables. Their values are summaries of the nonitalicized features listed below them, along the lines of Clauser et al. (1995).

For each of these features, an algorithm was written to score the student's work product to identify, evaluate, and summarize the quality of the work product in that aspect. For example, in Table 18.1, under the heading Troubleshoot, the "Sequence of targets" observable provides evidence of students' fault-locating behaviors. The log files of students' command sequences are parsed to determine the search pattern. That is, data are examined to see if the student (1) immediately visits the device on which there is a fault; (2) systematically searches devices, rarely (or never) returning to a previously visited network device; or (3) unsystematically "ping-pongs" among the devices, visiting many again and again. The different patterns are associated with different levels of competency.

All of the observables from a given scenario are modeled as conditionally dependent, in the manner described in Mislevy et al. (2002). These observables are used to update the student model and provide summary feedback to students and teachers. The features of the student work products on which the observables are based also contain more detailed information about students' performance on the task on which they are currently working, and used in providing task-level feedback. Hence the same evidence that is accumulated to make estimates of students' knowledge, skills, and abilities is also used, in a more detailed and timely manner for instruction in the form of task-level feedback. To illustrate, the following represents actual task-level feedback given to a student after attempting to solve a difficult design task (Create Network Diagram):

Check your diagram. You have forgotten a networking device or placed a networking device in the wrong location.

Check your diagram. You are missing a connection between two networking devices.

You have configured an incorrect IP address or you have left off an IP
address.

The question for us now is whether this type of stealth assessment approach,
employed in a simulation as described above, can similarly be used within
immersive gaming environments. We examine this question in a case study
involving a popular immersive game called *Oblivion*.

Application of the ECD Approach Using a Highly Immersive Game

Over the past 15 years, the gaming market has exploded due in the main
to advances in software and computer technology. With the advent of this
new technology, sophisticated graphics engines can now display breathtaking
graphics of landscapes, humans, and other real world and fantasy environments. Additionally, advances in artificial intelligence have enabled challenging environments that require players to adopt dynamic strategies for success.
Finally, millions of dollars now get invested in creating complex plots and
problems requiring hours of time to solve. All of these components set the
stage for highly immersive game play.

The purpose of this case study is to test the viability of our approach within
an existing immersive game and to identify knowledge, skills, and abilities that
may be learned during game play. Gee (2003) has asserted that the secret of
an immersive game as an engaging teaching device is not its 3D graphics but
its underlying architecture. Each level "dances around the outer limits of the
player's abilities," seeking at every point to be hard enough to be just doable.
Similarly, cognitive psychologists (e.g., Falmagne, Cosyn, Doignon, & Thiery,
2003; Vygotsky, 1987) have long argued that the best instruction hovers at the
boundary of a student's competence.

In the case study that follows, we describe the typical game play of a popular
game called *Elder Scrolls IV: Oblivion*. This game is a first person role-playing
game set in a 3D medieval world. The user can choose to be one of many
characters (e.g., knight, mage, elf), each of whom possesses various strengths
and weaknesses. Each character also has (or can obtain) a variety of weapons,
spells, and tools. The primary goal of the game is to gain rank and complete
various quests in a massive land full of castles, caves, virtual characters, monsters, and animals. There are multiple mini quests along the way, and a major
quest that results in winning the game. Players have the freedom to complete quests in any order they choose. Quests may include locating a person
to obtain information, eliminating a creature, retrieving a missing item, or
finding and figuring out a clue for future quests.

Character Skill Modification (Persistence)

There are many character skills to improve in *Oblivion*, and each skill improvement is frequency based, evidenced by the number of successful actions in relation to the particular skill. For instance, successfully hitting creatures with a sword in combat will increase the skill of "blade" over time. Additionally, successfully convincing someone to talk to you will increase the skill of "speechcraft," which defines the probability that a stranger will respond to you in conversation in the future. To improve these skills and thus gain rank requires many hours of game play, and many hours of game play implies persistence. This involves sticking with some activity both in the face of success and failure. Each time a player successfully engages some activity, the frequency and hence probability of subsequent success in the future is increased. In education, the attributes of persistence and self-discipline have been shown to significantly predict students' academic achievement—both in the near- and far-term (e.g., Duckworth & Seligman, 2005; Dweck, 1996).

Quest Completion (Problem Solving)

There are over 100 quests in *Oblivion*. The key challenge in these quests is to stay alive and to defeat creatures that try to harm you. For instance, during the course of game play, a player can contract vampirism while exploring caves around the land. In order to find a cure for vampirism, one must find a witch who will then provide information regarding key ingredients needed to make a potion for a cure. Each key ingredient is then marked on the map, which is used by the player to travel around in order to obtain the ingredients. Since the player has vampirism, many new obstacles enter into the quest. For example, as a vampire, one cannot travel during the day without dying (with certain exceptions), and the level for the attribute "charisma" decreases, which leads to difficulty in conversing with people, and so on.

Problem solving (which can range from simple to complex) plays a key role in quests since the player has to figure out what to do and how to do it (e.g., locate pertinent information that will provide clues to carry out a current quest). In the case of contracting vampirism, one must determine how and where to obtain information concerning a cure. In addition to problem solving skills, the player's background (or "folklore") knowledge is often helpful (e.g., knowing about likely places to find useful information, such as within chapels, from mages, etc.). This knowledge may be acquired over time with the game, or transferred from other games of this type.

In education, problem solving is often viewed as the most important cognitive activity in everyday and professional contexts (e.g., Hiebert et al., 1996; Jonassen, 2000; Reiser, 2004). However, learning to solve complex problems is too seldom required (or rewarded) in formal educational settings. As with persistence, we believe that assessment and support of problem solving skills are vitally important to improve students' long-term learning potential.

Combat (Attention and Multitasking)

Combat scenarios represent one way to keep the user engaged in game play. In *Oblivion*, combat requires the user to attend to several factors: health, magic level, fatigue, enemy maneuvering, enemy health, and escape plan. Like many games in general, and combat games in particular, concentration and attention play key roles in success. Additionally, there are many heuristics that can be used to more easily defeat particular creatures. The player must be aware of which creatures pose a serious threat (i.e., those that inflict massive amounts of health damage) and which ones can be easily defeated. In many cases, retreat is an option which enables a more strategic combat plan for difficult creatures.

In education, the central role of attention in learning has been clearly demonstrated for decades (e.g., Kruschke, 2001; Nosofsky, 1986; Trabasso & Bower, 1968). One of the main benefits of gaming environments is that they tend to capture and sustain attention. Thus attention represents another variable we view as educationally valuable.

Other Learning Components

Reading

Since much of *Oblivion* involves interaction with other people, reading and listening skills are essential to success in quests. Additionally, there are many books that give clues to quests and recipes for potions.

Creativity

There are many ways to solve a quest or defeat enemies in *Oblivion*. This freedom allows players to be creative in how they advance in the game. For example, if the player needs to obtain an object to aid in a quest, one can steal the object, buy the object, or persuade someone to relinquish the object. Each choice has various advantages and disadvantages.

Figure 18.3 illustrates some possible educationally relevant competencies that might be assessed during game play in *Oblivion*. This CM, with its "cognitive" and "noncognitive" variables, should be viewed as illustrative only. To show how we can create stealth assessments for one of the competencies cited above using an ECD approach, we focus on the attribute labeled *creative problem solving*.

Illustrating the Stealth Assessment Idea

Creative problem solving can be viewed as the aggregate of two abilities: creativity and problem solving. Creativity is a mental process involving the generation of new ideas or concepts, or new associations between existing ideas or concepts. The products of creative thought are usually considered to have both

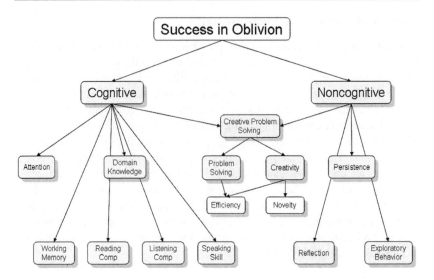

Figure 18.3 Illustration of a competency model for success in the game *Oblivion*.

originality (novelty) and appropriateness (relevance). However, while creativity has been studied from many different perspectives (e.g., cognitive science, artificial intelligence, philosophy, history, design research, social psychology, management, and so on), there is no single, authoritative definition of creativity, nor is there any standardized measurement technique. Problem solving generally refers to higher-order cognitive processes invoked to advance from an initial state to a goal state. And like creativity, problem solving has been studied extensively (see Newell & Simon, 1972), in areas as diverse as mathematics, political science, writing, and game playing.

Putting these two constructs together, we define creative problem solving (CPS) as the mental process of creating a solution to a problem. It is a special form of problem solving in which the solution is independently created rather than learned with assistance. Creative problem solving always involves creativity, but creativity often does not involve creative problem solving (e.g., in the arts). Creativity requires novelty as a characteristic of what is created, but does not necessarily imply that what is created has value or relevance. Thus to qualify as CPS, the solution must be relevant and clearly solve the stated problem (Sternberg, 2006). Solving school-assigned homework problems does not involve creative problem solving because such problems usually have well-known solutions.

Conceptual Framework for Creative Problem Solving

Whereas creativity can be seen in the products, it can also be considered in terms of processes. For example, Weisberg (1986) proposes that creativity can be defined by the novel use of tools to solve problems. Given the importance of relevance in CPS, creative contributions should be defined in some context (Sternberg, 1999). If an individual's CPS ability is judged within a context, then it will help to understand how the context interacts with how the person is judged. In particular, what are the types of creative contributions a person can make within a given context? Most theories of creativity concentrate on attributes of the individual, but to the extent that creativity is in the interaction of person and context, one would need as well to concentrate on the attributes of the person and his or her work relative to the environmental context—like the gaming environment.

Based on the work of Sternberg (1999), we adopt a notion of CPS that is measured within a context—as defined through a particular scenario or quest within a game. By focusing our definition of creativity to problem solving, one can assess novel and efficient contributions toward goals. Figure 18.4 shows a fragment of the ECD models for this CPS variable. Notice that competency model and evidence model are the same terms used in our previous ECD example, but here we use the term *action model* instead of *task model*. Action model reflects the fact that we are dynamically modeling students' action sequences. These action sequences form the basis for drawing evidence and inferences and may be compared to simpler task responses as with typical assessments. Finally, note that scene is used to define a particular quest in the game.

Competency Model

As shown earlier in Figure 18.3, we joined together problem solving and creativity to form the creative problem-solving competency. Efficiency is shown as informing both problem solving and creativity, but novelty only informs creativity in this model. Novelty is defined in relation to choosing less common (i.e., low frequency) actions in the solution of problems, while efficiency is defined in relation to the quantity and quality of steps taken toward a solution. Both novelty and efficiency are constrained by relevance. That is, the problem-solving space per scene is limited to only those actions explicitly linked or relevant to the particular problem or quest.

Evidence Model

The evidence model defines the connections between specific observables and their underlying competencies—novelty and efficiency. These connections are represented as little distribution tables within Scene 1 of the evidence model in Figure 18.4. In particular, the evidence model includes: (1) scoring rules for extracting observables from students' game play indicators found in log files; (2) the observables (i.e., scored data); and (3) measurement rules for accumulating evidence from the observables, which are then used to update the student model variables. For simplicity, our illustration includes just two

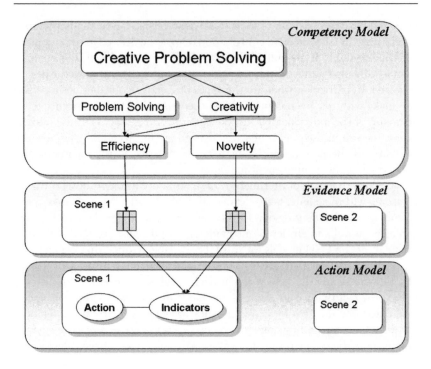

Figure 18.4 ECD models (conceptualization) applied to games.

observables, each informing either novelty or efficiency. Both of these, in turn, inform the CPS variable through intermediate variables (i.e., problem solving and creativity). The degree to which variables differentially inform their parent nodes is represented in a Bayes net (discussed in the next section, and illustrated in Figure 18.5).

Action Model

The action model is similar to the task model in ECD, but we have modified it for use in existing games to define particular sequences of interactions from which to extract our observables. Interactions consist of actions and their specific indicators. An action represents anything a player does within the context of solving a particular problem (contained within a scene), such as crossing a river and exploring a cave. Each action that a player takes to solve a given problem may be characterized along two dimensions: novelty and efficiency, illustrated in more detail in the next section. A list of indicators is explicitly linked to each action. These are the things that can be directly measured and reside within the player's log file.

For players in immersive gaming environments such as *Oblivion*, we can monitor their performance across many and varied problems and quests in terms of particular constructs. To assess the latent construct of creative problem solving, we can define indicators of actions for, say, efficiency and novelty, which are ultimately combined into a general estimate of creative problem solving.

Creative Problem Solving Instantiation

To illustrate how this methodology would actually work inside of a game (*Oblivion*), we have implemented each of the ECD models (competency, evidence, and action) using a Bayesian network approach. We begin by illustrating our action model. Consider the problem of attempting to cross a raging river full of dangerous fish in *Oblivion*. Table 18.2 contains a sample list of actions one can take to solve this problem, as well as the indicators that may be learned from real student data, or elicited from experts. For the system to learn the indicators from real data, estimates of novelty may be defined in terms of the frequency of use across all players. For instance, swimming across the river is depicted as a high frequency, common solution, thus associated with a low novelty weight. An estimate of efficiency may be defined in terms of the probability of successfully solving a problem given a set of actions. To illustrate, swimming across the river is associated with a low efficiency weight because of the extra time needed to evade the piranha-like fish that live there. On the other hand, digging a tunnel under the river to get to the other side is judged as highly novel, but less efficient than, say, freezing the water and simply sliding across; the latter being highly novel and highly efficient. The indicator values shown in Table 18.2 were obtained from two *Oblivion* experts, and they range from 0 to 1. Higher numbers relate to greater levels of both novelty and efficiency.

Actions can be captured in real time as the player interacts with the game, and associated indicators can be used to provide evidence for the appropriate competencies. Again, this is accomplished via our evidence model. Figure 18.5 shows a Bayesian model (using Netica software) linking evidence indicators (i.e., *ObservedEfficiency* and *ObservedNovelty*) to various competencies. Note that Figure 18.5 represents an instantiation of our ECD conceptual framework (see Figure 18.4). That is, the upper five nodes (boxes) show a fragment of our competency model for CPS. The bottom two nodes represent a simple evidence model linking actions to competencies via their associated probability distributions. Each node has two or more discrete states (e.g., low and high). Marginal probabilities are presented for each state. The lower two evidence-model nodes represent continuous variables that have been discretized into four states, ranging from 0 to 1, that will be used to model the actions depicted in Table 18.2. The same Bayesian model can be used to illustrate a variety of actions in the game.

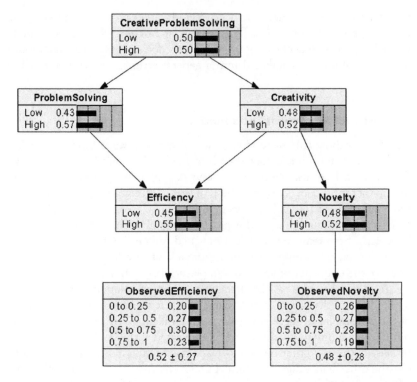

Figure 18.5 Bayesian model used to instantiate our ECD-based conceptual framework.

Prior and conditional probabilities can be elicited from experts and refined using players' data. In our case, conditional probability tables for *Observed-Efficiency* and *ObservedNovelty* have been initialized based on a normal distribution whose parameters can be eventually adjusted using real data. Means and standard deviations are shown at the bottom of each observable box.

Using the general model shown in Figure 18.5, we now illustrate various actions to show how the Bayesian model integrates evidence from particular cases. First, suppose a player chose to cross the river by digging a tunnel under it. As noted earlier, this represents an action that is classified as low in efficiency

Table 18.2 Examples of Action Model with Indicators for Novelty and Efficiency

Action	Novelty	Efficiency
Swim across river filled with dangerous fish	$n = 0.12$	$e = 0.22$
Levitate over the river	$n = 0.33$	$e = 0.70$
Freeze the water with a spell and slide across	$n = 0.76$	$e = 0.80$
Find a bridge over the river	$n = 0.66$	$e = 0.24$
Dig a tunnel under the river	$n = 0.78$	$e = 0.20$

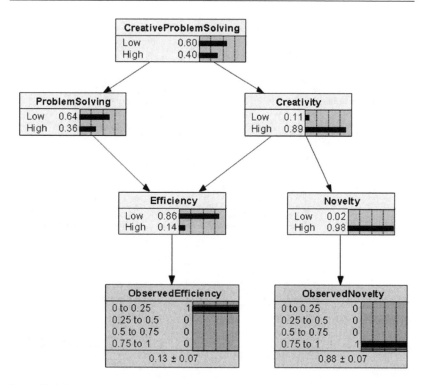

Figure 18.6 Bayes model depicting marginal probabilities after observing a low efficiency and high novelty action such as crossing the river by digging a tunnel under it.

(e = 0.20; linked to the lowest of four discrete states for *ObservedEfficiency*) and high in novelty (n = .78; linked to the highest state for *ObservedNovelty*). This evidence is added to the model shown in Figure 18.5 and propagated throughout the CM producing a new model with updated marginal probabilities for competency nodes and observed states for evidence nodes presented in Figure 18.6. Some of the marginal probability values are shown below while the full range of probability values are shown in Figure 18.6.

Pr(Efficiency = High | evidence) = 0.14
Pr(Novelty = High | evidence) = 0.98
Pr(Creativity = High | evidence) = 0.89
Pr(ProblemSolving = High | evidence) = 0.36
Pr(CPS = High | *evidence*) = 0.40

We can see that even though the player evidenced very high novelty in her solution, the parent node of CPS is still inferring that she is more low than high on this attribute—illustrating that efficiency is a more valued competency than novelty, based on the way the CM was set up.

Our second case is shown in Figure 18.7 where a player has successfully used

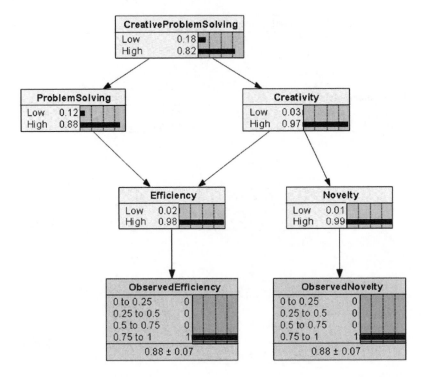

Figure 18.7 Bayes model depicting marginal probabilities after observing a high efficiency and high novelty action such as freezing the river and sliding across it.

a magical spell to freeze the river and slide across it. This action is associated with high efficiency and high novelty levels, resulting in the following marginal probability values:

Pr(Efficiency = High | evidence) = 0.98
Pr(Novelty = High | evidence) = 0.99
Pr(Creativity = High | evidence) = 0.97
Pr(ProblemSolving = High | evidence = 0.88
Pr(CPS = High | *evidence*) = 0.82

These two cases illustrate that different actions taken within *Oblivion* can be used to infer quite different levels of CPS, which could be used to inform teaching and learning—the "grow" part of the story, and described as part of our next steps.

Next Steps

Extending the example described in this chapter, we could build actual (as opposed to illustrative) ECD models for the various competencies shown in Figure 18.3, which (1) are presumed to have educational value, and (2) may be monitored via stealth assessment during game play with *Oblivion*. The justification for modeling creative problem solving as we did herein is that it is generally critical to success in many real world settings (e.g., school, business, the military). Stealth assessment within serious games offers the opportunity to inform and support a wider variety of knowledge, skills, and thinking needed for the 21st century.

Additionally, we feel there are numerous and valuable constructs that cannot be measured except in complex immersive games like *Oblivion*. For instance, many of the novel problem solving tasks that have been studied in the past (e.g., Tower of Hanoi) do not have the external validity found in immersive games. In *Oblivion*, the task of finding objects in the environment matches obstacles one would find in searching for objects in the real world (i.e., using focused attention coupled with heuristic search strategies). Data collected by measuring progress in these types of problems yields a richer source of information that can be used in formative feedback to ultimately improve learning. While we have not yet mapped the learning that can occur in our stealth assessment approach, the concept of dynamic feedback in game play lays the initial groundwork for such a framework. More work is needed to decide how dynamically changing the game play itself can best accommodate the proficiency levels of players. Currently, *Oblivion* enemies do become more difficult to defeat as the player gains rank (i.e., an approach to keep the game from actually getting easier), but no one has yet investigated how these changes in game difficulty can actually lead to increased learning of valued constructs. By developing a framework of dynamic stealth assessment, we hope to investigate its obvious extensions to learning.

Finally, we would like to apply the ideas presented in this chapter to another game to show proof-of-concept and generalizability of the approach. If that exercise was successful, the next step would be to use players' data (log files) to inform decisions concerning the adaptation of game play—such as increasing or decreasing challenges, introducing new characters, and so on. Ideally, and in subsequent projects, we would employ ECD to design games from scratch, in conjunction with game designers. This is because the fit between many current immersive games and education is not very good—particularly given "objectionable content" in many games, such as violence and sex. If we can clearly identify the essential elements in games that induce flow, learn how to efficiently and effectively cull learning indicators from series of actions, and use the information to support learning, we will be in a position to design valid (and more suitable) immersive games. Squire, Giovanetto, Devane, and Durga (2005) have begun the process of identifying such design features and analyzing emergent learning.

Summary and Discussion

The U.S. spends hundreds of billions of dollars per year on K-12 education, but students (particularly disadvantaged ones) are not adequately learning (Shute,

2007). For instance, performance on mathematics problem solving, reported by the Program for International Student Assessment (PISA Report, 2004) shows that students in 25 out of the 30 most developed countries in the world outperformed U.S. students. We really need to bolster our students' problem-solving skills to compete effectively at international and national levels. Along the same lines, Kirsch, Braun, Yamamoto, and Sum (2007) describe the "perfect storm" in this country in relation to enormous educational challenges. They contend that student engagement is a factor that can help close the achievement gap, noting that our top students do compare favorably (or at least comparably) to their non-U.S. counterparts.

To address these educational challenges and harness the potential of immersive games, we presented an ECD-inspired idea which involved the following steps: (1) specify educationally valuable competencies believed to contribute toward successful game play; (2) define evidence models that link game behaviors to the competencies; and (3) update the student model at regular intervals. Ultimately, we would like to be able to adapt content in the game to fit the current needs of the player based on student model information. The approach described in this chapter involved retrofitting ECD models to an existing game which has certain implications, such as the need to gather valid assessment information without getting in the way of the engaging features of the game (i.e., the flow). Bayesian models were used in our illustration to monitor actions, integrate evidence on players' performance, and update the student model in relation to emerging competencies. Bayes' models can also be used to support learning by generating progress reports for various educational stakeholders (e.g., teachers, students, parents). For example, reports could be used by teachers to recommend specific activities, or by students to work on a particular skill that needs improvement.

Information about students' competencies may also be used by the system to select new gaming experiences. For instance, more challenging quests could be made available for students that exhibit high CPS abilities. Up-to-date estimates of students' competencies, based on assessment information handled by the Bayes nets, can also be integrated into the game and explicitly displayed as progress indicators. Players could then see how their competencies are changing based on their performance in the game. *Oblivion* already includes status bars, representing the player's current levels of health, magic, and fatigue. These bars reside in the lower-left corner of the screen, and by clicking a bar, the player can view more detailed information on a particular variable (e.g., spells and potions currently possessed). Imagine adding high-level competency bars that represent attributes like CPS. As with the current set of bars, more detailed information could be accessed by clicking the bar to see current states of lower-level variables, such as efficiency, novelty, and problem solving. And like health status, if any competency bar gets too low, the student needs to act to somehow increase the value. Once students begin interacting with the bars, metacognitive processes may be enhanced by allowing the player to see game-

or learning-related aspects of their state. Viewing their current competency levels and the underlying evidence gives students greater awareness of personal attributes. In the literature, these are called "open student models," and they have been shown to support knowledge awareness, reflection, and learning (Bull & Pain, 1995; Kay 1998; Hartley & Mitrovic, 2002; Zapata-Rivera & Greer, 2004; Zapata-Rivera, Vanwinkle, Shute, Underwood, & Bauer (2007).

In conclusion, learning takes place naturally within the storyline of a well-designed game. The key, then, is seamlessly aligning story and lesson, a nontrivial endeavor (see Rieber, 1996). We presented a two-stage approach to address the problem: (1) analyze existing games to determine the kinds of activities that support learning, and then (2) use the knowledge to inform the development of design principles and practices for creating new games for 21st century skills. These new games would be as fully engaging as their predecessors, but would additionally be founded on research from cognitive science, educational measurement, and artificial intelligence. Furthermore, these new games would contain valid and reliable stealth assessments capable of accurately monitoring students' cognitive and noncognitive abilities over time and adjusting the game environment to support learning—in other words, seamlessly aligning the story and lesson. This chapter presented the first methodological step towards harnessing student engagement induced by flow to promote learning of valuable and life-long skills.

Author Note

We would like to gratefully acknowledge the following people for their ideas and editorial suggestions in relation to this paper: Gary Bente, Eric Hansen, Irv Katz, Jody Underwood, and Dan Eignor.

Notes

1. Note that other significant obstacles exist with regard to employing serious games in education. These were summarized and elaborated in the *Summit on Educational Games, 2006* (http://www.fas.org/gamesummit), hosted by the American Federation of Scientists. Those issues, however, are beyond the scope of this chapter.
2. Because all observables come from the same scenario (i.e., "task") there are a number of ways the context and activities can create dependencies among the observables. They are not known to be independent and they share a context, so we assume there is some degree of conditional dependence.

References

Almond, R. G., & Mislevy, R. J. (1999). Graphical models and computerized adaptive testing. *Applied Psychological Measurement, 23*(3), 223–237.

America's army 3. [Digital game]. (2009). U.S. Army. Retrieved March 9, 2009, from http://www.americasarmy.com/

Bangert-Drowns, R. L., Kulik, C. C., Kulik, J. A., & Morgan, M. T. (1991). The instructional effect of feedback in test-like events. *Review of Educational Research, 61*(2), 213–238.

Bauer, M., Williamson, D., Mislevy, R. & Behrens, J. (2003). Using evidence-centered design to develop advanced simulation-based assessment and training. In G. Richards (Ed.), *Proceedings of World Conference on E-Learning in Corporate, Government, Healthcare, and Higher Education* (pp. 1495–1502). Chesapeake, VA: Association for the Advancement of Computing in Education.

Black, P., & Wiliam, D. (1998a). Assessment and classroom learning. *Assessment in Education: Principles, Policy & Practice, 5*(1), 7–71.

Black, P., & Wiliam, D. (1998b). Inside the black box: Raising standards through classroom assessment. *Phi Delta Kappan, 80*(2), 139–148.

Blunt, R. D. (2006). *A causal-comparative exploration of the relationship between game-based learning and academic achievement: Teaching management with video games.* Doctoral dissertation. Walden University, Minneapolis, MN.

Bull, S., & Pain, H. (1995). "Did I say what I think I said, and do you agree with me?" Inspecting and questioning the student model. *Proceedings of the Artificial Intelligence in Education* (pp. 501–508). Charlottesville, VA: Association for the Advancement of Computing in Education.

Cannon-Bowers, J. (2006, March). *The state of gaming and simulation.* Paper presented at the Training 2006 Conference and Expo, Orlando, FL.

Carey, R. (2006). *Serious game engine shootout: A comparative analysis of technology for serious game development.* Retrieved March 23, 2007, from http://seriousgames-source.com/features/feature_022107_shootout_1.php

Civilization IV. [Digital game]. (2008). Hunt Valley, MD: Firaxis Games.

Clauser, B. E., Subhiyah, R., Nungester, R. J., Ripkey, D., Clyman, S. G., & McKinley, D. (1995). Scoring a performance-based assessment by modeling the judgments of experts. *Journal of Educational Measurement, 32,* 397–415.

Clarke, S. (2001). *Unlocking formative assessment.* London: Hodder & Stoughton.

Csikszentmihalyi, M. (1990). *Flow: The psychology of optical experience.* New York: Harper Perennial.

Dance dance revolution. [Digital game]. (1999). Tokyo, Japan: Konami.

de Freitas, S., & Oliver, M. (2006). How can exploratory learning with games and simulations within the curriculum be most effectively evaluated? *Computers and Education, 46,* 249–264.

Diner Dash [Digital game]. (2008). New York: Gamelab.

Duckworth, A. L.., & Seligman, M. E. P. (2005). Self-discipline outdoes IQ in predicting academic performance of adolescents. *Psychological Science, 16*(12), 939–944.

Dweck, C. S. (1996). Implicit theories as organizers of goals and behavior. In P. M. Gollwitzer & J. A. Bargh (Eds.), *The psychology of action: Linking cognition and motivation to behavior* (pp. 69–90). New York: Guilford Press.

Education Arcade, The. [Digital game]. (2008). *Revolution.* Retrieved March 9, 2009, from http://www.educationarcade.org/node/357

Elder Scrolls IV: Oblivion. [Digital game]. (2006). Rockville, MD: Bethesda Softworks/ ZeniMax Media.

Falmagne, J. C., Cosyn, E., Doignon, J. P., & Thiery, N. (2003). The assessment of knowledge, in theory and in practice. In R. Missaoui & J. Schmid (Eds.), *ICFCA, Vol. 3874 of lecture notes in computer science* (pp. 61–79). New York: Springer.

Finn, J. D., & Rock, D. A. (1997). Academic success among students at risk for school failure. *Journal of Applied Psychology, 82*(2), 221–234.

Fredricks, J. A., Blumenfeld, P. C., & Paris, A. H. (2004). School engagement: Potential of the concept, state of the evidence. *Review of Educational Research, 74*(1), 59–109.

Fredricks, J. A., & Eccles, J. S. (2006). Is extra participation associated with beneficial outcomes? Concurrent and longitudinal relations. *Developmental Psychology, 42*(2), 698–713.

Gee, J. (2003). High score education. *Wired Magazine, 11*(5). Retrieved on August 5, 2008, from http://www.wired.com/wired/archive/11.05/view.html

Grand Theft Auto IV. [Digital game]. (2008). Rockstar Games.

Hartley, D., & Mitrovic, A. (2002) Supporting learning by opening the student model. *Proceedings of ITS 2002* (pp. 453–462).

Hiebert, J., Carpenter, T. P., Fennema, E., Fuson, K., Human, P., Murray, H., et al. (1996). Problem solving as a basis for reform in curriculum and instruction: The case of mathematics. *Educational Researcher, 25*(4), 12–21.

Hoska, D. M. (1993). Motivating learners through CBI feedback: Developing a positive learner perspective. In J. V. Dempsey & G. C. Sales (Eds.), *Interactive instruction and feedback* (pp. 105–132). Englewood Cliffs, NJ: Educational Technology.

Jonassen, D. H. (2000). Toward a design theory of problem solving. *Educational Technology, Research and Development, 48*(4), 63–85.

Kay, J. (1998). *A scrutable user modelling shell for user-adapted interaction.* Unpublished doctoral dissertation. University of Sydney, Sydney, Australia.

Kirsch, I., Braun, H., Yamamoto, K., & Sum, A. (2007). *America's perfect storm: Three forces changing our nation's future* (ETS Policy Information Report). Princeton, NJ: Educational Testing Service.

Koller, D., & Pfeffer, A. (1997). Object-oriented Bayesian networks. In D. Geiger & P. P. Shenoy (Eds.), *Proceedings of the Thirteenth Annual Conference on Uncertainty in Artificial Intelligence* (UAI-97) (pp. 302–313). Providence, RI: Morgan Kaufmann.

Kruschke, J. K. (2001). Toward a unified model of attention in associative learning. *Journal of Mathematical Psychology, 45*, 812–863.

Kulik, J. A. (2002). School mathematics and science program benefit from instructional technology. (InfoBrief, NSF-03-301). Washington, DC: National Science Foundation. Retrieved March 9, 2009, from http://dwbrr.unl.edu/iTech/TEAC859/Read/KulikTech.pdf

Lepper, M. R., & Malone, T. W. (1987). Intrinsic motivation and instructional effectiveness in computer-based education. In R. E. Snow & M. J. Farr (Eds.), *Aptitude, learning, and instruction: Vol. 3. Conative and affective process analyses* (pp. 255–286). Hillsdale, NJ: Erlbaum.

Lieberman, D. A. (2006). What can we learn from playing interactive games? In P. Vorderer & J. Bryant (Eds.), *Playing video games: Motives, responses, and consequences.* Mahwah, NJ: Erlbaum.

Malone, T. W. (1981). Towards a theory of intrinsically motivating instruction. *Cognitive Science, 4*, 333–369.

Meier, S. (2004). *Civilization III.* [Digital game]. Retrieved March 9, 2009, from http://www.civ3.com/civ3.cfm

Messick, S. (1994). The interplay of evidence and consequences in the validation of performance assessments. *Education Researcher, 32*(2), 13–23.

Mislevy, R. J., (1994). Evidence and inference in educational assessment. *Psychometrika, 59*, 439–483

Mislevy, R. J., Steinberg, L. S., & Almond, R. G. (2003). On the structure of educational assessment. *Measurement: Interdisciplinary Research and Perspective, 1*(1), 3–62.

Mislevy, R. J., Steinberg, L., S., Breyer, F. J., Almond, R. G., & Johnson, L. (2002). Making sense of data from complex assessments. *Applied Measurement in Education, 15*(4), 363–389.

Newell, A., & Simon, H. A. (1972). *Human problem solving.* Englewood Cliffs, NJ: Prentice-Hall.

Nosofsky, R. M. (1986). Attention, similarity and the identification-categorization relationship. *Journal of Experimental Psychology: General, 115*, 39–57.

Pausch, R., Gold, R., Scaly, T., & Thiel, D. (1994, April). What HCI designers can learn from video game designers. In *Conference companion on human factors in computing systems* (pp. 177–178),. Boston: ACM Press.

Pearl, J. (1988). *Probabilistic reasoning in intelligent systems: Networks of plausible inference.* San Mateo, CA: Kaufmann.

PISA Report. (2004). *International outcomes of learning in mathematics literacy and problem solving: PISA 2003 results from the U.S. Perspective.* Retrieved May 4, 2007, from http://nces.ed.gov/pubsearch/pubsinfo.asp?pubid=2005003

Ranney, M. (1988). Changing naive conceptions of motion. *Dissertation Abstracts International, 49*, 1975B.

Rieber, L. (1996). Seriously considering play: Designing interactive learning environments based on the blending of microworlds, simulations, and games. *Education and Technology Research & Development, 44*, 42–58.

Reiser, B. J. (2004). Scaffolding complex learning: The mechanisms of structuring and problematizing student work. *Journal of the Learning Sciences, 13*(3), 273–304.

Shute, V. J. (2007). Tensions, trends, tools, and technologies: Time for an educational sea change. In C. A. Dwyer (Ed.), *The future of assessment: Shaping teaching and learning* (pp. 139–187). New York: Erlbaum/Taylor & Francis Group.

Shute, V. J. (2008). Focus on formative feedback. *Review of Educational Research, 78*(1), 153–189.

Shute, V. J., Hansen, E. G., & Almond, R. G. (2008). You can't fatten a hog by weighing it—Or can you? Evaluating an assessment for learning system called ACED. *International Journal of Artificial Intelligence and Education, 18*(4), 289–316.

Simon, H. A. (1995). The information-processing theory of mind. *American Psychologist, 50*, 507–508.

Squire, K. D. (2006). From content to context: Videogames as designed experience. *Educational Researcher, 35*(8), 19–29.

Squire, K. D., Giovanetto, L., Devane, B., & Durga, S. (2005). From users to designers: Building a self-organizing game-based learning environment. *TechTrends: Linking Research & Practice to Improve Learning, 49*(5), 34–43.

Squire, K. D., & Jenkins, H. (2003). Harnessing the power of games in education. *Insight, 3*(5), 7–33.

Steinberg, L. S., & Gitomer, D. G. (1996). Intelligent tutoring and assessment built on an understanding of a technical problem-solving task. *Instructional Science, 24*, 223–258.

Sternberg, R. J. (1999). A propulsion model of types of creative contributions. *Review of General Psychology, 3*, 83–100.

Sternberg, R. J. (2006). Creating a vision of creativity: The first 25 years. *Psychology of Aesthetics, Creativity, and the Arts, S*(1), 2–12.

Stiggins, R. J. (2002). Assessment crisis: The absence of assessment FOR learning. *Phi Delta Kappan Professional Journal, 83*(10), 758–765.

Trabasso, T., & Bower, G. H. (1968). *Attention in learning.* New York: Wiley.

Vygotsky, L. S. (1987). *The collected works of L. S. Vygotsky.* New York: Plenum.

Weisberg, R. W. (1986). *Creativity: Genius and other myths.* New York: Freeman.

Zapata-Rivera, D., & Greer, J. E. (2004). Interacting with inspectable Bayesian models. *International Journal of Artificial Intelligence in Education, 14*, 127–163.

Zapata-Rivera, D., Vanwinkle, W., Shute, V. J., Underwood, J. S., & Bauer, M. (2007). English ABLE. In R. Luckin, K. Koedinger, & J. Greer (Eds.), *Artificial intelligence in education—Building technology rich learning contexts that work* (pp. 323–330). Amsterdam, The Netherlands: IOS Press.

Chapter 19

Making the Implicit Explicit
Embedded Measurement in Serious Games

Gary Bente and Johannes Breuer

Serious games are a relatively new approach to mediated learning. They have broadened the thematic and methodological scope of former concepts of entertainment education and are already used in various educational contexts, such as healthcare, political education, and others. As compared to more traditional modes of mediated teaching and learning, serious games have changed the situation of the learner in many respects, challenging her active participation, stimulating direct experience via learning by doing, fostering immersion and involvement, and, based on this, increasing fun, motivation, and effort. In this experiential process, the role of teachers is certainly undergoing a fundamental change. The traditional role of the instructor is giving place to the roles of game developers, in-game coaches or advisors and expert coplayers. These teaching teams are tasked with providing situations for learning which are complex enough to be challenging but not threatening, using tools to track the learners' performance, identify obstacles, and adapt game difficulty. After all, learning with serious games remains a goal-directed process aimed at clearly defined and measurable achievements. As such, serious games have to implement assessments to inform teachers and learners about the progress and outcome of the learning process. As game developers Sande Chen and David Michael (2005) state: "Serious games, like every other tool of education, must be able to show that the necessary learning has occurred. Specifically games that teach also need to be games that test" (p. 2). The issue of assessment in serious games is prominently addressed by Shute, Ventura, Bauer, and Zapata-Rivera (this volume, chapter 18). The authors develop the concept of "stealth assessment," which describes a way of seamlessly embedding a dynamic and formative type of assessment in a game-based learning setting, thus gathering relevant information without interfering with performance, involvement, or game enjoyment. To further explore the possibilities of (stealth) assessment in serious games, this chapter takes a closer look at the definition and characteristics of serious games and the scope of methodologies to monitor and evaluate the learning process and its results, including aspects of data collection, interpretation, and feedback.

Starting from the concept of stealth assessment (cf. Shute et al., this volume, chapter 18) we will broaden the view of embedded in-game assessment with respect to exploiting sources of information relevant to the learning process beyond those which are directly task-related or conceptually linked to the targeted cognitive skills. The focus here will be on variables which tell us more about the players' momentary psychological situation, including arousal, attention, and work load, as well as about their mutual affiliations, transactions and social relations. The latter factors are of crucial importance in multiuser games in which learning may come about primarily through collaboration with others or through socioemotional pathways. Guidelines for such an approach have been set up in the European Union-funded project Psychologically Augmented Social Interaction over Networks (PASION). Its central idea of "making the implicit explicit" stresses the fact that the use of media for communication, collaboration, and learning purposes provides unique opportunities to augment social interactions with unprecedented possibilities of assessment, measurement, and feedback. Not only do digital media allow for the logging of user and system actions, they also provide interfaces for including additional sensing and measurement devices, such as eye-tracking or psychophysiological arousal monitoring. Whether they will be subsumable under the heading of stealth measurement depends on the level of integration they reach with respect to the rules of the game and the control interfaces and user data it relies on.

Although we are going to widen the scope of stealth measurement in this direction, we want to underpin the importance of theory-driven modeling approaches as provided by Shute et al. (this volume, chapter 18). In fact, more data does not necessarily mean more information. In particular, when the information obtained should have diagnostic value, it has to be analyzed and interpreted along theoretically founded and empirically established concepts relevant to the learning process. Although aiming at the provision of highly motivating learning tools for the future, scientific efforts, some of which are presented in this volume, have a basic research value as well. Beyond promising pedagogical applications, serious games can definitely be a most valuable research tool as well (Donchin, 1995). They can help to understand individual learning styles and problem-solving strategies under ecologically valid but nevertheless highly controlled conditions, while offering unprecedented possibilities for monitoring learner activities.

The Nature of Serious Games

What is a serious game, and what is it that makes some games serious, or at least more serious than others? Michael and Chen (2006) offer a working definition of serious games: "A serious game is a game in which education (in its various forms) is the primary goal, rather than entertainment" (p. 17). In entertainment games, success in the game is the intrinsic goal for the players, whereas serious games add the normative layer of learning goals. The occurrence of learning, however, is not a sufficient criterion to define a serious game. All kinds of games involve some type of cognitive or motor learning (e.g. learning the rules and controls, or acquiring game-relevant knowledge or skills; Gee, 2007; Liebermann, 2006). Many different forms of learning take place also within most entertainment games. This learned knowledge can be explicit but socially undesirable, such as the acquisition of deviant attitudes (Brady & Matthews, 2006) or the learning of maladaptive social behavior (Anderson & Bushman, 2001), or it can be implicit and well acceptable or even beneficial, such as the incidental learning of relevant content (Squire & Jenkins, 2003), the training of perceptual and motor skills (Green & Bavelier, 2000; Greenfield, Brannon, & Lohr, 1994; Griffith, Voloschin, Gibb, & Bailey, 1983; Subrahmanyam & Greenfield, 1994), the development of general problem-solving capabilities and cognitive meta-skills (Doolittle, 1995; Oyen & Bebko, 1996), or generalized learning attitudes (Liebermann, 1997). Moreover, serious games are not serious because players take them seriously (they also take ego-shooters very seriously); serious games are serious because they pursue explicit, a priori defined, measurable learning goals. While entertainment games can include chances for incidental learning of knowledge or skills, which might be transferable to life outside the game world, serious games endorse intentional learning according to predefined learning goals, which can be implicit as well as explicit.

Classifying (Serious) Games

Serious games are the successors and a further development of the concept of edutainment or entertainment education, which became major buzzwords in the 1990s. According to Michael and Chen (2006), however, serious games are "more than entertainment" (p. xv). Indeed, recent games have expanded the possible content as well as the range of teaching and learning methods that can be implemented. Classical educational games are only one segment of serious games. An exemplary list of types of serious games includes military games, government games, educational games, corporate games, healthcare games, political games, religious games, and art games (Michael & Chen, 2006). Shute et al. (this volume, chapter 18) broaden this definition and add entertainment games, which have the potential to be used for educational purposes. This addition is sensible, since in this case concepts and effect measures are applied ex post, trying to match the reality of the game. Hence, the research strategy here is more descriptive and correlational. Serious games, however, start from explicit goals and learning concepts. The serious game can be considered a treatment applied to achieve these goals. Here, concepts and measures have to be predefined, even before development and experimentally tested for their effects. The research strategy clearly follows prescriptive mechanisms and aims at causal relations and experimental designs (Campbell & Stanley, 1966).

Furthermore, serious games can be classified along the line of their modes of learning. While some serious games are constructed for training purposes, others are made to convey knowledge about a certain subject or just to create awareness for topics, brands, organizations etc.[1] Therefore, the possible learning goals or outcomes are quite diverse. Apart from these distinctions, which are specific for serious games, it is also meaningful to align such a classification with general distinctions of games as far as they are able to differentiate basic modes of operation and player experience which are potentially relevant to the learning process. A very popular and useful typology of games was formulated by the French sociologist Roger Caillois (2001). He basically describes four categories of games:

1. *Agôn* (Competition): This category includes sport games and other forms of games that stress the aspect of contest.
2. *Alea* (Chance): Examples of this group are all gambling activities.
3. *Mimicry* (Simulation): This refers to theater, disguises.
4. *Ilinx* (Vertigo): A rather open category which subsumes activities like dancing, climbing, or skiing.

All games in these categories can again be charted along the line of the two poles "Paidia" and "Ludus," reflecting the common distinction between play and game. While the first is mostly open-ended and doesn't have too many rules, the latter has a prescribed definition of win and loss and obeys a strict set of explicit rules and regulations.

Two further psychologically relevant dimensions which could be named luck vs. skill and competition vs. cooperation can be extracted from Caillois' typology, leading to a three-dimensional coordinate system, in which games in general and serious games in particular can be located (see Figure 19.1). In our view, this system provides an alternative to the problematic division of genres,

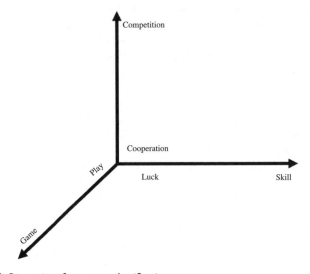

Figure 19.1 Dimensions for a game classification system.

which is mainly based on game content and technical features. The advantage of the dimensional approach is that it enables the researcher to classify games with respect to the mindsets and action resources of the players (which are activated by the logic of the game), and to target assessments to the particular psychological variables which characterize the very specific cognitive, social, emotional, and behavioral challenges of an application. We consider such differentiations to be crucial for future research, as they would allow us to separate effects of the game as such from those of the learning process.

Dimensions of the Player Experience

Immersion (Biocca, 1992) and flow (Csikszentmihalyi, 1990) are phenomena which affect the experience of fun while playing (digital) games (Rheinberg & Vollmeyer, 2003; Sweetser & Wyeth, 2005). Although fun and flow are conceptually hardly separable, it might be important to acknowledge the existence of potentially distinct motivational aspects relying on different game dimensions. A study by Petersen and Bente (2001) suggests that task characteristics are more important for the experience of engagement and fun in games than the degree of realism in graphics and sound. A series of studies conducted by Klimmt (2006) also revealed that the influence of realism is less pronounced than that of the relation of possibilities and necessities to act (which concern the task level). Flow thus might be more determined by task factors than by the realism of a game.

Beyond the conceptual problems inherent in the definition of flow, there are also measurement issues to be considered. Flow is a process variable which can only be measured indirectly by means of unobtrusive instrumentation as the measurement procedure itself otherwise might interrupt the flow state. Applying sensors or prompting subjective judgments can be expected to interfere with flow and thus neutralize the positive motivational effect of playful learning. In this sense, the challenge for integration is not simply to hide the measurement, but to give it a meaningful and acceptable place in the game. Therefore, alternative but related concepts which have been established empirically and which allow for continuous assessments without creating such interferences should be examined here. A promising approach is based on the opposition of challenge vs. threat (Blascovich & Mendes, 2000). The definition of challenge and threat is based on the relation of situational or task demands and personal resources; in contrast to flow, however, the concept of challenge and threat is clearly measurable via psychophysiological correlates (Blascovich, Seery, Mugridge, Norris, & Weisbuch, 2004; Wright & Kirby, 2003).

Ahdell and Andresen (2001) identify a series of motivational factors relevant to learning in general and to game-based learning in particular, which go beyond the experience of flow: willingness to learn, expectations, content, learning design, engagement, mentoring, and collaboration. The first two can be classified as pregame motivational factors, the next three as in-game factors, and the final two as social factors. In every game, however, a feeling of self-efficacy (Bandura, 1977) or effectance motivation (White, 1959)[2] is a prerequisite for engagement and motivation, as it promotes enjoyment and motivates the player/learner to keep on playing/learning (Klimmt & Hartmann, 2006). The repeated experience of self-efficacy or effectance increases the likelihood of a future use of the corresponding media (Klimmt, 2006). The implementation of challenging, tasks that are yet not overdemanding or threatening, is also important to avoid a low amount of invested mental effort (Salomon, 1984), because the amount of invested mental effort depends on the interaction of perceived self-efficacy and media characteristics. Therefore, creating motivating and challenging serious games can counteract the popular notion of digital games as a "light" or "easy" medium.

Also closely related to flow is the concept of presence, which Lombard and Ditton (1997) define as the "perceptual illusion of non-mediation" (p. 31). Accordingly, presence can only be experienced, if the attention of a player is fully (or at least to a major proportion) allocated to the content presented by the medium. The medium as a perceptual object ideally has to become "transparent" (i.e., it should not require the intentional allocation of attention and cognitive resources). As for flow, in-game measurement of presence thus poses problems as it would most likely ask for special attention and thus interrupt presence, which in turn might invalidate the measure itself. Again stealth measures, which are seamlessly integrated into the game, could be a desirable solution. Operationalizations which allow the use of game-inherent behaviors as indicators for presence, however, are lacking. Alternatively, measurement concepts could make use of the psychological responses to the interruptions of the game, measuring for example arousal states or the urge to resume playing. An interesting behavioral approach following this logic has been described in the concept of "Breaks in Presence" (Slater & Steed, 2000), which should be tested for its applicability in serious game research.

Monitoring the Learning Process

"Assessment is the future of serious games.... [Serious games] will not grow as an industry unless the learning experience is definable, quantifiable and measurable" (Kevin Corti, PIXELearning, cited by Chen & Michael, 2005, p. 7).

Jonathan Ferguson, a developer of serious games for educational purposes, poses two core questions for the design of serious games: How do you show that students are learning what they should learn? How do you know that what you are measuring is what you think you are measuring? While the first question can be answered by implementing appropriate assessments of learning goals and their fulfillment, the second question concerns the validity and depends on issues of measurement techniques in general (cf. Shapiro & Peña-Herborn, this volume, chapter 22; Ravaja & Kivikangas, this volume, chapter 23). The following sections will address these questions in order to identify which dependent and moderating variables should be assessed/measured in learning with serious games and how.

To ensure that learning occurs in a serious game, some sort of assessment has to be implemented within cycles of teaching and testing. The assessment of learning progress or achievement concerns the dependent variables of learning with serious games. While the classic form of learning assessment (which is predominant in many older edutainment applications) is the well-known principle of question and answer (Q&A), today's serious games offer the opportunity to employ alternative, less obvious, and less obtrusive forms of assessment. The general problem of classical tests, such as multiple choice questionnaires, is that they function as an add-on, which interrupts the learning process and which mainly tests memorization rather than understanding or the creative usage of acquired knowledge. Digital games usually include their own types of integrated assessment like tutorial tasks or high score lists, which provide feedback regarding the players' achievement, but are nonetheless part of the game (Chen & Michael, 2005). According to Shute et al. (this volume, chapter 18), these principles of in-game assessment ideally should be used to monitor learning processes and achievements in serious games. Not only can the assessment procedures stay unrecognized, but they can also become a game element themselves. The skills or knowledge which the serious game targets can become an in-game objective themselves or be relevant for these.

Different tasks, however, require different types of assessment. McGrath (1984), for instance, categorizes four basic kinds of tasks: creative tasks, problem solving and decision making, conflict resolution, and the execution of activities. While it is relatively simple to develop a grading system for judging the quality (or quantity) of executed actions and solutions for problem solving tasks, which can be defined before the task is implemented, it can be difficult to evaluate (and assess) the results of creative tasks or decision making.

The assessment of task performance can be either summative (i.e., it is given at the end of a learning process and evaluates the overall achievements of a learner), or formative (i.e., it is repeatedly implemented throughout the learning process to constantly survey the progress and failures, Boston, 2002). In serious games it is particularly useful to make use of formative assessments (see Shute et al., this volume, chapter 18). The idea of formative assessment implies that assessment can constitute a learning experience of its own, whereas a summative assessment grades the results of a completed learning process. According to Shute et al., formative assessments can be integrated into the structure of serious games since they allow not only the acquisition of outcome but also of process data, which can be decisive for the understanding and improvement of learning settings in serious games. If the assessments are "seamlessly woven into the fabric of the learning environment" (Shute et al., chapter 18), they should become virtually imperceptible. This, then, is the essence of stealth assessment.

Since serious games are a relatively new medium for learning, there still are several issues concerning assessment, which are addressed by Chen and Michael (2005). First, the emphasis in serious games is (or should be) less on rote memorization; hence assessment methods are needed that properly reflect the kind of learning prevalent in serious games. Second, (serious) games can be open-ended, thus raising the question how achievements may be best assessed in such games. Other questions also concern the measurement of rather abstract skills like teamwork or leadership or the issue of cheating, which can cause the circumvention of anticipated game responses (Consalvo, 2007). According to Chen and Michael (2005), serious games mainly use three principles of assessment: (1) completion assessment, which controls whether a player could finish a lesson or pass a test—this mostly corresponds to summative assessment; (2) in-process assessment, which evaluates how, when, and why players made their choices and accords to the idea of formative assessment; and (3) teacher assessment, which relies on observations and judgments made by the instructors. Teacher assessment, again, can be summative—if it only considers the final results—or formative—if it constantly judges single sequences in the game.

In order to design a viable way of creating and implementing stealth assessments and to make sense of the gathered data, Shute et al. (this volume, chapter 18) suggest the use of a so-called evidence-centered design (Mislevy, Steinberg, & Almond, 2003). Since in games the actions of players/learners often depend on each other, it makes sense to take this into consideration for assigning assessments. This means that the process of the learner's/player's interaction with and in the game has to be assessed, rather than just the outcomes of this interaction. To model the characteristics of (inter-)dependent actions that change dynamically, evidence-centered design is ordered into three model types: (1) the competence model, which represents the constellation of relevant knowledge, skills, and abilities; (2) the evidence model, which describes what specific behaviors or "observables" are indicative of different levels of skills in the competence model; and (3) the task model, which provides a framework for characterizing and constructing situations with which a student will interact.

Applied to serious games, the competence model defines what kinds of knowledge are needed to meet the challenges of the game; the evidence model can help to identify observable player actions or statements which give information about the required competencies; and the task model can describe which situations in the game can provide evidence for the application of the identified relevant abilities. The model of evidence-centered design is useful for the general conception of valid assessment and feedback in serious games. As assessment, however, is not a purpose on its own, the diagnostic function (primarily included in the evidence model) has to be linked to adaptive measures. Thus, we would suggest introducing an intervention or adaptation model as a further level which indicates measures to be taken to adapt task level and/or launch help functions (see Figure 19.2). While Shute et al. (this volume, chapter 18) stress the importance of dynamic models, it is possible to enhance their

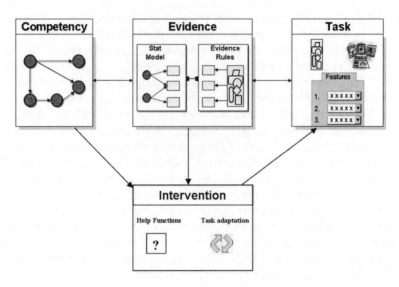

Figure 19.2 Evidence-centered design model by Shute, Ventura, Bauer, and Zapata-Rivera with additional layer.

concept with further measurements which can update and adjust the models mentioned above according to an intervention or adaptation model.

Measuring Intervening and Moderating Variables

Formative stealth assessment as proposed by Shute et al. (this volume, chapter 18) can be seen as a stepwise, or even continuous monitoring, of specific task-related player skills or competencies, which can be indexed by levels of goal achievement or by the use of particular problem solving strategies. Apart from these directly outcome-related variables, it might also be useful to monitor moderating and intervening variables known to influence human learning, such as activation, attention, vigilance, mood, etc. For many of these variables, psychology has provided measurement tools issuing objective indicators while leaving the learning process unaffected. Psychophysiology is one viable way to objectively measure such phenomena which can provide insights into aspects of emotional arousal and modes of information processing during media usage as well (e.g., Clariana, 1992; Fairclough, Venables, & Tattersall, 2005). Also aspects of visual behavior, such as eye movement, pupil dilation, or blink rates can be objectively measured to capture cognitive processes accompanying the learning process, such as mental workload, attention, and information processing (Partala & Surakka, 2003; Veltman & Gaillard, 1996).

The manifold possibilities of in-game measurement of emotional and cognitive processes cannot be explored here in detail. What we would like to underpin, however, is the fact that serious games imply the use of media, mostly computers, and that this fact allows us to use media capacities, and those of peripheral sensors and devices to record, store, and analyze psychological phenomena which are out of scope in nonmediated learning environments. Electronic media as an integral part of serious games thus not only can enhance motivation and facilitate the learning process, but also augment the learners' and teachers' experience by providing relevant psychological information which under normal conditions remains implicit, because it is hidden (e.g., arousal states, evaluations, moods, thoughts, attitudes), out of perceptual range (e.g., remote location, contextual information, personal history), hard to aggregate (e.g., interaction patterns, group structures), or ambiguous (e.g., nonverbal behavior, facial displays, silence).

There are multiple sources of implicit information which might be accessible during serious gaming by means of appropriate measurement tools. Table 19.1 depicts different levels of implicit information, also hinting at the different methodologies that might be applied. On the individual level, objective measures of cognitive and emotional processes, such as eye-tracking and psychophysiology, could be useful, as well as prompted ratings of mood, workload, and stress level. Data on the interindividual level could be extracted from records of the various messages (audio, video, text, pictures, and emoticons) by means of content analysis. Group structural information could be derived from log-file data and modeled via social network analysis (SNA; e.g., Huisman & van Duin, 2004; Wasserman & Faust, 1994) Contextual data could also be based on log-files (e.g., with respect to the current task type or difficulty level), but could also rely on GPS data or prompted information about workspace facilities. Altogether, access to these different levels of implicit information could help to increase group awareness (Dourish & Bellotti, 1992) and social presence (e.g., Biocca, Burgoon, Harms, & Stoner, 2001; Short, Williams, & Christie, 1976) when used for adaptive measures or feedback (see Table 19.1). For the implementation of any kind of sensible and helpful feedback we suggest a three-step approach of testing and validating. First, potentially relevant indices (e.g., galvanic skin response) and measurement methods for these have to be studied in terms of standard research criteria like reliability and validity. They especially have to be tested in specific settings to identify the relations between indices and typical situations in a task. In a second step the feasibility

Table 19.1 Levels of Potentially Relevant Implicit Information in Multi-User Serious Games

Intrapersonal level	Interpersonal level	Group level	Contextual level
Emotions	Messages	Structure	Social Context
Attention	Verbal	Relations	Situation
Attitudes	Paraverbal	Coherence	Location
Intentions	Nonverbal	Hierarchies	Tasks

of the measured indices as cues has to be tested. This means that the measured variables have to be processed for (real-time) feedback and the relevance and meaning of the feedback has to be clear for the players. Finally, modes of displaying the feedback information have to be designed which present the cues in a comprehensible and appealing way. For all these steps to work it is important to find a way to coherently and automatically collect and transform data. To make data useful for the learning process and the monitoring of it, modeling and interpreting the gathered data should be considered a central point.

Making Sense of In-Game Data: Modeling and Interpretation

Data is not necessarily equivalent to information. The transformation of data into comprehensible information requires analysis and interpretation on the basis of valid theoretical concepts and the modeling of causal relations between independent and dependent variables. For this purpose, Shute et al. (this volume, chapter 18) suggest the use of Bayesian networks (concerning the concept of Bayesian networks, see e.g., Heckerman, 1996). The Bayesian modeling approach bridges the gap between hidden layers of cognitive processing and observable behavior. Theory-driven operationalization of psychological outcome and process variables is usually quite a challenge. Bayesian modeling works well for measurements aimed at meta-cognitive functions and the detection of problem-solving heuristics because it allows for abstraction from concrete behavior (indicators) and tasks. However, sometimes observable behavior is the learning goal itself (e.g., mounting a device or reproducing specific content). Even then, modeling of cognitive processes can be helpful to assess learning progress, diagnose problems and adapt task demands and support strategies. Furthermore, Bayesian modeling can enable the inference of implicit variables from behavioral data.

In a study with the commercial role-playing game *Oblivion*, Shute et al. (this volume, chapter 18) demonstrated how indicators for the evidence model can be generated. For this, creative problem solving was characterized by the factors novelty and efficiency. Estimates of novelty were defined "in terms of the frequency of use across all players," while estimates of efficiency were conceptualized as "the probability of successfully solving a problem given a set of actions." Problem solving and creativity were defined as relevant competencies. Evidence for these can be found in the degrees of novelty and efficiency of a solution. Specific in-game actions, again, are observable indicators for these. To make valid predictions, one can elicit both prior and conditional probabilities "from experts and refined using players' data." In order to adapt teaching and learning procedures, corresponding evidence-centered design models could be built for each educationally relevant competency in a serious game. States and changes of these competencies can be surveyed with the help of stealth assessment.

Hidden layers of problem solving, in particular in collaborative efforts, how-ever, are not only existent on the individual level, but also on the group level. Bayesian modeling could be applied to these processes as well (e.g., by using counts of transactions, messages, convergent actions, etc.) as indicators for col-laborative effort. Powerful tools which can extract indicators of implicit social processes and structures are provided within the growing literature on social network analysis (e.g., Carrington, Scott, & Wassermann, 2005; Scott, 2000). Social network analysis allows elaboration on qualitative and quantitative aspects of group interaction, particularly in medium and large groups as typical for the massive multiuser online games (MMOGs). Beyond graphical represen-tations of networks, which can be fed back into the group process, SNA issues indices for social phenomena such as centrality, cohesion, reciprocation, or dominance (Wasserman & Faust, 1994), which can be used again within Bayes-ian systems to model, for example, collaborative instead of creative problem solving. SNA can rely on objective log-file information containing transactions among all possible dyads, but could also be based on subjective evaluations or other relational measures (e.g., derived from behavioral similarities).

For other informational levels (intra- and interindividual or contextual) in learning with serious games, valuable models still have to be defined. For psychophysiology, for instance, measurement scenarios for stress management and concentration in learning situations could be modeled. If stress manage-ment is understood as a valuable skill for learning with serious games, evidence for this competency could be found in game situations that induce stress (e.g., challenges induced by speed or complexity). If GSR and PPG are measured, changes in pulse volume amplitude or skin conductance can be described as observables. However, to make use of these observables for feedback purposes, these implicit indicators have to be changed into explicit and socially relevant cues, thereby augmenting the playing and learning experience. In a study con-cerning a remote teaching setting, Chen (2003) showed that the tracking of communicative actions in a remote classroom using a videoconferencing sys-tem helped teachers to better evaluate the learning process within the student group. The system automatically assessed whether students were speaking, ges-turing, or moving in their seats and grouped this data into a visualization of the classroom interaction dynamics, thereby modeling (non-)verbal behavior, which affects or is part of the learning process. Concepts like this give hints for possible ways to sensibly model and interpret implicit information, which can then be fed back to teachers and/or learners.

Making Use of Information: Feedback Loops

Feedback is an essential mechanism in both gaming (Gee, 2007; Liebermann, 2006) and learning (Webb, Stock, & McCarthy, 1994). Just like the learner, the player needs information about what she has achieved in order to plan the next possible or necessary steps. In serious games, player and learner roles are fused, and we should expect the importance of feedback to be even higher. Feedback in general is a powerful means to influence motivation (Kluger & DeNisi, 1996). This influence depends on the quality, complexity, accuracy, and context of the given feedback. Ilgen, Fisher, and Taylor (1979) defined source credibility, provision time, frequency and receiver's personality traits as decisive factors for the effectiveness of feedback. In serious games, feedback is needed to indicate "whether the players are on the right way" (Gee, 2007, p. 36). A central issue that connects games and learning in this respect is the importance of success. If a player or learner is successful, she enjoys the process of playing or learning and hence is likely to continue with this activity. Feedback can help players to sustain enjoyment and eliminate frustration, if it is individualized and constructive (Liebermann, 2006; Ritterfeld & Weber, 2006) and helps the players in achieving the goals in a game. Since the modes of rewards in digital games have undergone major changes throughout the last decades from the provision of mere quantitative feedback like high score lists in early arcade games to elaborate in-game reward systems which offer, for instance, items the players can use in the game, bonus levels, or a ranking system, it is desirable to adapt mechanisms of feedback and reward in serious games to the standards of current entertainment games. Mere evaluative feedback is usually not enough to keep players motivated in the long run. To maintain or even increase the necessary feeling of self-efficacy, feedback has to be aligned with the reward mechanisms. This can basically be realized in two ways: Either feedback provides information about how players/learners can attain a certain reward, or the feedback data can be a criterion for gaining a gratification of some sort. The latter would mean that players/learners only receive incentives if the feedback shows certain values. Good examples of this are biofeedback games which will be discussed later in this chapter. This option should be the preferred one since it smoothly merges feedback representations with the rules of the games and helps to avoid the impression that measurements and feedback are just artificial add-ons to the actual game.

There are multiple types of feedback and multiple ways to provide them in general as well as in serious games specifically. Feedback can, for example, be displayed either immediately or with a delay (Webb et al., 1994). Other relevant aspects are the source and the recipient of feedback, since it may be given by and to the teacher, a colearner, a digital agent (the game engine), respectively or the game developers (Gamberini, Martino, Scarpetta, Spoto, & Spagnolli, 2007; Liebermann, 2006; Michael & Chen, 2006). Feedback can be presented in different modalities (visual, auditory etc.) and codes (text, graphics etc.). The parallel use of a great number of feedback channels in one serious-gaming application enables the multimodality and multicodality (e.g., Weidenmann, 2002) of digital games. In addition to that, feedback can also address several aspects or levels of learning and playing like the task, the learner, the (learning) context, or the game mechanisms and can have a varying granularity as it can be provided for an individual, or a group (DeSchon, Kozlowski, Schmidt,

Milner, & Wiechmann, 2004). There are specific group-level feedback mechanisms which might be provided by SNA (e.g. Wasserman & Faust, 1994 for an overview of this topic). A study by Gamberini et al. (2007) suggested that correct SNA-based feedback concerning the reciprocity and density of player interactions in a collaborative digital game helps to increase communicational flow and symmetry and overall performance of the players.

The format in which feedback is displayed to the users can be manipulated; the data can be directly displayed as more or less raw data or it can be interpreted prior to presentation. Psychophysiological indices like skin conductance or heart rate could be processed and displayed as an arousal or stress indicator in a special feedback window. Moreover, arousal states or moods can be represented by bar charts or icons, such as smileys (e.g., Sánchez, Kirschning, Palacio, & Ostróvskaya, 2005) or even mapped onto a virtual character (e.g., if games are taking place in a shared virtual environment, game elements can become carriers for relevant feedback data). The same holds true for the assessment of achievement since the use of a scoring system is already an interpretation of certain actions. In this context, Shute et al. (this volume, chapter 18) suggest designing status bars for serious games that are analogous to those already in use in entertainment games like health status bars. Instead of health points these bars could represent attributes from the competency model. In some cases it might, however, also be useful to directly transmit information like the number of clicks.

Which types of feedback should or can be implemented in a serious game depends on hard- and software specifications and on the learning context in which it is embedded. For example, single-player games cannot provide real-time feedback from other players and a game that is not used in a blended-learning setting where a teacher is present cannot make use of direct feedback from teacher to learner. This, however, is not necessarily a disadvantage: As a study by Kluger and Adler (1993) suggests, people more actively seek feedback provided by a computer than feedback provided by a human being. Serious games, moreover, make possible the use of real-time feedback, which directly reacts to the players' actions. Thus, readjustments of feedback strategies become realizable. Shute (2007) suggests this kind of formative feedback as a promising strategy in serious games. The cycle of feedback and (re)adjustment is crucial for a serious game to function, because the game needs to "adapt to the players [sic] level of expertise and provide feedback appropriate to his or her level" (Arnseth, 2006, paragraph 41). In serious games feedback can and should be dynamic and adaptive or adaptable.

By assessing the state of the learners/players' competencies and giving relevant feedback, skills/knowledge of the player and the game's challenges can be matched or approximated. Thus the impression of control can be created or sustained, and the task can be considered a challenge instead of a threat (Gregoire, 2003). The assessment of the actual knowledge state of a learner is a necessary prerequisite for the provision of meaningful and helpful feedback as well as possible (re)adjustments of instructions. During the design and implementation of serious games, it is important to always keep in mind that there are players/learners with different levels of expertise. If this is not heeded, a learning procedure that is effective for novices may become ineffective for more advanced learners which leads to the "expertise reversal effect" (Kalyuga, Ayres, Chandler, & Sweller, 2003). To keep players/learners engaged, serious games have to be "pleasantly frustrating" (Gee, 2007, p. 36); that is, they must challenge the users to improve their skills without being boring or overburdening. Accordingly, it is important to design tasks and feedback options in serious games which suit their target audience, taking into consideration influential player characteristics like age and cognitive and motor abilities. As serious games are often used for very specific application areas (e.g., job training, school education, or political campaigns), the specific assumed and targeted competencies of players have to be defined as clearly as possible to create appealing and effective concepts for serious games.

As mentioned above, feedback can be essential for increasing both players' self-awareness and group awareness. Feedback about stress level and learning progress can help the players to identify problematic situations and to evaluate their own performance properly. This can endorse self-assessment in learners, which is a valuable way to improve meta-cognitive skills or even lead to a more realistic self-construal. For these purposes, Shute et al. (this volume, chapter 18) suggest the implementation of so-called open student models, which are dynamic and show learners the changes in their actual competencies. The use of these models may help students to improve their self-assessment skills (Mitrovic & Martin, 2007). Furthermore, feedback about colearners can create a sense of awareness of the social nature of the learning situation and provide a basis for social comparison processes (Festinger, 1954). According to Gutwin, Greenberg, and Roseman (1996), group awareness in computer-mediated contexts can be divided into different subcategories: informal awareness, social awareness, group-structural awareness, and work-space awareness. Informal awareness concerns the general idea of who is present and what the other group members are doing. Social awareness refers to information about the social or conversational context (e.g., mutual attention, emotional states, etc). Group-structural awareness contains aspects like roles and relations within the group. Finally, workspace awareness relates to the group members' interactions with the work environment or, in case of serious games, in the learning and playing environment. According to this, a multiplayer game can create informal awareness by representing the player's online status and activities; social awareness can be facilitated by disclosing intraindividual data (e.g., emotional states, cognitive workload), or providing additional nonverbal channels for interpersonal communication; group structural awareness and workspace awareness can be provided by SNA and context information.

There already are some examples of augmentation media, which are currently developed or already available (e.g., in the field of collaborative knowledge work). For instance, augmented awareness tools have been developed to enhance computer-supported collaborative learning by contribution evaluations (Buder & Bodemer, 2005). The users mutually rate the contributions in an online discussion regarding novelty of and agreement with the contributions. The tool aggregates and transforms the ratings visually in order to feed them back to the group. This raises awareness of potential conflict and emphasizes the novelty of contributions of minorities, which helps to prevent a majority-minority conflict and strengthen the influence of the minority group in a collaborative learning setting. Furthermore, findings indicate that the learners using the awareness support tool discuss longer and make fewer, but more significant, contributions (Buder & Bodemer, 2005).

Another example is a graph-based knowledge management system named "SkillMap" (Hertlein, Meyer, & Spiekermann, 2005) that provides feedback about coworkers' (or colearners') competencies. The goal of this application is to make the knowledge in organizations transparent and to facilitate organizational knowledge communication. One part of the network displays the working areas and the participants' fields of expertise, whereas another part visualizes the routes of knowledge exchange. Each user enters her interests and fields of expertise, as well as data concerning the exchange of knowledge and social relationships. The data can be refreshed continuously. The two networks (skill inventory and exchange database) are linked and can be scanned by the users. Hence, the participants of the network can easily retrieve information about who knows what and who knows whom. This knowledge allows the identification of parallel work processes. Furthermore, the system informs the users automatically if another research group is engaged in the same topic, and knowledge exchange is triggered. Thus the development of common ground is facilitated on basis of the shared knowledge, and so-called communities of practice (e.g., Wenger, McDermott, & Snyder, 2002) are built. Feedback applications originally designed for knowledge work settings can easily be transferred to serious games.

An intriguing example of objective in-game measurement and feedback of psychophysiological data being smoothly integrated into game play can be seen in biofeedback games. In these games, the players can influence the game by controlling their body functions such as breathing or pulse rate. Biofeedback games have e.g., been used to train children suffering from asthma to consciously control their breathing (Raposa, 2003). Following this idea, biofeedback training could be utilized in other serious games. Since digital games are known to capture the attention of children and teenagers quite easily, feedback on arousal and attention allocation (from GSR, PPG, and eye-tracking) could be a way to help students who suffer from attention deficit disorder (ADD). Likewise, biofeedback concepts can be implemented to teach learning strategies and meta-cognitive skills and foster auto-adaptive processes for stress regulation and coping (e.g., by giving feedback about arousal levels and making the conscious control of arousal part of the game).

Just like in biofeedback games for health training, data from stealth measurements in serious games can be directly used to influence the game environment. Changes in arousal or attention can be made explicit by altering the speed or the complexity of the game. A group structure can determine communicational possibilities (like availability of channels) in a game to coordinate cooperation for tasks to be solved. As soon as the players/learners are made aware of implicit information, they can react to it and adapt their behavior. Such an approach can help learners to acquire the skills and knowledge the game aims at, while at the same time learning about the learning process itself in order to train meta-cognitive skills and general learning attitudes or strategies. A broad but manageable combination of different measurements—with feedback which is meaningful and credible within the game world—is a useful way to test new ways of learning. Stealth measurement, together with feedback that makes implicit processes explicit and comprehensible for the learners, can thereby augment learning and help to research learning processes in mediated contexts at the same time.

Conclusion

In this chapter we tried to widen the concept of stealth assessment as introduced by Shute et al. (this volume, chapter 18) and to further explore possibilities for in-game measurement which also include relevant intervening or moderator variables in the learning process, such as individual emotions, attitudes, or group structures and processes to evaluate and facilitate the learning process in serious games in the sense of "flow and grow." We built on their modeling approach of an evidence-centered design and added an intervention layer to this which serves to control the type of measures to be taken and feedback to be supplied based on the output of diagnostic procedures issued by the Bayesian networks.

In the future, research in the field of serious games will have to be refined to identify relevant variables which affect the learning process, to develop corresponding and unobtrusive measures, and to define ways of data modeling and efficient feedback modes. The concept of augmenting learning in serious games by making relevant implicit information explicit through data gathered by stealth measurement is a promising starting point. In this effort game research could benefit from already existing tools validated in other areas of research, such as eye-tracking and psychophysiological measurement. New game designs and solutions for input/output devices are needed to realize a successful implementation of these principles. Concepts like biofeedback games can be modified and applied to serious games, while taking into consideration the necessities of assessing specific outcome and moderating/intervening variables. The proper connection of stealth measurement and assessment together with theory-driven modeling and feedback that makes relevant implicit information explicit can be an important step to reach the goal of aligning flow and grow in serious games.

Acknowledgments

This work was supported by the European Community, IST project "PASION – Psyhologically Augmented Social Interaction Over Networks" (Contract #027654).

Notes

1. An extensive list of currently available and projected serious games is offered on http://www.socialimpactgames.com/, which divides them into the categories of education and learning games, public policy games, political and social games, health and wellness games, business games, military games, advergames, and commercial games.

2. The difference between Bandura's concept of self-efficacy and White's term *effectance*, is that the former is conceptualized as a relatively stable character trait, whereas effectance or rather effectance motivation describes the idea that every human being strives to affect his or her environment since experiencing effectiveness causes pleasure.

References

Ahdell, R., & Andresen, G. (2001). *Games and simulations in workplace eLearning.* Unpublished master's thesis, Norwegian University of Science and Technology, Trondheim.

Anderson, C. A., & Bushman, B. J. (2001). Effects of violent video games on aggressive behavior, aggressive cognition, aggressive affect, physiological arousal and prosocial behavior: A meta-analytic review of the scientific literature. *Psychological Science, 12*(5), 353–359.

Arnseth, H. C. (2006). Learning to play or playing to learn—A critical account of the models of communication informing educational research on computer gameplay. *Game Studies,* 6 Retrieved October 13, 2007, from http://gamestudies.org/0601/articles/arnseth

Bandura, A. (1977). Toward a unifying theory of behavioral change. *Psychological Review, 84*(2), 191–215.

Biocca, F. (1992). Communication within virtual reality: Creating space for research. *Journal of Communication, 42*(4), 5–22.

Biocca, F., Burgoon, J., Harms, C., & Stoner, M. (2001, May). *Criteria and scope conditions for a theory and measure of social presence.* Paper presented at the 4th International Workshop on Presence, Philadelphia.

Blascovich, J., & Mendes, W. B. (2000). Challenge and threat appraisals. The role of affective cues. In J. P. Forgas (Ed.), *Feeling and thinking: The role of affect in social cognition* (pp. 59–82). New York: Cambridge University Press.

Blascovich, J., Seery, M. D., Mugridge, C. A., Norris, R. K., & Weisbuch, M. (2004).

Predicting athletic performance from cardiovascular indexes of challenge and threat. *Journal of Experimental Social Psychology, 40*(5), 683–688.

Boston, C. (2002). The concept of formative assessment. *Practical Assessment, Research & Evaluation, 8.* Retrieved October 13, 2007, from http://PAREonline.net/getvn.asp?v=8&n=9

Brady, S. S., & Matthews, K. A. (2006). Effects of media violence on health-related outcomes among young men. *Archives of Pediatrics & Adolescent Medicine, 160*(4), 341–347.

Buder, J., & Bodemer, D. (2005, September). *Augmented group awareness tools for collaborative learning.* Paper presented at the Second Joint Workshop of Cognition and Learning through Media-Communication for Advanced E-Learning, Tokyo, Japan.

Caillois, R. (2001). *Man, play and games* (M. Barash, Trans.). Urbana: University of Illinois Press.

Campbell, D. T., & Stanley, J. C. (1966). *Experimental and quasi-experimental designs for research.* Chicago: Rand McNally.

Carrington, P. J., Scott, J., & Wassermann, S. (2005). *Models and methods in social network analysis.* New York: Cambridge University Press.

Chen, M. (2003, November). *Visualizing the pulse of a classroom.* Paper presented at the ACM International Conference on Multimedia, Berkeley, CA.

Chen, S., & Michael, D. (2005). Proof of learning: Assessment in serious games. Retrieved August 25, 2007, from http://www.cedma-europe.org/newsletter%20articles/misc/Proof%20of%20Learning%20-%20Assessment%20in%20Serious%20games%20(Oct%202005).pdf

Clariana, R. B. (1992). *Media research with a galvanic skin response biosensor.* Paper presented at the Annual Convention of the Association for Educational Communications and Technology, Washington, DC.

Consalvo, M. (2007). *Cheating. Gaining advantages in videogames.* Cambridge, MA: MIT Press.

Csikszentmihalyi, M. (1990). *Flow: The psychology of optimal experience.* New York: Harper Perennial.

DeSchon, R. P., Kozlowski, S. W., Schmidt, A. M., Milner, K. R., & Wiechmann, D. (2004). A multiple-goal, multilevel model of feedback efforts on the regulation of individual and team performance. *Journal of Applied Psychology, 89*(6), 1035–1056.

Donchin, E. (1995). Video games as research tools: The Space Fortress game. *Behavior Research Methods, Instruments & Computers, 27*(2), 217–223.

Doolittle, J. (1995). Using riddles and interactive computer games to teach problem-solving skills. *Teaching of Psychology, 22*(1), 33–36.

Dourish, P., & Bellotti, V. (1992, November). *Awareness and coordination in shared workspaces.* Paper presented at the ACM Conference on computer-supported cooperative work, Toronto, Canada.

Fairclough, S. H., Venables, L., & Tattersall, A. (2005). The influence of task demand and learning on the psychophysiological response. *International Journal of Psychophysiology, 56*(2), 171–184.

Festinger, L. (1954). A theory of social comparison processes. *Human relations, 7*(2), 117–140.

Gamberini, L., Martino, F., Scarpetta, F., Spoto, A., & Spagnolli, A. (2007). Unveiling the structure: Effects of social feedback on communication activity in online multiplayer videogames. In D. Schuler (Ed.), *Online communities and social computing* (Vol. 4564, pp. 334–341). Berlin: Springer.

Gee, J. P. (2007). *Good video games + good learning: Collected essays on video games, learning and literacy.* New York: Lang.

Green, C. S., & Bavelier, D. (2000). Action video game modifies visual selective attention. *Nature, 423*(6939), 534–537.

Greenfield, P. M., Brannon, C., & Lohr, D. (1994). Two-dimensional representation of movement through three-dimensional space: The role of video game expertise. *Journal of Applied Developmental Psychology, 15*(1), 87–103.

Gregoire, M. (2003). Is it a challenge or a threat? A dual-process model of teachers' cognition and appraisal processes during conceptual change. *Educational Psychology Review, 15*(2), 147–179.

Griffith, J. L., Voloschin, P., Gibb, G., & Bailey, J. R. (1983). Differences in eye-hand motor coordination of video-game users and non-users. *Perceptual and Motor Skills, 57*(1), 155–158.

Gutwin, C., Greenberg, S., & Roseman, M. (1996, April). *Workspace awareness in real-time distributed groupware: Framework, widgets and evaluation.* Paper presented at the International Conference on Human-Computer Interaction, Vancouver.

Heckerman, D. (1996). *A tutorial on learning with Bayesian networks* (No. MSR-TR-95-06). Redmond, WA: Microsoft Research.

Hertlein, M., Meyer, B., & Spiekermann, S. (2005). skillMap: Identification of unrecognized parallel developments and of communities of practice in distributed organizations. Retrieved Sept 16, 2007, from http://ioe-skillmap.hu-berlin.de/download/skillMap_poster.zip

Huisman, M., & van Duin, M. A. J. (2004, August). *Software for statistical analysis of social networks.* Paper presented at the Sixth International Conference on Social Science Methodology, Amsterdam.

Ilgen, D. R., Fisher, C., & Taylor, M. S. (1979). Consequences of individual feedback in behavior in organizations. *Journal of Applied Psychology, 64*(4), 349–371.

Kalyuga, S., Ayres, P., Chandler, P., & Sweller, J. (2003). The expertise reversal effect. *Educational Psychologist, 38*(1), 23–31.

Klimmt, C. (2006). *Computerspielen als Handlung: Dimensionen des Erlebens interaktiver Unterhaltungsangebote* [The action of playing computer games: Dimensions of the experience of interactive entertainment contents]. Cologne, Germany: Halem.

Klimmt, C., & Hartmann, T. (2006). Effectance, self-efficacy and the motivation to play video games. In P. Vorderer & J. Bryant (Eds.), *Playing video games. Motives, responses and consequences.* Mahwah, NJ: Erlbaum.

Kluger, A. N., & Adler, S. (1993). Person- versus computer-mediated feedback, *Computers in Human Behavior, 9*, 1–16.

Kluger, A. N., & DeNisi, A. (1996). The effects of feedback interventions on performance: A historical review, a meta-analysis, and a preliminary feedback intervention theory. *Psychological Bulletin, 119*(2), 254–284.

Liebermann, D. A. (1997). Interactive games for health promotion: Effects on knowledge, self-efficacy, social support and health. In R. L. Street, W. R. Gold, & T. Manning (Eds.), *Health promotion and interactive technology: Theoretical applications and future direction* (pp. 103–120). Mahwah, NJ: Erlbaum.

Liebermann, D. A. (2006). What can we learn from playing interactive games? In P. Vorderer & J. Bryant (Eds.), *Playing video games. Motives, responses and consequences* (pp. 379–397). Mahwah, NJ: Erlbaum.

Lombard, M., & Ditton, T. (1997). At the heart of it all: The concept of presence. *Journal of Computer-Mediated Communication, 3*. Retrieved September 23, 2007, from http://jcmc.indiana.edu/vol3/issue2/lombard.html

McGrath, J. E. (1984). *Groups: Interaction and performance*. Englewood Cliffs, NJ: Prentice-Hall.

Michael, D., & Chen, S. (2006). *Serious games: Games that educate, train and inform*. Boston: Thomson.

Mislevy, R. J., Steinberg, L. S., & Almond, R. G. (2003). On the structure of educational assessment. *Measurement: Interdisciplinary Research and Perspective, 1*(1), 3–62.

Mitrovic, A., & Martin, B. (2007). Evaluating the effects of open student models on learning. *International Journal of Artificial Intelligence in Education, 17*(2), 121–144.

Oyen, A. S., & Bebko, J. M. (1996). The effects of computer games and lessons contexts on children's mnemonic strategies. *Journal of Experimental Child Psychology, 62*(2), 173–189.

Partala, T., & Surakka, V. (2003). Pupil size variation as an indication of affective processing. *International Journal of Human Computer Studies, 59*(1–2), 185–198.

Petersen, A., & Bente, G. (2001). Situative und technologische Determinanten des Erlebens Virtuelles Realität [Situational and technological determinants of the experience of virtual reality]. *Zeitschrift für Medienpsychologie, 13*(3), 138–145.

Raposa, J. (2003). *Biofeedback in educational entertainment*. Unpublished master's thesis, Domus Academy, Milan, Italy.

Rheinberg, F., & Vollmeyer, R. (2003). Flow-Erleben in einem Computerspiel unter experimentell variierten Bedingungen [Flow experince in a computer game under experimental conditions]. *Zeitschrift für Medienpsychologie, 15*(4), 161–170.

Ritterfeld, U., & Weber, R. (2006). Video games for entertainment and education. In P. Vorderer & J. Bryant (Eds.), *Playing video games. Motives, responses, and consequences.* (pp. 399–413). Mahwah, NJ: Erlbaum.

Salomon, G. (1984). Television is "easy" and print is "tough": The differential investment of mental effort in learning as a function of perceptions and attributions. *Journal of Educational Psychology, 76*(4), 647–658.

Sánchez, J. A., Kirschning, I., Palacio, J. C., & Ostróvskaya, Y. (2005, October). *Towards mood-oriented interfaces for synchronous interaction*. Paper presented at the Latin American Conference on Human-Computer Interaction, Cuernavaca, Mexico.

Scott, J. (2000). *Social network analysis: A handbook*. London: Sage.

Short, J., Williams, E., & Christie, B. (1976). *The social psychology of telecommunications*. London: Wiley.

Shute, V. J. (2007). *Focus on formative feedback*. Princeton, NJ: Educational Testing Service.

Slater, M., & Steed, A. J. (2000). A virtual presence counter. *Presence: Teleoperators and Virtual Environments, 9*(5), 413–434.

Squire, K., & Jenkins, H. (2003). Harnessing the power of games in education. *Insight, 3*, 5–33.

Subrahmanyam, K., & Greenfield, P. M. (1994). Effect of video game practice on spatial skills in girls and boys. *Journal of Applied Developmental Psychology, 15*(1), 13–32.

Sweetser, P., & Wyeth, P. (2005). GameFlow: A model for evaluating player enjoyment in games. ACM *Computers in Entertainment, 3*(3), 1–24.

Veltman, J. A., & Gaillard, A. W. K. (1996). Physiological indices of workload in a simulated flight task. *Biological Psychology, 42*(3), 323–342.

Wasserman, S., & Faust, K. (1994). *Social network analysis: Methods and applications.* Cambridge, England: Cambridge University Press.

Webb, J. M., Stock, W. A., & McCarthy, M. T. (1994). The effects of feedback timing on learning facts: The role of response confidence. *Contemporary Educational Psychology, 19*(3), 251–265.

Weidenmann, B. (2002). Multicodierung und Multimodalität im Lernprozess [Multicoding and multimodalities in the learning process]. In L. Issing & P. Klimsa (Eds.), *Information und Lernen mit Multimedia und Internet* [Information and learning with multimedia and the Internet] (pp. 45-64). Weinheim, Germany: BeltzPVU.

Wenger, E., McDermott, R., & Snyder, W. M. (2002). *Cultivating communities of practice.* Boston, MA: Harvard Business School Press.

White, R. W. (1959). Motivation reconsidered. The concept of competence. *Psychological Review, 66*(5), 297–333.

Wright, R. A., & Kirby, L. D. (2003). Cardiovascular correlates of challenge and threat appraisals: A critical examination of the biopsychosocial analysis. *Personality and Social Psychology Review, 7*(3), 216–233.

Chapter 20

Evaluating the Potential of Serious Games

What Can We Learn from Previous Research on Media Effects and Educational Intervention?

Marco Ennemoser

The idea of using game technology for nonentertainment purposes is anything but new. Rapid technological progress in past years has extended the scope of possible applications far beyond plain edutainment software, and we currently observe an almost euphoric optimism concerning the tremendous possibilities of serious games. A major challenge for serious games research is to thoroughly investigate if and under what conditions they meet these overwrought expectations. Concerning this matter, there are several requirements that can be derived from prior (and partially still persistent) shortcomings in related fields of research, especially research on media effects and educational interventions. Thus, a closer look at several decades of corresponding research should be useful to spare serious games researchers from blundering into the same conceptual, methodological, and practical deficiencies.

In the present chapter, I first summarize some major problems in these two related research areas and argue that they are very likely to plague serious games research as well. Second, I illuminate the outlined problems against the background of serious games characteristics and highlight that some of the particular strengths of serious games (e.g., interactivity or facilitation of deliberate learning) at the same time represent severe methodological problems in terms of intervention integrity. Third, I suggest a solution to deal with these challenges by systematically conceptualizing serious games effects as a product of mediated moderation or moderated mediation, respectively. Fourth, I discuss particular requirements for serious games research from a developmental point of view. In the final section, I present a framework for evaluation in serious games research that should permit reliable conclusions about the potential impact of serious games on development. This framework certainly does not entail any fundamentally new methodological approaches. However, it may help in establishing scientifically credible research in the field of serious games and, ideally, a standard of more evidence-based serious games development.

Problems in Related Fields of Research

The Problem of Naïve Assumptions in Media Effects Research—How Poor Theory Leads to Poor Methodology

What can we learn from media effects research? A comparison between research on serious games and media effects in general may seem to be flawed, at least with respect to the highly interactive nature of serious games and their explicit focus on training and learning. Nevertheless, it appears especially appropriate to call attention to a prejudicial tradition that serious games research is clearly at risk to continue: namely, the danger of naïve assumptions. Few fields of research have been more characterized by this problem than media effects research, it is a prime example of how naïve assumptions can lead to severe methodological shortcomings, which in turn may impede research progress for decades.

The Naïve Assumption of Specific Media Effects: What Does Work?

The most prominent example of this problem is research on television that was mainly determined by popular apprehensions about negative effects on children's learning, academic achievement, or cognitive development (e.g., Postman, 1984). Although research on the assumed effects has been carried out for more than 5 decades, the evidence is still unclear. Judging from the available literature, the problem is primarily rooted in poor theory, especially in the naïve assumption that (negative) effects are caused by inherent attributes of the medium (cf. Hornik, 1981). The deficiency of this approach becomes most evident against the background of research focusing on educational programs, such as *Sesame Street* or *Between the Lions*. Regardless of popular concerns about television, corresponding studies have consistently demonstrated the potential of television to stimulate cognitive development in children (e.g., Bryant, Alexander, & Brown, 1983; Linebarger, Kosanic, Greenwood, & Doku, 2004; Rice, Huston, Truglio, & Wright, 1990). Interestingly, both research directions have coexisted in the literature for several decades, although focusing on opposing effects (i.e., either positive or negatives) and at least partially supporting their respective assumptions. The simple conclusion to be drawn is that the medium is surely not the message (cf. Clark, 1994; Kozma, 1991); neither positive nor negative effects are caused by inherent or somehow self-acting attributes of the medium. Considering this, the challenge for current research on serious games is to avoid the naïve assumption that simply incorporating an intervention into a digital game format will automatically enhance learning. Instead, researchers first have to define the distinctive characteristics of a serious game and thoroughly explain how they can be utilized to produce the assumed facilitative effects (see Klimmt, this volume, chapter 16).

The Naïve Assumption that Underlying Mechanisms Are Trivial: How Does It Work?

Of course most media effects researchers at least implicitly had a theory of how the medium exerts influence. With respect to the assumed negative effects of television viewing on reading achievement, for example, there were four major inhibition hypotheses that gave fairly plausible explanations for such effects (cf. Beentjes & van der Voort, 1988). The most popular assumption was introduced as the *displacement hypothesis*, arguing that time spent watching television displaces reading time, and, in the long run, this trade-off would negatively affect reading performance (Neuman, 1988). Two other inhibition hypotheses assumed that television influences information-processing habits. According to the *passivity hypothesis*, the low level of mental effort children usually invest in watching television may lead to reduced effort when learning to read or write (Salomon, 1984). In comparison, the *concentration-deterioration hypothesis* assumed that the fast pace and rapid context changes in television programs may negatively affect children's ability to concentrate on a given task, with negative consequences for reading acquisition (Gadberry, 1980). Finally, the *reading-depreciation hypothesis* claimed that children's pleasant experiences with television would reduce their motivation to invest energy in school contexts, for instance, lowering their willingness to learn to read (see Beentjes & van der Voort, 1988; Koolstra, van der Voort, & van der Kamp, 1997). As illustrated in Figure 20.1, all hypotheses postulate indirect effects on reading achievement mediated by a third variable, thus including not only one but two assumptions: Television causally affects the mediating variable, which in turn has an impact on reading achievement.

Given that some of these hypotheses sound rather plausible, the majority of studies did not consider it necessary to address them empirically (Hornik, 1981). Indeed, a good deal of research was even content with calculating negative correlations, speculatively attributing them to a particular inhibition hypothesis, and thereby implying a causal television effect—despite the absence of any empirical evidence. In contrast, other studies directly assessed the hypothesized mediating variables, such as daily amount of leisure reading. Yet, with the exception of two longitudinal studies, they did not comprehensively examine the complete causal chain illustrated in Figure 20.1. For instance, some of them only examined whether or not television was associated with the particular mediating variable and simply ignored the second part of the causal path. This approach is obviously not suited to verify whether or not an observed effect of television on the mediating variable subsequently causes a decline in reading achievement.

Why is it important to scrutinize mediating effects so painstakingly in the field of serious games, when facilitating mechanisms seem so obvious and plausible? Note that even trivial assumptions may be wrong or deceptive, as the following example illustrates: In a recent longitudinal study investigating the

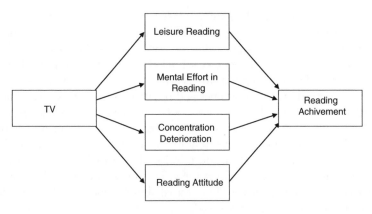

Figure 20.1 Hypothesized mediating effects of television on reading achievement.

effects of television on the development of reading achievement, relevant mediating hypotheses were examined more thoroughly than in previous research (Ennemoser & Schneider, 2007). First, the assumption of negative correlations between the amount of (noneducational) television and reading achievement was confirmed. Structural equation modeling techniques provided supporting evidence for substantial hindering effects in a sample of 6-year-old kindergartners who participated in the study over the course of four years. Moreover, there was some evidence for a displacement effect (i.e., prior television viewing was negatively associated both with the amount of parent–child reading and with subsequent leisure reading). However, as indicated by structural equation models, the (potentially television-induced) decline in reading achievement could not be attributed to the displacement effects reported above. Surprisingly, one of the two implications of the displacement hypothesis could not be confirmed: Although leisure reading and reading achievement were positively associated, the causal direction was quite unexpected (i.e., how much time young children spent reading depended on their prior reading abilities rather than the other way round). Thus, the hypothesized causal chain as illustrated in Figure 20.1 could not be confirmed. Furthermore, although inhibitory effects were substantial, none of the other inhibition hypotheses examined in this study was appropriate to explain the underlying causal mechanism.

The Naïve Assumption of Homogenous Effects: Are Effects Valid For Everyone and Under All Conditions?

A further shortcoming of previous media effects research is the insufficient consideration of moderating variables. Given that there is a good deal of evidence indicating that media effects may not be valid for everybody or under all conditions, this seems quite surprising. To give an example, stimulating effects of parental picturebook reading seem to fade as soon as children become able to read on their own and thus, positive effects are restricted to young kinder-gartners (Bus, van Ijzendoorn & Pellegrini, 1995). In a similar vein, Neuman (1988) found—for young elementary school children—a nonlinear relation-ship between television viewing and school achievement (i.e., correlations were positive for short viewing times and negative for longer viewing times). For high school children, however, the function was generally negative, regard-less of differences in viewing times. Of course, age or developmental trends are not the only potential moderators in this field. There is evidence that media effects also vary as a function of other third variables, such as social background (Comstock & Scharrer, 1999; Ennemoser, Schiffer, Reinsch, & Schneider, 2003; Fetler, 1984) or intellectual ability (Morgan & Gross, 1980; Schiffer, Ennemoser & Schneider, 2002).

As indicated by these findings, serious games research has to control for differential effects and moderating variables. Examples of variables that poten-tially moderate the effectiveness of serious games can be derived from previous studies on (multi-)media learning. They include, for instance, variables like prior knowledge, computer literacy, gender, attitudes toward multimedia learn-ing, or digital game experience (e.g., Richter, Naumann, & Groeben, 2000). Moderating variables must be taken into account in order to ensure that the effects of a serious game are valid for everybody (or at least for the particular target audience) and to determine under what conditions it will work.

Problems in the Field of Educational Intervention Research

What can we learn from the current situation in educational intervention research? Educational intervention research is characterized by several prob-lems that appear to be extremely relevant to serious games, even though the link between the two areas may not be self-evident at first glance. One major challenge concerns the relation between research and practice. Further, there are a number of methodological shortcomings, a large part of which concern basic empirical standards. The issues involved range from measurement qual-ity, to the inclusion of appropriate control or comparison groups, to questions of effect size and transfer. Because most of these items are actually well-known, I will only briefly summarize them in the framework presented in the final section. However, in addition to these basic issues there are three further chal-lenges that should be addressed here more carefully. Two of them have already been discussed in the context of research on media effects: the questions of mediation (How does it work?) and moderation (Does it work for everybody and under all conditions?). The third one is usually referred to as *treatment integrity* or *intervention integrity*, which concerns the question of internal and external validity of an intervention ("Does it—really—work?"), and thus rep-resents a severe problem in any field of intervention research (Shadish, Cook, & Campbell, 2002).

The Failure of Educational Intervention Research to Impact Educational Practice

As noted above, educational interventions are usually designed to influence particular domains of development (e.g., learning or social skills), and include general teaching methods as well as training programs for children with special needs. First, the good news: there is an abundance of methods and programs available that claim to have beneficial effects on development. However, the majority of these methods are rather a conglomeration of teaching aids and worksheets than a theoretically substantiated intervention program (Shavelson & Towne, 2002). Thus, one of the major challenges for users in the field of educational intervention is to choose programs or methods that are particularly suited for their concern. Certainly, the most recommendable criterion for this selection is whether or not the assumption that the program effectively facilitates development is supported by empirical evidence. Unfortunately, most available intervention programs do not provide such information, which points us to one of the most striking problems in educational intervention research: a sustained lack of evaluation studies (Pressley & Harris, 1994). Obviously, a good deal more effort is put into designing interventions than to carefully evaluating if and under what conditions interventions work. As a consequence, there is a conspicuous gap between the large amount of available intervention programs and the low number of evaluation studies, and, as pointed out by Hsieh et al. in their 2005 review, the situation seems to be getting worse.

The problem is not only a matter of quantity but also the quality of educational intervention research. Indeed, the sparse intervention studies published in relevant periodicals often fail to meet basic methodological standards described by Campbell and Stanley (1966), and thus do not allow for reliable conclusions. In this regard, there is a consensus in the literature that "the reputation of educational research is quite poor" (Shavelson & Towne, 2002, p. 23; see also Levin & O'Donnel, 1999).

The paucity of credible intervention research is regarded as one of the reasons for what Richard Mayer (2005) calls "the failure of educational research to impact educational practice." He concludes that "educational practice is remarkably uninformed by scientific evidence" (Mayer, 2005, p. 68). This lack of evidence-based practice seems especially problematic because the available literature regularly confirms that positive evaluation results are all but trivial. Indeed, even an elaborate theoretical foundation is no guarantee for the effectiveness of an intervention program (Pressley & Harris, 1994). In reference to the problems in media effects research, we could conclude that naïve assumptions are at work here as well (i.e. the naïve assumption that a prettily designed intervention will necessarily work).

Mediation and Moderation in Educational Research

As already pointed out in the section on media effects, educational researchers should avoid being content to demonstrate that there is an effect. Rather, they have to provide theories about underlying mechanisms and use appropriate statistical procedures to test whether or not the particular effect is exactly mediated as hypothesized (cf. Levin & O'Donnell, 1999). Unfortunately, only a minority of empirical studies explicitly conduct mediation analyses, as suggested by Baron and Kenny (1986). Thereby, researchers sacrifice the opportunity to promote further development of theory and, as a consequence, to successively develop even more effective interventions by systematic empirical investigation. In this regard, it seems important to note that a comprehensive understanding of how an intervention works is essentially figuring out moderation effects, (i.e., to determine for whom and under what conditions it works). But, very similarly as in the field of media effects research, moderator analyses are rather scarce and usually conducted in corresponding meta-analyses at best (e.g., Rohrbeck, Ginsburg-Block, Fantuzzo, & Miller, 2003; Rosenshine & Meister, 1994; Bus et al., 1995; Kulik & Kulik, 1991).

Considering the Interplay between Mediation and Moderation

Although there is a consensus that mediation and moderation have to be addressed more thoroughly in future educational research, scant attention is dedicated to the interplay between the two of them. However, this might be the key to figuring out what exactly happens between cause and effect, which finally enables us to (1) successively optimize the potential of a medium or an intervention and (2) determine for whom or under what conditions this potential takes effect.

To illustrate how considering this interplay provides a deeper understanding of facilitative potentials, I will give an example from a field where media effects research meets educational intervention research: It is widely believed that parental picture-book reading is beneficial for children's subsequent literacy development (Bus et al., 1995). As a consequence, parents are frequently recommended to apply this valuable "intervention" and read books to their children. However, although the empirical evidence is confirmative, the magnitude of positive effects is generally smaller than expected (Scarborough & Dobrich, 1994). Against this background, Meyer, Wardrop, Stahl, and Linn (1994) particularly criticize the belief of a "magic" improvement of reading abilities by parent–child reading (i.e., the naïve assumption of a media specific effect). Whereas the results of their longitudinal study confirmed positive effects of print media use, the benefits were observed only for reading activities actually done by the children themselves. Parent–child reading, however, did not substantially contribute to the development of reading ability.

Of course, it would be premature to conclude that parent–child reading doesn't have any potential to foster children's reading development. One major reason for the deflating evidence is that the causal chain of the hypothesized effect has not been considered carefully enough. To begin with, it seems plausible that parent–child book reading is primarily more suited to foster the development of oral language than of subsequent reading, because children do not practice reading in this situation. Indeed, the evidence is more supportive for this assumption (Bus et al., 1995). Hence, as oral language is a relevant predictor of later reading comprehension, the assumed effect of parental reading might be mediated by stimulated oral abilities (see Figure 20.2). However, there is still a missing link in this model. The questions to be answered are "How exactly does parent–child book-reading impact oral language?" or, more precisely, "What are the beneficial features of this situation?" Obviously, this is neither the medium (the book) nor is it exclusively the language input children receive in this event.

As suggested by a series of intervention studies, the gain of joint picture-book reading substantially increases if parents are trained to optimize parent–child interactions during reading (Arnold, Lonigan, Whitehurst, & Epstein, 1994; Whitehurst et al., 1988). This indicates that the main potential of parental reading lies outside of the medium itself by simply offering a platform that is especially suited to establish stimulating parent–child interactions, (i.e., dialogic reading.) Thus, it might be hypothesized that beneficial effects of parental reading are moderated by the degree to which parents succeed in creating such interactions. The theoretical model that results from these considerations is illustrated in Figure 20.2 and can be described as a model of mediated moderation (Baron & Kenny, 1986; Muller, Judd, & Yzerbyt, 2005). That is, positive effects of parent–child reading on subsequent reading comprehension are moderated by the quality of parent–child reading (dialogic reading). This moderation does not take an effect directly, but is further mediated by oral language ability.

As a conclusion, the weak and sometimes nonsupportive evidence for the potential of joint book reading is due to the failure to (1) comprehensively explain this potential in theory, (i.e., to explicate the facilitating mechanism); (2) assess relevant mediator and moderator variables, (e.g., oral language development and parent–child interactions, respectively); and finally, (3) to conduct statistical analyses that are suited to investigate the hypothesized processes of mediated moderation, (e.g. Edwards & Lambert, 2007; Muller et al., 2005).

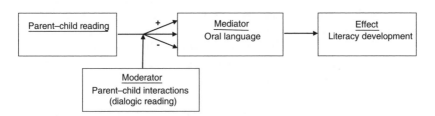

Figure 20.2 Mediated moderation model on the effects of parent–child reading on literacy development.

The regular neglect of involved processes of mediation and moderation is a characteristic hindrance of progress in educational research. As will be argued in the following sections, a systematic consideration of the interplay between these processes seems even more important and particularly beneficial for the field of serious games research.

The Problem of Intervention Integrity In Educational Research

Intervention integrity, sometimes also referred to as treatment integrity or treatment fidelity, is defined as the faithful delivery of an intervention (cf. Shadish et al., 2002). Ensuring that an intervention is implemented in the precise manner in which it was intended is critical for both internal and external validity of intervention research. Intervention integrity is threatened, for example, if the persons who carry out the treatment, (e.g., teachers), do not comprehensively adhere to the program. They might change the intervention schedule by giving additional or modified instructions, providing different materials, or varying the sequence and number of lessons. There might also be more practical problems, such as insufficient financial, spatial, or personal resources hindering the proper implementation of an intervention. If this is the case, the results of a study may be severely biased. To be precise, there are two problems to distinguish. First, if external validity is threatened, it might happen that an intervention works fine in a well-controlled laboratory experiment, but cannot exploit its facilitative potential under less controllable conditions in "real life." Ignoring this problem (i.e., neglecting implementation research to ensure that an intervention also works in practice), undermines the trustworthiness of educational research as described above. Second, if internal validity is violated, it is not even possible to draw conclusions about whether or not the intended intervention has any facilitative potential at all (i.e., none of the effects observed, or not observed, can unambiguously be attributed to the intended intervention).

Although treatment integrity is a most important issue in educational intervention research, the problem is hardly considered in empirical studies. Snyder, Thompson, McLean, and Smith (2002) reviewed the literature on childhood intervention programs and found that only 13% of the studies presented data that allow readers to evaluate whether the intervention was properly implemented. Similar reviews in related fields of research confirm the finding that the vast majority of intervention studies fail to report information on treatment integrity (Gresham, MacMillan, Beebe-Frankenberger, & Bocian, 2000; Wolery & Garfinkle, 2002).

Conceptualizing Serious Games Effects as a Process of Mediation and Moderation

Treatment integrity is a very special challenge in serious games research. There are two particular violations to integrity. Basically, both of them arise from one distinctive feature of serious games, which clearly differentiates them from common educational interventions: serious game players have, in two regards, "the choice." As opposed to conventional forms of interventions, serious games are interactive (i.e., individuals have considerable influence on what they do during their play). In addition, they can—at least outside institutional settings—decide themselves about the extent to which they use the serious game. In regard to intervention integrity (or the validity of experimental manipulations) both items represent a serious problem.

The "Problem" of Interactivity

In the field of serious games research, intervention integrity could be preserved quite easily with regard to the intervention procedure per se because content is provided by personal computer which allows for perfect step-by-step delivery of an intervention. However, while this may work fine in a conventional drill-and-practice program, the same approach would at least partially eliminate what is considered one of the major advantages of serious games, (i.e., the feature of interactivity). In an interactive game environment, it is hard to determine if the player of a serious game really does what he is supposed to do. Because players interact with the game in different ways depending on numerous variables like motivation, prior knowledge, or preferences for particular contents and sequences, all participants of a study might actually receive a different intervention. Thus, the most severe threat to treatment integrity in serious games is inherent in the intervention itself. Ironically enough, this "threat" represents one of the very features believed to provide a substantial contribution to the potential of serious games.

Several Approaches to Deal with the Problem of Interactivity

Current literature more and more frequently addresses the problem that interactivity undermines experimental designs. Although useful approaches are being suggested, a comprehensive solution to cope with this challenge is not in sight (e.g., Bucy & Tao, 2007; Klimmt, Vorderer, & Ritterfeld, 2007). In serious games research this problem can be addressed in several ways:

1. *Ignore Interactivity: The "horse race" approach.* From a pragmatic point of view it might be useful to simply compare the effects of an intervention or a serious game, respectively, with effects of conventional methods. In this case, the serious game is evaluated as a whole and treatment integrity is regarded as ignorable because—whatever players do while interacting with the game— results will tell us if it works better than alternative interventions. This is what Pressley and Harris (1994) describe as a horse race. Horse races are either won or lost and the prize for the winner is to be introduced to educational practice as the most valuable method. However, this approach tells us nothing about the strengths and weaknesses of serious games, and it is not really

useful to further optimize their potential. Horse races don't provide any deeper insight into underlying mechanisms, and the superiority of the winner might be alternatively explained by numerous other variables than by the particular characteristics of a serious game. Inversely, if the serious game unexpectedly happens to lose the race, there is no possibility to determine if this is due to a poor pedagogical concept, the overestimated potential of the "game factor", or simply to the fact that subjects did whatever was fun for them, thereby undermining the originally intended intervention.

2. *Restrict interactivity: The bias approach*. In educational research, violations to intervention integrity are generally treated as a source of bias. These violations have to be controlled in order to warrant that the intervention takes place as originally intended. Applied to the interactivity problem of serious games research, this would mean restricting some selected interactivity options of the game, thereby ensuring that the facilitative content will be received by all participants (Klimmt et al., 2007). Such an approach requires the researcher to have a well-elaborated theory of how to produce the intended outcomes. Interactivity might be allowed where deviations from the treatment plan are not regarded as crucial. For example, subjects may have the choice to complete some tasks in an arbitrary sequence, whereas this should be avoided when the order is theoretically important. Similarly, there may be the option to solve several problems in very different ways, but only if the kind of solution is not expected to impact the intended effects. Following this approach helps to ensure that players cannot go through the game without receiving the (theoretically) facilitative content.

Although there is, of course, still some compromise with respect to intervention integrity, deviations from the treatment plan should be within an acceptable range. Hence, restricting interactivity may allow for somewhat more reliable conclusions about effectiveness of a serious game even within a horse race approach. However, it implicates neglecting or, at least to some extent, sacrificing a specific attribute of serious games that is regarded as an important component of their very potential. Furthermore, the approach still leaves a lot of questions open that might be addressed more adequately by other solutions described below.

3. *Experimentally manipulate interactivity: The independent variable approach*. In serious games research, interactivity is often regarded as a facilitative attribute of the medium rather than a threat to intervention integrity. From this point of view it seems useful to treat interactivity as an independent variable in order to verify the assumption that higher levels of interactivity are associated with desirable effects. Indeed, the literature confirms that media effects vary as a function of interactivity, although results are not comprehensively supportive and sometimes paradoxical (Bucy, 2004).

The major problem of the independent variable approach is that effects of interactivity level are still confounded (i.e., intervention integrity is still violated). As mentioned above, higher levels of interactivity allow for more deviations from the treatment plan, especially with regard to the theoretically relevant content the player is supposed to receive. A study by Wong et al. (2007) gives an example of how this problem can be dealt with. Participants in one group (interactive condition) played a serious game whereby the whole game session was recorded. Participants in a second group (noninteractive condition) did not play the game themselves but received a replay of the game session of a matched counterpart. This procedure allows for testing the effect of interactivity while avoiding confounding effects through varying content.

The crucial point within this approach is to create appropriate control conditions that allow for less confounded conclusions about the effects of interactivity as a whole, or, maybe more recommendable, of particular interactivity features, respectively. Instead of constraining interactivity in the control condition to zero, it might also be useful to adopt the less restrictive bias approach suggested in the section above (i.e., to create a serious game version where interactivity options are no more restricted than necessary to warrant that theoretically relevant content is received by all participants). If a restricted serious game turned out to be superior to a nonrestricted version, this would provide evidence that interactivity is a threat to intervention integrity (i.e., uncontrolled interactivity undermines the treatment plan which, in the end, reduces the intended effects). In contrast, superiority of the nonrestricted version would confirm the inherent facilitative potential of interactivity (even if the precise mechanism is neglected). No differences between the two versions would at least allow for the conclusion that interactivity induced violations to treatment integrity are negligible with respect to the intended outcomes.

Further research approaches create gradually different levels of interactivity; however, experimental manipulations are more complicated than originally expected and often fail. An example of this problem is reported by McMillan, Hwang, and Lee (2003) who found individuals to be most interactively engaged in a Web site with the fewest interactive attributes. Obviously, some interactive attributes are more appealing and engaging than others, thereby confounding experimental manipulations in which different levels of interactivity are distinguished by the mere quantity of interactivity features.

One major advantage of the independent variable approach is that it directs attention away from investigating effects of serious games as a whole to the portion of effects that are attributable to specific characteristics of a serious game, in this particular case, to interactivity. However, as indicated by findings like those of McMillan et al. (2003), it seems still insufficient to examine the effects of interactivity as a whole. Rather, studies are needed that thoroughly investigate the role of particular interactivity features in detail by systematic experimental manipulations.

4. *Investigate causal pathways and differential effects of interactivity: The mediated moderation approach.* The main focus of the three approaches described above is on determining the effects of serious games or interactive features, respectively, on intended outcome variables. In doing so, they neglect the

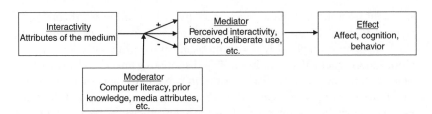

Figure 20.3 Mediated moderation model of interactivity (modified from Bucy & Tao, 2007).

causal path between treatment and effect, and consequently, the mediating variables involved. That is, they don't pay much attention to the question of how or why the assumed effects should be obtained. Moreover, they clearly fail to illuminate the intricate dual role of interactivity as both a violation of intervention integrity and facilitative potential of a serious game.

A helpful approach might be derived from an article by Bucy and Tao (2007). The authors address the dissatisfactory situation in interactivity research and conclude, "After three decades of analysis and investigation, we scarcely know what interactivity really is, let alone what it does, and we have scant insight into the conditions in which interactive processes are consequential for individual technology users" (Bucy & Tao, 2007, p. 647). In order to advance corresponding research, they suggest a "mediated moderation model" of interactivity that interposes two third-variables between causes (interactivity attributes) and effects (intended outcomes): a mediator and a moderator (see Figure 20.3). And we have to recognize by this point at the latest that dealing with interactivity and its violations to treatment integrity leads us to precisely the same essential requirements that have been identified in the section above: Serious games researchers have to pay attention to what exactly happens between cause and effect and have to theorize about the involved processes in terms of mediation and moderation.

Mediator Variables

As already discussed, media usually do not impose an influence directly. With regard to interactivity, effects may be mediated by third variables such as presence, entertainment experience, or perceived interactivity, as suggested by Bucy and Tao (2007). At this point, it seems important to note that mediating processes are indeed explicated in a good deal of studies. But, as with media effects research in general, the underlying mediating hypotheses are usually not directly addressed in the statistical analyses.

Moderator Variables

In addition to mediation, the model takes into account that the effects of interactivity may vary as a function of third variables. Tremayne and Dunwoody (2001), for instance, found that the relationship between level of inter-activity (the number of hyperlinks on a Web site) and knowledge acquisition was moderated by the subjects' Internet experience. While experienced users outperformed their novice counterparts in a high interactivity condition, nov-ices were the superior group when interactivity was low.

Mediated Moderation

Mediated moderation describes a situation in which a moderating effect (i.e., the effect of an interaction between two variables) is transmitted through a mediator variable (Baron & Kenny, 1986). As illustrated in Figure 20.3, Bucy and Tao (2007) propose that effects of interactivity (conceptualized as tech-nological attributes of the medium) are mediated by perceived interactivity, which may be considered as an example but is certainly not the only variable to serve as a potential mediator. Concepts like entertainment experience, self-efficacy, or presence are plausible candidates, as mentioned above. Further, the authors argue that the relationship between interactivity and the mediator is moderated by individual differences, especially Internet self-efficacy. Again, it must be pointed out that there are additional variables which seem notewor-thy as potential moderators (e.g., prior knowledge in the particular content domain, computer literacy, and motivational variables). Evidently, the medi-ated moderation approach draws attention away from interactivity (defined as attributes of the medium) to the players' responses to interactivity (actions, cognitions, emotions). Rather than considering these responses as a threat to intervention integrity (i.e. as a potential deviation from the treatment plan), it highlights their particular functions in a hypothesized process of mediation and moderation. To be precise, the model suggests (1) assessing exactly what individuals do while playing a serious game, with available logging techniques; (2) explicating and evaluating how these responses contribute to the intended outcomes; (3) investigating how the players' relevant interactive responses vary as a function of individual differences or experimentally manipulated interac-tivity features; and finally (4) determining the consequences of the mediated moderation processes for the intended outcomes. The resultant evidence from corresponding studies should be most valuable for further improvements of serious games.

Mediated Moderation or Moderated Mediation?

There are also—depending on the underlying conceptual framework—alternative ways to model the interplay between mediation and moderation. These models are referred to as moderated mediation and describe a situa-tion in which a mediation effect is moderated by some other variable (Baron & Kenny, 1986). Moderation might occur here at different points or, more precisely, concern different paths that are involved in the mediation process.

For example, the path between mediator and outcome variable (e.g., between entertainment experience and knowledge gain) might be moderated by motivational variables like goal orientation. Such a model would predict that serious gaming increases entertainment experience for all participants, but this increase facilitates knowledge gains only for learning-goal-oriented individuals but does not work for performance-goal-oriented users.

However, there is a good deal of confusion surrounding the distinction between moderated mediation and mediated moderation. A comprehensive review of this issue is beyond the scope of this chapter. In short, the discussion about whether or not a clear distinction is reasonable is mainly raised by partial overlaps between the two conceptualizations (from an analytical point of view they are indeed partially equivalent; cf. Edwards & Lambert, 2007). In this regard, Muller et al. (2005) come to the conclusion that "these two processes are in some sense the flip sides of the same coin" (p. 862). Edwards and Lambert (2007) address this question in depth and recommend forgoing further attempts to determine whether results support mediated moderation or moderated mediation. Rather, they suggest a general path analytic framework to investigate processes in which both moderation and mediation are involved. Thereby, the question as to whether results are finally interpreted in terms of mediated moderation or moderated mediation is left to the underlying theory.

The "Problem" of Deliberate Use

As mentioned above, intervention integrity refers to the question of whether an intervention is implemented into practice exactly in the manner as it was originally intended. In this regard, however, we have to distinguish between two different contextual conditions. First, there are institutional settings where individuals are assigned to participate (e.g., schools). The problem of intervention integrity in this context mainly arises from interactivity and from boundary conditions that might hinder implementation, as discussed above. Apart from institutional settings, however, serious games are hardly an intervention in a classical sense (i.e., they are not usually prescribed to a "patient"). Rather, individuals can decide by themselves to what extent they make use of it. Hence, it is possible that a serious game works fine in the laboratory but cannot exploit its facilitative potential under real-life conditions because individuals do not use it frequently enough. Again, the mediated moderation model described above should be useful to illuminate the particular role of deliberate use as both a strength and a methodological weakness. The difference is merely that deliberate use is not located in the model as an independent variable but rather serves as a mediator.

For example, as illustrated in Figure 20.3, it might be hypothesized that the entertainment value of a serious game on the topic of physiology stimulates the deliberate use of this game, and thereby increases the time spent on learning physiology, which finally results in higher knowledge gains. Indeed, this is a common assumption in serious games research (see Klimmt, this volume, chapter 16) but, as discussed above, this does not imply that its validity is trivial and that it doesn't need to be confirmed by empirical evidence. A corresponding study might, for instance, systematically manipulate entertainment value (i.e., particular entertainment features) in order to determine which attributes most effectively stimulate deliberate use. Dependent on the particular research question, it might additionally be examined if the observed increase in deliberate learning time is altered by third variables, such as interests or prior knowledge.

Major Advantages of the Mediated Moderation Approach

The major advantage of the mediated moderation (or moderated mediation) approach is that it helps in reaching a more precise understanding of interactive processes and consequential effects. It provides the opportunity to go beyond fruitless research perspectives whereby interactivity is either just treated as a threat to experimental designs (treatment integrity) or naïvely regarded as a facilitative feature that will—"somehow"—be uniformly beneficial for everybody under all conditions. Moreover, the additional focus on moderation effects points us to another facilitative potential of serious games that can then be addressed more appropriately in future research. This is the feature of adaptivity that enables us to individualize an intervention such that it meets the demands of the particular subject (by taking into account knowledge about mediated moderation effects) instead of strictly adhering to a fixed treatment plan.

Focus on Development

The discussion above makes clear that development is a complex process, and investigating the impact of influencing factors such as educational interventions, media use, or serious games on development is not an easy challenge. Thus, we have to consider third variables, include mediating variables, in order to explain and further optimize the potential of an intervention, and we must take into account moderating variables that govern the magnitude or direction of effects. However, a sharper focus on the continuously progressive nature of development highlights some additional challenges. Again, these challenges can be exemplified by research on media effects and educational intervention. And again, it can be stated that consequential conceptual and methodological requirements have been insufficiently addressed in both of these areas.

Consider the Durability of Effects

One persistent problem in educational intervention research is that development is often treated as something that happens in between the pre- and posttest of a laboratory experiment. As criticized by Pressley and Harris (1994), or more recently by Hsieh et al. (2005), the majority of studies assesses effects only immediately after an intervention. However, a lot of individual development has taken place long before the particular intervention (or the use of a serious game) and it has been influenced and moderated by numerous variables. And the same development will continue afterwards, again being influenced by many factors other than the particular intervention. Against this background, it seems a debatable point whether the short-term effects of a (typically brief) intervention persist for a longer time span after its completion. Hence, a minimum requirement for credible research claiming to investigate methods which are designed to impact development is to demonstrate that observed effects are durable. This can be done quite easily, simply by including follow-up assessments after a certain period of time (Hsieh et al., 2005).

Consider the Stage of Development

In the discussion on mediation and moderation it was argued that the effects of an intervention may be altered by individual differences. Certainly, one of the most important sources of individual differences is development per se (i.e., the stage of development itself may represent a moderator of effects). Empirical evidence for this notion, which is actually self-evident, is often provided by meta-analytical reviews (e.g. Bus et al., 1995; Rohrbeck et al., 2003). Results like these underscore the importance of taking a developmental perspective in serious games research. Features of an intervention or a medium (e.g., content and pedagogical and didactical features) potentially interact with age-related characteristics of the user, including developmental processes in numerous domains. This requires the researcher not only to include different age groups in his or her study design but also to consider developmentally changing needs of individuals in the design of the particular serious game.

Consider How Serious Games Are Involved in the Developmental Process

Utilizing an experimental perspective, serious games are perceived as an independent variable and aspects of development are taken into account either as a dependent variable (such as durability) or as a source of moderation (such as stage of development). However, from a developmental point of view this perspective is not sufficient to illuminate comprehensively how the use of serious games is entangled in the developmental process. A more thorough study of developmental questions in this field requires, first of all, considering the (deliberate) use of serious games as something that is itself susceptible to the influence of third variables, such as social background, gender, interests and motivation, cognitive abilities, or parental guidance. A perception of serious games as interactively involved in the developmental process is closely related to the issue of intervention integrity and it entails two major requirements:

1. *Investigate the interplay between the use of serious games and relevant third variables.* The use of serious games might depend on third variables (e.g., characteristics of the family background, such as educational orientation or financial resources). Potential consequences are (a) that "laboratory-proven" serious games work only for particular groups of individuals who actually use them (i.e., effects are moderated), or (b) that serious games do not have any additional effect at all, because only those individuals make use of them who would have yielded the same outcomes anyway (i.e., serious games are not the true cause of observed effects). Examples of similar findings were reported above with media effects research.

2. *Consider the development of interrelations.* Considering how serious games are involved in the developmental process also means taking into account reciprocal relationships between the use of serious games and intended outcomes over the course of time. Research on educational television, for example, has not only demonstrated the facilitative potential of educational programs but also confirmed the reverse direction (i.e., children with higher academic achievement scores subsequently tended to watch more educational television; Wright et al., 2001). Furthermore, the nature and direction of such interrelations might themselves underlie developmental changes. For instance, Ennemoser and Schneider (2007) pointed out that inhibitory effects of entertainment television on subsequent achievement were restricted to the younger one of two cohorts (last year of kindergarten at the outset of the study). For the older cohort (2nd graders), however, relations were not only less impressive, but the causal direction of effects turned out to be reversed (i.e., a hindering effect of television could not be confirmed in this age group). Instead, poor readers subsequently tended to watch more entertainment programs.

The two requirements described above raise the question of appropriate study designs. Of course, experimental research is irreplaceable to investigate and further optimize the potential of serious games. However, as illustrated by the examples above, a comprehensive investigation of serious games under a developmental perspective makes additional demands. Especially, it requires supplementing experimental evidence by externally more valid study designs, preferably longitudinal field studies, that focus on the (potentially interactive) interplay between serious games and development. An advantage of this supplement is that the resultant evidence should be less restricted to the mere impact serious games might have if they were "properly" implemented. In this regard, longitudinal studies will also provide a substantial contribution to the issue of intervention integrity (i.e., to the question of whether or not the effectiveness of serious games ranges beyond the scope of the laboratory).

Developmental Questions Require Developmental Research: Include Multiple Age Groups and Conduct Longitudinal Analyses

As mentioned above, developmental questions like that of varying effects for different age groups are often not addressed by related studies. Rather, a big part of the evidence stems from aggregated findings obtained within the framework of meta-analyses. However, researchers should take care not to rely exclusively on this source of evidence. Previous research on the impact of television on school achievement provides a prominent example of the (sometimes) questionable trustworthiness of meta-analytic findings.

Based on data obtained from more than 1 million students, Razel (2001) described the relationship between television and achievement as an inverted checkmark. That is, for small amounts of viewing, achievement increased with viewing, but as viewing increased beyond a certain point, achievement decreased rapidly. Although this function was found for each of the three age groups studied, optimal viewing times (the apex of the function) varied as a function of age. At age 9, 2 hours of television per day was associated with the best achievement scores, but, for older children, optimal viewing time gradually decreased. That is, with increasing age the inverted checkmark function successively turned into a nearly linear negative relationship.

The problem is that these findings are clearly contradicted by the results of well-controlled longitudinal studies that include multiple age cohorts and can be considered as methodologically outstanding in this field. Neither Ennemoser and Schneider (2007) nor Koolstra et al. (1997) found any evidence for the assumption of a curvilinear relationship in such a way that moderate viewing was associated with better achievement scores. In further contrast to Razel (2001), negative relations were not more pronounced in the older cohorts and (cross-sectional) relations did not increase over time. Most contradictory, Ennemoser and Schneider (2007) found that the amount of daily television in their younger group of German "heavy viewers" was precisely in the range of Razel's optimal viewing time for this age cohort[1] (i.e., this group should have performed best but actually demonstrated the lowest achievement scores). These findings are closely paralleled by the results of another well-controlled longitudinal study from the United States (Wright et al., 2001), and thus, cannot merely be explained by cultural differences in television viewing.

It should be noted that meta-analytical techniques represent an important and valuable research tool that is not called into question here in general. However, as illustrated by the examples above, there are more appropriate ways to investigate developmental questions within a given research field than leaving the answer to meta-analytical reviews. Concretely, this means addressing developmental questions directly by using appropriate study designs. One possibility to do this is to include multiple age cohorts (or groups that differ in age-related characteristics) in the same study. The most recommendable way, however, is to follow longitudinal research designs, which allow the researcher to investigate developmental trajectories directly.

A Framework for Serious Games Research

In the previous sections several shortcomings in two areas of related research were discussed with the objective of avoiding similar drawbacks in serious games research. Of course, there is a common arsenal of methodological strategies, already developed a few decades ago, to cope with (the majority of) these problems (e.g., Campbell & Stanley, 1966). However, despite decades of more or less extensive research activities in educational intervention and media effects research, the utilization of these strategies is still unsatisfactory. With regard to serious games research there are two important lessons to be learned out of this.

1. *The danger of naïve assumptions.* Research dealing with the potentials or effects of media has always been at the particular risk of being debased by poor theoretical conceptualizations (naïve assumptions), which in turn has led to poor research designs that are inappropriate to draw reliable conclusions. Considering the euphoric optimism concerning the potential of serious games, there is a danger that upcoming work in this field will inherit similar naïve assumptions. Thus, serious games research must go beyond postulating tremendous possibilities. That is, researchers have to elaborate carefully on assumptions about the potential of serious games and to generate testable hypotheses about underlying mechanisms and differential effects. Admittedly, first and foremost this is a conceptual rather than a methodological challenge. However, especially in the field of media effects research, a considerable portion of methodological shortcomings is primarily rooted in poor theory (e.g., Holbert & Stevenson, 2003).

2. *The need to establish a standard of scientifically credible research.* Current momentum in serious games research predominantly pushes the development and dissemination of serious games rather than troublesome theory-driven (evaluation) research. This may lead to the same situation as in educational intervention: a small amount of methodologically poor evaluation research that is certainly not suited to establish the evidence-based development of serious games as a standard. In contrast, serious games research needs to establish methodological standards, preferably at an early stage of research progress, in order to increase sensitivity to, and use of, scientifically credible research.

The following section suggests a possible framework for evaluation research in the field of serious games (see Figure 20.4). Methodological requirements are derived on the basis of some core research questions that have already been discussed above and will only briefly be summarized here. The suggested framework also includes considerations concerning the practical importance of effects as well as developmental questions.

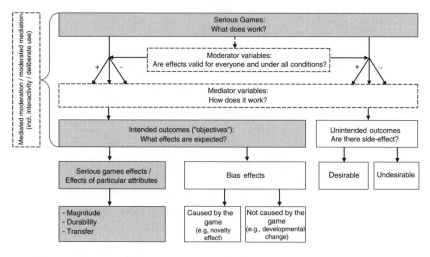

Figure 20.4 Evaluating the effects of a serious game.

Core Questions on Effectiveness: Does It Work?

Of course, one of the most important questions to be answered by serious games research is whether or not a program is effective with respect to its goals. Simply relying on the much-cited potential of serious games, we could decide to ignore the dashed boxes in Figure 20.4 (mediation and moderation) within our study design and investigate whether or not the serious game package is effective as a whole. That is, the validity of theoretical assumptions is either entirely neglected, or at least not addressed empirically. As described above, this horse race approach (Pressley & Harris, 1994) merely requires the inclusion of a control group that receives a competing conventional method.

Admittedly, such a verification of effectiveness may be considered valuable from a pragmatic point of view. However, with respect to the promotion of further developments it is surely not enough to demonstrate that it works. Shortcomings in media effects research highlight the need "to spend more effort on understanding how programs work" (Chen & Rossi, 1983). This requires taking into account all variables that are involved in the path from cause to effects, as illustrated in Figure 20.4. Following this path makes clear that there is not only one question to be answered (Does it work?), but there are actually six.

1. *What does work?* First, researchers must carefully elaborate on assumptions about the facilitative potential of serious games and identify particular attributes that should be beneficial. In this regard, it seems not exclusively, but especially important to investigate the relevance of those features that dis-

tinguish the serious games from conventional computer-aided learning tools and to demonstrate the supplementary gain that is provided by "playing" as opposed to "working at" it. That is, research has to thoroughly explain what exactly constitutes "the game factor" and to prove (or falsify) the assumed additional benefits of its components (e.g., game-specific features or interactivity). From a methodological point of view, an in-depth study of particular facilitative potentials requires the inclusion of multiple control conditions whereby the relevant attributes are systematically manipulated within the experimental design.

2. *How does it work?* The second requirement is to explicate the causal mechanism (i.e., to identify relevant mediator variables). Actually, this is done in the current literature more and more thoroughly (e.g., Klimmt, this volume, chapter 16). However, as argued in the sections above, it would be insufficient to make use of this theoretical progress simply by conducting horse races and explaining the results on the basis of this theory. Rather, it is essential to evaluate the validity of corresponding mediation hypotheses as well. In this regard, it is necessary to (a) assess the mediating variables that are involved by means of reliable and valid measures, and (b) to include these variables in appropriate statistical analyses to investigate whether or not gaming-induced growth (or decline) in these variables subsequently leads to the assumed changes in the outcome measures (Baron & Kenny, 1986; Preacher & Hayes, 2004). If one variable that is involved in the causal path is omitted (e.g., deliberate use—the increase of which is considered as a major strength of serious games), it will not be possible to draw reliable conclusions on the mediation hypothesis under consideration.

3. *Does it work for everybody under all conditions?* This third question may be helpful in explaining (or even avoiding) inconsistent findings. Elaborated theories about causal mechanisms offer the opportunity to derive hypotheses about plausible moderators that interact with particular attributes of the medium or cause nonlinear relations, respectively. Corresponding considerations have to be modeled within a framework of mediated moderation or moderated mediation. Involved variables must be assessed and the specified model has to be evaluated by the use of appropriate statistical procedures as suggested in the current literature (Bucy & Tao, 2007; Edwards & Lambert, 2007; Muller et al., 2005). An additional advantage of this approach is that the consideration of interactivity and deliberate use within such a framework largely (although not entirely) circumvents the problem of intervention integrity in serious games research.

4. *What are the expected effects?* Starting from the causes (What does work?) and further following the illustrated path in Figure 20.4 over the processes that are put in motion by them (moderation, mediation) finally leads us to one of the core questions that should actually be answered as one of the first: What effects do we expect? That is, the particular goals and intended outcomes of

a serious game have to be defined precisely in advance (Rossi, Lipsey, & Freeman, 2004). Examples of potential criteria are learning outcomes, attitudes, motivational aspects, the amount of voluntarily invested learning (or playing) activities, but also more economic considerations such as the cost-benefit ratio of the game. Further, sensitive, reliable and valid measures have to be chosen (or to be created) to assess these criterion variables.

5. *Are there unintended side-effects?* Unintended effects (see Figure 20.4) are not predominantly important for the basic question of effectiveness, but with respect to the "point balance" of an evaluation, they may have essential practical implications. For example, if excessively playing a serious game enhances learning outcomes in a particular domain, but at the same time takes learning efforts from other important subjects, the implementation of this program might be debatable. In general, unintended effects may be positive or negative and, though sometimes difficult to anticipate, are worth considering (Rossi et al., 2004; see also Ritterfeld, Cody, & Vorderer, this volume, chapter 1).

6. *Are there alternative explanations for observed effects?* As a matter of course, most attention is dedicated to the intended outcomes of a program. The challenge is to estimate the proportion of change in the outcome variables that can be attributed to serious gaming. This requires controlling for the ratio of changes in the outcome variables that are due to events or experiences *other* than the intervention program. As illustrated in Figure 20.4 we can distinguish between two sources of bias which might serve as alternative explanations for observed effects. The first one refers to changes that would have taken place even without any treatment. For example, natural maturational and developmental processes can produce considerable growth in learning outcomes, thus serious games effects may appear considerably larger than they really are.

The second subcategory comprises changes that are not caused by specific aspects of the particular serious game but by the mere fact that there has been an intervention at all (e.g., Hawthorne or placebo effects). Depending on the particular study design there are several well-established ways to deal with this problem. Experimental designs (laboratory experiment, randomized field experiment) partially permit researchers to disentangle different proportions of effect through the inclusion of appropriate control conditions. In study designs where it is not feasible to assign participants randomly to experimental conditions (quasi experiments), the possibilities to rule out alternative explanations for observed effects are limited. Most common approaches are the construction of equivalent control groups by matching procedures or the inclusion of statistical controls (for a more detailed discussion of this problem, see Rossi et al., 2004).

One source of bias that might be worth considering in more detail is the so-called novelty effect (cf. Clark & Sugrue, 1989) which poses a particular problem in the field of computer-assisted learning. Learning with a new medium or technology usually tends to increase the learner's interest, at least temporarily.

Thus, short-term performance gains may be attributed to a rapidly fading novelty effect rather than to particular features of the learning technology. There are several ways to deal with that problem. One possibility is to add intermediate assessments between pre- and posttests in order to determine if effects are limited to introductory sessions. Mediation analyses might be used to ascertain whether the introduction is followed by a decrease in motivational variables that subsequently leads to a decline in training gains. Further, we might provide two different content areas within the same game format and have two groups work on them in reversed order. If both groups outperform the other one in their first topic, respectively, this would indicate a novelty effect. If both groups outperform a third (alternative treatment) group in their second topic, we can conclude that the serious game is effective beyond novelty. Another way to investigate the novelty effect is to make individuals in a control group familiar with the game format in advance. This can be done by implementing an introductory (habituation) phase into the game which addresses content that is irrelevant for the intended outcomes. The effects of this supplemented version might be compared to those of the original game. In the worst case, benefits would completely vanish as a consequence of the habituation phase (i.e., gains could be entirely explained by the novelty effect). However, it seems to be a particular characteristic of serious games that researchers can always take a different perspective and turn a presumed problem into an advantage. Instead of treating novelty as a source of bias, it might be worthwhile recognizing and making use of its very potential (in the sense of being a mediator) by implementing regular changes in the game format that seem suited to produce the novelty effect.

The Practical Importance of Effects

In addition to the core questions discussed above, other questions about intervention effects are often neglected in serious games research discussions.

1. *Is the magnitude of effects important in practical terms?* A statistically significant effect is not necessarily practically important. For this reason, serious games research has to determine the magnitude of effects or of additional gains, respectively. This is usually done in terms of effect size that expresses the mean difference in outcome variables between an intervention and control group in standard deviation units.

2. *Are effects durable?* The magnitude of an effect is not the only criterion that matters in the evaluation of practical significance. As already pointed out by Belmont and Butterfield (1977), there is a need to ensure that the effects of an intervention do not fade immediately afterwards but persist for a certain period of time. This can be done by conducting follow-up assessments.

3. *Are there transfer effects as intended?* One further issue that is critical for serious games research is the question of transfer (e.g. Royer, 1979; Velada,

Caetano, Michel, Lyons, & Kavanagh, 2007). With transfer, the effects of an intervention generalize in two ways: First, observed effects are not limited to the particular task formats that were used during the intervention. Rather, they carry over to different tasks which require the same abilities. Second, acquired abilities are observable in situational contexts other than the intervention. For example, a serious game designed to promote prosocial attitudes and behavior is not very useful if positive effects do not generalize to other contexts besides those presented during the game, or even more importantly, to situations outside the game. In a broader sense, transfer means that what was learned during the intervention is actually beneficial under real-life conditions. With regard to serious games, it is a crucial question whether or not skills that were acquired by training in a digital game format really transfer to real life performance. Thus, maybe even more than in conventional intervention research, it is essential for serious games research to confirm the assumption of transfer. This entails including relevant but more distant outcome measures, and investigating whether or not effects really transfer to these variables.

Development

Many of the issues discussed above are more or less implicitly related to developmental questions; however, there are two further questions remaining.

1. *Does the serious game fit the developmental stages?* As argued above, serious games research has to consider that effects may vary as function of age-related variables. This problem can be addressed in two ways: (a) by the inclusion of different age groups (in the sense of a moderator), and (b) by taking developmentally changing needs into account in the particular serious games design (i.e. including an adaptivity feature for different age groups, or tailoring the game for the particular target group).

2. *How are serious games involved in the developmental process?* Uses and consequences of serious games may be interactively involved in the developmental process, at least in situational contexts where individuals are not assigned to make use of them (e.g., outside institutional settings or experimental studies). Such a view requires investigating the interplay with developmentally relevant third variables as well as (potentially changing) patterns of causal relationships over the course of time. This valuable supplement to experimental evidence is best provided by longitudinal field studies that allow for a direct assessment and, subsequently, for sophisticated statistical analyses of developmental changes.

The Bridge from Interactivity to Adaptivity

A systematic approach of conceptualizing serious games effects as a product of mediated moderation (or moderated mediation) should provide a better understanding of what individuals do during the game, how their (inter-) actions, emotions, or cognitions vary as a function of media attributes or third variables, and which consequences we can expect with regard to the intended outcomes. This understanding is exactly what we need to individualize a serious game in such a way that it meets the particular demands of an individual. From this standpoint, a comprehensive and theory-guided investigation of serious games effects seems to be a prerequisite for the evidence-based implementation of adaptivity features in serious games. For example, if we know that the optimal (i.e., the most beneficial) level of interactivity varies as a function of web expertise, we can provide the appropriate level for each participant, respectively.

How Can We Take Advantage of a More Sophisticated View of Interactivity with Regard to Adaptivity?

For the purpose of investigating the effectiveness of adaptivity, we might compare two versions of the same game (i.e., a nonadaptive original and a version that contains a carefully selected adaptivity feature). It might be expected that the nonadaptive condition will confirm available evidence about underlying mediation and moderation processes. The adaptive version, however, ought to reduce the overall moderation between serious game and outcome variables considerably. This process of homogenization must not take place at the cost of those individuals who would have done best in the nonadaptive version, but should benefit participants whose original scores are lower.

Considerations of appropriate adaptivity options are not necessarily restricted to single paths in the theoretical model. Rather, more complex approaches (after a good deal of corresponding research) might even utilize entirely different processes of mediation and moderation to produce the same outcomes for different individuals. To be precise, the same effects might be yielded by different attributes of the medium. Further, these effects might be mediated by different variables and undergo different moderation processes.

Conclusions

Colleagues reacted to preliminary versions of this chapter with the question: "Why do you derive conceptual and methodological challenges from other related fields, rather than directly from available serious games research?" The answer is that corresponding research in our field is just in its infancy and thus entirely unsuitable to illustrate the very point of this section. Most of the problems that were identified in this section are well known, some even border on common knowledge. Methodological as well as sophisticated statistical solutions are (for the most part) already at hand. But nevertheless, two prominent areas of research dealing with very similar topics have not succeeded in utilizing this knowledge over the course of several decades. That is, the challenge first and foremost is to successfully establish empirical standards at an early stage of the research progress. Therefore, a sound theory of what happens in between cause and effect is a necessary condition, and an elaborate conceptualization of moderation and mediation processes appears to be a useful approach to circumvent (or even capitalize on) some particular problems in the serious games arena discussed in this chapter. With regard to the practical implications, the resultant evidence from corresponding studies should be valuable for the utilization and further improvements of serious games. In this regard, the main object of research in the field should be not only to establish methodological standards, but also to establish evidence-based development of serious games as a standard.

Note

1. The moderate overall amount of television viewing was considerably below the American average in this age group, but representative for the German children sampled.

References

Arnold, D. H., Lonigan, C. J., Whitehurst, G. J., & Epstein, J. N. (1994). Accelerating language development through picture book reading: Replication and extension to a videotape-training format. *Journal of Educational Psychology, 86,* 235–243.

Baron, R. M., & Kenny, D. A. (1986). The moderator-mediator variable distinction in social psychological research: Conceptual, strategic, and statistical considerations. *Journal of Personality and Social Psychology, 51,* 1173–1182.

Beentjes, J. W. J., & van der Voort, T. H. A. (1988). Television's impact on children's reading skills: A review of research. *Reading Research Quarterly, 23,* 389–413.

Belmont, J. M., & Butterfield, E. C. (1977). The instructional approach to developmental cognitive research. In R. Kail & J. Hagen (Eds.), *Perspectives on the development of memory and cognition* (pp. 437–481). Hillsdale, NJ: Erlbaum.

Bryant, J., Alexander, A., & Brown, D. (1983). Learning from educational television programs. In M. J. A. Howe (Ed.), *Learning from television: Psychological and educational research* (pp. 1–30). London: Academic Press.

Bucy, E. P. (2004). The interactivity paradox: Closer to the news but confused. In E. P. Bucy & J. E. Newhagen (Eds.), *Media access: Social and psychological dimensions of new technology use* (pp. 47–72). Mahwah, NJ: Erlbaum.

Bucy, E. P., & Tao, C. (2007). The mediated moderation model of interactivity. *Media Psychology, 9*(3), 647–672.

Bus, A. G., van Ijzendoorn, M. H., & Pellegrini, A. D. (1995). Joint book reading makes for success in learning to read: A meta-analysis on intergenerational transmission of literacy. *Review of Educational Research, 65,* 1–21.

Campbell, D. T., & Stanley, J. C. (1966). *Experimental and quasi-experimental designs for research.* Chicago: Rand McNally.

Chen, H., & Rossi, P.H. (1983). Evaluating with sense: The theory-driven approach. *Evaluation Review, 7,* 283–302.

Clark, R. E. (1994). Media will never influence learning. *Educational Technology Research and Development, 42*(2), 21–29.

Clark, R. E., & Sugrue, B. M. (1989). Research on instructional media: 1978–1988. In D. Ely (Eds.), *Educational media and technology yearbook* (pp. 19–36). Denver, CO.: Libraries Unlimited.

Comstock, G., & Scharrer, E. (1999). *Television: What's on, who's watching, and what it means.* San Diego, CA: Academic Press.

Edwards, J. R., & Lambert, L. S. (2007). Methods for integrating moderation and mediation: A general analytical framework using moderated path analysis. *Psychological Methods, 12*, 1–22.

Ennemoser, M., Schiffer, K., Reinsch, C., & Schneider, W. (2003). Fernsehkonsum und die Entwicklung von Sprach- und Lesekompetenzen im frühen Grundschulalter: Eine empirische Überprüfung der SÖS-Mainstreaming-Hypothese [Television and the development of language and reading skills in elementary school: An empirical examination of the SES-mainstreaming hypothesis]. *Zeitschrift für Entwicklungspsychologie und Pädagogische Psychologie, 35*, 12–26.

Ennemoser, M., & Schneider, W. (2007). Relations of television viewing and reading development: Findings from a 4-year longitudinal study. *Journal of Educational Psychology, 99*, 349–368.

Fetler, M. (1984). Media effects on the young: Television viewing and school achievement. *Journal of Communication, 34*(2), 104–118.

Gadberry, S. (1980). Effects of restricting first graders' TV viewing on leisure time use, IQ change, and cognitive style. *Journal of Applied Developmental Psychology, 1*, 45–57.

Gresham, F. M., MacMillan, D., Beebe-Frankenberger, M. E., & Bocian, K. M. (2000). Treatment integrity in learning disabilities intervention research: Do we really know how treatments are implemented? *Learning Disabilities Research and Practice, 15*, 198–205.

Holbert, R. L., & Stephenson, M. T. (2003). The importance of indirect effects in media effects research: Testing for mediation in structural equation modeling. *Journal of Broadcasting & Electronic Media, 47*, 556–572.

Hornik, R. C. (1981). Out-of-school television and schooling: Hypotheses and methods. *Review of Educational Research, 51*, 193–214.

Hsieh, P., Acee, T., Chung, W., Hsieh, Y., Kim, H., Thomas, G. D., et al. (2005). Is educational intervention research on the decline? *Journal of Educational Psychology, 97*, 523–529.

Klimmt, C., Vorderer, P., & Ritterfeld, U. (2007). Interactivity and generalizability: New media, new challenges. *Communication Methods and Measures, 1*(3), 169–179.

Koolstra, C. M., van der Voort, T. H. A., & van der Kamp, L. J. T. (1997). Television's impact on children's reading comprehension and decoding skills: A 3-year panel study. *Reading Research Quarterly, 32*, 128–152.

Kozma, R. B. (1991). Learning with media. *Review of Educational Research, 61*, 179–211.

Kulik, C., & Kulik, J. A. (1991). Effectiveness of computer-based instruction: An updated analysis. *Computers in Human Behavior, 7*, 75–94.

Levin, J. R., & O'Donnell, A. M. (1999). What to do about educational research's credibility gaps? *Issues in Education, 5*(2), 177–230.

Linebarger, D. L., Kosanic, A. Z., Greenwood, C. R., & Doku, N. S. (2004). Effects of viewing the television program Between the Lions on the emergent literacy skills of young children. *Journal of Educational Psychology*, 96, 297–308.

Mayer, R. E. (2005). The failure of educational research to impact educational practice: Six obstacles to educational reform. In G. D. Phye, D. H., Robinson, & J. R. Levin (Eds.), *Empirical methods for evaluating educational interventions* (pp. 67–81). San Diego, CA: Academic Press.

McMillan, S. J., Hwang, J.-S., & Lee, G. (2003). Effects of structural and perceptual factors on attitudes toward the website. *Journal of Advertising Research*, 43, 400–409.

Meyer, L., Wardrop, J., Stahl, S., & Linn, R. (1994). Effects of reading storybooks aloud to children. *Journal of Educational Research*, 88, 69–85.

Morgan, M., & Gross, L. (1980). Television viewing, IQ and academic achievement. *Journal of Broadcasting*, 24, 117–133.

Muller, D., Judd, C. M., & Yzerbyt, V. Y. (2005). When moderation is mediated and mediation is moderated. *Journal of Personality and Social Psychology*, 89, 852–863.

Neuman, S. B. (1988). The displacement effect: Assessing the relation between television viewing and reading performance. *Reading Research Quarterly*, 23, 414–440.

Postman, N. (1984). *Amusing ourselves to death: Public discourse in the age of show business*. London: Heinemann.

Preacher, K. J., & Hayes, A.F. (2004). SPSS and SAS procedures for estimating indirect effects in simple mediation models. *Behavior Research Methods, Instruments, & Computers*, 36, 717–731.

Pressley, M., & Harris, K. R. (1994). Increasing the quality of educational intervention research. *Educational Psychology Review*, 6, 191–208.

Razel, M. (2001). The complex model of television viewing and educational achievement. *Journal of Educational Research*, 94, 371–379.

Rice, M. L., Huston, A. C., Truglio, R. T., & Wright, J. C. (1990). Words from Sesame Street: Learning vocabulary while viewing. *Developmental Psychology*, 26, 421–428.

Richter, T., Naumann, J., & Groeben, N. (2000). Attitudes toward the computer: Construct validation of an instrument with scales differentiated by content. *Computers in Human Behavior*, 16, 473–491.

Rohrbeck, C. A., Ginsburg-Block, M. D., Fantuzzo, J. W., & Miller, T. R. (2003). Peer-assisted learning interventions with elementary school students: A meta-analytic review. *Journal of Educational Psychology*, 95(2), 250–257.

Rosenshine, B., & Meister, C. (1994). Reciprocal teaching: A review of the research. *Review of Educational Research*, 64(4), 479–530.

Rossi, P. H., Lipsey, M. W., & Freeman, H. E. (2004). *Evaluation—A systematic approach* (7th ed.). Thousand Oaks: Sage.

Royer, J. M. (1979). Theories of the transfer of learning. *Educational Psychologist*, 14, 53–69.

Salomon, G. (1984). Television is "easy" and print is "tough": The differential investment of mental effort in learning as a function of perceptions and attributions. *Journal of Educational Psychology*, 76, 647–658.

Scarborough, H. S., & Dobrich, W. (1994). On the efficacy of reading to preschoolers. *Developmental Review*, 14, 245–302.

Schiffer, K., Ennemoser, M., & Schneider, W. (2002). Die Beziehung zwischen dem

Fernsehkonsum und der Entwicklung von Sprach- und Lesekompetenzen im Grundschulalter in Abhängigkeit von der Intelligenz [Relationships among television viewing, intelligence, and the development of language skills and reading competencies in elementary school children]. *Zeitschrift für Medienpsychologie, 14,* 2–13.

Shadish, W. R., Cook, T. D., & Campbell, D. T. (2002). *Experimental and quasi-experimental designs for generalized causal inference.* Boston: Houghton Mifflin.

Shavelson, R. J., & Towne, L. (2002). *Scientific research in education.* Washington, DC: National Academy Press.

Snyder, P., Thompson, B., McLean, M. E., & Smith, B. J. (2002). Examination of quantitative methods used in early intervention research: Linkages with recommended practices. *Journal of Early Intervention, 25,* 137–150.

Tremayne, M., & Dunwoody, S. (2001). Interactivity, information processing, and learning on the World Wide Web. *Science Communication, 23,* 111–134.

Velada, R., Caetano, A., Michel, J. D., Lyons, B. D., & Kavanagh, M. J. (2007). The effects of training design, individual characteristics and work environment on transfer of training. *International Journal of Training and Development, 11,* 282–294.

Whitehurst, G. J., Falco, F. L., Lonigan, C. J., Fischel, J. E., DeBaryshe, B. D., Valdez-Menchaca, et al. (1988). Accelerating language development through picture book reading. *Developmental Psychology, 24,* 552–559.

Wolery, M., & Garfinkel, A. N. (2002). Measuring in intervention research with young children who have autism. *Journal of Autism and Developmental Disorders, 32* 463–478.

Wong, W.L., Shen, C., Nocera, L., Tang, F., Bugga, S., Narayanan, H., et al. (2007, June). *Serious video games effectiveness.* Paper presented at the International Conference on Advances in Computer Entertainment Technology (ACE2007), Salzburg, Austria.

Wright, J. C., Huston, A. C., Murphy, C., St.Peters, M., Pinon, M., Scantlin, R. M., et al. (2001). The relations of early television viewing to school readiness and vocabulary of children from low-income families: The early window project. *Child Development, 72,* 1347–1366.

Chapter 21

Improving Methodology in Serious Games Research with Elaborated Theory

James H. Watt

Marco Ennemoser (this volume, chapter 20) makes a strong and well-reasoned critique of current research methodology in studying serious games. He calls for better assessment of game-playing outcomes, more consideration of the specific mediating processes by which serious games produce effects, and for introduction of variables that moderate the impacts of game playing on individuals into serious games effects theories. These are all trenchant critiques of current practice, and his calls for improvement in games research methodology are right on target. In this chapter, I will try to expand on some of these themes.

But before addressing some of the more central issues he raises, let us examine the term that delineates the discussion. *Serious games* is a label that causes some discomfort among both researchers and practitioners (Schuller, 2006). *Serious* seems at odds with play, and *play* is central to games. Usually, when someone refers to a serious game, they mean that they intend the outcome of the game to achieve a serious or important purpose, not that the play of the game is serious. This is not just semantic sophistry; it is an important distinction. The intended result of playing the game defines it as serious, not the act of playing the game. An alternative and more accurate label might be "games with a purpose." This identifier has been used before to describe Web 2.0 social games that accomplish computational purposes by using a game format (cf. Ahn, 2006). But the term more broadly describes games that stem from the tutorial, persuasive, or behavioral change motives of the game designer. However, in the remainder of this chapter, out of deference to common usage, I will use the common term *serious games* to refer to games with a purpose.

Goals of Games and Outcomes Assessment

It is precisely the fact that serious games have a purpose that makes them particularly amenable to scientific research and that strongly links research in serious games to educational assessment research. Ennemoser (this volume, chapter 20) uses this related literature to illustrate some of the shortfalls of methodology in the current state of serious game research. In both educational assessment and games research the goals of the activity or message are (or should be) known beforehand. In fact, the more clearly these goals are stated, the more definitive are the answers that research can provide.

But it is well-established that this initial stage of establishing testable goals is sometimes the most difficult stage of educational assessment (Hutchings, 1993; Watt, Drennen, Rodrigues, Menelly, & Wiegel, 1993). Until you can state very clearly the effect you wish to achieve with the educational intervention, be it in the form of a game or via another medium, you cannot formulate a research design that will get at the bedrock question: "Does it work?" (Watt et al., 1993)

This means that the first agenda item on the serious game researcher's agenda should be the articulation of the goals of the game. These cannot be abstract (e.g., "The game will produce good eating habits"), at least in their final form. Global and abstract goals must be further explicated and made concrete (Chaffee, 1991; Hage, 1972) and focused into a set of empirically observable outcomes (e.g., "The game will improve players' ability to accurately estimate the amount of fat in their diets"; "The game will decrease perceived attractiveness of junk foods"; etc.). With these more concrete goals defined, operational measures of game impact follow with only a little additional effort. It is a lot easier to find something when you know what you're looking for.

If the primary focus of the research study is simply a measurement of the efficacy of a game, a well-explicated set of goals and a valid and reliable operationalization of them is sufficient. These will provide the means to answer the "Did it work?" question, with a reasonably confident "yes" or "no" answer provided by statistics. But this is a very limited and purely pragmatic kind of research. It contains no information about why or how the game produced (or failed to produce) its desired outcome. It is only when one asks "How did it work?" as noted by Ennemoser (this volume, chapter 20), that one travels from outcomes assessment, which is essentially summative research focused on a single instance, to scientific research, which is essentially formative research that illuminates general principles across many instances (Scriven, 1996). Moving from outcomes assessment to scientific research requires development of good theory from which testable hypotheses can be drawn.

Naïve Assumptions and Intertwined Theory and Methodology

In projecting the errors of educational intervention research into investigations of serious games, Ennemoser states a fundamental and critically important truth: inadequate theory leads to inadequate methodology. He might have added "…and vice versa" to this statement. Theory and methodology in all scientific research are inextricable. Implicit in the question "How…" are theoretical mechanisms, and in the question "Why…" are theoretical explanations. Only good research methodology that is based on good theory provides adequate answers that establish the likely truth or falsity of the theoretical propositions.

As Ennemoser notes, this is the place at which naïve theoretical assumptions too often replace critical investigation. It is falsely comforting to think "everyone knows this" and for that reason, it's not necessary to verify a presumed fact or process. But common sense and common knowledge are often wrong, and only empirical observation will uncover this error (cf. Cacioppo, 2004; Locke & Latham, 1991).

A much-too-common naïve assumption in serious game research is a direct parallel to the hoary mass media effects assumption sometimes called the "hypodermic needle theory" or "magic bullet theory" of mass media effects (Severin & Tankard, 2001). In this theory, the mere presence of an assertion or exhortation in a message is sufficient to assume its effect on an audience. After all, it is common sense to assume that a message that advocates a particular action will persuade the audience that this action is the correct one, particularly when the message is delivered in a powerful medium like television or digital games. However, as many years of media research have shown, there are a stupendous number of "buts," "ifs," and "nots," attached to this commonsense view. There are so many, in fact, that the magic bullet theory, which was the generally accepted commonsense view of media effects in the early- to mid-20th century, is now commonly used as an example of naïve and simplistic thinking.

Yet the equivalent proposition is still a dominant theory of serious games effects. If a game contains facts or advocates attitudes, and the player is exposed to these messages either overtly or through subtle game mechanics, then the player must have been educated or persuaded. But like many commonsense propositions ("women are emotionally more fragile than men"; "older people won't play digital games"), naïve assumptions like this are quite often wrong. Correcting this global naivety is simple: conduct the research that either verifies or repudiates the assumption of desired effects. But such research can be expensive and time consuming, both of which are formidable barriers to actually finding out if a serious game works.

Games research is not the first area of study to be forced to address this problem. Fifteen years ago Human-Computer Interaction (HCI) researchers faced the dilemma of being increasingly marginalized in the software design process because their usability studies took too long, were too expensive, and used an experimental paradigm borrowed from cognitive psychology that focused too much on low-level and isolated perceptual and behavioral issues, rather than on the overall success of the design in achieving its pragmatic goal. The reaction within the HCI usability community was to adopt radical (and still somewhat controversial) changes to HCI usability research procedures that stressed smaller numbers of subjects, more qualitative and holistic measurements, simple measurements that returned results to the design process very quickly, and less controlled but more realistic field observations instead of laboratory studies (Nielsen, 1993). While these procedural shifts introduced some significant problems of their own, they have succeeded in embedding human usability assessment more firmly into the design process of software applications. Serious games researchers may need to engage in a similar discussion of ways that serious games research can be accomplished more rapidly and cheaply, so that reliance on the naïve assumption of game effectiveness is no longer justified by pragmatic concerns, and so that their research can be incorporated in game design at early stages of the process.

Ennemoser identifies another widespread and problematic error in games research that he calls the "naive assumption of media-specific effects." Invoking and inverting McLuhan (1963) he counsels, "The medium is not the message. Don't study media-specific effects." This is a pretty strong statement, and one that I must partially challenge. The assumption that the impact of content delivered by a new technology is somehow different from the same content delivered via an earlier medium is certainly arguable, but it is not absolutely wrong. (Perhaps Ennemoser is following the example of McLuhan himself in simplifying the situation to make his quite valid point more dramatically).

Read carefully, McLuhan's argument was not really captured in his theatrical statement "the medium is the message." A calmer reading of his theses can be paraphrased as "the medium itself produces *an* effect." Granted, McLuhan implies that the effect of the technology of communication is dominant over that of content, but years of research have produced many skeptics of this "technological determinism," and it has largely fallen out of favor. But this is not to say that research has completely debunked the idea that a communication technology itself can have a significant impact on its users.

It is interesting that McLuhan's original statement parallels very closely another dominant assumption about games of many commentators, politicians, and much of the lay public, namely that the game form itself produces effects that transcend, or at least amplify, the effects of the content of the game. There is some supporting evidence for the belief that at least part of the impact of technology is separate from the content of the medium, when one considers research with media other than games.

For example, there are results from computer-mediated communication (CMC) and human-computer interaction (HCI) research that support the idea of a communication technology's ability to modify the human-to-human communication process and change its outcomes. For example, in a study of Web advertising, Watt and Kimelfeld (2002) found that the widely accepted conventional advertising hierarchy of attitudinal and behavioral intention effects was much stronger during passive viewing when the Web site user had no real navigation alternatives and simply viewed a sequential set of Web pages than it was when the Web site user had to interact with the site to select a desired page. In this case, interactivity changed the nature of the persuasion process. Other examples involve changes in a medium's communication effectiveness according to the ability to provide social cues (Sproull & Kiesler, 1986), a rich sensory experience (Daft & Lengel, 1986), or synchronous feedback (Nowak, Watt, & Walther, 2005).

Probably the most pervasive, but as yet mostly unverified, assumption about the technological superiority of serious games over other media might be summarized in the statement "interaction intensifies effects." The engrossing nature of game interaction is presumed to magnify message effects or to produce new effects entirely. For example, Wartella and Jennings (2000) say "… the increased level of interactivity now possible with computer games and with the communication features of the Internet has heightened both the promise of greatly enriched learning and the concerns related to increased risk of harm."

This assumption of intensified effects due to interactivity is very evident in concerns about the effects of violent games, particularly by political or advocacy groups. For example, a June 2007 press release by the Campaign for a Commercial-Free Childhood (CCFC) has as its lead sentence "Citing concerns that harmful effects of ultra-violent video games on children will be magnified by playing them on the interactive Nintendo Wii system, the Campaign for a Commercial-Free Childhood (CCFC) is demanding that *Manhunt 2* (2007)—the most violent game available on Wii to date—be given an Adults Only rating by the Entertainment Software Rating Board (ESRB)." CCFC's cofounder, Dr. Susan Linn is quoted as saying "An Adults Only rating is the only way to limit children's exposure to this unique combination of horrific violence and interactivity" (CCFC, 2007). Clearly, there is an assumption that the particular kind of interactivity provided by the Wii controller will produce even stronger effects in players than the more traditional button-mashing controllers. While this may seem like a commonsense proposition, there is no evidence provided to support this assumption.

In fact, while the assumption of the power of interactivity in games has been repeated in various forms countless times, there is actually mixed evidence that interaction itself produces amplified impacts. For example, Wong et al. (2007) conducted a controlled experiment that held game content constant and manipulated interactivity. They concluded "(i)n contrast to the wide spread belief that interactivity is a crucial factor in media based learning, our findings cannot confirm this assumption" (p. 53). However, Tamborini and Skalski (2006) argue that interactivity produces a sense of presence that is likely to affect player experiences and outcomes, including learning.

Given the mixed evidence in the case of interactivity and other basic technological features of games, I would soften Ennemoser's entreaty to read, "Don't study medium-specific effects *exclusively or in isolation from other content factors*." The differential impact that game technologies can have on the effectiveness of serious games is one (but certainly not the only) important outstanding question about this medium. Further, the impacts of game technology may moderate effects of content. One might speculate that interactivity amplifies the impact of violence in games, but not of memory or learning processes. Research designs to investigate this speculation will necessarily involve presentation medium variables. As discussed below, it is probable that medium effects are not simple linear determinants of learning or persuasion outcomes, but interact with content variables to produce complex patterns of effects.

Research establishing the relative advantage of the game technology over alternative media in achieving the goals of a serious game is sorely needed, as Ennemoser states. Even a simple serious game can cost hundreds of thousands or millions of dollars to produce. If the game's success in producing learning or persuasion is no better than a book that costs one-tenth as much to produce, why would one bother with a game? Restated, the implied challenge to serious games researchers is to show with comparative research not only the effectiveness of particular serious games with well-designed outcomes assessments, but also to show the advantages that the game medium provides in achieving the goals.

Note that this kind of research implicitly tests the characteristics of the medium. If one contrasts the effectiveness of a game with that of the same content in another medium, the technological natures of both media are inextricably bound up in the comparison. One could argue that some capabilities of the games medium enabled by digital technology cannot be achieved in other media, so comparisons across media are inherently confounded. But this is precisely the point. The unique characteristics of games (e.g. interactivity, adaptation to the skill level of the player, discovery learning under the user's control) are exactly what are being contrasted with media that do not have these characteristics. If these technological features provide an advantage, then the case for the games medium is made. If they do not provide an observable advantage, then lower cost media are clearly preferred.

Expanding the Explanations of Serious Games Effects

A research agenda that establishes the technological advantages of serious games in producing the desired effects is essentially formative (Scriven, 1996). Formative research invokes the full scientific research paradigm in requiring a theory that explains as well as predicts. Outcomes assessment, which is an essentially summative research enterprise, simply predicts. While prediction is part of a full scientific approach, it is really a necessary, but not sufficient, condition of scientific explanation. The expansion of research perspective from prediction to explanation of the mechanism that produces the outcome illuminates general principles, and thus enables generalization of results to future game designs. But this requirement of a scientific theory is sometimes difficult to achieve.

Ennemoser's example of the competing explanations of television's effects on reading achievement clearly illustrates the problem of moving from prediction to explanation. He outlines several competing explanations of how television usage might have a negative impact on development of a child's reading abilities. A rock-ribbed pragmatist might ask, "Why should we care, as long as we can predict the effect." The answer is simple and compelling: If we wish to intervene in the process and produce the desired outcome, we need to understand the process involved in producing the effect. Using Ennemoser's example, if we want to improve reading abilities, and we know that more non-educational television use is associated with decreased reading abilities in older children, then simply reducing or eliminating noneducational television use should achieve this objective. But in a realistic situation, this may be impossible (ask a parent about this). Without knowing the actual process by which television use affects reading achievement, any attempt to use our predictive knowledge to affect the overall process by manipulating an intervening variable in the process is a shot in the dark.

For example, suppose one assumed that time displacement was the explanatory mechanism linking nonentertainment television use to lower reading achievement. If this was the case, counteracting television's negative effects on reading would be a matter of making more time available for reading from other activities (e.g., by eliminating activities like some organized sports and dancing classes from the child's schedule). This would make more time available for reading even if television usage remained constant, and thus should improve reading achievement. But Ennemoser's structural model indicates that time displacement is not the operational mechanism, so this attempt would fail, and might actually impair the child's development by eliminating other worthwhile activities. Understanding the intervening process opens the possibility of effectively manipulating intervening variables to achieve desirable goals. This calls for the elaboration of theories of serious games, as Ennemoser notes.

Elaborated Causal Theories

The process of elaborating theory that explains serious games' outcomes as well as predicting them takes us right into the heart of the problems of establishing causality in any scientific theory. At this point, it might be useful to review the general conditions for establishing a causal connection between two theoretical constructs or variables as these apply to the study of serious games.

Requirements of a Causal Relationship

There are four fundamental criteria for establishing a causal relationship between two theoretical constructs or variables: spatial contiguity, covariance, temporal order, and necessary connection (Watt & van den Berg, 1995).

Spatial Contiguity

The condition of spatial contiguity requires that the concepts must be connected "in the same time and space," as a system that rules out magical "effects at a distance" by requiring a physical connection between the cause and effect.

This condition is almost trivial in connection with social and behavioral research, as no researcher would present a theory in which, for example, the existence of a serious game is expected to produce an effect in a player who never actually is exposed to the game. We meet the condition of spatial contiguity when we specify the unit of analysis and require that both the causal construct and the effect construct be present in this same physical unit. For example, a hypothesized relationship between the time spent playing a serious game (the causal construct) and the amount of learning from the game (the effect construct) requires that both be present in the same physical brain— one can't relate the amount of playing time for Bob to the learning shown by Betty.

Covariance

The values of both the causal and effect variables must shift together in some systematic and predictable way, before we can say that they are causally related. This is the condition typically addressed by statistics. Covariance is a necessary, but not sufficient, condition for establishing causality. In outcomes assessment research that is focused on prediction rather than explanation, meeting the conditions of spatial contiguity and covariance are sufficient to establish the efficacy of the game. But scientific causality requires the presence of two additional conditions.

Temporal Ordering

Temporal ordering requires that a change in the variable which we call the cause must happen *before* the related change in the effect variable. It also requires that any modification of the effect variable must not be associated with change in the cause variable. Difficulty in establishing a temporal order in purely observational research like single time-point surveys is a consistent research problem. For example, does a high level of aggressiveness in adolescents lead to their playing more violent digital games, or does playing violent digital games lead to aggressiveness? To eliminate this difficulty, a researcher may use an experimental design in which the presumed causal variable is manipulated at a time preceding measurement of the presumed effect variable. There is no temporal ambiguity here, but controlled experiments often suffer from poorer external validity (Campbell & Stanley, 1963) than do observational studies, making generalization to actual game use conditions more problematic. In fact, Ennemoser emphasizes this issue as a major concern in serious games research.

Structural equation modeling (SEM), such as that presented by Ennemoser, can provide a test of plausibility of different temporal orders in observational research, but cannot unambiguously establish the time ordering. Temporal orders can be tested by simply reversing the cause and effect variables in the theoretical structural model, and comparing the predictions of the model to the actual observed data. This procedure is powerful and fairly simple to do with easy-to-use statistical analysis tools like AMOS. But it is quite possible for two models with contradictory temporal orders to be plausible. While SEM evidence is a much more persuasive than a simple assumption of temporal order, SEM is used much too infrequently in games research studies.

Necessary Connection

This is the most problematic condition of causality, and the one most controversial from the standpoint of classic philosophy of science (Hume, 1748/1957). The necessary connection is a statement which specifies how a change in the cause variable can bring about a covariant change in the effect variable. This statement gives a plausible explanation for the mechanism or procedure that connects the cause and effect. It is important to understand that the necessary connection is a verbal statement that describes an unobserved process that occurs between two observed variables. As such, it can never be directly tested because there is no measurement of the theoretical constructs involved in the process being described. The unobservability of the process has caused some philosophers of science, like Karl Pearson (1900), to reject it as a condition of causality. But such a rejection comes at a steep price.

One purpose of the necessary connection is elimination of spurious relationships that meet the other tests of causality, but in which the levels of the presumed cause and effect variables are actually determined by a third, unmeasured, variable. For example, there is the famous stock market "hemline index" (Pal, 2007). Changes in the length of women's hemlines precede corresponding changes in the stock market indexes. But there is no convincing mechanism that one could describe that directly links hemline changes to changes in financial markets, even though the other conditions of causality are met. If there was, economic prosperity could be achieved by convincing fashion designers that short skirts were de rigueur. But as Pal notes, both hemline and market changes are likely the result of changes in some third variable, possibly something like the general psychological state of optimism in a society. The lack of a good necessary connection rules out calling the length of hemlines the cause of market changes, even though the other conditions of causality are met.

Elaborating Necessary Connection into Testable Propositions

All causal statements have at least one expressed or implied necessary connection statement. But in some cases, the theoretical relationship has multiple competing necessary connection processes that are very different, but equally plausible. In this case, there is a clear need to extend empirical research to the intervening processes in order to understand what is happening in better detail. Ennemoser illustrates this step in his report of alternative mechanisms linking television usage and reading achievement. By defining the intervening process variables theoretically and operationally, competing processes can be critically tested against each other, as he shows in his example. The result is clearer understanding of how the initial cause construct and the final effect construct are mediated by the intervening process.

But we must recognize that explicating and measuring a concept like "time displacement" does not remove necessary connection among causal variables. In fact, it replaces one necessary connection with two. As an illustration, consider the original theoretical formulation:

$$(+)\text{TV Viewing} \rightarrow (-)\text{Reading Achievement}$$

Ennemoser then outlines several competing necessary connections that could explain how this effect is produced. One example is the displacement hypothesis: Time spent viewing TV replaces time spent reading, and that affects reading achievement negatively. Ennemoser then introduces the empirical variable (Time Spent Reading) necessary to move this statement from a necessary connection to an empirical test:

$$(+)\text{TV Viewing} \rightarrow (-)\text{Time Spent Reading} \rightarrow (-)\text{Reading Achievement}$$

Note that there are now two causal relationships, each of which has its own implied necessary connection. The first might be stated as "TV Viewing reduces time reading because children have a fixed time for voluntary activities in a fixed-sum manner" and the second as "More practice reading improves reading achievement." These are much less abstract and probably more generally accepted than the original necessary connection, so if evidence is found for this causal sequence, we can be more confident that we have, as Ennemoser suggests, "explained the mechanism."

Note that these more concrete statements of necessary connection are still assumed, not observed, processes, like all necessary connections. They can still be challenged. The first statement assumes that a fixed-sum time allocation occurs; it is quite possible that this is not correct. Further explication of the process to replace this necessary connection with empirical validation will introduce additional observed variables with causal links, and their own set of necessary connections in an infinite regress of growing complexity. As the necessary connections are expanded into empirical theoretical propositions, the theory becomes more complex, nuanced, and explanatory, assuming the propositions are supported by data.

But this example also illustrates a pragmatic limit to "explaining the mechanism." It is impossible to fully observe all possible intervening variables; these are infinite in number. But the process of further explicating and testing intervening processes in a controversial causal link is critical to advancement of theory in many areas of game studies. Let us look at one major example.

The educational value of most serious games depends on a presumed process of observational or participative learning. The details of this learning process are very important in understanding how both serious and entertainment games produce intended and unintended effects in players. For example, Anderson and colleagues contend that learning from violent digital game content is the critical process linking game exposure to subsequent aggression, and that this can be generalized into a learning model that applies to most serious games (Buckley & Anderson, 2006). As it stands, this learning model is a complex, but essentially untested, necessary connection statement. But the expansion of the learning model from a presumed process into a complex and empirically observable structure of causal statements would allow the games researcher to test the adequacy of Anderson's basic model.

There are certainly alternatives to the learning model of game effects as the necessary connection linking violent digital game exposure to effects on players. Some of these are outlined in Weber, Ritterfeld, and Kostygina (2006). Explicating these alternative intervening processes into testable propositions provides the basis for critical comparison of these mechanisms against the Anderson learning processes. This kind of critical comparison advances scientific explanation by requiring that competing theoretical views support their propositions with reproducible empirical data.

More Complexity: Moderating Variables, Interaction, and Other Nonlinearities

Ennemoser follows his call for explaining the detailed mechanisms of game effects with another very relevant, but very demanding, request: Investigate moderating variables in the effect process. Moderating variables are, in statistical terms, interaction components of two or more variables in which particular combinations of levels of the variables produce effects beyond the linear, proportional effect of either variable in isolation. For example, suppose a serious game to teach economic principles is presented to two randomly chosen groups of students. One group has minimal play time of 2 hours in two consecutive days; the other group has play time of 8 hours in 2 days. At the end of the second play period, each group is given a test of factual material presented in the game. The hypothesis is that increased exposure to the game produces increased learning. To further explore the learning process, we subdivide the groups before playing into two subgroups: one group is given a competitive challenge ("see if you can get the highest point score ever on a test to follow playing") while the other subgroup is not.

We thus have crossed two independent variables, each having two levels: time of play (low and high) by competitive incentive (present or none), producing four experimental groups. If we find that learning in the low-exposure no-incentive group is similar to learning in the high-exposure no-incentive group, while learning in the low-exposure incentive group is much lower than in the high-exposure incentive group, we conclude that an incentive moderates the time of exposure. In the absence of an incentive, time of playing has no effect. But in the presence of an incentive, time of playing does have an effect. This kind of nonlinear interaction is probably the rule, rather than the exception, in games research.

In simple examples like the above, there are statistical tools (primarily ANOVA) that are commonly available and easy to use. But when the models become more complex, as they will if we respond to Ennemoser's entreaty to incorporate intervening game effects mechanisms more explicitly into overall theories, advanced procedures and tools are needed. The procedures for testing hypotheses involving interactions and operational nonlinearities are certainly available (cf. Cohen, Cohen, West, & Aiken, 2003) but like structural model analysis, games researchers are frequently not trained in their use. Common statistical packages like SPSS do not provide easy-to-use tools that would facilitate this process, either. The result is the common and conventional reliance on simpler linear models of effects that partition effects of causal variables into independent and noninteracting components. Even structural modeling tools like LISREL and AMOS handle interactions only with some effort. This lack of tools inhibits development of sufficiently complex theories that adequately represent serious games processes.

The lack of analysis tools also impedes the methodological training of new games researchers. Most new PhD graduates have very little experience with nonlinear and interaction hypotheses. This impedes more powerful theoretical understanding of serious games. There is a clear need to improve both the analysis tools available to games researchers and to improve the training of games researchers in research methodologies that make use of these more powerful tools. Both of these needs are important challenges to the serious games research community.

Summary and Prescriptions

So what does all this mean for the study of serious games? Ennemoser makes a general appeal to establish standards of systematic scientific evaluation as a basic requirement of serious games research. While these standards really are not different from research standards in other areas of scientific inquiry, summarizing his critique and its implications (and adding my own) leads to the following prescriptions when applied to serious games research. This very general list is a combination of a call for best practices in research methodology, theory development, tool development, and educational reform for games researchers.

1. Develop detailed and well-explicated goals for any serious game under investigation. Use these to develop valid and reliable measures of goal achievement. Conduct comparative media research to establish the relative advantage of the games medium.
2. Don't rely on naïve assumptions of effect. Challenge these with empirical outcomes assessment. Support assertions of effect with data, not political positions.
3. Find ways to cut the cost and time lag of summative research so that research results are incorporated into the design cycle of serious games. It is more effective to guide games design than to simply evaluate an existing design. The current HealthGames Research initiative of the Robert Wood Johnson Foundation (Lieberman, 2007) to fund research into the principles of effective design of serious games is an excellent example of the growing realization of this fact.
4. Investigate "commonsense" assumptions about the basic characteristics that define computer game technology (like interactivity) that presumably make games more effective in teaching and persuasion. Use this research to justify (or not justify) serious games applications.
5. Improve the external validity of games research by studying the principles of game design with multiple methods that include observation, experimentation, and implementation of games to be investigated in realistic settings.
6. Possibly the most important prescription is to reform graduate curricula in games research so that students are educated in advanced analytical techniques like structural equation modeling, interaction analysis, and advanced mathematical modeling of game effects. The current lack of use of advanced statistical and mathematical tools in games research is likely the product of graduate educational curricula in academic departments like communication, psychology, and computer science that produce academic games researchers. The research methods curricula in these departments are typically restricted to courses covering only basic principles and methods, with novice researchers left to discover and teach themselves the more advanced techniques. This is a serious problem. Traditional research methodology is not going to be able to deal with the complexity of multiple nonlinear effects that serious games present.
7. Concurrent with educational reform, attention and resources need to be targeted at development of research tools that make investigation of complex nonlinear relationships much easier than the current generation of statistical packages do. The current packages are grounded in an essentially reductionist view of causality that focuses on the linear addition of simple, isolated effects. Complex phenomena like human reactions to games are a poor fit to this paradigm. It is much more likely that nonlinear relationships, which include moderating interaction effects and multiple

mediating variables, are the reality. Analysis tools need to mirror this reality.

All games research, and serious games research in particular, present very important and potentially illuminating problems for media researchers. These are as interesting as the problems presented to television researchers a generation ago. With the proper perspective and training in appropriate research skills, the current generation of researchers will be able to understand the potential of this medium and bend it toward serious purposes.

References

Ahn, L. v. (2006). Games with a purpose. *Computer, 39*(6), 92–94.

Buckley, K. E., & Anderson, C. A. (2006). A theoretical model of the effects and consequences of playing video games. In P. Vorderer & J. Bryant (Eds.), *Playing Video Games: Motives, responses, and consequences* (pp. 363–378). Mahwah, NJ: Erlbaum.

Cacioppo, J. T. (2004). Common sense, intuition, and theory in personality and aocial psychology. *Personality & Social Psychology Review, 8*(2), 114–122.

Campaign for a Commercial-Free Childhood (CCFC). (2007). *CCFC demands adults only rating for Manhunt 2*. Retrieved November 18, 2007, from http://www.commercialfreechildhood.org/pressreleases/manhunt2.htm

Campbell, D. T., & Stanley, J. C. (1963). *Experimental and quasi-experimental designs for research*. Chicago: Rand McNally.

Chaffee, S. H. (1991). *Explication (communication concepts)*. Newbury Park, CA: Sage.

Cohen, J., Cohen, P., West, S. G., & Aiken, L. S. (2003). *Applied multiple regression/correlation analysis for the behavioral sciences* (3rd ed.). Mahwah, NJ: Erlbaum.

Daft, R. L., & Lengel, R. H. (1986). Organizational information requirements, media richness and structural design. *Management Science, 32*, 554–571.

Hage, J. (1972). *Techniques and problems of theory construction in sociology*. New York: Wiley.

Hume, D. (1957). The idea of necessary connection (from an inquiry concerning human understanding). In M. Mandelbaum, F. W. Gramlich, & A. R. Anderson (Eds.), *Philosophic problems: An introductory book of readings* (pp. 68–75). New York: Macmillan. (Original work published 1748)

Hutchings, P. (1993). Principles of good practice for assessing student learning. *Assessment Update, 5*(1), 6–7.

Lieberman, D. (2007). *HealthGames research: Advancing effectiveness of interactive games for health*. Retrieved December 10, 2007, from http://www.healthgamesresearch.org/

Locke, E. A., & Latham, G. P. (1991). The fallacies of common sense "truths": A reply to Lamal. *Psychological Science, 2*(2), 131–132.

McLuhan, M. (1963). *Understanding media: The extensions of man*. New York: McGraw-Hill.

Manhunt 2. [Digital game]. (2007). New York: Rockstar Games (subsidiary of Take Two Interactive Software).

Nielsen, J. (1993). *Usability engineering*. Boston, MA: Academic Press.

Nowak, K. L., Watt, J., & Walther, J. B. (2005). The influence of synchrony and sensory modality on the person perception process in computer-mediated groups. *Journal of Computer-Mediated Communication, 10*(3), Article 3. Retrieved from http://jcmc.indiana.edu/vol10/issue3/nowak.html

Pal, M. (2007). Funny money. *Business Standard Online.* Retrieved November 25, 2007, from http://www.businessstandard.in/general/storypage.php?&autono=279571

Pearson, K. (1900). *The grammar of science* (2nd ed.). London: A. & C. Black.

Schuller, D. (2006). *C# game development.* Retrieved from http://einfall.blogspot.com/2006/08/irked-serious-games.html

Scriven, M. (1996). Types of evaluation and types of evaluator. *Evaluation Practice, 17*(2), 151–162.

Severin, W. J., & Tankard, J. W. (2001). *Communication theories: Origins, methods and uses in the mass media.* New York: Addison-Wesley.

Sproull, L., & Kiesler, S. (1986). Reducing social context cues: Electronic mail in organizational communication. *Management Science, 32,* 1492–1512.

Tamborini, R., & Skalski, P. (2006). The role of presence in the experience of electronic games. In P. Vorderer & J. Bryant (Eds.), *Playing video games: Motives, responses, and consequences* (pp. 225–240). Mahwah, NJ: Erlbaum.

Wartella, E. A., & Jennings, N. (2000). Children and computers: New technology—Old concerns. *Future of Children, 10,* 31–43.

Watt, J. H., Drennen, N., Rodrigues, R. J., Menelly, N., & Wiegel, E. (1993). Building assessment programs in large institutions. In T. W. Banta (Ed.), *Making a difference: Outcomes of a decade of assessment in higher education* (pp. 103–120). Jossey-Bass: San Francisco.

Watt, J. H., & Kimelfeld, Y. (2002). *Web advertising and the rear view mirror: Viewing an active medium with passive theory.* Troy, NY: Rensselaer Social and Behavioral Research Laboratory.

Watt, J. H., & van den Berg, S. (1995). *Research methods for communication science.* Boston: Allyn & Bacon.

Weber, R., Ritterfeld, U., & Kostygina, A. (2006). Aggression and violence as effects of playing violent video games? In P. Vorderer & J. Bryant (Eds.), *Playing video games: Motives, responses, and consequences.* Mahwah, NJ: Erlbaum.

Wong, W. L., Shen, C., Nocera, L., Carriazo, E., Tang, F., Bugga, S., et al. (2007). Serious video game effectiveness. In *Proceedings of the international conference on advances in computer entertainment technology* (Vol. 203, pp. 49–55). New York: ACM.

Chapter 22

Generalizability and Validity in Digital Game Research

Michael A. Shapiro and Jorge Peña

One goal of media research is to be able to say something beyond the particular circumstances of our studies—to be able to generalize. The notion of generalizability is inherently complex, depending on the goals of investigation as well as the social system of scholarship. Computer and console digital games present a number of challenges difficult to imagine when many of our extant approaches to generalizability and validity were conceived.

One challenge is the inherent difficulty of investigating extremely dynamic stimuli. While the basic nature and structure of a television or movie story has remained relatively stable for decades, the nature and structure of digital games changes far more rapidly. The difference between *Ozzie and Harriet* and *The Simple Life* is in many ways much smaller than the difference between *Pong* and *World of WarCraft* (*WoW*). Games are also dynamic in another way. As a player plays a particular game, the game interacts with the player's behavior so that events and other features can change with each playing. Indeed, the player usually becomes a character, rather than watching a character (see contributions in Vorderer & Bryant, 2006).

A second challenge is that players not only come to the games with widely varying skills, but the players themselves change as they gain experience with specific games and games in general (see, for example, Gee, this volume, chapter 5). How an adult might interpret a television program changes with maturity, but virtually all adults possess the basic skills to watch virtually any television show or movie. For digital games in complex online environments, a "newbie" often requires considerable instruction and support before he or she can truly enjoy the game.

In this chapter we will outline a view of generalizability, discuss in more detail some challenges to generalizability in doing digital game research, and suggest some future directions for generalizability and validity in game research.

What is Generalizability?

Our definition of generalizability is simple and follows the definition adopted by Lee and Baskerville (2003) that generalizability is the ability to say something beyond the particular. This definition is consciously broad compared to the common definition of external validity—the ability to generalize to particular target persons, settings, and times or across target persons, settings, and times (Cook & Campbell, 1979).[1] The most common manifestation of this definition of external validity focuses on statistical sampling from a population as the key to generalizability. Of course it is often important to estimate the value of some parameter(s) in some population(s)—the age distribution of game players in a population, the prevalence of sexual situations in the content of games, how many 11- to 14-year-olds access health Web sites at home—with the expectation that a parameter observed in some random sample from that population is likely to hold true for the entire target population of people. When estimating the actual value of a parameter in a population (or the equivalent across situations and settings) then a statistical approach to generalizability is essential. However, parameter estimation is not critical to every investigation of digital games, and focusing on a statistical definition of generalizability is problematic and may lead to lost opportunities for understanding digital game phenomena in at least a couple of ways.

One problem with the statistical definition of generalizability is that it tends to reify social categories as a cause of behavior (Berkowitz & Donnerstein, 1982), focusing on visible categories that can easily be counted such as sex, age, or ethnicity. For example, females and the elderly are typically not digital game players. A recent consumer survey indicated that 38% of U.S. digital game players were female, and only 2% of digital game players were over the age of 50 (Entertainment Software Association [ESA], 2006). But that probably has less to do with age and gender than with the socialization of the current generation of players and the paucity of games oriented to the needs and interests of these groups. For example, female characters in digital games are underrepresented and often sexualized in comparison to their male counterparts, and this may affect females' involvement with digital games (Dietz, 1998; Ivory, 2006). All of that is likely to change. The digital game industry is attempting to expand their consumer base to female users with more creative games (Gaudiosi, 2007), and almost certainly today's game players will continue to be interested throughout their lifespan and that will motivate the creation of games that reflect their changing interests and needs. It seems likely that today's teenage game players will be interested in some form of digital game when they are elderly, unless games are replaced by some newer form. Not only does focusing on visible categories rather than thinking about the underlying causes lead to the possibility of misunderstanding the current situation, but it may also lead us to unwarranted expectations about the future, both potentially larger problems of generalization than any here-and-now parameter estimate.

In addition, as Lee and Baskerville point out (2003): "this [statistical] notion of generalizability eliminates access to the insights that many information systems researchers offer in their research findings" (p. 222). Focusing on statistical generalizability privileges the set of procedures for estimating parameters in a population. While these procedures are valuable in many cases, a number of authors (Berkowitz & Donnerstein, 1982; Mook, 1983) maintain that understanding a social phenomenon and understanding human behavior is a better path to generalizability than describing its surface manifestations (for a review, see Shapiro, 2002). While some of these authors focus on the role of experiments in developing good theory, the same point can be made about a wide variety of kinds of observations and studies. A study contributes to generalizability if it leads, directly or indirectly, to an enhanced understanding of social phenomenon and human behavior. A case study that detects a phenomenon among game players can't be generalized in the statistical sense. From a case we don't know how widespread the phenomenon is. However, observing that phenomenon may contribute to generalizability in the long run by alerting us to something that current theory doesn't explain or to a possibility that hadn't previously occurred to us.

In the long run, what matters is our ability to explain the effect of social and psychological variables in the form of coherent theories. For example, at the psychological level our ability to explain the meaning people attach to situations and the behaviors people carry out is more important to generalizability than sample representativeness (Berkowitz & Donnerstein, 1982). If a case study leads to a new understanding of a phenomenon and advances theory, that case study contributes more to our ability to generalize than a statistically valid description that does not lead to such a new understanding. A similar case can be made for many other kinds of studies that may fall short of statistical generalizability but may contribute to our understanding of social phenomenon and contribute to the goodness of our theories and thus our broader ability to generalize.

Creativity also plays an important role in a broader definition of generalizability (Shapiro, 2007). From the small imaginative leaps that allow investigators to put forward normal science hypotheses confirming well-established theories, to the rarer, bold, original insight that allows us to look at an area in new ways, creativity plays an important role our ability to generalize.

Thus a broad definition of generalizability has a number of advantages. Rather than restricting the kinds of studies that confer generalizability, arguably any empirical study or program of empirical studies has the potential to say something beyond the particular—and thus add to generalizability.[2] This is particularly important in studies of digital games. The dynamic nature of gaming media challenges our methods and our ability to construct theories.

The Challenge of Digital Games

Until recently, most new communication technologies quickly became relatively stable in form, with most users in a culture at least minimally skilled in their use.[3] For example, while the content of movies and television can be more or less challenging, almost all viewers have the visual, aural, attentional, and intellectual skills to successfully and nearly effortlessly understand the vast majority of television shows and movies on at least a basic level. Viewers also learn the conventions required to discern commercials from movies, and movies from news (Gunter & McAleer, 1997; Kunkel, 2001; Van Evra, 1998). While there may be effects of the proliferation of cable channels, effects of improvements in video and audio fidelity, and effects of changing content (e.g., reality shows), there is little evidence that these changes or the skills of viewers challenge our fundamental ability to draw conclusions from our research about movies and television. While cable channels, the advent of high definition television, and content innovations may lead us to modify some media theories, it seems unlikely they will force us to fundamentally rethink many notions of media theory.

One cannot say the same about computer media in general or digital games in particular. Playing digital games represents a radically unstable stimulus in a number of ways. First, today's digital games are quite different from yesterday's games. A key difference is that digital game technology nowadays has better bandwidth (improved graphics and sounds) compared to the games examined in previous studies. Over the years, the digital game industry has developed newer digital game hardware capable of drawing more and more detailed polygons on a screen, augmenting their capability to deliver more realistic and lifelike graphics (Williams, 2002). Also, the music and sound effects of digital games now approaches the quality of the best film and television material, thus providing aural cues to players about in-game events and moods and enhancing psychological feelings of immersion into the game (Zehnder & Lipscomb, 2006).

This fact has inspired numerous researchers to hypothesize how increases in digital games' audiovisual bandwidth affects the findings uncovered in older studies employing earlier digital game technologies. In response, many researchers tend to generalize the effects uncovered yesterday (and augment them) to today's social and technological landscape. For instance, Funk and Buchman (1996, p. 20), argued that digital games of the 1990s were much more realistic and often more violent than their predecessors, and these characteristics enhance the negative effects of violent digital games. Along these lines, Tamborini and Skalski (2006) hypothesize that the effects of current digital games may be larger than the impacts uncovered by earlier studies, since new games are more vivid and interactive. Indeed, early studies examined games with crude graphics to depict actions (e.g., dots, lines, boxes) to test their hypotheses, while recent studies use graphically realistic digital games with anthropomorphic characters (Sherry, 2001, p. 414).

Thus, explicitly or not, many digital game researchers agree that an increase in the medium's audiovisual capabilities is not trivial. Increased bandwidth should affect players' cognitive, emotional, and behavioral responses more powerfully than earlier and cruder digital games. Some research supports this claim. In an empirical review, for example, Sherry (2001) found that older digital game studies have smaller effect sizes than newer studies, and hypothesized that aggressive outcomes have increased perhaps due to the more active, arousing, and graphic nature of newer games. Digital games' enhanced bandwidth has been linked to enhanced feelings of *presence* or "being there" among users (e.g., Eastin, 2006), which facilitates not only more involvement and immersion in the game, but also enhanced feelings of self and partner presence within gaming contexts where people employ virtual "bodies" or avatars (e.g., *The Sims 2; EverQuest;* Tamborini & Skalski, 2006).

Other aspects of digital games have changed as well. *Pong* was at best an analogy of table tennis with only one dimension of control (up-down). On the other hand, *WoW* is a combination of a complex role playing game, such as *Dungeons and Dragons* (1974), and a real-time costume party in which players can interact in multiple ways including collaborate, chat, exchange virtual goods, specialize in a profession, fight, and take part in other activities that mirror real life—including a funeral (to our knowledge pregnancy and birth does not take place in *WoW,* but does in *The Sims 2,* 2004). Pretty much any human behavior can be mimicked in contemporary digital games.

The future is likely to produce even more significant changes in digital game technology—many of them impossible to anticipate. For example, Nintendo stormed the market by introducing a console with a controller that acts as a remote controller, band, baton, or sword (Gaudiosi, 2007). This highlights the haptic experience of digital games and makes the user–console interface more transparent, as the swinging movements of the controller are mirrored within the games.

The dynamic nature of digital games makes it unwise to place all of our trust in media effects models (Bryant & Zillmann, 2002) or any framework that depends on the relative stability of its object of study. Such models tend to inspire relatively deterministic hypotheses that favor progressively finer, feature-at-a-time evaluations of technology, and its effects that may yield no clear-cut pattern of outcomes (DeSanctis & Poole, 1994). Traditional effects studies are a solid contribution to our understanding of digital games, and play an important role in expanding the generalizability of our knowledge. And yet the dynamic nature of digital game research challenges us to consider a variety of other ways of developing knowledge in this area.

Interactivity and Duct Tape on Mars

Perhaps the most radical difference between digital games and traditional forms of entertainment media is the control and interactivity afforded by digital games (Grodal, 2000). Digital games, as with other computer programs, are essentially interactive technologies that require active engagement of a user who negotiates processes and achieves goals (Rafaeli, 1988; Salomon, 1990; Tamborini & Skalski, 2006; provide more detailed discussions about interactivity). The interactive relationship between users and technology is often overlooked in effects digital game research.

One aspect of this relationship between the technology and the user is the ability of the user to change the stimulus itself. For example, when *Doom 3* was introduced in 2004, the enhanced audiovisual experience was very immersive and scarier than earlier versions. The dimly lit Martian environment in 2145 was filled with monsters, ambient music, noises, whispers, and maniacal laughter. To enhance fear, designers arranged the game so players could not illuminate and shoot at the same time. Weapons did not have a flashlight attached and there was no way to do so. A technically proficient player developed and released a modification or "mod" (Lowood, 2006) of *Doom 3* that allows players to attach a flashlight to their machine guns (http://ducttape.glenmurphy. com/). Although video editing programs have become more common, few if any viewers spend time altering the props in their favorite television show.

Digital game "modding," that is, modification of games in new, original, and unanticipated ways by players, suggests a new way of looking at interactions with media. Salomon (1990) suggests there might two distinguishable and complementary aspects of the effect of computer technologies. One aspect is the psychological influences of the technology over the user (e.g., higher visual acuity, aggression, learning), which has received the most attention. Salomon (1990) calls these the *effects of computer technology*. Modding is more like the second aspect "effects with"—how technologies may allow people to carry on activities they could not undertake before using a medium. Such activities include planning, writing, designing, or communicating with computer software.

Modifying existing games is common among experienced players, ranging from relatively minor modifications, like the addition of duct tape, to enabling new abilities, to more significant modifications such as building new scenarios and constructing what amounts to new versions of the game (e.g., *Counter-Strike*). These observations suggest a range of human behaviors that now must become part of our theories of digital games. This may include why and how people bother to modify digital games such as *Doom* (Lowood, 2006). Perhaps some modders have a high need for achievement (McClelland, Atkinson, Clark, & Lowell, 1953), think modding is fun, and possess high levels of intrinsic motivation (Parker & Lepper, 1992), or perhaps they are high in need for cognition (Cacioppo, Petty, & Kao, 1984).

Among other factors, current technological advances and the imaginations of both designers and players make digital games a dynamic object of study. While there is a role for traditional effects studies, they don't fully capture this complexity. The need to enhance the generalizability of gaming research requires considering a variety of established theoretical and methodological approaches.

Undoubtedly, many approaches to the issue of producing generalizable knowledge in such a dynamic environment are useful. We discuss two in detail below because they strike us as having considerable merit and are well established in the communication literature. One is to focus on human cognition, behavior, and emotion while playing games and not on the features of the technology itself. The advantage of this approach is that it both draws on and builds theory in multiple areas of communication that may or may not involve games. We illustrate that approach by using the research on games and social relationships in online digital games. For the second approach we draw on the attempts in organizational communication to model dynamic processes to suggest that dynamic modeling during game play may be a productive way to look at digital games.

Gaming and Relationships

Recently, investigators have examined how people communicate and form social relations through digital games. Most of this research focuses on how this occurs in online digital games (see Axelsson & Regan, 2006; Chan & Vorderer, 2006) that constitute virtual worlds, allowing for synchronous or real-time interactions between geographically dispersed users. Examples of this include multiuser dungeons (MUDs), persistent virtual worlds such as *WoW*, *EverQuest*, or simpler "shooter" online games in which players are allowed extended interaction time.

A main finding of these studies is that online digital games offer new social contexts and opportunities for relationship formation and informal sociability (e.g., Parks & Roberts, 1998; Steinkuehler & Williams, 2006). For example, an early study indicates that most participants who used a MUD-like text game formed personal relationships with other users, including close friendships, acquaintanceships, and romantic relations (Parks & Roberts, 1998). The time users employed networked computer technology strongly predicted online relationship formation. Simply put, those who spend more time employing networked computer technologies meet and befriend other online users (Parks & Floyd, 1996).

Recent studies seem to confirm that networked digital games are extraordinarily social under certain conditions. Among MUD players, the use of paralanguage such as emoticons (:-), ^_^) increases over time in text communications, and, as users learn to employ such conventions, they also develop relationships (Utz, 2000). Sociability among online players has been linked to spending more time playing (Parks & Floyd, 1996) and to how players write messages. For instance, a recent content analysis of players' text messages in an online multiplayer game showed that despite the game's aggressive goals (i.e., kill others for points), players communicated mostly with positive socioemotional messages (i.e., verbalizations of laughter, greetings, jokes) instead of negative socioemotional messages (i.e., insults, disapproval) (Peña & Hancock, 2006). Players who spent more time in the game expressed more positive and less negative socioemotional messages and, congruently with Utz (2000), employed more contextual language conventions (Peña & Hancock, 2006). Finally, a survey of *EverQuest* players indicated that half of the players believed their gaming relationships were comparable to their real-life relationships, and that players engaged in short-term (i.e., players banding together to tackle tougher objectives, such as killing a Dragon) and longer-term online group dynamics (i.e., creating or joining a player "clan"; Yee, 2001).

Why are online games so social? One possibility is that certain kinds of people are sociable players. For instance, some researchers have linked personality traits to the motivation to play digital games in general (Hartmann & Klimmt, 2006), and social outcomes in online gaming in particular. More specifically, Yee (2001) found that players who feel that their *EverQuest* relations were better than their real-life relations scored lower on extraversion and higher on neuroticism. Also, players who were less skeptical about the possibility of making friends in MUDs made more friends (Utz, 2000).

However, these dispositional explanations do not consider situational variables such as the built-in sociability aspects of some games (e.g., *WoW*), and how repeated encounters among online game players fosters sociability even in games that had not been optimized for social interactions, including highly competitive and aggressive games (e.g., *Quake, Doom*). Some games have been "socially engineered" to support relation formation among players. Examples of this include Multiuser Object Oriented dungeons (MOOs) (Curtis, 1997; Parks & Roberts, 1998), and the newer *EverQuest, WoW*, and *Second Life*. But social engineering is not all there is to gaming sociability. Field studies report social developments among players of games that are far less optimized for social interaction than *WOW or EverQuest*, such as shooters and role-playing games (Peña & Hancock, 2006; Williams & Skoric, 2005). Furthermore, building sociability into a game may backfire. For instance, a frequent complaint on Internet game player forums is how *EverQuest* was designed to force players to band to survive and achieve goals, instead of allowing players to "solo" or do things on their own.

A more established explanation stems from social information processing (SIP) theory (Walther, 1992, 1996; Walther & Parks, 2002). Social information processing has been frequently invoked as an explanatory mechanism for the findings in gaming and sociability research (see Parks & Floyd, 1996; Parks & Roberts, 1998; Peña & Hancock, 2006; Utz, 2000; Yee, 2001). Social information processing theory states that people are motivated to reduce uncertainty in computer-mediated contexts lacking in social cues. Examples of this lack of cues include geographically distributed interactions, anonymity, and lack of individuating cues such as physical appearance—all of which are conditions that normally apply to online gaming. Social information processing theory states that people employ the content and the form of messages to develop and test impressions of others and thus reduce partner uncertainty under these conditions. Over time, this fosters more refined interpersonal knowledge, and may prompt a shift from impersonal to interpersonal relations (Walther, 1992, 1996). From this standpoint, relation-formation among online game players is facilitated by people's uncertainty about partners and repeated within-game encounters, even in games with little optimization for sociability (Peña & Hancock, 2006).

Games as a Process

For decades modern media researchers have recognized that messages are not things with fixed meanings and effects (Bauer, 1971; Dervin, 1981). Processing any message in any medium is a dynamic process, even if we focus only on one user. That user must choose a medium, process the stimulus (sometimes making important choices, such as which article to read in a newspaper), and bring to bear a variety of abilities and experiences in choosing messages and constructing the meaning of that message. This becomes an even more dynamic process as social, cultural, and institutional factors are added.

Much research on media uses techniques that fix variables across instances in some way, including survey methods and experiments. For example, a typical media experiment manipulates a variable of interest in order to see what outcome that produces in another set of variables of interest. Like snapshots, assembling sets of such studies is a time-tested way of producing a model or theory of the processes involved. In addition, techniques such as time-series analysis and longitudinal studies use observations over relatively long periods of time to capture one dynamic aspect of how people used media.

More recently, some investigators have attempted to capture change as it occurs. At the psychological level Lang's limited capacity model (Lang, 2000; Lang, Chung, Lee, Schwartz, & Shin, 2005) is built on the notion that when the structure of a message controls how it is processed, such as television messages, it is important to look at the trade-offs that occur when viewers must simultaneously process the form and structure of a message. To do that Lang and her colleagues use traditional experimental manipulations as well as continuous psychophysiological measures of attention, arousal, and valenced response. This has produced a rich set of results about how messages are processed and remembered aimed at a more dynamic model of message processing. Observing digital game players in this way, Lang and her colleagues found that while playing *Quake* physiological arousal increased over game playing for the fighting phases of the game and decreased for the hunting sequences, although there are differences between men and women (Lang, Schneider, & Deitz, 1999). These investigators also found that digital game narratives influence emotional responses while playing (Schneider, Lang, Shin, & Bradley, 2004).

Organizational communication has also used process models to explain why people develop uses of technology not intended by designers. In particular, adaptive structuration theory (AST) (DeSanctis & Poole, 1994) is concerned with explaining technology's role in organizational change. Adaptation structuration theory recognizes that technologies do provide social structures by offering rules and bundled capabilities (e.g., recording of ideas, e-voting, etc.) and a spirit, or the goals and underlying values of the technology (e.g., to promote efficiency and rational consensus). Other sources of structure for people's actions are the purpose of interaction (e.g., task or play), environmental contingencies, and norms that emerge in social interactions. In this context, structuration refers to people applying and re-creating the influence of the bundled features and spirit of a technology (e.g., a group striving for efficiency). Critically, users also appropriate a technology when they decide to use or not use, blend, mix, or replace structural and spiritual features of a technology. People's appropriations can have faithful or unfaithful natures, depending on whether an appropriation upholds or not the spirit of a technology. Finally, other factors influencing appropriation of the structure provided by technology are users' interaction styles, experience with the structural and spiritual dimensions of technology, in situ values and attitudes, and people's agreement with appropriating technology in a given way (DeSanctis & Poole, 1994). Methodologically, AST emphasizes the study of the interaction process, including microlevel and temporal analyses of sentences, communication sequences, documents, and speeches to look for instances of structuration and appropriation.

Adaptation structuration theory seems applicable to digital game research. For example, although *Doom* has been primarily linked to aggressive effects (e.g., Uhlmann & Swanson, 2004), as a piece of software it can be characterized as having a modification-friendly spirit, with bundled or downloadable editing capacities for users to create and modify content (Lowood, 2006). As such, the "duct-tape mod" described above appears to be a faithful appropriation of technology, as it embraces the history and potential for modification embedded in *Doom* as a software. But people's agreement on the duct-tape mod's faithfulness has been disputed. Some users argue that the mod takes away from the game, since having a flashlight attached to a weapon does not allow for those milliseconds of terror occurring when people spot a monster and switch from flashlight to weapon (e.g., http://www.idlethumbs.net/display.php?id=43.).

In gaming contexts, AST highlights how users' actions negotiate between the appropriation of the designers' spirit (i.e., darkness enhances *Doom 3*'s fun) and the views of proficient users (i.e., duct tape now exists and will continue to exist in the future). Also, the methodological tools applied to digital game studies, which usually include experiments, surveys, interviews, and covert and participant observations (for reviews see Lee & Peng, 2006; Subrahmanyam, Kraut, Greenfield, & Gross, 2001) can be complemented by analyses emphasizing the gaming process. For example, AST's focus on microlevel and longitudinal analyses of conversations and other behavioral records may illuminate what people do as they appropriate digital game technologies, and how this unfolds over time. For example, an analysis of online game players' text transcripts suggests that digital games intended for violence and competition were instead appropriated as a forum for social communication (Peña & Hancock, 2006; see also Steinkuehler & Williams, 2006).

Conclusions

Digital games are one of many new entertainment and learning technologies that challenge the ways in which investigators try to go beyond specific observations, studies, and sets of studies to build a picture of human behavior with these technologies. We have outlined a broad view of generalizability that accepts but goes beyond surface similarities and statistical procedures to try and capture the multiple and complex ways that investigators can use to accumulate knowledge about human behavior. The particular challenges of computer and console game research is to develop methods, models, and theories that capture a stimulus that seems to (1) change fairly dramatically every few years, and (2) invites the user to interactively complete game objectives, sometimes even allowing users to create gaming content. We suggested two ways for research to capture the complexity of games—focusing on common human behaviors while playing games and developing techniques for conceptualizing the process of game playing.

We have identified two ways in which digital games in particular challenge our ability to generalize and suggested some strategies for coping with those complexities. Our aim in doing this is to start a conversation rather than exhausting the subject. It is worthwhile to point out that all communication is a complex process. New technologies, in which the characteristics discussed here are perhaps more salient, should sensitize us to these aspects of traditional media. Television viewers may not be participants in the program, but the mental processes that enable understanding of plot, character, causality, and other aspects of the program are dynamic and complex. Procedures that are developed to assess digital games and other interactive technologies may also be profitably applied to older media. A main benefit of this is that digital game researchers may someday strongly contribute to the discussion in their main disciplines with cutting edge models and methods.

Generalizability is not a function of any one technique, any one study or any one investigator. Rather, issues of generalizability at the broad level defined here are a function of a complex discourse among scholars in an area of investigation (Kvale, 2002; McGrath & Brinberg, 1983; Mook, 1983; Shapiro, 2002). We hope we have started a conversation in this particular area of inquiry.

Notes

1. Some communication scholars have added the ability to generalize to messages as well as across messages (Jackson, 1992; Reeves & Geiger, 1994).
2. We define *empirical* here in the broad sense as any study based on systematic observation. This would include, but is not limited to, experiments, surveys, quasi-experiments, field observation, participant observer studies, interviews, ethnomethodology, and studies guided by grounded theory. We exclude from the scope of this paper studies based exclusively on rhetorical, literary, or cultural analysis because these represent a complex set of concerns that are beyond the scope of this article and beyond the capabilities and expertise of the authors.

3. Obviously it is possible to radically experiment with the form. But the vast majority of stories told in movies and television are basically chronological with well-established deviations from that form (flashbacks, fantasy segments) that are easily understood by the vast majority of adult viewers. Of course viewers construct a variety of meanings from the same stimulus, and some stories are more open to varied interpretation than others. While relevant to our consideration of games, the meaning of all messages is constructed and thus this is not a special problem of any communication technology.

References

Axelsson, A. S., & Regan, T. (2006). Playing online. In P. Vorderer & J. Bryant (Eds.), *Playing video games: Motives, responses, and consequences* (pp. 291–306). Mahwah, NJ: Erlbaum.

Bauer, R. A. (1971). The obstinate audience. In W. Schramm & D. F. Roberts (Eds.), *The process and effects of mass communication* (pp. 326–346). Urbana: University of Illinois Press.

Berkowitz, L., & Donnerstein, E. (1982). External validity is more than skin deep: Some answers to criticisms of laboratory experiments. *American Psychologist, 37*(3), 245–257.

Blizzard Entertainment. [Computer software]. (2004). World of warcraft Los Angeles: Vivendi games.

Bryant, J., & Zillmann, D. (2002). *Media effects: Advances in theory and research.* Mahwah, NJ: Erlbaum.

Cacioppo, J. T., Petty, R. E., & Kao, C. F. (1984). The efficient assessment of need for cognition. *Journal of Personality Assessment, 48*(3), 306–307.

Chan, E., & Vorderer, P. (2006). Massively multiplayer online games. In P. Vorderer & J. Bryant (Eds.), *Playing video games: Motives, responses, and consequences* (pp. 77–88). Mahwah, NJ: Erlbaum.

Cook, T. D., & Campbell, D. T. (1979). *Quasi-experimentation design and analysis for field settings.* Boston: Houghton Mifflin.

Counter-Strike [Digital game]. (2000). Valve Software. Los Angeles, CA: Vivendi games.

Curtis, P. (1997). Mudding: Social phenomena in text-based virtual realities. In S. Kiesler (Ed.), *Culture of the Internet* (pp. 121–142). Mahwah, NJ: Erlbaum.

Dervin, B. (1981). Mass communicating: Changing conceptions of the audience. In R. E. Rice & W. J. Paisley (Eds.), *Public communication campaigns* (pp. 71–87). Beverly Hills, CA: Sage.

DeSanctis, G., & Poole, M. S. (1994). Capturing the complexity in advanced technology use: Adaptive structuration theory. *Organization Science, 5*(2), 121–147.

Dietz, T. L. (1998). An examination of violence and gender role portrayals in video games: Implications for gender socialization and aggressive behavior. *Sex Roles, 38,* 425–442.

Doom 3 [Digital game]. (2004). id Software. Mesquite, TX: Activision.

Dungeons & Dragons [Digital game]. (1974). Gigax, G., & Arneson, D. Lake Geneva, WI: Tactical Studies Rules.

Eastin, M. S. (2006). Video game violence and the female game player: Self- and opponent gender effects on presence and aggressive thoughts. *Human Communication Research, 32*(3), 351–372.

Entertainment Software Association (ESA). (2006). *Essential facts about the computer and video game industry.* Retrieved March 20, 2007, from http://www.theesa.com/archives/files/Essential%20Facts%202006.pdf

EverQuest [Digital game]. (1999). San Diego, CA: Sony Online Entertainment.

Funk, J. B., & Buchman, D. D. (1996). Playing violent video and computer games and adolescent self-concept. *Journal of Communication, 46*(2), 19–32.

Gaudiosi, J. (2007). *How the Wii is creaming the competition.* Retrieved April 24, 2007, from http://money.cnn.com/magazines/business2/business2_archive/2007/05/01/8405654/index.htm

Grodal, T. (2000). Video games and the pleasures of control. In D. Zillmann & P. Vorderer (Eds.), *Media entertainment: The psychology of its appeal* (pp. 197–213). Mahwah, NJ: Erlbaum.

Gunter, B., & McAleer, J. (1997). *Children and television* (2nd ed.). New York: Routledge.

Hartmann, T., & Klimmt, C. (2006). The influence of personality factors on computer game choice. In P. Vorderer & J. Bryant (Eds.), *Playing video games: Motives, responses, and consequences* (pp. 133–145). Mahwah: Erlbaum.

Ivory, J. D. (2006). Still a man's game: Gender representation in online reviews of video games. *Mass Communication & Society, 9*(1), 103–114.

Jackson, S. (1992). *Message effects research: Principles of design and analysis.* New York: Guilford Press.

Kunkel, D. (2001). Children and television advertising. In D. G. Singer & J. L. Singer (Eds.), *Handbook of children and the media* (pp. 375–393). Thousand Oaks, CA: Sage.

Kvale, S. (2002). The social construction of validity. In N. K. Denzin & Y. S. Lincoln (Eds.), *The qualitative inquiry reader* (pp. 299–325). Thousand Oaks, CA: Sage.

Lang, A. (2000). The limited capacity model of mediated message processing. *Journal of Communication, 50*(1), 46–70.

Lang, A., Chung, Y., Lee, S., Schwartz, N., & Shin, M. (2005). It's an arousing, fast-paced kind of world: The effects of age and sensation seeking on the information processing of substance-abuse PSAs. *Media Psychology, 7*(4), 421–454.

Lang, A., Schneider, E. F., & Deitz, R. (1999, August). *Emotional experience and physiological arousal during violent video game playing: Gender, experience, and presence matter.* Paper presented at the Association for Education in Journalism and Mass Communication, New Orleans.

Lee, A. S., & Baskerville, R. L. (2003). Generalizing generalizability in information systems research. *Information Systems Research, 14*(3), 221–243.

Lee, K. M., & Peng, W. (2006). Massively multiplayer online games. In P. Vorderer & J. Bryant (Eds.), *What do we know about the social and psychological effects of computer games? A comprehensive review of the current literature* (pp. 325–345). Mahwah, NJ: Erlbaum.

Linden Research Inc. (2003). Second life [Computer software]. Retrieved March 20, 2006, from http://secondlife.com/community/downloads.php

Lowood, H. (2006). A brief biography of computer games. In P. Vorderer & J. Bryant (Eds.), *Playing video games: Motives, responses, and consequences* (pp. 25–41). Mahwah: Erlbaum.

McClelland, D. C., Atkinson, J. W., Clark, R. A., & Lowell, E. L. (1953). *The achievement motive.* New York: Apple-Century-Crofts.

McGrath, J. E., & Brinberg, D. (1983). External validity and the research process: A comment on the Calder/Lynch dialogue. *Journal of Consumer Research, 10,* 115–124.

Mook, D. G. (1983). In defense of external validity. *American Psychologist, 38,* 379–387.

Parker, L. E., & Lepper, M. R. (1992). Effects of fantasy contexts on children's learning and motivation: Making learning more fun. *Journal of Personality and Social Psychology, 62*(4), 625–633.

Parks, M. R., & Floyd, K. (1996). Making friends in cyberspace. *Journal of Communication, 46,* 80–97.

Parks, M. R., & Roberts, L. D. (1998). Making MOOsic: The development of personal relationships on-line and a comparison to their off-line counterparts. *Journal of Social and Personal Relationships, 15,* 517–537.

Peña, J., & Hancock, J. T. (2006). An analysis of socioemotional and task-oriented communication in an online multiplayer video game. *Communication Research, 33*(1), 92–109.

Pong [Digital game]. (1972). New York: Atari.

Quake [Digital game]. (1996). id Software. Mesquite, TX: Activision.

Rafaeli, S. (1988). Interactivity from new media to communication. In R. P. Hawkins, J. M. Wiemann, & S. Pingree (Eds.), *Advancing communication science: Merging mass and interpersonal processes* (pp. 110–134). Newbury Park: Sage.

Reeves, B., & Geiger, S. (1994). Designing experiments that assess psychological responses to media messages. In A. Lang (Ed.), *Measuring psychological responses to media messages* (pp. 165–180). Hillsdale, NJ: Erlbaum.

Salomon, G. (1990). Cognitive effects with and of computer technology. *Communication Research, 17*(1), 26–44.

Schneider, E. F., Lang, A., Shin, M., & Bradley, S. D. (2004). Death with a story: How story impacts emotional, motivational, and physiological responses to first-person shooter video games. *Human Communication Research, 30*(3), 361–375.

Second Life [Digital game]. (2003). Linden Research. Retrieved March 20, 2006, from http://secondlife.com/community/downloads.php.

Shapiro, M. A. (2002). Generalizability in communication research. *Human Communication Research, 28*(4), 491–500.

Shapiro, M. A. (2007). Values, creativity, and imagination in generalizability. *Communication Methods and Measures, 1*(3), 207–213.

Sherry, J. L. (2001). The effects of violent video games on aggression: A meta-analysis. *Human Communication Research, 27*(3), 409–431.

Sims 2, The [Digital game]. (2004). Maxis. Redwood City, CA: Electronic Arts.

Steinkuehler, C. A., & Williams, D. (2006). Where everybody knows your (screen) name: Online games as "third places." *Journal of Computer Mediated Communication, 11*(4), 885–909.

Subrahmanyam, K., Kraut, R., Greenfield, P., & Gross, E. (2001). New forms of electronic media: The impact of electronic games and the Internet on cognition, socialization, and behavior. In D. G. Singer & J. L. Singer (Eds.), *Handbook of children and the media* (pp. 73–100). Thousand Oaks, CA: Sage.

Tamborini, R., & Skalski, P. (2006). The role of presence in the experience of electronic games. In P. Vorderer & J. Bryant (Eds.), *Playing video games: Motives, responses, and consequences* (pp. 225–240). Mahwah, NJ: Erlbaum.

Uhlmann, E., & Swanson, J. (2004). Exposure to violent video games increases automatic aggressiveness. *Journal of Adolescence, 27*(1), 41–52.

Utz, S. (2000). Social information processing in MUDs: The development of friendships in virtual worlds. *Journal of Online Behavior, 1*(1). Retrieved February 2, 2003, from http://www.behavior.net/JOB/v2001n2001/utz.html

Van Evra, J. (1998). *Television and child development.* Mahwah: Erlbaum.

Vorderer, P., & Bryant, J. (2006). *Playing video games: Motives, responses, and consequences.* Mahwah, NJ: Erlbaum.

Walther, J. B. (1992). Interpersonal effects in computer-mediated interaction: A relational perspective. *Communication Research, 19*(1), 52–90.

Walther, J. B. (1996). Computer-mediated communication: Impersonal, interpersonal, and hyperpersonal interaction. *Communication Research, 23*(1), 3–43.

Walther, J. B., & Parks, M. R. (2002). Cues filtered out, cues filtered in: Computer-mediated communication and relationships. In M. L. Knapp & J. A. Daly (Eds.), *Handbook of interpersonal communication* (3rd ed., pp. 529–563). Thousand Oaks, CA: Sage.

Williams, D. (2002). Structure and competition in the U.S. home video game industry. *The International Journal of Media Management, 4,* 41–54.

Williams, D., & Skoric, M. (2005). Internet fantasy violence: A test of aggression in an online game. *Communication Monographs, 72*(2), 217–233.

World of warcraft [Digital game]. (2001). Irvine, CA: Blizzard Entertainment.

Yee, N. (2001). The Norrathian scrolls: A study of EverQuest (version 2.5). Retrieved October 12, 2002, from http://www.nickyee.com/eqt/report.html

Zehnder, S. M., & Lipscomb, S. D. (2006). The role of music in video games. In P. Vorderer & J. Bryant (Eds.), *Playing video games: Motives, responses, and consequences* (pp. 241–258). Mahwah, NJ: Erlbaum.

Chapter 23

Designing Game Research
Addressing Questions of Validity

Niklas Ravaja and Matias Kivikangas

In chapter 22 of this volume, Michael Shapiro and Jorge Peña aptly highlight the challenges present in the research on digital games and note the potential problems associated with the statistical definition of generalizability (i.e., external validity). They suggest a simple, broad definition of generalizability that it is "the ability to say something beyond the particular." We argue, however, that the statistical approach to generalizability is essential for experimental game studies and also for surveys. The peculiar characteristics of digital games influence generalizability, and this should be taken into account when designing game research studies. In this chapter, we look deeper and focus on internal validity, external validity, the validity of measures (e.g., psychophysiological measures), and the ecological validity used in experimental game research.

Internal Validity in Game Studies

According to Maxwell and Delaney (2004), the issue of internal validity is whether there is a causal relationship between variable X and variable Y, regardless of what X and Y are theoretically supposed to represent. Threats to internal validity are often related to the problem of a confounding variable—an extraneous variable that is correlated with the levels of the variable of interest. Internal validity can be regarded as the most important form of validity, because other forms of validity are meaningless if the study does not first possess internal validity.

Both internal and external validity are dependent on how treatment differences are created. Basically, there are two ways to create stimulus variance when studying games: (1) different games can be sampled within each level of the treatment (e.g., using a pretest procedure); or (2) the same game can be altered to produce two or more versions (cf. message sampling and message altering; Ravaja, 2004; Reeves & Geiger, 1994). In the case of game sampling, selecting many games for each level of a treatment suggests that systematic error due to confounds in the game (i.e., extraneous game attributes that could influence subject responses), becomes smaller. However, given the complexity of games, this does not guarantee that all confounding variance is eliminated.

As noted by Shapiro and Peña (this volume, chapter 22), digital games are extremely dynamic stimuli compared to traditional media stimuli; that is, the game is not the same for all players or the same across playing sessions for a single player. This makes it difficult to assess how, in general, the dynamic nature of games influences internal validity when using game sampling. For example, if the games have been selected on the basis of a feature (e.g., violent games versus nonviolent games), but this feature does not manifest itself for all players, this may decrease internal validity of a study. In particular, some games (e.g., role-playing games) involve very heterogeneous tasks and the player may freely choose what kind of tasks he or she undertakes, creating an experience unique to that particular player. On the other hand, the fact that a given game is not the same for all players would be expected to reduce systematic error due to game confounds; that is, to the extent that the game characteristic of interest is always present (when different players play a given game), the dynamic nature of games is likely to result in the same outcome as game sampling, thereby, in effect, increasing internal validity. Game sampling may be the method of choice when the game feature of interest cannot be manipulated as a unit (Ravaja, 2004). However, it should be noted that game sampling in particular and experimental game research in general may be problematic when studying games with long playing times. The duration of an experimental session can hardly exceed 3 hours, including the administration of questionnaires, but many games, such as role-playing games are normally played during several or many consecutive days and the gaming experience may evolve during this period.

Treatment differences can also be created by altering the same game to produce two or more versions. The advantage of game altering is that, when a single feature of interest is changed in two versions of the same game and all other features are equivalent between the versions, the problem of possible game confounds is largely eliminated. Game altering can be realized by using the game's own settings (e.g., difficulty level), or by designing modifications (mods) of existing games. For both game sampling and game altering, an important practical question is how many different games there should be within a given treatment level. Although one cannot give a definitive answer to this question, it is apparent that at least more than one game within each treatment level is needed (cf. Jackson, 1992).

External Validity in Game Studies

External validity refers to the stability across other contexts of the causal relationship observed in a given study (Maxwell & Delaney, 2004); that is, can the finding be generalized across different experimental settings, procedures, participants, or time (cf. Brewer, 2000; Shadish, Cook, & Campbell, 2002)? In game research, the ability to generalize across different games is an important issue for external validity (cf. Reeves & Geiger, 1994). To increase external validity, one should take steps, where possible, to assure that the study uses a heterogeneous group of persons, settings, games, and times. Although heterogeneity makes it more difficult to obtain statistically significant findings, once they are obtained, it allows generalization of these findings with greater confidence to other situations (Maxwell & Delaney, 2004). Thus, when creating treatment differences using game sampling, it is usually advisable to sample heterogeneous games within each level of the treatment.

The importance of external validity depends on the type of study (e.g., basic research vs. applied research), and the specific research questions. In basic research, the central interest is in the relations among variables and why the variables are related as they are. Thus, when using games in basic psychological research, one can argue that it is not important whether the finding can be generalized across different games. In this case, the suggestion by Shapiro and Peña holds true: "What matters is our ability to explain the effect of social and psychological variables in the form of coherent theories" (this volume, chapter 22). However, external validity is usually important in digital game research, given that many game studies involve applied aspects. That is, in applied research, the central interest forces more concern for generalizability, because one certainly wishes to apply the results to the other persons and to other games, for example.

Game mods can be used to test specific research hypotheses and, given the high experimental control afforded by mods, they may also be a tempting tool for basic research on emotions and social psychological research. However, to the extent that external validity is integral to the aims of the study, it is important to ensure that the players still perceive mods as real games. Social psychological research (e.g., studies on social interaction), has utilized highly dynamic stimulus conditions for a long time, in which the importance of external validity has usually been acknowledged, suggesting that this may also be important for similar game research involving mods.

Validity of Measures

The characteristics of digital games also pose challenges regarding the validity of the measures used when studying games. Psychophysiological measures are a good example of this. Given that digital games are a dynamic object of study, Shapiro and Peña suggest two ways for research to capture the complexity of games: (1) researchers should focus on human cognition, behavior, and emotion while playing games (and not on the features of the technology itself); and (2) techniques should be developed for conceptualizing the process of game playing. In view of these suggestions, psychophysiological measures would be expected to hold a particular promise for the research on digital games. The advantages of psychophysiological measures include: (1) measurements can be performed continuously with high temporal resolution; (2) processes of interest can be covertly assessed; and (3) these measures may provide information on emotional and attentional responses that are not available to conscious awareness (Ravaja, 2004). In basic psychological research, psychophysiological measures, (e.g., electrodermal activity [EDA], facial electromyography [EMG], and frontal electroencephalographic [EEG] asymmetry), have successfully been used to index emotional responses, defined in terms of emotional valence and arousal, to discrete stimuli (e.g., static emotional images, presented to passive participants; see Lang, Greenwald, Bradley, & Hamm, 1993). Likewise, media studies have used psychophysiological measures when examining emotional and attentional responses to media messages (e.g., video, television, radio, and textual messages; Bolls, Lang, & Potter, 2001; Ravaja, Kallinen, Saari, & Kelti-kangas-Järvinen, 2004; Ravaja, Saari, Kallinen, & Laarni, 2006; for a review, see Ravaja, 2004). However, digital games differ from traditional psychological and media stimuli in important ways, the most important difference being that digital game play involves active, dynamic interaction (including motor activity) and a motivated performance situation (i.e., active coping task, Grodal, 2000; Ravaja, Saari, Salminen, Laarni, & Kallinen, 2006). In digital games, the player is typically an active participant in the dynamic flow of events and action. In fact, we know quite little of the use of psychophysiological measures in the context of games: do they really index emotional and attentional processes during game playing? In our theorizing and research designs, constructs (e.g., emotion or attention), must be differentiated from their measures or ways to identify them. Unlike measures, constructs are always hypothetical and not directly observable.

The concept of construct validity is important here. Construct validity refers to whether a measure, such as a self-report scale or electrodermal activity, measures the unobservable construct that it purports to measure (Kerlinger, 1986). Evaluation of construct validity requires examining the correlation of the target measure with variables that are known to be related to the construct purportedly measured by the target measure or for which there are theoretical grounds for expecting it to be related (Campbell & Fiske, 1959). Correlations that fit the expected pattern provide evidence of construct validity. In construct validation, both convergence and discriminability are required (Kerlinger, 1986). Accordingly, there are two important variations of construct validity: (1) convergent validity and (2) discriminant validity. A measure has convergent validity when other measures that purport to measure the same construct correlate well with the target measure. A measure has discriminant validity when it does not correlate with measures that purport to measure different constructs.

Psychophysiological measures have not been properly construct-validated in the context of digital game play. That is, their convergent and discriminant relations with other measures, (e.g., self-report measures and other psychophysiological measures), purportedly measuring the same or different constructs, have not been established. The problem is underscored by the well-known fact that there is often a many-to-one relation between psychological processes and psychophysiological measures (Cacioppo, Tassinary, & Berntson, 2000). That is, a given psychophysiological measure can potentially be linked to several psychological constructs (e.g., emotion and attention), and the interpretation of psychophysiological measures is highly dependent on the context and research paradigm. In order to establish convergent validity when using psychophysiological measures as measures of emotional processes during game play, a psychophysiological measure that purports to measure emotional valence, for example, should covary with self-reported emotional valence during game play, as well as with other psychophysiological measures that would be expected to index emotional valence. Accordingly, Ravaja and coworkers have recently shown that EMG activities of the zygomaticus major (cheek), corrugator supercilii (brow), and orbicularis oculi (periocular) muscle areas covary during digital game playing for both phasic and tonic responses (Ravaja, Saari, Salminen, Laarni, & Kallinen, 2006; Ravaja, Saari, Turpeinen, Laarni, Salminen, & Kivikangas, 2006). These convergent relationships provide evidence for the validity of the facial EMG measures as measures of emotional valence during game play. However, there is also evidence that corrugator EMG activity may increase not only when experiencing negative emotions, but also during periods of heightened effortful attention (Cohen, Davidson, Senulis, Saron, & Weisman, 1992). Thus, it would also be important to show that corrugator EMG responses to game play do not covary strongly with established indices of attention, such as reduced EEG alpha power. This would provide evidence for discriminant validity of corrugator activity as a measure of (negative) emotions during game playing. The process of construct validation may also involve testing hypotheses, such as that corrugator EMG responses will be greater during games known to be frustrating compared to games known to elicit flow experiences. Confirming such a hypothesis would provide further evidence for the construct validity of corrugator EMG activity as a measure of negative emotions.

Ecological Validity

Digital games are now increasingly played with mobile devices in different contexts, such as coffee bars, subway stations, or buses, which may be quite different from a laboratory setting. Prior research on emotional responses to games has, however, been carried out exclusively in the laboratory, which raises questions about the ecological validity of laboratory research. The issue of ecological validity is: do the methods, material, and setting of the experiment approximate the real-life situation that is under study? A study may possess external validity but not ecological validity, and vice versa, although improving ecological validity often improves external validity as well (cf., Shadish, Cook, & Campbell, 2002). The availability of very small mobile psychophysiological data collection systems (e.g., Varioport-B, Becker Meditec, Germany), now makes it possible to examine emotion-related psychophysiological responses (e.g., EEG, facial EMG, EDA, heart rate, and respiration) elicited by game play in the real-world context. Some of these systems can also collect data on environmental parameters, such as ambient noise, illumination, and temperature. This makes it possible to examine how these parameters influence emotional responses to games. In moving our research designs from the laboratory to the real world, we lose some of the tight experimental control available in the psychophysiological laboratory, but we gain ecological validity.

Conclusion

Given the heterogeneity of digital games, researchers should examine how the characteristics of the particular games they plan to use may influence the internal and external validity of a study. For example, with regard to the internal validity of experimental game studies, one cannot categorically conclude that one should use a larger number of stimuli within each treatment level when studying games than when studying more traditional media; however, there should be more than one game within each treatment level. In addition, although external validity may not be critically important when games are used as stimuli in basic psychological research, it is important in applied research, and many game studies involve applied aspects. Moreover, the peculiar characteristics of digital game playing may have a profound influence on psychophysiological measures of emotion and attention. Thus, although psychophysiological measures are clearly promising from the perspective of game studies, they have to be construct-validated in connection with digital game playing.

Acknowledgments

This work was supported by the European Community, NEST project "FUGA—The fun of gaming: Measuring the human experience of media enjoyment" (NEST-28765).

References

Bolls, P. D., Lang, A., & Potter, R. F. (2001). The effects of message valence and listener arousal on attention, memory, and facial muscular responses to radio advertisements. *Communication Research, 28,* 627–651.

Brewer, M. B. (2000). Research design and issues of validity. In H. T. Reis & C. M. Judd (Eds.), *Handbook of research methods in social and personality psychology* (pp. 3–16). New York: Cambridge University Press.

Cacioppo, J. T., Tassinary, L. G., & Berntson, G. G. (2000). Psychophysiological science. In J. T. Cacioppo, L. G. Tassinary, & G. G. Berntson (Eds.), *Handbook of psychophysiology* (2nd ed., pp. 3–23). New York: Cambridge University Press.

Campbell, D. T., & Fiske, D. W. (1959). Convergent and discriminant validation by the multitrait–multimethod matrix. *Psychological Bulletin, 56,* 81–105.

Cohen, B. H., Davidson, R. J., Senulis, J. A., Saron, C. D., & Weisman, D. R. (1992). Muscle tension patterns during auditory attention. *Biological Psychology, 33,* 133–156.

Grodal, T. (2000). Video games and the pleasures of control. In D. Zillmann & P. Vorderer (Eds.), *Media entertainment: The psychology of its appeal* (pp. 197–212). Mahwah, NJ: Erlbaum.

Jackson, S. (1992). *Message effects research: Principles of design and analysis.* New York: Guilford Press.

Kerlinger, F.N. (1986). *Foundations of behavioral research* (3rd ed.). Fort Worth, TX: Holt Rinehart & Winston.

Lang, P. J., Greenwald, M. K., Bradley, M. M., & Hamm, A. O. (1993). Looking at pictures: Affective, facial, visceral, and behavioral reactions. *Psychophysiology, 30,* 261–273.

Maxwell, S. E., & Delaney, H. D. (2004). *Designing experiments and analyzing data: a model comparison perspective* (2nd ed.). Mahwah, NJ: Erlbaum.

Ravaja, N. (2004). Contributions of psychophysiology to media research: Review and recommendations. *Media Psychology, 6,* 193–235.

Ravaja, N., Kallinen, K., Saari, T., & Keltikangas-Järvinen, L. (2004). Suboptimal exposure to facial expressions when viewing video messages from a small screen: Effects on emotion, attention, and memory. *Journal of Experimental Psychology: Applied, 10,* 120–131.

Ravaja, N., Saari, T., Kallinen, K., & Laarni, J. (2006). The role of mood in the processing of media messages from a small screen: Effects on subjective and physiological responses. *Media Psychology, 8,* 239–265.

Ravaja, N., Saari, T., Salminen, M., Laarni, J., & Kallinen, K. (2006). Phasic emotional reactions to video game events: A psychophysiological investigation. *Media Psychology, 8,* 343–367.

Ravaja, N., Saari, T., Turpeinen, M., Laarni, J., Salminen, M., & Kivikangas, M. (2006). Spatial presence and emotions during video game playing: Does it matter with whom you play? *Presence: Teleoperators and Virtual Environments, 15,* 381–392.

Reeves, B., & Geiger, S. (1994). Designing experiments that assess psychological responses to media messages. In A. Lang (Ed.), *Measuring psychological responses to media messages* (pp. 165–180). Hillsdale, NJ: Erlbaum.

Shadish, W. R., Cook, T. D., & Campbell, D.T. (2002). Experimental and quasi-experimental designs for generalized causal inference. Boston: Houghton Mifflin.

Part IV

Applications, Limitations, and Future Directions

Chapter 24

Three-Dimensional Game Environments for Recovery from Stroke

Younbo Jung, Shih-Ching Yeh, Margaret McLaughlin, Albert A. Rizzo, and Carolee Winstein

In the United States, more than 780,000 people annually suffer a new or recurrent stroke, which has emerged as one of the leading causes of severe and long-term disability (American Heart Association, 2008). This health crisis reflects considerable human suffering as well as an enormous economic burden. According to the American Heart Association (2008), the health care costs of caring for stroke victims is estimated to cost about $65.5 billion in 2008 alone. The poststroke disability manifests itself in functional impairments such as difficulty in handling multiple activities of daily living (e.g., dressing, preparing and eating a meal, bathing, etc.). Quality of life tends to be severely impacted by stroke (Jonsson, Lindgren, Hallstrom, Norrving, & Lindgren, 2005; Mayo, Wood-Dauphinee, Cote, Durcan, & Carlton, 2002).

Fortunately, some of the motor functioning lost due to stroke can be recovered or improved via task-oriented motor training that facilitates activities by targeting specific relevant movements (Taub, Uswatte, & Morris, 2003). It is important to note that a good motor training task should be designed to target a specific functional deficit (e.g., pointing, grasping, twisting, or stretching). And the intensity of such a task should be based on both the ongoing status of the impairment and desired therapeutic goals, such as increased speed, accuracy, efficiency, extent, or orientation of movements (Lee & Maraj, 1994; Schmidt & Lee, 1999). However, the motor training tasks used for conventional therapy are limited in that they are usually highly repetitive (e.g., move a soda can from a table to a shelf and back 20 times) and do not allow therapists to capture motor-response performance of patients in real time accurately and systematically (e.g., performance evaluations depend on the therapist's subjective intuition and experience). Potential problems with these limitations include unmotivated and disengaged poststroke patients and a subsequent obligation on the therapist's side to encourage patients, evaluate their performance, and provide easy-to-understand feedback for improvement. As a consequence, with conventional therapy it is very challenging for physical therapists to provide patients with a tailored rehabilitation program based on the patients' level of impairment and progress towards improvement. The adjustment of environmental parameters to modulate the intensity of practice (e.g., adjusting the difference in height between table and shelf in the reaching task, or increasing the weight of the object being moved back and forth) can be labor intensive and tedious work for therapists, not to speak of the inconvenience of timing each practice with a stop watch, recording the elapsed time for a particular movement, and providing feedback to the patient. Therefore, it is a high priority to develop more efficient and engaging methods for motor rehabilitation after stroke.

In this regard, integrating digital game features such as audiovisual effects, immediate performance feedback (e.g., scores), systematic variation in difficulty levels, and automatic database logging of players' performance into the motor training task could benefit both the patient and therapist (Holden, 2005; Jung, Yeh, Stewart, & USC-UT Consortium, 2006; Weiss & Katz, 2004). In this chapter, we introduce ongoing interdisciplinary efforts, involving researchers from the fields of communication, electrical engineering, computer science, psychology, and physical therapy, to develop three-dimensional game environments for poststroke recovery. We briefly describe how various game environments have developed and show the results from our clinical trial. Finally, we discuss implications and direction of future research for the use of three-dimensional digital games in motor training and other therapeutic applications.

Developing Game Environments for Motor Rehabilitation

Serious Games in Motor Training

Recently in the field of stroke rehabilitation, much attention has been paid to interactive digital games (i.e., serious games) that could provide numerous assets for rehabilitation beyond what is currently available with traditional methods (Holden, Todorov, Callahan, & Bizzi, 1999; Weiss & Katz, 2004). In fact, studies have demonstrated the positive effects of using serious games with virtual reality technologies on motor-skill improvement for functional deficits in poststroke rehabilitation, including reaching (Holden et al., 1999), hand function (Merians et al., 2002), and walking (Deutsch, Latonio, Burdea, & Boian, 2001; You et al., 2005).

Advantages of using advanced interactive games in motor rehabilitation include: (1) The capacity for systematic delivery and control of game parameters, such as difficulty levels or task requirements: This capacity ensures the hierarchical delivery of challenges in digital games (i.e., difficulty levels), based on gradual improvement or varying levels of impairment in each patient. (2) The ability to simulate realistic environments inside digital games: By designing game environments that not only "look like" the real world, but actually incorporate challenges that require real world functional behaviors, the ecological validity of rehabilitation methods could be enhanced. (3) The collection of advanced interactive data such as reaching trajectories from game play: Through a patient's play, a large quantity and wide variety of high quality data could be captured to serve as important information to assess the rehabilitation process. (4) The ability to embed game features into serious tasks: Game features such as real-time visual, auditory, and haptic feedback could not only motivate the patient but also make the patient feel present within the digital game world.

In spite of potential benefits of serious games for motor training after stroke, it is very challenging to develop any specific digital game that could be used in a real motor training session. In the following sections, we identify potential challenges in the development stage, as well as complicated issues in the evaluation stage, with examples from our interdisciplinary project in which we developed gamelike environments for motor rehabilitation after stroke.

Human Factors Design

Human factors design in engineering is very similar to social marketing, in that design of technology begins by identifying human needs, followed by tailoring the technology to needs of the target audience (Kreuter, Farrell, Olevitch, & Brennan, 2000; Vincente, 2004). Having human factors design in mind, we started our design of three-dimensional game environments for motor rehabilitation by identifying two important groups of users; namely, patients poststroke and therapists. Although often neglected in research, therapists play a very important role in the successful implementation of game-enhanced motor rehabilitation in the real world because (1) in all likelihood the therapist will use digital games more frequently than a stroke patient (cf., although the therapist is not the player, the therapist will use serious games to help the patient play); and (2) therapists can identify patients' needs with respect to the recovery of their lost motor function. Thus, we worked very closely with physical therapists from the very beginning stage of game development by creating a clear road map of the design process (see Figure 24.1).

The first step was to identify common everyday-life activities that people are unable to perform after stroke. Then, the goals and patterns of movements in corresponding training tasks from traditional therapy were analyzed in order to transform these training tasks into digital games in three-dimensional environments (cf., this process is also known as mapping; see Norman, 1988). Unlike entertainment games, the first step is very critical for the development of serious games aimed at specific goals such as motor rehabilitation, because random movements will not be beneficial in promoting recovery of motor function.

Based on the design process, we identified three different movement patterns for stroke patients who suffer from motion deficits in the upper extremity and mapped real-life tasks into four different types of digital games (see Table 24.1 for how we derived four digital games from identifying movement

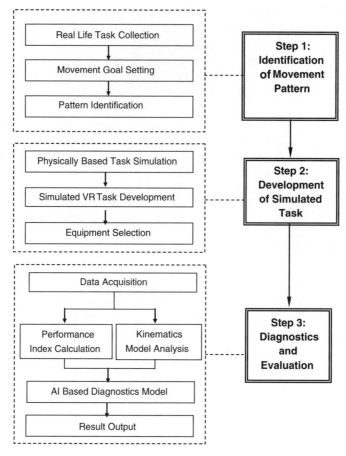

Figure 24.1 Design process for game development (adapted from Yeh et al., 2005).

patterns and goals). In the following sections, we describe four digital games (*Spatial Rotation, Ball Shooting, Reaching,* and *Pinch*) and important game features embedded within the four games.

Table 24.1 Development Process for Four Digital Games

Movement Pattern	Movement Goal	Real-Life Tasks	Digital Games
Coordinated thumb and index finger	Pinch or squeeze	Pinch or squeeze a plastic bag	Pinch
Pronation and supination	Twist	Twist a screw driver	Spatial Rotation
Coordinated arm and shoulder movement	Extend or stretch	Hang a map on the wall	Reaching & Ball Shooting

Figure 24.2 Screenshot of four digital games: Spatial Rotation, Ball Shooting, Reaching, and Pinch from left.

Digital Games Developed

In general, all games are presented to patients via three different types of three-dimensional display: a CRT monitor and shutter glasses (StereoGraphics); a head mounted display (eMagin); and an autostereoscopic display (see the section on display types for a detailed description). To provide interactivity in three of the four digital games (i.e., *Spatial Rotation, Ball Shooting*, and *Reaching*), a 6 degree-of-freedom (DOF) magnetic tracker (Flock of Birds, Ascension Technology) is attached to the patient's hands or to a held object. The fourth game, *Pinch*, is performed using two PHANToM devices (SensAble Technologies) reconfigured to work together. PHANToM 1 was a Premium 1.5/3 DOF model fit with a thimble gimbal replacing the stylus and attached to the end of the index finger. PHANToM 2 was a 6 DOF model with the stylus placed in the web space of the hand and secured to the thumb with an elastic band (see Figure 24.2 for screen shots of the four digital games). With two PHANToM devices, a patient could receive tactile (haptic) feedback when grasping and lifting up a virtual cube in a digital game environment. For this game, the weight and the texture (slippery, rough) of the cube can be manipulated by the therapist to address current patient strengths and needs. Games were programmed using C++ with Open GL and Ghost libraries.

Spatial Rotation

This game requires a patient to perform a combined movement of supination/pronation and shoulder ab/adduction by superimposing a three-dimensional cube configuration onto a rotated version of itself. A patient could use either a handheld object (e.g., PVC tube) or a band strip around the player's hand to which a motion tracker was attached, in order to play the game. Both the number of angles within the cube configuration as well as the degree of superimposition could be systematically altered by therapists to adjust difficulty levels.

Ball Shooting

This game requires a patient to reach and intercept a ball shot from a wall. Both *Ball Shooting* and *Reaching* were developed for the patient to reach either a dynamically moving or stationary target with synchronized forearm and hand movement on the patient's paretic side. Simultaneously, coordination of eye and hand is required so as to drive the forearm tracking a moving target. The concept is derived from daily life tasks, such as reaching for a moving object in the air while someone passes it to you. The environmental parameters for these two games could be tailored to individual patients' particulars, such as arm length and height of the shoulder, and eyes in a sitting position, which ensures personalized presentation of game stimuli relative to the patient's physical characteristics.

Reaching

Similar to *Ball Shooting*, *Reaching* requires the patient to reach for static cubes and "hit" one cube at a time in a patient-selected order, then to return to the start position between each hit. In this game, the target cubes are stationed in a preset distance range such as 70 or 80% of the patient's arm length. This range is determined by the therapist with respect to the level of patient's impairment. It is important to note that the distance should be long enough to challenge the patient's paretic arm for maximum possible extension, and yet short enough to enable the patient's successful reach upon effort.

Pinch

Pinch enables a precision grasp between the thumb and index finger and requires the patient to pick up a cube and lift it to a certain height by using the combination of two Phantom force-feedback devices. Upon a successful trial, the patient receives audiovisual feedback, such as an applause and color changes in the cube. The patient can also check the summary of game play after the completion of each practice block (10 to 20 trials) to learn about his or her trial success rate and total elapsed time.

Important Game Features

There are important game features that need to be integrated into game-based motor rehabilitation. In this section, we briefly describe those features with examples from our four digital games.

Interface for Interaction

The interface is the crucial factor determining the forms of interaction and the quality of interaction. We developed digital game environments that could best utilize our hardware equipment (e.g., various display types, a motion tracker, PHANToMs, etc.) to accommodate corresponding real-life tasks (see Figure 24.3 for examples). In addition, the interface was designed in a user-friendly

Figure 24.3 A poststroke patient playing digital games in the clinical trial: (a) A patient using a CRT monitor and shutter glasses for Ball Shooting; (b) A patient using two PHANToMs for Pinch.

way so that even a therapist with little in the way of computer skills could control the digital games with a brief training session. Step-by-step manuals, as well as written scripts to explain digital games to patients are provided.

Visual and Audio Feedback

Visual and audio feedback is one of the most essential game features that can make digital games interesting, interactive, and exciting. We designed synchronized visual and audio effects to increase the patient's immersion and engagement in digital game environments. In addition, instant performance feedback, such as the number of successful trials, is provided to the patient to motivate and challenge continuous play.

For example, in *Ball Shooting* the virtual hand of a patient is required to be positioned or returned to the start position to activate the game. The color of the start position changes from white to red to indicate the proper position of the virtual hand (see Figure 24.4). Simultaneously, a sound effect, "beep," indicates a successful return to the start position. Another visual and audio feedback is that a bird will fly out with a "cawing" sound when the patient does reach the moving target successfully. Alternatively, the patient hears a spring-oscillation like sound effect when he or she misses the moving target.

Figure 24.4 Screen shots of visual effects in Ball Shooting.

Display Types for Three-Dimensional Perception

The effect of three-dimensional stereo helps patients perceive the distance in depth and virtual location of their hands or objects in digital game environments. Shutter glasses or an autostereoscopic display are possible choices for displaying the three-dimensional effect. The advantage of the autostereoscopic display is that the patient does not have to wear anything to get the three-dimensional effect as long as he or she remains in a "sweet spot," or at least this is the case with the less expensive and hence more generally useful versions. The drawback is that a limited sweet spot might cause the patient to easily lose three-dimensional perception with even a minor head movement. A head mounted display (HMD) could be a solution to this problem since an HMD allows the patient to perceive the three-dimensional environment regardless of head movements. However, a HMD is not a perfect solution since the patient has to wear it over his or her head, which could be disorienting or uncomfortable.

In fact, the results from our clinical trial with three patients poststroke indicated that most of the patients preferred the CRT monitor with glasses, followed by the autostereoscopic monitor, and the HMD. Preferences for the display were not influenced by the novelty of technologies, but affected by comfort issues particular to this patient population and the nature of their therapeutic regimen. More specifically, two of the three patients wore glasses, and one patient was reluctant to wear anything over the head after his brain surgery, which together could result in relatively negative evaluation of the HMD. These results include limitations in that there were a small number of samples due to the pilot nature of our clinical trials, and some potentially influential factors such as screen size and resolution were not controlled. Nevertheless, the results imply two important issues: (1) user characteristics should be considered in selecting an interface (the latest technology does not always win); and (2) different display types could influence the effectiveness of motor rehabilitation using digital games. Since preparation for various display types could be achieved at relatively low cost, it is recommended that options to select the most preferred display type be granted to patients in order to maximize training efficiency and effectiveness.

Mapping Mechanism for Interaction

A mapping mechanism is the process for converting measures from the physical world to the digital game environment. In other words, mapping transforms intended therapeutic activities into actual operations when the patient plays digital games through the interactive interface. Thus, mapping is essential for interaction and successful motor rehabilitation in digital game environments in two ways. First, an accurate mapping can ensure that the system will drive the patient's activity in the way that is intended by the therapist's rehabilita-

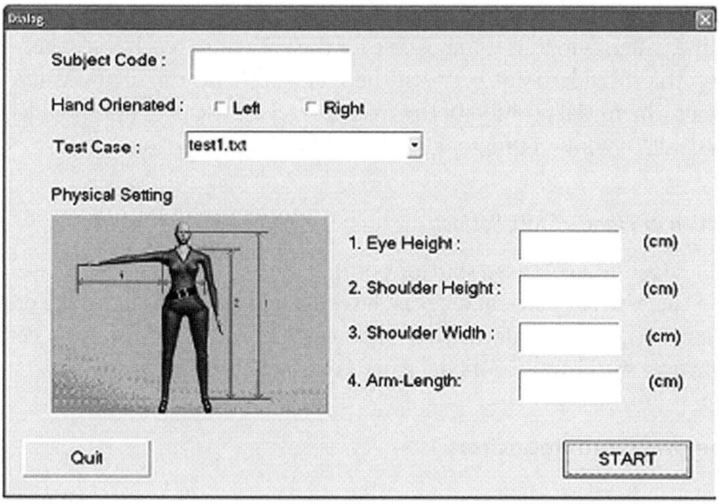

Figure 24.5 User interface for the entry of physical attributes.

tion goals. Second, it can assure an exact reconstruction of the movement trajectory to provide valuable kinetic information about performance and progression to the therapist and patient for assessment.

For example, in *Reaching*, four physical attributes are measured from the patient and entered into the database (see Figure 24.5 for the data-entry interface). The environmental parameters (e.g., position of virtual camera, and allocation of target position and hand-start position) in *Reaching* are automatically personalized to meet the individual patient's physical attributes.

Allocation of Virtual Camera

The allocation of the virtual camera (i.e., the position of eyes inside the digital game through which game scenes are shown in the screen) is to guarantee that each patient has an appropriate view, with respect to the patient's physical attributes, of all items inside the digital game environment. Once the virtual camera is allocated, the relationship between the eye and hand in the physical world can be rebuilt in the digital game environment, which makes all interactions more intuitive.

Allocation of Target Position

To allocate the target position of cubes in *Reaching*, a physical measure of the patient's arm length is needed. In addition, the position of the patient's shoulder joint needs to be calibrated because the derivation of target position should be based on the combined information of the arm length and where the shoulder joint stands (e.g., if the position of a cube is within an arm length from the patient's foot, it is impossible for the patient to reach the cube). Thus, to map the shoulder joint between the real world and the digital game environment, the initial position of the tracker is set on the patient's shoulder joint upon the activation of program for the calibration, as shown in Figure 24.5.

Allocation of Hand's Start Position

The hand must have a fixed starting position in the physical world for each trial so that the patient's performance can be compared among trials for the progress assessment. This setup also ensures the mapping in the start position between the physical world and the digital game environment (see Figure 24.6).

Automatic Data Repository

Another important game feature is the systematic record of the game performance that could be very useful information to assess patients' progress. For our digital games, a Web-based online data repository system was developed to provide a single interface for accessing the data acquired from the intervention, which archived mainly performance outcome measures derived from raw sensor data streams, as well as questionnaire data for the game evaluation. Two primary functionalities provided are uploading and browsing or searching data. By allowing the therapist to easily browse the previous performance of a patient, prior to initiating the next session the therapist could tailor digital game environments to match the current capabilities or progress of the patient throughout the course of motor rehabilitation (e.g., adjust the level of difficulty in games). As such, the patient could experience more optimized and challenging practice in digital game environments.

Evaluating Game Environments for Recovery from Stroke

Evaluating the effectiveness of serious games in motor rehabilitation or other medical intervention is not an easy task in many aspects. First of all, the evalu-

Figure 24.6 Mapping for the allocation of target and hand-start position in Reaching.

ation process is a longitudinal field experiment due to the nature of clinical trials. This type of research cannot be conducted with college students, unlike usual experimental research. Besides, using digital games for motor rehabilitation is still in its infancy, so there is no single standardized measure to evaluate such medical interventions. In this section, we briefly introduce various types of measures that together could be used to assess the effectiveness of serious games in motor rehabilitation with examples from our clinical trial.

Overview of the Clinical Trial

Six individuals with hemiparesis were recruited through the screening process. One participant out of six dropped out of the clinical trial after one session due to the patient's depression that was unrelated to the study. Each participant attended 11 to 12 training sessions lasting 1 or 2 hours per day, over approximately 3 weeks. A physical or occupational therapist was present during each session to run diagnostic tests and adjust game parameters accordingly. If necessary, the therapist provided assistance to protect participants' joint structures or promote their movement quality during game play. Each participant chose the order of digital games that he or she wanted to play to promote performer-based motor learning.

Various Measures

Clinical Evaluation of Behavioral Assessments

Clinical assessment is very important since the major purpose of playing digital games is to regain motor functions that have been lost due to stroke. The clinical evaluation of behavioral assessments was conducted at three points through the clinical trial: pretraining, midtraining (between the 6th and 7th visits) and posttraining. Motor performance was evaluated via a standard arm function test: TEMPA. Severity of motor deficit was determined with the upper extremity portion of the Fugl-Meyer (Fugl-Meyer, Jaasko, Leyman, Olsson, & Steglind, 1975), a measure of motor function. Finally, the Stroke Impact Scale (SIS; Duncan, Wallacem, Lai, Johnson, Embretson, & Laster, 1999) was applied to assess the participation and the quality of life. Although the pattern of some clinical evaluation of behavioral assessment showed gradual improvement throughout the trial, this pattern was observed only among participants with moderate level of impairments. Two participants who had severe impairment level did not show any pattern of improvement (see Stewart et al., 2007 for a detailed discussion).

Usability Assessment

Usability refers to the user's subjective assessment of any given system in terms of ease of use, effectiveness, and satisfaction. In our trial, usability was measured with a combination of a 5-item questionnaire with 7-point semantic differential scales and 13-item questionnaire with independent 7-point scales (Cronbach's α = .97). The usability test was conducted twice: at the beginning of the intervention period (day 1 or 2) and at the end (day 11 or 12).

For data analysis, paired samples t-tests were conducted to compare the means from the beginning and ending points, and ANOVA for the means among different games within individual participants. Results indicated that the participants differed in terms of their preferences for the digital games. For example, one participant with a relatively severe level of impairment evaluated *Ball Shooting* more positively than *Reaching* in terms of usability at the beginning point, $t(17)$ = 2.22, $p < .05$ and at the ending point, $t(17)$ = 2.28, $p < .05$. The participant evaluated *Reaching* more positively than *Spatial Rotation* at the ending point, $t(17)$ = 4.29, $p < .001$, but there was no significant difference at the beginning, $t(17)$ = .76, *n.s.* This participant could not play *Pinch* due to the severity of impairment. In addition, there was no significant difference between the beginning- and ending-point usability ratings, except for *Spatial Rotation*. The usability of *Spatial Rotation* dropped dramatically from 4.5 (*SD* = 2.64) at the beginning point to 2.4 (*SD* = 1.58) at the ending point, $t(17)$ = 4.11, $p < .01$

On the other hand, the other participant with a relatively moderate level of impairment evaluated *Ball Shooting* more positively than *Reaching*, $t(17)$ = 5.05, $p < .001$, *Reaching* than *Spatial Rotation*, $t(17)$ = 5.58, $p < .001$, and *Spatial Rotation* than *Pinch*, $t(17)$ = 10.43, $p < .001$ at the beginning point. However, *Spatial Rotation* was evaluated more positively than *Reaching*, $t(17)$ = 2.73, $p < .05$, and *Reaching* than *Pinch*, $t(17)$ = 7.58, $p < .001$, at the ending point. There was no significant difference between *Ball Shooting* and *Spatial Rotation* at the ending point. Interestingly, the usability of *Ball Shooting* and *Reaching* dropped dramatically throughout the trial. The decreased perception of the games' usability could be due to the increased level of difficulty for the games during the trial. The therapists aimed to keep the success rate of patients' game play at 80%. Thus, patients might feel frustrated to see no visible improvement in their game play since the difficulty level of the games increased as patients' game skills improved. This implies the importance of optimal match between patients' impairment level or skill level and games' difficulty level, which will be discussed further in a subsequent section.

Performance Measures in Games

Performance measures from digital games could be also a good indicator of the patient's progress in a clinical trial. Some of the examples include hit rate, and performance time.

Hit Rate

Hit rate is the percentage of successful completion of required tasks in digital games. A higher value of hit rate means more successful completion of each game such as superior accuracy in reaching, rotating, or pinching.

Performance Time

Performance time is the differential between the time when a new trial starts and the time when the trial ends in a digital game. For example, in *Pinch* it is the difference between the time when a new cube appears and the time when the cube is successfully lifted up to a certain height and brought back to the original position. A smaller value of performance time means greater accuracy for the successful completion of required tasks in the digital game.

Behavioral Measures: Kinematics

These measures are extracted from continuous position data with time stamps. Movement efficiency (ME) is defined as the ratio of the actual moving path of the patient's impaired arm to the shortest moving path (ideal path of a healthy user's arm assuming no impairment). For example, the actual moving path is the accumulation of linear distance with each time interval. The shortest moving path is the linear distance between the start position and the hit point of the virtual target in *Ball Shooting*. Movement efficiency is an indicator of the moving stability of an impaired arm. A lower value of ME represents a better moving stability.

Other kinetic measures include the trajectories that could be reconstructed over the time period of each game play, based on the data on position and orientation. Through the trajectories, more information, such as extreme moving rate, boundary of moving range, and oscillation of movement, can be further identified.

Discussion

In this chapter, we introduced an interdisciplinary project in which we developed four specific digital games for recovery from stroke, with respect to their design process, game features, and evaluation criteria. Evidence suggests that intense and task-specific training is effective for promoting recovery after a cerebrovascular accident. Three-dimensional digital game environments could simulate the real world using a human–machine interface and provide various and enjoyable practice environments without necessarily losing the intensity and task-orientation of motor training, compared with traditional approaches. Serious games are a promising tool for rehabilitation that allows customized and personalized progression. Additionally, the versatility of serious games allows the promotion of skill development that is generalizable to real world functional activities across a wide range of severity levels. In spite of all the touted benefits that serious games could provide, there are difficult challenges that need to be considered in developing and implementing serious games for recovery from stroke.

First of all, the usability results from our clinical trial suggest that there are differences in individual preference for the games. Overall, participants preferred *Ball Shooting* the most, followed by *Reaching*, and *Spatial Rotation*. The *Pinch* task was not included in the comparison due a small number of participants who were able to perform it. Interestingly, perceived usability of the three games decreased over the course of the intervention. A plausible explanation for the individual preference and decreased usability in general may be related to participants' level of impairment. For some participants a certain movement may be easier to perform, and that may affect their perceived usability of the game. For example, the impairment level of one participant was severe, so that the participant might not have been able to perform the supination and pronation exercise easily with the impaired arm, which is the primary movement requirement in *Spatial Rotation*. The challenge could induce frustration and may have led to relatively negative ratings for the usability of *Spatial Rotation* over time. This implies the importance of optimal matching between patients' skill and games' difficulty. Digital games need to be difficult enough to challenge patients' physical movements so that patients could regain some of their lost motor function but should be easy enough to be achievable with effort.

Further, the technological equipment for serious games is still expensive and bulky. New interactive interfaces such as three-dimensional displays or motion tracking devices need to become more portable and cheaper in order to facilitate the implementation of serious games in motor rehabilitation after stroke. Such technological evolution could pragmatically transform lab-based serious games into a home-based rehabilitation tool.

Based on our observations of the clinical trial, the usual hierarchical relationship between the physical therapist and the patient seemed to be less marked in game-based motor training sessions. There were frequent compliments and encouragements from the therapist (e.g., "it was so close," "Yeah, you got it," "Look at your score," etc.). By assisting the patient physically and mentally, the therapist coplayed three-dimensional games together with the patient, which, we believe, resulted in much laughter, intimacy through shared activities, and natural bonding between them.

The coplay perspective highlights three important issues with regard to serious games for medical applications. First, we often neglect how players could influence the effects of digital games (i.e., human factors) because we pay too much attention to what digital games could do for players (i.e., technology features). Game features such as interactivity or graphical enhancement are essential elements for the success of digital games in motor rehabilitation.

However, the way such digital games are played by players (e.g., coplay) could either intensify or attenuate desired outcomes, especially in medical applications. Second, researchers need to consider measuring effects at the dyadic level. Most research reports the usability and effectiveness of digital games in motor rehabilitation at the individual level of patients (e.g., how the level of impairment improved through the training sessions). Since the therapist is also a user of digital games for motor training, the therapist's perception and evaluation of such digital games, as well as his or her interaction with the patient, need to be taken into account in order to demonstrate more in-depth analyses. Third, digital games are indeed complementary tools for motor rehabilitation. Professional assists from the physical therapist are critical for appropriate posture and training of the patient even in digital game environments. This could go a long way toward alleviating the therapist's fear of "being replaced" that is often identified as the inevitable resistance from caregivers when a new technology-enhanced innovation is introduced (cf., Mair et al., 2004).

As a final remark, serious games clearly have great potential to provide engaging and interesting motor training environments to patients poststroke when they are carefully developed and cautiously exercised in the field with professional assistance from therapists. However, successful development of three-dimensional digital games for rehabilitation is very challenging due to its interdisciplinary nature and complexity. This is why we need more research in the areas of using serious games for recovery from stroke specifically, and for medical intervention in general.

Acknowledgment

This research was supported in part by National Institutes of Health Roadmap Initiative grant # P20 RR20700-01 and by the Integrated Media Systems Center, a National Science Foundation Engineering Research Center, Cooperative Agreement # EEC-9529152, with additional support from the Annenberg School for Communication, University of Southern California. We thank all our collaborators.

References

American Heart Association. (2008). *Heart disease and stroke statistics: 2008 update.* Dallas, Texas: American Heart Association. Retrieved February 15, 2008 from http://www.americanheart.org/downloadable/heart/1200082005246HS_Stats%20 2008.final.pdf

Deutsch, J. E., Latonio, J., Burdea, G., & Boian, R. (2001). Poststroke rehabilitation with the Rutgers Ankle System: A case study. *Presence, 10,* 416–430.

Duncan, P. W., Wallacem, D., Lai, S. M., Johnson, D., Embretson, S., & Laster, L. J. (1999). The stroke impact scale version 2.0: Evaluation of reliability, validity, and sensitivity to change. *Stroke, 30*(10), 2131–2140.

Fugl-Meyer, A. R., Jaasko, L., Leyman, I., Olsson, S., & Steglind, S. (1975). The post-stroke hemiplegic patient: A method for evaluation of physical performance. *Scandinavian Journal of Rehabilitation Medicine, 7,* 13–31.

Holden, M. K. (2005). Virtual environments for motor rehabilitation: Review. *Cyberpsychology & Behavior, 8,* 187–211.

Holden, M., Todorov, E., Callahan, J., & Bizzi, E. (1999). Virtual environment training improves motor performance in two patients with stroke: Case report. *Neurology Report, 23,* 57–67.

Jonsson, A. C., Lindgren, I., Hallstrom, B., Norrving, B., & Lindgren, A. (2005). Determinants of quality of life in stroke survivors and their informal caregivers. *Stroke, 36,* 803–808.

Jung, Y., Yeh, S., Stewart, J., & USC-UT consortium for interdisciplinary research. (2006). Tailoring virtual reality technology for stroke rehabilitation: A human factors design. Extended Abstracts on *Human Factors in Computing Systems* 929–934.

Kreuter, M., Farrell, D., Olevitch, L., & Brennan, L. (2000). *Tailoring health messages: Customizing communication with computer technology.* Mahwah, NJ: Erlbaum.

Lee, T. D., & Maraj, B. K. (1994). Effects of bandwidth goals and bandwidth knowledge of results on motorlearning. *Research Quarterly for Exercise and Sport, 65*(3), 244–249.

Mair, F. S., Hibbert, D., May, C. R., Angus, R., Finch, T., Boland, A., et al. (2002). Problems with implementation: The story of a home telecare trial. In P. Whitten & D. Cook (Eds.), *Understanding health communication technologies* (pp. 3–10). San Francisco: Jossey-Bass.

Mayo, N. E., Wood-Dauphinee, S., Cote, R., Durcan, L., & Carlton, J. (2002). Activity, participation, and quality of life 6 months poststroke. *Archives of Physical Medical Rehabilitation, 83,* 1035–1042.

Merians, A. S., Jack, D., Boian, R., Tremaine, M., Burdea, G. C., Adamovich S. V., et al. (2002). Virtual reality-augmented rehabilitation for patients following stroke. *Physical Therapy, 82,* 898–915.

Norman, D. A. (1988). *The design of everyday things.* New York: Doubleday

Schmidt, R. A., & Lee, T. D. (1999). *Motor control and learning: A behavioral emphasis* (4th ed.). Champaign, IL: Human Kinetics.

Stewart, J. C., Yeh, S., Jung, Y., Yoon, H., Whitford, M., Chen, S., et al. (2007). Pilot trial results from a virtual reality system designed to enhance recovery of skilled arm and hand movements after stroke. *Journal of NeuroEngineering and Rehabilitation, 4.* Retrieved from http://jneuroengrehab.com/content/pdf/1743-0003-4-21.pdf

Taub, E., Uswatte, G., & Morris, D. M. (2003). Improved motor recovery after stroke and massive cortical reorganization following constraint-induced movement therapy. *Physical Medicine and Rehabilitation Clinics of North America, 14,* 77–91.

Vincente, K. (2004). *The human factor.* New York: Routledge.

Weiss, P.L., Katz, N. (2004). The potential of virtual reality for rehabilitation. *Journal of Rehabilitation Research and Development, 41*(5), 7–10.

Yeh, S., Rizzo, A. A., Zhu, W., Stewart, J., McLaughlin, M.L., Cohen, I., et al. (2005). An integrated system: Virtual reality, haptics and modern sensing technique (VHS) for poststroke rehabilitation. *Proceedings of the ACM Symposium on Virtual Reality Software and Technology* (VRST 05), USA, 59–62.

You, S. H., Jang, S. H., Kim, Y. H., Hallett, M., Ahn, S. H., Kwon, Y. H., et al. (2005). Virtual reality-induced cortical reorganization and associated locomotor recovery in chronic stroke: An experimenter-blind randomized study. *Stroke, 36,* 1166–1171.

Chapter 25

Reducing Risky Sexual Decision Making in the Virtual and in the Real World

Serious Games, Intelligent Agents, and a SOLVE Approach

Lynn Carol Miller, John L. Christensen, Carlos G. Godoy, Paul Robert Appleby, Charisse Corsbie-Massay, and Stephen J. Read

Everyday millions of adolescents and young adults take potentially life-altering risks, including not using a condom when having sex. Sadly, nearly half of all new HIV infections are contracted in adolescence and young adulthood (Fisher, Fisher, Bryan, & Misovich, 2002). Although HIV is increasingly prevalent among heterosexual individuals, over 18,000 men who have sex with men (MSM) are newly diagnosed with HIV/AIDS annually, representing 70% of all male adults and adolescents diagnosed, and 51% of all newly diagnosed cases of HIV/AIDS in 2004 (Centers for Disease Control [CDC], 2006). Among those 18 to 30, younger MSM engage in more risky sexual behaviors (MacKellar, et al., 2005; Xia et al., 2006). Despite these numbers, progress in stemming new HIV cases seems stalled. One reason may be that a younger, tech-savvy generation of MSM may "tune out," or disregard conventional prevention messages (for a review, see Wolitski & Valdiserri, 2001, pp. 883–884).

Younger MSM may instead be responsive to interactive interventions (e.g., interactive video, intelligent agents/games) especially when delivered via the Internet—a "potentially powerful tool for use with HIV prevention interventions" (CDC, 2006, p. 4). Certainly, in educational domains, interactive media—compared to noninteractive media—has been shown to enhance transfer of learning (e.g., Moreno, Mayer, Spires, & Lester, 2001), but the literature on the effectiveness of interactive health interventions is more limited. Nevertheless, there are educational interventions that show promise for enhancing health education in a number of domains (e.g., Bartholomew et al., 2000; Lieberman & Brown, 1995; Reis, Riley, & Baer, 2000; Tingen, Grimling, Bennett, Gibson, & Renew, 1997) including diabetes management (e.g., Brown, et al., 1997) and dietary change (e.g., Brug, Campbell, & van Assema, 1999; Campbell, DeVellis, Strecher, & Ammerman, 1994; Kreuter & Strecher, 1996; Winett, Moore, Wagner, & Hite, 1991).

The challenge for researchers, however, is to design interactive interventions that (1) utilize theory that integrates the best intervention efforts from past literature and new opportunities for investigation and discovery that are enabled by interactive technologies, while enhancing our ability to predict future behavior and optimize risk reduction; (2) take advantage of the shared available features of interactive and gaming environments (e.g., the ability to create virtual choices that realistically map onto real-life, interactivity, personalization); and (3) take advantage of the special features of intelligent agent and gaming technologies available today and on the horizon. In this chapter, we discuss work funded by grants supported by the National Institutes of Health (NIH).[1] Our approach to changing risky behavior is called Socially Optimized Learning in Virtual Environments (SOLVE) using interactive technologies (interactive video [IAV] and intelligent agent and gaming technologies [IT] that address each of the above issues).

Socially Optimized Learning in Virtual Environments: SOLVE Theory

Traditional Approaches Help Reduce Risk-Taking: But More Needs to be Done

Guided by a variety of theoretical approaches, such as Bandura's (1994) cognitive social learning theory, cognitive behavior therapy (Beck, 1970), and the theory of planned behavior (Ajzen, 1985, 1991; Ajzen & Fishbein, 1980), various researchers (for reviews see DiClemente & Peterson (1994) and Fisher & Fisher (1992)) have demonstrated that extensive training in cognitive and behavioral skills can significantly reduce high risk sexual practices (e.g., anal sex without a condom). Based on this work, Kelly (1995) has identified a number of theory-based components that should be included in a behavioral intervention for changing risky sexual behavior for men who have sex with men. For example, intervention components should be designed to increase perceived self-efficacy for engaging in safer choices, support beliefs that those changes will reduce risk (Ajzen, 1991; Bandura, 1994), and form and bolster strong behavioral intentions to use safer sex behaviors when appropriate (Ajzen, 1985). Additional components should support the learning of behavioral skills (such as condom use and assertiveness skills), and enhance self-management skills for managing cognitions and behaviors relevant to risky situations (Beck, 1970; see also Kelly, St. Lawrence, & Betts & Brasfield, 1990; Kelly, St. Lawrence, Hood, & Brasfield, 1989).

Nevertheless, there are several major shortcomings to traditional interventions: (1) they are labor intensive, expensive to deliver, and require large participant time commitment at an intervention delivery site; (2) variance accounted for in risk reduction is typically small (Baron & Brown, 1991; Kirby, 2001; Romer, 2003) even with more sophisticated methodological approaches and prospective designs controlling for initial behavior/perceptions (e.g., Brewer, Weinstein, Cuite, & Herrington, 2004; Fishbein & Yzer, 2003; Gerrard, Gibbons, Benthin, & Hessling, 1996); and (3) these "kitchen sink" approaches do not tell us what (within the intervention) is (and is not) working for whom under what conditions, thereby making improvement difficult.

Interactive Environments Can Address Some of These Shortcomings

Consistent with research on factors that mediate HIV prevention for MSM (e.g., Kelly, 1995) SOLVE argues that changes in cognitions (e.g., self-efficacy; Bandura, 1994), behavioral intentions (Ajzen, 1985) and skills training that support safer sex can reduce risky behaviors (i.e., unprotected anal sex; UAI)—but does so by using virtual instead of one-on-one models and guides that are embedded in a cost-effective and sensory (i.e., visually and aurally) engaging lifelike intervention (for more detail see, Appleby, Godoy, Miller & Read, 2008; Read et al., 2006).

In SOLVE-IAV, MSM assume the role of a character on a "virtual date" who "hooks up" with an attractive other using interactive technology. As the lead character, MSM make choices regarding what to do on the virtual date (e.g., how to talk directly about using condoms), and those choices define the story as the drama unfolds. These guides and models use a variety of strategies to enhance learning and motivation to change risky behavior, which include modeling behavior to enhance procedural knowledge and skills (e.g., modeling condom use, condom initiation, negotiation, and risk, such as drugs, alcohol, UAI) refusal skills, and the incorporation of behavior, such as checking condom dates and bringing condoms on a date into "preparation" routines). If the user makes a particular choice for his agent (e.g., talk directly about safer sex), the user is simultaneously making decisions about what to do as well as watching the model that represents them; in essence, show them how to do that. In addition, the guides (peer mentors) may change beliefs by linking risky behavior to subsequent negative outcomes, thus reinforcing "implemental intentions" (Gollwitzer, 1999), addressing beliefs that undermine safer choices (e.g., discussing facts and beliefs about alcohol and drugs, and the relative risks of various sexual behaviors, differentially reinforcing safer and riskier choices), recapping the sequence of choices MSM make, and explaining real-life implications of such choices.

Need to Address the More Automatic Route to Decision Making

Decision makers rely on "nonconscious biases" that automatically guide behavior before conscious knowledge does (Bechara, Damasio, Tranel, & Damasio, 1997, p. 1293). With increasing life experience these nonconscious biases become more accurate—guiding more advantageous and less adverse decisions and outcomes. Such experience-based "gist" learning also keeps adults from being distracted by detail and irrelevant information (Reyna & Farley, 2006). Emotions are key mediators in decision-making processes (Damasio, 2000; Panksepp, 1998; Rolls, 1999); they adaptively elicit, in a highly efficient way, learned responses in social situations (Frijda, 1986; Keltner & Gross, 1999; Levenson, 1994; Oatley & Johnson-Laird, 1996; Plutchik, 1979). These emotional responses, which help mark the situation as "good" or "bad", assist decision making under circumstances of conflict or uncertainty, operating either consciously or nonconsciously.

Thus, adolescents and young adults may not consciously deliberate risks and benefits. Rather, they may have "unconscious emotional and cognitive reactions to environmental triggers" (Reyna & Farley, 2006, p. 33), making decisions reactively or intuitively. For example, adolescents' "willingness" to engage in risky behaviors, which they may later regret (e.g., in the heat of the moment), accounts for variance in behavior beyond intentions alone (Gibbons et al., 2004); these reactions are not easily explained by more deliberative models.

However, experience with risk cues is needed to develop accurate "gists" that provide the basis for adaptive automatic reactions. Without prior situational experience to accurately mark a situation as risky, decisions by today's youth can be catastrophic (see Baird & Fugelsang, 2004). But in many domains, such as HIV/AIDS, gaining the necessary experience can be extremely costly. Among young MSM (15 to 29) who had engaged in UAI, 59% of those testing positive for HIV perceived that they were at low risk for infection (MacKellar et al., 2005). If lack of prior negative outcomes increases risk-taking—until that catastrophic outcome occurs, then we need to find a way to provide the "risk avoidance cues" and the negative outcomes without real risks. Interventions that fully simulate that experience might enable safer learning of more automatic anticipatory emotions (i.e., fear) among young adults (Read et al., 2006). Preventing HIV among new generations of young MSM may require interventions that concurrently address the "two divergent paths to risk taking: a reasoned and a reactive route," taking into account the developmental trajectories involved in each (Reyna & Farley, 2006, p. 1).

SOLVE: Combining Reactive as well as Cognitive Routes to Decision Making

SOLVE simultaneously addresses the more traditional cognitive intervention strategies used in one-on-one counseling as well as the more reactive and more affect-based route to decision making (Bechara et al., 1997; Reyna & Farley, 2006). As indicated in Figure 25.1, our theoretical model suggests that, in the presence of cues associated with a potentially risky situation (including those in the virtual environment designed to simulate real life), both cognitions and affective biases (from prior experience) are activated and guide virtual decisions—both consciously and nonconsciously. Affect associated with these

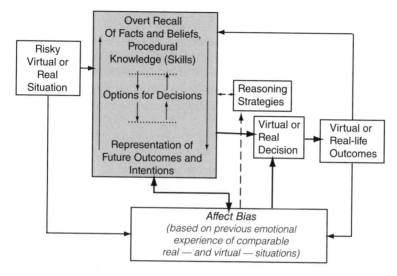

Figure 25.1   SOLVE Theoretical Model modified from Bechara et al. (1997).

virtual decisions then biases future decisions (virtual and real-life) that, in combination with cognitions and skills, impact virtual or real-life outcomes.

This SOLVE theoretical model suggests that to change a population's risky behavior, interventions need to incorporate the more experientially and affectively based aspects of learning. Because many of the details regarding the SOLVE components have been described elsewhere (see Appleby et al., 2008; Miller & Read, 2005; Read et al., 2006), we present the highlights of this approach that pertain to the use of interactive media, serious games, and intelligent agents in this chapter.

Is SOLVE-IAV Effective?

In recent experimental longitudinal findings we found that MSM in the interactive condition had lower levels of UAI 90 days postintervention (Miller & Read, 2005; Read et al., 2006) compared to those in a standard of care control group. In an additional longitudinal study with 18- to 30-year-old MSM (using IAVs targeted to African-American, Latino, and White MSM), preliminary findings suggest that SOLVE-IAV reduces UAI over time, especially for younger (18–24), high risk MSM (two or more instances of UAI with nonprimary partners in the past 3 months) compared to wait-list control, yoked control (passively viewing the IAV with the choices of another subject), and one-on-one human interaction conditions. SOLVE-IAV accounts for significant variance above and beyond traditional variables (e.g., intentions, self-efficacy) in predicting to future risk-taking. The question remains: What features of interactive environments facilitate the achievement of effective interventions?

SOLVE: Shared Technology-Enabled Possibilities

Since 1989, our research team has been engaged in developing interactive virtual environments using the most current technology with the goal of reducing risky sexual behaviors. Initially, we used CD-ROM and DVD technology. With the most recent advent of effective intelligent agents, we can advance our HIV prevention interventions using intelligent agents and gaming technologies.

These Interactive Environments

1. *Enable individuals to identify with, assume the role of, make decisions for, and learn from the modeled behavior of a character on a virtual date.* Because the user can select what decision the character will make (thereby "owning" the decision), the user can watch the "virtual self" model the resulting behavior and consequences; this enables scaffolding of new strategies for achieving goals (e.g., negotiating safer sex) in a specific context ("on the couch") and under specific conditions (e.g., romantic interest, sexual arousal). This provides modeling for a range of component skills including how to initiate, negotiate, refuse (to have sex without a condom), and use condoms under a range of conditions. Interestingly, the extent to which MSM identify with their self characters in the interactive condition is a significant predictor in our preliminary analyses of unprotected anal intercourse (UAI) risk reduction.

2. *Engage MSM at risk for contracting HIV, in part, because MSM can make and therefore "own" their decisions (instead of just passively observing another's behavior).* Engaging the attention of MSM and motivating them within an intervention is critical for learning (Grunwald & Corsbie-Massay, 2006). In dating and sexually intimate contexts, individuals are motivated to seek opportunities (e.g., for sex, emotional relationships) and avoid threats (e.g., physical, psychological). SOLVE environments allow for these dynamic interactions by making it possible to experience virtual interactive sexual encounters with attractive others: MSM in our focus groups viewed such environments as fun and engaging and our preliminary analyses with over 300 MSM reveal that participants in the interactive video condition (IAV) found our environments significantly more engaging than MSM who simply observed another MSM's choices.

3. *Afford opportunities for situated virtual learning in realistic narratives that map onto real-life contexts of risk and therefore are more likely to lead to a transfer of learning without having to experience risks first hand.* Preliminary findings from our NIAID grant indicate that virtual decisions (e.g., sexual position preference, choosing to kiss, cuddle, or use condoms) are significantly and positively correlated with decisions of a similar type within the past 3 months. We found similar significant patterns for predicting to specific future decisions from virtual decisions 3 months prior.

4. *Allow MSM to make virtual risky choices in contexts that are affectively and contextually similar to contexts of risk in real life.* In standard one-on-one or group behavioral interventions for HIV prevention, many of the affective and contextual cues that guide behavior in real life are missing or inadequate. In most sexual encounters, individuals who are attracted to their partners will experience very salient and immediate affective and motivational reactions (e.g., sexual arousal; fear of rejection) that can potentially lead to risky choices. Research on state dependent encoding and learning (Bower & Forgas, 2000) suggests that if individuals learn behavioral strategies while experiencing even a mild form of the relevant affect (e.g., sexual arousal), they may be better able to more automatically activate, retrieve, and use safer sexual strategies in similar contexts of risk in real life. That is, if interventions afford virtual decision-making opportunities leading up to safer choices under similar emotional conditions of encoding, we may enhance subsequent retrieval of cognitions, goals, and problem-solving skills in similar emotional contexts of risk. Standard interventions rarely take into account the physical context, circumstances, and cues that impact decision making. With interactive media, we can make the when, where, whom, and how of risky situations very concrete, relevant, and realistic for the target audience. For example, we can incorporate visual and acoustic signals from bars, clubs, apartments, and online connections that are typical "scripted" paths to risky choices for distinct populations of MSM.

5. *Provide required modeling opportunities through self and other characters* (e.g., all participants view the self and other characters pocketing condoms as part of the grooming activities in preparation for a date).

6. *Offer optional mentoring.* Interactive environments make it possible for MSM to ask for advice or seek out additional information during the video. Although MSM rarely sought advice, unfamiliar situations often prompted users to seek guide advice (e.g., decisions regarding methamphetamine for users who had never encountered the drug).

7. *Afford guides and mentors to interrupt risky choices and scaffold self-regulatory change.* As mentioned earlier, typical behavioral interventions do not contextualize the sequence of events leading up to risky decision points, and do not allow MSM to make risky choices. Interactive environments make these accommodations and incorporate more advanced components, including the use of ICAP (interrupt; challenge; acknowledge; and provide) framework:

   a. Interrupt risky choice before it is consummated (slowing it down, making it less automatic).

   b. Challenge and frame consequences of risky choice in terms of consideration of future consequences, thus reducing risky sex (Appleby, Marks, Ayala, Miller, Murphy, & Mansergh, 2005). In SOLVE (Read et al., 2006), we combined the social cognitive intervention with a message framing approach. That is, we (Miller & Read, 2005; Read et al., 2006) include framing elements that map onto prior research, tailoring, and framing guide responses to be responsive to the men's behavioral choices.

In SOLVE, messages are generally framed as gains (e.g., use condoms to stay safe, avoid HIV) because past research suggests that prevention messages are more effective if we focus on what the individual has to gain by engaging in the self-promoting behavior (Rothman, Bartels, Wlaschin, & Salovey, 2006). But when the individual is about to take a risk (e.g., have unprotected anal sex), the guides "popped up," challenging MSM with a loss-framed message (e.g., "Are you kidding? Anal sex without a condom? Don't you know how dangerous that is? Even if you are HIV positive you can still get other strains of the disease and get AIDS faster. Don't fool yourself into thinking being on top is safe. If you still want to have anal sex (and I know you do), you can still change your mind and put one on right now"). The guides challenge risky decisions using loss-frame messages (Salovey & Williams-Piehota, 2004).[2]

In fact, only loss-frame messages have been shown to reduce unprotected anal or vaginal sex for HIV positive individuals (Richardson, et al., 2004) and have recently been shown to evoke negative affect (Stark, Rothman, Bernat, & Patrick, 2007). In the latter study, Stark et al. measured facial EMG and skin conductance responses while individuals received framed-messages and determined that loss-framed messages elicited more negative affect compared to gain-framed messages.

c. Acknowledge motives and feelings motivating behavior. It is important to articulate the individual's emotions, motives, and goals and link them to decision making and the subsequent consequences. Consistent with work on scaffolding self-regulation (Read et al., 2006), guides acknowledge and make salient MSM's emotions and desires, both short- (e.g., "if you still want to have anal sex…and I know you do…" and long-term (e.g., "you can still…be safe"). The fear that loss-frame messages evoke has been shown to motivate behavior change when associated with a clear method of reducing the fear (Witte & Allen, 2000). The guides also provide a way to be self-efficacious to avoid the threat (fear), yet still achieve desires through statements such as, "…you can still change your mind and be safe…put on a condom right now."

d. Provide strategies for simultaneously achieving approach motives, avoiding immediate negative outcomes, and avoiding negative future consequences (contracting HIV) that may not have been adequately incorporated into decisions within the risk context. Interactive environments provide an alternative path to integrate complex motives—what can be done to achieve important goals (short- and long-term) in the same contextualized situation given one's motives and emotions. The self-character can model a safer strategy that better achieves the user's goals (if the user selects that choice). If the user does not select that safer choice, guides recap (see below) and review each choice at the end of the interactive experience to ensure that each user observes his character model a safer alternative strategy.

8. *Potentially evoke negative affect (i.e., fear, guilt).* As mentioned above, we used loss-framed messages that are likely to evoke negative affect. Bechara et al. (1997) have demonstrated that this affect may automatically self-guide MSM's future risky choices in similar situations, even outside of their conscious awareness.[3] Consistent with work on affect-based decision making, preliminary evidence indicates that negative affect (e.g., fear, guilt) immediately post SOLVE-IAV significantly predicts reduction in subsequent real-life UAI (Christensen et al., 2007). These negative affective reactions to decisions may then guide more automatic, subsequent real-world decision making by activating negative emotions triggered by similar risk contexts in the future.

9. *Afford Test, Intervention, and Local Evaluation (TILEs).* Interactive virtual environments afford local tests of whether MSM are likely to make risky sexual decisions in response to specific risky situations and cues, provide interventions designed to alter those specific contextualized decisions, and then formatively evaluate whether this specific intervention is virtually effective. We identify a series of TILEs within the intervention: a context specific set of Test (i.e., the user's choice in a risky situation), Intervention (i.e., a gain/loss-framed message from the guides regarding the user's choice), and Local Evaluation (i.e., whether the user chooses the same virtual decision again or a safer one). Interactive environments make it possible to create a landscape of these TILEs, affording discrimination and generalization of different "test" situations and subsequently evaluating the effectiveness of different interventions for a given MSM. This creates a "topology" of when, and under what conditions, a given MSM engages in risky behaviors and what interventions are most effective, for a given MSM.

10. *Provide TILEs for unexpected, but typical, obstacles that increase risk taking.* For example, we incorporated TILEs for interacting with a drug dealer at a club who was peddling methamphetamine, a popular drug in this population (Appleby, Storholm, Ayala, & Miller, 2007).

11. *Review the choices and events that unfolded within the virtual scenario, thus reinforcing good choices and providing models for better choices.* At the end of the intervention, MSM are led through their choices by the guides who highlight the safer and riskier choices that the user made. The choices are automatically recorded and can be repeated and reviewed automatically

by the guides. When choices were risky, guides provided a less risky alternative for the situation.

12. *Afford personalized risk reduction.* In SOLVE, MSM go on a virtual date and are provided with virtual decision-making experiences instead of real ones. The action proceeds, as it does in real-life, based on the decisions made by the user, including potentially risky choices, to form a narrative. These choice points are designed to be similar to real-life risky situations and can be viewed as "test stimuli" for TILEs, and all are recorded for future data analysis. How the intervention proceeds is a function of MSM's decisions, with respect to and within these TILEs.

Limitations and Future Directions: SOLVE-IT

IAV Limitations

Interactive video environments that simulate risky choices appear promising for providing a diagnostic test-bed for past behavior and future real-life risk taking. Despite its promise, the limitations of IAV technology restrict the number of test situations (e.g., venues, interaction partners, type of risk, risk scenarios, etc.), and this limits personalized risk reduction for MSM. For example, we could not (1) insure that there was at least one risky test situation that was relevant to all MSM; (2) assess whether different MSM exhibited different risk-taking profiles across various situations; (3) assess whether a given MSM's responses to specific types of test situations predicted similar real-life behavior; (4) assess whether a given MSM learned to self-regulate his initially risky choice (to make a safer choice) in a given virtual situation and whether that predicted subsequent real-life UAI risk-reduction in the same or similar situations; and (5) easily update and change the intervention—providing both an application and an updatable "test-bed" for to incorporate cumulative advances in personalized interventions.

Intelligent Agents in Serious Gaming Environments: Addressing IAV Limitations

SOLVE-IT (SOLVE using intelligent agent and gaming technologies) could address these limitations. In the field of artificial intelligence (AI), an intelligent agent is defined as a system that perceives and acts on its environment to maximize its ability to achieve its goals (Russell & Norvig, 2003). Intelligent agents can be embedded in multiplayer games where numerous intelligent agents and humans interact and in which a human can be substituted for an agent. Serious games are applications that utilize innovative gaming technologies to enhance learning and problem solving in domains such as education, national defense, or healthcare (Sawyer, 2007).

Intelligent agents and gaming technologies can provide a nearly infinite number of alternative realistic partners for humans. Given that intelligent agents also have goals, this provides a wealth of potential scenarios and test situations, thus making it possible to incorporate and readily test (with repeated trials) new interventions or updates in real-time, within the same game.

Members of our NIMH research team have developed, produced, and used these technologies for interventions in a variety of health, training, and educational applications (Johnson, Vilhjalmsson & Marsella, 2005; Marsella, Johnson, & LaBore, 2003). In Marsella et al.'s multiagent-based simulation environment, *PsychSim* (Marsella & Pynadath, 2004, 2005; Marsella, Pynadath, & Read, 2004; Pynadath & Marsella, 2004, 2005), a researcher can construct a social scenario where a diverse set of entities, either groups or individuals, interact and communicate among themselves.

Each entity has its own goals and policies of achievement, relationships with other entities (e.g., friendship, hostility, authority), private beliefs, and mental models about other entities that include recursive models of their beliefs and goals. That is, each agent has a "theory of mind" about themselves and about all other virtual and real interactants in the program. The simulation tool generates the behavior for these entities and provides explanations in terms of each entity's goals and beliefs. The rich entity model allows one to examine the potential consequences of minor variations in the scenario. The researcher can manually perturb the simulation by changing the models or specifying actions and messages for any entity to perform. Alternatively, the simulation itself can perturb the scenario to provide a range of possible behaviors that can identify critical sensitivities of behavior to deviations in modified goals, relationships, or mental models. Participants can fill out a variety of different individual difference measures tapping into beliefs, policies, goals, and values that can be used to model agents. For example, the extensive literature on attachment styles can be used to create the computational models.

Attachment Theory: Underlying Basis for the "Theory of Mind" of Agents

Our goal is to use intelligent agents to model individual realistic cases of MSM who take sexual risks (i.e., engage in UAI) with nonprimary partners. Attachment theory (Bowlby, 1969) elegantly describes how coherent beliefs about self and others broadly impacts sexual decision making and behavior (Miller & Fishkin, 1997); it suggests that one's mental model of others in close relationships as adults depends upon the beliefs and mental models and attachments that we form as children with our caregivers. A voluminous literature in developmental, personality, social, and clinical psychology, as well as in related social sciences, provides the basis for modeling individual agents with coherent differences in their models of the self and others, and their subsequent actions (e.g., Cassidy & Shaver, 1999; Hinde, 2005; Mikulincer & Goodman, 2006; Rholes & Simpson, 2004). Two dimensions underlie adult attachment styles or "mental models" (Brennan, Clark, & Shaver, 1998): (1) anxiety, with the high end associated with negative views of self (e.g., unlovable, unworthy), and (2) avoidance, with the high end associated with negative views of others (untrustworthy, undependable, unsupportive). These two dimensions form four attachment types: Secure (low avoid, low anxiety), Preoccupied (high anxiety, low avoid), Avoidant (low anxiety, high avoid), and Fearful (high anxiety, high avoid) (Fraley, Waller, & Brennan, 2000). Some risk-taking behaviors (e.g., substance use, participating in sex work) have been associated with the high end of the anxiety dimension (Gwadz, Clatts, Leonard, & Goldsamt, 2004) while poor partner communication that may therefore serve as an impediment to condom use has been associated with the high end of the avoidant dimension (Moore & Parker-Halford, 1999).

While more chronic attachment styles are predictive of risk, the nature of the relationship is also critical. For example, those with the greatest love for, trust in, commitment to, and interdependence with one's primary partner were more likely to engage in unprotected anal intercourse with him (Appleby, Miller, & Rothspan, 1999). Because there is a significant subgroup of these MSM who also had unprotected sex outside of their primary relationship, and because the base rates of HIV are high among MSM, those in committed relationships may paradoxically be at greater risk for HIV than those in non-committed relationships. These findings demonstrate the complex relationship between relationship status, attachment styles, and risky behavior. In our own current NAID R01 funded work, we have found that both avoidant and anxious dimensions predict risky sexual behaviors with nonprimary partners for MSM, and the nature of these predictions may depend upon the current status of one's romantic relationships.

Modeling Realistic Intelligent Agents

Intelligent agents provide lifelike interaction partners and "contexts of risk" by creating a range of characters that are realistic and differ in a host of physical and psychological characteristics, a significant advantage over the interactive video (IAV). As in real-life, in the virtual environment MSM will be able to choose virtual "intelligent agent" partners based on their characteristics and profiles, choose preferred venues, including Web sites, bars, and clubs with known demographics, or opportunistically interact with characters at various locations in the gaming environment.

With PsychSim, Marsella and Pynadath's system for creating intelligently realistic agents, SOLVE-IT intelligent agents will have humanlike physical characteristics and humanlike psychological attributes such as goals, beliefs, and policies that produce their behavior. We can populate a virtual environment with a realistic array of psychologically, and physically diverse MSM as potential partners because the underlying activation of various states, goals, beliefs, and policies of the agents differ, thus providing more realistic diverse interpersonal experiences. Each of our agents will be based on the data of real participants to create each "realistic" agent. Participants' responses to various individual difference measures and scenario-specific questions in our research studies will serve as a primary data source.

By gathering case-based data suitable for modeling an individual's own states, goals, beliefs, and policies, we can model individual cases as intelligent agents. This data will allow us to: (1) run simulations with the intelligent agents created from the data for a given case (e.g., attachment styles) and examine which virtual interactions for that agent are likely to lead to risky behaviors and which are not; (2) compare what the actual human does when interacting in that environment; and (3) if our simulated case accurately predicts the behavior demonstrated by the real individual, that case can be used in the future as a template for the game to choose scenarios that are most challenging for that MSM. Therefore, the modeled case based on an actual MSM becomes a realistic potential sexual partner within SOLVE-IT for another real life MSM interacting with this virtual agent.

Computational Approach to Modeling MSM and Predicting Risk

We model the responses of real-life MSM to create realistic virtual characters in the virtual environment. PsychSim's decision-theoretic agents not only provide agents with a theory of mind, but PsychSim has powerful automated fitting algorithms that allow agent models to be readily fitted to empirical data (Pynadath & Marsella, 2004), significantly facilitating its use in research. Therefore, we can use MSM's responses at baseline and in the virtual environment to computationally model the decisions that MSM are likely to make given the precipitating factors in the context (e.g., the type of venue, the partner's characteristics, etc.). With our team of social scientists, statisticians, and computer scientists—we will explore the following question: Can the computational model of PsychSim better predict who is likely to engage in UAI at follow-up, and under what circumstances, compared to conventional statistical tools? Can it also better predict change in real-life UAI? Virtual diagnosticity of behavior may provide an updatable "test-bed" that affords cumulative advances for the science of optimizing behavioral risk-reduction. If we can accurately measure each MSM's beliefs, policies, and goals in predicting the user's risky behaviors, this could shed light on how beliefs get activated and their effect on risky choices in given situations, and lead to subsequent work comparing the virtual choices of each real-life MSM against his modeled self.

Greater Personalization of Environments for Risk Reduction

Intelligent agents and games would allow another benefit: they can provide greater tailoring of the environment for each individual MSM, based on his baseline measures (e.g., Kreuter, Farrell, Olevitch, & Brennan, 2000; Skinner,

Campbell, Rimer, Curry, & Prochaska, 1999) and personalization within the environment, based on MSM's patterns of responses during the game and on our intelligent agent based modeling online of that MSM. Such personalization would be highly innovative. If intelligent agents (e.g., potential partners, guides in the game/gaming environment) can be more responsive to the behavior of a given MSM, and if we can "model" the user online in real time, we may greatly advance the science of optimizing personalized risk reduction—doing so online over the Web—thereby potentially providing extraordinary reach.

SOLVE-IT provides a virtual intelligent agent/game test-bed for the creation of a cumulative science of optimizing personalized diagnosis, intervention development, and risk reduction. This advance could revolutionize the way we as researchers conceptualize, understand, predict, and reduce risky behavior—personalizing it to optimize risk reduction for the individual case. Such an approach could simultaneously address health disparities within and across diverse at-risk target populations.

Notes

1. The project described was supported by Grant Number 1 R01AI052756 from the NIAID. Its contents are solely the responsibility of the authors and do not necessarily represent the official views of the NIAID. The current game and SOLVE theory development is supported by Grant Number R01 MH082671 from the NIMH. Its contents are solely the responsibility of the authors and do not necessarily represent the official views of the NIMH.
2. Prior research indicates that gain frames (e.g., what one stands to gain, such as avoiding AIDS, staying safe) if one engages in a behavior (e.g., uses condoms) are generally particularly effective for prevention promotion (Rothman & Salovey, 1997). But, in the face of greater risk taking, alternative frames (e.g., loss frames, emphasizing what you will lose if you engage in the risk), might be more effective for subsequent behavior change. Framing effects can exert a profound impact on health behavior (Rothman & Salovey, 1997) such that some frames (e.g., gain frames) work best for prevention while other frames (e.g., loss frames) work better when individuals confront more risky situations. Salovey and Williams-Piehota (2004), consistent with others (e.g., Kühberger, 1998; Tversky & Kahneman, 1981), have suggested that for HIV prevention, loss frame messages for high-risk individuals might be more effective (under high risk) than gain frame messages (focusing on what one has to gain).
3. In Bechara et al. (1997) this was indicated by learned changes in galvanic skin responses that anticipated risky choices in a gambling task before cognitions regarding the perceived risk could be articulated.

References

Ajzen, I. (1985). From intentions to actions: A theory of planned behavior. In J. Kuhl & J. Beckmann (Ed.), *Action-control: From cognition to behavior* (pp. 11–39). Heidelberg, Germany: Springer.

Ajzen, I. (1991). The theory of planned behavior. *Organizational Behavior and Human*

Decision Processes. Special Issue: Theories of Cognitive Self-Regulation, 50(2), 179–211.

Ajzen, I., & Fishbein, M. (1980). *Understanding attitudes and predicting social behavior.* Englewood Cliffs, NJ: Prentice-Hall.

Appleby, P. R., Godoy, C. G., Miller, L. C., & Read, S. J. (2008). Reducing risky sex through the use of interactive video technology. In T. Edgar, S. M. Norah, & V. S. Freimuth (Eds.), *Communication perspectives on HIV/AIDS for the 21st century* (pp. 379–384). New York: Erlbaum.

Appleby, P. R., Marks, G., Ayala, A., Miller, L. C., Murphy, S., & Mansergh, G. (2005). Consideration of future consequences and unprotected anal intercourse among men who have sex with men. *Journal of Homosexuality, 50*(1), 119–133.

Appleby, P. R., Miller, L. C., & Rothspan, S. (1999). The paradox of trust for male couples: When risking is a part of loving. *Personal Relationships, 6*(1), 81–93.

Appleby, P. R., Storholm, E. D., Ayala, A., & Miller, L. C. (2007, May). *Methamphetamine and risky decision making among men who have sex with men.* Poster Presented at the 19th Annual Convention of the Association for Psychological Science, Washington, DC.

Baird, A. A., & Fugelsang, J. A. (2004). *The emergence of consequential thought: Evidence from neuroscience.* New York: Oxford University Press.

Bandura, A. (1994). Social cognitive theory and the exercise of control over HIV infection. In R. J. DiClemente & J. L. Peterson (Eds.), *Preventing AIDS: Theories and methods of behavioral interventions* (pp. 25–59). New York: Plenum.

Baron, J., & Brown, R. V. (1991). *Teaching decision making to adolescents.* Hillside, NJ: Erlbaum.

Bartholomew, L. K., Gold, R. S., Parcel, G. S., Czyzewski, D. I., Sockrider, M. M., Fernandez, M., et al. (2000). Watch, discover, think, and act: Evaluation of computer-assisted instruction to improve asthma self-management in inner-city children. *Patient Education and Counseling, 39*(2–3), 269–280.

Bechara, A., Damasio, H., Tranel, D., & Damasio, A. R. (1997). Deciding advantageously before knowing the advantageous strategy. *Science, 275*(5304), 1293–1294.

Beck, A. T. (1970). Cognitive therapy: Nature and relation to behavior therapy. *Behavior Therapy, 1*(2), 184–200.

Bower, G. H., & Forgas, J. P. (2000). *Affect, memory, and social cognition.* New York: Oxford University Press.

Bowlby, J. (1969). *Attachment and loss: Vol. 1. Attachment.* New York: Basic Books.

Brennan, K. A., Clark, C. L., & Shaver, P. R. (1998). *Self-report measurement of adult attachment: An integrative overview.* New York: Guilford Press.

Brewer, N. T., Weinstein, N. D., Cuite, C. L., & Herrington, J. E., Jr. (2004). Risk perceptions and their relation to risk behavior. *Annals of Behavioral Medicine, 27*(2), 125–130.

Brown, S. J., Lieberman, D. A., Gemeny, B. A., Fan, Y. C., Wilson, D. M., & Pasta, D. J. (1997). Educational video game for juvenile diabetes: Results of a controlled trial. *Medical Information, 22*(1), 77–89.

Brug, J., Campbell, M., & van Assema, P. (1999). The application and impact of computer-generated personalized nutrition education: A review of the literature. . [Special Issue].*Patient Education and Counseling, 36*(2), 145–156.

Campbell, M. K., DeVellis, B. M., Strecher, V. J., & Ammerman, A. S. (1994). Improving dietary behavior: The effectiveness of tailored messages in primary care settings. *American Journal of Public Health, 84*(5), 783–787.

Cassidy, J., & Shaver, P. R. (1999). *Handbook of attachment: Theory, research, and clinical applications.* New York: Guilford.

Centers for Disease Control (CDC). (2006). *HIV/AIDS among men who have sex with men [fact sheet].* Retrieved October 2006, from http://www.cdc.gov/hiv/resources/factsheets

Christensen, J. L., Miller, L. C., Appleby, P. R., Godoy, C. G., Corsbie-Massay, C., & Read, S. J. (2007). *When it's good to feel bad: How responses to virtual environments predict real-life sexual risk-reduction.* Unpublished master's thesis, University of Southern California, Los Angeles.

Damasio, A. R. (2000). *The feeling of what happens: Body and emotion in the making of consciousness.* New York: Harcourt.

DiClemente, R. J., & Peterson, J. L. (Eds.). (1994). *Preventing AIDS: Theories and methods of behavioral interventions.* New York: Plenum.

Fishbein, M., & Yzer, M. C. (2003). Using theory to design effective health behavior interventions. *Communication Theory, 13*(2), 164–183.

Fisher, J. D., & Fisher, W. A. (1992). Changing AIDS-risk behavior. *Psychological Bulletin, 111*(3), 455–474.

Fisher, J. D., Fisher, W. A., Bryan, A. D., & Misovich, S. J. (2002). Information-motivation-behavioral skills model-based HIV risk behavior change intervention for inner-city high school youth. *Health Psychology, 21*(2), 177–186.

Fraley, R. C., Waller, N. G., & Brennan, K. A. (2000). An item response theory analysis of self-report measures of adult attachment. *Journal of Personality and Social Psychology, 78*(2), 350–365.

Frijda, N. H. (1986). *The emotions.* Cambridge, England: Cambridge University Press.

Gerrard, M., Gibbons, F. X., Benthin, A. C., & Hessling, R. M. (1996). A longitudinal study of the reciprocal nature of risk behaviors and cognitions in adolescents: What you do shapes what you think, and vice versa. *Health Psychology, 15*(5), 344–354.

Gibbons, F. X., Gerrard, M., Lune, L. S. V., Wills, T. A., Brody, G., & Conger, R. D. (2004). Context and cognitions: Environmental risk, social influence, and adolescent substance use. *Personality and Social Psychology Bulletin, 30*(8), 1048–1061.

Gollwitzer, P. M. (1999). Implementation intentions: Strong effects of simple plans. *American Psychologist, 54*(7), 493–503.

Grunwald, T., & Corsbie-Massay, C. (2006). Guidelines for cognitively efficient multimedia learning tools: Educational strategies, cognitive load, and interface design. *Academic Medicine, 81*(3), 213–223.

Gwadz, M. V., Clatts, M. C., Leonard, N. R., & Goldsamt, L. (2004). Attachment style, childhood adversity, and behavioral risk among young men who have sex with men. *Journal of Adolescent Health, 34*(5), 402–413.

Hinde, R. A. (2005). *Ethology and attachment theory.* New York: Guilford.

Johnson, W. L., Vilhjalmsson, H., & Marsella, S. C. (2005). Serious games for language learning: How much game, how much AI? *Proceedings of the 12th International Conference on AI in Education, Amsterdam.*

Kelly, J. A. (1995). *Changing HIV risk behavior: Practical strategies.* New York: Guilford.

Kelly, J. A., St. Lawrence, J. S., Betts, R., & Brasfield, T. L. (1990). A skills-training group intervention model to assist persons in reducing risk behaviors for HIV infection. *AIDS Education and Prevention*, 2(1), 24–35.

Kelly, J. A., St. Lawrence, J. S., Hood, H. V., & Brasfield, T. L. (1989). Behavioral intervention to reduce AIDS risk activities. *Journal of Consulting and Clinical Psychology*, 57(1), 60–67.

Keltner, D., & Gross, J. J. (1999). Functional accounts of emotion. *Cognition and Emotion*, 13, 467–480.

Kirby, D. (2001). Understanding what works and what doesn't in reducing adolescent risk-taking. *Family Planning Perspectives*, 33, 276–281.

Kreuter, M. W., & Strecher, V. J. (1996). Do tailored behavior change messages enhance the effectiveness of health risk appraisal? Results from a randomized trial. *Health Education Research*, 11(1), 97–105.

Kreuter, M. W., Farrell, D., Olevitch, L., & Brennan, L. (2000). *Tailoring health messages: Customizing communication with computer technology*. Mahwah, NJ: Erlbaum.

Kühberger, A. (1998). The influence of framing on risky decisions: A meta-analysis. *Organizational Behavior and Human Decision Processes*, 75(1), 23–55.

Levenson, R. (1994). Human emotion: A functional view. In P. Ekman & R. J. Davidson (Eds.), *The nature of emotion: Fundamental questions* (pp. 123–126). New York: Oxford University Press.

Lieberman, D. A., & Brown, S. J. (1995). Designing interactive video games for children's health education. In K. Morgan, R. M. Satava, H. B. Sieburg, R. Mattheus, & J. P. Christensen (Eds.), *Interactive technology and the new paradigm for healthcare* (pp. 201–210). Amsterdam: IOS Press.

MacKellar, D. A., Valleroy, L. A., Secura, G. M., Behel, S., Bingham, T., Celentano, D. et al. (2005). Unrecognized HIV infection, risk behaviors, and perceptions of risk among young men who have sex with men: Opportunities for advancing HIV prevention in the third decade of HIV/AIDS. *Journal of Acquired Immune Deficiency Syndrome*, 38(5), 603–614.

Marsella, S. C., Johnson, W. L., & LaBore, C. (2003). Interactive pedagogical drama for health interventions. *Proceedings of the 11th International Conference on Artificial Intelligence in Education* (pp. 1–8). Sydney, Australia.

Marsella, S. C., & Pynadath, D. V. (2004). PsychSim: Agent-based modeling of social interactions and influence. *Proceedings of the International Conference on Cognitive Modeling, Pittsburg, USA*.

Marsella, S. C., & Pynadath, D. V. (2005). Modeling influence and theory of mind. *Artificial Simulation of Behavior*, 1–8.

Marsella, S. C., Pynadath, D. V., & Read, S. J. (2004). *PsychSim: Agent-based modeling of social interactions and influence*. In *Proceedings of the Internal Conference on Cognitive Modeling* (pp. 243–248). Mahwah, NJ: Erlbaum.

Mikulincer, M., & Goodman, G. S. (Eds.). (2006). *Dynamics of romantic love: Attachment, caregiving, and sex*. New York: Guilford.

Miller, L. C., & Fishkin, S. A. (1997). *On the dynamics of human bonding and reproductive success: Seeking windows on the adapted-for human-environmental interface*. Hillsdale, NJ: Erlbaum.

Miller, L. C., & Read, S. J. (2005). Virtual sex: Creating environments for reducing risky sex. In S. Cohen, K. Portnoy, D. Rehberger, & C. Thorsen (Eds.), *Virtual decisions: Digital simulations for teaching reasoning in the social sciences and humanities* (pp. 137–160). Mahway, NJ: Erlbaum.

Moore, S., & Halford, A. P. (1999). Barriers to safer sex: Beliefs and attitudes among male and female adult heterosexuals across four relationship groups. *Journal of Health Psychology, 4*(2), 149–163.

Moreno, R., Mayer, R. E., Spires, H. A., & Lester, J. C. (2001). The case for social agency in computer-based teaching: Do students learn more deeply when they interact with animated pedagogical agents? *Cognition and Instruction, 19*(2), 177–213.

Oatley, K., & Johnson-Laird, P. N. (1996). The communicative theory of emotions: Empirical tests, mental models, and implication for social interaction. In L. L. Martin & A. Tesser (Eds.), *Striving and feeling: Interactions among goals, affect, and self-regulation* (pp. 363–393). Mahwah, NJ: Erlbaum.

Panksepp, J. (1998). *Affective neuroscience.* New York: Oxford University Press.

Plutchik, R. (1979). *A psychoevolutionary synthesis.* New York: Addison-Wesley.

Pynadath, D. V., & Marsella, S. C. (2004). Fitting and compilation of multiagent models through piecewise linear functions. In *Proceedings of the International Conference on Autonomous Agents and Multi Agent Systems* (pp. 243–248).

Pynadath, D. V., & Marsella, S. C. (2005). PsychSim: Modeling theory of mind with decision-theoretic agents. In *Proceedings of the International Joint Conference on Artificial Intelligence* (pp. 1181–1186).

Read, S. J., Miller, L. C., Appleby, P. R., Nwosu, M. E., Reynaldo, S., Lauren, A. et al. (2006). Socially optimized learning in a virtual environment: Reducing risky sexual behavior among men who have sex with men. *Human Communication Research, 32*(1), 1–34.

Reis, J., Riley, W., & Baer, J. (2000). Interactive multimedia preventive alcohol education: An evaluation of effectiveness with college students. *Journal of Educational Computing Research, 23*(1), 41–65.

Reyna, V. F., & Farley, F. (2006). Risk and rationality in adolescent decision making. *Psychological Science in the Public Interest, 7*(2), 1–44.

Rholes, W. S., & Simpson, J. A. (2004). *Attachment theory: Basic concepts and contemporary questions.* New York: Guilford.

Richardson, J. L., Milam, J., McCutchan, A., Stoyanoff, S., Bolan, R., Weiss, J. et al. (2004). Effect of brief safer-sex counseling by medical providers to HIV-1 seropositive patients: A multi-clinic assessment. *AIDS, 18*(8), 1179–1186.

Rolls, E. T. (1999). *Brain and emotion.* Oxford: Oxford University Press.

Romer, D. (2003). *Reducing adolescent risk: Toward an integrated approach.* Thousand Oaks, CA: Sage.

Rothman, A. J., Bartels, R. D., Wlaschin, J., & Salovey, P. (2006). The strategic use of gain- and loss-framed messages to promote healthy behavior: How theory can inform practice. *Journal of Communication, 56*(Suppl. 1), S202–S220.

Rothman, A. J., & Salovey, P. (1997). Shaping perceptions to motivate healthy behavior: The role of message framing. *Psychological Bulletin, 121,* 3–19.

Russell, S. J., & Norvig, P. (2003). *Artificial intelligence: A modern approach* (2nd ed). Upper Saddle River, NJ: Prentice-Hall.

Salovey, P., & Williams-Piehota, P. (2004). Field experiments in social psychology: Message framing and the promotion of health protective behaviors. [Special issue] *American Behavioral Scientist, 47*(5), 488–505.

Sawyer, B. (2007). Serious games: Broadening games impact beyond entertainment. *Computer Graphics Forum, 26*(3), xviii–xviii.

Skinner, C. S., Campbell, M. K., Rimer, B. K., Curry, S., & Prochaska, J. O. (1999). How effective is tailored print communication? *Annals of Behavioral Medicine, 21*(4), 290–298.

Stark, E. N., Rothman, A. J., Bernat, E., & Patrick, C. (2007, January). *Using facial EMG and skin conductance response to detect determinants of the framing effect.* Poster Presented at the Society for Personality and Social Psychology, Memphis.

Tingen, M. S., Grimling, L. F., Bennett, G., Gibson, E. M., & Renew, M. M. (1997). A pilot study of preadolescents to evaluate a video game-based smoking prevention strategy. *Journal of Addictions Nursing, 9*(3), 118–124.

Tversky, A., & Kahneman, D. (1981). The framing of decisions and the psychology of choice. *Science, 211*, 453–458.

Winett, R. A., Moore, J. F., Wagner, J. L., & Hite, L. A. (1991). Altering shoppers' supermarket purchases to fit nutritional guidelines: An interactive information system. *Journal of Applied Behavior Analysis, 24*(1), 95–105.

Witte, K., & Allen, M. (2000). A meta-analysis of fear appeals: Implications for effective public health campaigns. *Health Education & Behavior, 27*(5), 591–615.

Wolitski, R. J., Valdiserri. (2001). Are we headed for a resurgence of the HIV epidemic among men who have sex with men? *American Journal of Public Health, 91*, 883–888.

Xia, Q., Osmond, D. H., Tholandi, M., Pollack, L. M., Zhou, W., Ruiz, J. D., et al. (2006). HIV prevalence and sexual risk behaviors among men who have sex with men: Results from a statewide population-based survey in California. *Journal of Acquired Immune Deficiency Syndromes, 41*(2), 238–245.

Chapter 26

From Serious Games to Serious Gaming

Henry Jenkins, Brett Camper, Alex Chisholm, Neal Grigsby, Eric Klopfer, Scot Osterweil, Judy Perry, Philip Tan, Matthew Weise, and Teo Chor Guan

Popular accounts of the serious games movement have often fallen back on the image of the computer as a "teaching machine" that "programs" its users—for better or for worse. The fantasy is that one can just plant kids in front of a black box and have them "learn" as if learning involved nothing more than absorbing content. Picture that sequence from *The Matrix* where Neo has new skills downloaded directly into his head and can use them instantly. Those who fear that games may turn normal youth into psycho killers similarly hope that serious games might transform them into historians, scientists, engineers, and tycoons. At the same time, teachers express anxiety that their pedagogical labor will be displaced by the game console.

Putting the emphasis on the program to deliver content has often led to highly rigid and prestructured play experiences, carefully regulated to conform to various state and national curricular blueprints, with little chance for emergent play or creative expression by the players. Elsewhere, Education Arcade researcher Scot Osterweil (2007) has contrasted the playful and open-ended learning associated with *Scrabble* to the rigid rules and strict competition of the spelling bee, a contrast which hints at the limits of our prevailing models of serious games.

For the better part of a decade, researchers associated with the MIT Comparative Media Studies Program (through Games to Teach, The Education Arcade, and The Singapore-MIT GAMBIT Game Lab) have been researching the pedagogical potentials of digital games. We have adopted a range of different models for what an educational game might look like—from mods of existing entertainment titles to augmented reality games, from role-playing games to collectible cards—and how they might be produced—including several recent collaborations with commercial media producers and professional game designers. Our games straddle academic fields, including history (*Revolution*, 2005) and current events (*iCue*, 2008), math and literacy skills (*Labyrinth*, 2008), science (*Palmagotchi*, 2007), even waste management (*Backflow*, 2007). What links these various projects together has been a design philosophy that focuses less on serious games and more on serious gaming. We see games not so much as vehicles for delivering curricular content as spaces for exploration, experimentation, and problem solving. We do not simply want to tap games as a substitute for the textbook; we want to harness the meta-gaming, the active discussion and speculation that take place around the game, to inform other learning activities. Researchers have documented the ways that conversations around recreational game play reshape the player's perceptions of violence and the social bonds being expressed through play (Wright, Boria, & Breidenbach, 2002), and they have described the informal learning communities that have grown up around games, such as *Civilization III* (2001; Squire & Giovanetto, 2008), enabling participants to learn world history even as they improve their game performance. Many of our games rely on the mechanics of meta-gaming to get students to articulate what they have learned from the play experience.

Play as a learning process is not a new idea: consider the model United Nations as a well-established pedagogical practice in American social sciences. Essentially, the model United Nations is a role-play activity where students are assigned to represent delegates from different countries and work through current policy debates. Students don't show up and start playing: the role-play motivates library and classroom activities leading up to the formal event. Nor do they just stop playing: a good teacher builds on the role play by having students report back on what they learned through presentations, classroom discussions, or written assignments. A hallmark of our serious games projects is that we factor the context and process of play into our game design, insisting that much of the learning takes place outside the box as the experience of gaming gets reflected upon by teachers and learners in the context of their everyday lives.

The model United Nations is a game that was designed to function within the context of our existing educational system—though often the game play takes place outside of school hours and requires students from multiple schools to gather at a shared location. Play also can enable learning outside of school, as occurs when students play a range of currently available educational titles, and many serious games advocates are encouraging us to use the prospect of educational games to reimagine what the schooling process might look like. We are all for exploring alternative possibilities, but as a team, we have focused our energies on developing models that factor in education as it is currently being conducted, and that means working around some of the conflicting expectations that burden our schools.

We expect our schools to be inclusive of all types of learners, while demanding a unitary measure of student success and a one-size-fits-all curriculum. We expect teachers to be talented professionals while paying them low salaries and even lower levels of respect. We expect schools to overcome problems of poverty, class, and ethnic background while we have no solutions for these problems in the society at large. And we demand that all our schools be above average (displaying our own failure to grasp math and statistics).

Game-based learning is similarly burdened by conflicting expectations. Educational games must be open-ended and exploratory, but they must "cover" the curriculum. They should be content-rich, but they can't cost much to produce. They should be engrossing, but shouldn't take too much time from classroom instruction. Children should enjoy them as much as entertainment games, even though they address topics that students don't appear to be interested in. All of these contradictions are enough to send a game designer screaming from the room. The good news is that educators are finally paying attention to the power of games for learning; the challenge of all good design is to find solutions for competing needs.

In this chapter, we look back on some key milestones in our program's exploration of serious gaming. In each case, we will explore how our understanding of instructional activities rather than curricular content shaped our design choices. We focus on what players do when they are playing our games—seeing these activities as enabling learning—rather than focusing on simply exposing them to classroom content. Each project represents a different model for how a pedagogical game might work in relation to current educational practices; each also reflects a shared vision that sees play as a key component of learning.

Revolution: A Historical Simulation of Colonial America

Revolution was a total conversion mod of the popular PC game *Neverwinter Nights* (2002) modeled on Colonial Williamsburg. In this classroom-based multiplayer experience, each student would take on the role of a different resident on a single day in the spring of 1775. Players would adopt a variety of classes, races, genders, and political perspectives as they relived the debates surrounding the American Revolution.[1]

The starting idea was broad: to create an online historical simulation for classroom use. We knew we wanted the game to be online, allowing students to learn together socially. And we knew we wanted to base the game on Colonial Williamsburg, which has a long tradition of historical learning through role-play. We felt such a game would be a great opportunity to apply our values of learning as exploration and expression rather than eliciting rote memorization only.

Revolution was designed by people who were players first and educators second: if a game is not fun, its educational goals do not matter. We wanted to leverage design principles from successful entertainment games. If we could create a game that looked and sounded on par with store-bought games, and that used familiar interface and game play concepts, we could create an experience that escaped the negative image of edutainment while leveraging new media literacies for pedagogical ends.

From the start, one of our biggest challenges was to design for the time constraints of the typical class period. Public school teachers typically have an hour or less to get the students settled down, introduce the game, teach the students how to play, have the students play the game, get the students to stop playing, and have a coherent discussion afterward. So how might we design a complete and compelling game play experience under these constraints? We were intrigued by commercially successful games that use fixed time limits to shape player experience, compressing complex processes into finite units of game time. *The Legend of Zelda: Majora's Mask* (2000), for example, is about helping people as they go about their daily lives in a single town over the course of a fixed time period. The time limit focuses the player on the social space of the game, since the game's protagonist, Link, only has a short time to affect events that will happen with or without him. Inspired, we focused *Revolution*'s time frame into a single day. This day in our virtual Williamsburg would equal 40 minutes of class time, and would represent a key turning point in the Revolutionary War. We wanted players to log into the game and find themselves in a living, functioning simulation of colonial America. Students could explore the era's social and political norms by trying to shape events, or they could simply sit back and observe.

Game scholar Ian Bogost identifies what he calls "procedural rhetoric" (Bogost, 2007, p. 3)—the notion that a game system's design can impart a persuasive point of view. We wanted students to learn how a colonial society worked by interacting with a system designed to embody the ideas we intended. Students should learn about history by mastering the rules of the game, because the rules were abstracted from historical research. We wanted to get away from the drill-and-test model of public education and to challenge the master narrative of history. Instead, we wanted to focus on the choices historical agents made and the conditions under which they made them.

Our first decision was to forego coding *Revolution* from scratch and make it as a mod of an existing game. Using an existing engine enabled rapid prototyping and design. Using an existing engine also improved production quality—graphics and sound would already be at a level students would associate with professional games. Since many game companies offer modification tools to consumers for sharing new content, we wanted to explore the advantages of modding for developing serious games.

After much consideration, we settled on the *Neverwinter Nights* toolset. *Neverwinter Nights (NWN)* is a role-playing game (RPG) series for the PC that was specifically designed by its makers, Bioware Corp., to support modding projects. There was already a very robust culture of player-made *NWN* mods, which we could tap for inspiration and experience. We wanted to create a socially dynamic world where students would interact with both player-controlled and non-player-controlled characters, and *NWN* was built for character conversation, a feature we felt was crucial to the social world we wanted to model.

Yet we didn't want the conventions of the *NWN* toolset (shaped by the commercial role-playing game genre) to transform our historical content in undesired ways; some of this involved making compromises—such as accepting that our characters would not be able to remove their hats when entering a house, as was historical practice, because hats and heads come attached in the original toolset. Some of this involved adding features to respond to elements we could not disable: unable to prevent students from certain disruptive activities, we built in consequences so that constables would extract unruly players for a time-out before returning them to the game. Given that there was so much of *NWN* we could not change, we wanted to at least ensure that the conversation system would enhance the fidelity of our historical simulation. Luckily, it turned out to work better than we ever imagined. *Revolution's* conversation system evolved from a critique of how knowledge transfer typically occurs within the RPG genre. In many RPGs, information passes between characters as if by magic with no focus on the mechanisms of human communications. One of our development team members described a situation in *The Elder Scrolls: Morrowind* (2002), in which he killed a man, who claimed with his dying breath that his son would avenge him. When the player walked immediately to the son's house, he was promptly attacked. We understood the designers of *Morrowind* wanted actions in the game to have social consequences. But these consequences simply flipped on and off like a light switch. We wanted students to focus on how information flowed through a colonial society and what factors blocked information from passing between different social circles.

NWN's conversation system was well equipped to produce this desired effect. We started by making computer-controlled characters remember what they were told. Then, when they were within a specific range of another character, they would go over to them and share the knowledge they had previously received. A player could pass one piece of information to a nonplayer character and then watch the news spread virally across town. Once we realized that we could make such a "gossip" system work, we saw all sorts of new pedagogical possibilities. While we originally envisioned a game focused around trades and jobs, much like a visit to Colonial Williamsburg, we began to recenter *Revolution* around the social and informational mechanisms of the era. In effect, we made *Revolution* a game about the oral culture of late 18th-century America. In order to play *Revolution* effectively, students would need to understand how this oral culture was shaped by the social, political, racial, and gender strata of the time

A player's reputation, for example, could be adversely impacted by gossip surrounding her beliefs or actions, increasing the stakes of political choices. Revolutionaries could pass word to their supporters without information falling into the hands of the Redcoats or their Loyalist supporters. Because information would not pass certain social barriers easily, players had to figure out how to inform everybody about a local rally. If the player's avatar had an upper-class status, the information would spread more easily among the upper class. Gender and race would have similar effects. In this way, different players could work together or against each other in trying to manipulate the flow of information.

Other affordances of NWN allowed us to build in opportunities for students to reflect back on their experiences. Russell Francis, a researcher from Oxford University, asked *Revolution* players to write diaries or construct machinima (animations produced using the game engine) recounting the events from the perspective of their fictional characters. This process allowed them to share their very different experiences in the game with classmates and gave researchers insights into what they learned and how they learned through their role-play. Francis found that players often combined things they learned in the game with insights from their own lives or things they had read in other accounts of the period (Francis, 2006, p. 7). For example, one student, who played the part of a house slave, described feelings of isolation or tension with field slaves as a result of her privileged access to the master. This sense of alienation emerged as much from what she brought to the game as from anything we had programmed into the simulation. Such accounts helped us to better appreciate the ways that the mechanics of role-play enabled students to consolidate what they had learned about the period and communicate it with others.

In *Revolution*, players learned about American social history through their exploration of the game world, through observing and participating in the ongoing activities of the town, by making choices about how to align themselves within existing political factions, by helping to shape the circulation of information and by paying the consequences of their choices in terms of how other characters viewed their "reputation," and by reflecting back on their play experience by creating in-character accounts of the action. Learning how to play the game involved learning how a colonial society operated with tacit knowledge embedded in the design of rule sets, communication networks, and reputation systems.

Labyrinth: Playing with Math and Literacy

Labyrinth is a puzzle adventure game in which the player wanders the corridors of an underground factory populated by monsters. These monsters have been kidnapping people's pets, apparently for nefarious purposes. The player's job is to uncover the monsters' secret plans, free the pets, and restore order to the world. Along the way the player solves a host of confounding puzzles, which are designed to provide them opportunities to work through core mathematical principles.

Our mandate with *Labyrinth* was to create a game that addressed middle school math and literacy.[2] Our design goals emerged from our focus group conversations with middle school teachers. Needing to prepare their students for high-stakes tests, teachers were leery of committing precious class time to new technology, but they identified math principles that were not being learned through traditional means and expressed the hope that games might offer a better platform for teaching them. They did not want to introduce technologies they could not manage themselves, but they often lacked the time to learn how to master the new technologies. In addition, teachers recognized the attraction of games to their students, but they could not justify games—with all the negative connotations the word implies—to administrators and parents.

No single game can treat every subject in a given curriculum, but *Labyrinth* adheres to the standards developed by the National Council of Teachers of Mathematics (NCTM). We know from our work with educators that many prescribed concepts are never fully mastered by struggling math students. All but the best curricula, even those that adhere to the NCTM standards, teach math procedures without promoting real understanding of the underlying concepts. *Labyrinth* concentrated on the "big ideas" of mathematics, including proportionality, variables, graphing, geometry and measure, and rational numbers. For example, students encounter a vending machine, and have a set of coins of unmarked denominations. They must develop strategies for feeding the coins into the machine so that they can figure out which coins have which values (i.e., solving for variables). While playing, they develop mental models of variables and devise strategies for solving such problems. They are building a scaffolding of ideas, models, and habits of mind that they will be able to apply to their formal schoolwork and to their lives as thinking adults.

Teachers told us that in a high-stakes testing environment, their days are full just covering the mandated curriculum. They cannot imagine spending large blocks of time on a game. For this reason, *Labyrinth* can largely be played as homework. It is Web-served, so no matter where students play the game, teachers can log on and assess how they are progressing through the challenges. If students play the game on their own, they are apt to engage with it in a spirit of discovery and experimentation. Children need the opportunity to approach mathematical problems with the same determined inventiveness they exhibit when mastering somersaults or shooting hoops. *Labyrinth* players will be exposed to a host of new skills to master at their own pace and in their own fashion. When the core concepts underlying the puzzles are eventually introduced in school, the players will be "ready to learn," having achieved mastery over the same concepts through the game.

Imagine a teacher coming into a classroom and saying, "Today I'd like to introduce *variables*. I know I have never used the word here before, but I also know you students are already experts on the subject, because you have all mastered this puzzle." She then projects a *Labyrinth* puzzle and discusses how it relates to the topic. She gets the students comparing notes about how they solved the puzzle and maps various solutions to math concepts. The teacher deploys the puzzle as a visualization tool to make textbook ideas more concrete, and perhaps this process actually fortifies her own understanding, improving her teaching along the way. Far from asking her to devote hours to the game, we have given her a way to quickly incorporate the game into the lesson she was already preparing to teach.

While *Labyrinth* is primarily a math game, it is also designed to promote media literacy. Literacy in the 21st century will not just be about reading and understanding text, but about making sense of a whole range of communications media and learning to become a producer of new media content and a participant in online communities (Jenkins, Purushotma, Clinton, Weigel, & Robison, 2006).

Two features of the game target these media literacy skills. *Labyrinth* replaces cut scenes with comics, using sequential storytelling to relay back story and other information needed to navigate through the game world. Comics employ a wide variety of powerful visual devices, while still giving children the freedom to read and reflect at their own pace. Comics are the perfect bridge between watching and reading. And we wanted young people to develop better skills at understanding the interplay between words and images.

Labyrinth also promotes writing. We know that children who otherwise spend little time writing may spend hours posting hints and solutions to game frequently asked questions (FAQ) Web sites. Accordingly, we built the FAQ right into the game, and gave players the incentive to write. Students playing the game are enrolled in teams with fellow students. To improve the team's overall performance, players will aid lagging members by writing messages that help them solve the game challenges. The puzzles have different solutions every time they are played. To give effective aid to their teammates, players cannot just share answers, but need to communicate problem-solving strategies. We contend that if students read and write about their thinking, there will be benefits to their reading, their writing, and their thinking.

Disadvantaged youth do not uniformly have access to the same technologies at home. They are most likely to have video game consoles, but development licenses for the Xbox and Playstation are prohibitively expensive, and are not usually granted to educational game producers. The same licensing difficulties apply to popular handheld devices like the Nintendo DS or Sony PSP, though there are signs that "thinking games" are gaining acceptance on these platforms. Cell phones are mobile, but not ubiquitous with our target audience, and the proliferation of incompatible platforms makes cell phone development extremely expensive.

Thanks to after-school programs and libraries, as well as the rapid penetration of broadband, the Internet-enabled computer seems to be the device likely to reach the most children through more hours of the day. A Web-served game can be accessed anywhere, and thus affords all players, including the underserved, maximum mobility.

A game developed in Flash can be played on almost any connected computer and will not be blocked by school or library networks because it will not need to be downloaded. There is not a better platform if we are serious about bridging the technology gap. A Flash game will also be stable on the widest range of devices. We are researching the potentials of playing *Labyrinth* on handheld computers and hope, by the end of our funding cycle, to identify and develop specifications for the specific handheld technology that has the broadest reach. In the not-too-distant future it should be possible to port Flash games to devices like the Nintendo DS, which at this moment looks like the handheld with the greatest potential penetration of the market.

Labyrinth makes few demands on teachers. Once the teacher has input a class list, students can log on directly without teacher assistance. As with any other good electronic game, built-in tutorials let players gradually master challenges without additional instruction. Teachers can turn their students loose on the game, and then wait a week and ask the children to teach them how to play. In doing so, students will display competencies teachers don't realize they possess. Although we hope teachers will also play and master the game, we want to respect the constraints under which they work. If teachers do not have time to learn the game, there will still be a mode in which they can play single puzzles and introduce them into class discussion.

We hope that *Labyrinth* will be both entertaining and thought provoking, capturing young people's imaginations while still earning the acceptance of teachers and the approval of parents. Our approach respects all that is inventive and exploratory in play while challenging students to grow intellectually. *Labyrinth* players learn through doing: they acquire familiarity with math principles by working through engaging puzzles and challenges; they master basic literacy skills through a similar process—reading game-related comics and by sharing advice with other players. Only later do teachers help students to map what they have done in the game with concepts from their textbooks.

Thinking Outside the Classroom: Two Mobile Simulation Approaches to Enhance Student Learning

As mobile devices become more accessible and affordable, more and more students are carrying mobile technologies such as personal digital assistants, cell phones, portable gaming systems, iPods, and iPhones in their backpacks. What will learning look like when these powerful handheld computers are as ubiquitous as calculators? In the following we describe two software applications designed by the MIT Scheller Teacher Education Program for handheld computers: *Palmagotchi*, a networked evolutionary biology simulation, and *Handheld Augmented Reality Games*, a toolkit for creating location-based role-playing simulations.[3] Simulation games, in particular, can leverage the anywhere/anytime nature of mobile computing, extending student engagement with content beyond face-to-face classroom time, and asking learners to synthesize digital information with real-world observations.

Our synthesis of the constructivist (Glasersfeld, 1995) and situated learning (Lave & Wenger, 1991) paradigms leads us to design activities that are social, authentic, and meaningful, connected to the real world, open-ended, and containing multiple pathways, being intrinsically motivating, and filled with feedback. While many technologies can foster some of these design elements, mobile learning games are particularly well suited to supporting them all. Guiding principles that inform our designs include:

- **Fostering deep personal engagement through role-playing immersion:** Each student plays an integral part in a larger system (a fruit fly in a population, a potential carrier in a viral disease model). Many off-the-shelf entertainment games are designed around extrinsic rewards—points or award structures that are easy to measure. In role-playing games this could be wealth, as well as the level of your character. In our games, personal investment provides an intrinsic motivator to explore and master game strategies, and therefore better understand scientific models and curricular content.

- **Engaging students in highly social settings that encourage multiplayer collaborative problem solving:** Students using our games interact with their classmates in real time, discussing observations and negotiating interactions through both open and moderated discussion. Students typically spend only a fraction of their time actually looking at the screen of the PDA. In one study (Klopfer, Yoon, & Rivas, 2004), which analyzed student behaviors using our handheld simulation games, "looking at the screen" was not one of the top five most common behaviors. Instead, students were talking, writing notes, interacting with other students, analyzing data, and walking around. This approach engages a wider range of students, including those who are not typically engaged by the individualistic structure of traditional coursework and homework.

- **Encouraging active participation and knowledge building:** During game play, students are active, often walking around, or moving from player to player to observe and compare data. Game actions require both digital and face-to-face interaction.

- **Providing teachers with a flexible model of implementation:** The overly structured materials of science kits or packaged software do not typically allow teachers to express their creativity and use the skills that led many into the profession. On the other hand, giving teachers a tabula rasa is unworkable. The majority of teachers do not have the time or expertise to design entire lessons. Our game designs provide teachers without software programming backgrounds with well-formed and easily customizable activities. Teachers can feel a sense of ownership over materials that match their specific instructional needs.

- **Enabling cognitive flow:** In these games, the reward is *flow* (Csikszentmihalyi, 1997), or "being completely involved in an activity for its own sake" (as cited in Geirland, 1996, pp. 160–161). Flow is marked by extreme concentration, pleasure, focus, reward, and even exhaustion. Activities that lead to flow display clear goals, high concentration, feedback, appropriate challenge, personal control, and intrinsic reward.

Palmagotchi: Participating in Coevolution

"Casual games" are the fastest growing and perhaps largest genre of digital games. Casual games can be played a few minutes at a time, typically during down time (waiting for the bus, for a few minutes over lunch, etc.). Casual games are often played on PDAs (handheld computers like the Palm or Pocket PC), the Nintendo DS, Sony PSP, and increasingly on smart phones (e.g., Windows Mobile phones and iPhones) and cell phones. *Tamagotchi*, a game involving virtual pets, offers one powerful model for the educational use of these platforms. *Tamagotchi's* (1996) simple design, along with the emotional bond between player and pet, results in a game that is simple to learn, allows for increased mastery, can be played casually a few minutes at a time, and yet sustains interest and interaction. Such an approach doesn't interrupt or impede the "business" of the school day.

Palmagotchi, a ubiquitous multiplayer handheld game, is based on a flexible networked platform called myWorld, and builds off of past work developing mobile peer-to-peer participatory simulations, such as *Virus* (2004). *Palmagotchi* allows students to become part of a dynamic biological process referred to as coevolution. *Palmagotchi's* underlying model is loosely derived from Darwin's observations of finches in the Galapagos Islands. The "virtual pets" in *Palmagotchi* are birds and flowers that live within a larger simulated ecology that also includes predators and changing climate patterns. Students gain a deeper understanding of fundamental ecological, genetic, and coevolutionary processes as they nurture their creatures.

The player's goal is to keep the lineage of his or her birds alive within the larger ecosystem, mating with other birds to produce and raise independent offspring before the parent bird dies. Each participant's handheld computer (a Windows Mobile device) starts with a small number of birds and flowers. Each bird has its own unique set of genetically determined traits (e.g., beak length, metabolism, ability to flee from predators, survival during cold weather, etc.). Ultimately, individual flowers' and birds' survival demonstrate their interdependence within the ecosystem. An accelerated "game time" allows students to observe and analyze general trends across multiple generations.

The game does not just convey specific information; playing the game allows students to conduct thoughtful, collaborative scientific inquiry. Initial implementations show that students (and teachers) are highly engaged in the process of maintaining their virtual pets over several days of play, learning the underlying science to improve their performance. They regularly find time outside of class to engage deeply in the game. Class time has been used effectively to discuss data and related biological processes, meeting the content standards required of students and teachers while maintaining high engagement and interest by all. The platform upon which *Palmagotchi* is based is being used to develop other new games for the science curriculum.

Augmented Reality

Augmented Reality (AR) devices superimpose a virtual overlay of data and experiences onto a real-world context. Augmented Reality can employ a variety of technologies, ranging from head-mounted displays to simple mobile devices. We have focused our research and development on "lightly" augmented realities, which require a small amount of virtual information and can be performed on handheld computers, and more recently on cell phones. These technologies support explorations and learning in the students' natural context, their own community and surroundings.

For example, *Charles River City* (2008), loosely based on Chris Dede's MUVE *River City* (2005), was one of our early augmented reality games. In this game, students follow an outbreak of illness coinciding with a topically relevant event in the Boston Metro Area. One of the first runs started out like this: The July 1, 2004 headline of the *Boston Globe* reads "26 More Fall to Mysterious Illness as DNC Looms." A rash of disease has swept through Boston; and—with the Democratic National Convention coming to the city in a few weeks—citizens, politicians, and health officials are all concerned. What is the source of the illness? Is this an act of bioterrorism or a naturally occurring event?

Players are told that a team of 20 experts is brought in to investigate the problem, including epidemiologists, physicians, public health experts, laboratory scientists, biologists, computer scientists, and environmental specialists. This group must work together to evaluate case reports and available surveillance data, investigate the cause and source of the outbreak, assess risk, communicate with the professional and public communities, and identify and implement effective remedies. The teams collect and analyze environmental samples, hospital records, patient histories, clinical samples, and testimony from community members. The team must determine its findings and propose actions very quickly in order to assess the risk, diminish societal fears, and solve the problem. Our initial research on AR simulations (Klopfer & Squire, 2007; Klopfer, Squire, & Jenkins, 2002) demonstrates that this technology can effectively engage students (notably, female students have responded very well) in critical thinking about authentic scientifically based scenarios and enhance their interest in IT.

In order to scale our research and enable AR games to reach a wider audience, we have developed an AR Toolkit that allows designers, teachers, and even students to develop their own games. Using this toolkit, we have already built AR simulations in many content areas over the last few years. Games have been implemented in such diverse areas as environmental science, colonial American history, epidemiology, math, and English. These activities also support students' development of critical 21st-century IT skills including computer-mediated collaboration and information sharing, managing uncertainty, and analyzing complex systems.

The power in AR lies in truly augmenting the physical landscape, creating digital content closely tied to real-world locations, and thus supporting direct observation as well as data analysis. To extend these learning opportunities, we are enhancing our software and experimenting with new classroom practices to make it easier for teachers to localize and customize their games. This will enable educators to focus their efforts on meaty "curricular" tasks of narrative, data analysis, and even game design, with minimal effort spent on the technological aspects. This nearly invisible technology embodies the principle of technology adapting to the classroom, though in this case, the classroom is the entire world.

The Future of Educational Handheld Games

A user-centered—and thus "teacher-centered"—design approach greatly enhances the likelihood that teachers (on whom the success of these experiences ultimately lies) will be able to successfully integrate these technologies into the classroom. Educational software designs like *Palmagotchi* leverage the portability of mobile devices to integrate learning across students' everyday lives, allowing teachers to tap game-based learning without losing valuable classroom time. Similarly, our AR toolkits allow teachers to customize games to local conditions, setting their own pedagogical goals and moving learning beyond the school walls. Such games engage students in multisensory, kinesthetic, collaborative experiences. Such games offer students engaging and motivating experiences (managing a virtual ecology, exploring real world spaces, working in teams to solve complex problems), while enabling students and teachers to investigate important ideas (evolution, public health).

Backflow: Learning Through Designing an Environmentally Conscious Mobile Game

Inspired by our work on participatory simulations, *Backflow* used a mobile phone platform to model choices modern cities face as they manage waste and garbage, weighing the economic and environmental consequences of different options. The original concept had the player directing the flow of sewage through a series of pipes using switches, with the option of shunting the waste to his or her neighbor, helping to clear the game screen but potentially inviting retaliation. The game would simulate a system of environmental exchange and the interdependencies of environmental actors. The basic mechanic also offered the possibility to support a fun, casual-style single-player game themed around recycling, in which the player's frantic button mashing would direct recyclables in the waste stream to the correct recycling bins.

Backflow was one of the first games to emerge from the newly launched Singapore-MIT GAMBIT Lab. The Singapore-MIT GAMBIT Game Lab was established in 2006 between the Program in Comparative Media Studies at MIT and the Media Development Authority of Singapore as a 5-year project to sponsor new research about digital games, to develop new and innovative games, and to train students from Singapore's tertiary education institutions in preparation for entering the game industry. In 2007, over 30 Singaporean students were flown to Cambridge, Massachusetts, to participate in the equivalent of a professional internship. Over a 9-week period, they worked closely with MIT students and faculty to develop six new games, each designed to tackle a specific research challenge head-on. GAMBIT was designed both as a research center, which incubates new approaches to game design, and as a training program, which helps prepare students for work in game companies around the world.

Existing mobile participatory simulations such as *Palmagotchi* use the peer-to-peer connective capabilities of Palm and Windows Mobile handheld computers to embed a group of players inside a simulation. While each individual device is inexpensive, purchasing enough devices for an entire classroom can be a prohibitive expense for many schools. To address this, researchers from the MIT Scheller Teacher Education Program worked with the GAMBIT team to develop a game for a platform more popular among teachers and students: the mobile phone. Mobile phones are a challenging game development platform in comparison to dedicated gaming consoles or the PC, with relatively tiny screens, low system memory, and low-powered microprocessors. However, every mobile phone is a communications device, incorporating networking technologies that are well suited for participatory simulations.

To that end, the GAMBIT students were given a number of new mobile phones from a variety of manufacturers, and set to the task of developing a game that would run reliably across at least two of the devices. Working with the MIT Scheller Teacher Education Program, the team chose to address environmental issues in their simulation. Other than the title of the game, *Backflow*,[5] everything else in the original design had to change in order to accommodate testing feedback and hardware realities. A game in which players flushed waste to each other in real time required the mobile phones to be constantly connected to the Internet and maintain synchronization between all players. Network latency limitations and subscription costs made such a system very difficult to realize. Furthermore, game testing suggested that a multiplayer game based on "tragedy of the commons" would not be very fun to play.

The basic single-player mechanic of sorting garbage by flipping switches on pipes remained, but the multiplayer aspect was scaled back to work asynchronously, with interactions between players recast as an exchange of resources in a stock market-like system. Instead of dumping garbage on each other willy-nilly, players would negotiate to share waste capacity. The development team hoped to use this waste market to simulate the process of "cap and trade" emissions credit trading, a strategy that has been used successfully in the real world to limit greenhouse gas emissions in a free market. Additional testing revealed that this concept was difficult for players to grasp. The team had to revise the design of the game continuously in order to strike a balance between playability, legibility, and realism.

The final game is best described as a hybrid of several genres: a casual puzzle game, a city simulation, and a resource trading and management game. The player begins by registering a new account and creating a new city. New cities start at 45,000 residents, a value that will change with the success or failure of the player's ability to properly recycle. A maze of pipes extends from the city at the top of the screen to several recycling bins and a sewer near the bottom. The player uses the keys on the mobile phone number pad to direct items to the right place: glass to the glass recycling, organic waste to the sewer, and so on. If the player sends a recyclable item to the correct bin, the game rewards some raw materials of that type. Instead of emissions credit trading, these materials can be used to build efficiency upgrades for the player's system. But if the player makes a mistake and sends waste to the wrong bin, the pollution level for the city rises.

At the end of a round, the game calculates the city's pollution level, and adds or subtracts residents accordingly (based on the assumption that clean cities are more attractive living spaces than polluted ones). Between rounds, the player may decide to buy system upgrades or trade resources. Players soon realize that they can easily build up a scarcity of one type of material and a surplus of another, making trading necessary for advancement. Urban growth increases the complexity of the pipe system and the speed of the waste stream. "Winning" the game means finding a balance of population and waste processing ability that a player can manage.

Despite the challenges of a new and constrained platform, the students successfully created an online mobile phone game in 9 weeks. Much of the success of *Backflow* is a testament to the team's adaptability: they faced the limitations of the technology and the feedback from real players and adjusted the game design and development plan to make a functional, playable, and engaging game faithful to the spirit of the MIT Scheller Teacher Education Program. GAMBIT students learned how to think like game designers by working under similar conditions, embracing a process of rapid prototyping within deadline pressures that forced them to confront constraints of time, resources, and energy. *Backflow* players similarly learn through making a series of choices and exchanges, optimizing their performance while operating under less than optimum circumstances. Playing the game well forces the students to work through a series of constraints and incentives that are similar to those faced by real world governments if they are to make environmentally responsible and economically viable decisions.

iCue: Tapping Social Networks to Foster Civic Awareness

NBC News has been working with the Education Arcade to develop *iCue*, a Web-based educational media product that is at once a media archive, a portal for learning activities and games, and a social network connecting teachers and students around the country in shared learning activities designed to enhance their understanding of current events and American history.[4] The project seeks to address the seismic shifts in the ways young people acquire news and information about the world around them, shifts which are having an adverse impact on the markets for network news. Gone are the early evenings when families gathered around the television to catch up on the day's events as narrated by genteel anchormen such as John Chancellor, David Brinkley, and Walter Cronkite. Today's audiences, especially young people, consume news and information through channels that are available 24/7 across the Web, mobile phones, and other handheld digital media devices. One need only glance at year-to-year Nielsen ratings data to recognize the steep downward trend in viewers of the evening network news broadcasts. During the May 2007 television sweeps period, network news viewers across the "Big Three"— ABC, CBS, and NBC—totaled roughly 21 million per night or just less than 7% of the U.S. population. By contrast, Apple sold 21 million iPods during the 2006 holiday shopping season. NBC has embraced the *iCue* project in hopes of better understanding how this generation of news consumers will relate to their content, while providing a resource for teachers and students to enhance critical thinking and writing skills across the curricula of U.S. history, government and politics, and English language and composition.

Designed initially as a resource for students taking courses as part of the College Board's Advanced Placement (AP) Program, *iCue* includes video clips from the NBC News and Universal radio and film archives to support teaching and learning of core concepts, people, and places. In subsequent years, NBC plans to support additional subjects in world history, literature, language learning, science, and mathematics across the K-12 curriculum. *iCue* deploys an innovative media player modeled upon a technology students have used for decades in the classroom, in the library, and at the kitchen table: the index card. NBC has designed its "CueCard," a two-sided media player that plays video on its face and then "flips" onscreen to enable students to annotate, comment, share, and discuss multimedia materials as part of online discussion groups organized around their own social or learning networks. Students collect CueCards in their online digital portfolio for reference, cataloging them for use in their online writing exercises, activities, and games.

How does this card technology fit in the domain of gaming? First, there are the traditional card games such as *Go Fish*, a matching game, or *Poker*, a complex strategy game. Then, there are the collecting of baseball and other sports cards and the fantasy sports games that are fueled by players' performance statistics. Or, consider the global collecting, role-playing, and strategy card games such as *Pokémon* and *Yu-Gi-Oh!*, which have inspired a generation of kids to master and manipulate hundreds of fictional characters and their attendant powers and properties the way a NASA systems analyst might analyze complex data sets.

Each card represents a unique set of people, places, things, and ideas—

embodying information students need to master for their coursework. The CueCards interface allows students not only to view and annotate media arti-facts, but also to share and play with those cards to map connections among the represented concepts. In one challenge, students are asked to put into chronological order a series of CueCards that represent different events in the Civil Rights era, encouraging students to think about timelines in the U.S. History course. In another, students are challenged to match video clips and newspaper articles of Japanese internment camps of the 1940s with reports of suspected "terror" suspects at Guantanamo Bay after 2001. In yet another, stu-dents are asked to make connections between the suffrage campaign of Susan B. Anthony and the presidential campaign of Hillary Rodham Clinton.

Through our formative research, we have observed students drawing on pre-existing knowledge, new ideas presented via the CueCards, and peer-to-peer discussions to generate new conceptual maps; their "answers" draw on differ-ent kinds of evidence—video, newspaper, and primary documents—to dem-onstrate solutions. Students share the pathways they have found with teachers and peers, inspiring both online and classroom discussion around important events and concepts. The process shows history not as something fixed, which is often the impression after reading a traditional textbook or encyclopedia entry, but as a dynamic and evolving discipline as students draw many differ-ent links between events and agents and resolve conflicting perspectives.

We are mapping and analyzing the thinking processes that shape students' use of *iCue*. Do they focus on one type of resource over another in solving the game's challenges? How do they integrate information from several media sources and how does this affect what they learn? How will teachers use *iCue* to supplement their classroom and homework assignments? How do different socioeconomic levels, urban vs. rural geographies, and varied pre-AP educa-tional offerings affect students' *iCue* experience? To qualify this, we are eval-uating student understanding in several ways: (1) concept mastery exercises (e.g., fill in the blanks, multiple choice questions, etc.) both within and out-side of the game; (2) group discussions with students; (3) player performance, where awareness and mastery of important concepts can be measured by stu-dent advancement through game levels and scoring; and, finally (4) natural language-based research tools that enable us to analyze forum discussions and blogs.

Our aim is to tap students' interest in games, participatory culture, and collective intelligence to get them to engage more closely with history and cur-rent events. While *iCue* enhances student and teacher access to a rich archive of media materials, players do not simply sit back and watch these news clips; they draw on them as resources for their game play activities, shuffling them and reordering them like index cards, exchanging them and deploying them like *Pokémon* cards. The learning occurs as players map their own connec-tions between key events and concepts over time, comparing notes with each other, and mastering challenges that require them to rethink core assumptions and consider the processes by which we come to shared understandings and meanings.

Conclusion

Over the past decade, researchers associated with MIT's Comparative Media Studies Program have been exploring the pedagogical potential of digital games. Rather than adopt a one-size-fits-all solution, we have explored different models for what might constitute the ideal learning game. In the process, we have tested different genres and delivery platforms and mapped alternative models of collaboration between academic institutions and commercial partners.

Underlying these games have been some core principles:

1. Our games are designed to fit within specific learning contexts, addressing the real-world problems that educators confront. Each represents a different strategy for addressing such factors as the structure of the school day, limited access to technology, the teacher's unfamiliarity with games, and integration within existing curricular frameworks, all of which might prejudice teachers, parents, or principles against game-based learning. Our goal is to develop games that can be used widely across a range of schools and communities, not simply prototypes for laboratory research.

2. Our games are part of a sequence of learning activities, introducing new concepts or providing experiences that can become the basis for further discussions and writing exercises. Game play often occurs outside of the classroom, much as homework extends and supports schoolroom learning. For example, *Palmagotchi* encourages kids to keep an eye on their evolving ecosystems at odd moments throughout the day, while teachers can work through problems from the games to explain basic principles. Increasingly, our games are designed to support customization and localization, so teachers can adopt the games to their own instructional goals.

3. We share a belief that play represents a meaningful strategy for making sense of the world around us: the best games inspire a process of exploration and experimentation. As students play games, they test hypotheses about how the world works, revising them based on their experiences; they develop new strategies for solving problems; and they make new connections between previously isolated bodies of knowledge. These games are designed to tap what students already know (as occurs when they get into character for a role-playing game like *Revolution*), and they help young people master complex problems that might otherwise seem insurmountable (as when they cite multimedia materials to draw connections between current and historic events in *iCue* or when they tap different kinds of expertise to solve the real world challenges posed by *Charles River City*).

4. We seek to make every element of the game design intellectually mean-ingful and personally rewarding: from the knowledge transfer system in *Revolution* to the puzzle design in *Labyrinth*, from the card-based interface of *iCue* to the exchange mechanisms in *Backflow*. We want to make sure that students and teachers spend more time acquiring valued skills and knowledge and less time mastering the game technology.

5. We see game play as a social rather than an individual learning opportu-nity. We build into these games opportunities for students to share insights with each other (through, for example, the exchange of theories within the AR simulations or of strategies in the in-game FAQ in *Labyrinth*), and in the process, to foster peer-to-peer learning. Students are most likely to master information when they use it to solve problems and share it with others, articulating what they have learned.

6. Last, but certainly not least, we design our games to be fun. These games were designed by players and we've learned what we can from existing entertainment titles. A game that fails to engage the student will fail to motivate learning, no matter how rich its intellectual content may be.

Taken as a whole, these principles shift our focus away from the design and deployment of serious games and onto the processes and resources that support serious gaming.

Notes

1. The idea for *Revolution* emerged as part of the Games to Teach Project, funded by a Microsoft iCampus grant, and later became the flagship project for the Edu-cation Arcade. It was a complicated project spanning five semesters, starting in Fall 2002 and extending through Fall 2004. It was designed by a team of graduate and undergraduate students, working part time while taking classes. Participants included Philip Tan (Producer), Matthew Weise (Game Designer), Brett Camper (Lead Programmer), David Lee (3D modeling), Giovanni Mendoza (Art), Cassie Huang (Character Design), James Tolbert (Animation), Nicholas Hunter (Pro-grammer), and Bertha Tang (Art).

2. *Labyrinth* is the product of a partnership between MIT's Education Arcade, Maryland Public Television, Macro International, and Johns Hopkins Univer-sity, funded by a grant from the U.S. Department of Education. The ongoing project began in early 2006. Participants in the design process included Kristina Drzaic, Dan Roy, Alec Austin, Ravi Purushotma, Elliot Pinkus, Evan Wendel, and Lan Le, under the leadership of Scot Osterweil. The game was designed and storyboarded by students and staff of the Comparative Media Studies Program, with final development handled by Fablevision, a publisher and software devel-oper. The completed game will be distributed by Maryland Public Television, which has also taken on responsibility for teacher training.

3. *Palmagotchi* was built by the Teacher Education Program with the help of lead developers, including Victor Costan and Kyle Fritz. Development of the Hand-held Augmented Reality Games is largely supported by a grant from the U.S. Department of Education StarSchools initiative, in collaboration with the

University of Wisconsin and Harvard University. Lead developers on the Augmented Reality project include Ben Schmeckpeper, Tiffany Wang, Kirupa Chinnathambi, R. J. Silk, and Lisa Stump.

4. *iCue* emerged from conversations between the MIT Education Arcade and NBC News in early 2006. Product development is being managed by NBC News and the NBC Technology Growth Center in New York, with portions of the information architecture, technical implementation, and game engine being executed with iFactory in Boston. The MIT Education Arcade continues to work with NBC News to research user behavior and performance, supporting NBC's product and educational programming development. Project leaders include Alex Chisholm, Eric Klopfer, Scot Osterweil, and Jason Haas (MIT); Adam Jones, Nicola Soares, Laura Sammons, Michael Levin, Kathy Abbott, Soraya Gage, Mark Miano, and Beth Nissen (NBC); and Glenn Morgan, Sean Crowley, and Ruth Tannert (iFactory).

5. Under the guidance of Eric Klopfer, Judy Perry, and Marleigh Norton, *Backflow* was developed by Zulfiki bin Mohamed Salleh, Neal Grigsby, Chen Renhao, Nguyen Hoai Anh, Wang Xun, Fabian Teo, Brendan Callahan, Guo Yuan, and Hoo "Fezz" Shuyi from the Singapore-MIT GAMBIT Game Lab.

References

Backflow. [Digital game]. (2007). Grigsby, N., Salleh, Z. B. M., Norton, M., Klopfer, E., Perry, J., Nguyen, H. A., et al. Cambridge, MA: Singapore-MIT GAMBIT Game Lab.

Bogost, I. (2007). *Persuasive games: The expressive power of videogames*. Cambridge, MA: MIT Press.

Charles River City. (2008). Klopfer, E. Augmented learning. Cambridge, MA: MIT Press.

Civilization III, Sid Meier's [Digital game]. (2001). Briggs, J. L., & Johnson, S. New York: Infogrames.

Csikszentmihalyi, M. (1997). *Creativity: Flow and the psychology of discovery and invention*. New York: HarperCollins.

Elder Scrolls III: Morrowind. [Digital game]. (2002). Howard, T., Rolston, K., Walton, C., Carofano, M., & Meister, C. Rockville, MD: Bethesda Softworks.

Francis, R. (2006, March). *Towards a theory of a games based pedagogy*. Paper presented at the JISC Innovating e-Learning 2006: Transforming Learning Experiences Online Conference.

Geirland, J. (1996). Go with the flow. *Wired, 4*(9). Retrieved December 1, 2007, from http://www.wired.com/wired/archive/4.09/czik.html

Glasersfeld, E. v. (1995). A constructivist approach to teaching. In L. P. Steffe & J. E. Gale (Eds.), *Constructivism in education* (pp. 3–15). Hillsdale, NJ: Erlbaum.

iCue. [Digital game]. (2008). Chisholm, A., Klopfer, E., Osterweil, S., Haas, J., Jones, A., Soares, N., et al. New York: NBC News.

Jenkins, H., Purushotma. R., Clinton, K., Weigel, M., & Robison, A. J. (2006). *Confronting the challenges of participatory culture: Media education for the 21st century*. Chicago: MacArthur Foundation.

Klopfer, E., & Squire, K. (2007). Environmental detectives—The development of an augmented reality platform for environmental simulations. *Educational Technology Research and Development, 56*(2), 203–228.

Klopfer, E., Squire, K., & Jenkins, H. (2002). Environmental detectives: PDAs as a window into a virtual simulated world: Wireless and mobile technologies in Education, 2002. *Proceedings of the IEEE International Workshop*, 95–98.

Labyrinth. [Digital game]. (2008). Lau, T., Meneses, S. F., Osterweil, S., Grossman, B., Drzaic, K., Roy, D., et al. Owings Mills, MD: Maryland Public Television.

The legend of Zelda: Majora's mask. [Digital game]. (2000). Miyamoto, S., Aonuma, E., & Koizumi, Y. Kyoto, Japan: Nintendo.

Lave, J., & Wenger, E. (1991). *Situated learning: Legitimate peripheral participation*. New York: Cambridge University Press.

Neverwinter nights. [Digital game]. (2002). Oster, T., Holmes, M., Greig, S., Moar, D., Brockington, M., Knowles, B., et al. New York: Infogames, Inc.

Osterweil, S. (2007). What makes a good software game for children? *Parents Choice*. Retrieved December 1, 2007, from http://www.parents-choice.org/article.cfm?art_id=191&the_page=consider_this

Palmagotchi. [Digital game]. (2007). Costan, V., Fritz, K. P., Klopfer, E., & Perry, J. Cambridge, MA: Teacher Education Program, MIT.

Pokémon Trading Card Game. (1996). Renton, WA: Wizards of the Coast.

Revolution. [Digital game]. (2005). Tan, P., Weise, M., Camper, B., Hunter, N., Lee, D., Mendoza, G., et al. Cambridge, MA: The Education Arcade.

River city. [Digital game]. (2002). Dede, C., Clarke, J., Dieterle, E., Metcalf, S., Dukas, G., Garduño, E., et al. Cambridge, MA: Harvard University Graduate School of Education.

River city. Nelson, B., Ketelhut, D. J., Clarke, J., Bowman, C., & Dede, C. (2005). Design-based research strategies for developing a scientific inquiry curriculum in a multi-user virtual environment. *Educational Technology*, 45(1), 21–27.

Squire, K. D., & Giovanetto, L. (2008). The higher of education of gaming. *eLearning*, 5(1), 2–28

Tamagotchi. [Digital game]. (1996). Maita, A. Tokyo: Bandai.

Virus. (2004). Klopfer, E., Yoon, S., & Rivas, L. Comparative analysis of Palm and we arable computers for participatory simulations. *Journal of Computer Assisted Learning*, 20(5), 347–359.

Wachowski, A., & Wachowski, L. (Writers). (1999). *The Matrix*. USA: Warner.

Wright, T., Boria, E., & Breidenbach, P. (2002). Creative player actions in FPS online video games: Playing Counter-strike. *Game Studies: The International Journal of Computer Game Research*, 2(2).

Chapter 27

Immersive Serious Games for Large Scale Multiplayer Dialogue and Cocreation

Stacey Spiegel and Rodney Hoinkes

This chapter is an overview of over 15 years of exploration and development in the domain of large scale interactive and entertainment-based serious games. The approach has been to combine advanced immersive technologies with social interactive content for use with the public in educational and museum environments. Our initial goal was the enhancement of participant engagement in serious topics, initially through a focus on dialogue and later with the addition of cocreation. This chapter will explore a series of international museum installations created by collaborative teams of expert content specialists, educators, game designers, and technical innovators. The results of these collaborations provide insight into the different forms serious games may take with respect to personal engagement, community involvement, and long-term stickiness of ideas and interaction.

Through the development and exhibition of interactive edutainment products, our team, which is working with the immersion technology, came to understand three identifiable characteristics that were considered highly desirable in order to achieve a compelling and emotionally involving educational experience. These critical characteristics include an opportunity for dialogue, an expression of personal relevance in relation to the subject matter, and the opportunity for cocreation.

Over a 10-year period, we refined a model for large-scale immersive serious games we dubbed Immersion Cinema, utilizing the combination of a cinematic nonlinear narrative storyline interwoven with a series of games. Immersion Cinemas explore this content within large-scale physical environments including 135° immersive screens, surround sound, and touch-screen networked computers providing interactivity for each of up to several hundred participants. These environments and content experiences focused upon dialogue and interactivity to demonstrate and promote personal relevance. The popularity of these highly produced dramatic experiences created an excellent short-duration motivation and learning environment, but lacked in support for the ongoing stickiness we felt was a key goal of the networked digital era of learning and engagement. The immersive and interactive characteristics of the early models we explored proved their value, but were severely limited by physical location and time constraints. With the introduction of broadband Internet allowing for the types of group engagement with rich media environments we had previously only attained in custom-designed intranets, we were able to add persistence to support stickiness. We use the term *stickiness* to refer to the attributes of an experience which encourage people to stay or continually participate. This combination of immersion, interactivity, and persistence clearly pointed us strongly in the direction of virtual worlds, while the need for more comprehensive rich media and interactivity modes pointed out that new solutions were needed beyond that pursued by the digital game industry.

We are in the early stages of this next-step evolution of the original goals and ideas—now taken into what we refer to as the parallel world. The increased scale of participation possible enhances dialogue opportunities and supports the formation of social networks with high personal relevance—our definition of a community. The increased time available, along with the foundation concept of persistence, supports the third key concept we have found to be critical—that of cocreation. The biggest issue in the support of this concept is the availability of tools for simple and powerful creative expression at meaningful levels of rich media.

Taken together, we suggest a model adapted from the Center for Advanced Media Research Amsterdam (CAMeRA) to demonstrate the critical real/virtual world characteristics required for deep learning in the context of a

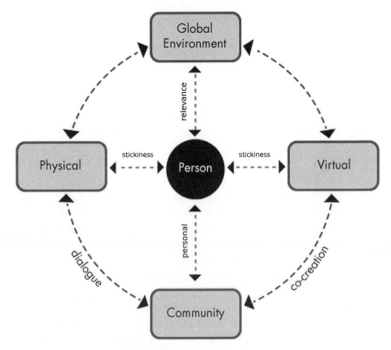

Figure 27.1 Deep Learning Model, adapted from the Center for Advanced Media Research Amsterdam (CAMeRA)

social network (See Figure 27.1). We begin with a community of users having a shared interest in a global topic. The intensity of the user's personal relevance may be enhanced through dialogue that occurs in addressing a physical manifestation of that topic, while their ability to be expressive is supported through cocreation in the virtual.

The Germ of an Idea

The history of the Immersion Cinema concept begins with the early and extensive work done in advanced visualization. By connecting to early experiments with Computer Aided Design (CAD), Geographic Information Systems (GIS), and visual simulation environments, we began experimental creations of information landscapes that held user-contributed rich media databases. In the earliest manifestations the projects were seed-funded as artistic experiments looking at the influence of technology on culture. These innovative opportunities resulted in a series of projects done in a variety of countries across Western Europe and North America.

The first project of note was called *Crossings* and was developed in Karlsruhe, Germany, as part of an artist-in-residence opportunity at the Zentrum für Kunst und Medientechnologie. The resulting project was an immersive (6-screen projection) interactive experience exhibited as part of the Multimediale exhibit in 1994. The virtual world that was created was based on a landscape derived from GIS data constituting an area connecting France and Germany along a mountainous corridor. The concept of this environment was to establish a social and art/design dialogue around the ideas of networking, communication, culture, and space (both real and virtual). Once the landscape was generated, an international group of artists, designers, and design students were invited to populate the environment with information environments and objects that were set in the landscape. Each space, place, or object represented a fully functional database of specific information, spatial structure, and information-space interface that the contributors wanted to share within this exploratory community. This environment was used to test methods of collaboration, dialogue, and feedback in virtual worlds, cocreation amongst the participants, and public reaction to virtual worlds as information spaces. Dialogue was strongly evident amongst public participants, and the immersive visual environment was clearly of value to group engagement. At the same time, cocreation was limited to the original designers and artists, each largely operating on their own vision within the overall project concept. This resulted in cocreation largely as an early design input but without a strong feedback loop to take advantage of the collective input of the participating public, all of whom were contributors to the evolution of key virtual world concepts.

In the following year, a second formative project called *Oasis* was undertaken to focus more upon public cocreation in an experimental real time artwork. This was based on a series of networked machines which allowed up to

10 simultaneous participants the opportunity to navigate and contribute to building a cocreated knowledge terrain. As participants navigated the landscape, they would walk over painted sections of the terrain, each linking to some thematic information on the World Wide Web. If they found the topic of interest and knew of additional resources, they could share it immediately with all other inhabitants of the landscape by painting a nearby patch of the terrain. The act of painting immediately linked the Web site in their web browser to that spot on the landscape. In this experiment, little emphasis was placed upon truly immersive environments or a strong conceptual framework for the landscape; rather, cocreation of a knowledge environment was the primary focus. We found this resulted in very interesting contributions but far less dialogue, motivation, and reduced time of engagement.

We reviewed the feedback from these initial productions and decided that the seeds of the ideas from *Crossings* itself were far more compelling to participants. This included a strong sense of immersion, dialogue, and engagement in the subject matter. This resulted in the development of a second manifestation of *Crossings*, a far more involved application of the core technology done in conjunction with the V2 organization in Rotterdam. The virtual landscape was regenerated as a fully immersive 3D world and the software coded to run in the world's largest 360° simulator at Marine Safety International in Rotterdam. This simulator included 12 SGI Super Graphics Workstations, a computer-controlled motion platform, spatial sound computing system, and networked computers on the ship bridge to handle real-time navigation, rich media display, and complete system coordination. Some of the original content from the first *Crossings* and *Oasis* were included, the landscape aesthetically strengthened and unified, but one of the biggest steps forward was the introduction of the strongly emotive portion of the experience known as the tolerance space. While most of the original *Crossings* environments and that of *Oasis* were experiments in representing grounded cyberspaces, the tolerance space introduced an implicit narrative to the work, providing a very strong impetus for dialogue empowered by a completely immersive environment. The environment created by *Crossings* Version 2 demonstrated a new type of system, including a virtual world, narrative, and modes of interaction that worked together to significantly empower dialogue and participation in a topic area to a level rarely seen before. As a result of the public success of this project, an opportunity arose to develop a far more advanced application using the simulator again to interact in a shared 3D environment. This Dutch-based project was called *Safe Haven* and was once again mounted in the Marine Safety International simulator in Rotterdam.

The context for this project was developed with an even stronger narrative, building on the feedback seen from *Crossings* Version 2. The environment focused upon an exploration of cultural diversity in the city of Rotterdam. In these early days of digital video, a documentary videographer taped the streets of Rotterdam and interviewed 180 people of diverse cultural background living within this Dutch community. Individuals were asked a series of questions regarding their cultural heritage and how they came to the city, and what their lives were like within it. We edited these stories into digital clips and embedded each clip into one of four chambers of a real time 3D representation of a human heart, which the audience would explore in the simulator. The chambers of the heart formed a biological representation of the city in opposition to the traditional architecturally-oriented virtual reality views, and were specifically based on the interviewee's concerns and interests, providing an organic cocreated environment in which to explore cultural diversity. The motion platform in the Marine Safety International simulator had been designed as a navigation bridge to teach ship captains and crew the navigational aspects of Rotterdam Harbor. For *Safe Haven* we converted the bridge systems from ship navigation equipment to interactive stations allowing up to six people simultaneously to interact in the narrative storylines embedded in our 3D world. The participants entered the bridge and went on a 30-minute real time journey exploring the diversity of cultures living within their own community. As the person navigating in the 3D world approached the image of an individual, that person's story popped up and played on one of six interactive stations on the ship's bridge. While interested players would watch that story, someone else could take over and navigate to a thematically related video in the same space which would be played out on another of the screens, or take the entire audience to a new space and its theme expressed by the city's inhabitants. Players on the ship's bridge interacted with the virtual world and not only engaged in dialogue with other players on the bridge, but by proxy with the city itself through the videos, many of which (having similar, opposing, or diverse viewpoints) could be playing at one time. In this way an intimate and immersive exploration of the cultural diversity in Rotterdam was expressed in a highly emotional manner, and audience members, after concluding their journey, were found to be deeply moved by the layering of stories they had chosen to see and hear.

Participant feedback and continuous capacity crowds illustrated that we had succeeded in providing a computer-mediated means of engaging a broad spectrum of the public in a topic, extending engagement to rich dialogue and motivation to pursue the topic areas presented. The outgrowth of these large-scale art and technology projects was the commercial foundation of a new media company whose primary goal evolved as the creation of social interactive environments that combined games and movies together for entertainment-based educational purposes.

Immersive Serious Games

We founded the Canadian company Immersion Studios in 1997 just as the Internet and World Wide Web was entering its first phase of exponential growth. While the dreams and vision for the future were being pushed to commercial reality, in fact it was still too early for the general public to easily access media-rich content and truly immersive environments. The vision of a ubiquitous broadband world capable of this type of experience was certainly imagined, though it would take 10 years before the functionality could be practically applied. The phenomenal public response to the projects in Europe, culminating with the *Safe Haven* project in Rotterdam, provided a basis for pursuing a commercial approach. Early commercial explorations were based upon a strong entertainment focus, while in fact we found the strongest market interest existed in a hybrid educational and entertainment context that became known as edutainment. Immersion Studios set out to establish a network of interactive and immersive cinemas where audiences could become motivated and engage in a personally relevant dialogue on complex issues of science communication.

The desire to combine together narrative and interactivity gave rise to a number of experimental interactive experiences. The first Immersion Cinema show created was called *My Canada*. It was shown in a theater environment on a large format screen (24 meters wide by 6 meters high) with 50 interactive consoles spread throughout the audience space. The show itself took the audience on a scripted travelogue through a real time 3D landscape of each province in Canada. While moving through each location of travel, the audience would spend time on their interactive consoles exploring the images, text, and video that described the history and character of that location. The choice of provinces to explore was decided by popular vote on the interactive consoles amongst the two-hundred person audience. Approximately 55,000 people explored *My Canada* (1997) during an exhibition period of three weeks. In this period we interviewed hundreds of players who had experienced *My Canada* to gain an understanding of the role interactivity played in the enjoyment and emotional involvement of the experience. Amongst other insights we learned that *My Canada* was not fun enough, had limited interactivity, and the content layered within the environment did not allow the audience to do anything more than randomly browse through it. We also heard that while the audience was stunned by the quality and scale of the immersive environment, they were missing deeper emotional involvement, as there was no concrete storyline for engagement.

In response to this feedback we created a new show called *Monsters of the Deep*. This show stood as a counterpoint to *My Canada*. It was created as a fully animated prerendered nonlinear narrative that used the interactive feedback from the audience on their consoles to determine the outcome of the storyline. This storyline was a completely fictional notion of what lay hidden in the depths of the ocean and the audience was taken on an adventure ride to the bottom of our virtual ocean. The most relevant aspect of this production was the application of a game-based solution for controlling or impacting the interactive narrative. Multiple story alternatives were created and could be accessed at key junction points in the show based on audience interaction on their consoles. Audience members were situated directly within a fictional submarine and could take on a variety of roles on the boat. Alternative sequences of the narrative were played out in different shows as a consequence of audience skill and involvement. The feedback we received from a survey of over a thousand players demonstrated that *Monsters of the Deep* proved to be far more successful in engaging the audience, and fostered our increased focus on interactive games as a solution for deep learning when structured within a nonlinear narrative.

Taken together, there were a number of key elements that we were able to derive from these early examples in immersive edutainment technology:

- The time and cost to produce entertainment-quality real-time 3D Visual Simulation environments, compared with nonlinear prerendered video, was prohibitive.
- Immersive environments are an excellent means to suspend disbelief and establish presence.
- A strong story with relevant interactivity was powerful in establishing engagement, and interactivity without a clear purpose was meaningless.
- Multiuser interactivity in a physical setting creates an environment that encourages dialogue amongst players (as opposed to passive cinematic environments).

The strongest interest generated from this experience came from the emerging edutainment market. These environments were facing direct competition from a resurgence of digital game consoles, the lure of the Internet and World Wide Web, and dominance of traditional modes of entertainment. An equal or more compelling immersive and interactive platform that encouraged dialogue was seen by many educators as a potential way to drive engagement in educational concepts.

Narrative and Game Play

Prior to the new millennium museums emerging around the world, we were looking for meaningful ways to bring the complex ideas of contemporary science to the general public. As their content evolved to a higher degree of complexity, the demand for new ways to educate the public became critical. The first series of Immersion Cinema experiments in social interaction were evidence that interactivity used as a control element within a narrative storyline constituted a social dialogue that engaged the audience more deeply in the meaning of the content.

The first large-scale field test of this approach was in a collaborative partnership between U.S. Federal agency NOAA and the New England Aquarium in Boston to produce a show titled *Storm Over Stellwagen* (1999). The issues these groups wanted to highlight were the impact of climate change and human behavior in a particularly sensitive marine sanctuary near Boston called Stellwagen Bank. The target we developed was the combination of a fictional storyline with a scientifically accurate marine environment, a host of accurately represented marine species, and a unique simulation engine based on environment and sustainability. The storyline set the stage for the audience to interactively determine the combined impact of environmental, climatic, and human intervention on Stellwagen Bank. The culmination of the factors chosen by the audience (which was expressed interactively) was processed by the simulation engine. The resulting parameters were evaluated and matched to a set of potential future scenarios, with the cinema system calling up a sophisticated prerendered animated sequence of what Stellwagen Bank would look like under the projected future. After several years of running this show the New England Aquarium found that audiences were often deeply involved emotionally in the impact they had caused and returned to test out alternative solutions. Students responded particularly well to the association they experienced between cause and effect, recognizing the complexity each solution entailed. In this particular show the imbedded interactive games were all text and simple simulation parameter controls rather than the real-time 3D graphical games we would later come to employ. One notable finding was the level of dialogue amongst the audience members as they experienced the show. It was often a noisy experience with people engaging those around them to discuss alternative answers and debate potential strategies to the simulation.

Simulation was the key new addition to the interactivity in this experience. A key characteristic of the simulation used in this show was that the results were shown on two levels: the results of the individual's choice—the private—and the result that would occur if the group's cumulative inputs were considered—the public. These public–private interactions became a common characteristic in many of the following productions, providing a specific result that encouraged dialogue both during and after the experience. This was also the first show where we recognized the highest achievers through a scoring system, something we carried forward in all our future productions as an additional means of encouraging participation at a high level. Scores were shown throughout the experience to the individual game players, increasing with interaction and content discovery, and top performers highlighted to the whole group at the end of the experience.

Early in the development of these immersive and interactive cinematic experiences we realized that one of the biggest values of such a system was the ability to combine highly detailed and complex information in a narrative storyline. The goal was to make available a wide range of scientific information and allow the players to move to their own level of exploration of the content woven into a shared storyline. The best example of how this was done was an experience we developed called *Vital Space* (2000), which was a story of an astronaut in a Mars-based International Space Station who, through an accident, becomes contaminated by something in a Martian dust sample. The astronaut isolates herself to save the rest of the crew and turns to the audience on Earth to utilize the latest technology to cure her. This fictional advanced technology provided the players with a means to navigate the body of the sick commander with nanobots. These nanobots could be directed by the audience exploring the gross organs all the way down to the DNA structure in search of the virus. This exploration took place through a collaborative effort of up to 200 audience members but also allowed for individual exploration of the body and its functions. As the set of nanobots under player control traversed the body, individuals could investigate particular elements of the systems to unearth clues to a diagnosis of the problem. Once the symptoms were discovered, the audience performed a diagnostic assessment which revealed the location of a parasite in the astronaut's body. The players as a collective would then compete in the destruction of the parasite in order to save the astronaut. The competitive element established the ranking of individual players as the group achieved success within the game. An important question that was raised through the technique of collaborative and competitive game play was the value of each of these forms of interaction in providing an educational experience. Even though this experience was shown in multiple countries in the world, no consensus was arrived at as to the competitive element in contrast to the individual exploration or the social interaction. The anecdotal feedback that we received through the various educational institutions that played this experience was that in some cases the competitive element was a distracting feature, where others saw it as a primary compelling element in motivation, encouraging the pursuit of the educational values.

While the *Storm Over Stellwagen* experience added value to interactivity via simulation, the *Vital Space* show extended this with some direct game play elements. In each case this was woven into a strong narrative and was used to amplify the sense of personal engagement in the story, encourage interaction through personal scoring and rewards, and a feeling of consequence in the group's success or failure at the end of the experience. The resultant balance between passive cinematic storytelling and fully interactive games was clearly established with a model that was well received by students, educators, parents, and the general public. However, this was seen as simply a beginning and not an end state. Rather than simply staying within one model that was considered successful, we set out to test the breadth of interactivity that would work within this platform for edutainment.

Pushing the Limits

Another example pointing to the challenge of changing contemporary thinking processes was a show called *Sharks: Predator/Prey* (2001). Marine science had evolved and it had become evident how important it was to communicate to the general public the relationship between species which in earlier times was called the food chain but now was more accurately understood as the food web. *Sharks: Predator/Prey* was a fully 3D real-time game that could be played by a hundred or more people simultaneously. The experience began with players starting as the smallest creature in the ocean, a type of phytoplankton, and maturing through the game to try and become a great white shark. Success resulted in players taking the role of more complex creatures in the ecosystem and trying to meet increasingly complex goals for survival. Each step of the way one had to discover who is a predator and who is a prey and strive to survive in an ocean of creatures formed by the people in the audience. The game is set in a very competitive environment against the backdrop of a large-format screen showing high-resolution animations of who is eating who—in graphic detail. The players were not led in a narrative; they were thrust with a minimal introduction into the simulation/game and allowed to unearth the relationships more deeply through game play. This particular game was found to be more popular with typical game-playing audience members and more of a challenge for multigenerational audience members who needed too much time to absorb game control concepts instead of focusing upon game content. *Sharks: Predator/Prey* represented a good example of a group experience for the gamer generations, which they equated to providing self-built understanding and motivation. *Sharks: Predator/Prey* was the first show to push the concepts of an immersive experience beyond the cinema. Immersion Cinema shows had shown tremendous motivational value, rich dialogue, and exceptional value in communicating scientific, cultural, and historical concepts, but were fundamentally limited to their short-form cinema experiences of typically 30-minute duration. The *Sharks: Predator/Prey* experience could easily be extended in time, and expanded in scope, as simulation and game play were at the core instead of the narrative. This also allowed for more ready adaptation to broadband Internet use, and with it the potential for extended interaction, motivation, and personal engagement in the topic area beyond the experience in an Immersion Cinema.

This era represented the height of experimentation in viable immersive group experiences. We continued with the development of numerous distinctly different experiences that further pushed the envelope from the narrative cinema/game hybrid we had pioneered. Another small but meaningful experiment known as *Ring Road* (2001) was undertaken involving the underwater habitat of Monterey Bay in California, developed in conjunction with Mystic Aquarium in Connecticut. This project connected a real remotely-operated vehicle (ROV) and multiple live cameras in Monterey Bay via Internet2 to audience members across the country in an Immersion Cinema in Mystic. In this experiment players were interacting in a simulated undersea environment on consoles that matched the actual underwater world captured by the ROV and displayed on the large format screen in Mystic. This experience was not driven by a preprogrammed narrative or explicit simulation. The environment was entirely dynamic and allowed instructors to take the players on a personal investigation of the animal and plant species in the virtual habitat in relation to what was observable in the actual natural habitat. Instructors also had options to activate simple trivia gaming into the experience and allow winning students to control the actual ROV in Monterey Bay. If actual underwater conditions were poor on a particular day, alternative video recordings of the live environment could be called up as a comparison for the audience. The live environment inputs and controls were seen as very compelling and made the message real to the players in a way that virtual environments and game play could not entirely achieve. However, reliance on the instructor to make the situation work well in the midst of the number of interactive options was a real challenge that often did not fit together smoothly. A different approach to integrating live and virtual was needed if the benefits were to be retained and limitations minimized.

Another example which combined live experiences and the virtual was done in conjunction with Bob Ballard, the scientist who discovered the *Titanic*. Running an annual educational program called the JASON Project, Ballard's team offered a telepresence solution to highlight scientific exploration to school groups across America. *Exploration: Sea Lions* (2003) was an Immersion Cinema experience that offered a significant expansion to Ballard's proposition of telepresence as an educational tool. By inserting an experiment connecting students interactively, over 1,000 students across America in immersive cinemas and classrooms had the opportunity to explore a complex scientific problem of why sea lions were dying in the Channel Islands of California. Real-time interactive interfaces allowed students to research and simulate real life scenarios of the sea lions and develop a hypothesis which they could share amongst each other through dialogue and database sharing. Students put together presentations which represented their conclusions as to why the sea lion population was decreasing. Participants could then reflect upon their hypotheses after viewing each of the alternatives or supporting presentations to make a final assessment of the cause of the problem. In the end, the addition of interactive exploration of the scientific issues indicated to be a powerful means for more active concern and discovery among the students. One of the unique features introduced in this project was the use of avatars to represent the students and their identity. This introduction of a representation of themselves added to the value of play and personal identity in the pursuit of an educational problem. As students mastered their chosen area of inquiry in this show, they could directly offer assistance to other students through their avatars and assist in advancing the collective understanding of all the players.

Exploration: Sea Lions, like the *Ring Road* experience one before it, connected to live on-site experiences and virtual investigations but with very different results. *Ring Road*, which tried to weave the live into the virtual directly, found itself challenged by constant context-switching to establish strong enough presence for the players, thereby reducing the motivation and engagement level and ultimately the learning outcomes. *Exploration: Sea Lions* put the live and virtual experiences next to one another but left them each to their format and was by far the more successful approach. The live broadcast helped to situate the interactive production but left it with room to take on its own identity and potential for establishing presence. Students and teachers each rated the *Exploration: Sea Lions* experience very highly, noting that it encouraged dialogue, was of strong value to weaker students, and motivated students about the subject area (Ritterfeld, Weber, Fernandes, & Vorderer, 2004).

State of the Art in Immersive Gaming

Three final examples of the state of the art in blending narrative and game play are worth highlighting here. The first of these is *Dolphin Bay (2005), a* strong action adventure production examining human impacts upon dolphin habitat that is a very tight integration of game play and narrative throughout. The second is a production called *Dinosaurs: Beyond Extinction* (2003), which focused upon the complex issue of adaptation of species and examined the potential for episodic and cross-media experiences. Finally, a show interwoven with a whole exhibition called *Sparking Reaction* (2002) looked at issues of energy and nuclear power generation that demonstrated the value in extending a cinema experience to the virtual.

The most intriguing and complex development for a marine biology application is called *Dolphin Bay* and plays today in Mote Marine in Sarasota, Florida. This highly evolved storyline interweaves a series of complex games that take the viewer to a personal interaction in the role of a marine biologist trying to save dolphins within a fictitious bay. The production utilized movie directors, screenwriters, and Hollywood actors combined in a sophisticated game development. This experience blurred the line between cinema and game to an extent that a player would not be able to identify either as the clear driving factor. Emotion and intense action fostered engagement with the story and acting but clearly pushed audience dialogue to occur during game play portions of the experience only. This understanding of how narrative and game play serve key roles in aspects of participation was most evident in this production due to the highest quality of each aspect.

Dinosaurs: Beyond Extinction was developed in consultation with the Smithsonian Institute Museum of Natural History. This production focused on adaptation of species in pursuing what no longer could be referred to as evolution. The players needed to discover what characteristics were necessary in creatures to remain vital and persistent through history. The story line takes place in the future where, instead of vacation by flying in an airship from one physical location to another, we would vacation by time travel back into history, experiencing the unique moments that framed human invention. The players as a collective decide to go on a voyage back into time, choosing a location in a time period, which inevitably gets bungled by the robotic host, Bob. On take-off, the time machine becomes disabled at some point in prehistory, and through a series of games to identify species in the environment, we unearth the fact that the players are stuck 480 million years back in the Permian period. Once the ship is repaired and jumps back to the present, the players find that dinosaurs have taken over and humankind is no longer in existence. Bob determines that the players have accidentally caused some types of adaptation in their investigations of the past habitats which have allowed dinosaurs to survive events such as the K2 asteroid. The players are quickly taken back to before this event and given the task of understanding what adaptations might have occurred such that they can correct or stop them. The audience's success or failure determines what type of future is returned to—friendly to them or not. The point of this edutainment experience was to sensitize the players to the highly complex interweaving of mutation as a fundamental force of life. Through game play, a very complex and important idea about what sits at the core of the continuation of terrestrial life could be communicated. Complexity that exists in understanding science and natural history can only be explored and expressed by utilizing new technology that combines narrative storyline with game play. *Dinosaurs: Beyond Extinction* sits as a powerful experience, rated highly by players for presence, engagement, fun, and learning, but it was conceived for multiple additional purposes that also set it apart from many Immersion Cinema productions. By selecting a show structure, time travel, that is universal and lead characters, robots, that are sympathetic and consistent, we established a narrative base that could serve multiple interactive shows, and in fact other show types. *Dinosaurs: Beyond Extinction* spawned investigations into television show production and a series of digital games as means of extending the ideas and developing a community around the characters and history exploration.

Many institutions struggle with a way to teach new scientific values by exploring issues-based science communication. It is believed that a deeper understanding might be achieved in the role of science and how it shapes our world. An example of an issues-based scientific experience was a visitor center created for British Nuclear Fuels Ltd. (BNFL). This was done in collaboration with the London Science Museum as the content partner. This corporation was at a crossroads in finding its future area of focus and business practice. With most of its holdings in atomic energy generation, BNFL was contemplating a new role in fuel reclamation. *Sparking Reaction* explored the role of energy production from the perspective of the nuclear industry through a series of games. The players were challenged to build reactors, generate the fuel, power the grid, and dispose of the waste. The outcome of the players' choices and their skill left the toxic problem difficult to resolve. Alternative solutions in looking at renewable resources were contrasted with the same power demands and challenges for production. At the end of this show the players were asked which of the various solutions they would choose and for their attitude to nuclear energy. This experience, combined with a series of interactive exhibitions and a participatory Web site, provided the company with direct public feedback as to what corporate roles and responsibilities the company should have in the nuclear industry. Ultimately, BNFL got out of the energy production business and moved its primary focus to the reprocessing of spent nuclear fuels.

While these three experiences were significantly different, they each significantly aided in evolving the thinking and understanding surrounding the limitations and potential directions and value of fully realized interactive cinema experiences. At the most successful, Immersive Cinema experiences established a strongly engaging interactive and sensory experience, while providing time and impetus for significant dialogue during and after the experience. The clear long-term weakness of these experiences is the lack of a sustained impact or stickiness to follow along from the energy and value they establish. Experiences such as *Sparking Reaction* show the potential when the spark of relevance is ignited by an interactive and immersive experience, and allowed to grow and extend through user participation and engagement in virtual-only environments.

Moving into the Parallel World

With a change in the broadband paradigm, the opportunity to become more deeply involved in online social networking was at hand. Our first experiment in combining some of the key characteristics for deep learning—personal relevance, dialogue, and cocreation—was *Virtual Canada*, created as part of the World Expo 2005 in Japan.

Built on the 3D Torque Game Engine and our own next-generation multiuser software, *Virtual Canada* was the first virtual country to be created as an Massive Multiplayer Online (MMO) community. The goal of the project was to provide an opportunity for dialogue on cultural diversity at the Japan Expo 2005. It was a companion product to the Canada Pavilion which exposed the same topics through noninteractive means. *Virtual Canada* was made out of 3D models of cities set in the vast landscape that includes natural parks, historic and tourist sites, and cultural centers spread across the country. The database was constructed to reflect a wide diversity of Canadian economic, social, and cultural interests. Tools were created to provide the user community with the opportunity to interact at the highest possible level. Dialogue was achieved through a real-time translation solution between English, French, and Japanese. Players took on their identity with avatars and went on quests in search of cultural facts and individuals' stories on diversity. The identity of individuals could be shared by occupied homes within *Virtual Canada* and by using the toolset provided to upload persistent rich-media assets to decorate their homes and then share that experience with others. The same toolset was provided to museums across the country as well as schools. The country soon became populated with a variety of user-created content that filled out the database of rich media assets. Streaming video, sound, text, and image constituted the substance for communicating the Canadian perspective on cultural diversity. *Virtual Canada* ran on desktop PCs but also networked hardware systems that were provided to a series of museums and were mirrored in the Canadian pavilion in Japan. This provided an international perspective with users exploring, engaging in a dialogue, and cocreating both locally and abroad. *Virtual Canada*, as a serious game, opened the door for alternative solutions for edutainment. This sits in contrast to the strictly fantasy-based MMOs and unstructured free-for-all social communities such as *Second Life*, *Alphaworld*, and *There*. The public response to the Canada Pavilion and the opportunity to use an MMO game as a tool for enhancing social communication and cultural expression was shown to now be viable.

We now had an edutainment system that provided the strong excitement and motivation of a physically based immersive experience and the dialogue that it can promote. This system was also able to extend this to virtual worlds that allowed for ongoing user dialogue and cocreation, providing the means to evolve each player's understanding and promoting broader communication and change.

Serious Games in the Parallel World

The core software developed for *Virtual Canada* was made available to the open source community in 2007 as a means to open the exploration of parallel worlds to a wider audience of researchers, and those wishing to cocreate future creative experiences with us. We are now focused upon the next generation of serious game environments that can bridge between the power of immersive dialogue and the ongoing relevance of cocreated social software.

By building on this powerful set of tools, a new project in Scandinavia was able to leap frog the evolution of a social network into a serious game. The project known as *Virtual Rockheim* (2009) represents the first phase in the realization of the actual Norwegian National Center for Rock and Popular music called *Rockheim*. The online version was launched in the fall of 2008 while the physical center will open in Trondheim in 2009. *Virtual Rockheim* represents a significant development focusing on creative expression in music as a primary communication and navigation tool. The solution developed for *Virtual Rockheim* is to contemplate a way in which music could be used as a navigational tool in a ubiquitous software environment accessible on any networked machine anywhere. Thinking of Norwegian music in terms of geographical space led to the conclusion that Google Earth would be an appropriate platform to organize the database of music content through time and space. The approach is to organize the artists by when they created the music and where they actually played it, mapping 3D links to these activities into their appropriate cities and towns within the Norwegian landscape.

Virtual Rockheim is an online social community that uses music as the navigational metaphor to link to a rich-media *Rockipedia* and the virtual museum.

This prototype environment evolved from the previously discussed open source solution that encourages contribution and cocreation from the broader social community. The user community contributes to and explores musical performers within the virtual landscape. The Wiki-style *Rockipedia* is an enormous community feed database including video, images, and text featuring the important artists of each generation.

Opening the door of the virtual museum leads you into the 3D real time world of *Virtual Rockheim*. Log in, download the software, choose an avatar, and explore the Internet radio holodeck, a tribute room, and virtual concerts. Each decade of musical history is represented through a 3D environment. Clickable-rich media assets embedded in the world can be explored and experienced through your avatar and stored in your play list. The virtual museum also offers live real-time 3D virtual concerts which will feature artist avatars and avatar audience-members participating from around the world. These concert events will be user-generated experiences made possible through a selection of open source tools available only in *Virtual Rockheim*. At its heart, *Virtual Rockheim* represents the next generation of MMO educational technology, allowing for thousands of players to inhabit and explore a virtual/cultural world together. This is only the starting point, however; as *Virtual Rockheim* integrates the latest in Web 2.0 cocreation tools to extend its stickiness across the virtual landscape right back into the real world. The virtual world of concerts, holodeck play lists, and so on links to other shared popular communities such as *Myspace*, *YouTube*, *Flickr*, and *Last.fm*. The key difference is this MMO exists to extend a cultural form of expression into a shared national identity. It is hoped this project paves the way toward what we understand are the components that constitute deep learning. A player's musical experiences can be woven into a personal story of music engagement alongside the artists themselves.

Serious Social Games

Throughout the projects, platforms, and study/feedback we have explored in the past 15 years, we have pushed the envelope of engagement from the personal to social. We have often explored concepts that are far from simple and involved scientific phenomena, historical events, or cultural knowledge combined with moral and societal values. These areas necessitate collective knowledge to be pursued wisely toward action. We believe that one of the most promising areas in which to pursue this challenge is that of the MMO, combining personal engagement, encouraged and supported by social interactions, and affording vast opportunities for cocreation. Many MMOs are emerging on a daily basis, though most are purely game/entertainment or commercially oriented. The few that are more open to creativity, dialogue, and cocreation have thus far been so technical and open-ended that a user often does not know where to begin, or why to participate. Our experience has shown us that the value of nonlinear narrative experiences explored in an immersive environment enhances engagement, the first step in social participation. Serious topics, simulation and game activities that provoke thought and dialogue foster personal relevance leading to enhanced stickiness. Finally, thematically focused content and intuitive creative tools provide the means for cocreation, which in turn allows the social community to evolve from increased personal relevance and stickiness, into the strong community of deep learners we promote with the deep learning model elaborated above (see Figure 27.1).

References

Alphaworld. (n.d.). Available at http://www.activeworlds.com/worlds/alphaworld

Exploration: Sea Lions. (2003). Mystic, CT: Mystic Aquarium/The JASON Foundation.

Dinosaurs. (2003). Washington, DC: The Smithsonian Institution

Dolphin Bay. (2005). Sarasota, FL: Mote Marine Laboratory.

My Canada. (1997). Canadian National Exhibition.

Ring Road / Monterey Sanctuaries. (2001). Mystic, CT: Mystic Aquarium/The JASON Foundation.

Ritterfeld, U., Weber, R., Fernandes, S., & Vorderer, P. (2004). Think science! Entertainment Education in interactive theaters. Computers in Entertainment, 2(1), 11.

Second Life. (n.d.). Available at http:// www.secondlife.com

Sharks: Predator/Prey. (2001). Toronto, Canada: Immersion Studios, Inc.

Sparking Reaction. (2002). London: The Science Museum.

Storm Over Stellwagen. (1999). Washington, DC: NOAA.

There. (n.d.). Available at http://www.there.com

Virtual Rockheim. (2009). Bergen, Norway: The Royal Norwegian Ministry of Culture.

Vital Space. (2000). Toronto, Canada: Immersion Studios, Inc.

Chapter 28

The Gaming *Dispositif*

An Analysis of Serious Games from a Humanities Perspective

Joost Raessens

According to the French philosopher Gilles Deleuze, concepts are meaningless unless they are helpful to the understanding and solution of significant contemporary problems (Deleuze & Parnet, 1989). In line with Deleuze, I introduce the concept of the *dispositif*[1] as a heuristic tool for studying the political–ideological coloring of serious games. Such a tool is important because, to date, much of the debate on serious games has been merely framed in terms of effectiveness without paying attention to their political–ideological interest. And when theorists do pay attention to the political–ideological interest of games, they barely involve the different ways in which the player is addressed or positioned by the game in their analyses.

In the first paragraph, I analyze the concept of the cinematographic *dispositif* as it was originally conveyed within film studies by the French film theorist Jean-Louis Baudry and offer a further critical development of the concept. In the second paragraph, I show what it means to analyze serious games as a *dispositif*. To discuss the possible political-ideological tendencies of the playing of serious games, I focus on the unconscious desires involved in this phenomenon, drawing on the work of the Slovenian philosopher Slavoj Žižek. I show that these tendencies may or may not be actualized, depending on the different ways in which the player is addressed or positioned, respectively, by the game's technical base, the game text, and the context in which the game is played. Queries into the political-ideological meaning of a specific serious game can, thus, only be answered by taking into account all the elements of the gaming *dispositif* as I describe them in this chapter. In the third paragraph I show in more detail how this works on the basis of a close reading of two serious games: *Food Force* (2005) and *Darfur is Dying* (2006). The last paragraph contains my conclusions.

Cinematographic *Dispositif*[2]

Jean-Louis Baudry

One of the founding fathers of apparatus theory—a dominant theory within film studies during the 1970s—is the French psychoanalytic film theorist Jean-Louis Baudry. In the early 1970s, Baudry published two influential articles about the question of the cinematographic apparatus: "Ideological Effects of the Basic Cinematographic Apparatus" (1970/1986a) and "The Apparatus: Metapsychological Approaches to the Impression of Reality in the Cinema" (1975/1986b). In his text of 1970, Baudry theorizes the arrangement (in French: *disposition*) of the screening situation of the film spectator in analogy with the prisoner in Plato's cave (Figure 28.1):[3]

> The arrangement [*disposition*] of the different elements—projector, darkened hall, screen—in addition from reproducing in a striking way the mise-en-scène of Plato's cave... reconstructs the situation necessary to the release of the "mirror stage" discovered by Lacan. (1970/1986a, p. 294)

In his text of 1975, Baudry actually refers to this screening situation as a specific kind of *dispositif*:

> Plato's prisoner is the victim of an illusion of reality, that is, of precisely what is known as a hallucination, if one is awake, as a dream, if asleep; he is the prey of an impression, of *an impression of reality*.... Plato...would imagine or resort to an apparatus [*dispositif*] that doesn't merely evoke but quite precisely describes in its mode of operation the cinematographic apparatus [*dispositif*] and the spectator's place in relation to it. (1975/1986b, p. 302)

Baudry's argument as formulated in the titles of and quotes from both articles can be divided into three parts: (1) he argues *that* the film spectator is a victim and defines *of what* he is a victim; (2) he describes the *desires* and *pleasures* attached to this victimhood;[4] and (3) its ideological *effects*.

First, Baudry compares the *dispositif* of cinema to the *dispositif* of Plato's

Figure 28.1 Plato's cave

cave. As is the case with Plato's prisoner, the film spectator sits immobilized in a darkened room as the victim or prey of an impression of reality evoked by the images projected on the screen in front of him.

Second, Baudry compares the state of mind of a film viewer with that of a dreamer, arguing that both are characterized by a desire for and regression to an infantile state: "the 'mirror stage' discovered by Lacan" (Baudry, 1970/1986a, p. 294). The mirror stage:

> represents a fundamental aspect of the structure of subjectivity.... The moment of identification, when the subject assumes its image as its own, is described by Lacan as a moment of jubilation, since it leads to an imaginary sense of mastery. (Evans, 2001, p. 115)

Just like a child who identifies with his or her own image in the mirror, the film spectator identifies "with what stages the spectacle, makes it seen, obliging him to see what it sees; this is exactly the function taken over by the camera...which constitutes and rules the objects in this 'world'" (Baudry, 1970/1986a, p. 295).[5] The desire for and the pleasures attached to the cinematic experience are closely related to the desire to return toward "a mode of relating to reality which could be defined as enveloping and in which the separation between one's own body and the exterior world is not well defined" (Baudry, 1975/1986b, p. 313). According to Baudry (1975/1986b), "cinema, like dream, would seem to correspond to a contemporary form of regression, but whereas dream, according to Freud, is merely a 'normal hallucinatory psychosis,' cinema offers an artificial psychosis" (p. 315).[6]

Third, Baudry (1970/1986a) discusses the ideological effects of this artificial psychosis. As the victim of an "impression" of reality and not of an "objective reality" (p. 287) with an "open and indeterminate horizon" (p. 292), the film spectator is forced to identify not only with an ideologically colored, but also with a homogeneous image of reality where heterogeneity, difference, openness, and indetermination are eliminated. According to Baudry (1970/1986a), this is the case because the meaning of a film:

> does not depend only on the content of the images but also on the material procedures by which an illusion of continuity...is restored from discontinuous elements.... We could say that film...lives on the denial of difference: difference is necessary for it to live, but it lives on its negation. (p. 290)

Beyond Baudry

To make Baudry's concept of the *dispositif* productive for the analysis of contemporary media in general, and serious games in particular, we need to further develop this concept in three closely related ways. This is in line with Baudry's (1970/1986a) own words: "We would like to establish for the cinema a few guidelines which will need to be *completed, verified, improved* " [italics added] (p. 287).

The first element of Baudry's theoretical framework that needs to be 'verified' concerns his assumed technological determinist position. According to Carroll (2004), Baudry is not particularly interested in "the content of the images or the stories of particular films or even of particular kinds of films," but only in "a network which includes the screen, the spectator, and the projector…the projection situation itself, irrespective of what is being screened" (pp. 224–225). When we conduct a close-reading of Baudry's articles, it is striking to see that he does not argue against the importance of specific film forms— their content, their narrative continuity or discontinuity, their positioning of the spectator. What he does argue against is the exclusive attention to these forms which ignores the importance of their technical bases:

> It is strange…that emphasis has been placed almost exclusively on their [contemporary media] influence, on the effects they have as finished products, their content…. The technical bases on which these effects depend and the specific characteristics of these bases have, however, been ignored. (Baudry, 1970/1986a, p. 287)

Moreover, according to Philip Rosen (1986), Baudry's focus on the *dispositif* does not necessarily neglect the importance of "the questions of textuality" (p. 281). Even if one would agree with Baudry that the cinematographic *dispositif* has certain tendencies, it seems possible that "certain kinds of deployment of narrative can be set in contradiction to these tendencies" (p. 282), according to Rosen. In order to avoid an exclusive interpretation of the concept of the *dispositif* as referring to the machinery or the technical aspects of cinema, it is useful, as Frank Kessler (2006) proposes, to use the French term *dispositif* instead of the English translation *apparatus*. This English term runs the risk of being confused with another of Baudry's concepts, namely the "basic cinematographic apparatus" (*l'appareil de base*) which concerns "the ensemble of the equipment and operations necessary to the production of a film and its projection" (Baudry, 1975/1986b, p. 317). A second advantage of the French term *dispositif* is that it implies "the idea of a specific arrangement or tendency (*disposition*)" (Kessler, 2006, p. 60) which the English translation *apparatus* does not.

So, the concept of *dispositif* allows us to conceptualize the interplay of five elements that play a leading part in the production of media meaning, and their interrelationships: The (1) technical base of media that helps to shape (2) specific positionings of the user (spectator/player), based upon (3) specific unconscious desires to which correspond (4) different media forms/texts with their specific modes of address, and (5) different institutional and cultural contexts and viewing situations.

The second element of Baudry's theoretical framework that needs to be 'improved' concerns his claim that a technical phenomenon such as the restoration of the illusion of continuity from discontinuous elements lays the foundation of cinema's ideological effects of continuity and homogeneity. This claim is far from convincing for many reasons, two of which I refer to here. First, as was argued by David Bordwell and Kristin Thompson (1986), spatial, temporal, as well as narrative continuity are the result of "continuity editing" (p. 210) and "classical narration" (Bordwell, 1985, p. 156) both of them having all sorts of alternatives.[7] Second, as Stuart Hall—one of the most influential representatives of the active audience theory—argued, texts are open to various reading strategies.[8] So, the way in which a film spectator reads a film is not only determined by the technical phenomenon referred to by Baudry. But this leaves unimpeded the "possible" ideological consequences of the *dispositif* as such. As Baudry (1975/1986b) rightly argues:

> Instead of considering cinema as an ideologically neutral apparatus…the impact of which would be entirely determined by the content of the film (a consideration which leaves unsolved the whole question of its persuasive power and of the reason for which it revealed itself to be an instrument particularly well suited to exert ideological influence)…it is necessary to consider it from the viewpoint of the apparatus that it constitutes. (p. 312)

The third element of Baudry's theoretical framework that needs to be 'completed' concerns Baudry's use of the myth of Plato's cave to persuade us that the invention of cinema is a manifestation of a long-standing and transhistorical desire. Both from a synchronic and diachronic perspective, we can argue against Baudry and claim that contemporary media all have different media *dispositifs* with different configurations of technology, user positioning, desire, media text, and context. In the next section I analyze how this configuration takes shape in relation to serious games.

Serious Games as *Dispositif*

Dutch cultural theorist Mieke Bal (2002) argues that "the travelling nature of concepts is an asset" (p. 25) because concepts travel between disciplines and *do* things, that is, they "offer miniature theories, and in that guise, help in the analysis of objects" (p. 22). The concept *dispositif* has only recently traveled from film studies to game studies. One of the reasons why concepts originating from film studies stayed out of the focus of game scholars for so long is, one could argue, the impact of Espen Aarseth's (2001) opening article in the first issue of the online journal *Game Studies*: "Computer Game Studies, Year One." Though he states that "We all enter this field from *somewhere else*, from anthropology, sociology, narratology, semiotics, film studies, etc., and the political and ideological baggage we bring from our old field inevitably determines and motivates our approaches," he advocates a new discipline, computer game studies, warning us as follows: "Games are not a kind of cinema, or literature, but *colonising* [italics added] attempts from both these fields have already happened, and no doubt will happen again."[9] Now that computer game studies is a well-established field, game scholars do not worry so much anymore about these "colonising attempts," but are trying to make concepts coming from somewhere else productive for their work.[10] Nevertheless, they have to take into account that "no concept is meaningful for cultural analysis unless it helps us to understand the object better *on its*—the object's—*own terms*" [italics in original] (Bal, 2002, p. 8). When Sue Morris (2002), for example, uses Baudry's concept *dispositif* in her analysis of the first-person shooter game genre, she implicitly refers to this debate:

> From the outset, it is important to emphasize that film, television and computer or video games are completely distinct and different media— both as textual systems and in terms of their mechanisms of engagement. My goal here is not one of applying film and television theory directly to computer games, but rather to see how some of the concepts developed in the study of other media may assist in an exploration of this relatively new and unexplored medium. (pp. 81–82)

Morris's argument is in line with what Bal (2002) writes about concepts that travel: "Between disciplines, their meaning, reach, and operational value differ. These processes of differing need to be assessed before, during, and after each 'trip'" (p. 24).

Analyzing serious games as a *dispositif* means studying the five elements that I have used above to characterize such an approach: The (1) technical base of serious games that shape (2) specific positionings of the player, based upon (3) specific unconscious desires to which correspond, (4) different game forms or texts with their specific modes of address, and (5) different institutional and cultural contexts and playing situations.

As a starting point of this second paragraph, I will analyze the third element, the unconscious desires attached to the playing of serious games. I raise the question if "artificial psychosis" (Baudry, 1975/1986b, p. 315) is the best, or the only, conceivable concept one could use for describing the state of mind of the serious game player.

Slavoj Žižek's Range of Unconscious Desires

An alternative, or better, a broader range of unconscious desires, stem from another Lacan-inspired theorist, the Slovenian philosopher Slavoj Žižek (1999) in his analysis of cyberspace. In this section, I summarize Žižek's framework and the ways in which Caroline Pelletier translated this framework into the field of educational gaming. My most important contribution to this debate is to interpret the four kinds of unconscious desires (element 3 of Baudry's dispositif)—which Žižek as well as Pelletier refer to—as *virtual tendencies* that may or may not be actualized, depending on the different ways in which the player of the game is positioned by the technical base (elements 1 and 2), by the game text itself (element 4) and by the context in which the game is played (element 5). Questions about the political–ideological effects of specific serious games, as we will see in my case studies of *Darfur is Dying* (2006) and *Food Force,* (2005) can, thus, only be answered by taking into account all five elements of the gaming *dispositif* as I describe them in this chapter, and not, as Žižek and Pelletier tend to do, by exclusively referring to the four different unconscious desires.

Žižek (1999) starts his analysis of unconscious desires by addressing the following question: "What are the consequences of cyberspace for Oedipus—that is, for the mode of subjectivization that psychoanalysis conceptualized as the Oedipus complex and its dissolution?" (p. 110). Pelletier (2005) describes the well-known Oedipus story as a way to communicate to individuals that they are no longer at one with their respective mothers, while they also identify with and fear castration by the father. Universally, the father represents symbolic authority through which individuals gain access to sociosymbolic signifiers such as language, social status, and gender.

What makes this question important to the study of serious games is that, framed within a Lacanian perspective, educational/serious games deal with the player's entry into the game's symbolic order. In contrast to the three standard reactions toward cyberspace —that cyberspace involves the end of Oedipus (whether in a dystopian or utopian form) or, on the contrary, that cyberspace entails the continuation of Oedipus—Žižek advocates a fourth way, which he defines as *interpassivity*.

Pelletier uses Žižek's framework to formulate the political–ideological functions of educational games. This can be resumed in Table 28.1.

According to Žižek, the first two standard reactions toward cyberspace are that it involves the end of Oedipus. This can be a dystopian development (1, see Table 28.1)— Žižek is referring here to Jean Baudrillard and Paul Virilio:

> Individuals regressing to pre-symbolic psychotic immersion, of losing the symbolic distance that sustains the minimum of critical/reflective attitude

Table 28.1 Four Reactions Toward Cyberspace and Educational/Serious Games

| | 1. 2. End of Oedipus | | 3. Continuation of Oedipus | 4. In between: interpassivity |
	1. Dystopia	2. Utopia		
Žižek	Psychosis	Perversion	Hysteria	Perversion
Pelletier	Games as sensual temptations	Games as pain relievers	Games as replicas of non-virtual life	Games as dramatic stages for reality construction

(the idea that the computer functions as a maternal Thing that swallows the subject, who entertains an attitude of incestuous fusion towards it). (Žižek, 1999, p. 111)[11]

On the other hand, there are theorists—here Žižek refers to Sandy Stone and Sherry Turkle—who emphasize the liberating utopian potential of cyberspace (2, see Table 28.1):

Cyberspace opens up the domain of shifting multiple sexual and social identities, at least potentially liberating us from the hold of the patriarchal Law.... In cyberspace, I am compelled to renounce any fixed symbolic identity, the legal/political fiction of a unique Self guaranteed by my place in the socio-symbolic structure.... Cyberspace opens up the liberating perspective of globalized multiple perversion. (Žižek, 1999, p. 112, 116) [12]

According to the third standard reaction toward cyberspace, the oedipal mode of subjectivization continues, albeit by other means:

Yes, in cyberspace, "you can be whatever you want", you're free to choose a symbolic identity (screen-persona), but you must choose *one* which in a way will always betray you, which will never be fully adequate; you must accept representation in cyberspace by a signifying element that runs around in the circuitry as your stand-in. (p. 114) [13]

Finally, at the end of his article when Žižek puts the question on the table which of these three reactions toward cyberspace is the right one, he comes up with a fourth one. I would like to reconstruct the three steps he takes to explain this fourth reaction. In the first step, Žižek argues the standard reactions to cyberspace—cyberspace is involving a break from or a continuation with Oedipus—are wrong and that we need to conceptualize a middle position. This in-between is "a perversion like the second one, but on condition that one conceptualizes perversion in a much stricter way" (p. 116). The Žižekian pervert not only violates the rules of normal behavior, as we have seen earlier (2, see Table 28.1), but, at the same time, effectively longs for the symbolic Law, for its regulation and rules. To make clear what he has in mind, Žižek gives the example of people—mostly highly paid executives—who, sick of having to be in charge all the time, work for a New York agency called *Slaves Are Us* where they can enjoy being brutally ordered to do their job; that is, to clean apartments for free. This example is what Žižek calls a "fantasy-scenario of interpassivity" (p. 118).

In the second step, Žižek argues that both interactivity and interpassivity are ways in which digital technologies position people as responders. They are not oppositional, but mutually constitutive. According to Žižek, interactivity is currently used in two senses: "(1) *interacting with* the medium—that is, not being just a passive consumer" [italics in original] (p. 105). Interactivity in this sense is a player clicking and moving a mouse, and tapping the keys of the keyboard. The second form of interactivity occurs when these actions lead to in-game actions: "(2) *acting through* another agent, so that my job is done, while I sit back and remain passive, just observing the game" (pp. 105–106). This is the case when the player observes an avatar on the screen acting. What Žižek means by interpassivity is a reversal of the second meaning of interactivity: "the distinguishing feature of interpassivity is that, in it, the subject is incessantly—frenetically even—*active*, while displacing on to another the fundamental passivity of his or her being"[italics in original] (p. 106).[14] We see this interpassive mechanism at work when the player is passionately clicking and tapping while his avatar is fulfilling the game's demands. A prime example of interpassivity is the Japanese electronic toy, the *tamagochi*.[15] The *tamagotchi* is a virtual pet that captivates its carers by issuing orders:

> The interesting thing here is that we are dealing with a toy…that provides satisfaction precisely by behaving like a difficult child bombarding us with demands. The satisfaction is provided by our being compelled to care for the object any time it wants—that is, by fulfilling its demands.… The whole point of the game is that *it always has the initiative*, that the object controls the game and bombards us with demands [italics in original]. (pp. 107–108)

But, and this is crucial, the carers play this interpassive game under the condition of disavowal: "'I know very well that this is just an inanimate object, but none the less I act as if I believe this is a living being'" (p. 107).[16] This moment of distancing plays an important role in the discussion about serious games as we will see later on.

In the third step, Žižek claims that, although generally our fundamental fantasies remain unconscious and thereby inaccessible to us, artists such as film makers are able to do what the analysand can do during a psychoanalytic session, that is "to 'traverse the fundamental fantasy'" (p. 61).[17] Cyberspace, in other words, offers artists—and game designers—the possibility "to realize (to externalize, to stage) our innermost fantasies" (p. 121).

> Far from enslaving us to these fantasies, and thus turning us into de-subjectivized blind puppets, it [cyberspace] enables us to treat them in *a playful way* [italics added], and thus to adopt towards them a minimum of distance—in short what Lacan calls la traverseé du fantasme ("going-through, traversing the fantasy"). (p. 121)

Traversing our—for example, psychotic, hysteric, or perverse—fantasies or, as Žižek refers to it, *overidentifying* with them, means that we can follow the Other's orders while simultaneously having a critical, reflexive relation with them. The question if such a critical distance exists or needs to exist, is, as we will see in the next section, a crucial element in the debate about the political–ideological impact of serious games.

Serious Games

These four reactions toward cyberspace as explicated by Žižek are translated by Pelletier into the field of the educational sciences. What makes Pelletier's approach important is that she tracks down these reactions in the literature about educational games. According to Pelletier (2005), elements of the "end of Oedipus" reaction—either its dystopian or utopian mode—can be traced in those theories which define games as *sensual temptations* or as *pain relievers*. The games-as-sensual-temptations argument (1, see Table 28.1) goes like this: "when using games as part of classroom teaching, teachers should interrupt the play process on a regular basis to prevent students immersing themselves in the game and losing sight of the learning objectives" (p. 320). Pelletier says, "learning is seen to take place not through play but rather through reflection on the game's content" (p. 320).

At first sight this argument seems to be contradicted by those studies that show that we can learn from the playing of games (Lieberman, 2006; Ritterfeld & Weber, 2006). But there are other examples that show that reflection on the game's content is an important component of learning as well. For example, as I argue in a study of the Dutch game *Frequency 1550* (Raessens, 2007), reflection is an important aspect of the learning process:

> On the third day, after two days of playing, all teams gathered at HQ [Head Quarters] to see what they did best, and to collectively reflect on the media produced, their answers to the questions, and the strategic decisions taken during the game. These aspects became even more meaningful to them when they had to present their results to a wider audience of classmates. By discussing the results, their choices, and the challenges they overcame with team members, but also with "outsiders," they learned to reflect better on the creative process in which they were involved. (Raessens, 2007, p. 211)

Elements of the games-as-pain-relievers argument (2, see Table 28.1) can be traced back to the work of Mark Prensky. His digital games-based learning approach combines two aspects and it is precisely this combination of the two arguments that we need to be critical about. First, Prensky (2001) defines active learning in terms of breaking with traditional forms of education and giving greater agency to learners. Second, he conceptualizes learning and training as pleasurable activities after the pain of learning is removed:

> Training and schooling is finally throwing off the shackles of pain and suffering which have accompanied it for so long.… At its very best, even

the hard part goes away, and it all becomes fun, a really good time from which, at the end, you have gotten better at something, through a process [called] "stealth learning." (pp. 4, 8)

Prensky's argument as described by Pelletier (2005) goes as follows: if we want to retrieve the original pleasure of learning, we have to break with "the rule of Law or symbolic authority" (p. 319). But as Pelletier argues, this narrative is a misleading one because he is "challenging one form of authority in order to replace it with another—the global economy" (p. 320). What Prensky does is simply reinstate authority elsewhere: "So it is precisely Prensky's playful attitude towards learning which initiates the supremacy of a consumer-oriented and fast-paced brand of capitalism" (p. 320).

The games-as-replicas-of-non-virtual-life argument (3, see Table 28.1) deals with those theories in which the Oedipal narrative is continued by other means. James Paul Gee's comments on David Williamson Shaffer's (2006) *How Computer Games Help Children Learn* are in line with Pelletier's analysis of this argument. Shaffer shows how computer and video games can help students learn to think like engineers, urban planners, journalists, and lawyers. Gee characterizes Shaffer as having "a deeply conservative vision...his goal is to put pressure on schools to prepare children to be productive workers, thoughtful members of society, and savvy citizens" (Shaffer, 2006, p. xii). According to Gee and Shaffer, schools are "not preparing children to be innovators at the highest technical levels—the levels that will pay off most in our modern, high-tech, science-driven, global economy" (Shaffer & Gee, 2005). Their solution to "our crisis" as Gee and Shaffer call it—the fact that the United States runs the risk of being overshadowed by countries like China and India—is epistemic games, which "are about having students do things that matter in the world by immersing them in rigorous professional practices of innovation" (Shaffer & Gee, 2005). In doing so, a game player is trained to become a member of a certain community and to adopt its epistemic frame: "we call a community's distinctive ways of doing, valuing, and knowing its *epistemic frame*. We use this term because an epistemic frame 'frames' the way someone thinks about the world—like putting on a pair of colored glasses" (Shaffer & Gee, 2005).[18]

The meaning of the fourth argument—games-as-dramatic-stages-for-reality-construction (4, see Table 28.1)—becomes clear when we compare the playing of serious games to playing with a *tamagotchi*. When we play a serious game, according to Pelletier (2005), the same two characteristics emerge as when we play with a *tamagotchi*. On the one hand, the game captivates the player by issuing orders: "Playing a game involves following orders; the game sets the objectives, the sequence in which they are to be completed, and usually the winning conditions" (p. 322). The pleasure of gaming consists, therefore, of what I described above in terms of interpassivity: "being able to 'do what you are told,' in other words, fulfilling the desires of another" (p. 322). On the other hand, playing serious games always incorporates a moment of disavowal—of distancing—specific to games. "In playing games...we perform actions in the full knowledge that we are doing this within the constraints set by someone else" (p. 323). According to Pelletier, this is exactly the process on which gaming is based: "Because the rules are already set, the goals already decided, we can be playful around them" (p. 323).

Translating these four reactions toward cyberspace into the field of educational/serious game studies makes us understand the different ways in which the player relates to the game's symbolic order. To decide which of these virtual tendencies of the gaming *dispositif* become actualized in a specific situation, we have to analyze the different ways in which serious game players are positioned.

Positioning of the Player

In this last section of the second paragraph, I focus on the different forms of player positioning: the game's technical base, the game text itself, and the (institutional, cultural) environment in which these games are played.

When we look closely at the technical base of serious games and how this technical base positions the player, we immediately become aware of the enormous differences, not only between the different game platforms (such as PC, console, Wii, GameBoy, and cell phone), between single- and multi-player games, but also between playing and making games whether they are new games or modifications of existing ones (inside or outside the mainstream gaming industry).

Both *Food Force* (2005) and *Darfur is Dying* (2006), for example, were made outside the mainstream gaming industry. They are Web-based, single-player PC games which means that a single person is sitting at a desk or table in front of a PC screen. The player is playing against the computer software using a mouse and a keyboard and listens to the sound and music via the music boxes or headphones attached to the computer. Although the PC screen is much smaller than a cinema screen, most of the player's visual field is nevertheless taken up by the image on the screen, because the player is situated much closer to the computer screen than is the case in the cinema. Most players play at home, either in a shared space such as a living room—playing Wii multiplayer games for example—or, to minimize distractions when playing a single-player game, in a private room such as the bedroom. Contrary to cinema viewers, game players generally do not play in a darkened room. Sound is also important, which increases the immersiveness of the gaming experience.[19]

The most striking difference with film spectators is that game players are highly active while remaining immobilized in terms of physical location. With the exception of pervasive games, game players sit in a chair in front of their computer screen with both hands occupied—one clicking and moving a mouse, the other tapping the keys of the keyboard—to control the activity in-game. When we recall how Baudry characterized the film spectator, the differences with the game player become instantly obvious. According to Baudry, "no more that in dream does he [the film spectator] have means to act in any way upon the object of his perception, change his viewpoint as he would like" (Baudry, 1975/1986b, p. 314). Cinema does not offer "the dreamer the possibility of exercising any kind of immediate control" (p. 315).

We also have to take into account how the player of the game is addressed or positioned both by the game text itself and by the institutional and cultural context in which the game is made and played. By defining a pragmatic approach as one that takes into account the role of the spectator (in film studies) or the player (in game studies), we characterize textual positioning as an immanent and contextual positioning as an extrinsic form of pragmatics.[20] The immanent film pragmatist Franceso Casetti (cited in Buckland, 1995) developed three fundamental principles: "that the film signals the *presence* of the spectator; that it assigns a *position* to him/her; that it makes him follow an *itinerary*" (p. 115). Extrinsic film pragmatist Roger Odin (1995), on the other hand, is of the opinion that a film spectator is primarily subjected to social institutions. A reading of a film "does not result from an internal [textual] constraint, but from a cultural constraint" (p. 213).

As mutually constitutive of each other, the concept of interpassivity runs the same risk as interactivity, namely that the cultural aspects of media become neglected. As Henry Jenkins (2007) noted, technologies offer a particular form of interactivity whereas participation refers to what the culture does with these media resources. So, serious games scholars should not only focus on how serious games bring about a critical, reflexive relation towards its content—as Pelletier (2005) suggests in her analysis of interpassivity—but also on the apparent contradictory trends that shape the media landscape (Jenkins, 2007). On one hand, media technologies today have lowered production and distribution costs, have widened the number of available delivery channels and have enabled individual's unprecedented access to content. On the other hand, the ownership of mainstream media rests in the hands of only a few multinational conglomerates who dominate more and more sectors of entertainment industries. What makes Jenkins's position interesting is that he avoids both an attitude of refusal and an attitude of blind acceptance toward the cultural industries but opts for an in-between position: an open, negotiating relation in which consumers demand a share of popular culture by appropriating its content for their own purposes.

These forms of player-positioning play a role in actualizing the virtual tendencies of the serious gaming *dispositif,* and I will now analyze this in more detail in relation to *Darfur is Dying* and *Food Force.*

Food Force **and** Darfur is Dying

In this third paragraph, I firstly introduce both *Food Force* and *Darfur is Dying.* Then I describe which of the four unconscious desires or dispositions of the gaming *dispositif* are at the basis of these two specific games. Finally, I analyze how these virtual desires or dispositions become actualized by discussing the ways in which the game player is positioned by the games' technology, the game texts, their institutional contexts and cultural settings.

Food Force and Darfur is Dying: An Introduction

Food Force is a serious digital game that was released by the UN World Food Programme (WFP). Its target group is children aged 8 to 13. The game, which takes approximately 30 minutes to play, tells the story of a food crisis on the fictitious island of Sheylan. Players can play the game after downloading it for free from the *Food Force* Web site. WFP released the game in April 2005, and, in their annual report for 2005, claimed that:

> The adventure [launching the game] turned out well: international media immediately picked up the story and by June one million people were play-ing the game. Now, 12 months on, *Food Force* has been downloaded nearly 4 million times, and the www.food-force.com website averages over 18,000 unique visitors per week. (UN World Food Programme, 2006, p. 43)

Darfur is Dying was the winner of the Darfur Digital Activist Contest launched by mtvU in partnership with the Reebok Human Rights Founda-tion and the International Crisis Group during the Games for Change (G4C) conference in October 2005.[21] The goal of the student contest was the design of a digital game that raised awareness about the humanitarian crisis in the Darfur region of Sudan where civilians run the risk of being killed or raped by militias backed by the Sudanese government. By playing the game, the player becomes involved in this world. The game was released in April 2006, at the *Darfur is Dying* Web site where it can be played for free. In September, 2006, game director Susana Ruiz stated in an interview:

> According to mtvU's traffic numbers, more than 800,000 people have played the game over 1.7 million times since its launch on April 30th. Of those, tens of thousands have participated in the activist tools woven into the game play—such as sending emails to friends in their social networks inviting them to play the game and become informed about Darfur, as well as writing letters to President Bush and petitioning their Represen-tatives in Congress to support legislation that aids the people of Darfur. (Parkin, 2006)

From the perspective of pragmatics that I advocate in this chapter, the political–ideological interest of serious games can only be determined by tak-ing into account the interplay between the four possible unconscious desires I discussed before and the different ways in which the player of the game is addressed or positioned by the game's design and technology,[22] by the game itself (text), as well as by the institutional and cultural setting in which the game is played (context). This is the kind of analysis I will apply to *Darfur is Dying* and *Food Force*.

Unconscious Desires

When we look more closely at the four unconscious desires or dispositions both Žižek and Pelletier refer to, it seems to be a *contradictio in terminis* to think that serious games in general and *Darfur is Dying* and *Food Force* in particular, would be able or willing to put an end to Oedipus; that is, refrain the player from entering the symbolic order of the game. This means that both the psychosis (based on the games-as-sensual-temptations argument) and the perversion (based on the games-as-pain-relievers argument) would be desires that are foreign to the seriousness of these games. That does not mean, however, that Pelletier's reflections related to both dispositions are useless here. The games-as-sensual-temptations argument makes clear that not only the playing of the game, but also the reflection on the gaming experience is an important component of learning as well. The games-as-pain-relievers argument makes us aware of the risks of what Vance Packard once labeled as a *hidden persuader*.[23] Claiming that the gamer is in power, as theorists often do, can hide a specific symbolic order from view in which the gamer is inscribed when playing the game, as we have seen is the case in Prensky's argument. What we finally need to decide is whether the playing of serious games, such as the two games under discussion, leads to a hysteric continuation of Oedipus or to a "perverse" interpassive relationship with them.

Continuation of Oedipus

To analyze which symbolic order the player enters when playing *Darfur is Dying* and *Food Force*, I recall Shaffer and Gee's (2005) reference to the game's epistemic frame: "an epistemic frame 'frames' the way someone thinks about the world—like putting on a pair of colored glasses." To understand how this process works, George Lakoff's concepts of "framing" and "metaphor" are useful. According to Lakoff and Johnson (2003), metaphors frame our understanding of the world: "Our ordinary conceptual system, in terms of which we both think and act, is fundamentally metaphorical in nature…. *The essence of metaphor is understanding and experiencing one kind of thing in terms of another*" [italics in original] (pp. 3, 5). Applying this idea to the field of politics, Lakoff (2004) argues that political discourses frame the facts of the world.

> Frames are mental structures that shape the way we see the world. As a result, they shape the goals we seek, the plans we make, the way we act, and what counts as a good or bad outcome of our actions. In politics our frames shape our social policies and the institutions we form to carry out policies. To change our frames is to change all of this. Reframing *is* social change. (p. xv)

In order to increase our understanding of both games' symbolic order, it is productive to approach them from a family values perspective. According to Lakoff, "we all have a metaphor for the nation as a family...because we usually understand large social groups, like nations, in terms of small ones, like families or communities" (p. 5). Both *Darfur is Dying* and *Food Force* are trying to persuade their players to adopt what Lakoff describes as "a [Democratic, progressive] nurturant parent family model" (p. 6). According to the metaphor of the nurturant parent, "in foreign policy the role of the nation should be to promote cooperation and extend these values to the world" (p. 40) and to focus on "international institutions and strong defensive and peacekeeping forces" (p. 63). Caring and responsibility equals "caring about and acting responsibility for the world's people; world health, hunger, poverty...rights for women, children...refugees, and ethnic minorities" (p. 92). This metaphor goes against the metaphor of the (Republican, conservative) strict father family model that, in foreign affairs, leads to the following: "The government should maintain its sovereignty and impose its moral authority everywhere it can, while seeking its self-interest (the economic self-interest of corporations and military strength)" (p. 41).

Before I analyze in more detail how both *Food Force* and *Darfur is Dying* involve players in these nurturant parent values by addressing or positioning them in specific ways, we need to understand how pervasive these values are in world politics. In *The WFP Mission Statement*[24] and in their *Annual Report 2005*, the World Food Programme refers to the responsibility the international community has for primary health care, access to clean water, proper hygiene; to the fact that food aid is essential for social and humanitarian protection; to the importance of helping people survive and rebuild their lives. James T. Morris, Executive Director of World Food Programme, refers to "the United Nations family" and "the whole UN family" (World Food Programme, 2006, pp. 5–6). In their *Mission Statement*[25] and their *New Challenges, New Horizons: Year in Review 2006*, the UN Peace Operations also refers to "the United Nations family" (2007, p. 24); to the international community's "duty of care"; to its responsibility to support health care missions; to the protection of community and minority rights; and to the protection of human rights.

Darfur is Dying and *Food Force* represent the UN Peace Operations and the UN World Food Programme as organizations able to—literally—"nurture" their family members. Therefore, both games express the values, and let the player enter the symbolic order, of the nurturant parent family model.

In Between: Interpassivity

Pelletier notes in analyzing the interpassive aspects of playing both games, that we have to focus on the moment of disavowal or distancing that is specific to games. The question we need to answer is whether playing serious games entails having a critical, reflexive relation toward them. According to the Dutch Cultural Council (2005), looking through and exposing the hidden, naturalized, ideologically presupposed rules of a medium is an important aspect of "media wisdom." Ted Friedman (1995) calls this process "demystification":

> Learning and winning...or "reaching one's goals at" a computer game is a process of demystification: One succeeds by discovering how the software is put together. The player molds his or her strategy through trial-and-error experimentation to see "what works"—which actions are rewarded and which are punished. (p. 82)[26]

Darfur is Dying rests on the premise that the UN Security Council has the right and the duty to authorize military intervention to stop serious abuses of human rights in regions all over the world. *Food Force* rests on the premise that fighting hunger is a responsibility of the international community. The "baseline ideological assumptions that determine which strategies will win and which will lose" (Friedman, 1999, p. 144) become apparent through actually playing the games. That is why Friedman claims that "to win...you have to figure out what will work within the rules of the game" (p. 136). This is because a digital game, as opposed to, for example, the normal mode of consumption of a film, is played over and over again until all of the game's secrets have been discovered.

Friedman's claim is problematic, because he overlooks the three interpretative strategies that may be activated in the player as a reaction to what Sherry Turkle (1996) calls the seduction of simulation: players can either surrender to the seduction of *Food Force* and *Darfur is Dying* by interpreting the game more or less according to the encoded UN-ideological frames (simulation resignation); or players, as Friedman claims, may understand these frames by demystifying or deconstructing the assumptions or frames that are built into the simulation (simulation understanding); or they can completely disavow the social and political importance of these kinds of games (simulation denial).

These three strategies do, indeed, describe the reactions of players and critics of both games. For example, game critic and Water Cooler Games forum editor Gonzalo Frasca writes about *Food Force*: "Finally! An educational game that rocks! Informative, well produced and very enjoyable to play with. Go United Nations!... Overall, I am extremely happy for this game, it is an excellent example of the way edutainment should be."[27] Most of the other comments on this forum reflect this view: "This was a wonderful game...successful at teaching the player about a few things, such as what foods are important, where investment is more valuable, etc. Great stuff!" and "Very nice game indeed." Simulation resignation is also the dominant reaction toward *Darfur is Dying* on other game review Web sites: "Fortunately, this game is refreshingly smart about its subject and effective in its delivery."[28] According to Parkin (2006) the game is one of the first to focus attention on a real survival-horror situation requiring players to fight to stay alive not from space invader aliens, but from real world bullets in a parched and barren landscape. Vargas (2006) further noted that the vast majority of young people were in fact clueless about the Darfur situation until they experienced the game.

Simulation understanding and simulation denial are in the minority among posted reviews. On the Water Cooler Games forum, some players deny *Food Force*'s importance by criticizing the UN for spending money on digital-game development while thousands starve.[29] And the BBC news cites Ian Bogost: "Bogost worries that MTV's involvement makes the game seem more like a marketing tool" (Boyd, 2006). Others criticize the built-in assumptions of *Food Force* because the game does not refer to forms of misconduct by UN personnel: "How much like the real U.N is it?"[30] They also raise the question whether the WFP's difficult work lends itself well to minigames: "It seems more like a MMO (ex. *Everquest*). Or a Sim where you control the WFP."[31] *Dafur is Dying* is criticized for the same reason: "It seems to trivialize the problem" (Vargas, 2006) and "He [Bogost] also wonders whether *Darfur is Dying* oversimplifies an incredibly complex conflict" (Boyd, 2006).

What these reactions to both games make clear is that it is, indeed, possible for players and critics to have the kind of critical, reflexive relation to these games, as described by Žižek and Pelletier. But looking through and exposing the hidden, naturalized, ideologically colored rules of serious games is, however, not commonplace. Players of *Darfur is Dying* and *Food Force* seem to be more superficial than both Žižek and Pelletier hope for, at least when we define superficiality as remaining on the surface of the game's symbolic order as opposed to the in-depth process of deconstruction.

Player Positioning By Technology, Text, and Context

Player Positioning By Technology

First of all, players of both games are positioned by the game's technology. Both games have similar assets: both are accessible through the Internet (*Darfur is Dying* can be played via de game's Web site while *Food Force* must be downloaded first to your own computer); both can be played for free; both game Web sites provide access to activist tools and offer the player all kinds of background information. Both games do not offer multiuser environments in their game play, maybe because of financial restrictions. Both games also lack a constructive mode of participation in the sense that players are denied a possibility for game modification.[32]

Player Positioning By Text

Repeating Casetti's argument but now in relation to serious games, the analysis of player positioning by the game itself must focus on three elements: how the game signals the *presence* of the player; how it assigns him a *position*; how it makes him follow an *itinerary*.[33] The player of *Darfur is Dying* is assigned a position that can be described as a third-person perspective on the game's world. In this world, the player controls an avatar that is visible on-screen. At the beginning of this game the player selects one out of eight Darfurian avatars to represent a refugee camp. The game has a simple two-level structure. On the first level, the player has to explore or itinerate in the game space—that is the area outside the refugee camp—foraging for water. The avatar has to provide water for the community, but because the well is 5 kilometers from the refugee camp, the player runs the risk of being captured and possibly killed by the militias during this itinerary. The player can move his or her avatar by using the arrow keys of the keyboard and the spacebar to hide from the militias. After having reached the well and having been able to return to the camp, the player may decide to go foraging again (as long as there are avatars left to do so) or to enter the second level inside the refugee camp. Here the player has a *SimCity*-style, top-down view of the camp. The player has to explore the camp and complete urgent tasks, such as obtaining food, building shelters, and staying healthy.

The basic rule of the game is clearly an ideologically motivated one: players can win the game by supporting Darfuri civilians. The goal of the game is to safeguard the refugee camp, keep it up and running for 7 days, and protect as many adults and children as possible from being killed by the Janjaweed militia. At the end of the game, players can put their name on a high score list on the game's Web site. A screen with "Goal Accomplished" pops up when the avatar successfully brings water to his or her family and community. The message of the game is communicated most clearly in its rhetoric of failure. If captured by the militia, the avatar faces realistic consequences. This is a moment where the game signals the presence of the player: "You will likely become one of the hundreds of thousands of people already lost to this humanitarian crisis." When a female avatar is captured the consequences are heartbreaking: she faces "abuse, rape and kidnapping by the Janjaweed."

The game is programmed in such a way that a player is not only unhappy with a negative outcome, but also with a positive one. When a player succeeds in accomplishing the goal of the game, he is informed that this will not end the real conflict: "The men, women, and children of Darfur have been living under harrowing conditions since 2003."[34] Though the game does not have real-life consequences for the player, it does have consequences for the Darfurian avatars of the player. Because the player identifies with the onscreen avatar, she or he becomes engaged in the problematics of the game.

In contrast, in the virtual world of *Food Force*, the player's engagement does not come from identification with an onscreen avatar, but from the personal experience of playing the game. From Casetti's perspective, the player of *Food Force* is assigned a position that can be described as a first-person point of view on the game world: he or she is required to adopt a minimal degree of characterization; that is, the young rookie is addressed by the game as "you." In the beginning of the game, this young rookie is briefed on a humanitarian crisis on the fictitious island Sheylan in the Indian Ocean. It is the player's mission to deliver food as quickly as possible to Sheylan's residents. Guided by a team of experts, in a race against the clock, the player has to accomplish six missions or minigames in a linear order, delivering food to an area in crisis. In one of the itineraries, the Air Surveillance mission, the player has to explore the crisis area by helicopter and count the number of people who need help by selecting one of the preprogrammed actions: fly to the right, left, up or down.

The basic rule of *Food Force* is also an ideologically motivated one: players win the game by completing the six missions and in doing so, help to fight hunger. The goal of the game is directly conveyed to the player: "You can learn to fight hunger.... Millions of people are now depending on you for help. This is more than just a game. Good luck!" Players receive positive feedback on their performance from computer-controlled team members if their missions are successful. At these moments, the game signals the presence of the player. If the mission fails, the player is encouraged to try again. After playing the game, a player can summit his or her final score to a worldwide high score list on the game's Web site. Though the game does not have real-life consequences for the player, he is constantly reminded of the fact that in real life the WFP-missions have huge consequences for these hungry people. Before and after each mission, the player can watch animated video clips providing background information on the importance of the WFP's work.

Player Positioning By Context

In line with Odin's (1995) extrinsic form of pragmatics and Jenkins's analysis of the current media landscape (2006, 2007), we have to take into account that players of both *Darfur is Dying* and *Food Force* are also addressed or positioned by the institutional context or cultural setting in which these games are played. Three aspects are of importance. First, both games are played in the context of a Web site that provides the player with background information about the social issues these games deal with. This situation is quite different from that of the film spectator: "No exchange, no circulation, no communication with any outside. Projection and reflection take place in a closed space" (Baudry, 1970/1986a, p. 294). Whereas the linearity of (the screening of) a film makes it undesirable to make the film spectator go in and out of the diegesis, aspects such as the nonlinearity of a game and the possibility of pausing, makes this much easier to do for a game. The *Food Force* Web site provides the player with information about the reality behind the game: "In the world today hundreds of millions of people suffer from chronic hunger and malnutrition." Furthermore, the player can learn about WPF's mission to fight hunger worldwide and learn how he or she can actively support the WFP's activities outside the game world. Players can help by giving money to the WFP, by teaching others about famine, and by organizing fundraising activities at school or at home. "Joe's blog" on the *Food Force* Web site links the game world with the outside reality in interesting ways. Joe Zake, the fictional Sheylanese nutritionist character of the game, asks Web site visitors: "to spread the word about hunger using this blog: read, comment and link."

On the *Darfur is Dying* Web site, the player can not only play the game ("Help stop the crisis in Darfur: Start your experience"), but also receive background information about the crisis in Darfur ("In the Darfur region of western Sudan, a genocide is occurring") and the different ways in which she or he can try to stop the crisis ("Do something now to stop the crisis in Darfur"). Players can educate themselves on the crisis in Darfur, send messages to (former) President Bush, ask their representatives to support funding for African Union peacekeepers, and start divestment movements on their campus.

Second, both games are often played in the context of a class-room situation. On the *Food Force* Web site, teachers can find all the information they need to use the game as a classroom tool for teaching about hunger. Apart from the game, the Web sites make other educational resources available: "The WFP Food Force educational video game and the.... Feeding Minds, Fighting Hunger education initiative are important tools for preparing and encouraging young people to work together to help create a world free from hunger."[35] From a pragmatic perspective, both elements can be seen as a framework of cultural constraints that regulate the players' understanding of these games and thereby helps them in entering the games' symbolic order.

Third, as part of today's media transformations, users are increasingly able to use different media technologies to design their own games (as is the case with *Darfur is Dying*) and to use the activist tools woven in the game's Web site (both games). Relevant here is the critique of the Italian philosopher Gianni Vattimo on the work of Horkheimer and Adorno. According to Vattimo (1992), Max Horkheimer and Theodor Adorno thought that the mass media would produce "a general homogenization of society" in which "the diffusion of slogans, propaganda (commercial as well as political) and stereotypical worldviews" would dominate (p. 5). Vattimo, on the other hand, is much more optimistic about the role of the mass media. According to him, they have played a crucial role in "a general explosion and proliferation of 'Weltanschauungen,' of worldviews" (p. 5). All kinds of minorities and subcultures have seized the opportunity to express their views in the relative chaos of today's media. According to Vattimo, this is a development that has contributed to the rise of the postmodern society characterized by relativity, contingency, heterogeneity, and diversity. The fact that both *Food Force* and *Darfur is Dying* were made outside the mainstream gaming industry and succeed in raising issues that the mass-news media do not always consider newsworthy, shows the relevance of Vattimo's approach.

Conclusion

In this chapter I examined how serious games are ideologically colored. I analyzed the different forms of player positioning that contribute to the production of meaning, one of the central points of interest within a humanities approach. To be able to do so, I analyzed, critiqued, and further developed the concept of the *dispositif* as it was conveyed within film studies, from the perspective of pragmatics and cultural analysis. The advantage or productivity of using this concept within game studies is that it helps to articulate the understanding that the process of making meaning is deeply influenced by the ways in which configurations of technology, user positioning, desire, media text, and context take shape in specific games. It is not only productive, I would say, to make the concept of the *dispositif* travel to game studies, but also back again to film studies where Baudry introduced it in a more limited sense. And although this study is not primarily empirical, I argue that the analysis of the concept of the *dispositif* can be helpful in the design of future empirical research in both fields.

I questioned the impact of serious games by analyzing the if and how of the player's entry into the game's symbolic order. I described the four kinds of unconscious desires—Žižek and Pelletier refer to—as *virtual tendencies* that may or may not become actualized, depending on how the player of a specific game is positioned or addressed. In *Food Force* and *Darfur is Dying*, the games-as-replicas-of-non-virtual-life argument seemed to be dominant. The ideologically colored construction is not automatically revealed by the mere activity of play as Friedman presupposes. Furthermore, it turned out to be almost a *contradictio in terminis* to presume that serious games in general, and *Darfur is Dying* and *Food Force* in particular, would be able or willing to put an end to Oedipus; that is, discourage the player from entering the symbolic order of the game. This would mean that there seems to be little room for a critical, reflective attitude toward the game's ideology while playing these games.

The question whether such a critical distance needs to exist in the first place is up for discussion. It is of course a legitimate aspiration to teach children about hunger (*Food Force*) and to raise awareness about the humanitarian crisis in the Darfur region of Sudan (*Darfur is Dying*). But at the same time it is also legitimate to teach children how to understand (Turkle) or demystify (Friedman) the frames and values of which a specific serious game wants to convince its player. I agree with Turkle (1996) when she advocates the importance of an attitude of simulation understanding: "Understanding the assumptions that underlie simulation is a key element of political power" (p. 71). It could be a task of media literacy education, not only to teach children *through* but also *about* digital games. As Kurt Squire argues, "students might be required to critique the game and explicitly address built-in simulation biases" (Squire, 2002).

According to Henry Jenkins (2007), the fact that in the new media landscape children are becoming participants, and not only spectators or consumers, also means that they should be aware of their "ethical responsibilities" (p. 1); for example, by asking "about the motives or accuracy of the ways games depict the world" (p. 15) or by asking what kind of (ideologically colored) games they would want to design themselves. Professional serious game designers as well as serious game theorists also have an ethical–political responsibility when they make decisions about the ways in which they design serious games and construct theories about them. Which of the virtual tendencies become actualized is not directly inscribed into the game's technical properties. They are the "possibilities opened up by cyberspace technology, so that, ultimately, the choice is ours, the stake in a politico-ideological struggle (Žižek, 1999, p. 123).

Acknowledgments

This research has been supported by the GATE project, funded by the Netherlands Organization for Scientific Research (NWO) and the Netherlands ICT Research and Innovation Authority (ICT Regie); see http://gate.gameresearch. nl. This chapter has been written as part of the Utrecht Media Research project (UMR), Utrecht University, The Netherlands; see http://www2.hum.uu.nl/ Solis/umr. I would like to thank Frank Kessler for his helpful comments on an earlier version of this chapter and Christien Franken for editing this chapter. I also would like to thank the members of the Utrecht Media Seminar for their suggestions.

Notes

1. For reasons I will explain later, I consider the French term *dispositif* more accurate than the English translation 'apparatus'.
2. This paragraph is partly based on Kessler (2006, part II). For a detailed discussion of the *dispositif* as a theoretical concept, see Kessler (2006, 2007); see the Utrecht Media Research program Web site for more details: http://www2.hum. uu.nl/Solis/umr.
3. Noël Carroll (2004) describes the mise-en-scène of Plato's cave as follows: "Those prisoners are chained in a darkened vault. Behind and above them, fires burn. As passersby walk between the prisoners and the flames, the strollers' ambulating shadows are cast upon the wall of the cave. The prisoners see these moving shadows and take them for reality" (p. 229).
4. Žižek's alternative for this concept of victimhood is interpassivity. See a further description in the "Slavoj Žižek's Range of Unconscious desires" section of this chapter.
5. This form of primary identification must be distinguished from "secondary" identification, which refers to processes of identification with the characters of a film.
6. "Psychosis involves immersion in the imaginary (in other words, the visual and the sensual), with no symbolic authority to enable critique and a sense of self separate from one's sensations" (Pelletier, 2005, p. 325).
7. For the alternatives to continuity editing, see Bordwell and Thompson (1986, pp. 220–227); for the alternatives to classical narration—such as art-cinema narration, historical-materialist narration and parametric narration—see Bordwell (1985, pp. 205–310).

8. For an analysis of the active-audience theory in relation to computer games, see Raessens (2005).

9. For an analysis of this discourse of colonization, see Raessens (2006).

10. For a productive interplay between film studies and computer game studies, see for example King and Krzywinska (2002), and the Digital Games Researchers Association (DiGRA) Special Interest Group (SIG) Games and Film (http://www.gamefilmsig.wordpress.com).

11. See also note 6.

12. According to Žižek, the pervert is a "'transgressor' *par excellence* who purports to violate all the rules of 'normal,' decent behavior" (Žižek, 1999, p. 118). Pelletier (2005) proposes that, "Perversion is characterized by actions that aim to deviate from norms in order to disavow the authority of these norms" (p. 325).

13. Pelletier (2005) notes that Žižek sees cyberspace as hystericizing the subject in the sense that "The hysteric is characterized by an obsessive concern with the subject's identity and where they stand in relation to the Other" (p. 325).

14. "The opposite of the first mode of interactivity is also a kind of 'interpassivity', the mutual passivity of two subjects, like two lovers passively observing each other and merely enjoying the other's presence" (Žižek, 1999, p. 106).

15. Interpassivity is by no means limited to digital culture. Other examples of interpassivity that Žižek refers to are the role of the Chorus in Greek tragedy: "Your emotions are taken charge of by...the Chorus" (Žižek, 1999, p. 104) and "so-called canned laughter (where laughter is included in the sound-track, so that the TV sets laughs for me)," (pp. 104–105).

16. Here Žižek is referring to an expression of Octave Mannoni (2003): "I know well, but all the same" ("Je sais bien, mais quand meme"). The mechanism of disavowal characterizes itself by this doubleness. Although Mannoni developed this expression in relation to theatre, it is also fundamental to an understanding of film spectatorship as described by psychoanalytical film theorists.

17. This is what Žižek demonstrates in the DVD *The Pervert's Guide to Cinema. Parts 1, 2, 3* (Fiennes, 2006). According to Žižek: "Cinema is the ultimate pervert art. It doesn't give you what you desire, it tells you how to desire.... The art of cinema consists in arousing desire, to play with desire. But, at the same time, keeping it at a safe distance, domesticating it, rendering it palpable."

18. See also Squire (2005): "It is critical to note—especially in business and training—that what is desired is getting participants to adopt a very particular viewpoint. In terms of corporations, this means adopting the point of view desired by the organization" (p. 19).

19. For a detailed description of the gaming *dispositif*, see Morris (2002).

20. For both characterizations, see Simons (1995, p. 210).

21. The winning student team received $50.000 to develop the game.

22. Also see Lauwaert (2007): "Norms and values, knowledge and experiences, rules and requirements are embedded into the design and promote specific user behavior" (p. 78).

23. For an analysis of how advertisers tap into our unconscious desires in order to persuade us to buy the products they are selling, see Packard (1984).

24. See http://www.wfp.org/policies/policy/mission.

25. See http://www.un.org/Depts/dpko/dpko/info/page3.htm.

26. Baudry, 1975/1986a, argues that this moment of critical reflection is generally absent from the cinematic experience. Film only functions "on the condition that the instrumentation itself be hidden or repressed" (p. 295).

27. See http://www.watercoolergames.org/archives/000381.shtml.

28. See http://www.gameology.org/node/1013.

29. See note 27.
30. See note 27. In 2005, the UN established an Ethics Office with the objective to "ensure that all staff members observe and perform their functions consistent with the highest standards of integrity," see http://www.un.org/reform/ethics.
31. See note 27. Massively multiplayer online role-playing game (MMO or MMORPG); a sim is a simulation game, like *SimCity*.
32. I define as "construction" the addition of new game elements, that is "the making of new games or—and this is much more common—the modification of existing games" (Raessens, 2005, p. 381). The fact that both games were made outside the mainstream gaming industry, I will discuss in the "Player Positioning by Context" section.
33. Following an itinerary I call "reconfiguration." It consists of "the exploration of the unknown, in the computer game represented worlds" and the selection of "objects and actions from a fixed set of system-internal possibilities" (Raessens, 2005, p. 380). It is the dominant mode of participation in *Darfur is Dying* and *Food Force*. I discussed Casetti's work in the "Positioning of the player" section.
34. The reason for this is probably because, after a few attempts, an experienced player is able to accomplish the missions without any problems, and he or she might get the idea that the Darfurian people only need to try harder to be successful. In this case, the game play would clearly contradict the desired message of the game.
35. See http://www.food-force.com/index.php/teachers. Information about the Feeding Minds, Fighting Hunger initiative can be found at http://www.feedingminds.org.

References

Aarseth, E. (2001). Computer game studies, year one. *Game Studies, 1*(1).

Bal, M. (2002). *Travelling concepts in the humanities. A rough guide*. Toronto: University of Toronto Press.

Baudry, J. L. (1986a). Ideological effects of the basic cinematographic apparatus. In P. Rosen (Ed.), *Narrative, apparatus, ideology* (pp. 286–298). New York: Columbia University Press. (Original work published 1970)

Baudry, J. L. (1986b). The apparatus: Metapsychological approaches to the impression of reality in the cinema. In P. Rosen (Ed.), *Narrative, apparatus, ideology* (pp. 299–318). New York: Columbia University Press. (Original work published 1975)

Bordwell, D. (1985). *Narration in the fiction film*. Madison, WI: University of Wisconsin Press.

Bordwell, D., & Thompson, K. (1986). *Film art. An introduction*. New York: Knopf.

Boyd, C. (2006, July 6). Darfur activism meets video gaming. *BBC news*. Retrieved March 16, 2009, from http://www.news.bbc.co.uk/2/hi/technology/5153694.stm

Buckland, W. (Ed.). (1995). *The film spectator: From sign to mind*. Amsterdam, The Netherlands: Amsterdam University Press.

Carroll, N. (2004). From *Mystifying Movies*: Jean-Louis Baudry and "The Apparatus." In L. Baudry & M. Cohen (Eds.), *Film theory and criticism: Introductory readings* (pp. 224–239). New York: Oxford University Press.

Darfur is dying [Digital game]. (2006). York, A., Stein, M., Keating, N., & Santiago, K. Retrieved from http://www.darfurisdying.com

Deleuze, G., & Parnet, C. (1989). H comme histoire de la philosophie. In *L'Abécédaire de Gilles Deleuze* [Documentary]. Paris: Vidéos Editions Montparnasse.

Dutch Cultural Council. (2005). *Mediawijsheid. De ontwikkeling van nieuw burgerschap* [Media wisdom. The development of new citizenship]. The Hague: Author.

Evans, D. (2001). *An introductory dictionary of Lacanian psychoanalysis.* London: Routledge.

EverQuest [Digital game]. San Diego, CA: Sony Online Entertainment.

Fiennes, S. (Director) (2006). *The pervert's guide to cinema. Part 1, 2, 3.* [DVD]. Presented by Slavoj Žižek.

Food Force [Digital game]. (2005). Rome: UN World Food Programme. http://www.food-force.com

Friedman, T. (1995). Making sense of software: Computer games and interactive textuality. In S. Jones (Ed.), *CyberSociety. Computer-mediated communication and community* (pp. 73–89). Thousand Oaks, CA: Sage.

Friedman, T. (1999). Civilization and its discontents: Simulation, subjectivity, and space. In G. Smith (Ed.), *On a silver platter: CD-ROMs and the promises of a new technology* (pp. 132–150). New York: New York University Press.

Jenkins, H. (2006). *Convergence culture. Where old media and new media collide.* New York: New York University Press.

Jenkins, H. (2007). *Media literacy. Who needs it?* Retrieved March 16, 2009, from http://www.projectnml.org/yoyogi

Kessler, F. (2006). The cinema of attractions as dispositif. In W. Strauven (Ed.), *The cinema of attractions reloaded* (pp. 57–69). Amsterdam: Amsterdam University Press.

Kessler, F. (2007). Notes on *dispositif.* Retrieved March 16, 2009, from http://www.let.uu.nl/~Frank.Kessler/personal

King, G., & Krzywinska, T. (2002). *ScreenPlay: Cinema/videogames/interfaces.* London: Wallflower Press.

Lakoff, G. (2004). *Don't think of an elephant! Know your values and frame the debate.* White River Junction, VT: Chelsea Green.

Lakoff, G., & Johnson, M. (2003). *Metaphors we live by.* Chicago: University of Chicago Press.

Lauwaert, M. (2007). *The place of play. On toys, technological innovations and geographies of play.* Doctoral dissertation published by Maastricht University, The Netherlands.

Lieberman, D. (2006). What can we learn from playing interactive games? In P. Vorderer & J. Bryant (Eds.), *Playing video games: Motives, responses, and consequences* (pp. 379–397). Mahwah, NJ: Erlbaum.

Mannoni, O. (2003). "I know well, but all the same…" In M. Rothenberg, D. Foster & S. Žižek (Eds.), *Perversion and the social relation* (pp. 68–92). Durham, NC: Duke University Press.

Morris, S. (2002). First-person shooters—A game apparatus. In G. King & T. Krzywinska (Eds.), *ScreenPlay: Cinema/videogames/interfaces* (pp. 81–97). London: Wallflower Press.

Odin, R. (1995). For a semio-pragmatics of film. In W. Buckland (Ed.), *The film spectator: From sign to mind* (pp. 213–226). Amsterdam, The Netherlands: Amsterdam University Press.

Packard, V. (1984). *The hidden persuaders.* New York: Pocket.

Parkin, S. (2006, September 4). Interview—*Darfur is dying. Eurogamer.* Retrieved March 16, 2009 from http://www.eurogamer.net

Pelletier, C. (2005). Reconfiguring interactivity, agency and pleasure in the education and computer games debate—Using Žižek's concept of interpassivity to analyse educational play. *E-Learning, 2*(4), 317–326.

Prensky, M. (2001). *Digital game-based learning.* New York: McGraw-Hill.

Raessens, J. (2005). Computer games as participatory media culture. In J. Raessens & J. Goldstein (Eds.), *Handbook of computer game studies* (pp. 373–388). Cambridge, MA: MIT Press.

Raessens, J. (2006). Playful identities, or the ludification of culture. *Games and Culture: A Journal of Interactive Media, 1*(1), 52–57.

Raessens, J. (2007). Playing history: Reflections on mobile and location-based learning. In T. Hug (Ed.), *Didactics of micro-learning: Concepts, discourses, and examples* (pp. 200–217). Münster, Germany: Waxmann Verlag.

Ritterfeld, U., & Weber, R. (2006). Video games for entertainment and education. In P. Vorderer & J. Bryant (Eds.), *Playing video games: Motives, responses, and consequences* (pp. 399–413). Mahwah, NJ: Erlbaum.

Rosen, P. (1986). Introduction part three: Apparatus. In P. Rosen (Ed.), *Narrative, apparatus, ideology* (pp. 281–285). New York: Columbia University Press.

Shaffer, D. W. (2006). *How computer games help children learn.* New York: Palgrave MacMillan.

Shaffer, D. W., & Gee, J. P. (2005). *Before every child is left behind: How epistemic games can solve the coming crisis in education.* Retrieved March 16, 2009, from http://www.epistemicgames.org

SimCity [Digital game]. Emeryville, CA: Maxis Software.

Simons, J. (1995). Introduction. In W. Buckland (Ed.), *The film spectator. From sign to mind* (pp. 209–212). Amsterdam: Amsterdam University Press.

Squire, K. (2002). *Cultural framing of computer/video games.* Retrieved on March 16, 2009, from www.gamestudies.org/0102/squire

Squire, K. (2005). *Game-based learning: Present and future state of the field.* Retrieved March 16, 2009, from http://www.masieweb.com/dmdocuments/Game-Based_Learning.pdf

Turkle, S. (1996). *Life on the screen: Identity in the age of the Internet.* London: Weidenfeld & Nicolson.

UN Peace Operations. (2007). *New challenges, new horizons: Year in review 2006.* New York. Retrieved March 16, 2009, from http://www.un.org/Depts/dpko/dpko/pub/year_review06/YIR2006.pdf

UN World Food Programme. (2006). *Annual report 2005.* Rome. Retrieved March 16, 2009, from http://www.wfp.org/policies/annual_reports/documents/2005_wfp_annual_report.pdf

Vargas, J. A. (2006, May 1). In *Darfur is dying*, the game that's anything but. *Washingtonpost.com.* Retrieved March 16, 2009, from http://www.washingtonpost.com

Vattimo, G. (1992). The postmodern: A transparent society? In *The transparent society* (pp. 1–11). Cambridge, England: Polity Press.

Žižek, S. (1999). Is it possible to traverse the fantasy in cyberspace? In E. Wright & E. Wright (Eds.), *The Žižek reader* (pp. 102–124). Malden, MA: Blackwell.

Index

Page numbers in italic refer to figures or tables.